SOCIAL WORK

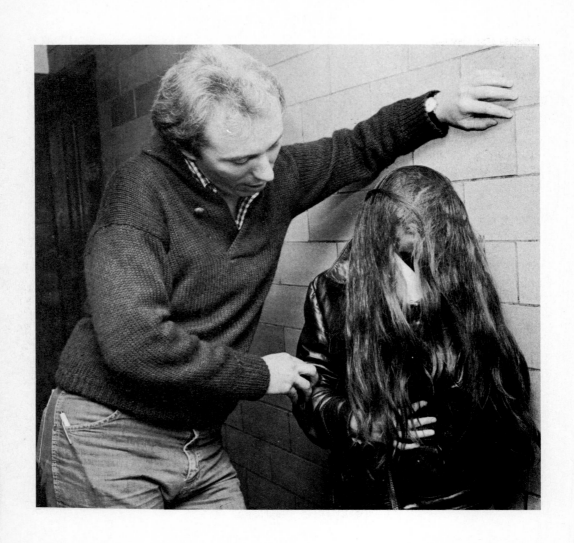

SOCIAL WORK
A Profession of Many Faces

FIFTH EDITION

Armando Morales
University of California at Los Angeles

Bradford W. Sheafor
Colorado State University

ALLYN AND BACON

Boston London Sydney Toronto

Photo Credits:

Frontispiece, Stock, Boston, Inc. / J. Berndt; Chapter 1, Stock, Boston, Inc. / John Maher; Chapter 2, AP/Wide World Photos; Chapter 3, Woodfin Camp & Associates, Inc. / Lynne Jaeger Weinstein; Chapter 4, Stock, Boston, Inc. / Steve Hansen; Chapter 5, Magnum Photos, Inc. / Paul Fusco; Chapter 6, Stock, Boston, Inc. / Judy S. Gelles; Chapter 7, Stock, Boston, Inc. / Bohdan Hrynewych; Chapter 8, The Picture Cube / Marianne Gontarz; Chapter 9, The Picture Cube / Ellis Herwig; Chapter 10, Stock, Boston, Inc. / Paul Fortin; Chapter 11, Archive Pictures, Inc. / Earl Dotter; Chapter 12, Magnum Photos, Inc. / Paul Fusco; Chapter 13, The Bettmann Archive; Chapter 14, Stock, Boston, Inc. / Addison Geary; Chapter 15, Archive Pictures, Inc. / Michael O'Brien; Chapter 16, Magnum Photos, Inc. / Leonard Freed; Chapter 17, The Picture Cube / Frank J. Staub; Chapter 18, Woodfin Camp & Associates, Inc. / Jim Anderson; Chapter 19, Monkmeyer Press Photo Service / Michael Heron; Chapter 20, Archive Pictures, Inc. / Jeff Jacobson; Chapter 21, Archive Pictures, Inc. / Abigail Heyman; Chapter 22, Magnum Photos, Inc. / Eli Reed; Chapter 23, The Bettmann Archive.

Series Editor: Karen Hanson
Cover Administrator: Linda K. Dickinson
Manufacturing Buyer: Bill Alberti
Text Designer: Deborah Schneck
Editorial-Production Service: Kathy Smith

Library of Congress Cataloging-in-Publication Data

Morales, Armando.
    Social work : a profession of many faces / Armando Morales and
Bradford W. Sheafor.—5th ed.
        p.   cm.
    Bibliography: p.
    Includes index.
    ISBN 0-205-11888-7
    1. Social service—United States.   2. Social work education–
–United States.   3. Social case work—United States.   4. Social
service—Vocational guidance—United States.   5. Social work with
minorities—United States.   I. Sheafor, Bradford W.   II. Title.
HV91.M67   1988
361'.973—dc19   88-7504
                                                                       CIP

Printed in the United States of America

10 9 8 7 6 5 4 3 2 1   93 92 91 90 89

DEDICATED TO

Our mothers
and
Roland, Gary, and
Tio Juan Acevedo who introduced me
to social work and gangs,
and
Nadine,
Christopher, Perry, Brandon, and Laura

Contents

Part Five   The Future of Social Work   588

Preface

In his recent best seller, *Cultural Literacy: What Every American Needs to Know*, E. D. Hirsch, Jr. convincingly makes the point that one of the greatest problems that Americans, and especially our youth, experience today is that many have a very limited awareness of their cultural background. In Hirsch's terms, they lack adequate cultural literacy to comprehend a substantial amount of important communication. The person, for example, who does not appreciate the meaning of Supreme Court decisions such as *Brown* v. *Board of Education* or the "Gault Decision," who fails to recognize the dangers associated with the label "Three Mile Island" or destruction of the ozone, who does not understand the significant contributions of Abraham Lincoln, Franklin D. Roosevelt, or Martin Luther King, Jr. to American society, or who is not knowledgeable about the implications of such major events as the Great Depression, the Vietnam War, or Watergate, cannot fully comprehend much of what is reported. Unless one is culturally literate, it is not possible to fully participate in and contribute to society.

Borrowing from Hirsch's thesis, this book is intended to prepare the reader with a beginning social work literacy. It presents an overview of the social work profession that introduces many of the terms, concepts, people, and critical events that have shaped this profession. To be "social-work literate," one must appreciate the contributions of Jane Addams and Mary Richmond; understand the reasons social work exists in this society and the purpose of the "Code of Ethics" in preserving social work's professional integrity; know the role of the National Association of Social Workers and the Council on Social Work Education in maintaining and strengthening social work; recognize the importance of the social welfare institution in American society and the function of human service agencies in fostering or diminishing the quality of services provided; and have some empathy for what it is like to be poor or to experience the impact of institutional racism, sexism, or ageism.

While we were not familiar with Hirsch's concept of cultural literacy when we wrote the prior editions of *Social Work: A Profession of Many Faces*, we now recognize that our underlying intent has been to provide sufficient general content to prepare the reader to consume other social work literature that addresses these topics in more depth. In other words, this book intends to give the reader a sufficient working knowledge of social work to intelligently read, comprehend, and begin to understand the literature of this profession.

The context of culture in which social work is practiced has changed during the years we have been engaged in writing and rewriting this book. We began the first edition just as Richard Nixon took office for his second term and concluded this edition as Ronald Reagan was ending his second term. We have seen a decline of social concern in the United States as resources for human services have been exchanged for military build-ups and as many of the Great Society programs have been dismantled. We have seen an economy apparently headed for another depression in the 1980s strengthened by new and more prudent fiscal policies. Unfortunately, fiscal solvency was achieved primarily through sacrifices extracted from the poor. As we indicate in Chapter 4, for example, the lowest one-fifth of the American families lost 8 percent in real disposable income during the first term of the Reagan Administration, while the upper one-fifth gained 9 percent. On the more positive side, we have seen the incidence of poverty among the aging population significantly reduced. In fact, the rate of poverty among the elderly declined by more than ten percent between 1980 and 1983. Further, while we have not seen gains in regard 'to human rights issues (e.g., the Equal Rights Amendment failed to gain ratification), the institutionalized programs to protect civil rights withstood efforts to erode their effectiveness.

The changes we have observed in the social attitudes of American society have been mirrored by the students who attend our colleges and universities, and ultimately those who elect to prepare for careers in social work. We have observed in students that their concern in the mid-1970s over the plight of the poor, the ill, and the aged; their militant campaigns against racism and sexism; and their outrage over U.S. military actions in Vietnam have all too often been replaced by social apathy and a narrow vocational approach to careers. The question often heard by the university faculty member, "What can I do to help people?" has too often been replaced by "What can you do to prepare me for a career that offers good pay and job security?" Admittedly decent pay and job security are desirable, but the shift in motivation and loss of idealism reflected in many of today's students concerns us.

Certainly the change in intensity of social concern has not been limited to students. We have also seen a rather dramatic shift in social work practice as many social workers have moved away from work with the poor and most vulnerable members of society and into private practice with the middle class. We have seen the zeal for social change as a prime activity of social work erode in favor of an overemphasis on clinical skills for practice with individuals and families. While we believe that private practice is an appropriate model for social work and that the use of clinical skills is a valid means of providing human services, we decry the fact that these approaches have expanded at the expense of social work's historical commitment to social action and direct services for the most vulnerable members of society.

During the years we have worked on this book, we believe that social work has made great strides in clarifying its unique role among the helping professions and stabilizing a relatively clear path that embraces baccalaureate, master's, and doctoral level preparation. In addition, remarkable shifts have occurred in the places where social workers provide their services. Occupational social work, for example, has expanded rapidly while some traditional practice areas like public assistance, community organization, and corrections have experienced an exodus by professional social workers. As it has done throughout its history, social work has adapted to the prevalent conservative public attitude that seeks to restrict human services by leaving the streets and, we believe temporarily, finding safety in the less controversial clinical aspects of social work practice. However, by maintaining its clear focus on the interaction between people and the world around them, social workers are poised to again become more actively engaged in social change activities when the political climate supports more aggressive work in that area.

We frankly seek to appeal to the social conscience of those who examine these pages. We strive to project the social worker as one who maintains a balanced perception of person *and* environment as targets of change. Our view of the social worker is that of one who serves individuals, families, groups, organizations, and communities with an "informed passion" for improving the quality of life for all people, but especially the most vulnerable members of our society. We are firm in our conviction that social work has an essential role to perform in helping people deal more effectively with the world around them and conclude that few occupations could offer us the personal satisfaction that we have experienced as social workers.

This book, then, provides the basic information for becoming literate in social work. It is an overview of social work—past and present. It is intended for the person who wants to learn about social workers—what they do and why they do it. As an introduction to this important profession, *Social Work: A Profession of Many Faces* helps the newcomer to this discipline or the person considering a career in social work to acquire a solid grounding. Although the title reflects the important point that this is a profession composed of people from widely diverse backgrounds, which serves people with a range of social problems, and is practiced in a wide variety of social agencies using quite varied knowledge and techniques, social work practice has many common features that help to bind social workers together into one profession.

The authors themselves reflect some of the different faces of social work. One has devoted most of his practice experience to working with individuals, families, and groups, while the other has worked mostly with organizations and communities. Both are employed by universities. However, one is primarily engaged in direct clinical practice with the poor, and in teaching and training psychiatric residents and psychology and social work interns in a department of psychiatry. The other is engaged in teaching baccalaureate and master's level students in a professional social work education program. One is a member of a minority group, and the other is a part of the majority. One has always lived in a large urban area on the West Coast, while the other is the product of smaller communities in the Midwest and Rocky Mountain region. Despite the different faces these two social workers reflect, we are in substantial agreement in our enthusiasm for social work and our perception of the factors that make this profession essential to American society.

We have made a number of changes in the fifth edition of *Social Work: A Profession of Many Faces* that we believe have resulted in a substantial improvement over prior editions. Our intent was to maintain the features that our past readers have found helpful and to address new and emerging areas that we anticipate will be of concern to social workers.

First, we updated the factual information in this book. New data on social work salaries (Chapter 1), employment projections for social workers and other helping professions (Chapter 3), student enrollment patterns and characteristics of social work education programs (Chapter 3), the results of the Reagan Administration's efforts to dismantle the "Great Society" and human rights programs (Chapter 4), and the social conditions experienced by the special population groups (including AIDS victims) addressed in this book (Chapter 11) are all included.

Second, we extensively revised several chapters. In Chapter 2, we have extended our historical review of social work's emergence through the mid-1980s and introduced material on an evolving effort by social work and other helping professions to strengthen collaborative interprofessional practice and education. We have taken a new look (Chapter 6) at the settings where social workers practice—both social agencies and private or proprietary practice—and the influence of each on the ability of the social worker to conduct effective practice. A section on the knowledge required for ethnically and culturally sensitive social work practice was introduced in Chapter 7; Chapter 8 was completely rewritten to reflect new information and understanding of the values that influence social workers and social work practice; and Chapter 9 includes new materials on developing social work assessment skills. Our concluding chapter (Chapter 23), which is based on the evolving, promising concept of *prevention*, now highlights the important role social work can perform in addressing the timely, critical issue of urban gang violence and homicide prevention.

Finally, we added four new chapters to this edition. Chapter 13 addresses the medical and psychiatric needs of the homeless, and expands our understanding of one of America's most perplexing social problems. Chapters 15 and 16 provide a comparative view of social work in rural and urban America. One identifies the special characteristics of social work practice in rural areas and illustrates that uniqueness with a case study of the Appalachian region, while the other provides an in-depth look at the etiology of homicide in general and the growing and disturbing problem of urban gang violence and its causes. And last, Man Keung Ho has prepared an insightful and informative chapter on "Social Work with Asian Americans" (Chapter 20).

Many people directly and indirectly influenced our ideas and gave support that made the preparation of this work possible. We wish to acknowledge our universities, the University of California at Los Angeles and Colorado State University, as well as our colleagues and students who have in countless ways helped by sharing ideas and offering critical reviews of these materials. Their critique has led to revisions that improved the quality and readability of the material.

Finally, our families and loved ones must be thanked for sacrificing some of our precious time together so that the activity of preparing this book could be included in our already crowded schedules. Their love, support, and encouragement provides meaning to our work and our lives.

SOCIAL WORK

Part One

The Profession
of Social Work

If the world were a perfect place, it would provide for everyone warm and safe housing, an adequate supply of nutritious food, challenging jobs, good health care, and love and caring from friends and family. It would be a world with minimal stress, crime, and suffering. All people would find their lives satisfying and fulfilling. Social work exists because the world is less than perfect. Social workers serve people and the institutions of society as they confront this imperfection.

Social work is a humanizing profession and social workers are action-oriented people. The social worker is not satisfied with this imperfect world that sends too many children to bed hungry at night, has effectively declared too many older people useless, restricts too many physically handicapped people from productive living, allows too many women and children to be physically and sexually abused, deprives too many members of minority groups of the full opportunity to share in the benefits of this affluent society, has too many sin-gle parents trying to raise children in substandard housing without enough money for proper nutrition and food, and deprives too many emotionally and intellectually impaired people of satisfying lives because they behave or learn differently from the majority in the society. In fact, when even one person is a victim of loneliness, hunger, discrimination, poor housing or clothing, domestic violence, or emotional upset, there is a need for social work.

Social work emerged during the twentieth century as an important profession in U.S. society. Its development has paralleled a seeming roller coaster of public interest in human welfare and social services. At times when the national political climate placed a high priority on human welfare, jobs were plentiful and the number of people entering social work increased dramatically. These social workers found it refreshing to be part of a profession that addressed the overall well-being of people. In a world where terrorist attacks have become commonplace and where

3

nuclear stockpiles grow annually, it is little wonder that social work, a profession concerned with the enhancement of human potential, has attracted many bright and socially concerned young people.

However, the tides of the political climate periodically yield a conservative orientation more concerned with defense than human welfare, with big business than human rights, and with cutting social programs to balance the budget rather than increasing the taxes of the wealthy. In such times the appeal of social work to many young people declined and the supply of competent social workers prepared to help people lead more satisfying lives was reduced. Paradoxically, the decline in support for human services has occurred at times when social and economic conditions dictated the greatest need for the services of social workers. When the demand for human services by needy citizens has increased within the society, social work positions have been viewed as a luxury that can be reduced when it is time for budget cutting. In effect, when there is a poorly functioning economy society increases the burden on its most vulnerable members by reducing the supports available to them.

Since it does not appear that the world will become perfect any time soon, it is reasonable to assume that large numbers of social workers will continue to be needed. Employment opportunities may decline or shift from public to private auspices and there may be variations in the number of human service programs the public is willing to support, but the need for the services the social workers can provide will still exist. Although employment cannot be assured for the new social worker, professional education programs con-

tinue to graduate fewer social workers than the U.S. Bureau of Labor Statistics projects will be needed.

Why is social work important to American society? Social workers provide important services to help people solve problems that limit their social functioning and enhance the quality of their lives. Social workers provide these services in a variety of ways.

Sometimes the social worker offers a *direct service* or helps individuals, families, or other groups on a face-to-face basis. In some situations they help people solve specific problems, while at other times social workers counsel people to solve problems or engage in activities that will enhance the quality of their lives—whether or not they experience an identifiable problem.

The services of the social worker might also be provided on behalf of individuals or groups of people. These *indirect services* help to make social institutions such as organizations, neighborhoods, communities, or even the policies of a government or laws of a country more responsive to the needs of people.

Employment opportunities are an important factor for an individual to consider when making a career choice. Yet, as a review of the development of social work will indicate, the political climate has acted like a swinging pendulum that affects the availability of social-work jobs. As it has swung from a conservative to a liberal climate and back, social work has adapted its employment patterns to these changes and has continued to provide needed services. The combination of attrition and the creation of new arenas of social work practice has always enabled the competent and professionally prepared social worker to find satisfying employment.

Providing needed human services and contributing to an improvement of the quality of life for all people is a personally rewarding experience. A social worker can make a small but important contribution to the well-being of society. When one makes a career choice, these personal rewards must be considered.

This book presents an overview of social work for the person considering this profession as a possible career choice. It does not attempt to "sell" social work but to portray it honestly, and with its strengths and limitations in clear view. Because we are interested in recruiting qualified people to our profession—a profession in which we take great pride—we hope this book will enable people to discover whether social work is for them. Social work is not easy work. It can be as emotionally draining as it is rewarding. It can be as frustrating as it can be satisfying. The prerequisite to developing the knowledge, values, and skills necessary for competent social work practice must be a basic commitment to social betterment and a willingness to invest oneself in facilitating the process of change.

Part One is devoted to the excitement, promise, and realities of social work's growth in the United States during this century. It provides a general review of the profession and stresses the commonality of purpose in this diverse field.

Wherever possible we present conceptions of social work that enjoy general acceptance in the field rather than those that reflect our exclusive biases. Although we may be accused of presenting a "consensus" view of social work, we do so because of our belief that familiarity with the field should begin in the "mainstream." Once this material is mastered, then the tributaries can be explored.

To understand the current status of social work, one must perceive the field within the context of its historical development. Particular chapters include brief historical perspectives relevant to the subject of the chapter. In addition, case materials are used to illustrate the more academic parts of the book. A concerted effort was also made to avoid jargon or technical language unfamiliar to the reader.

Chapter 1 provides a general framework for viewing the profession. It describes and defines this field so the reader may have a base on which to build a more thorough knowledge of social work. In subsequent chapters many of these points are examined more thoroughly.

Chapter 2 combines an understanding of the many helping professions with the specific place social work occupies among them. The chapter demonstrates how the motivation to establish social work as a profession has contributed both positively and negatively to the field.

Chapter 3 is especially geared to the person considering social work as a career. Using the National Association of Social Workers' classification system for identifying the several levels of social service personnel as an organizing theme, the chapter examines entry points, qualifications, expected competencies, and termination points for each level. The three chapters in Part One, then, provide an orientation to the social work profession—its purpose, its growth and development, its structure.

C H A P T E R

1

Social Work: A Comprehensive Helping Profession

The profession of social work is made up of people dedicated to helping others change some aspect of their social functioning. In simplest terms social workers help people improve their interaction with various aspects of their world—their children, parents, spouse, family, friends, co-workers, or even organizations and whole communities. Social work is a profession committed to improving the quality of life for people through various activities directed toward social change.

UNDERSTANDING THE SOCIAL WORKER

Social work is a profession that is full of contradictions. Social workers may deal with very successful people, but more often they work with the more vulnerable members of our society. They relate to problems ranging from marital conflict to juvenile delinquency and from mental illness to unsafe housing. They provide services that vary from counseling to group therapy, to fund raising, and even social action. Social work itself strives for professional status that inherently restricts the number of people who can be recognized as professional, yet is philosophically anti-elitist.

How does one understand this complex profession? Five themes serve to characterize social work and provide a foundation on which to build more in-depth understanding of this profession.

Commitment to Social Betterment

The fundamental importance of improving the quality of life, i.e., *social betterment* must be a central value in the belief system of the social worker. As a profession social work has maintained an idealism about the ability and responsibility of this society to provide opportunities and resources that allow each person to lead a full and rewarding life. It has seen its mission as being particularly concerned with the underdog—the most vulnerable people in the society. This idealism must not be confused with naïveté. Social workers are often the most knowledgeable people in the community about the plight of the poor, the abused, the lonely, and others who for a variety of reasons are out of the mainstream of society or experiencing social problems. When social workers express that perspective, it is often an uncomfortable one for people who wish to protect the "status quo." At times criticized as "bleeding heart do-gooders," social workers would contend that if this label implies that they care for and advance the cause of the less successful members of society, then they proudly wear it.

Desire to Enhance Social Functioning

A second theme that provides an understanding of social work is the focus of this profession on helping to improve *social functioning*. Social functioning is the manner in which people interact with their environments—with the people and social institutions with which they come into contact. Social workers help to facilitate change in the social functioning between people and social institutions in order to solve problems or to enhance the quality of already adequate functioning.

The social work profession emerged to help people change in relation to a rapidly changing world. Where once change was more gradual, today the world in which we live has become a dynamic and rapidly changing environment. The technology explosion, information explosion, population explosion, and even the threat of nuclear explosion dramatically impact our lives. Those people who can readily adapt to these changes—and are not limited by discrimination due to race, cultural background, gender, age, or physical, emotional, or intellectual abilities—seldom use the services of social workers. Other have become victims of this too rapidly changing world and its unstable social institutions. They require help from the social worker in dealing with this change.

An Action Orientation

Moreover, it is a profession of doers. Social workers are not handwringers who contemplate social issues in hopes that they will disappear. Rather, they take action to prevent problems from developing and to help people deal effectively with situations that cannot be changed, as well as to attack those situations that can be changed. Hubert Humphrey captured the view of many social workers when he said, "The purpose of life is action."

Social work is an applied science. While social workers draw on considerable knowledge about people and various social groups and institutions, their primary activity is not the development of this knowledge. They tend to borrow their basic knowledge from other disciplines such as cultural anthropology, economics, political science, psychology, human physiology, and sociology. Selecting carefully from the important work of these and other disciplines, social workers translate that knowledge into action, or services, that will benefit their clients and the institutions of society.

Appreciation for Human Diversity

To deal effectively with such a wide range of individual and institutional change, social work has become a profession characterized by diversity—diversity of clientele, diversity of knowledge and skills, and diversity of services provided. In addition, the social workers themselves come in all sizes, shapes, colors, ages, and descriptions.

Social workers view diversity as a strength. They consider human difference desirable and appreciate the richness that can be offered a society through the culture, language, and traditions of various racial, ethnic, and cultural groups. They value the unique perspectives of persons of different gender, sexual preference, or age groups and they recognize and develop the strengths of persons who have been disadvantaged.

What's more, social workers view their own diversity as an enriching quality that has created a dynamic profession that can respond to human needs in an ever-changing world. Indeed, social work *is* a profession of many faces!

A Versatile Practice Perspective

The wide range of human problems with which social workers deal, the variety of settings in which social workers are employed, the extensive scope of the services they provide, and the diverse populations that they serve make it unrealistic to expect that a single practice approach could adequately serve the social worker. Rather, the social worker must have a comprehensive repertoire of knowledge and techniques that can be used to meet the unique needs of individual clients or client groups. The social worker who is locked into a limited helping approach simply lacks the versatility to be of maximum effectiveness.

The versatile social worker, then, must have a solid foundation of knowledge about the behavior of people and their social institutions in order to understand adequately the situations that their clientele bring to them. They also need to understand that differing beliefs may affect the way people will understand and react to those situations. And, finally, they must have mastered a number of helping techniques they can imaginatively select and skillfully use to help individuals, families, groups, organizations, and communities improve their social functioning.

How can we characterize the social worker? As we have seen, the social worker must possess a fundamental commitment to social betterment, a basic desire to use his or her talents to enhance social functioning, the ability to translate concerns into action, an appreciation of human diversity, and the ability to be versatile in approaching practice situations.

A GLANCE AT SOME SOCIAL WORKERS IN ACTION

Examining the day-to-day work of members of a profession helps one to appreciate the manner in which the goals of that profession are operationalized. Perhaps observing some case examples of social workers as they apply their knowledge and skills will reveal a clearer picture of this profession. Consider the following social workers as they go about their work.

In twenty minutes Nadine Harrison, a social worker with the local welfare department, has an appointment with Ms. Kim Lee. Ms. Lee is terribly worried about her future and that of her two small children. Her husband was killed two months ago in a construction accident. In addition to her grief and loneliness, Ms. Lee found that, after paying funeral expenses, little money was left for raising the children. She asked Ms. Harrison for help.

Brandon Ford is a social worker employed in a psychiatric hospital. Although he works with some patients individually, this afternoon he will meet with a group of adolescent boys who expect to be released from the hospital in a few weeks. Mr. Ford will help the boys explore their feelings about leaving the hospital and their friends and will discuss problems they may face when they return to their homes.

Laura Jackson is executive director of the Council on Aging in her community. This council identifies and seeks solutions to problems experienced by older people in that community. As executive director, Ms. Jackson provides leadership to the citizen board as it considers new programs. Tonight the board will consider initiating a new program for older people: a telephone hook-up between shut-ins.

Perry Garcia is a social worker at a storefront neighborhood center in a large city. His job is to help residents rectify substandard housing conditions in the area. Tonight Mr. Garcia is helping a group from the neighborhood plan a strategy for pressuring some of the landlords to improve the quality of housing.

This afternoon Christopher Warren will testify before a committee of the state legislature that is considering the need for new laws and programs related to the state parole system. After seven years as a probation officer for a large juvenile court and now as parole officer for the district court, Mr. Warren is well-prepared to serve as an expert witness.

In each of these situations, the social worker is planning to provide some form of help that will enable a person or a group of people to make a change in their social functioning. Nadine Harrison's primary concern is for an *individual,* while Brandon Ford's responsibility is for a *group* of boys. Laura Jackson is helping an *organization* respond to the needs of older people, and Perry Garcia works to help a *neighborhood* and *community* improve the quality of housing. At the more comprehensive *state* or *national* levels, Christopher Warren is helping to improve the laws affecting people on parole. In these examples one can see that social workers are involved with a variety of *client systems,* or work with a number of different levels of clientele.

They also are employed by a variety of social agencies. They were found working in a public welfare department, a psychiatric hospital, a local council on aging, a neighborhood center, and a parole office. Clearly, social workers serve a very diverse group of people experiencing a wide range of problems.

Although social workers usually begin helping at one particular practice level, they often reflect their versatility of approach by moving to other levels in order to be of maximum help to their clients. For example:

Brandon Ford learned from the group discussion that one of the boys, Artie Chambers, was afraid to leave the hospital because he believed his father was "mad at me for acting crazy." Mr. Ford met several times with Artie and his parents to help them examine Artie's fear and understand his improved behavior since hospitalization. Also, several boys in the group talked about what a drastic change it would be to leave the hospital, where life is highly structured, and go home to a life with a great deal of freedom. Taking his cue from this discussion, Mr. Ford gained permission to plan several excursions into the community and a few weekend visits home for the boys. He also learned that three of the boys could have been released several weeks earlier if there had been supportive mental health services in the small town where their parents lived. This information led him to convene a group of interested citizens in that town for considering ways in which the community could make such services available.

The work of Brandon Ford reflects that of a generalist social worker. He views the problems presented from a perspective that is not encumbered by any single practice approach or by working at any single client level. He began with a group of clients, but soon found it necessary to deal with both a child's family as well as a community in order to reduce or eliminate the problems in social functioning that he encountered.

THE MISSION OF SOCIAL WORK: SOCIAL BETTERMENT

While social work can be characterized by its variability, it has maintained a fundamental purpose for its nearly one century of existence in the United States: directly serving people in need and, at the same time, making social institutions more responsive to all people. However, the ability to specify this fundamental purpose clearly in precise terms has been difficult as the social work profession has evolved several patterns of operation through the years. Meyer notes:

The development of social work as a profession has been a tortuous effort to develop boundaries within which an integral identity could be carved out while maintaining an open exchange with society. All enduring professions adapt to social change and pursue their interests, but they maintain the same purposes at the core. Architects design buildings, doctors deal with sickness and health, lawyers practice law, and educators teach. Social workers are concerned with _____ . With what? Fill in the blank. With people? Psychosocial functioning? Delivery of social services? Management of human service agencies? Policy analysis? Social change? Developmental services over the life span? Residual services to people with defined problems? All of these or some of these?[1]

The mission of social work can be expressed in a number of different forms. To understand this mission, it is useful to examine briefly the historical development of social work.

Influences from Practice Roots

Social work sprang from the need to institutionalize the response of U.S. society to an increasing number of people who were experiencing social problems in the late 1800s. Although some form of human service, people helping people in need, has no doubt always been present, the rapid social changes partially created by industrialization and urbanization required that these services be formalized. It was evident that many basic needs could not be met by the traditional resources of the market economy or the family.

Human services took shape within various organizations, or social agencies, that were created in response to these problems. While volunteers played an important role in the provision of services, it was soon learned that many social needs were most effectively met by paid personnel who were trained in the best methods of providing services. These emerging professionals, social workers, took their orientation from the agencies in which they were employed and only much later developed a professional identification that would transcend the scope of any one agency. Because social work began from this agency orientation, the roots of social work's mission can be found in the three dominant agencies in which social workers were first employed.

One development began in 1863 with the founding of the Massachusetts State Board of Charities. That organization, the forerunner of the present public human services agencies, was quickly imitated in other states and provided a base of operation for social work practice. The purpose of the state boards was to supervise the *care* given by the state-supported institutions responsible for the poor, the physically and mentally ill, and prisoners. The boards also collected information on all financial relief activities in the state in an effort to understand the problems and improve the quality of services.

Another development was the Charity Organization Society (COS) movement, which began in Buffalo, New York in 1877 and spread to about 125 other cities in the United States in the late nineteenth century. The COS offered a range of services aimed at *curing* individuals who experienced problems in social functioning (or perhaps, more accurately, helping people cure themselves) and, at the same time, coordinating and evaluating existing services throughout the community.

Finally, the settlement house movement emerged in urban areas, beginning in New York with the Neighborhood Guild in 1886 and in Chicago with Hull House in 1889. Settlement houses originally focused on providing services to European immigrants who were flooding into the metropolitan centers and were ill-prepared for the demands of this urban environment. Many were subjected to inhumane treatment in factories and other workplaces. The settlement house workers were actively engaged in social reform aimed at *changing* laws and conditions that created these hardships.

From these and other social agencies that developed during this time, social work established its commitment to serving the more helpless and vulnerable members of society. The means of achieving this mission—caring, curing, and changing—have continued to characterize social work practice activities to the present time. Today, however, the range of agencies in which social workers are employed is much more varied. Richan and Mendelsohn comment that:

> At first glance it is surprising to discover that the arena is so wide and varied in size and depth. Social workers are all over the society; they turn up everywhere. Some are self-employed, engaged in private practice, but the bulk of them are employed in private or public agencies. You meet social workers in schools, hospitals, welfare departments, correctional institutions, residential treatment settings, adoption agencies, community service organizations, veterans' bureaus, the military, nursing homes, and children's services. They work in courts, in prisons, in literally all types of service agencies; they are even found tucked away in private industry. Social workers populate government bureaus and civil service at every level; many are involved in social work education as well.[2]

Although the degree of emphasis on the different aspects of the social work mission varies according to the type of agency in which social workers are employed, important commitments continue to be shared by most social workers.

Social Work's Three Purposes

Social work emerged with not just one, but three, purposes that reflect its particular mission among the helping professions: caring, curing, and changing.

Caring At the heart of the social work value system is a concern for the well-being of all people. From the efforts to enhance the quality of life in prisons and poorhouses more than a century ago to the effort to humanize services in nursing homes and juvenile detention facilities today, social workers have continually sought to improve care for limited or helpless groups in the population. At times this caring role has taken a back seat to social change and treatment efforts in social work. Keeping this vital function in the conscious view of the profession is essential if social work is to perform its role adequately in society. Robert Morris has provided a clear summary of this situation:

> Social work in the United States began by filling a very basic, caring function. The need for this function has increased over time, and social work has flourished beyond the expectations of its founders. But . . . we have become attracted to new physical and psychological sciences that have led us to believe that we can prevent or cure, and this has become a central dynamic

for our professional growth, displacing the earlier caring function. But the curative powers we have embraced have proved less than adequate. We now need to consider whether our historic contribution lies in restoration of the caring function, while relegating the search for a cure for social problems to the exploratory and experimental frontier.[3]

The best knowledge we can muster is inadequate to prevent or cure the many social problems encountered by the disabled, elderly, and other persons with limited capacity for social functioning. Adequate care to make people comfortable and help them cope with limitations is, at times, the most important service a social worker can provide. In addition, there is an important leadership role for social work in helping communities create the necessary services to provide such care. This fundamental purpose continues to be a part of the mission of social work.

Curing In recent years, the dominant thrust of social work practice has been to treat people experiencing problems in social functioning. A variety of helping techniques have been developed for providing direct services to individuals, families, and groups. These range from general counseling techniques to more specialized approaches such as transactional analysis, family therapy, behavior modification, reality therapy, and gestalt therapy. In addition, a variety of lesser known approaches such as neurolinguistic programming, psychomotor therapy, existential therapy, and psychodrama are also used by some social workers.

These individually focused approaches do not necessarily cure problems in social functioning. Much depends on the ability of the social worker to use these techniques and the appropriateness of the technique for a given client and situation. In fact, most social workers would argue that at best they can only help clients cure themselves. Having the ability to make appropriate judgments, knowing how to engage clients in the helping process, and having a suitable environment for the provision of services are essential to good social-work practice. Research on the effectiveness of social-work helping activities concludes that the broad range of helping services loosely classified as social casework is effective to the degree that the interventions selected are related to the client's problems.[4]

Changing Social change has always been a part of social work. Many of the pioneer social workers were active reformers who worked to improve conditions in slums, hospitals, prisons, and poorhouses. Today social workers actively seek to impact social legislation related to social programs . . . conditions that maintain or increase racism, sexism, and poverty. They make efforts to reform, that is, to incrementally improve the existing system—to tinker with laws, procedures, and attitudes until these are more responsive to human needs.

There is an increasing amount of literature from social workers who identify their perspective as radical. These social workers conclude that the present structure of society is not capable of incorporating the changes necessary to improve significantly the quality of life for most people. Galper summarizes the radical philosophy:

> It is practice that attempts to respond fully both to social work's humanitarian concerns and to the distorted, exploitative realities of the society. Radical social work is little more than social work that has not compromised its own commitment to human welfare. It is social work that takes very seriously the dilemma of a people-serving profession in a people-denying society and tries to resolve that dilemma by finding ways for the profession to be of real service rather than by accommodating itself to conventional arrangements.[5]

Unless the United States experiences a major economic crisis in the next few years, it is doubtful that the major overhaul in social programs proposed by the radical approach will occur. Rather, the more gradual reform efforts that have characterized social work's approach to change will continue, although there are frequently calls for greater activity related to the activist/advocate role for social workers in facilitating the empowerment of the poor and other more vulnerable people. Nevertheless, the final purpose in social work's historic mission, changing the society and its institutional structures, is alive and well today.

DEFINING SOCIAL WORK: SOCIAL FUNCTIONING

Social work has been a product of an increasingly complex world that makes it difficult for people to meet their needs effectively through conventional interaction with family, friends, neighbors, and the various social institutions. As a profession that emerged in response to these changes, its public sanction evolved gradually and a clear conceptualization or professional definition was elusive.

Early Efforts to Define Social Work

The definition of social work has gone through several cycles. The early efforts to describe social work were perhaps best exemplified by Mary Richmond in her classic book, *Social Diagnosis*,[6] in 1917. Roy Lubove summarizes her contribution as follows:

> She interpreted social diagnosis as "the attempt to make as exact a definition as possible of the situation and personality of a human being in some social need—of his situation and personality, that is, in relation to the other human beings upon whom he in any way depends or who depend upon him, and in relation to the social institutions of his community." The social worker's unique skill—in contrast to the physician, minister, lawyer, teacher, friend, neighbor, or ordinary layman—involved her ability to base treatment upon the expert collection and interpretation of social evidence.[7]

While Mary Richmond's work began to tease out some unique features of the practice of social work, at least in relation to individuals and families, it was far from a suitable definition. Social workers, or those who wanted to identify themselves with this emerging profession, tended to identify themselves by level of practice and setting. Thus, the social worker might characterize himself or herself as a psychiatric caseworker, a hospital group worker, or a community organizer. Not only did a certain amount of elitism develop around these entities, but they also distracted social workers from recognizing the common elements in these various forms of practice.

To address this problem, the American Association of Social Workers convened a meeting of agency executives in Milford, Pennsylvania in 1923, in order to define "social casework" (i.e., practice with individuals, couples, and families). Because these representatives of a range of settings were not immediately successful in their effort, four subsequent meetings of the "Milford Conference" were held and each successive year the commonalities hidden among differing expressions of social work became clearer. Still, the committee was unable to conceptualize social work in a manner that would provide a satisfactory umbrella for social work practice.[8]

The 1950s brought another surge of interest in developing a clear conceptualization of social work. A merger of several specialized social work practice organizations (e.g., American Association of Hospital Social Workers, American Association of Visiting Teachers, American Association of Psychiatric Social Workers and the more generic American Association of Social Workers) into the National Association of Social Workers (NASW) was completed in 1955. A spirit of unity dominated the social work profession, and the effort to find a definition of social work that would reflect the commonality in the diverse practice activities began in earnest. A critical step was the publication of the "Working Definition of Social Work Practice" in 1958. Although not actually providing a definition of social work, the efforts of this committee yielded an important basis for subsequent definitions by identifying fundamental areas of commonality in the purpose of all social work practice:

1. To assist individuals and groups to identify and resolve or minimize problems arising out of disequilibrium between themselves and their environment.

2. To identify potential areas of disequilibrium between individuals or groups and the environment in order to prevent the occurrence of disequilibrium.

3. In addition to these curative and preventive aims, to seek out, identify, and strengthen the maximum potential in individuals, groups, and communities.[9]

Current Definitions of Social Work

In the 1970s and early 1980s NASW published three special editions of *Social Work* that presented substantial debate and discussion, but not conclusions, about the nature of social work.[10] While this activity yielded fruitful discussion and enhanced understanding of the central features that characterize social work, the profession has not yet generated a definition of social work that has either general acceptance or official sanction. Thus, a definition of social work adopted by the NASW Board of Directors in 1970 represents the latest official definition of this profession.[11] The definition (Box 1–1) contains three sentences that provide a useful overview of social work.

> *A General Definition of Social Work:* Social work is the professional activity of helping individuals, groups, or communities enhance or restore their capacity for social functioning and creating societal conditions favorable to that goal.

This sentence provides a concise description of social work appropriate for use in giving a one-sentence "dictionary" definition of the profession. At this level of abstraction, general boundaries are drawn around social work. It is *professional activity* that requires a particular body of knowledge, values, and skills, as well as a discrete purpose, to guide the practice of the social worker.

  BOX 1–1   NASW DEFINITION OF SOCIAL WORK

Social Work Is

the professional activity

of helping individuals, groups, or communities enhance or restore their capacity for social functioning and

creating societal conditions favorable to that goal.

Social Work Practice Consists of

the professional application of social-work values, principles, and techniques to one or more of the following ends:

helping people obtain tangible services;

counseling and psychotherapy with individuals, families and groups;

helping communities or groups provide or improve social and health services; and

participating in relevant legislative processes.

The Practice of Social Work Requires Knowledge

of human development and behavior;

of social, economic, and cultural institutions; and

of the interaction of all of these factors.

Community sanction to provide this professional activity is assumed to be present and social work is, in turn, expected to be accountable to the public for the quality of services provided.

The remainder of the sentence captures the uniqueness of social work. It makes it clear that social workers serve a range of client systems that include individuals, families or other household units, groups, organizations, neighborhoods, communities, and even larger units of society. However, the unique preparation and competence of the social worker is directed toward helping those systems interact more effectively with persons or social institutions that have an impact on them. The term *social functioning* captures the social worker's effort to help people, whether individuals or collectives, change their functioning to create more satisfactory forms of social interaction. William Gordon describes this viewpoint more precisely:

> The central social work focus is placed at the interface between or the meeting place of person and environment—at the point where there is or is not matching with all its good and bad consequences for the person and environment. The phenomenon of concern at this interface is the "transaction" between person and environment. Transaction is "exchange in the context of action or activity." This action or activity is a blend of person-activity and impinging environment-activity.[12]

Social functioning is a helpful concept because it takes into consideration both the developmental characteristics of the person and the forces from the environment. It suggests that a person brings to the situation a set of behaviors, needs, and beliefs that are the result of his or her unique experiences from birth. Yet it also recognizes that whatever is brought to the situation must be related to the world as that person confronts it. It is in the transactions between the person and the parts of that person's world that the quality of life can be enhanced or damaged.

Herein lies the uniqueness of social work. The social worker is prepared to work with both the person and the relevant environment to improve the quality of their interaction. In contrast, the physician is primarily prepared to treat physical aspects of the individual, and the attorney is largely concerned with the operation of the legal system in the larger environment (although both the physician and the attorney must give secondary attention to other, related systems). The social worker, however, gives secondary attention to the individual and environment separately, and directs primary attention to the manner in which they relate to each other. In other words, the social worker is primarily engaged in facilitating transactions between the person and the environment. Figure 1–1 depicts this unique focus of social work and will be developed more fully in later chapters to illustrate the dimensions of social work in more detail. It should be noted that this figure overstates the sharpness of the focus of social work to highlight the point that social-work intervention involves both person and environment. Figure 10–1 portrays this perception of social work in greater detail by identifying

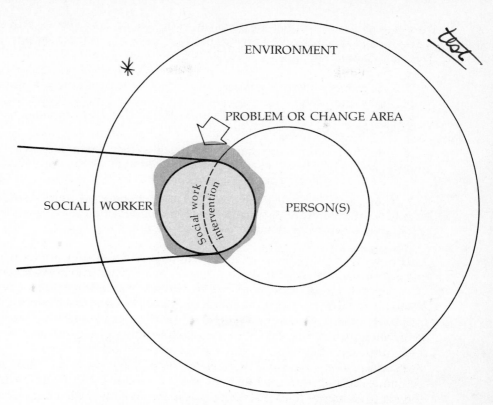

Figure 1–1 *Focal point of social work intervention*

the specific person(s), social worker, problem or change activity, and relevant environmental forces as they pertain to a case example.

> *A Description of Social Work Practice:* Social work practice consists of the professional application of social work values, principles, and techniques to one or more of the following ends: helping people obtain tangible services; counseling and psychotherapy with individuals, families and groups; helping communities or groups provide or improve social and health services; and participating in legislative processes.

This part of the NASW definition directs attention to what social workers do. However, doing must be preceded by a purpose. The *purpose of social work* is neatly summarized in a "Working Statement" on the purpose and objectives of social work.

> The purpose of social work is to promote or restore a mutually beneficial interaction between individuals and society in order to improve the quality of life for everyone.[13]

That statement implies that the purpose is dependent on the beliefs that social workers hold about the relationship between people and their environment. The statement summarizes those beliefs as follows:

> The environment (social, physical, organizational) should provide the opportunity and resources for the maximum realization of the potential and aspirations of all individuals, and should provide for their common human needs and for the alleviation of distress and suffering.
>
> Individuals should contribute as effectively as they can to their own well-being and to the social welfare of others in their immediate environment as well as to the collective society.
>
> Transactions between individuals and others in their environment should enhance the dignity, individuality, and self-determination of everyone. People should be treated humanely and with justice.[14]

The payoff for the clients of social workers, whether they are individuals, groups, or various social institutions, is in the services provided. These services might take the form of providing access to *social provisions* or tangible items such as food, housing, clothing, or financial assistance. They might also include *social services* or more intangible forms of helping, such as using counseling or group process skills to help people solve problems or to improve their functioning relative to their interactions with other people or with various social institutions. Finally, social workers engage in the use of *social action* techniques to improve the functioning of community groups and organizations or to influence the legislative process to make the laws more responsive to human needs.

> *Knowledge Requirements for the Social Worker:* The practice of social work requires knowledge of human development and behavior; of social, economic, and cultural institutions; and of the interaction of all of these factors.

The NASW definition of social work concludes with a recognition that social work practice must also be guided by knowledge. The social worker is obligated to provide the best service possible. To improve the success rate with clients over one's natural helping abilities, it is necessary to draw on the best knowledge of human behavior and of the larger society. First, the social worker must gain both general knowledge about aspects of the human condition and specific technical knowledge required for social work. This can be gained through completing one of the baccalaureate and/or master's level educational programs accredited by the Council on Social Work Education (CSWE). The knowledge one would expect to acquire in these programs includes a liberal arts perspective as well as a professional foundation that includes the basic knowledge, values, and skills required for competent social work practice.[15] Second, the social worker must be dedicated to a lifetime of study as a skillful reader of the professional literature and as a student in staff development, continuing education, or advanced degree programs.

SOCIAL WORK PRACTICE APPROACHES: VERSATILE AND ACTION-ORIENTED

Social work also has had difficulty in arriving at a practice approach that was sufficiently flexible and encompassing to relate to this complex profession. In fact, social work can be characterized during much of its history as a profession in search of a practice approach. That search included the development of several distinct practice methods, i.e., casework, group work, community organization, administration, and research, as well as the more recent emergence of a generalist perspective and the development of a number of specialized practice approaches.

The Traditional Practice Methods

As part of its drive to become identified as a unique profession, social work sought to identify a distinctive method of practice that would distinguish it from the other helping professions such as law, medicine, and psychology. The first practice method to develop, *social casework*, had its roots in the Charity Organization Society movement and was expressed in the first significant publication on social work practice, *Social Diagnosis*.[16] In this book Mary Richmond focused on the requirements for effective practice with individuals and families, regardless of the type of problem presented, and filled an important void in social work by introducing a practice literature. The principles of social casework identified by Richmond were enthusiastically adopted by social workers and the profession moved to an almost exclusive focus on individuals and families. The popularity of Freudian psychology in the 1920s and 1930s, coupled with conservative opposition to more aggressive social change strategies, directed social work toward less controversial individual approaches. Edith Abbott noted that Richmond later had expressed concern over the exclusive nature of this trend and had stated that social workers should simultaneously be concerned with preventing problems.

> The good social worker, says Miss Richmond, doesn't go on helping people out of a ditch. Pretty soon she begins to find out what ought to be done to get rid of the ditch.[17]

Social workers concerned with providing services to groups took longer to develop a set of guiding principles, partially because those social workers involved in the Settlement House Movement disagreed as to whether they should identify professionally with the emerging fields of social work, recreation, or continuing education. This disagreement among the *social group workers* was resolved in the 1930s in favor of identifying with social work and thus a second distinct method evolved.

The third practice method to develop was *community organization*. The Charity Organization Societies provided a coordinative and evaluative function among the emerging agencies in most communities, a function that was later moved to more autonomous councils of social agencies and is now frequently a United Way function. This form of practice was concerned with the distribution of financial resources and services within communities. Specific practice approaches that emerged within these organizations gradually were identified with social work.

In addition to using one of these three primary practice methods in their work, many social workers also found themselves responsible for administering social agencies and conducting research on the effectiveness of social work practice. Their experience and education usually left them with little preparation for these indirect service activities. By the late 1940s *administration* and *research* had evolved as practice methods in social work. Viewed as secondary methods, they were seen as a supplement to one's ability as a caseworker, group worker, or community organizer.

The Multi-Method Practice Approach

Concurrent with the development of these five distinct practice approaches was the growing commitment to the identification of social work as one profession with a unifying practice method. A major study of social work and social work education, the Hollis–Taylor Report, was concluded in 1951. It recommended that because the breadth of social work practice required social workers to intervene in more than one level of client system, social work education should prepare students with a beginning level of competence in each of the five practice methods.[18]

The multi-method practice approach proved a better fit with the varied demands for social work practice, but failed to yield the unifying practice theme the profession needed. Practitioners continued to identify with a dominant method and use the others sparingly. Elitism within the profession based on practice method and setting interfered with the search for commonality and unity within social work.

The Generalist Practice Approach

Supported by concepts drawn from social systems theory, the generalist approach to practice began to emerge in the late 1960s. As Balinsky has stated, "The complexity of human problems necessitates a broadly oriented practitioner with a versatile repertoire of methods and skills capable of interacting in any one of a number of systems."[19] The generalist model provided that versatility and met the requirement for a flexible approach to social work practice demanded by the increasing complexity and interrelatedness of human problems.

Generalist practice contains two components. First, it provides a perspective from which the social worker views the practice situation. Social system theory helps the social worker to maintain a focus on the interaction between systems—i.e., the person-environment transactions. Second, rather than attempting to make the client's situation fit the methodological orientation of the social worker, the situation is viewed as determining the practice approach to be used by the social worker. Thus, the social worker is required to have a broad knowledge and skill base from which to serve clients or client systems, and to have the ability to appropriately select from that base to meet the needs of the clients.[20]

The Specialist Practice Approach

Along with the emergence of the generalist approach has come the development of a number of specialized practice approaches. Typically these specializations are built on the assumption that the social worker has mastered the generalist elements of practice and can then add depth in a single dimension of practice.

While education for generalist practice usually is offered in baccalaureate social work programs or the early part of master's level programs, specialist education has increasingly been designated as the prerogative of the latter part of a master's degree. The Curriculum Policy Statement of the Council on Social Work Education that guides the accreditation of these programs identifies the following specializations that schools might offer:

Fields of Practice: Services to families, children, and youth; services to the elderly; health; mental health; developmental disabilities; education; business and industry; neighborhood and community development; the justice system; and income maintenance and employment.

Population Groups: Children, youth, adults, middle-aged adults, the aged, women, men, families, ethnic populations, groups defined by income levels, migrants.

Problem Areas: Crime and delinquency, substance abuse, developmental disabilities, illness, family violence, neighborhood deterioration, poverty, racism, sexism.

Practice Roles and Interventive Modes: Practice with individuals, families and groups, consultation, training, community organization, social planning, program planning and development, administration, policy formulation, implementation and analysis, and research.[21]

In addition, schools might offer an opportunity for students to concentrate in "advanced generalist" practice where the student adds both more detailed information about the practice competencies learned in the generalist model and greater breadth of knowledge, values, and skills required for practice.

Today, like many disciplines, social work embraces both generalist and specialist approaches to practice. The generalist viewpoint supports the commonality that unites social work into one profession; the specialist approach helps to delineate unique areas for in-depth social work practice. In tracing the history of this generalist-specialist issue, Leighninger notes that "debates of optimum levels of breadth and depth in social work education and practice, and the relationship between these, recur in each decade."[22] At this point social work appears to have achieved a reasonably comfortable position regarding the balance of generalist versus specialized practice.

THE SOCIAL WORKERS: THEIR MANY FACES

It is possible to understand the diversity of social workers better by knowing their competencies, their career patterns, and their personal characteristics. The colleagues with whom one works and the trends in one's profession are important considerations when one is making a career choice.

The Competencies of Social Workers

We have seen that to practice social work effectively, one must be able to provide a variety of helping services. The social worker not only must be able to work directly with a client or clients, but also must be prepared to understand and work to change the environment of these clients. One must understand the culture in which the practice occurs, the cultural background of the people served, and the functioning of the social agency where the services are provided as well as know what other services are available in the community, the reasons the clients have sought services, and alternative means by which to provide these services. In short, the social worker must be competent in knowledge, values, and skills to help clients resolve a broad range of existing or potential problems in social functioning.

What are the basic competencies that are fundamental to social work practice? Depending on the particular job a social worker occupies, the type of agency, client capabilities, problems being addressed, and resources available, the social worker will need to have differing competencies. With a generalist perspective and a repertoire of helping techniques,[23] the social worker is prepared to begin most social work jobs. As one becomes experienced and jobs become more specialized, additional skills may be required.

As social work gradually reached greater consensus regarding how it should be defined, it has become possible to be more precise about the competencies required to fulfill that role. Throughout social work's recent history several efforts have been made to identify the critical tasks performed by social workers.[24] The primary limitation of these approaches was their reliance on experts to describe what social workers do in their daily practice. Too often these descriptions were more assertions about what social workers should be doing than factual statements of what tasks social workers actually perform. In the early 1980s NASW conducted a project designed to address its concern that many human service agencies were reducing the professional education requirements for many social work jobs and, therefore, reclassifying them to lower level positions (see Chapter 3). In an effort to establish a method to determine if there is a valid relationship between the content of professional education programs and social work practice activities, the NASW Classification Validation Project constructed a "job analysis" approach for studying social work practice that yields important empirical data about the activities of social work practitioners.[25]

The "job analysis" strategy invites frontline social workers to rate a series of approximately 135 different tasks typically performed by social workers according to their importance in their work and a profile of their work activity is obtained through analysis of these answers. Through the statistical technique of cluster analysis it is possible to reduce the many tasks into a few groupings of activity performed by social workers with the specific tasks that are correlated with each cluster serving as the basis for its definition. This self-reported analysis of the work of social workers yields perhaps the best description available of the type of activities in which social workers actually engage.

Several studies have been completed in which the "job analysis" methodology has been used.[26] The most recent study, reported in 1987, using this methodology yielded the following sixteen clusters of practice activity of social workers from both governmental and voluntary social agencies.

1. *Formal Intervention with Individual Clients.* Use specific assessment or intervention techniques to provide support, improve client functioning, or bring about changes in the presenting needs of individual clients and their immediate support groups.

2. *Ongoing Case Management for Specific Clients.* Organize work and make arrangements for carrying out an ongoing plan of services for a specific client. . . . Activities include dictating and recording actions, reviewing files prior to client contact, carrying out procedures to protect client rights, and establishing a working relationship with clients.

3. *Teaching of Adaptive and Daily Living Skills.* Give informal instruction to help clients, volunteers, and agency personnel acquire adaptive skills for daily living. These areas include hygiene, basic communications, money management, orientation to new living arrangements and communities, and insight into human development processes.

4. *Linking Clients to Resources.* On behalf of clients, engage in interactions with agency personnel, natural helpers, and potential employers in order to connect clients with resources. These linkages involve using established connections. They include making contacts with professionals for purposes of team building and networking as well as putting clients with similar backgrounds and problems in contact with one another.

5. *Resource Assessment and Aggressive Client Brokering.* Identify service providers, services, and resources and assess their suitability for use by clients. Aggressively solve delivery problems and mediate on behalf of specific clients to insure eligibility and protect their rights.

6. *Initiation and Adjustment of Service Plan.* Carry out activities, for individual or multiple clients, to develop a service plan (at intake) or change it at strategic points in the episode of service. Activities include arranging for resources inside or outside the agency, assessing the need for changes, and evaluating progress.

7. *Assessment of the Need for Protective Services.* Observe children and adults and assess the hazards associated with their living conditions or placement settings in order to determine whether various types of abuse or neglect (psychological, sexual, or physical) have occurred or are likely to occur.

8. *Arrangement of Specific Services for Clients.* Make referrals and engage clients and family members in making various types of linkages (e.g., transportation, medical care, appointments). Conduct case follow-ups and prepare individuals and families for changes in living arrangements.

9. *Formal Intervention with Groups.* Use formal interventive techniques with groups in order to teach skills in group participation to group members or to improve social functioning by taking part in the group process.

10. *Self Development/Information Transmission.* Engage in activities designed to develop self-awareness with regard to one's knowledge, skills, and values as such self-awareness relates to improvement in job functioning. Keep current by reading various materials, attending workshops, and exchanging various types of information.

11. *Quality Assurance Monitoring.* Communicate organizational performance expectations in order to insure compliance with organizational standards. Activities include reviewing agency records, conducting job performance evaluations of workers, carrying out orientation and training, and holding performance review conferences with workers.

12. *Staff Management.* Clarify job duties and agency rules, establish work schedules, and assign cases and other responsibilities to staff members.

13. *Internal Paper Flow.* Fill out and/or sign vouchers, requisitions, or standard data collection forms to purchase materials, pay vendors, or provide data for agency records.

14. *Ongoing Program/Unit Administration.* Perform tasks associated with day-to-day operation of a program or administrative unit. Activities include budgeting, monitoring, and documentation of expenditures, keeping track of supplies and inventory, monitoring the status of buildings and equipment, and summarizing information about staff.

15. *Management of Organizational Change/External Relations.* Propose and negotiate plans for implementing program and other organizational changes. Internal activities include recruiting and screening program personnel and conducting staff meetings. External activities involve serving as a buffer to protect staff from external pressures, negotiating with consumers, and interpreting programs to the community in order to maintain their viability.

16. *Program Planning/Design/Evaluation.* Assess the need for new services, establish program goals, design programs, plan service delivery mechanisms, secure support and resources, prepare staff, and evaluate program differences.[27]

Analysis of rankings of the importance of each of these sixteen clusters of practice tasks indicated that persons engaged in direct service jobs were most likely to engage in the activities described in clusters 1–9 while those in supervisory or administrative jobs were likely to find clusters 11–16 most important in their work. All workers were somewhat evenly involved in cluster 10, Self Development/Information Transmission.[28] It is evident from these data that social workers have varied jobs that require competence to perform many tasks. It takes rigorous professional education to master the necessary competencies to enter social work practice prepared to provide the services required by persons in need.

The professional social worker, then, differs from the *natural helper*.[29] Before reaching a social worker or other professional helpers, clients often have asked for or have been given help by family, friends, neighbors, or volunteers. When that help is successful, people usually do not seek out professional help. Natural helping is an important resource for problem solving. It is based on a mutual relationship among equals and the natural helper draws heavily on intuition and life experience to guide the process. Professional help is different. It is a disciplined approach focused entirely on the needs of the client that requires the helper consciously to apply specific knowledge, values, and skills in the helping process. Both natural and professional helping are valid means of helping people resolve problems in social functioning. In fact, at times the social worker will help activate natural helping systems in order to supplement professional help and maintain support for clients after the services of the social worker have been terminated, but they are not a substitute for competent professional help in addressing serious problems or gaining access to needed services.

Career Patterns of Social Workers

Varying social work career patterns have evolved as demands for social workers have changed over time. The early social workers were volunteers or paid staff who required no specific training or educational program to qualify for the work. When formal educational programs were instituted at the turn of the century, they were training programs located in the larger social agencies. In fact, it was not until 1939 that standards required that all recognized social work education must be offered in institutions of higher education. There was also controversy over whether appropriate social work education could be offered at the baccalaureate level as well as at the more professionally acceptable master's level. The reorganization, or perhaps more accurately organization, of social work into a single professional association (the National Association of Social Workers) and one professional education association (the Council on Social Work Education) in the 1950s yielded a single-level profession. At that time, only the master's degree from an accredited school of social work was considered "legitimate" social work preparation. In 1961 the NASW established another level of professional recognition by creating the Academy of Certified Social Workers (ACSW). It was the first step in creating a multilevel career pattern.

Although today the MSW is considered the terminal practice degree in social work, an increasing number of social workers are also completing doctoral degrees in social work (DSW or Ph.D.). The number of persons completing the doctorate at a school of social work in the United States increased from 33 in 1965 to 155 in 1975, and stood at 181 in 1985.[30] Most doctoral level social workers are employed in teaching or research positions, but an increasing number of doctoral programs aimed at preparing people for direct social work practice are emerging.

It was not until 1970 that the NASW recognized baccalaureate level social workers as members of the Association when they had completed a social work major approved by the Council on Social Work Education. By 1985 there were a reported 23,533 social work majors in 351 accredited programs in the United States.[31] Another career level had evolved.

In 1981 the NASW published a classification system that helps to clarify the various entry points to social work and defines the educational and practice requirements at each level. This system helps to sort out the somewhat mixed practice levels that have evolved in social work over the past thirty years.

Basic Professional	Requires a baccalaureate degree from a social work program accredited by the Council on Social Work Education (CSWE)
Specialized Professional	Requires a master's degree from a social work program accredited by CSWE
Independent Professional	Requires an accredited MSW and at least two years of post-master's experience under appropriate professional supervision
Advanced Professional	Requires special theoretical, practice, administrative, or policy proficiency or ability to conduct advanced research or studies in social welfare, usually demonstrated through a doctoral degree in social work or a closely related social science discipline.[32]

This classification scheme has several benefits. First, it identifies and clarifies the practice levels existing in social work, and it distinguishes the competencies that both clients and employers can expect (see Chapter 3 for a more complete specification of the competencies). Second, it describes a continuum of social work education with several entry points for the person wishing to make a career in social work. Finally, it suggests a basis for job classification that can increasingly distinguish among the various levels of social work competence in task and salary.

Characteristics of Today's Social Workers

In 1982 the National Association of Social Workers conducted an extensive survey of its members. The 1982 study, repeating a 1972 membership survey,

TABLE 1–1 Characteristics of Social Workers: Comparison of 1972 and 1982 NASW Membership Surveys[33]

MEMBER CHARACTERISTIC	1972	1982
Gender		
Female	59.4%	73.0%
Male	40.6	27.0
Minority Group Member	10.0	11.4
Age		
30 years and under	No Data	21.3
31 through 50 years	No Data	55.7
51 years and over	No Data	22.7
Unemployed	No Data	8.3
Annual Salary		
Under $17,500	No Data	30.5
$17,500 to $24,999	No Data	36.8
$25,000 and over	No Data	32.5
Auspice of Primary Employment		
Public Agency	56.0	45.7
Private Agency	40.7	42.4
Private (for profit) practice	3.3	12.0
Primary Practice Function		
Consultation	No Data	1.9
Direct Service	No Data	63.7
Education/Training	No Data	5.6
Management/Administration	No Data	19.9
Planning	No Data	0.7
Policy Development/Analysis	No Data	0.4
Research	No Data	0.6
Supervision	No Data	7.2
Primary Practice Setting		
Children and Youth	11.8	15.5
Community Organizing	3.1	1.8
Family Services	10.8	11.2
Criminal Justice	2.4	1.7
Group Services	No Data	0.4
Medical or Health Care	16.5	18.1
Mental Health	16.3	26.6
Mental Retardation	1.7	13.3
Occupational	0.1	0.4
Public Assistance	8.2	1.0
School Social Work	6.7	3.4
Services to Aged	2.1	4.5
Substance Abuse	0.6	2.9
Other	10.0	9.3

drew 57,000 responses and represents the most comprehensive survey of social workers and their work conducted to date. Some striking changes appear between the two studies that are summarized in Table 1–1 on page 29.

The data in Table 1–1 provide an informative profile of the people who have selected social work as a career, their employment patterns, and their practice activities. Several trends are of note. First, there has been a substantial increase in the percentage of female social workers. Statistics regarding enrollment in both baccalaureate and master's level programs in social work reflect the same pattern and suggest the percentage of women in social work will continue to increase at least through the remainder of the 1980s.[34]

Second, although the number of minority group members in social work increased during the decade between the 1972 and 1982 membership surveys, it is doubtful that this trend will continue because of the reduction of federal support for higher education and the substantially reduced availability of financial assistance for social work students. This has already impacted enrollments in master's level programs and eventually will affect the make-up of the social work profession. During the five-year period from 1981 to 1985, for example, the percentage of minority students in MSW programs declined from 17.3 percent to 15.6 percent.[35]

Third, the membership survey was conducted in 1982 and, therefore, does not reflect current salary levels for social workers. However, salary data from 26,338 social workers who initiated or renewed their NASW memberships between July 1986 and June 1987 updates this information revealing a mean annual salary of $27,800.[36] Recognizing that the NASW membership includes relatively few baccalaureate level graduates, the data most accurately reflect the salary levels of MSW social workers. The data do indicate that the baccalaureate level social workers reporting their salaries earned 21 percent less than the average for the MSWs, while those with the DSW or Ph.D. degree earned 28 percent more than those with the MSW degree.

These salary data reflect regional differences. Social workers in the West earned an average salary of $29,700 compared to $28,300 in the Northeast, $27,000 in the Midwest and South Central regions, and $26,100 in the Southeast. One's salary is also related to his or her primary function in social work practice. Social workers involved primarily in indirect service activities had the highest salaries. Specifically, managers and administrators averaged $35,200, policy developers and analysts $33,600, persons involved in education and training earned an average of $32,300 annually, while those in planning, research, and supervisory positions averaged $29,000. The direct service workers, on the other hand, averaged $25,300. As suggested by Julia Rauch in Chapter 12, "Gender as a Factor in Practice," these positions are also associated with gender. The contention that women are less likely to hold the higher paying indirect service positions is confirmed by a salary differential of 30.5 percent reflected in this study.[37]

Finally, this study also revealed a clear salary differential based on the practice setting where a social worker is employed. The following data reflect those differences:[38]

Practice Setting	Average Salary	Percent of Respondents
Colleges and Universities	$32,300	4.5%
Private Practice (Self-employed)	31,100	11.1
Courts/Criminal Justice	30,000	1.5
Private Practice (Partnership)	29,900	4.2
Elementary/Secondary Schools	28,700	5.4
Institution (Nonhospital)	28,000	3.1
Hospital	27,900	20.9
Social Service Agency	26,800	24.9
Outpatient Facility	25,800	17.7
Group Home/Residential	22,500	1.9
Nursing Home/Hospice	21,800	2.0
Other	xxx	3.0

Fourth, the NASW membership survey indicates there was a dramatic shift from public agency employment to private practice between 1972 and 1982. It would appear that the conservative approach to human services of the Reagan Administration has reduced the number of positions held by social workers in public agencies, but that they have maintained employment through adopting a more entrepreneurial approach to practice. Where private agency employment stayed approximately the same, employment in public agencies declined by more than 10 percent and the number of social workers engaged primarily in private practice increased almost that same amount.

Finally, these data reflect substantial shifts in the employment patterns of social workers during this ten-year interval. Observing the changes of percentages of social workers employed in different practice settings in Table 1–1, shows there have been decreased employment in practice settings that involve community organizing, criminal justice, public assistance, and school social work. Social workers, instead, shifted their employment pattern toward providing services related to mental health, mental retardation, services to the aged, and substance abuse.

What are the employment prospects for social workers in the future? It is especially difficult to project future social work employment patterns because social workers are usually lumped with other human service providers when the U.S. Bureau of Labor Statistics makes its labor force projections. In addition, due to the fact that social work practice is intertwined with the larger society and subject to political and economic swings, projections require assumptions that may not hold up well in relation to short-term trends. Over the long term, however, social work employment has been rather steady, constituting .004 percent of the civilian labor force.[39]

Recognizing the inherent limitations in making projections of future social work employment, one can construct a general picture of the future. The U.S. Bureau of Labor Statistics projects a 22 percent growth rate for social work between 1985 and 1995. That projection places social work as an occupation that is expected to grow "faster than average" for all occupations during that period.[40] In 1986 335,000 positions were classified as social work jobs and an estimated 49.3 percent were filled by people with professional social work education. The Bureau of Labor Statistics data suggest that there will be an increase of 7,370 social work positions each year and that attrition will amount to 16.3 percent or roughly 54,605 annual replacements. If we project that the ratio of the professionally-educated to other persons classified as social workers does not change, the social work education programs will need to graduate a minimum of 30,500 persons per year (7,370 + 54,605 replacements × .493) to meet the demand. In 1985 there were 6,347 baccalaureate graduates, 8,790 MSW graduates, and 181 doctoral level graduates for a total of 15,326 new professionally-prepared social workers ready to enter the employment market in the United States.[41] Thus, it is reasonable to conclude that social work education is producing only about one-half the anticipated supply of professional social workers that will be needed for the next decade. Although jobs may not be plentiful for social workers in a particular year, geographic location, or type of employment, the long-range projections for those with professional social work education are encouraging.

CONCLUDING COMMENT

Since its inception almost a century ago, social work has emerged as a comprehensive helping profession. From the beginning social workers have sought that elusive common denominator that would make a clear conception of this diverse discipline possible. It is quite possible that social work might have developed into several different disciplines, but the common task of helping people negotiate a more satisfying and productive existence with the world around them served to make the profession a cohesive entity.

The basic mission of social work has been to provide a combination of caring, curing, and changing activities in order to help people improve their social functioning—that is, to help people and their social environment change to enhance the quality of life for all. In addition to helping people deal with their environments, social workers are also charged to bring about social change in order to prevent problems or make social institutions more responsive to the needs of individuals.

To accomplish these goals, social workers are employed in settings that provide services ranging from child welfare to mental health to corrections work. An increasing number are employed in private practice where they contract directly with clients to provide services. Some are generalist in their practice perspective, while others are specialists and provide in-depth services related to particular helping activities.

The social workers themselves are prepared with the knowledge, values, and skills, or the competencies, to respond to a great variety of human problems. They are professionally educated at both the baccalaureate and master's levels of education and have evolved a career pattern that prepares them to provide this broad range of human services. Despite the conservative political/economic climate in the 1980s, employment projections for the next decade continue to be above the capacity of the professional social work programs to produce. The future for the person choosing a career in social work looks quite positive.

SUGGESTED READINGS

Bartlett, Harriet M. "Toward Clarification and Improvement of Social Work Practice." *Social Work* 3 (April 1958): 3–9.

Billups, James O. "Unifying Social Work: Importance of Center-Moving Ideas." *Social Work* 29 (March–April 1984): 173–180.

Gordon, William E. "A Critique of the Working Definition." *Social Work* 7 (October 1962): 3–13.

Gordon, William E. "Social Work Revolution or Evolution?" *Social Work* 28 (May–June 1983): 181–185.

Leiby, James. "Moral Foundations for Social Welfare and Social Work: A Historical View." *Social Work* 30 (July–August 1985): 323–330.

Meyer, Carol H. "Social Work Purpose: Status by Choice or Coercion?" *Social Work* 26 (January 1981): 69–75.

Minahan, Anne N. "Purpose and Objectives of Social Work Revisited." *Social Work* 26 (January 1981): 6.

Morales, Armando. "Beyond Traditional Conceptual Frameworks." *Social Work* 22 (September 1977): 387–393.

National Association of Social Workers. *Social Work* 19 (September 1974), 22 (September 1977), and 26 (January 1981). Three issues devoted to conceptual frameworks for the profession.

Rosenfeld, Jona M. "The Domain and Expertise of Social Work: A Conceptualization." *Social Work* 28 (May–June 1983): 186–191.

Weick, Ann. "Reframing the Person-in-Environment Perspective." *Social Work* 26 (March 1981): 140–143.

ENDNOTES

1. Carol H. Meyer, "Social Work Purpose: Status by Choice or Coercion?" *Social Work* 26 (January 1981): 71–72.

2. Willard C. Richan and Allan R. Mendelsohn, *Social Work: The Unloved Profession* (New York: New Viewpoints, 1973): p. 20.

3. Robert Morris, "Social Work Function in a Caring Society: Abstract Value, Professional Preference, and the Real World," *Journal of Education for Social Work* 14 (Spring 1978): 83.

4. Katherine M. Wood, "Casework Effectiveness: A New Look at Research Evidence," *Social Work* 23 (November 1978): 437–458 and Ray J. Thomlison, "Something Works: Evidence from Practice Effectiveness Studies," *Social Work* 29 (January–February 1984): 51–56.

5. Jeffry H. Galper, *The Politics of Social Service* (Englewood Cliffs, N.J.: Prentice-Hall, 1975), p. 189.

6. Mary E. Richmond, *Social Diagnosis* (New York: Russell Sage Foundation, 1917).
7. Roy Lubove, *The Professional Altruist* (Cambridge, Mass.: Harvard University Press, 1965), p. 47.
8. American Association of Social Workers, *Social Casework: Generic and Specific* (Washington, D.C.: National Association of Social Workers, 1929), p. 11.
9. Copyright 1958, National Association of Social Workers, Inc. Reprinted with permission from Harriet M. Bartlett, "Towards Clarification and Improvement of Social Work Practice," *Social Work* 3 (April 1958): 5–7.
10. See *Social Work* 19 (September 1974); *Social Work* 22 (September 1977); and *Social Work* 26 (January 1981).
11. National Association of Social Workers, *Standards for Social Service Manpower* (Washington, D.C., 1973), pp. 4–5.
12. William E. Gordon, "Basic Constructs for an Integrative and Generative Conception of Social Work," in Gordon Hearn, ed., *The General Systems Approach: Contributions Toward an Holistic Conception of Social Work,* (New York: Council on Social Work Education, 1969), p. 7.
13. Anne N. Minahan, "Purpose and Objectives of Social Work Revisited," *Social Work* 26 (January 1981): 6.
14. Ibid.
15. Council on Social Work Education, *Handbook of Accreditation Standards and Procedures,* rev. ed., (New York: Council on Social Work Education, 1984): Appendix 1.
16. Richmond, *Social Diagnosis.*
17. Edith Abbott, "The Social Caseworker and the Enforcement of Industrial Legislation," in *Proceedings of the National Conference on Social Work, 1918* (Chicago: Rogers and Hall, 1919), p. 313.
18. Ernest V. Hollis and Alice L. Taylor, *Social Work Education in the United States* (New York: Columbia University Press, 1951).
19. Rosalie Balinsky, "Generic Practice in Graduate Social Work Curricula: A Study of Educators' Experiences and Attitudes," *Journal of Education for Social Work* 18 (Fall 1982): 47.
20. Bradford W. Sheafor and Pamela S. Landon, "Generalist Perspective" in Anne E. Minahan, ed., *Encyclopedia of Social Work,* 18th ed. (New York: National Association of Social Workers, 1987), pp. 660–669.
21. CSWE, *Handbook of Accreditation,* Appendix 1.
22. Leslie Leighninger, "The Generalist-Specialist Debate in Social Work," *Social Service Review* 54 (March 1980): 1.
23. Bradford W. Sheafor, Charles R. Horejsi, and Gloria A. Horejsi, *Techniques and Guidelines for Social Work Practice* (Boston: Allyn and Bacon, 1988).
24. Herbert Bisno, "A Theoretical Framework for Teaching Social Work Methods and Skills," *Journal of Social Work Education* 6 (Winter 1970): 5–17; Harold L. McPheeters and Robert M. Ryan, *A Core of Competence for Baccalaureate Social Welfare and Curricular Implications* (Atlanta: Southern Regional Education Board, 1971), pp. 9–26; Morton L. Arkava and E. Clifford Brennen, eds., *Competency-Based Education for Social Work Evaluation and Curriculum Issues* (New York: Council on Social Work Education, 1976); Morton L. Arkava, David E. Cummins, John C. Johnson, and Nancy S. Dodd, *Montana Social Work Competence Scales: A Summative Examination for Baccalaureate Social Workers* (Missoula: University of Montana Department of Social Work, 1976); Council on Social Work Education, *Teaching for Competence in the Delivery of Direct Services* (New York: Council on Social Work Education, 1976) and Betty L. Baer and Ronald Federico, *Educating the Baccalaureate Social Worker,* Vol. 1 (Boston: Ballinger, 1978), pp. 86–89.
25. Robert J. Teare et al., *Classification Validation Processes for Social Service Positions,* Vols. I–VII, (Washington, D.C.: National Association of Social Workers, 1984).
26. Robert J. Teare, "Validation of the ACSW Examination: Status Report to the Na-

tional Association of Social Workers," (unpublished manuscript, 1984); Bradford W. Sheafor, Robert J. Teare, Mervyn W. Hancock, and Thomas P. Gauthier, "Curriculum Development Through Content Analysis: A New Zealand Experience," *Journal of Education for Social Work* 21 (Fall 1985), pp. 113–124; and Robert J. Teare, *Validating Social Work Credentials for Human Service Jobs: Report of a Demonstration* (Silver Spring, Md.: National Association of Social Workers, 1987).

27. Robert J. Teare, Bradford W. Sheafor, and Thomas P. Gauthier, "Establishing the Content Validity of Social Work Credentials," (Photocopy materials accompanying paper presented at 33rd Annual Program Meeting of Council on Social Work Education, St. Louis, Missouri, March 9, 1987.)

28. Ibid.

29. Shirley L. Patterson, "Toward a Conceptualization of Natural Helping," *Arete* 4 (Spring 1977): 161–171, Alice H. Collins and Diane L. Pancoast, *Natural Helping Networks* (Washington, D.C.: National Association of Social Workers, 1976), and James K. Whittaker and James Garbarino, *Social Support Networks: Informal Helping in the Human Services* (New York: Adeline de Gruyter, 1983).

30. Allen Rubin, ed., *Statistics on Social Work Education in the United States: 1985* (Washington, D.C.: Council on Social Work Education, 1986), p. 40. (Data reflect reports from 85.5 percent of the DSW/Ph.D. programs.)

31. Ibid., p. 53. (Data reflect reports from 83.5 percent of the accredited BSW programs.)

32. Reprinted with permission from *NASW Standards for the Classification of Social Work Practice*, Policy Statement 4 (Silver Spring, Md.: 1981), p. 9.

33. National Association of Social Workers, "Membership Survey Shows Practice Shifts," *NASW News* 28 (November 1983): 6–7.

34. Rubin, *Statistics, 1985*, 53–54.

35. Ibid., p. 54.

36. "First-Time Look at Members' Salaries Finds Their Average Income is $27,800," © 1988 National Association of Social Workers, Inc. Reprinted with permission from *NASW News*, Vol. 33, January, 1988, pp. 1 and 18.

37. Ibid.

38. Ibid., p. 18.

39. Sheldon Siegel, Remarks presented at the Seventh NASW Professional Symposium, November 20, 1981.

40. William M. Austin, "The Job Outlook in Brief," *Occupational Outlook Quarterly* (Spring 1986), 13.

41. Rubin, *Statistics, 1985*, 53–54.

CHAPTER 2

The Emergence
of Social Work
as a Profession

The growth and development of social work has not been a planned event. It just happened. It is a response to human suffering that began in several different parts of American society and eventually coalesced into a single, diverse profession.

Because its development has not been guided by a clear master plan, social work has been heavily influenced by a variety of factors. It has been pushed in one direction by external forces such as periods of political and economic conservatism, the stress of wars and other major international events, and by competition from other emerging helping disciplines. At the same time, social work has been pulled in other directions by its own goals and aspirations, such as the need for a coherent concept of the profession that could incorporate its different roots and its intense desire to be recognized as a legitimate profession.

In order to understand and appreciate social work more fully, it is useful to trace its emergence and identify key historical events and professional actions that have shaped the profession. While one could gain insight into the emergence of social work by examining the influence of external events, this chapter is guided by an examination of social work's internal professional development. It begins with a review of professions, particularly the helping professions, in U.S. society. It traces the emergence of social work during the past century with emphasis on the choices made that affected its acceptance as a profession and concludes with an analysis of its current professional status.

THE NATURE OF PROFESSIONS

A field of sociological inquiry has developed that is devoted to the definition and description of the nature of professions. One of the central figures in this field is Wilbert Moore who concludes that "to have one's occupational status accepted as professional or to have one's occupational conduct judged as professional is highly regarded in all post industrial societies and in at least the modernizing sectors of others."[1]

Professions are highly regarded because they have been granted sanction to perform essential services that ensure survival and enhance the quality of

life. For individuals, professionalism is usually personally satisfying, financially rewarding, and productive of high social status. For professions, this
recognition is essential: it enhances the ability to recruit qualified people and
ensures the respect of other professions and the general public. From the
clients' point of view, the designation of professionalism signals those persons
who are qualified to provide particular services and provides protection
against incompetent and unethical behavior by practitioners. Recognition
as professional, then, has been an important motivation driving many
occupations.

How is it determined whether or not an occupation is a profession? One
approach to the study of professions, known as the *absolute approach,* has been
to examine the traditional professions of medicine, law, the ministry, and
higher education to isolate their fundamental elements. These studies revealed that professions could be characterized by such factors as their requirements for specialized skill and training, a specific base of knowledge,
the formation of professional associations, and the development of codes of
ethical behavior governing professional practice.[2] Other occupations were
then evaluated to determine whether they, too, contained these elements and
could be considered professions. Using this approach, occupational groups
were classified in one of two categories: professional or nonprofessional.

More recently the prevalent approach to the study of professions has been
to identify the key attributes common to professions and assess the degree
to which any other occupational group possesses these attributes. This *relative
approach* to professionalism allows for the placement of any occupational
group along a continuum from nonprofessional to professional. Using this
approach, Moore, for example, identifies the primary characteristics of a
profession as a full-time occupation, commitment to a calling, identification
with peers, specified training or education, a service orientation, and autonomy restrained by responsibility.[3] Using such criteria, it is possible to place
each occupational group on a scale of professionalism relative to other occupations. The point at which an occupation sufficiently meets the criteria to
be considered a profession is not absolute, but determined by judgment.
While some sociologists have labeled occupations that have not reached the
top of the scale on all items as "semi-professions" or emerging professions,
others have judged them to be fully accepted professions.

As more has been learned about professions, three elements have been
delineated to help explain the unique characteristics of the occupations that
are considered to be professions.

First, professionals must be free from constraints that might limit their
ability to act in the best interests of their clients. The protection of this *professional autonomy* has been most successful in professions that contract directly
with clients to provide services on an entrepreneurial or private practice basis.
In these situations few constraints are imposed on the manner in which practice is conducted. In agency-based professions, however, the organizations
employ the professionals and contract with the clients to provide service. The

agency's rules and regulations, intended to improve organizational efficiency and accountability, limit the professional's autonomy to exercise completely independent judgment regarding the manner in which services are provided.

Second, professions possess a monopoly in their field of expertise. Society has granted *professional authority* to a few people who have acquired the necessary knowledge and skills to provide the needed services in a given area of professional practice. Society grants this authority because it has in effect determined that it is inefficient, if not impossible, for every person to acquire all the knowledge and skill needed to meet complex human needs. Thus, these professionals are given the exclusive right to make judgments and give advice to their clients. In granting this professional authority, society, in essence, gives up the right to judge the competence of these professionals except in extreme cases of incompetent or unethical practice. Society depends on the members of that profession to determine the requisite entrance preparation and be sure those who are practicing as members of that profession do so competently.

To be able to operate within the authority of a given profession, each member must master the knowledge and skills the profession has determined to be essential. Through the accreditation of its educational programs and the content of examinations that govern entry to a profession, the technical information and competencies fundamental to that profession are assured. However, human problems typically extend beyond the purview of any one profession. To be of maximum effectiveness it is important that the professional not only has the technical training required for his or her profession, but must also possess a fund of general knowledge gained from the study of history, literature, philosophy, theater, and other fields that will help to provide a broad understanding of the human condition. In short, professionals must be both technically and generally educated.

Third, when the right to judge practice is relinquished, the public becomes vulnerable and rightfully expects the professions to protect them from abuses that may accrue from the professional monopoly. Everett C. Hughes indicates that the motto of the professions must be *credat emptor* ("buyer trust"), as opposed to the motto of the marketplace, *caveat emptor* ("buyer beware").[4] For example where the layperson would rarely question the prescription of a physician, that same person might be very cautious when buying a used car and might have it thoroughly tested by an independent mechanic before making a purchase. To maintain this buyer trust, the professions must be accountable to the public that has granted them the sanction to perform these services. In order to establish and maintain this *professional responsibility,* professions develop codes that identify the expected ethical behavior of practitioners and establish mechanisms for policing their membership regarding unethical or incompetent practice.

In a sense, the professions and society struck a deal. In exchange for responsible service in sensitive areas of life, the professions were granted exclusive authority, i.e., a professional monopoly, to offer these services.

THE HELPING PROFESSIONS: A RESPONSE TO HUMAN NEED

All helping professions began as a response to unmet human need. As people experienced suffering or insufficient development in some aspect of life, when natural helping networks were not sufficient to meet the resulting needs, various forms of professional help emerged. Physicians, teachers, clergy, and other professional groups began to appear and to be given approval by the society to perform specific helping functions. The buyer's, or client's, vulnerability was intensified in the area of helping services because they dealt in especially sensitive areas where unwitting persons could be harmed by the incompetent or improper actions of the professional. In addition to the codes of ethics and bodies established to investigate situations where abuses of this monopoly were alleged, the helping professions also characteristically have had external sources of client protection. For the entrepreneurial professions and private practitioners, this additional protection has taken the form of licensing professional practice, while clients of agency-based professions are usually considered to have adequate supplemental protection through the monitoring of practice by the agencies and organizations.

It was soon realized that the effectiveness of these helpers was increased when their skills were supported by specific knowledge and values that could guide their interventions into the lives of clients or groups of clients. As this professional knowledge expanded through the development of theories and concepts, as well as through experience, trial and error, or practice wisdom, the professions expanded their technical knowledge requirements and their membership became increasingly exclusive. There was a time when each profession could respond to a number of human needs. For example, the clergy traditionally provided help for both spiritual and social needs. However, the increasingly specialized knowledge necessary to provide effective helping services has led to a proliferation of helping professions, each with its own specializations.

What are these needs to which the helping professions have responded? In simplest form, people have two fundamental needs. The first is to possess security; that is, to love and be loved, to relate to others, and to have material comforts. The second is to experience growth by achieving maturity and developing one's maximum potential.[5] Such broad definitions of need did not provide sufficient focus for emerging professions. Too much knowledge and skill was required of any individual to meet these broad needs adequately. A more precise description of needs, provided by Naomi Brill, helps to clarify the primary focus of the several helping professions as they exist today.[6]

Physical Needs: functioning of the physical structures and organic processes of the body. (Medicine and Nursing)

Emotional Needs: feelings or affective aspects of the consciousness that are subjectively experienced. (Psychology)

Intellectual Needs: capacity for rational and intelligent thought. (Education)

Spiritual Needs: desire for a meaning in life that transcends one's life on earth. (Religion)

Social Needs: capacity for satisfying relationships with others. (Social Work)

While the helping professions have tended to organize around a single need, there are exceptions, such as psychiatry, in which both emotional and physical needs—and their interaction—are the focus of professional service.

The increase of helping professions from few to many, and their overlap when providing services to people who experience more than one need, has inevitably led to problems in defining professional boundaries. As newer professions like social work, occupational therapy, and music therapy have emerged, they have devoted considerable energy to staking out their professional boundaries. That activity is important because it identifies for each profession, the other professions, and the public the unique contribution made by each to meeting human needs. It also helps to focus their education and training programs, research activities, and the development of appropriate professional knowledge.

How a profession stakes out its professional boundaries has significant influence on that profession. The more elitist professions limit the people they claim as their target of service to those with narrowly defined problems, typically charging high fees to the few people who require that service. These professions usually require extensive and highly technical training; few people acquire the credentials to be recognized as part of that profession. This limited supply of professionals yields high prestige and financial reward for those who hold the proper qualifications. Other professions have been far more open in their membership requirements and more general in the type of issues for which they provide service. This lack of exclusiveness has at times been viewed as less professional and has resulted in lower prestige and less financial remuneration for the persons identified with these professions.

Two models of professionalism have developed in the United States. One is the *private model* where the individual client contracts directly with the professional for service. Law and medicine are clear examples of professions that have followed this model. A second model, typified by teachers and city planners, is the *public model of professionalism* in which the professionals primarily operate under the auspice of formal organizations and direct their services to the common good. Howe notes:

> For any given profession, the pattern of whether it serves primarily individual clients, the public, or both groups equally is determined in large part by the nature of the service it provides and by whether its beneficiaries are individuals or larger groups. When the beneficiary is one individual client, the service would be what an economist would call a private good; if the service benefits the collectivity, it would be a collective or public good.[7]

For social work, with its dual focus on person and environment, both the private and public models of professionalism apply. It must balance concern for the individual client and the public welfare.

Thus, it is evident that the nature of the services provided, the needs of the clientele served, and the professional model adopted will influence the orientation of any emerging profession. In addition the aspirations of that profession for a particular place among the professions will have a significant impact on the choices it makes at various points during the development.

How, then, has social work emerged? Where does it fit among the helping professions?

SOCIAL WORK AS A PROFESSION: AN HISTORICAL PERSPECTIVE

From Volunteers to an Occupation (Prior to 1915)

The roots of social work may be found in the extensive volunteer movement during the formative years of the United States. In the colonial period, for example, it was assumed that individuals or families would care for themselves, but if further difficulties existed, friends, neighbors, or representatives of the community would volunteer to meet their needs. A description of such voluntary service is given by William Bradford, Governor of Massachusetts, concerning the smallpox epidemic of 1620:

> In ye time of most distress, there was but 6 or 7 sound persons, who to their great comendations be it spoken, spared no pains night nor day, but with abundance of toyle and hazard of their owne health, fetched them woode, made them fires, drest them meant, made their beads, washed their loathsome cloaths, cloathed and uncloathed them; in a word did all ye homly and necessarie offices for them . . . all this willingly and cherfully, without any gruding in ye least, shewing herein true love unto their friends and brethern.[8]

These voluntary acts of service gradually became more formalized as numerous social agencies were formed. Some organizations carried such descriptive names as the Home for Little Wanderers, the Penitent Females Refuge, and the Home for Intemperate Women. In the early 1800s, Alexis de Tocqueville commented on this development:

> Americans of all ages, all conditions, and all dispositions constantly form associations. . . . The Americans make associations to give entertainments, to found seminaries, to build inns, to construct churches, to diffuse books, to send missionaries to the antipodes; in this manner they found hospitals, prisons, and schools.[9]

The volunteer activities of some of these organizations involved interaction with the needy, the ill, and those with other social problems. These volunteer efforts were, however, frequently marked by a condescending attitude toward recipients of these services.

Developing out of this background came social work as an *occupation*. What are recognized as the first paid social work positions in the United States were jobs in the Special Relief Department of the United States Sanitary Commission.[10] Beginning as a voluntary agency and then receiving public support, the Special Relief Department and its agents served Union soldiers and their families experiencing social and health problems in the Civil War. Because of the pressures for service during the war, women were allowed to enter the social service arena, and their outstanding performance helped pave the way for their continuing participation in meaningful positions in social work.[11] Following the war this department ceased functioning, and social workers temporarily disappeared.

Social work reappeared as a paid occupation a few years after the establishment of the Massachusetts Board of Charities in 1863. Founded under pressure from Samuel Gridley Howe this agency coordinated services in almshouses, hospitals, and other institutions in the state. Although its powers were limited to inspection and advice, the Board gained wide acceptance under the leadership of Howe and its paid director, Frank B. Sanborn.[12] The concept of state boards spread to other states in the 1870s, and many achieved greater administrative responsibilities—although responsibility for program management was not achieved until the early 1900s. In an effort to reflect the enlightened approach of the Massachusetts Board of Charities, its secretary focused on identifying the causes of poverty. The causes identified were "first, physical degradation and inferiority; second, moral perversity; third, mental incapacity; fourth, accidents and infirmities; fifth, unjust and unwise laws, and the customs of society."[13] To deal with problems of such complex roots, paid staff members who could specialize in these areas were required.

Another significant development leading to the emergence of social work as an occupation was the establishment of the Charity Organization Society (COS) of Buffalo in 1877. Copied after a similar organization in London, a number of these societies were founded for the dual purposes of finding means to help the poor and of preventing the poor from taking advantage of the numerous uncoordinated social agencies that had developed in many communities. After several years of mixed success with "friendly visitors," the Buffalo COS began using trained people to contact clients. In 1893 Nathaniel S. Rosenau of the Buffalo Society questioned the right of the superannuated clergyman, unsuccessful merchant, or political favorite to serve as manager of a charitable society or institution. He concluded that it was necessary that persons in charge of this work be specially trained, have a calling for the work, and intend to devote themselves to it.[14]

This interest resulted in the formation of the New York School of Philanthropy in 1898. Under the guidance of Edward T. Devine, secretary of the New York COS, the New York School began with a six-week summer session to train paid workers. Later the training time was extended to one year and eventually to two years.

Another development leading to the emergence of social work as an occupation was the initiation of the settlement movement in 1886. Patterning settlement houses after London's Toynbee Hall, people such as Stanton Coit and Jane Addams established settlements in New York and Chicago. Within fifteen years, about a hundred settlement houses were operating in the United States. Robert H. Bremner sums up the impact of the settlement movement:

> Through friendly contact with the poor, settlement workers acquired not just a knowledge, but an understanding of the daily life and trials of the urban masses. The best of them identified their own interests with the welfare of their neighbors. Where others thought of the people of the slums as miserable wretches deserving either pity or correction, settlement residents knew them as much entitled to respect as any other members of the community. Numerous young men and women who lived and worked in the settlements during the 1890's carried this attitude with them into later careers in social work, business, government service, or the arts. It was the most important single contribution of the settlement movement; and it was destined to exert a great influence on the course of both social work and social reform in the 20th century.[15]

Social work practice in institutional settings developed primarily in the Massachusetts General Hospital in 1905.[16] Under the guidance of Richard C. Cabot, physician to outpatients, Ida Cannon established the first medical social work department in a hospital in the United States. Once again there was a precedent for this service in London. However, social workers in the United States refused to identify with nursing, because of nurses' subordinate status, and attempted to develop a professional identity based on the model of the physician:

> The enlistment of medical social workers marked an important stage in the development of professional social work. A casework limited to the charity organization and child welfare societies provided too narrow a base for professional development, associated as it was with problems of relief and economic dependency. Medical social work added an entirely new institutional setting in which to explore the implications of casework theory and practice.

> Medical social service invigorated the quest for professional skill and technique. Here was a "new and special service that demands new and special instruction and expertness." Ida Cannon and others, determined to secure a useful and respected place in the hospital hierarchy, insisted that "human kindness alone cannot solve tangled social problems."[17]

Medical social workers became interested in professional education as a means of moving beyond the "warm-heart" position into an understanding of the psychic or social conditions at the base of patient distress. Furthermore, with professional education it would be possible to move into a colleague relationship with the physician. By 1912 a one-year course in medical social work was established in the Boston School of Social Work.

One other significant development in this preprofessional period was the formation of an occupational association, the National Conference on Charities, in 1873. This conference, later called the National Conference on Charities and Corrections, brought volunteer and professional staff members of social agencies together to exchange ideas about the provision of services, to discuss social problems, and to "give more intensive study to 'practical' work."[18] By the end of this period social work as an occupation was distinguishable from the many volunteer groups concerned with social welfare.

Professional Emergence (1915–1950)

With social work firmly established as an occupation rather than a volunteer activity, attention then turned to its development as a profession. At the 1915 meeting of the National Conference on Charities and Corrections, Abraham Flexner addressed the group on the subject, "Is Social Work a Profession?" Dr. Flexner, an authority on graduate education, had made a penetrating study that led to major changes in medical education. The organizers of this session apparently hoped Flexner would assure them that social work was, or was about to become, a full-fledged profession. However, that was not in the cards. Flexner, using an "absolute approach" to his study of professions, spelled out six criteria for identifying a profession:

1. Professions are essentially intellectual operations with large individual responsibility.
2. They derive their raw material from science and learning.
3. This material is worked up to a practical and clear-cut end.
4. Professions possess an educationally communicable technique.
5. They tend to self-organization.
6. They become increasingly altruistic in motivation.

After evaluating whether social work met these criteria—but not evaluating to what degree they were met—Flexner concluded that social work had not yet made it into the professional elite.[19] Following Flexner's admonition to "go forth and build thyself a profession," social workers busily attended to these functions over the next thirty-five years.

One effort was to develop a code of ethics. In 1921 Mary Richmond indicated that, "we need a code; something to abide by, or else we will have low social standing."[20] One code, the "Experimental Draft of a Code of Ethics for Social Case Workers," was discussed at the 1923 meeting of the National Conference on Social Welfare. Although this proposal was never acted upon, it represented a beginning effort at formulating a statement of professional ethics.

Probably the greatest effort was devoted to building a professional organization. The National Social Workers Exchange was opened in 1917 to provide vocational counseling and placement and later became actively involved in the identification and definition of professional standards. In 1921 its functions were taken over by the broader American Association of Social Workers, which made significant efforts to develop a comprehensive professional association. This effort was later weakened by attempts of some specialties to develop their own professional organizations. A chronology of the development of these specialized groups follows:

- 1918 American Association of Hospital Social Workers
- 1919 American Association of Visiting Teachers
- 1926 American Association of Psychiatric Social Workers
- 1936 American Association for the Study of Group Work
- 1946 American Association for the Study of Community Organization
- 1949 Social Work Research Group[21]

Evidence of the relatively-low status of social work early in this period was reflected in a Russell Sage Foundation salary study in 1926, which indicated that the $1,517 average annual salary for social workers was 18 percent less than that of elementary school teachers and 38 percent less than that of secondary school teachers.[22] The need for a unified thrust for professional status was evident.

Another development during this period concerned the methods of preparation to enter the social work profession. Social work education had begun in agency-based training, but a concerted effort was made during this period to transfer it to colleges and universities, where other professions had located their professional education. In 1919 the Association of Training Schools for Professional Social Workers was established with seventeen charter members—both agency and university affiliated schools.[23] The purpose of that organization was to develop professional standards in social work education. By 1927 considerable progress toward that purpose had been made and the Association of Training Schools reorganized into the American Association of Schools of Social Work (AASSW). Where the education programs had been offered in agencies as well as at both undergraduate and graduate levels in colleges and universities, the AASSW determined that by 1939 only university affiliated programs with two-year graduate programs would be recognized as professional social work education.[24]

That action led to a revolt by schools whose undergraduate programs prepared professionals to meet the staffing needs of the social agencies in their states. A second professional education organization was formed in 1942, the National Association of Schools of Social Service Administration, made up largely of public universities in the midwest that offered baccalaureate and one-year graduate level professional education programs. Harper described this development as "a protest movement against unrealistic and premature insistence upon graduate training and overemphasis upon professional case-work as the major social work technique."[25]

With leadership from governmental and voluntary practice agencies, the two organizations were later merged (1951) into the Council on Social Work Education (CSWE) following the landmark Hollis–Taylor study of social work education.[26] The outcome of that decision favored the two-year master's program as the minimum educational requirement for full professional status. Undergraduate social work education temporarily faded from the scene.

Another important area of concern that was given only limited attention during this period was strengthening the knowledge and skill base of social work practice. Richmond's rich contribution, *Social Diagnosis,* was the first effort to formalize a communicable body of techniques applicable to the diverse settings in which social caseworkers were found.[27]

Momentum from this thrust, however, was lost as social work slipped into the grasp of the popular psychoanalytic approach. Nathan Cohen comments, "The search for a method occurred just at the time the impact of psychoanalysis was being felt. Did social work, in its haste for professional stature, reach out for a ready-made methodology for treating sick people, thus closing itself off from the influence of developments in the other sciences?"[28] This question must be answered in the affirmative. By adopting the helping methodology that was currently in vogue, social work became firmly, but perhaps inappropriately, wedded to the private model of professionalism. Writing in *Harper's Magazine* in 1957, Marion K. Sanders accurately criticized social work for "floating with the ghost of Freud."[29] One might speculate about what would have happened if the model adopted had been the one for public education or public health.

Consolidating the Gains (1950–1970)

The move to consolidate the accrediting bodies for the schools of social work into the CSWE set an important precedent for the field and was part of a broad movement to treat social work as a single and unified profession. In 1950 the several specialized associations and the American Association of Social Workers agreed to form the Temporary Inter-Association Council of Social Work Membership Organizations (TIAC). The purpose behind the formation of TIAC was the organization of one central professional association. After considerable efforts by the specialties to maintain their identities, TIAC proposed a merger of the several groups in 1952. By 1955 this was accomplished, and the National Association of Social Workers (NASW) was formed. The purposes of the NASW were:

1. To improve administration of social work services.

2. To advance research in social work.

3. To improve social work practice.

4. To improve social work education.

5. To recruit to the profession.

6. To improve social conditions.

7. To gain public understanding of social work.

8. To improve salaries and working conditions.

9. To develop, promulgate, and enforce a Code of Ethics.

10. To certify the competence of social workers.

11. To promote the development of the profession in other countries.[30]

The basic membership requirement for the NASW was graduation from a school of social work accredited by the CSWE and, of course, payment of dues. By 1964, 88.7 percent of NASW members held at least a master's degree, and 4.1 percent had completed the two-year educational program but had not completed all degree requirements.[31] The remainder were members under the "grandfather clause" for non-degree members of the predecessor organizations.

NASW membership rose from 28,000 to 45,000 between 1961 and 1965, largely because of the formation of the Academy of Certified Social Workers (ACSW), which required both NASW membership and a two-year period of supervised experience. Many job descriptions were revised to require membership in the Academy, forcing social workers to join the NASW and obtain certification.

The late 1950s were a time of great introspection, and the professional journal, *Social Work*, was filled with articles such as "The Nature of Social Work,"[32] "How Social Will Social Work Be?"[33] and "A Changing Profession in a Changing World."[34] Perhaps the most significant work was Ernest Greenwood's classic article, "Attributes of a Profession," in 1957.[35] Greenwood, using the "relative approach" to the study of professions, identified five critical attributes of professions which, depending on the degree to which they have been accomplished, determine the degree of professionalism for any occupational group:

1. A systematic body of theory.

2. Professional authority.

3. Sanction of the community.

4. A regulative code of ethics.

5. A professional culture.

He related the development of social work to each of these five criteria and placed social work on a scale of professionalism. He concluded:

When we hold up social work against the model of the professions presented above, it does not take long to decide whether to classify it within the professional or non-professional occupations. Social work is already a profession; it has too many points of congruence with the model to be classifiable otherwise. Social work is, however, seeking to rise within the professional hierarchy, so that it, too, might enjoy maximum prestige, authority, and monopoly which presently belong to a few top professions.[36]

To the credit of social workers, they were as stimulated by Greenwood's declaration that they had become a profession as they were by Flexner's conclusion that they were not yet in the select circle. In 1958 the NASW published the "Working Definition of Social Work Practice," a valuable beginning to the difficult task of identifying professional boundaries.[37] This was followed by William E. Gordon's excellent critique, which helped strengthen and clarify some parts of the working definition, particularly in relation to knowledge, values, and practice methodology.[38] In 1960 the NASW adopted a Code of Ethics to serve as a guide for ethical professional practice,[39] thus completing the steps to become a fully recognized profession.

At what price has professional status been attained? Marion K. Sanders pointedly noted that social work had become a profession but had lost a mission. She indicated that social work had avoided controversial issues to keep its image clean, had become rigid in efforts to control service provision, and had developed jargon to maintain exclusiveness.[40]

Turning Away from the Elitist Professional Model (1970 to present)

From the turn of the twentieth century to the late 1960s, social work displayed a pattern typical of an emerging profession. It created a single association to guide professional growth and development, adopted a code of ethical professional behavior, provided for graduate-level university-based professional schools and acquired recognition to accredit those educational programs, successfully obtained licensing for social work practice in some states, conducted public education campaigns to interpret social work to the public, achieved recognition for social work among the helping professions, and moved in the direction of other professions by increasing specialization and limiting access to the profession. Indeed, social work was on its way to carving its niche among the elite group of helping professions.

However, social work did not vigorously pursue the path that would lead to even greater professional status. The 1970s and 1980s have been a time in which social work displayed ambivalence about several matters that might make it seem more "professional."

First, with the increased social awareness that developed in the late 1960s and early 1970s, social workers became much more active in social change activities than at any time during the previous several decades. A legacy from Lyndon Johnson's "Great Society" programs was federal support in the form of jobs and other resources to make efforts to eliminate social problems and to alleviate human suffering. Social work already was committed to those goals and social workers were prepared to move away from their clinical orientation and onto the front lines of social action. In 1966 Alvin Schorr reflected on this change:

> For one reason or another, the dazzle that once hovered over casework— especially psychiatric social work—now lights up social policy. Those interested in social policy ten years ago could have held their conventions in a telephone booth (if they had a dime); today they deliver the major addresses at our national conferences.[41]

For social workers bent on achieving higher professional status, the activitist social workers were sometimes unpopular. Their somewhat controversial activities at times created an unwelcome public image of the profession characterized by activists on the front lines of social change. This change in the balance of activities performed by social workers helped to bring social work back to its roots and reestablish the "change" orientation in its mission of caring, curing, and changing (see Chapter 1).

The more liberal political climate that supported the resurgence of social work activism was short-lived. The federal support for programs that encouraged social change dwindled and was nearly nonexistent by the time Ronald Reagan moved toward the conclusion of his second term. Social workers had again turned toward a more clinical orientation and the social policy addresses at their national conferences were more nostalgic than immediately applicable.

Second, in 1970 NASW made a dramatic move by revising its membership requirements to give full membership privileges to anyone who had completed a baccalaureate degree in social work from an undergraduate program approved by CSWE. In opposition to the more common pattern, in which professions become more exclusive in their membership, social work opened its membership to more people. Professional qualification could be gained by obtaining professional education at the undergraduate level. However, social work has been uneasy about operating as a multilevel profession and, although the NASW classification system is clear about the "Basic Social Worker" being viewed as fully professional, the social worker at this level has never been accepted by many MSW social workers. Advocates for the baccalaureate social worker contend that NASW has not devoted sufficient attention to this practice level and that its program priorities in the 1980s "centered too much on licensing, vendor payments, private practice and other issues that were not sufficiently relevant to the baccalaureate worker."[42]

Rather dramatic changes were also seen in social work education during this period. In 1974 the Council on Social Work Education was granted approval to implement a full accreditation process for baccalaureate social work education programs. Initially, 135 schools met the undergraduate accreditation requirements and by 1987, more than 350 schools throughout the United States and Puerto Rico had achieved accredited status. Of particular importance was the increased accessibility of these programs to persons wishing to become social workers. Where the eighty-nine MSW programs tended to be located in the more urbanized areas, the undergradute programs could also be found in colleges and universities in suburban and rural areas. People working in human service jobs without the requisite social work education, as well as people wanting to enter this field for the first time, could have access to social work education without moving to the few communities where the master's level programs were located. The emergence of professionally-sanctioned baccalaureate level social work education programs especially increased the opportunity for members of minority and lower socioeconomic backgrounds to enter this profession as it was possible to complete the requisite educational preparation without completing both undergraduate and graduate level programs. For example, in 1985, 28.6 percent of the 23,500 baccalaureate social work majors were of minority background as opposed to only 15.6 percent of the 14,055 full-time MSW students.[43]

The return of a conservative political climate in the United States contributed to a general perception that few jobs would be available in social work when the Reagan Administration completed its objective of dismantling the "Great Society" programs. After peaking at nearly 28,000 undergraduate majors in the late 1970s, that number had declined by more than one-fourth in 1983. Enrollments have increased gradually each year since that time. Similarly, the number of full-time MSW students declined by one-fifth between 1978 and 1983 but has remained relatively stable since.[44] It is noteworthy that during this same period the U.S. Bureau of Labor Statistics upgraded social work in its projections from an occupation that would grow "as fast as average" to one that would grow at a rate that is "faster than average" for all occupations through 1995. The changed enrollment patterns, then, increase the problems social agencies experience in obtaining qualified social workers to serve their clients as even fewer people with professional social work education are available to enter the growing labor market. The increasing divergence between the supply and demand for social workers is moderating the gains that were being made in increasing the ratio of professional social workers to persons requiring services.

A third trend occurring in the past two decades has been the growing acceptance of a generalist orientation as a basis for social work practice. Where professions have tended to become increasingly specialized, social work made a distinct move in the opposite direction. The search for a common practice approach that could embrace the breadth of social work practice has at least temporarily ended with general agreement that the generalist perspective is a viable approach for beginning level social workers. This approach directs the social worker to address practice situations unencumbered by specific methods and select the most appropriate intervention techniques to fit the unique needs of the client or client group.[45] This practice model is seen as compatible with the increasingly accepted concept of social work as the helping profession concerned with the transactions between people and their environments.

The generalist approach is reinforced by the accreditation standards of the

Council on Social Work Education, which require that the baccalaureate level programs make preparation for generalist practice their primary educational objective. As the same time the master's level programs characteristically devote some or all the first year of the two-year programs to preparation for generalist practice. The adoption of this approach, however, has not meant that social work has given up the development of specialized practice. Specialized master's level programs build on the generalist base but then extend to a variety of concentrations or to advanced generalist practice. Reports from the schools indicate that in relation to their practice method concentrations, 61 percent of the graduate students select direct practice, another 18 percent choose generic or advanced generalist methods, and the remainder are spread among various combinations of administration/management or community organization/planning concentrations.[46] In regard to fields of practice or social problem areas selected by the graduate students, 22 percent selected mental health or community mental health, 16 percent elected health settings, 14 percent chose family services, and 11 percent elected to enter child welfare practice.[47] These concentrations reflect a continued emphasis on traditionally popular and professionally acceptable areas of social work practice.

The Emergence of Interprofessional Practice and Education

With their own identity as a profession firmly established, social workers have begun to join other professions in efforts to strengthen interprofessional practice and education. The vehicle for this development is the National Consortium on Interprofessional Practice and Education where the Council on Social Work Education and the National Association of Social Workers have joined parallel associations from medicine, law, theology, education, nursing, psychology, and the several "allied health disciplines" to explore ways of improving human services through cooperation among the professions. As opposed to previous attempts to create a new professional group blended from disenchanted members of existing professions (i.e., the "human services" movement), the major professions are beginning to explore means to better prepare practitioners to work collaboratively in the provision of services in a manner that builds on the unique contributions of each profession.

As U.S. society has become increasingly complex, the single profession approach to meeting human needs has increasingly been recognized as inadequate. Richard Snyder identifies several factors that have contributed to the need for a major effort to discover appropriate areas for interprofessional collaboration in service delivery and social policy development.

> Cumulative complexity and change have produced conditions and trends that call into question the adequacy of monoprofessional practice in a growing number of cases and for a growing number of patients/clients. Among the more important dimensions of complexity are: pervasive specialization and the challenge it presents to the orchestration of knowledge and skills

in behalf of cases whose contours do not fit the boundaries of specialties; the number of causal factors and the many patterns of relationship among them that may be involved in diagnosing particular cases; the ramifications of alternative treatments—how far these extend, in what directions, and how ascertainable this is; and the fragmented system of policy making that affects health care and human services.[48]

On the front lines of practice the problems of turf skirmishes, the expansion of one profession into the competence areas of another, and the risk that clients may not have access to professionals who have the most appropriate knowledge and skills for their specific needs threatens to erode the public's faith in the professions. Van Bogard Dunn and Mary Janata capture the perception of many social workers, as well as members of other professions, when they identify the day-to-day experience of many professionals.

In attempting to meet human need, professionals find that problems often exceed the competence of one profession alone, and they are pressed to search for new ways of approaching them. Rapid technological advances and the resulting increase in the knowledge pool require new modes of problem solving and new collaboration among the professions in the delivery of services. Thus, today's practitioner who is committed to compassionate and effective service is challenged to develop a rationale and a program for interprofessional dialogue and cooperation.[49]

Clients of human service agencies are the primary losers when there is professional specialization without interprofessional collaboration.

CONCLUDING COMMENT

For nearly three-fourths of a century social work has tried diligently to become recognized as a profession. It has made substantial progress in meeting the generally accepted criteria for professions. Consensus about its unique purpose among the professions has been reached and social work has achieved sanction as the appropriate profession to help people resolve problems in their interaction with their environments. Social workers have been granted the professional autonomy to provide the necessary helping services for people in need, although social workers are constrained by the fact that most are employed in social agencies that further limit their ability to exercise professional judgment. Increasingly, they are entering private practice where these constraints are less severe.

Social work has taken its authority to provide these professional services seriously. Its national professional organization, the National Association of Social Workers, has consistently worked through the decades to clarify social work's knowledge, value, and skill base. Social work has developed educational programs that prepare new people to enter this profession and established a process for accrediting the programs that meet qualitative educational standards at both the baccalaureate and master's levels. These educational programs have been well-received. Since 1958, the first year of MSW accreditation under the Council on Social Work Education, and 1974 when baccalaureate level accreditation was implemented, more than 250,000 persons have completed accredited social work degrees.[50]

Social work has also adopted a comprehensive "Code of Ethics" (see Chapter 8) and established procedures for dealing with social workers who may violate that code. Social work has established a process through the National Association of Social Workers to carry out its professional responsibility to protect clients and the general public from abuses that might arise from the professional monopoly it has achieved.

One might expect social workers to feel satisfied with these accomplishments. While most social workers believe the progress made in becoming a recognized profession is desirable, as the 1990s approach it is evident that controversy continues over social work's professional status. Philosophically uncomfortable with the inherent elitism in the professional model but committed to the protection it provides clients, social workers continue to search for the appropriate degree of professionalism desirable or, perhaps, to discover a professional model more appropriate to the public professions. The emerging interprofessional collaboration approach has the potential of modifying some of the issues of exclusiveness that affect clients and concern social workers.

SUGGESTED READINGS

Alexander, Chauncy. "History of Social Work and Social Welfare: Significant Dates," in Anne Minahan, ed., *Encyclopedia of Social Work*, 18th ed. Silver Spring, Md.: National Association of Social Workers, 1987, pp. 777–788.

Austin, David M. "The Flexner Myth and the History of Social Work," *Social Service Review* 57 (September 1983): 357–377.

Austin, David M. *A History of Social Work Education*. Austin: University of Texas at Austin, School of Social Work, 1986, Social Work Education Monograph Series, 1.

Brieland, Donald. "History and Evolution of Social Work Practice," in Anne Minahan, ed., *Encyclopedia of Social Work*, 18th ed. Silver Spring, Md.: National Association of Social Workers, 1987, pp. 739–754.

Greenwood, Ernest. "Attributes of a Profession." *Social Work* 2 (July 1957): 45–55.

Howe, Elizabeth. "Public Professions and the Private Model of Professionalism." *Social Work* 25 (May 1980): 179–191.

Kirchner, Don S. *The Paradox of Professionalism: Reform and Public Service in Urban America, 1900–1940*. Westport, Conn.: Greenwood, 1986.

Leighinger, Leslie. *Social Work: Search for Identity*. Westport, Conn.: Greenwood, 1987.

Lubove, Roy. *The Professional Altruist*. Cambridge: Harvard University Press, 1965.

Moore, Wilbert E. *The Professions: Roles and Rules*. New York: Russell Sage Foundation, 1970.

Poppel, Philip R. "The Social Work Profession: A Reconceptualization." *Social Service Review* 59 (December 1985): 560–574.

The Ohio State University College of Education. *Theory Into Practice* 24 (Spring 1987): entire issue.

Trolander, Judith Ann. *Professionalism and Social Change: From the Settlement House to Neighborhood Centers, 1886 to the Present.* New York: Columbia University Press, 1987.

ENDNOTES

1. Wilbert E. Moore, *The Professions: Roles and Rules* (New York: Russell Sage Foundation, 1970), p. 3.
2. A. M. Carr–Saunders and P. A. Wilson, *The Professions* (Oxford: Clarendon Press, 1933), pp. 3–31.
3. Moore, *Professions,* pp. 5–6.
4. Everett C. Hughes, "Professions," *Daedalus* (Fall 1963): 657.
5. Naomi I. Brill, *Working With People: The Helping Process,* 2nd ed. (Philadelphia: Lippincott, 1978), p. 10.
6. Ibid., pp. 6–8.
7. Elizabeth Howe, "Public Professions and the Private Model of Professionalism," *Social Work 25* (May 1980): 181.
8. Ralph E. Pumphrey and Muriel W. Pumphrey, eds., *The Heritage of American Social Work* (New York: Columbia University Press, 1961), p. 12.
9. Alexis de Tocqueville, *Democracy in America* (New York: Alfred A. Knopf, 1945 reprint), p. 106.
10. John C. Kidneigh, "History of American Social Work," in *Encyclopedia of Social Work,* edited by Harry L. Lurie, 15th issue (New York: National Association of Social Workers, 1965), p. 4.
11. Walter I. Trattner, *From Poor Law to Welfare State* (New York: Free Press, 1974), pp. 69–71.
12. Ibid., p. 6.
13. Pumphrey and Pumphrey, *Heritage,* p. 146.
14. Roy Lubove, *The Professional Altruist* (Cambridge: Harvard University Press, 1965), p. 19.
15. Robert H. Bremner, *From the Depths* (New York: New York University Press, 1956), p. 66.
16. Lubove, *Altruist,* pp. 24–25.
17. Ibid., p. 32.
18. Pumphrey and Pumphrey, *Heritage,* pp. 161–163.
19. Ibid., pp. 301–307.
20. Ibid., p. 310.
21. Kidneigh, *History of Social Work,* pp. 13–14.
22. Lubove, *Altruist,* p. 133.
23. Bradford W. Sheafor and Barbara W. Shank, *Undergraduate Social Work Education: A Survivor in a Changing Profession* (Austin: University of Texas at Austin School of Social Work, 1986), Social Work Education Monograph Series, 3, p. 4.
24. David M. Austin, *A History of Social Work Education* (Austin: University of Texas at Austin School of Social Work, 1986), Social Work Education Monograph Series, 1, p. 8.
25. Herbert Bisno, "The Place of Undergraduate Curriculum in Social Work Education," Vol. II, in Werner W. Boehm, ed., *A Report of the Curriculum Study* (New York: Council on Social Work Education, 1959), p. 8.
26. Ernest V. Hollis and Alice L. Taylor, *Social Work Education in the United States* (New York: Columbia University Press, 1951).
27. Mary E. Richmond, *Social Diagnosis* (New York: Russell Sage Foundation, 1917).

28. Nathan E. Cohen, *Social Work in the American Tradition* (New York: Holt, Rinehart & Winston, 1958), pp. 120–121.
29. Marion K. Sanders, "Social Work: A Profession Chasing Its Tail," *Harper's Monthly* 214 (March 1957): 56–62.
30. David G. French, "Professional Organization," in Harry L. Lurie, ed., *Encyclopedia of Social Work*, 15th issue (New York: National Association of Social Workers, 1965), p. 576.
31. Ibid.
32. Werner W. Boehm, "The Nature of Social Work," *Social Work* 3 (April 1958): 10–18.
33. Herbert Bisno, "How Social Will Social Work Be?" *Social Work* 1 (April 1956): 12–18.
34. Nathan E. Cohen, "A Changing Profession in a Changing World," *Social Work* 1 (October 1956): 12–19.
35. Ernest Greenwood, "Attributes of a Profession," *Social Work* 2 (July 1957): 45–55.
36. Ibid., p. 54.
37. Bartlett, "Toward Clarification," pp. 5–7.
38. William E. Gordon, "Critique of the Working Definition," *Social Work* 7 (October 1962): 3–13; and "Knowledge and Values: Their Distinction and Relationship in Clarifying Social Work Practice," *Social Work* 10 (July 1965): 32–39.
39. National Association of Social Workers, *Code of Ethics* (Washington, D.C.: The Association, 1960).
40. Sanders, "A Profession Chasing Its Tail," pp. 56–62.
41. Alvin L. Schorr, "Editorial Page," *Social Work* 11 (July 1966): 2.
42. Sheafor and Shank, *Undergraduate Social Work Education*, p. 25.
43. Allen Rubin, ed., *Statistics on Social Work Education in the United States, 1985* (Washington, D.C.: Council on Social Work Education, 1986), pp. 53–54. (Data based on reports from 83.5 percent of the accredited baccalaureate programs and 96.6 percent of the accredited MSW programs.)
44. Allen Rubin, *Current Statistical Trends in Social Work Education: Issues and Implications* (Austin: University of Texas at Austin School of Social Work, 1986), Social Work Education Monograph Series, 4, pp. 3–6.
45. Bradford W. Sheafor and Pamela S. Landon, "Generalist Perspective," in Anne Minahan, ed., *Encyclopedia of Social Work*, 18th ed., (Silver Spring: Md.: National Association of Social Workers, 1987): 660–669.
46. Rubin, *Statistics on Social Work Education, 1985*, p. 79.
47. Ibid., p. 81.
48. Richard C. Snyder, "A Societal Backdrop for Interprofessional Education and Practice," *Theory Into Practice* 24 (Spring 1987): 94.
49. Van Bogard Dunn and Mary M. Janata, "Interprofessional Assumptions and the OSU Commission," *Theory Into Practice* 24 (Spring 1987): 99.
50. David A. Hardcastle, *The Social Work Labor Force* (Austin: University of Texas at Austin School of Social Work, 1987), Social Work Education Monograph Series, 7, p. 8.

CHAPTER 3

Entry to the Social Work Profession

Selecting a career is one of the most important decisions a person must make. Whether that decision is to become a homemaker, physician, salesperson, teacher, chemist, or social worker, it should be based on a thorough understanding of the physical, emotional, and intellectual demands of the field and a close look at one's own suitability for that type of work. Whatever the choice, it will dictate how a person spends a major part of each day. It will also spill over into other aspects of life, including life style,[1] general satisfaction with self, and quality of life.

Making a career choice is difficult because of the wide range of careers to choose from but, more importantly, because of the problems an outsider experiences in gaining an adequate and accurate understanding of a career. Too often, only after a person has made substantial commitments in time, energy, and money or has cut off other opportunities by taking steps to enter a career, does he or she find that it is not what was expected or wanted.

Another difficulty lies in having a clear perception of one's own needs, interests, and abilities. Personal introspection, occupational preference testing, guidance counseling, and experience in activities related to the career are all resources for making this choice.

The person contemplating a career in social work must consider a number of factors. It is evident that social work is extremely broad in scope—ranging from social action to individual therapy—and is constantly changing, with a *knowledge base* that is far from stable or well developed. Thus, explicit guidelines for social work practice do not exist, leaving the social worker with the responsibility for exercising a great deal of individual judgment.

The *value base* calls for a view of the human condition compatible with the social work approach of helping people improve their social functioning. Furthermore, the *skills* demanded of the social worker vary widely and require a flexible, creative, and introspective person to practice them. The pressures of a social work job are great since the outcome of the work is critically important to the clients. In addition social workers are regularly criticized by both clients and the general public, frequently in regard to programs social workers administer but over which they have little policy-making influence.

If a person can tolerate the ambiguity, responsibility, pressures, and criticism that are a part of social work; if the values, skills, and interests required of social workers are compatible; and if it is rewarding to work constructively to help people improve their level of social functioning, social work offers a rich and satisfying career. Before selecting social work as a career, one needs a general knowledge of this profession. In addition, volunteer experience, summer or part-time jobs in social agencies, and personal interaction with social workers may also help to determine one's suitability for a career in social work. The information contained in this chapter provides an orientation to a social work career.

ISSUES IN SOCIAL WORK PREPARATION AND EMPLOYMENT

Membership in any profession requires that the persons aspiring to enter that discipline acquire the specified qualifications. The very act of defining professional membership is inherently elitist in that, wherever the boundaries are drawn, some persons who provide closely related services or operate with similar knowledge and values will be excluded. In social work, for example, completion of the education and practice experience specified by the National Association of Social Workers (NASW) in its membership qualifications is necessary to gain professional recognition. However, social workers are cognizant that many other helping people with different education and experience make important contributions to the broader social welfare institution, but should not be identified as social workers.

Education and Accreditation

The social work profession contends that a person must have the requisite social work education, that is, either a bachelor's degree with a major in social work or a master's degree in social work (MSW) from an accredited social work program, as a minimum for professional recognition. The accreditation process is administered by the Council on Social Work Education (CSWE) and has become a significant factor in social work because the graduate of the accredited program is assumed to be prepared to enter practice as a beginning-level professional social worker—ready to apply the appropriate knowledge, values, and skills in the service of clients. For all practical purposes education is the primary gatekeeper of the profession. This does not mean that all graduates are equally prepared to enter practice, that some people who do not have all the required social work courses are unable to perform many tasks of a social worker, or even that all schools offer the same opportunity for learning the essentials of social work. Rather, accreditation attests to the fact that the public can have confidence that graduates are at least minimally prepared for beginning-level social work practice because they have completed an instructional program that is soundly designed and taught by competent faculty. Berengarten states that:

The overriding principle of accreditation is based on the belief that a public

service is performed by identifying and publicizing those programs and institutions which merit public confidence.[2]

Job Classification

Does completion of the accredited social work degree in fact prepare people
for social work jobs? Social workers contend that accreditation standards are
related sufficiently to the demands of practice so as to represent sound preparation for the broad scope of social work practice. However, some social agencies that employ large numbers of social workers, such as state welfare departments, have been concerned that education in social work may not
necessarily be suitable preparation for their particular jobs. Because of court
decisions in related fields that held that, if challenged, an employer must be
able to prove that any requirement for a job is indeed valid, a number of
agencies began to redefine social work positions so as to make them open to
people with other preparation. This activity, known as declassification, or
perhaps more accurately as reclassification, has been of major concern to social
workers. They are concerned that the reclassification trend will mean that
clients will receive services from less qualified persons and that other disciplines will attempt to take over what has been social work's professional turf.

In 1979 the U.S. Children's Bureau began funding NASW to conduct a
three-year project that would help employers determine if a social work degree was required for a particular job. The project reviewed court decisions
and the research literature relative to job classification and produced a recommended set of procedures for validating the relationship between social
work education and specific jobs.[3]

Like many other important federally funded projects in the 1980s, the
NASW Classification Validation Project was terminated before it was completed. The final year of the project, for which funding was cut by the Reagan
Administration, was to be devoted to field testing. Despite the inability to
field test at that time, two subsequent projects have successfully tested this
methodology.[4] There is clear indication that this approach, although complex
and somewhat expensive to administer, measures the content of social work
jobs and relates that to the level of preparation for those positions given by
educational programs. Now that there is a procedure to validate social work
education as relevant for social work practice, it is possible to reverse the
declassification trend and more consistently employ practitioners with the
necessary knowledge and skills for the jobs they are performing.

Licensing or State Regulation of Social Work Practice

With the active encouragement of social workers and considerable effort by
the National Association of Social Workers, many states have adopted legislation that provides for the licensing of social work practice—particularly
for social workers engaged in private or nonagency-based practice. In 1987

forty-five jurisdictions had approved some form of regulation for social workers[5] and several others were considering such legislation.

For clients, licensing identifies those social workers who are appropriately prepared with professional education and experience to provide client services. The American Association of State Social Work Boards accurately describes the purpose of licensing as being primarily for the protection of clients:

> Licensure is a process by which an agency of state government or other jurisdiction acting upon legislative mandate grants permission to individuals to engage in the practice of a particular profession or vocation and prohibits all others from legally doing so. By ensuring a level of safe practice, the licensure process protects the general public. Those who are licensed are permitted by the state to use a specific title and perform activities because they have demonstrated to the state's satisfaction that they have reached an acceptable safe level of practice.[6]

Where licensing for social work exists, the person who does not have the requisite preparation who elects to advertise or perform services using the title of social worker is in violation of the law. Moreover, if a licensed social worker is found to be incompetent or engages in unethical practice activities, the state can withdraw his or her license.

For social workers licensing gives legal sanction to their work and is viewed as another indicator of social work's professional maturity. There is, of course, self-interest involved in licensing. The NASW policy statement on licensure includes the following benefits for the profession:

1. Establishing a public, legal definition of the profession that recognizes the differential levels of social work practice.

2. Protecting consumer and clientele rights and raising standards of service competence of practitioners in both agency and independent practice.

3. Establishing a public accountability in the delivery of social services based on professional standards rather than inconsistent, private standards of performance, and that protects the practitioner in the performance of social work tasks.

4. Providing a basis for the development and enhancement of the profession within the context of other social institutions and professions.[7]

Licensing has had an important side effect for many social workers. Since licensing identifies persons the state has judged to be qualified to practice as social workers, it provides third-party vendors (e.g., health insurance companies) with a basis for reimbursing individuals and families for services provided by these social workers. Thus, licensing has directly benefited private practitioners and social workers in agencies that provide direct clinical services. Although most states also make licensing available for social workers engaged in indirect service provision (for example, community planning, administration, and social policy development), people in these positions have experienced only limited value from being licensed.

The precise language required for the laws that license social workers raises the problem identified in Chapter 1 of defining a profession that is both clinical and social change oriented. Since the legislation is primarily intended to protect individual clients, some states have adopted legislation that addresses only the social workers primarily engaged in clinical practice. For example the California law specifies that social workers are licensed to practice "psychotherapy of a nonmedical nature."[8] Some minority group members have had difficulty passing what they consider irrelevant, traditionally clinical, psychotherapy-focused tests and complain their exclusion as practitioners and formulators of licensing standards will not allow the minority communities to receive the quality services to which they are entitled.[9] New York State, on the other hand, defines the purpose of licensed social work practice as "helping individuals, groups and communities to prevent or resolve problems caused by social or emotional stress."[10] This definition is broad enough to embrace the full range of social work services—both clinical practice and social change.

The National Association of Social Workers has developed a model statute to guide the state chapters as they press for licensing legislation. Like the New York law, the Model Licensing Act for Social Workers defines social work in comprehensive terms that include service and action to affect human behavior and the social condition of individuals, families, groups, organizations, and communities, which are influenced by the interaction of social, cultural, political, and economic systems. It describes social work as the disciplined application of social work knowledge, values, principles, and methods in a variety of ways, including, but not restricted to, the following:

1. Counseling and the use of applied psychotherapy with individuals, families, and groups, and other measures to help people modify behavior or make personal and family adjustment.

2. Providing general assistance, information, referral services, and other supportive services.

3. Explaining and interpreting the psychosocial aspects of a situation to individuals, families, or groups.

4. Helping organizations and communities analyze social problems and human needs and provide human services.

5. Helping organizations and communities organize for general neighborhood improvement or community development.

6. Improving social conditions through the application of social planning and social policy formulation.

7. Meeting basic human needs.

8. Assisting in problem-solving activities.

9. Resolving or managing conflict.

10. Bringing about change in the system.[11]

Although some state legislatures have not adopted this broad description of social work practice activities, the NASW model statute identifies an appropriate range of services a social worker should be able to perform. In addition the model statute also calls for licensing at both the generalist baccalaureate and specialist master's levels, although multilevel licensing has not been adopted in all jurisdictions.

Just as the effort to achieve professional status has created a dilemma for social workers (see Chapter 2), so, too, has the issue of licensing. Social workers appreciate the fact that legal sanction of the people qualified to provide social work services protects the public and and recognize that sanction places social work on a solid economic base by allowing social workers to be paid for their services by private insurance companies. At the same time such payment for social work services has tended to increase private practice aimed at middle- and upper-class clients. Few poor people have health insurance. The result has been a diversion of social work from its primary mission of service to vulnerable populations—especially the poor. In addition, the practical benefit of licensing is primarily related to clinical practice for which vendor payments are made. Health insurance programs do not finance social action. Thus, licensing also risks further erosion of social work's historical commitment to social change.

Professional Standards

As indicated in Chapter 2, a profession is required by society to take responsibility for protecting the public from those members who abuse the professional monopoly. To conduct this self-policing, the profession must establish standards and develop procedures for evaluating complaints and imposing sanctions if a member has been found guilty of incompetent or unethical practice.

NASW has devoted considerable attention to matters of professional standards. The most important single document for specifying social work practice expectations is the *Code of Ethics* adopted by NASW in 1979. The code identifies expected behaviors of the professional social worker in the following areas:

1. Conduct and Comportment

2. Ethical Responsibility to Clients

3. Ethical Responsibility to Colleagues

4. Ethical Responsibility to Employers and Employing Organizations

5. Ethical Responsibility to the Social Work Profession

6. Ethical Responsibility to Society[12]

When a social worker joins NASW, he or she must profess willingness to practice within the limits prescribed by the Code of Ethics. The Code, then, serves as the baseline for evaluating the professional behavior of social workers.

Because social work is primarily an agency-based profession, NASW has also established standards for appropriate personnel practices in agencies that employ social workers. These guidelines identify personnel standards and practices that provide for the fair treatment of social workers in the hiring process, adequate working conditions when employed, and proper procedures for the termination of employment.[13] The standards serve as the basis for judging the validity of claims by social workers that they have been wrongfully treated by their employers.

The process established for complaints begins with the local chapter of NASW. An individual or organization may lodge a formal complaint about the practice of a social worker or the personnel practices of an agency. The appropriate committee of the chapter will then conduct an investigation of the complaint and make a determination that the complaint is or is not substantiated. Either party has the right to appeal to the NASW National Committee on Inquiry that reviews the charges and makes a final judgment. When the judgment is that standards have been violated, an individual's membership in NASW may be suspended, and the action taken against either the individual or agency is published in the *NASW News*. The sanctions remain in effect until the terms established by the Committee on Inquiry are satisfied.

RELATED HUMAN SERVICE PRACTICE

Because social work has been late in identifying the particular services that social workers are best prepared to provide among the helping professions, much of the general public is not clear about who should and should not be considered social workers. Further, because the complexity of human needs requires a range of service providers equipped with a variety of knowledge and skills, many people who are providing some form of human services— from volunteers to members of related disciplines—are part of the social service delivery system. The person considering a career in social work should carefully compare social work with these related human service disciplines.

Volunteers

One cannot fully examine the human services without recognizing the important role played by volunteers. For many people who have other vocations, one way to be involved with human services is to volunteer. The willingness to give of oneself, without monetary reward, in order to help others is characteristic of human societies and is expressed in the activity of millions of people who give their time, energy, and talents to make this a better world. It was from efforts to prepare volunteers to provide more effective human services that social work became a paid occupation and, later, a significant helping profession.

Today, social workers work closely with volunteers in many agencies. Their jobs often include the recruitment, selection, training, and supervision of volunteers.[14] Although most commonly found in youth-serving agencies, such as scouting organizations, or the YMCA, volunteers also serve on the boards of, or in a direct working capacity in, every human service agency imaginable—from nursing homes to crisis hotlines to mental hospitals.

The qualifications of volunteers vary from activity to activity. At times professionals volunteer their services beyond their jobs in their own agencies or to help in other agencies. These volunteer activities may use their professional abilities but may also require skills unrelated to professional training. Like any other good citizen, the social worker has an obligation to donate his or her talents in order to improve social conditions.

Most volunteers, however, are not professionals. They are housewives, bankers, auto mechanics, or retired persons, to name but a few. They receive personal gratification from helping others. It is important that volunteers are engaged in activities that fall within their competence and that the experience is personally satisfying.

Nonprofessional Service Providers

All human service practice does not require the competencies of a social worker or someone with related professional skills. Many important services can be provided by persons who bring to the helping situation the perspective of the client population. These people have been referred to in the literature as *indigenous workers*. They may be clients, former clients, or others who have rapport with low-income or other client groups based on having similar experiences to the client population. At times indigenous workers can build relationships with clients when professionals have difficulty establishing working relationships with these people.

Indigenous workers can be found in human service organizations ranging from neighborhood centers to welfare agencies. A sample of tasks an indigenous worker may be expected to perform includes:

- Interviews applicants for services to obtain basic data and provide information on services avilable.

- Interprets programs or services to special cultural groups and helps such groups, or individuals, express their needs.

- Assists people in determining eligibility for services and assembling or obtaining required data or documentation.

- Participates in neighborhood surveys, obtaining data from families or individuals.

- Conducts casefinding activities within the community, encouraging people to make use of available services.

- Provides specific instructions or directions concerning the location or procedures involved in obtaining help.

- Serves as liaison between an agency and special groups or organizations in the community.[15]

The indigenous worker's own life experience and knowledge of the individuals or groups being served are his or her most important qualifications. As the same time the worker is employed in a rewarding job that has the potential through additional education and experience to advance to professional status.

Another important source of nonprofessional personnel for human service agencies are the *graduates of community colleges*. These Associate of Arts (AA) degree programs vary considerably from school to school but focus on preparing for very specific human service jobs with titles such as mental health technician, community service aide, child welfare worker, case aide, or eligibility worker.

The AA degree programs usually include the study of human growth and behavior, social problems, the social service delivery system, personal values and self-awareness, and basic communication skills. These programs may provide field experiences so students have an opportunity to apply knowledge acquired in the classroom. The tasks the AA graduate can be expected to perform are very concrete and require limited individual judgment. They include such activities as fact finding relative to specific cases, interviewing to obtain data, locating sources of assistance, organizing community groups around specific issues, making social provisions (for example, money, food stamps, and housing) available to people, and screening applicants for service.

Other Baccalaureate Level Disciplines

Several disciplines offer majors in colleges and universities that are closely related to social work. Completing these degrees can serve as helpful preparation for some human service jobs and can also be good preparation for a subsequent degree in social work. However, these programs of study should not be confused with social work degree programs that, if accredited, carry professional recognition.

The Social Science Disciplines   Social work has traditionally had a close relationship with the social science disciplines for two reasons. First, social work has drawn on basic knowledge from the fields of psychology, sociology, anthropology, economics, and political science as it developed its theoretical base for understanding the individual, family, group, organization, community, and the impact of culture on all these. Second, in higher education, social work has had close administrative ties with these disciplines at the baccalaureate level. It is not uncommon to find a social work major housed in a sociology department or in a multidisciplinary social science department.

Moreover, the social work student frequently completes a double major or minor in one of the social sciences. Although master's level social work education has traditionally isolated itself from other units of the universities in which it is located, in recent years there has been movement toward developing working relationships and joint master's degree programs with other disciplines.

With the exception of the clinical branch of psychology and the small branch of applied sociology, the social sciences do not intend to engage in the provision of human services. Their purpose is to develop and test theories that will help people understand the aspects of life with which they are concerned. Take sociology for example, the social science discipline most commonly confused with social work. Eighty percent of the 15,000 sociologists in the United States are teachers of sociology at two- or four-year colleges or universities.[16] In addition to their instructional activity, these faculty members are heavily involved in research and theory development. Summarizing a 1975 study of sociologists, Wilson and Selvin state that the 20 percent in nonacademic positions are primarily engaged in research.

> It seems clear that the sociologists' work in business, industry, and government, and private agencies entails, above all, the design and carrying out of research guided by appropriate theory pertinent to a particular field (such as demography) in collaboration with others; and exploiting skills in oral and written communication.[17]

Because most social science jobs are in higher education, employment forecasts are influenced by the projected decline in the number of positions expected to be available in colleges and universities during the next decade. The U.S. Bureau of Labor Statistics defines as social scientists the following occupational groups: anthropologists, economists, geographers, historians, political scientists, psychologists, sociologists, and urban/regional planners. The Bureau estimates the social science disciplines will grow "as fast as average" for all occupations through the mid-1990s, but the demand will come from replacements as opposed to new jobs being created. The number of graduates is expected to exceed the number of new positions creating "strong competition for jobs" in most of these disciplines.[18]

Related Helping Professions When making a career choice within the helping services, a person should examine a wide range of helping professions that might fit his or her individual talents and interests. The more well-known professions are medicine, law, nursing, teaching, and psychology. Some of the less well-known professions such as music therapy, speech pathology, occupational therapy, recreation therapy, urban planning, and school counseling also offer challenging and rewarding careers.

Each of these is an established profession and has prescribed and accredited educational programs a person must complete to be recognized as a member of that profession. Like social work, these professions identify standards for competent and ethical practice and take responsibility for policing the membership for compliance with these standards. The clientele of these professions, then, have some protection from the possible misuse of professional authority. Employment opportunities in these professions vary considerably, but most jobs are defined as requiring the requisite professional education for entry. It is instructive to compare estimates of the demand for social workers with that of other helping professions. Table 3–1 provides a comparison of selected helping professions based on the projections of the U.S. Bureau of Labor Statistics.

Emerging Human Service Occupations   During the 1970s a new occupational group began to emerge in the social services field known generally as *human services* or *human development*. Human services differ from the helping professions we have reviewed because they intend to be nonprofessional. Most people giving leadership to this developing occupation are professionally trained in other disciplines and have been largely involved in corrections and mental health services—although they branch into every aspect of the social services.

The development of the human services field was stimulated by dissatisfaction with the service delivery system. Fundamental to the philosophy behind this field are two viewpoints:

1.   The human services have been fragmented by division into problem areas (e.g., public welfare, mental health, corrections, developmental disabilities, public health, and vocational rehabilitation) that create barriers to client services because, to receive help, the client is often required to work with multiple agencies and multiple professionals. The human services philosophy calls for the integration of services through the development of "umbrella agencies" that will offer a wide range of services with a single staff member providing the help to a client.

2.   The integration of services blurs the boundaries between professions and, therefore, requires that a professional orientation be abandoned in favor of a more generic service orientation. The approach is pragmatic. It is oriented to task completion as opposed to treatment; it is concerned with worker skill development as opposed to knowledge acquisition; it is interested in worker flexibility as opposed to worker professional identification; and (like social work) it is interested in the impact of social institutions, social systems, and social problems on clients.[19]

Social workers would agree that the fragmented methods of delivering social services have made it difficult for clients to obtain these services. However, the profession does not regard service integration as a solution (division lines can exist just as rigidly within one large agency as in several smaller agencies) and believes the professional model, with all its limitations, continues to be a valuable means of identifying persons prepared with the knowl-

TABLE 3–1 Employment Projections Among the Helping Professions

PROFESSION	ESTIMATED WORKERS 1984[1]	ESTIMATED ANNUAL GROWTH RATE[1]	ESTIMATED ANNUAL REPLACEMENT RATE[2]	ANNUAL NEW WORKERS NEEDED	ANNUAL SUPPLY ESTIMATE[2]	ANNUAL SUPPLY AS % OF DEMAND
Much Faster Than Average						
Physical Therapists	58,000	4.2%	10.0%*	8,236	2,948[3]	35.8%
Lawyers	490,000	3.6	4.8	41,160	35,991[7]	87.4
Registered Nurses	1,377,000	3.3	10.2	185,895	116,686[3]	62.8
Occupational Therapists	25,000	3.1	10.0*	3,275	1,918[4]	58.6
Faster Than Average						
Dentists	156,000	2.5%	1.2%	5,772	5,282[7]	91.5%
Physicians	476,000	2.3	1.4	17,612	16,861[7]	95.7
Social Workers	335,000	2.2	16.3	61,975	21,970[4]	35.5
Psychologists	97,000	2.2	7.9	9,797	10,571[5]	107.9
Recreational Workers	123,000	2.1	26.3	34,932	15,084[4]	43.2
Elementary Teacher	1,381,000	2.0	10.6	174,006	69,188[6]	39.8
As Fast As Average						
School Counselors	152,000	1.9%	13.5%	23,000	18,299[4]	78.2%
Speech Pathologists/ Audiologists	47,000	1.7	10.0*	5,499	6,632[4]	120.6
More Slowly Than Average						
Urban Planners	17,000	.9%	10.0%*	1,853	1,638[4]	88.4%
Secondary Teachers	1,045,000	.5	9.3	102,410	74,143[6]	72.4

[1] William M. Austin, "The Job Outlook in Brief," *Occupational Outlook Quarterly* (Spring, 1986), 13–16.
[2] Bureau of Labor Statistics, *Occupational Projections and Training Data, 1984 Edition*, (Washington, D.C.: Government Printing Office, 1984), 13–32.
[3] Includes pre-baccalaureate/baccalaureate, master's/Ph.D. degrees
[4] Includes baccalaureate/master's/Ph.D. degrees
[5] Includes master's/Ph.D. degrees
[6] Includes baccalaureate degree only
[7] Includes professional degree only
* Projections not provided by Bureau of Labor Statistics. A 10 percent annual replacement rate is estimated by authors.

edge, values, and skills to respond to particular human needs. Social work would argue for improving the existing approach to providing social services and for increased interdisciplinary practice, rather than encouraging the development of an occupational group that has no clear service approach, no standards for ethical conduct, no professional responsibility for quality control, no standardized educational preparation, and no professional orientation.

At this time the human services or human development fields seem to identify people who hold a common service philosophy rather than constitute a valid occupational category. The person considering these fields should be advised that the emerging educational programs do not have professional accreditation, do not lead to jobs that can be clearly classified for employment purposes, and do not offer the advantages of the professional model to both the consumer and the worker.

LEVELS OF SOCIAL WORK PRACTICE

As has been seen, social work emerged as a single-level profession—the MSW level—and in the past twenty-five years has evolved into a multiple-level profession. To help bring some order to this patchwork of entry points and differing levels of practice expectations, NASW has developed a helpful classification plan. That scheme is used as a format for the remainder of this chapter. It defines four practice levels: Basic Professional, Specialized Professional, Independent Professional, and Advanced Professional; establishes the requirements of each, and differentiates them on the basis of the following factors:

1. Knowledge required by the position.
2. Responsibility for own practice (autonomy).
3. Type and complexity of skills required.
4. Complexity of the situations faced by clientele.
5. Social consequences of service to society or community.
6. Degree of client vulnerability.
7. Social function (that is, inherent value of the service to the individual and community).[20]

Table 3–2 provides a means of comparing these four practice levels on the basis of descriptions of the expectations for the practitioner and the requisite education and experience preparation at each level.

Basic Professional

The practice at this first level has been formally recognized as "professional" only since 1970, when the NASW first admitted to full membership persons

TABLE 3–2. Levels of Social Work Practice

PRACTICE LEVEL	DESCRIPTION OF LEVEL	PREPARATION FOR PRACTICE
1. Basic Professional	Practice requiring professional practice skills, theoretical knowledge, and values that are not normally obtainable in day-to-day experience but that are obtainable through formal professional social work education. Formal social work education is distinguished from experiential learning by being based on conceptual and theoretical knowledge of personal and social interaction and by training in the disciplined use of self in relationship with clients	Requires a baccalaureate degree (BSW) from a social work program accredited by the Council on Social Work Education (CSWE).
2. Specialized Professional	Practice requiring the specific and demonstrated mastery of therapeutic technique in at least one knowledge and skill method, as well as a general knowledge of human personality as influenced by social factors, and the disciplined use of self in treatment relationships with individuals or groups, or a broad conceptual knowledge of research, administration, or planning methods and social problems.	Requires a master's degree (MSW) from a social work program accredited by the CSWE.

3. Independent Professional

Achievement of practice based on the appropriate special training, developed and demonstrated under professional supervision, which is sufficient to ensure the dependable, regular use of professional skills in independent or autonomous practice. A minimum of two years is required for this experiential learning and demonstration period following the master of social work program. This level applies both to solo or autonomous practice as an independent practitioner or consultant and to practice within an organization where the social worker has primary responsibility for representing the profession or for the training or administration of professional staff.

Requires an accredited MSW and at least two years of post-master's experience under appropriate professional supervision.

4. Advanced Professional

Practice that carries major social and organizational responsibility for professional development, analysis, research, or policy implementation, or is achieved by personal professional growth demonstrated through advanced conceptual contributions to professional knowledge.

Requires proficiency in special theoretical, practice, administration, or policy or the ability to conduct advanced research studies in social welfare; usually demonstrated through a doctoral degree in social work or a closely related social science discipline.

Source: Copyright © 1981, National Association of Social Workers, Inc. Reprinted with permission from *NASW Standards for the Classification of Social Work Practice* (Washington, D.C.: The Association, September 1981), p. 9.

with a BA or BSW from a social work program approved by the Council on Social Work Education. This recognition not only reflected a movement away from professional elitism but also reinforced the increased quantity and quality of undergraduate social work programs that had emerged since the mid-1960s.

Some baccalaureate-level social work education has existed for many years.[21] A few schools offered social work courses at this level as early as the 1920s. However, the thrust of social work was toward graduate education. In 1932 the American Association of Schools of Social Work (AASSW) declared that, to be recognized as professional, a social worker must graduate from a four-year college and complete at least one year of graduate education. In 1937 this position was revised to establish two years of graduate education as the minimum level for professional practice.

In response to the AASSW policy, several schools created in 1942 a competing organization, the National Association of Schools of Social Administration (NASSA), for the purpose of having undergraduate programs recognized as professional preparation. After several years of conflict over the legitimacy of undergraduate education, thirteen organizations interested in the resolution of this issue and in the overall enhancement of social work education formed the National Council on Social Work Education. As an initial activity of this organization, the Hollis–Taylor study of social work education was commissioned.[22]

The Hollis–Taylor report, released in 1951, urged that undergraduate education maintain a broad focus and avoid teaching social work skills or preparing students for social work practice upon graduation. However, the process by which this study was conducted created harmony between the AASSW and the NASSA, which then merged with the National Council in 1952 to create what is now the single accrediting body for social work education: the Council on Social Work Education (CSWE).

The CSWE offered membership to both undergraduate and graduate schools and undertook a thirteen-volume curriculum study of social work education at both levels. One volume of this study recommended establishment of professional social work education at the undergraduate level with a continuum developed from undergraduate to graduate programs.[23] This recommendation was initially rejected by the CSWE and was not implemented until the NASW and CSWE took action in 1970 to recognize that quality undergraduate programs could prepare professional-level social workers.

During most of the 1960s, undergraduate programs operated under CSWE guidelines based on the following objectives:

1. To contribute to liberal education by developing a citizen who is knowledgeable about social work and other human service professions;

2. To improve the preparation of persons who wish to enter schools of social work;

3. To train personnel who can perform social welfare functions for which a baccalaureate degree is sufficient.[24]

These programs might best be described as a traditional liberal arts education oriented toward social welfare. They were usually taught in departments of psychology or sociology, offered no more than three or four social work courses, and often had no social workers as faculty. With little independent identity on their campuses, and with the failure of both employers and graduate social work programs to give preference or credit for completion of these programs, they were not popular—even among students who planned to enter social work. It is still not uncommon for the social worker who is unaware of the significant developments in undergraduate education in the 1970s to recommend that college students interested in social work complete a major in psychology or sociology. This viewpoint reflects the disrepute of undergraduate programs in the 1960s and fails to recognize improvements of the past two decades.

Disenchantment of students, employers, and professional social workers with undergraduate education contributed to the establishment of a Joint CSWE–NASW Ad Hoc Committee on Manpower Issues in 1968. The Committee's recommendations contributed to concurrent actions in 1970 by NASW members to grant full membership to graduates of approved undergraduate programs and by the CSWE to establish standards for approval of these programs. The standards adopted were essentially structural: they contributed to the visibility of social work programs, required that social workers be included in faculty, and demanded specification of educational objectives.[25] CSWE curriculum guidelines recommended—but did not require—the inclusion of content in the following areas:

1. Man and his environment.

2. Social welfare services and social welfare practice: philosophical and historical perspectives.

3. Policies, programs, and issues related to social welfare institutions and services.

4. Scientific method.

5. Communication skills.

6. Social work practice.

7. Field instruction.

CSWE "approval" was granted to 220 schools by 1973, but was at best a limited and informal type of accreditation. It was primarily concerned that the schools have an adequate structure for the growth and development of a baccalaureate program. Specification of curriculum content was slower to develop because a workable division between baccalaureate- and master's-level education had not evolved. One study indicated that most approved programs offered courses introducing the student to the social welfare institution and to social work as a profession, with at least one social work practice course, while about one-half offered a social welfare policy course, one-third offered courses in human behavior and the social environment, and all required a practicum or field experience, which varied from four hours per week for one term to as much as twelve hours per week for four terms.[26]

In 1973 CSWE took the second step to complete legitimate accreditation: it adopted much more substantial standards for baccalaureate degree programs, placing the primary focus on preparation for professional social work practice.[27] By 1987 there were 349 fully accredited baccalaureate programs with 22 more in candidacy status.[28] Reports from 83.5 percent of the accredited programs for the 1985–86 academic year indicated that they had more than 23,500 full-time students and approximately 3,000 part-time students enrolled as majors in social work. After peaking in 1978 with about 30,000 full-time majors, undergraduate social work education programs experienced a severe decline in the early 1980s, which reached a low of 20,000 in 1983 but now is generally increasing each year.[29]

In 1984 a significant step to further upgrade the quality of baccalaureate social work education was taken when the Council on Social Work Education operationalized a new set of accreditation standards and a much more substantive Curriculum Policy Statement. The Standards spell out the expectations for each program relative to its purpose, structure, and resources. The Standards also require that each school's curriculum be consistent with the Curriculum Policy Statement.[30] While the latter does not dictate how any school shall organize its curriculum, it is considerably more explicit than the 1974 Accreditation Standards about the content of the student's learning experience.

With NASW recognition has come the gradual acceptance of baccalaureate-level social work, both by employers as preparation for practice and by the graduate programs as preparation for advanced standing. Increasingly, jobs have been defined to recognize the competence and abilities of social workers who have completed this type of educational program, and salary and work assignments have been differentiated from those without this preparation. Furthermore, in 1972 CSWE granted approval for graduate schools to accept up to one full year credit for special groups of students. By 1985, fifty-six graduate programs offered some form of *advanced standing* to graduates of accredited programs that typically amounted to waiving one to two terms of graduate work.

The NASW classification system presents expectations for the basic social worker in relation to the seven factors that characterize social work practice. Clearly, the developments in the 1970s and 1980s enhance the conclusion that the social worker who has completed an accredited undergraduate social work program should be prepared with the competencies for the level of professional practice identified in Box 3–1.

BOX 3–1   ILLUSTRATIVE PRACTICE COMPETENCIES FOR THE BASIC PROFESSIONAL SOCIAL WORKER

Knowledge

Basic and general knowledge of human behavior, social systems, and social institutions.

Awareness of social problem areas—their cause and impact on individuals, families, and communities, and the appropriate resources and methods involved in dealing with them.

Knowledge of basic theories and methods of casework or group work.

Working knowledge of at least one specific method of intervention or treatment.

Working knowledge of basic research techniques and sources of specialized, professional knowledge.

Specific knowledge of social planning and community organization methods.

Responsibility

Functions under direct and regularly provided professional supervision.

Is instructed in specific details of tasks, assuming a general knowledge of professional methods, functions, and objectives.

Casework or other professional judgments must be renewed to confirm decisions that affect clients in complex situations.

Acts professionally on one's judgment within an assigned scope of practice.

Determines client's or community's needs for service within one's practice area. Initiate or terminate one's own or another's services.

Supervises others in services they are qualified to provide.

Is advised of administrative requirements or consultative supervision.

Requires regular direct supervision. Requires regular direct supervision for learning specialized practice.

Skill

Ability to relate in positive or appropriate relationships under adverse conditions.

Ability to recognize primary behavior dysfunction of individuals and groups.

Ability to make a basic social assessment and service plan.

Awareness of community resources relevant to identified needs.

Ability to relate as a professional participant in an agency program.

Ability to carry out basic techniques of social research.

Ability to conduct or participate in methods of community organization and planning.

Ability to conduct a comprehensive social study or treatment plan within a given service.

Ability to initiate and develop community-group programs within given standards.

Situational Complexity

Routine service or tasks whose goal is easily achievable.

Single function of limited difficulty.

Clear expectation of clients.

Clients with noncompetitive interests when resources are available.

Temporary, uninvolved helping relationship.

Identified emotional and social needs with only limited or potential resources.

Some degree of unconscious motivation.

Service goals are achievable.

Social Consequences

Minor potential effect, the impact being limited to one or a small number of clients.

Potential errors or shortcomings limited in scope.

Benefits significant, but not essential to health or life.

Service or program involves a significant social problem.

Client Vulnerability

Minimal risk to persons or groups.

Potential risks temporary or correctable.

Client or groups with a clear and valid expectation of service.

Actions closely or regularly supervised or evaluated.

Actions or decisions governing a client's situation subject to prior approval.

Actions or activities have no significant impact on costs.

Significant health or emotional need or risk of injury involved.

Service or treatment errors not readily corrected or ameliorated.

Clear identifiable impact on the client or community.

Administration and planning of a program have a minor impact on costs.

Social Function

To provide information on rights, benefits, and services.

To obtain social and personal information or data within specified limits of ethics and confidentiality.

To advise the public or clients of social expectations and requirements in a constructive, helping relationship.

To develop data or other research information for the analysis or study of social problems.

To deal with negative or mildly hostile persons or groups on behalf of society.

To enable clients or persons seeking aid to understand, accept, or use help in relation to a social problem.

To interpret and build trust among resident individuals or groups in services designed to provide help.

To enable individuals or groups to involve themselves in socially-constructive activities or changes in conduct.

To work with hostile persons or groups to achieve or improve understanding or cooperation.

Source: Copyright © 1981, National Association of Social Workers, Inc. Reprinted with permission from *NASW Standards for the Classification of Social Work Practice* (Washington, D.C.: The Association, September 1981), pp. 20–21.

Specialized Professional

Prior to the re-emergence of baccalaureate-level social work education and the basic social worker, the generally accepted level of preparation for social work practice was that of the specialized social worker. At this level the social worker must have completed a master's degree from one of the ninety-two accredited master's level social work education programs or one of the seven programs in pre-accreditation status. Although it is expected that the MSW social worker, too, will make use of professional supervision, he or she should have sufficient competence to appropriately exercise independent judgment and initiative.

Historically, social work education began as a similar version of the more sophisticated in-service training programs of today. The first formal education program was initiated under the auspices of the New York Charity Organization Society in 1898. This school, the New York School of Philanthropy, began with a six-week summer course for social workers. It evolved into a one-year program in 1904 and expanded into a two-year program in 1911. From the settlement house movement, another root of social work, cooperative extension courses were offered for college graduates, beginning in 1901, by the Chicago Commons Settlement in cooperation with the University of Chicago. In 1907 these courses became part of the Chicago School of Civics and Philanthropy and in 1920 became affiliated with the University of Chicago—the first school of social work entirely under university auspices. The first full-time school of social work was established as a joint program between Simmons College and Harvard University in 1904. Harper summarized the situation in the early 1900s when he stated that "at the beginning of the present century education for social work was predominantly at the undergraduate level."[31]

As Chapter 2 indicates, the growing interest that social work become a profession was an important factor in the development of educational programs at the graduate level. In 1915 the first fully-graduate school was established at Bryn Mawr. Further, as many of the undergraduate and agency-based educational programs matured, they were elevated to the master's level.

The early curricula of these schools involved preparation for a range of services from individual helping approaches to economic and reform theory. They included a heavy investment in internships or field experience as a tool for learning practice skills and tended to be organized around practice settings, such as hospital social work and school social work. Their greatest emphasis was on preparation for the services offered by private social agencies and they tended to neglect the growing demand for social workers in the public social services.

By the 1940s the two-year MSW had become the minimum requirement for professional practice, although a few schools with strong undergraduate programs were resisting that requirement. The two-year programs were organized around what was known as the "Basic Eight," in reference to the eight primary divisions of social work practice: public welfare, social casework, social group work, community organization, medical information, social research, psychiatry, and social welfare administration. Although each school did not offer all the Basic Eight, these practice divisions reflected the major areas of social work practice and education.

The period from 1950 through 1965 was one of rapid growth in the number of MSW programs and the relative standardization of these programs. By 1965 there were sixty-seven accredited graduate schools and nearly 9,000 students.[32] The schools had largely abandoned programs structured on the basis of practice setting and instead organized curricula around the practice methods of casework, group work, community organization, administration, and research.

Several significant developments have occurred in social work education at the graduate level since 1965. There has been a general movement by CSWE toward allowing individual schools more flexibility in determining curriculum content, provided the content is consistent with the educational objectives of the school and is within the general parameters of the Curriculum Policy Statement. The graduate programs have typically built the first year of the two-year programs on the basis of a generalist practice model and added their unique specializations to the second-year curricula. The establishment of advanced standing programs based on the student's prior experience, usually completion of a bachelor's level social work program, encouraged the graduate programs to keep their programs carefully articulated with baccalaureate education. Prior to the last two decades, students considering MSW programs could expect pretty much the same basic curriculum regardless of which school they attended. The reasons for selecting a school were usually based on geography, quality of faculty, or availability of financial assistance. Today, this selection is appropriately based on the specialization the student desires to have developed by the time the MSW is completed. In a real sense graduate social work education is becoming what has traditionally been the expectation of graduate level work, that is, it is more substantive and specialized than that which one would find at the baccalaureate level.

The number of MSW programs has continually increased through the years, but beginning in 1979–80 MSW programs began a marked decline in full-time enrollments, which leveled out in 1983–84 and have remained relatively constant since.[33] For persons interested in obtaining a master's degree in social work, the chances of being admitted to a graduate school are quite good with two-thirds of the applicants being accepted in 1985. For students completing undergraduate social work education programs and seeking advanced standing in MSW programs, more than 75 percent were accepted allowing these students a shortened period of graduate education.[34] The number of part-time students in graduate social work programs increased by nearly 30 percent between 1981 and 1985 and make up more than one-third of all MSW students.[35]

What accounts for the decline in applications to MSW programs during this period? We can only speculate, but several factors appear to be involved. While there has been a decline in the number of full-time students, there has been an almost equal increase in the number of part-time MSW students. This information suggests that although the job market for social workers is tighter than it was several years ago, there continues to be a substantial number of people who desire graduate education in this profession. It would appear that the conservative political climate and the subsequent decrease in financial aid for graduate students in social work, as well as the increasing share of the costs of higher education being borne by the consumer, has led some students to pursue this degree on a part-time basis while working elsewhere. Other potential students have undoubtedly been priced out of the market for graduate social work education and have not applied.

The difference between the basic social worker and the specialized social worker has been a point of contention in social work. A comparison of Box 3–1 and Box 3–2 reveals that the specialized or master's-level prepared social worker has a more extensive knowledge base in one or more areas of specialization and operates with greater autonomy in more complex practice situations. Although the NASW classification system begins to clarify these differences, an important next step in understanding these two levels is to utilize carefully controlled research and analysis to determine the degree to which social workers at these levels do, in fact, differently perform the functions identified in this classification scheme.

Independent Professional

This classification identifies the experienced specialized social worker. It requires no additional academic preparation but assumes a person has achieved greater competence from increased experience and professional supervision.

**BOX 3–2   ILLUSTRATIVE PRACTICE COMPETENCIES
FOR THE SPECIALIZED PROFESSIONAL SOCIAL WORKER**

Knowledge

Knowledge of personality theory, interpersonal communications, social group relations, or community organization theory.

A working knowledge of several methods of interpersonal helping or treatment. Knowledge of at least one psychotherapeutic technique.

A broad and beginning specialized knowledge of at least one such knowledge area.

Knowledge of the theory and techniques of professional and personnel supervision and organizational administration.

Basic knowledge of the administration of social programs.

Knowledge of the appropriate techniques and methods of research or planning.

Responsibility

Normally functions under periodic or consultative supervision. Requires learning for specialized practice.

Is advised of administrative requirements and expected to adhere to them adequately.

Requires instruction only in highly complex, specialized, or new methods or procedures.

Directs or administers a program staffed by professional social workers and other personnel.

Reviews work of subordinate professional workers. Assigns and evaluates social work activities.

Skill

Ability to establish constructive relationships with resistant clients by overcoming strong initial resistance or dealing with conflict-laden or complex situations.

Ability to design and conduct research.

Ability to provide psychotherapeutic treatment under supervision.

Ability to administer a social service program of limited scope within a larger setting.

Ability to determine differential treatment needs.

Ability to provide professional social work training or supervision.

Ability to represent the discipline of professional social work within an interdisciplinary program.

Ability to develop and conduct a treatment-therapy program or service without direct supervision.

Ability to provide a specialized treatment or method of service.

Situational Complexity

Involves two or more clients with divergent interests.

Multiple service functions with responsibility for coordination of services or personnel.

Goals present major difficulties.

Clients who are emotionally confused or have conflicting social needs.

Resources not readily available.

Social Consequences

Activity requires interdisciplinary coordination.

Actions have a serious but temporary impact and involve more than one client.

Service or program involves a significant social problem.

Client Vulnerability

Actions involve the potential for a long-lasting but not life-threatening condition or a risk to mental stability.

Ability of client or groups to identify needs is severely limited.

Social Function

To overcome strong resistance to participation or use of socially required assistance or conduct involving the protection of others.

To achieve socially desirable changes in conduct involving significant emotional and mental growth and change.

To achieve long-lasting or broad-scale change toward socially desired objectives.

Source: Copyright © 1981, National Association of Social Workers, Inc. Reprinted with permission from NASW Standards for the Classification of Social Work Practice (Washington, D.C.: The Association, September 1981), p. 24.

The independent social worker is expected to have developed and integrated the knowledge, values, and skills of social work in at least one practice area. From this experience he or she should be able to develop sufficient expertise in that field to function independently and skillfully in sensitive situations. Furthermore, the independent social worker should be able to provide leadership in at least one practice arena and to supervise and consult with other social workers.

One indicator of reaching the independent professional level is membership in the Academy of Certified Social Workers (ACSW). The ACSW was established in 1960 to protect clients from the abuses and incompetence of inadequately-prepared practitioners. The ACSW also strives to establish a favorable public image, to obtain societal sanction, and to increase public confidence and understanding of social work.[36] Initially, the requirements for ACSW membership were completion of an MSW degree, employment for two years under the supervision of an ACSW-level social worker, membership in the NASW, and payment of dues. The organization made no attempts to evaluate one's social work practice or one's level of competence. Thus, membership really signified nothing more than certification of post-degree experience and dues payment. The ACSW was severely criticized by a number of social workers because of its lack of evaluative standards.

In 1969 the ACSW requirements were revised to incorporate qualitative standards for certification. Beginning in 1971, certification was granted only after evaluation of the following materials:

1.   An application form (incorporating a curriculum vitae).

2.   An objective multiple-choice written test.

3.   References from professional peers.

4.   An oral interview.[37]

Although data are not available to evaluate the effectiveness of the ACSW in achieving its goals, these revisions clearly represent a significant move in the direction of making the certification of social workers meaningful.

According to the *NASW Standards for the Classification of Social Work Practice*, the factors influencing practice reported in Box 3–3 reflect the expected level of competence for the independent professional.

BOX 3–3   ILLUSTRATIVE PRACTICE COMPETENCIES FOR THE INDEPENDENT PROFESSIONAL SOCIAL WORKER

Knowledge

Sufficient expert knowledge to teach or communicate social work practice and theory to professionals in other disciplines or in an interdisciplinary service.

A thorough knowledge of at least one method of professional practice and specialized knowledge of others.

Responsibility

Acts professionally on his or her judgment.

Determines clients' or the community's need for service within one's own practice area. Initiates or terminates one's own or another's services.

Requires instruction only in highly complex, new or specialized methods or procedures of treatment, research, planning, or other mode of work.

Obtains professional supervision on a consultative basis, as needed.

Skill

Ability to conduct a psychotherapy of a highly complex or demanding nature.

Ability to conduct differential diagnoses of individuals or groups, involving complex and unconscious factors.

Ability to administer an autonomous social work, health or mental health program of limited scope or one of major scope within a larger organization.

Ability to take full professional responsibility in a multidisciplinary setting or for general community development or services.

Situational Complexity

Severe conflicts between persons or groups served.

Multiple causative factors—major lack of resources.

Clear evidence of unconscious needs that restrict the ability of a client to change.

Highly complex emotional and social goals of service.

Social Consequences

Actions with the potential for a major or long-lasting impact.

Activities that provide the basis for reviewing, studying, or developing a policy.

Vulnerability

Administration, planning, or research involve moderate costs or risks.

Actions involve the potential for a risk to mental stability.

Inability of clients or groups to identify their own needs.

Social Function

To negotiate and mediate among deeply opposed persons or groups to achieve socially sanctioned objective.

To conduct broad-scale research studies that deal with specific social or community issues.

To provide treatment to overcome major problems involving social dysfunctions, behavior, or severe risk to others.

Advanced Professional

This classification represents the most highly-experienced and advanced education level of social work. It calls for extensive practice or research skills and implies the completion of either a doctoral degree in social work (DSW or Ph.D.) or a doctoral degree in a closely-related social science discipline. In contrast to many professions, few social workers achieve—or even aspire to achieve—the advanced professional level.

Doctoral education in social work was initiated nearly three quarters of a century ago, but experienced its major growth only relatively recently. Thomas Holland and Abbie Frost summarize the historical development of doctoral programs as follows:

> The early years of doctoral education in social work were marked by slow growth of programs. Expansion has accelerated in recent years. In the three decades after Bryn Mawr College accepted its first doctoral student (1915), five more universities began offering the doctorate in social work—the University of Chicago (1924), the Catholic University (1934), the Ohio State University (1934), the University of Pittsburgh (1945), and Saint Louis University (1947). In the 1950s, eight new programs were opened and in the 1960s seven more swelled the ranks. A sharp expansion occurred over the next decade— sixteen new programs were launched. Another eleven have opened their doors since 1980, and four more new programs are scheduled to open before this decade ends.[38]

The purposes for establishing doctoral programs in social work have been mixed. The organization formed to provide an arena for discussing common issues experienced by doctoral programs in the late 1970s, the Group for Advancement of Doctoral Education, has constantly wrestled with the problem of identifying an appropriate purpose for doctoral education. Should these programs be viewed as research or clinical? Should the research focus be academic or directed to social work practice? Should these programs devote their efforts to preparing the advanced practitioner or the teacher/researcher? Should the main goal be to credential social workers so they might more effectively compete with other professionals or should the main goal be to create a cadre of leadership that can further the development of this profession? Each program answers these questions in its own way. Since the doctorate is not viewed as an entry degree for the social work profession, these programs receive their sanction only from their universities and do not participate in a professional accreditation process. Therefore, the schools have considerable flexibility to determine the focus of their curricula and have taken on somewhat unique identities.

With 15 percent of the doctoral programs failing to report their enrollment data for 1985, the last year for which data are available, it is difficult accurately to report trends in social work doctoral education. A reasonable approximation would be that for any one year there are 800 to 900 full-time students enrolled, an equal number of part-time students, and 200 to 300 students who will graduate from a social work program with the DSW or the Ph.D.[39] This does not, however, establish the total number of social workers completing doctoral degrees, since some persons complete doctoral-level work in related fields such as sociology, psychology, higher education, and public administration.

At this time the advanced social worker represents a very small part of social work and is rarely recognized in job classification or licensing criteria. The competencies of this social worker are listed in Box 3–4, and are aspired to by social workers with increasing frequency.

BOX 3–4 ILLUSTRATIVE PRACTICE COMPETENCIES FOR THE ADVANCED PROFESSIONAL SOCIAL WORKER

Knowledge

Advanced and expert knowledge in practice, research, administration, planning, or teaching.

Highly specialized and expert knowledge in a social work content area.

A thorough knowledge of several types of vulnerable populations, corresponding service delivery systems, methods for assessing needs and planning to relate the service delivery systems to human needs that are high priorities.

Responsibility

Directs major research study involving design, staffing, management, technical responsibility, writing, and budget.

Has chief administrative responsibility for major social service or multiservice department or organization.

Has responsibility for a major planning or policy-setting function.

Skill

Ability to design and conduct complex or extended research or planning studies involving multiple or discordant factors.

Highly specialized expertise in at least one social work method.

Ability to administer a major social work, social welfare, mental health, or health program or department with broad management and budgetary responsibilities.

Situational Complexity

Multiple, complex technical operations.

Broad-ranging organizational and administrative requirements and policies.

Long-range planning for the development of resources.

Social Consequences

Actions that have major public or social consequences.

Client Vulnerability

Administration, planning, and research involve long-lasting or major public costs risks.

Social Function

To develop techniques or policies designed to further social objectives.

To conduct, write, and present social research studies of major scope.

Source: Copyright © 1981, National Association of Social Workers, Inc. Reprinted with permission from *NASW Standards for the Classification of Social Work Practice* (Washington, D.C.: The Association, September 1981), p. 24.

CONCLUDING COMMENT

The NASW classification plan represents an important step in the difficult task of differentiating practice at the several levels that have evolved in social work. Periodic revisions of these standards and research into the accuracy with which they portray social work practice will not only help to further define social work levels, but also will help to make a better distinction between social work and related disciplines.

There is no uniform acceptance within the social work field of these multiple practice levels nor of a range of professional levels extending from the basic to the advanced social worker. It may well be several more years before the public, social agencies, clients, and even social workers themselves fully appreciate this range of levels as legitimate parts of social work. When that happens, clients will have more ready access to social workers who are equipped to supply the specific services they need and social workers, hopefully, will devote more energy to strengthening the quality of practice at each level.

For the person considering a career in social work, knowledge of these levels of practice helps to identify possible entry and terminal points. The selection of a particular practice level as a goal for any individual must depend on personal interest, the desire to provide a particular type of service for which that level offers the necessary preparation, and the ability to arrange one's life to acquire the necessary professional education to prepare for practice at that level. Recognizing that a person's goals and aspirations may change, social work offers an advantage over many other professions by presenting the opportunity to enter at a basic practice level and build on that background to achieve more advanced levels.

SUGGESTED READINGS

Austin, David M. *A History of Social Work Education.* Austin: University of Texas at Austin School of Social Work, 1986, Social Work Education Monograph Series, #1.

Berengarten, Sidney. *The Nature and Objectives of Accreditation and Social Work Education.* Austin: University of Texas at Austin School of Social Work, 1986, Social Work Education Monograph Series, #2.

Holland, Thomas P., and Frost, Abbie K. *Doctoral Education in Social Work: Trends and Issues.* Austin: University of Texas at Austin School of Social Work, 1987, Social Work Education Monograph Series, #5.

Karl, Barry D. "Lo, the Poor Volunteer: An Essay on the Relation between History and Myth," *Social Service Review* 58 (December 1984): 493–522.

National Association of Social Workers. *NASW Standards for the Classification of Social Work Practice.* Washington, D.C.: The Association, September 1981.

Pecora, Peter J., and Austin, Michael J. "Declassification of Social Service Jobs: Issues and Strategies." *Social Work* (November–December 1983): 421–426.

Rubin, Allen. *Current Statistical Trends in Social Work Education: Issues and Implications.* Austin: University of Texas at Austin School of Social Work, 1986, Social Work Education Monograph Series, #4.

Sheafor, Bradford W., and Shank, Barbara W. *Undergraduate Social Work Education: A Survivor in a Changing Profession.* Austin: University of Texas at Austin School of Social Work, 1986, Social Work Education Monograph Series, #3.

ENDNOTES

1. Sigmund Nosow, "Social Correlates of Occupational Membership," in Sigmund Nosow and William H. Form, eds., *Man, Work, and Society,* (New York: Basic Books, 1962), pp. 517–535.

2. Sidney Berengarten, "Accreditation: Its Nature and Objectives," *Social Work Education Reporter* 29 (September 1981): 11.

3. Robert J. Teare, et al., *Classification Validation Processes for Social Service Positions,* Vols. I–VII, Silver Spring, Md.: National Association of Social Workers, 1984.

4. Bradford W. Sheafor, Robert J. Teare, Mervyn W. Hancock, and Thomas P. Gauthier, "Curriculum Development Through Content Analysis: A New Zealand Experience," *Journal of Education for Social Work* 21 (Fall 1985): 113–124 and Robert J. Teare, *Validating Social Work Credentials for Human Service Jobs: Report of a Demonstration,* Washington, D.C.: National Association of Social Workers, 1987.

5. "Licensure Law Enacted; Two Others Revisited," *NASW News* 32 (September 1987): 10.

6. Robert R. Wohlgemuth and Thomas Samph, *Summary Report: Content Validity Study in Support of the Licensure Examination Program of The American Association of State Social Work Boards,* Oak Park, Ill.: American Association of State Social Work Boards, 1983, p. 2.

7. "The 1975 Delegate Assembly Actions: Professional Issues; Legal Regulation of Social Work Practice Policies for a Continuing Effort," *NASW News* 20 (July 1975): 15.

8. David G. Phillips, "The Swing toward Clinical Practice," *Social Work* 20 (January 1975): 61.

9. Robert A. Salinas, "Licensing: Will It Protect the Chicano Community?" *Mano a Mano* 3 (January 1974): 2.

10. Phillips, "The Swing Toward Clinical Practice," p. 61.

11. National Association of Social Workers, "The Model Statute," in *Handbook on the Private Practice of Social Work* (Washington, D.C.: The Association, 1974), pp. 58–59.

12. *NASW News* 26 (January 1980): 24. See Chapter 8 for reprint of the entire Code of Ethics.

13. National Association of Social Workers, *Standards for Social Work Personnel Practices: Policy Statement #2* (Washington, D.C.: The Association, 1971).

14. Bradford W. Sheafor, Charles R. Horejsi, and Gloria A. Horejsi, *Techniques and Guidelines for Social Work Practice* (Boston: Allyn and Bacon, 1988), pp. 450–453 and Ralph G. Navarre, *Professional Administration of Volunteer Programs* (Madison, Wis.: "N"–Way Publishing, 1986).

15. National Association of Social Workers, *Standards for Social Service Manpower* (Washington, D.C.: The Association, 1973), p. 14.

16. Everett K. Wilson and Hanan Selvin, *Why Study Sociology: A Note to Undergraduates* (Belmont, Calif.: Wadsworth, 1980), pp. 9–10.

17. Ibid., p. 14.

18. U.S. Department of Labor, *1984–85 Occupational Outlook Handbook* (Washington, D.C.: Government Printing Office, 1984), pp. 100–101.

19. Joseph Mehr, *Human Services: Concepts and Intervention Strategies* (Boston: Allyn and Bacon, 1980), pp. 12–20.

20. National Association of Social Workers, *NASW Standards for the Classification of Social Work Practice.* (Washington, D.C.: The Association, September 1981), p. 8.

21. A comprehensive analysis of the growth and development of baccalaureate level social work can be found in Bradford W. Sheafor and Barbara W. Shank, *Undergraduate Social Work Education: A Survivor in a Changing Profession* (Austin: University of Texas at Austin School of Social Work, 1986).

22. Ernest V. Hollis and Alice L. Taylor, *Social Work Education in the United States* (New York: Columbia University Press, 1951).

23. Herbert Bisno, *The Place of Undergraduate Curriculum in Social Work Education*, Social Work Curriculum Study, Vol. 2 (New York: CSWE, 1959).

24. Council on Social Work Education, *Social Welfare Content in Undergraduate Education* (New York: CSWE, 1962), pp. 3–4.

25. Council on Social Work Education, *Undergraduate Programs in Social Work* (New York: CSWE, 1971).

26. Alfred Stamm, *An Analysis of Undergraduate Social Work Programs Approved by CSWE, 1971* (New York: Council on Social Work Education, 1972).

27. Council on Social Work Education, "Standards for the Accreditation of Baccalaureate Degree Programs in Social Work," (mimeographed, New York: CSWE, 1973).

28. Council on Social Work Education, *Colleges and Universities with Accredited Social Work Degree Programs*, (Washington, D.C.: CSWE, 1987).

29. Allen Rubin, *Statistics on Social Work Education in the United States, 1985*, (Washington, D.C.: Council on Social Work Education, 1986), p. 53.

30. Council on Social Work Education, *Handbook of Accreditation Standards and Procedures*, rev. ed., (Washington, D.C.: CSWE, 1984).

31. Ernest V. Harper, "The Study of Social Work Education: Its Significance for the Undergraduate Educational Institutions," *Social Work Journal*, 22 (October 1951): 179.

32. Raymond DeVera, ed., *Statistics on Social Work Education, 1965–66* (New York: Council on Social Work Education, 1966), p. 6.

33. Allen Rubin, *Current Statistical Trends in Social Work Education: Issues and Implications* (Austin: University of Texas at Austin School of Social Work, 1986), pp. 5–10.

34. Rubin, *Statistics on Social Work Education, 1985*, p. 73.

35. Ibid., p. 54.

36. Philip Klein, *From Philanthropy to Social Welfare* (San Francisco: Jossey–Bass, 1968), pp. 215–216.

37. "ACSW Certification: What, Where, When, Why, How?" *NASW News* 16 (March 1971): 4–5. As late as 1988 the proposal for an oral interview had not been implemented and no plans were on the horizon to initiate it.
38. Thomas P. Holland and Abbie K. Frost, *Doctoral Education in Social Work: Trends and Issues* (Austin: University of Texas at Austin School of Social Work, 1987), p. 1.
39. Rubin, *Statistics on Social Work Education, 1985*, p. 54.

Part Two

The Context
of Social Work

One characteristic of Western societies is their tendency to create social institutions to meet human needs. Two institutions have been dominant in U.S. society—the family and the market economy. During the past 150 years rapid change created by industrialization and urbanization has strained the ability of these two institutions to adequately respond to human needs. For example, specialization and the increased use of modern technology has made it more difficult for the physically and mentally handicapped person to find employment. Or, as individuals became more mobile in order to use their more highly specialized skills in business and industry, they also became isolated from the support of their extended families. Thus, the need for a social welfare institution that could help meet some of these social needs evolved.

Today a number of professionals deliver social programs that are intended to meet these human needs. These professionals include social workers, physicians, recreation specialists, public health nurses, occupational therapists, psychologists, and others. The social programs take the form of direct provisions, social services, and social action efforts. Most of these programs are delivered through not-for-profit social agencies that employ these professionals, but some are offered through profit-oriented organizations or through private practice situations.

Particularly in the social provision programs, such as those giving food, clothing, or money, volunteers and nonprofessionals provide valuable services. Among the nonprofessionals are receptionists, eligibility technicians, food stamp clerks, and homemakers, to name but a few. For most services, however, professional knowledge and skills are required. The different professional disciplines each bring their special knowledge, values, and skills to the helping process. In the various practice fields one also finds different roles performed by the disciplines. For example, in a family service agency the social worker is the primary professional, while teaching is the primary discipline in a school and other disciplines are viewed as supportive to this effort. In still other settings, such as a mental health center, several disciplines may be equal partners as a premium is placed on interdisciplinary teamwork.

The social programs, the various disciplines, and the human service agencies or entrepreneurial practice settings provide the context in which social work exists. Figure II–1 depicts this context as an important dimension of the social worker's focus on people interacting with their environment. The social worker helps the person and the relevant parts of the environment as they seek to improve their interaction. For the agency-based social worker, that agency becomes a part of the environment that can help or hinder the services given to the client. In addition, the social worker must help client(s) gain access to other agencies and the services and programs they offer. If the resources available are not adequate or if there are factors in the environment that contribute to potential or existing problems of social functioning, the social worker is charged to deal with these issues as well.

The social worker, then, not only

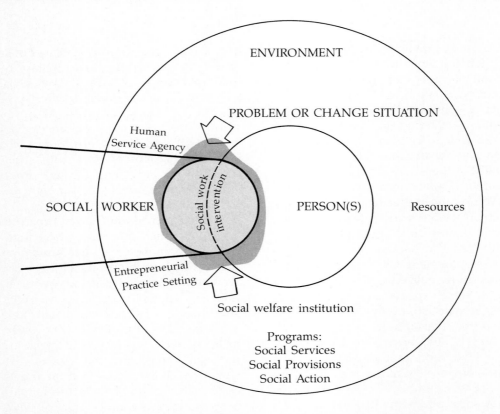

Figure II–1 *The context of social work practice*

must be prepared to deal with clients as individuals, families, or small groups on a face-to-face basis but also must acquire the necessary knowledge, values, and skills for enhancing the ability of social agencies to provide services. In fact, the social worker works within the context of the entire social welfare institution and must seek to make that institution more responsive to human needs.

Part Two helps the reader acquire a general understanding of the context in which social workers practice. Chapter 4 reviews the development of the social service delivery system in the United States. It discusses the various meanings of the term *welfare* and provides an understanding of the human needs that the social welfare institution is intended to meet. The chapter also examines social programs and services as they are now provided.

Chapter 5 surveys eleven unique fields in which social workers apply their trade. The selection of fields varies from social work with children to social

work in business and industry, from corrections to mental health settings, and from hospitals to group service agencies. Despite the differences in these fields of practice, a basic pattern of the social worker helping people interact more effectively with the world around them emerges.

Chapter 6 examines those public and private social agencies where most social workers are employed. Agency structure and functioning are discussed with special attention given to the inherent conflicts that exist between the professional practice model and the bureaucratic model of organization usually found in social agencies. Some social workers have adopted an entrepreneurial approach and many have opted for private practice, but that approach, too, is fraught with problems. It is possible, however, to minimize the problems of working within both the agency and the private practice in order to meet human needs more effectively.

CHAPTER 4

Understanding the Social Welfare Institution

The Constitution for the United States expresses a commitment to promote the "general welfare" of the people.

> We, the people of the United States, in order to form a more perfect Union, establish justice, insure domestic tranquility, provide for the common defense, promote the general welfare, and secure the blessings of liberty to ourselves and our posterity do ordain and establish this Constitution for the United States of America.
>
> Preamble for the Constitution

How does a nation go about achieving such lofty goals as "insuring domestic tranquility" and "promoting the general welfare" of the people? Indeed, through the more than 200 years since the Constitution was adopted there has been continuing debate and changing public policy regarding the requirements to meet this Constitutional imperative. Yet, the resolve to achieve this objective has remained unchanged. A nation must assure that certain basic human needs are met if it is to survive.

Since the adoption of the Constitution, U.S. society has undergone dramatic changes making it necessary to adapt the social institutions to fit emerging needs of the population. For example, moving from an agriculture-based economy to one based on machines, and then on electronic technology, radically altered the structure of the work force. The related movement from a rural to an urban society influenced the ability of the primary social institution, the family, to perform its traditional role in meeting the needs of family members. One result from these changes has been the growth of the social welfare institution from a relatively minor role in U.S. society to a central place in fulfilling the Constitutional commitment.

Social work emerged during this period as the profession sanctioned to bring the resources of the environment to bear on the needs of people. The person wishing to understand social work must understand this background as it is constantly evolving and will ultimately influence the social worker's ability to conduct effective practice.

HUMAN NEEDS

Each individual has his or her own special needs. The configuration of needs that each person experiences, the intensity with which they are felt, and the ability to discover ways to meet them is part of what makes human beings unique. Each person varies, for example, in the degree of need for expressions of affection, for approval from friends and colleagues, and for intellectual growth. Some people can manage pain and illness or limited financial resources quite satisfactorily, while others suffer greatly. Some ignore the many injustices that prevail, while others are motivated by injustice to seek corrections that create a more equitable society.

Society need not develop programs that are responsive to each and every human need. In fact, people are expected to develop their own means for satisfying most of their needs without help from others. If that fails, they look to family and friends, natural helpers in the community, and only then to the various human services to help meet these needs. The professionals who provide these services are often the "resource of last resort" for people seeking help.

Fundamental differences in viewpoint about the appropriate role of human services appear when the line is drawn between an individual's and society's responsibility for meeting need. A conservative philosophy leans toward placing the full responsibility on the individual; a liberal position favors a more substantial responsibility by society. The social work value system, as we shall see in Chapter 8, is weighted in the latter direction.

Although each of us has a unique constellation of needs, there are some common needs that affect all people. John Romanyshyn described these as needs of the flesh (survival and creature comforts), needs of the heart (love, intimacy, and exchange of tenderness), needs of the ego (sense of adequacy and self-assertiveness), and needs of the soul (transcending self to define the meaning of life beyond one's own biological existence).[1]

Human needs are not all of equal importance. Some must be fulfilled before people are able to address others. According to Maslow's research, people attempt to fulfill their needs in the following order:

Physiological survival needs: nourishment, rest, and warmth, for example.

Safety needs: preservation of life and sense of security.

Belongingness needs: to be part of a group and to love and to be loved.

Esteem needs: approval, respect, acceptance, appreciation, etc.

Self-actualization needs: to be able to fulfill our fullest potential.[2]

When sufficient numbers of people fail to have one or more of these needs met in the normal course of their lives, society must decide if it is to take responsibility for their well-being. If so, society must determine when and to what degree it will attempt to provide means for helping those people meet their needs. The more basic the need, the more likely it is that society will make some provision for meeting it. Human services for the hungry child are more likely to be supported than marital counseling for a middle-class couple—and marital counseling would gain more support than providing developmental or growth enhancing experiences to the "normal" or "healthy" person who wants to develop his or her potential more fully.

WHAT IS WELFARE?

In the literature on meeting human needs, the term *well-being* consistently appears. When needs are adequately met, people experience a sense of well-being, or a general satisfaction with their lives. An implicit goal of society is to facilitate the well-being of its members.

A dictionary definition of welfare expresses this same intent: "the good fortune, health, happiness, prosperity, etc., of a person, group or organization; well-being."[3] Social work has clearly accepted the role of promoting the well-being or welfare, in the sense of the above definition, of members of society and has placed particular emphasis on the most vulnerable members.

Everyone does not interpret welfare in the same way. The way some commentators and politicians speak of people "on welfare" would lead one to believe that welfare is the means by which a large number of "lazy and immoral people" are ripping off tax dollars contributed by a handful of upstanding citizens. From a different perspective, some would say social welfare is a tool used by those in power to keep impoverished a group of poor, mostly minority females, so they will be forced to do the menial work of society—yet not so impoverished they will be moved to overthrow those in power.[4]

Society places different value judgments on the reasons people receive welfare services. To many people, it is acceptable for the farmer facing fluctuation in the price of crops to receive welfare in the form of price supports or for the small business owner to receive a government subsidized loan. It is less acceptable for the deserted mother and her children to be recipients of welfare in the form of food stamps. It is even more unacceptable for the alcoholic who cannot hold a job to receive welfare in the form of public assistance, though the need here is just as great as in many other troubled situations.

Betty Mandell notes that "one's definition of social welfare depends partly upon one's conception of a society's responsibility to its citizens."[5] There are those who argue that each individual should be responsible for his or her own well-being. If that is not possible, at least the person's family should assume that responsibility, or in some cultures, a tribe, neighborhood, or community should assume that function. Historically, churches and synagogues have assumed some of this backup function, and residuals from this perception are still evident in the sponsorship of some social services. Others would argue that we live in a complex society in which people are highly interdependent and subject to difficulties that arise from malfunctions in the society itself (for example, a continuing 5–7 percent minimum unemployment rate). Therefore, they argue, society must make provision for preventing or resolving difficulties that arise from this situation by providing human services and must also seek to enhance the quality of life for members of that society. What, then, is welfare? In the broadest sense, welfare is human concern for the well-being of individuals, families, groups, organizations, and communities.

SOCIAL INSTITUTIONS

To promote the welfare of people, their needs must be met by themselves, their family and friends, or, at times, by others. When a society develops a formalized means of providing resources for helping to meet human needs, it has created an "institution." As the term is used here, an institution is "a formal, recognized, established and stabilized way of pursuing some activity in society."[6] Social institutions are the organized procedures societies create to meet the needs of the people.

The primary social institution of U.S. society and all other societies is *the family*. Robert Bierstedt notes that "the family . . . is a universal institution of society. There is no society anywhere on earth that does not have the institution of family: in all of them in all periods of history procreation has been institutionalized."[7] In most societies the family also performs the central functions of providing love and affection, safety, and facilitating child rearing. Relative to Maslow's hierarchy, the family provides a procedure for potentially meeting all the identified needs.

In the United States a second level of institutions exists for meeting specific needs. These institutions reflect the procedures adopted to help meet the needs that are high on Maslow's scale, or, in the case of religion, is central to the nation's belief system. At this level we find the *economic* institution that provides the system for exchange of goods and services, the *religion* institution that provides mechanisms for people to relate to the supernatural,[8] and the *public protection* institution that provides for defense of the nation as well as fire and police protection. Because of their importance in meeting the most basic human needs, these second-level institutions tend to receive priority over all other social institutions (except the family) in the law, public policy, and the allocation of resources.

The third level of institutions responds to some of Maslow's highest order needs, but relates more directly to those on the lower end of the scale. While addressing some survival and safety matters, these institutions emphasize procedures that are intended to improve the quality of life, i.e., self-esteem and self-actualization. They are found in their most developed forms in the more advanced societies and include the *education* institution, for example, which is concerned with the transmission of knowledge, skills, and culture from one generation to another. Further, the maintenance of wellness, the rehabilitation of the handicapped, and the treatment of illness reflect the goals of the institution of *health*. Also, the *social welfare* institution, as we shall examine more fully in later parts of this chapter, initially emerged to meet basic survival needs, but more recently has broadened its scope to include problem solving and enhancement goals. A variety of other important but less central institutions such as *recreation, sports, arts and humanities, entertainment, environmental management*, etcetera have emerged for the purpose of enhancing the quality of life.

In addition a set of facilitative social institutions has been created to provide processes through which the other institutions operate. These facilitative institutions include *government*, which determines how decisions in the society will be made, *communication*, which involves patterns for transmitting important information, and, as U.S. society has become increasingly dependent on the movement of goods and people, *transportation*.

Since social institutions are created to meet certain needs of society, they can be expected to change as the society changes. For example, as industrialization altered the manner in which goods were produced, the structure of the family unit and its functions in the production of food and other goods also changed. The role of the extended family was diminished and the nuclear family assumed a more central function. The ensuing stress on the nuclear family is well-documented and the negative fallout from this stress is reflected in the high incidence of divorce and family violence.

To achieve the goals of a social institution, a variety of programs, structures, and resources must be provided. These *programs* are the mechanisms through which the institution's purpose is carried out. Depending on the scope of an institution, a large number of programs may be required to achieve a goal. For example within the education institution (and higher education in particular) a number of programs are required for any college or university to fulfill its role. Each student must complete both a general education and a specialized curriculum in his or her major field. To support that process of education, the school must have an admissions procedure, advising system, tutoring support, library, media resources, dormitories, bookstore, and even faculty members. With all these programs, the student's education is not considered complete unless he or she engages in, or at least observes, various extracurricular programs such as plays, symposia, and sporting events that transmit aspects of this culture. A sample of the programs required to meet the goals of the social welfare institution are identified in Chapter 5.

Structures, too, must be created to provide vehicles for delivering the programs to the people in need. Some form of association or organization is required at either the national, state, or local level to administer the program. Where an institution is an intangible process or procedure, an association is a tangible structure. It is a group of people who are organized to carry out a specific function. For example a specific church is one expression of the institution of religion while a human service agency is an association created to physically deliver social welfare programs. According to Bierstedt the important characteristics of associations are that they have "(1) a specific function or purpose, (2) associational norms, (3) associational statuses, (4) authority, (5) tests of membership, (6) property, and (7) a name or other identifying symbols."[9] In other words, associations are formal organizations. Chapter 6 examines in more detail associations that are settings for social work practice.

Finally, *resources* in the form of people, money, and various social provisions, e.g., food, housing, and clothing, are required for the associations to fully implement the established programs. To actually reach recipients of the social welfare programs, professionals and other staff members, as well as volunteers, provide direct and indirect services.

THE SOCIAL WELFARE INSTITUTION

The social welfare institution should be viewed as a supplement, rather than a replacement, for individual expressions of caring. There have always been informal efforts to meet needs through individual caring by family, friends, and other natural helpers. This natural helping, however, does not bring the resources or concerns of society to bear on the helping process. It is an individual as opposed to an institutionalized response.

The social welfare institution finds expression in the form of laws, policies, services, human service agencies, volunteers, and the variety of professions and other occupational groups that make it possible to help people meet their needs. Social work is one of the professions that helps to carry out the function of the social welfare institution. It is concerned with the welfare of people and with creating an environment that supports their growth and development. It addresses what C. Wright Mills identifies as both "personal troubles" and "public issues."[10]

Development of the Social Welfare Institution

From Colonial Times to the Great Depression The emergence of social work is closely related to the development of the social welfare institution. There was no place for social work or most other human service disciplines until society formalized its response to meeting human needs. Depending on the commitment society makes to meet social needs, the demand for social workers will rise and fall. Understanding the development of the social welfare institution helps one recognize the changing role of social work today.

Picture life in rural America as the land was plowed and the family worked together to tame the wilderness. Few have been spared watching at least a few episodes of *Little House on the Prairie* or *The Waltons* that present us with a Hollywood image of a predindustrial society.

Although there were trials and tribulations in an agricultural society, the person with average intelligence and a willingness to work hard could usually succeed. Given an open frontier and liberal government policies for staking a claim to fertile land, an individual could readily acquire property to produce the necessities of life. Because the family was a strong institution and each member had sharply defined roles in support of efforts to conquer the land, people survived and, in time, prospered. The "American Dream" could be-come a reality for most—unless one was of African, Asian, Mexican, or Native American background—in this simple agrarian society.

The family, however, was not alone or completely self-supporting in this adventure. For mutual protection, social interaction, and the opportunity to trade the goods they possessed, families would band together into loosely knit communities. Trade centers emerged as small towns; a market economy evolved; and merchants opened stores, bought and sold products, and ex-tended credit to people until their products were ready for market.

These efforts to meet human needs can be characterized as "mutual aid." Members of the extended family (that is, grandparents, children, and other relatives) could be supported and were needed to work the farm or tend the store. Even the retarded or physically handicapped person could find mean-ingful ways to contribute to this simple and not too stressful environment. For the most part the family institution worked and the market economy, unencumbered by national and international trade conditions, also worked. When special problems arose, neighbors and the community helped. The barn that burned was quickly rebuilt; widows and orphans without extended families were cared for; and the sick were tended. People would share their products with needy friends and neighbors, knowing that the favor would be returned when conditions improved.

In this preindustrial society, the quality of life depended on the "grace of God" and hard work. Society rarely needed to take responsibility for re-sponding to unmet human needs; and when it did, the church often assumed that function. In short, the family, the church, and the market economy were the significant social institutions. Because people were acquainted with each other, services were highly individualized and personalized.

It is tempting to blame industrialization for the many problems that emerged in U.S. society in the 1800s and 1900s. Admittedly, industrialization is one important factor, but political, religious, international, and other factors also contributed to the pressures experienced by the family and market sys-tem. Nevertheless, industrialization did force a too-rapid change on society and exacerbated the problems of these institutions in adapting to serve human needs.

The movement from an agricultural society to an industrial society signif-icantly affected the family and market system. People congregated in cities where there were jobs; the individual breadwinner rather than the family unit became the key to survival; and interactions with others were increasingly characterized by impersonality. Those with handicapping conditions had little opportunity for satisfying employment in the specialized technological work environment.

As people's needs were met less by the family and market system, society stepped in to provide for meeting those needs, and the social welfare insti-tution emerged. Mayer Zald identifies the issues as follows:

> Modern society is an industrialized society, and the development of con-temporary welfare institutions is directly linked to industrialization. First,

as the level of industrialization increases, the over-all resources and standards of living increase. Thus, industrialization leads to higher minimum standards of human welfare. Higher minimum standards are reflected through the demands of potential recipients, professional groups, and the general public for greater welfare services. Second, as industrialization increases, many welfare functions that were previously handled by the family become the function of differentiated welfare institutions—"needs" that were previously met by the family, or not at all, become collective responsibilities. Third, as industrialization increases, the degree of societal interdependence and differentiation increases. On the one hand, welfare policies and programs become nationwide in scope. On the other hand, effective policies and programs must be adapted to the many types and categories of dependencies and needs created by the increased complexity of the social system.[11]

Industrialization began in Europe well in advance of the colonization of the United States. In England a series of laws were passed in the 1400s and 1500s that attempted to clarify the responsibility of the individual and the role of society in meeting human needs. These laws were drawn together into two significant pieces of legislation enacted by Parliament in 1601, the Statute of Charitable Uses and the Elizabethan Poor Law. The former became the basis on which U.S. philanthropy developed, and the latter was the basis for serving the poor.

The colonists had some respite from industrialization, since they were first concerned with developing their agricultural base. Open land in the West slowed the process of urbanization and many of the related social problems. The immigrants who came to this country to escape government authority stressed the dignity of the individual, social equality, and equality of opportunity in their philosophy. They believed only those with a major defect could fail in this land of opportunity, and according to Puritan reasoning, those who failed must suffer from moral weakness. Thus, those in need of services were viewed as morally weak, and a welfare philosophy, ably captured and labeled by William Ryan as "blaming the victim," emerged.[12]

The Puritan view that people needing help were sinful was counterbalanced by the perception, derived from the French Enlightenment in the eighteenth century, that people are inherently good. The fallout from these conflicting viewpoints, as applied to the poor, resulted in a perception that there are two classes of people needing help from society: the worthy poor and the unworthy poor. The worthy poor were viewed as good people who required help because they were afflicted by an ailment or were women or children left destitute by the death or desertion of the husband and father. The unworthy poor were able-bodied yet in need because they were thought to have flaws in character. As late as 1818 John Griscom, reporting to the managers of the Society for the Prevention of Pauperism in the City of New York, identified the following as causes of poverty: "ignorance, idleness, intemperance in drinking, want of economy, imprudent and hasty marriages, lotteries, pawnbrokers, houses of ill fame, the numerous charitable institutions of the city, and war."[13] Most of the responsibility for being poor, according to this reasoning, rested with the poor people themselves.

There were, of course, those who reflected a more sympathetic view of persons in need and who attempted to reform the punitive and uncaring approaches to providing services or, more accurately, providing custodial care in the almshouses or prisons. As early as 1776 the Society for Alleviating the Miseries of Public Prisons was formed in Philadelphia, the same city where Thomas Bond and Benjamin Franklin had founded the first general hospital in the United States. Later Dorothea Dix visited and chronicled the deplorable conditions in prisons and almshouses. Her efforts stimulated the passage of a bill in the U.S. Congress to grant "public lands to states to assist in financing care of the insane."[14] The veto of this bill in 1854 by President Franklin Pierce established a position that was to dominate thinking in this field for the next three-quarters of a century—the federal government has no appropriate role in the social welfare institution.

Although some state and county government services emerged, the federal government did not become seriously involved in the social welfare institution until President Franklin D. Roosevelt's New Deal program in the mid-1930s. As late as December 1930 President Herbert Hoover approved an appropriation of $45 million to feed livestock in Arkansas though he opposed the appropriation of an additional $25 million to feed the farmers who raised that livestock.[15] Although the provision of services through private philanthrophy experienced considerable support during this period, private philanthrophy alone could not weather the crisis created by the Great Depression of the 1930s. As Ralph and Muriel Pumphrey note:

> The depression of the thirties was an economic and social storm of such unprecedented proportions that established patterns had to be reconsidered. The Social Security Act represented an overriding of the Pierce Veto after the passage of eighty-one years. It was hailed by its supporters as a means of insuring sound democracy and as opening the door of opportunity for the social work profession to provide the leadership in a new era of humane, efficient, and constructive public welfare administration.[16]

From the Great Depression to the Present   The Great Depression was also a great equalizer. People who had previously been successful in the market system suddenly required help. These were moral, able-bodied people who needed help. Could they be blamed for their condition? Or do other factors in a society create or contribute to the troubles that individuals experience? For a period of time U.S. society became more sensitive to people in need and increasingly came to recognize that indeed there are structural factors in modern society that are responsible for many social problems.

The Second World War rallied the people of the United States to a common cause and helped them recognize their interdependence. In such periods of potential disaster, each person must be counted on to contribute to the common good. Under these conditions the nation could ill afford a system that created "throwaway" people by failing to provide for their basic needs. The Second World War also served to stimulate the economy, and, after a period of recovery, extend the scope of the social welfare institution.

The 1960s introduced a period of prosperity and unprecedented responsiveness to human needs. The Kennedy and Johnson administrations fostered the "War on Poverty" and "Great Society" programs, while simultaneously the "Human Rights Revolution" was at its height. These activities focused public concern on the poor, minorities, women, the aged, the handicapped, and other population groups that had previously been largely ignored. Legislation protecting civil rights and creating massive social programs was passed; court decisions validated the new legislation; and social workers sprang to the foreground to provide needed services.

The bloom on social concerns and social programs began to fade in the middle 1970s, and public apathy replaced public concern. A deteriorating economy fueled a growing conservatism, the U.S. trade balance began shifting to a negative position, and relationships with other countries that were strong as a result of the Second World War began to erode. Military buildup was placed in competition for scarce resources with human services. The time was ripe by the 1980s for the Reagan administration to dismantle the social programs that had developed over the last two decades. Echoing a political rhetoric that incorporated the distrust of government that had characterized the philosophies of presidents Franklin Pierce and Herbert Hoover, mixed with punitive, moralistic views regarding the recipients of human services and a belief that a strong defense against external attack should be the nation's highest priority, Ronald Reagan was swept into office.

High on the Reagan administration's agenda was the effort to reverse the growing federal role in the social welfare institution. John Palmer and Isabel Sawhill's careful analysis of the goals of Ronald Reagan's initial social agenda concludes:

> . . . the president proposed to reduce annual spending on social programs by nearly $75 billion, about 17 percent, below prior policy levels by FY 1985. The deepest cuts (nearly 60 percent) were proposed for the smallest component of social spending—the myriad of fixed-dollar grant programs that primarily fund the delivery of education, health, employment, and social services by state and local governments. Substantial cuts (28 percent) were also proposed for the somewhat larger category of benefit programs targeted on the low-income population, such as Food Stamps, Aid to Families with Dependent Children (AFDC), child nutrition, housing assistance, and Medicaid, while more modest reductions (11 percent) were slated for the social insurance programs, such as Social Security, Medicare, and Unemployment Insurance, which account for about two-thirds of all social program spending.[17]

President Reagan's disdain for the broadened scope of the social welfare institution and the recipients of social welfare programs was evident in his popularized statement that the resources were not going "to the needy, but the greedy." His goal of cutting federal expenditures was aimed at restricting governmental participation and shifting the financial support for a contracted social welfare institution to the states and the private sector. Early in Reagan's first term there was only limited replacement of these federal revenues by other sources, but increasingly "state and local governments, private organizations, and individuals have all shared in partially filling the gap left by federal cutbacks."[18]

In the following paragraphs Lee Bawden and John Palmer summarize the Reagan administration's success in implementing that agenda during his first term.

> The president clearly did seek to turn back the social policy clock, in some extreme cases (e.g., AFDC) to a pre-New Deal time. By and large, however, it was more recent history that sustained the most strenuous efforts at repeal. Given his way, the president would have eradicated most of the hallmarks of the Great Society and would have shrunk the social insurance programs to a scope more nearly approximating their New Deal origins. On the civil rights front the president would have scrapped the federal government's role as a "commanding general" in favor of something more like a reluctant sergeant; broad goals, quotas, and timetables would have been replaced by individual disciplinary action according to rather narrowly interpreted rules.
>
> As it turned out, Congress and the courts have been considerably moderating forces on the president's intentions. Congress acted to protect many of the Great Society programs and to hold together the bottom tier of the safety net. As a result, by and large, the most ineffective programs were deeply cut or eliminated, while the programs more generally acknowledged as effective were left unscathed or reduced only modestly. And, although the president had, as any president has, considerably more latitude in the civil rights area than in the social spending programs, Congress and the courts have provided a substantial check here, rejecting the administration's most ambitious efforts at narrowing the laws or their interpretation.[19]

ISSUES IN SOCIAL WELFARE

The commitment of a society to support the social welfare of its members is the first step toward responding to social needs. That commitment must, then, be translated into programs that respond to the needs that the society determines are appropriate to support. Making decisions about what needs, what type of response, and how many resources to commit creates several important issues. Since the social worker is responsible for implementing many programs, it is important for him or her to understand these issues. The manner in which they are resolved in relation to each program influences the ability of the social worker to respond to human needs.

Purpose of Programs

For some, the purpose of the social welfare institution is to facilitate the *socialization* of people to the norms and behaviors of society. Developing the knowledge and skills to become a full participating member of society is expressed in recreation programs and in the work of youth serving agencies. Others expect social welfare to provide a *social control* function by identifying and removing people from situations in which they are disruptive to society. These disruptive people can be found in mental hospitals and correctional institutions. Another view is that the social welfare institution has a *social integration* responsibility for helping people become more involved with the world around them. Counseling, therapy, rehabilitation, and other services are designed to achieve this purpose.[20] Finally, some consider social welfare to have a *social change* purpose, that is, to express the conscience of society by stimulating changes that will enhance the overall quality of life.

Can the social welfare institution accomplish all these purposes at the same time? One must question the effort to be responsive to such a broad range of human issues and suggest the social welfare institution might be more effective if its purpose were more sharply focused.

Conceptions of Social Welfare

Social programs reflect one of two philosophical views of social welfare in the manner in which they are designed. Wilensky and Lebeaux have identified these two approaches as residual and institutional.[21] The *residual* formulation is based on the premise that the proper sources for meeting a person's needs are the family and the market economy. If these sources fail to meet an individual's needs, the social welfare structure is brought into play on a temporary (residual) basis to help until the family or the economic system begins to work properly. The social agency guided by this conception would define its services as a response to a particular problem, a response that would terminate as soon as a pre-determined "normal" level of functioning is achieved. For example, many marriage counseling services assume there are problems with a marriage, and the couple using these services often carry the label and stigma of "serious marital problems" even though they may seek the service to strengthen an already satisfactory marriage.

The *residual*, or "safety net," view treats social welfare programs as a temporary backup to family, church, economic, and political institutions.[22] This approach dominated the early development of the social welfare institution and is evident in the philosophy of the Reagan administration today. Romanyshyn summarizes the situation as follows:

> Social welfare in the United States has fallen in a large measure within the residual concept, with its patchwork system of programs based on the assumption that social obligation extends only to meeting the emergency needs of that portion of the population that is regarded as incapable of meeting its own needs through the traditional means of the market and the family. The residual view accepts the poor as incompetent second-class members of society for whom second-class services may be provided.[23]

Society has changed so much that traditional institutions will no longer be able to meet adequately the needs of all people. For example, technological advances may create unemployment because employees are not needed and not because there is either a malfunction of the economic institution or an inadequate or unwilling labor force.[24] The recognition of this change has led to an additional perception of the role of the social welfare institution: that social welfare is one of society's first-line institutions for meeting needs. This *institutional*, or *developmental*, conception supports the view that social services are basic to the well-being of all people. Like the utilities of water and electricity, these *social utilities*, such as day care, recreation centers, and lunch programs for senior citizens, are available at the request of the users and carry no stigma or implication of personal inadequacy.

The social welfare institution in the United States reflects both the residual and institutional conceptions of social welfare. Frequently, even within a single social agency, there will be a confusing hodgepodge of programs embodying both residual and institutional philosophies. For example, a public welfare department administers a package of residual services, such as financial assistance, yet carries responsibility for Medicare, a program based on the institutional conception of social welfare.

Local versus Federal Responsibility

There is continuing disagreement concerning the level of society's responsibility for social welfare. The view that unmet human needs signify the failure of the individual or "normal" need-meeting institutions assigns the responsibility for correcting those problems to the local level. This position argues that the family, private social agencies, community, or state should develop and finance human services. Its supporters contend the services are more personalized and attuned to the needs of people when they are developed locally. It is a perception that longs for a return to the conditions of a preindustrial society.

Those supporting the other side of this issue seek a strong federal role in social welfare and argue the human needs to which the social welfare institution is prepared to respond are created, or at least intensified, by factors—such as chronic unemployment, the cost of energy to heat one's home, society's treatment of older people, or inflation and high interest rates—over which there is limited individual or local influence. Creating programs at a national level makes it possible to equalize the burden and the responsibility for taking corrective measures to help the people who experience these social problems. The disagreement over this issue has resulted in a complex system of services at all levels. Social workers have the responsibility for helping people find their way to services through this maze of programs.

Charity or Right to Service?

Another issue that regularly confronts the social welfare institution is the right of clients to receive or refuse services. Historically, social services were viewed as charity—a benevolent gift that a righteous public bestowed on the worthy poor and, begrudgingly, provided for the not-so-worthy. The recipient is expected to be forever grateful for any help given through social programs; and the donors, as well as the persons providing the services, expect to be appreciated.

As the institutional conception of social welfare became more accepted, the view of services as a right of the client emerged. Clients have come to believe they are entitled to services and increasingly have organized or sought legal remedy to ensure they are provided to meet their needs. Groups advocating for the rights of the poor, the aged, the developmentally disabled, and the physically handicapped are found throughout the United States. When one's right to receive services becomes an issue, the question of one's right to refuse services must also be addressed.

Individualization of Service

Another issue that social workers and other professionals confront in delivering social programs is adapting services to meet individual needs. The policies and procedures that guide the delivery of human services are defined to respond to the typical person or group experiencing an unmet need. Thus, social programs are designed for a class of people who experience similar problems or needs for service. However, the circumstances of any one poor family, a specific battered wife, or any particular group of tenants of a slumlord will be to a certain degree unique. Effective service requires a degree of flexibility to make interpretations of these policies and procedures so they might be stretched to cover unique situations. Legislators, agency boards, and administrators must be aware of the importance of allowing for leeway in policy interpretation by the service providers. At the same time, the service providers must avoid taking that flexibility as license to create their own eligibility requirements or service criteria.

Categories of Social Programs

It is useful to recognize that social programs can be divided into three distinct categories: social provisions, social services, and social action programs.

Social provisions are designed to meet the most fundamental needs of the population. These services can best be described as the tangible provisions given directly to persons with limited income. They include provisions that may be granted as either cash or in-kind benefits such as food, clothing, or housing.

Social provisions are the most costly programs in outlay of actual dollars. As the social welfare institution has evolved, the governmental agencies have assumed the primary responsibility for providing these services and the private sector has taken the role of providing backup for those people who are missed by the public programs. Meals and lodging for transients and the homeless, emergency food programs, financial aid in response to crisis programs, shelters for battered wives, and many other human service programs are provided by voluntary social agencies. Yet, as Michael Sosin found in his study of voluntary material aid programs, the basic social provision programs are too costly for the private sector.

> One anticipated finding is that government agencies are much more likely to deal with basic material needs. This is in keeping with the historical picture. Since the New Deal, the expectation has grown that material assistance is primarily a public activity.
>
> This expectation may have extended to emergency assistance, which is also more frequently provided in public than private agencies (although the differences are small). Homelessness and disaster problems are evenly distributed across public and private agencies. These results lead us to the possibility, as history suggests, that private agencies that provide emergency aid or continuing assistance still must face the issue of legitimating a service normally provided—and perhaps expected to be provided—by the public sector.[25]

What are the governmental social provisions? The list is extensive. A partial listing illustrates the broad array of such programs financed by the federal, state, and county governments. These social provision programs include: Aid to Families with Dependent Children (AFDC), Supplemental Security Income (SSI), Needy Veterans Pensions, General Assistance, Food Stamps, School Lunch, Nutrition for the Elderly, Low Income Housing Assistance, Low-rent Public Housing, Low-income Energy Assistance, and others. It is estimated that in 1984 the programs mentioned above served approximately 65,000,000 persons.[26] While some were recipients from more than one program, the programs nevertheless reached a substantial part of the U.S. population.

Social services reflect programs that are designed to help people resolve problems or enhance their social functioning. Kamerman and Kahn identify these as general or personal social services that include "family and child welfare; social services for the young and the aged; social care for the handicapped, frail, and retarded; information and referral services; and community centers."[27] These services can be analyzed more fully by placing them in the categories of: (1) social services for socialization and development; (2) social services for therapy, help, rehabilitation, and social protection; and (3) access services.[28] These categories are not mutually exclusive, however, and service to a single client or family might involve all three categories.

Many social service programs are designed to contribute to the *socialization and development* of various groups of people. These services may be for children or adults, for healthy or disabled people, or even for persons not seeking to be helped. Kahn describes these services as having a goal of "socialization into communal values, transmittal of goals and motivation, and enhancement of personal development."[29] These services might be found in day care centers, scouting programs, parent education groups, YMCA or YMHA activities, senior citizen centers, and many other programs.

Other social services are designed to provide *therapy, help, rehabilitation,* and *social protection*. These services are delivered in many different settings and with a variety of clients. They may be short- or long-term services, provided in homes or in social agencies, and provided on an outpatient or in-patient basis. The goal is to help people resolve a variety of issues that interfere with their desired functioning or give guidance to people whose behavior interferes with the functioning of others. These services might be found in family service agencies, mental health centers, probation and parole offices, child welfare programs (including foster care and adoption), hospitals, schools, and agencies offering protective services for older people.

Finally, an important aspect of social services is facilitating *access* to resources that meet needs. A number of factors can make it difficult for people to use already existing social provisions and services. Usually, they must have transportation to the place where service is provided, so they may need help finding a way to get to the help. They may need help finding what agency offers the programs they need and, once there, may require help to get through the complex requirements of the agency to receive service. Finally, clients may face forms of discrimination because of their income, race or ethnicity, sex, age, or handicap, and, as a result, may need the support of a helping person to get the desired services. Access services are provided in many different agencies and may range from informal suggestions to advocating for a client. As Kahn notes, "access services may include information, advice, referral, complaints, case advocacy, class advocacy, and legal services, all on both individual and group bases."[30]

Social action approaches recognize that it is often inadequate just to help a person or group deal with an unjust world. Efforts must be made to create a more just and supportive environment. It is not enough to help a woman understand and even cope with a job that discriminates against her because of her sex. Although these activities are important, they do not resolve the basic problem, and they place the burden of change and adjustment on the victim. It is essential that social programs be created and maintained that can help clients change conditions causing problems or, by recognizing the accumulated experience of a number of clients, can provide leadership to broader efforts to eliminate these problems.

The problems that lead to social action programs stem from a variety of sources and require a range of change efforts. We may be concerned with something as basic and subtle as institutional racism, which has crept into the very fabric of our culture. Programs that are informational or conscious-ness-raising or that directly challenge the existing situation may help eliminate, or at least reduce, the impact of this problem. The problem may even be the agency itself. Do all people have equal access to the services? Does each client receive the services the agency has to offer or that the law requires? Is the agency open the proper hours to make services available to all potential clients? Are there physical barriers that make it difficult for blind or physically handicapped clients to use the services? Are the policies of the agency or the laws that create the programs fair and just, relative to those who will be served and to what services will be given? These and many other questions the helping person should raise require various forms of social action.

Social action requires an aggressive stance by the helping person, coupled with an understanding of change processes in communities and organizations. The efforts involved in social action include "fact-finding, analysis of community needs, research, the dissemination and interpretation of information, organization, and other efforts to mobilize public understanding and support in behalf of some existing or proposed social program."[31]

EXPENDITURES ON SOCIAL PROGRAMS

The causes of human need for which people depend on the social welfare institution may range from rat-infested housing to emotional upset over the loss of a loved one. To respond to these needs, a large number and variety of social programs have been created through laws passed by legislative bodies and through policies established by the boards of directors of voluntary social agencies. In the final analysis, however, the effectiveness of these social programs depends on their implementation through the social agencies and the competence of the staff.

Total Expenditures in the United States

Social programs are offered under the auspices or sponsorship of federal, state, and local governments, private human service agencies (both nonprofit and "for profit" agencies), and through professionals engaged in private practice. A substantial amount of money is invested in these programs. The combined expenditures for all levels of government and private philanthropy, as depicted in Table 4–1, indicates a remarkable investment of the people of the United States in the social welfare institution. More than $700 billion was spent in 1984 on programs in health, education, and welfare. Throughout the remainder of this chapter, data for 1980 and 1984 are included to help identify the influence of the first term of the Reagan administration on the social welfare institution.

The expenditures for social welfare programs between 1960 and 1984 reflect a substantial increase in the amount of money invested in social welfare, although the reduced buying power of the dollar accounts for a part of the increase. Yet, when the share of the national wealth (i.e., the percentage of Gross National Product) spent on health, education, and social welfare programs is computed, it is evident that the substantial gains made through the Great Society programs between 1960 and 1970 have partially eroded.

The data on expenditures for health, education, and social welfare programs also reveals a considerably expanded government role in financing these programs in the past twenty-five years. Table 4–1 indicates that of all expenditures made by federal, state, and local governments, the money spent

TABLE 4–1 Total Health, Education, and Social Welfare Expenditures, 1960–1984

	1960	1970	1980	1984 (prel.)
Total Expenditures	$57.1 B	$155.4 B	$510.7 B	$700.5 B
Percent Gross Natl. Product	12.1%	21.0%	19.8%	18.8%[1]
Federal, State, and Local Govt. Expenditures	$52.3 B	$145.9 B	$492.8 B	$672.0 B
Percent Total Govt. Outlay	38.4%	48.2%	56.5%	52.8%
Private Philanthropy Expenditures	$ 4.8 B	$ 9.5 B	$ 17.9 B	$ 28.5 B
Percent Public Expenditures	9.2%	6.5%	3.6%	4.2%

[1] 1 percent of GNP was equivalent to $371.8 billion in 1984.

Source: U.S. Bureau of the Census, *Statistical Abstracts of the United States: 1987* (107th ed.) Washington, D.C., 1986: 340, 342, 368.

on these programs increased from 38.4 percent in 1960 to 56.5 percent in 1980—but declined to 52.8 percent in 1984 as the Reagan administration policies came into effect. Nevertheless, despite the substantial amounts of money spent on national defense, roads and highways, and other governmental services, these programs continue to consume more than one-half of all public expenditures.

Since 1960 a shift of responsibility from the private sector to government for funding social welfare programs has been apparent. Public funds spent on these programs increased nearly thirteen-fold during this period, while voluntary contributions increased slightly less than one-half that amount. Despite the conservative effort to "turn back the clock" on this matter, it is evident that the private sector cannot possibly fund the massive programs required to meet human needs. When computed as a percent of governmental expenditures, private philanthropy declined from 9.2 percent in 1960 to 4.2 percent in 1984. Nonetheless, the voluntary contribution of $28.5 billion to the well-being of people by individuals, businesses, and foundations is substantial. These funds have had an especially important influence on higher education, hospitals, national health organizations, and smaller social agencies in local communities.

For those of us accustomed to dealing with money in $10- and $20-dollar increments, the billions of dollars spent on these services is difficult to appreciate. It is, perhaps, helpful to translate this to per capita expenditures. In 1984 nearly $3,000 was spent through government and private philanthropy for the health, education, and social welfare needs for every person in the United States. With the average personal income in 1984 at $13,120 per person,[32] people in the United States contributed nearly 23 percent of their individual resources to these programs through taxes and voluntary donations.

Public Sector Social Welfare Expenditures

Although the U.S. government classifies all health, education, and welfare expenditures as "social welfare outlays," most people would not include the same items under this label as the U.S. Social Security Administration when it compiles its reports. To report that over $700 billion was spent on social welfare might be misleading to many people and inflate the perception of what is spent on the poor. For example nearly 75 percent of the federal, state, and local government expenditures were related to two items: social insurance and education. The former includes a variety of programs such as public employee retirement benefits, Old-Age, Survivors, and Disability, and Health Insurance (OASDHI or Social Security as it is better known), unemployment insurance, and worker's compensation. These are funded almost entirely by worker and employer contributions and not by tax revenues. The latter item, education, involves a considerable amount of money for school construction and adult and vocational education programs, which many would not consider "social welfare."

Table 4–2 provides a breakdown of the "social welfare outlays" by federal, state, and local governments in 1960, 1970, 1980, and 1984. Perhaps the most striking trend in these data is the growing share of the social welfare funds that are consumed by the social insurances. Between 1970 and 1984 the expenditures for the social insurance programs increased more than 500 percent and now account for more than one-half of all social welfare outlays.

We can gain further clarity about the influence of the Reagan administration on public expenditures for health, education, and welfare if we examine the following expenditures for the nonsocial insurance programs.

	1980		*1984*	
Public Aid	$ 71.8B	27.4%	$ 89.9B	27.3%
Health & Medical	27.9	10.6	37.9	11.5
Veteran's Programs	21.5	8.2	26.1	7.9
Education	121.1	46.2	152.0	46.1
Housing	7.2	2.8	10.4	3.2
Other Social Welfare	13.6	5.2	13.5	4.1

The increases in the dollars allocated reflect inflation and population growth in the United States, and the somewhat constant percentages allocated to each category suggest that the overall impact of Ronald Reagan's first term

TABLE 4–2 Federal, State, and Local Government Expenditures on Health, Education, and Social Welfare, 1960–1984

	1960		1970		1980		1984 (prel.)	
	$	%	$	%	$	%	$	%
Total	52.3 B	100	145.9 B	100	492.8 B	100	672.0 B	100
Social Insurance	19.3	36.9	54.7	37.5	229.8	46.6	342.3	50.9
Public Aid	4.1	7.8	16.5	11.3	71.8	14.6	89.9	13.4
Health and Medical	4.5	8.6	9.9	6.8	27.9	5.7	37.9	5.6
Veteran's Programs	5.5	10.5	9.1	6.2	21.5	4.4	26.1	3.9
Education	17.6	33.7	50.9	34.9	121.1	24.6	152.0	22.6
Housing	.2	.4	.7	.5	7.2	1.5	0.4	1.6
Other Social Welfare	1.1	2.1	4.2	2.9	13.6	2.8	13.5	2.0

Source: U.S. Bureau of the Census, *Statistical Abstracts of the United States: 1987* (107th ed.) Washington, D.C., 1986: 340.

was not substantial in changing the distribution of government funds among the health, education, and social welfare programs. The general pattern of distribution among these categories did not substantially change from prior administrations.

Through an analysis of the federal, state, and local governmental programs that are restricted to persons with limited income, one can gain a more in-depth understanding of the influence of Reaganomics on the poor. Not only were the "public aid" and "other social welfare" appropriations that directly impact poor people reduced as a proportion of government spending during the early 1980s, but as Table 4–3 reveals, the enhancement programs such as job training and social services experienced a greater reduction in social welfare dollars.

One goal of Reaganomics was to shift support of social programs from the federal government to state and local levels as a means of decreasing federal involvement in the social welfare institution. Between fiscal years 1980 and 1984, there was a small shift in that direction. In 1980 the federal share of the total government expenditures for persons with limited income was 76.6 percent, while in 1985 that share had been reduced to 74.8 percent.[33]

A second goal of Reaganomics was to shift as many social welfare programs as possible to voluntary social agencies or private enterprise. Leaders in industry have supported the Reagan view and have urged that corporations play an increased role in philanthropy. The position of the influential Business Roundtable (also endorsed by the U.S. Chamber of Commerce and the National Association of Manufacturers) reflects the business community's op-

TABLE 4–3 Public Cash and Noncash Benefits for Persons with Limited Income: 1980 and 1984

PROGRAM	1980 ANNUAL EXPENDITURES		1984 ANNUAL EXPENDITURES	
	$	%	$	%
Total	$104.6 B	100	$133.0 B	100
Medical Care	$ 32.2 B	30.8	$ 44.4 B	33.4
Cash Aid	29.4	28.1	36.6	27.5
Food Benefits	13.6	13.0	19.8	14.9
Housing Benefits	9.2	8.8	12.7	9.6
Education Aid	5.2	5.0	8.4	6.3
Jobs and Training	8.7	8.4	5.5	4.1
Social Services	4.6	4.4	3.5	2.7
Energy Assistance	1.7	1.6	2.1	1.6

Source: U.S. Bureau of the Census, *Statistical Abstracts of the United States: 1987* (107th ed.) Washington, D.C., 1986: 343.

position to the government's participation in the social welfare institution but
at the same time recognizes the importance of human services. It calls for
business and industry to increase its social responsibility by funding social
welfare programs more generously.

> The principal alternative to private philanthropy is government funding,
> which is considered to be inherently less efficient in the distribution and
> control of funds for these purposes. The sources of government funds, it
> must be emphasized, are tax-paying individuals and business enterprise.
> As businessmen and as individuals it is, therefore, in everyone's self-interest
> to support society through private social investments rather than through
> the complex and costly redistribution of tax dollars by government. Ac-
> cordingly, if the business community is serious in seeking to stem over-
> dependence on government and still allow the private not-for-profit sector
> to make the same contribution to society that it has in the past, business
> must itself increase its commitment.[34]

Private Sector Social Welfare Expenditures

Has the private sector increased its contribution to private charity? Table
4–4 indicates that the increase in total private philanthropy was fairly substantial in the total dollars contributed, i.e., from $48.7 billion to $93.7 billion
between 1980 and 1987. However, if just the health, education, and welfare
allocations are considered, there has been only a slight increase (i.e., from
3.7 to 5.0 percent) compared to the funds spent by federal, state, and local
governments.

Although it is not possible to disaggregate the data in Table 4–4 to identify
the sources of funds for each category of allocation, it is evident that the
increases in private philanthropy did not come from business and industry.
Business corporations gave only 4.8 percent of the 1987 total, the same as in
1980. The relative increases in charitable contributions between 1980 and 1987
were, in fact, in the form of gifts from foundations and charitable bequests—
the result of changed tax laws.

The decrease in government expenditures for enhancement programs had
a substantial influence on the nonprofit social agencies as many contract with
government agencies to either provide services or conduct research for which
they are reimbursed with public funds. Of the total revenues of these nonprofit organizations, 35 percent comes from the federal government, 20 percent from private contributions, 5 to 10 percent from other levels of government, and the rest from fees and earned income.[35] Therefore, nonprofit
agencies feel the impact of changes in governmental funding patterns.

Palmer and Sawhill summarize the impact of the Reagan administration's
first term on nonprofit social agencies as follows:

> President Reagan hoped that reductions in taxes and domestic expenditures
> would restore the vitality of the voluntary sector. However, these reductions
> have adversely affected the finances of nonprofit organizations and thus
> their ability to provide services for two reasons. To begin with, lower tax
> rates raise the cost of charitable donations because the deductions permitted

TABLE 4–4 Total Private Philanthropy, 1960–1987

	1960		1970		1980		1987	
Total	$10,926 (mil.)	100%	$20,887 (mil.)	100%	$48,739 (mil.)	100%	$93,680 (mil.)	100%
Source								
Individuals	9,160	83.8%	16,190	77.5%	40,710	83.6%	76,820	82.0%
Foundations	710	6.5	1,900	9.1	2,810	5.8	6,380	6.8
Businesses	482	4.4	797	3.8	2,359	4.8	4,500	4.8
Charitable bequests	574	5.3	2,000	9.6	2,860	5.7	5,980	6.4
Allocation								
Religion	5,010	45.9%	9,340	44.7%	22,230	45.6%	43,610	46.6%
Education	1,720	15.7	3,280	15.7	6,860	14.1	10,840	11.6
Social welfare	1,630	14.9	2,920	13.9	4,910	10.1	9,840	10.5
Health & hospitals	1,350	12.5	3,440	16.4	6,670	13.7	13,650	14.6
Arts and humanities	408	3.7	663	3.2	3,150	6.5	6,410	6.8
Civic & public	314	2.9	455	2.2	1,460	3.0	2,600	2.8
Other	502	4.6	932	4.5	3,460	7.1	3,890	4.6

Source: American Association of Fund-Raising Counsel Trust for Philanthropy, *Giving USA, 1988* (New York: 1988).

for this purpose are then worth less to the taxpayer. Over the period 1981–1984, the Reagan tax changes discouraged donations by an estimated $10 billion. What is more important, reductions in domestic spending have taken a heavy toll on some types of nonprofit organizations. By FY 1984, real federal spending for programs relevant to nonprofit organizations was below FY 1980 levels. . . .

. . . However, the effects have been quite uneven. Agencies established under the aegis of the Great Society and those focusing services on the poor have been hit especially hard by the federal cutbacks. Unable to close the funding gap with sufficient private donations or with charges for services, many agencies have had to reduce their activities, especially those engaged in housing and community development, legal services, social services, and employment and training.[36]

Impact on Individual and Family Income

Proponents of Reaganomics have argued that a reduction in taxes plus reduced federal expenditures (except for defense) would create a general prosperity that would "benefit all segments of society, poor and middle as well as upper class."[37] The data related to President Reagan's first term indicate that conditions have deteriorated for the most vulnerable members of the society—the poor. Examination of Table 4–5, using the government's definition of poverty (e.g., $10,178 for a family of four persons in 1983), suggests that from 1980 through 1983, 2.6 percent more of the U.S. population were poor. While income transfer programs have reduced the amount of poverty slightly for older people, the incidence of poverty increased for families and particularly for families headed by women. It has only been intervention by a more liberal Congress and the courts that has kept the reductions in human services for the poor from being as great as most experts had anticipated.

With the scorecard on the first term of Ronald Reagan's presidency in, Palmer and Sawhill again provide a clear analysis of the impact on families. While the wealthy families improved their position during this period, poor families lost ground.

TABLE 4–5 Percentage of Population Below the Poverty Level

	ALL PERSONS	PERSONS 65 YEARS AND OVER	MARRIED COUPLE FAMILIES	FAMILIES HEADED BY WOMEN
1980	10.4%	9.7%	5.8%	28.9%
1981	11.7	9.6	6.7	31.7
1982	12.7	9.3	7.5	33.9
1983	13.0	8.7	7.8	34.1

Source: U.S. Bureau of the Census, *Estimates of Poverty Including the Value of Noncash Benefits: 1979–1983*, Technical Paper 51, February, 1984 cited by Courtenay Slater, "Concepts of Poverty," *The Journal of The Institute for Socioeconomic Studies* 9 (Autumn 1984): 8.

Not all families shared in the income growth that occurred between 1980 and 1984. In fact, since 1980 the real disposable income of the poorest one-fifth (quintile) of all families declined by nearly 8 percent, while that of the top quintile rose by almost 9 percent. The income of the typical middle-class family (the middle quintile) grew by a scant 1 percent. Because of the underlying economic and demographic trends, some of this widening of the income distribution would have taken place regardless of who was president. But the particular tax and benefit reductions that President Reagan supported exacerbated the trend. His policies helped the affluent but were detrimental to the poor and middle class.

How a family fared over this period depended more on its income-level than on its other characteristics, but such factors as age, sex, and race also played a role. For example, the incomes of the elderly rose substantially; the elderly were also the major gainers from Reagan's policies. In contrast, female-headed and black families did poorly, and they were the major losers from the administration's policies.[38]

CONCLUDING COMMENT

Efforts to achieve the goals of the social welfare institution have yielded a rapidly increasing number of social programs at an escalating cost. On one side of the ledger are the dollars invested by governmental and voluntary associations to enhance the well-being of people. These costs can be calculated and regularly appear in the headlines: "Muhlenberg County Welfare Rolls Pass $5 M" or "United Way Reaches $750,000 in Fund Drive." The other side of the ledger for social programs is their impact on the quality of the lives of the people they serve. When basic human needs are being met, the quality of people's lives is enhanced and the social welfare institution is performing its proper function. When poverty, hunger, and homelessness are increasing, the social welfare institution as well as the society is failing.

After two decades of increasing commitment by the U.S. population to the social welfare institution, and particularly to people with limited income, the 1980s have been a period of changed direction. There has been a reduction of human services during the first term of Ronald Reagan, and, as evidenced by his landslide re-election to a second term, relatively little concern by the voting public about the harmful effects that these reductions have on the vulnerable members of the population. Will there be additional reductions in the support for human services during the remainder of the 1980s? If so, when will we reach the point that those who have carried this burden, the poor, mobilize their resources and rebel? What form will that rebellion take? What will social work's role be?

If social work is to achieve its mission of social betterment, especially for the most vulnerable members of society, it must have more adequate social programs to provide for people in need. The evidence indicates that the social programs in the United States have never adequately addressed the needs of the poor and, in fact, eroded during the Reagan administration's first term. Social workers face a dual challenge. They must search for new and more effective ways to provide services and at the same time promote welfare reform measures that will eliminate societal conditions that oppress or limit human functioning.[39]

SUGGESTED READINGS

Abramson, Alan J., and Salamon, Lester M. *The Nonprofit Sector and the New Federal Budget*. Washington, D.C.: The Urban Institute, 1986.

AuClaire, Philip Arthur. "Public Attitudes Toward Social Welfare Expenditures." *Social Work* 29 (March–April 1984): 139–144.

Axinn, June, and Levin, Herman. *Social Welfare: A History of the American Response to Need*. 2nd ed. New York: Harper and Row, 1982.

Axinn, June, and Stern, Mark J. "Women and the Postindustrial Welfare State." *Social Work* 32 (July–August 1987): 282–288.

Chambers, Donald E. *Social Policy and Social Programs: A Method for the Practical Public Policy Analyst*. New York: Macmillan, 1986.

Federico, Ronald C. *The Social Welfare Institution: An Introduction*, 4th ed. Lexington, Mass.: D.C. Heath, 1984.

Gilbert, Neil. "The Welfare State Adrift." *Social Work* 31 (July–August 1986): 251–256.

Jansson, Bruce S. *The Reluctant Welfare State: A History of American Social Welfare Policies*. Belmont, Calif.: Wadsworth, 1988.

Johnson, Barbara Brooks. "The Changing Role of Women and Social Security Reform." *Social Work* 32 (July–August 1987): 341–345.

Kamerman, Sheila B. "The New Mixed Economy of Welfare: Public and Private." *Social Work* 28 (January–February 1983): 5–10.

Levitan, Sar A. *Programs in Aid of the Poor*, 5th ed. Baltimore: The Johns Hopkins University Press, 1985.

McGovern, George. "Whose Responsibility Is Social Responsibility? An Opposing View." *Public Welfare* 39 (Fall 1981): 8–17.

Morris, Robert. *Rethinking Social Welfare. Why Care for the Stranger?* New York: Longman, 1986.

Ozawa, Martha N. "Nonwhites and the Demographic Imperative in Social Welfare Spending." *Social Work* 31 (November–December 1986): 440–446.

Palmer, John L. *Perspectives on the Reagan Years*. Washington, D.C.: Urban Institute Press, 1986.

Palmer, John L., and Sawhill, Isabel V. *The Reagan Record*. Washington, D.C.: Urban Institute Press, 1984.

Sosin, Michael. *Private Benefits: Material Assistance in the Private Sector*. Orlando, Fla.: Academic Press, 1986.

Trattner, Walter I. *From Poor Law to Welfare State*. 3rd ed. New York: Free Press, 1984.

ENDNOTES

1. John Romanyshyn, Victor Baez, and Bradford W. Sheafor, "Social Welfare, Organizational Structure, and Professionals" (Fort Collins, Colo.: Colorado State University, August 1976), videotape.
2. Abraham H. Maslow, *Motivation and Personality* (New York: Harper and Row, 1970), pp. 35–58.
3. *The Random House College Dictionary*, rev. ed. (New York: Random House, 1975), p. 1,493.
4. Gwendolyn C. Gilbert, "The Role of Social Work in Black Liberation, *The Black Scholar* (December 1974): 16–23.
5. Betty Reid Mandell, ed., *Welfare in America: Controlling the "Dangerous Classes"* (Englewood Cliffs, N.J.: Prentice-Hall, 1975), p. 3.
6. Robert Bierstedt, *The Social Order*, 3rd ed., (New York: McGraw-Hill, 1979), p. 320.

7. Ibid., p. 324.
8. Bernard Berelson and Gary A. Steiner, *Human Behavior: An Inventory of Scientific Findings*, (New York: Harcourt, Brace, & World, 1963), p. 384.
9. Bierstedt, *The Social Order*, p. 305.
10. C. Wright Mills, "Troubles and Issues," in Paul E. Weinberger, ed., *Perspectives on Social Welfare*, 2nd ed., (New York: Macmillan, 1974), p. 31.
11. Mayer N. Zald, *Social Welfare Institutions: A Sociological Reader* (New York: John Wiley, 1965), pp. 21–22.
12. William Ryan, *Blaming the Victim* (New York: Vintage, 1971).
13. Ralph E. Pumphrey and Muriel W. Pumphrey, eds., *The Heritage of American Social Work* (New York: Columbia University Press, 1961), p. 60.
14. Robert H. Bremner, *American Philanthropy* (Chicago: University of Chicago Press, 1960), p. 191.
15. Harold L. Wilensky and Charles N. Lebeaux, *Industrial Society and Social Welfare* (New York: Free Press, 1965), p. 42.
16. Pumphrey and Pumphrey, *Heritage of Social Work*, pp. 432–433.
17. John L. Palmer and Isabel V. Sawhill, eds., *The Reagan Record: An Assessment of America's Changing Domestic Priorities*, p. 13. Copyright 1984 by the Urban Institute. Reprinted by permission of Ballinger Publishing Company.
18. Ibid., p. 17.
19. D. Lee Bawden and John L. Palmer, "Social Policy: Challenging the Welfare State," in Palmer and Sawhill, *The Reagan Record*, pp. 213–214.
20. Yeheskel Hasenfeld and Richard A. English, eds., *Human Service Organizations* (Ann Arbor: University of Michigan Press, 1974), p. 2.
21. Wilensky and Lebeaux, *Industrial Society*, pp. 138–140.
22. Neil Gilbert and Harry Specht, *The Emergence of Social Welfare and Social Work*, 2nd ed., (Itasca, Ill.: Peacock, 1981).
23. John Romanyshyn, *Social Welfare: Charity to Justice* (New York: Random House, 1971), p. 33.
24. Alfred J. Kahn, *Social Policy and Social Services* (New York: Random House, 1973), p. 77.
25. Michael Sosin, *Private Benefits: Material Assistance in the Private Sector* (Orlando, Fla.: Academic Press, 1986), p. 37.
26. U.S. Bureau of Census, *Statistical Abstracts of the United States: 1987* (Washington, D.C.: U.S. Department of Labor, 1986), p. 343.
27. Sheila B. Kamerman and Alfred J. Kahn, *Social Services in the United States: Policies and Programs* (Philadelphia: Temple University Press, 1976), p. 3.
28. Kahn, *Social Services*, pp. 27–33.
29. Ibid., p. 29.
30. Ibid., p. 31.
31. Charles Zastrow, *Introduction to Social Welfare Institutions*, (Homewood, Ill.: Dorsey, 1978), p. 515.
32. U.S. Bureau of the Census, *Statistical Abstracts of the United States, 1987*, 107th ed., (Washington, D.C.: U.S. Bureau of the Census, 1986), p. 419.
33. Ibid., p. 343.
34. "The Business Roundtable Position on Corporate Philanthropy," issued March 26, 1981 by the Business Roundtable.
35. Palmer and Sawhill, *The Reagan Record*, p. 18.
36. Ibid., pp. 18–19. Also see Lester M. Salamon, "Nonprofit Organizations: The Lost Opportunity," in Palmer and Sawhill, *The Reagan Record*, pp. 261–286.
37. Ronald Jirovec, "Documenting the Impact of Reaganomics on Social Welfare Recipients," *Arete* 9 (Spring 1984): 36.
38. Palmer and Sawhill, *The Reagan Record*, p. 22.
39. Armando Morales, "Beyond Traditional Conceptual Frameworks," *Social Work* 22 (September 1977): 387–393.

CHAPTER 5

Fields of Social
Work Practice

One factor that makes social work different from many other professions is the opportunity to engage in helping people deal with a wide range of human problems without needing to obtain specialized professional credentials for each area of practice. During his or her lifetime, for example, a single social worker might organize and lead self-help groups in a hospital, deal with cases of abuse and neglect, develop release plans for persons in a correctional facility, plan demonstrations protesting racist or sexist injustices, arrange for foster homes and adoptions for children, secure nursing home placements for older people, supervise new social workers, and serve as the executive director of a human service agency. Regardless of the type of work performed, the social worker always has the same fundamental purpose—namely, to draw on basic knowledge, values, and skills in order to help achieve desired change in order to improve the quality of life for the persons involved.

Although there will be similarities in the tasks performed by social workers regardless of the practice setting, there will also be unique aspects of their practice in each place of employment. The very nature of the social programs developed to address different social problems requires that social workers in different settings use specialized terminology and some specialized helping techniques. For example the technical language and skills used by a social worker who is director of the local United Way should differ from those used by a social worker in the oncology unit of the local hospital. As social workers move from one setting to another, they must develop new competencies and adapt old ones to fit the practice needs. Social work provides a broad professional umbrella and social workers must be flexible as they move among the various settings where they are sanctioned to practice.

What kind of human problems do social workers address? To examine the many areas where the perspective and abilities of the social worker are needed would require many pages of description. In fact, many of the more than 2,000 pages of the *Encyclopedia of Social Work*[1] give general descriptions of social problems addressed by social workers and provide references to the most pertinent literature on the subject. The following list of fifty different social problems discussed in the *Encyclopedia* gives an indication of the range of issues social workers address:

Abortion
Adolescent pregnancy
Adoption
Aged
Alcohol use and abuse
Child abuse and neglect
Child sexual abuse
Child welfare services
Civil rights
Corrections
Disabilities: Developmental
Disabilities: Physical
Disasters and disaster aid
Divorce and separation
Domestic violence
Drug use and abuse
Emergency health services
Family: One parent
Family: Stepfamilies
Family and population planning
Foster care for adults
Foster care for children
General and emergency assistance
Group care for children
Health planning
Homelessness

Homosexuality
Housing
Hunger and malnutrition
Income maintenance
Infertility services
Information and referral services
Juvenile offenders and delinquency
Legal issues and services
Literacy
Long-term care
Loss and bereavement
Mental health and illness
Patients' rights
Poverty
Primary health care
Prostitution
Protective services for children
Protective services for the aged
Racial discrimination and inequality
Refugees
Runaways
Sex discrimination and inequality
Sexual dysfunction
Suicide
Unemployment and
    underemployment
Veterans and veterans' services[2]

The social programs designed to help people address these problems call for many different approaches to service delivery. As the helping profession with primary responsibility for helping connect people in need with the services in the community, social workers must have at least general knowledge of the full array of social programs. While detailed knowledge of each program and each human service agency may not be possible, the social worker should be familiar with all practice fields. With the help of directories of human service resources, and, in some communities, information and referral agencies, social workers are prepared to offer valuable assistance in locating specific sources of help.

The human service system is complex, and we cannot expect the layperson to successfully negotiate that system alone. The social worker is required to have considerable skill in matching people in need with resources. To reduce the client's sense of "getting the runaround" in securing services, and, perhaps, reduce the chance of the client becoming discouraged and not getting to needed help, the social worker must carefully check that the referral is to an appropriate resource. In addition, the professional at times may need to provide a variety of supports, such as encouragement, telephone numbers, names of individuals to contact, or even transportation to facilitate the client's getting to the correct resources.[3] Thus, the social worker not only must work within a single practice field but also must be prepared to help clients negotiate services among practice fields.

This chapter identifies some of the features of the primary fields of social work practice to familiarize the beginning worker with the range of settings. The particular position of social work in each field of practice is also described briefly. *Field of social work practice* is a phrase used to describe a group of practice settings that deal with similar client problems. Each field may include a number of different agencies or other organized ways of providing services. For example in any community, the social agencies concerned with crime and delinquency might include a juvenile court, a residential center or halfway house, a community corrections agency, a probation office for adult offenders, and/or a correctional facility where offenders are incarcerated. All work with people who have come to the attention of the legal system and would be considered part of the practice field of corrections. Although the fields discussed in the remainder of this chapter do not exhaust the full range where social workers might be employed, those identified suggest the great variety of settings in which the social worker is prepared to engage. One of this profession's strengths is the ability of its members to change employment from one practice field to another with only the need to adapt a part of one's knowledge and skills to the uniqueness of a new setting.

AGING

As industrialization increased, meaningful roles for older people decreased in our society. Because of improved medical care that extends life and inflation that reduces the buying power of savings and retirement funds, the elderly have become a large and vulnerable population. The problems typically experienced by this 11 percent of the U.S. population are related to health (86 percent must manage one or more chronic illnesses); housing (an estimated 30 percent live in substandard housing); loneliness because of loss of a mate, friends, and family members; change of lifestyle because of retirement and limited leisure time activities; and institutionalized living (more than 5 percent live in long-term care facilities requiring a loss of freedom and privacy).[4]

Social workers are involved with the problems of older people in a number of practice settings. Their work in income maintenance programs places them in contact with older people when financial supports are offered and when family services are provided to help older people deal with stress in their lives or make decisions about changing living arrangements. The role of social workers in medical hospitals and mental health centers also places them in direct contact with older people and their families as they seek to resolve some of the difficulties faced at this time of life.

In their efforts to enhance the quality of life for older people, approximately 3 percent of the social workers contribute to two other kinds of services to older people: those for persons requiring support to remain in their own homes and those for individuals residing in long-term care facilities.

Supports for People in Their Own Homes

A number of programs are available to help older people remain in their own homes as long as doing so is a safe and satisfying experience. Social workers help older people make links to community programs that bring health care, meals, and homemaker services into their homes; provide transportation services; and offer day-care or recreation programs. Increasingly, when older people are faced with a terminal illness, social workers help them deal with their impending death through counseling or referral to a Hospice program.[5]

Supports for People in Long-Term Care Facilities

For many older people some form of long-term care in a nursing home or other group living facility becomes a necessity. Social workers frequently help the individual and/or family select the facility and make moving arrangements; some are even staff members of the facility.

While much attention in a long-term care facility is directed toward meeting the basic physical and medical needs of the residents, social workers in these facilities contribute to the quality of life for residents by helping them maintain contact with their families and friends when possible, to develop meaningful relationships with other people within the facility, and to engage in a variety of activities both within and outside the facility. They also facilitate access to other social services when needed and help residents secure arrangements that protect their personal rights and ensure quality care while living in the long-term care facility.

BUSINESS AND INDUSTRY (OCCUPATIONAL SOCIAL WORK)

Social work has been practiced in business and industrial settings since the late 1800s.[6] Social workers have been employed both by management and labor unions to offer services and provide consultation about the development of employee programs. In recent years there has been a rapid growth of interest in this area of social work practice. Although only about one-half of 1 percent of social workers are currently employed in occupational social work positions, as the practice field is becoming known, the potential to make valuable services available to the general population is enormous. Jorgensen indicates that 64 percent of the population over age 16, or nearly 104 million people, are in the labor force.[7] Like schools and hospitals the workplace is an opportune place to identify social problems and provide needed services.

Although corporations are primarily interested in making a profit on the goods and services they produce, they are increasingly realizing worker productivity is closely related to the general welfare of the employees. The humanizing of big business has been a major theme in recent years.[8] Efforts to resolve or prevent employee problems in social functioning are seen as simply good business. Occupational social workers are a support for the managers of the companies and a resource to the employees.

Barbara Shank and Beth Jorve, drawing on a conceptual scheme developed at the University of Pittsburgh, identify three models of social work practice in business and industry: the employee service model, the consumer service model, and the corporate social responsibility model.[9]

The *employee service model* of occupational social work focuses on activities that provide direct service to the employees of a business or industry. The social worker using this model might develop and implement employee assistance programs and various supervisory training programs. In addition the social worker might provide counseling to individuals or families in relation to marital, family, substance abuse, aging, health and retirement problems, offer referral to other community agencies or self-help groups such as Alcoholics Anonymous, and consult with management on individual problems. Typical problems the social worker might also address would be the identification of job-related factors such as boredom or stress, an employee's desire to find resources to upgrade his or her job skills, the need for preretirement planning, or a linkage to Workman's Compensation or unemployment insurance programs.

The occupational social worker following the *consumer service model* might serve as the company's representative to various consumer groups and focus on identifying consumer needs and methods of meeting them. Typically found in banks, public utilities, and government agencies, these social workers help to provide liaison with consumer groups and social service agencies, develop outreach programs, and provide counseling to customers to meet unique needs.

The third model, the *corporate social responsibility model* of practice, places the social worker in the role of assisting corporations and businesses to make a commitment to the social and economic well-being of the communities in which they are located. The social workers consult with management on their policies concerning human resources, their donations to nonprofit organizations, and social legislation they may wish to support. In addition, social workers may administer health and welfare benefit programs for employees, represent the company in research and community development activities, and provide linkage between social service, social policy and corporate interests.

CHILD WELFARE

As society developed in the United States, the family became the primary social institution and was entrusted with the care and nurturing of children. U.S. law and custom mandated that other social institutions must not interfere with the rights and responsibilities of the family. It was assumed that parents would make choices that were in the best interest of both themselves and their children. For example, if parents thought it more important for children to work in industry or help with the farm work than to attend school or have time for play, that was their decision.

Because of this authority given to parents, children have become one of the most vulnerable groups in society. Although through the years there has been legislation that helped to protect children from some abuses, they continue to be somewhat hidden within the family and have little opportunity to protect themselves.

One of the first fields of social work practice to develop was child welfare. Social workers were instrumental in the passage of legislation to protect children and in the creation of the White House Conferences on Children and Youth. Here, in each decade since 1909, the overall condition of children and youth in the United States has been carefully reviewed and proposals for improving their condition promoted. Today, according to the NASW membership study, more than 15 percent of social workers are engaged in providing services related to children and youth.[10]

In most situations social workers seek to help both the parents and the children. The services that are provided recognize that not only the children need protection but also the parents may require help in changing their behavior in order to provide better care for their children. In addition, social workers not only respond to the problems that have developed but also promote laws, programs, and public understanding of the special needs of children. Five basic types of child welfare services are provided: adoption and services to unmarried parents, foster care, residential care, support for children in their own homes, and protective services for abused and neglected children and youth.

Adoption and Services to Unmarried Parents

The adoption process begins with the expectant mother, usually unmarried, who faces the difficult decision of whether to keep her baby or place the child for adoption. A few of the factors to be considered in this decision include the mother's plans for the future such as continuing school or securing employment and child care, the attitudes of the mother's family about the pregnancy, the feelings of the father and the mother's relationship with him, and where the mother will live while pregnant and after the baby arrives. Social workers use both individual and group counseling to help women think carefully and sensitively about their decisions. They also, at times, offer counseling to the "unmarried fathers" to help them deal with this situation.

If the decision is made to place the child for adoption, the social worker must screen and select adoptive parents carefully. Matching parents and children is a difficult task that requires considerable knowledge and skill. To gain the best information possible on which to make these decisions, the social worker might conduct group orientation meetings and develop thorough social histories of the prospective adoptive parents. Detailed information on the child's background and even special interests of the natural mother for the child's future (religious affiliation, for example) become a part of the basis for final adoptive placement.

Although there is an abundance of prospective adoptive homes, recent trends making it more socially acceptable for single parents to raise children have reduced the supply of infants available for adoptive placement. However, it continues to be difficult to secure satisfactory adoptive homes for older children or those who are physically or mentally handicapped. An important function of the social worker is to recruit parents for these "hard to place" children.

Foster Care

At times children may need to be removed from their own homes, but it is not possible or desirable to sever permanently the relationship with their natural parents in order to place them for adoption. In these cases, temporary (or sometimes long-term) foster care is required. The social worker must work with the parents, the child, and the courts to obtain a decision to remove a child from his or her own home and make a foster home placement. This process involves a careful assessment and a plan whereby the child can return home if conditions improve.

The social worker is also responsible for developing a pool of good quality foster homes. He or she must recruit, select, train, and monitor those families that are entrusted with the care of foster children. The placement of a child in a foster home often creates a severe stress on the child, the natural parents, and the foster parents. Considerable practice skill by the social worker is required if he or she is to help resolve these problems.

Residential Care

At times the appropriate placement for a child is a residential care facility, that is, a group home or a residential treatment center. These facilities are most likely to be chosen when the child exhibits antisocial behavior or requires intensive treatment to change behaviors that may create problems for him or her or others.

In these situations one role of the social worker is to select an appropriate residential care facility, which involves working with the child, the family, and often the courts. In addition, other social workers are usually staff members of such a facility, providing care and treatment for the children who are placed there. They are especially involved in helping to maintain positive contact between the child and the family and in making plans for the child to return home when appropriate. The fact that these residential care facilities require licensing creates another role for the social worker—evaluating facilities for the purpose of licensing.

Support in Own Home

Much child welfare work involves providing support services in order to keep children in their own homes. These support services can take the form of counseling or linking clients with outside resources.

Counseling may involve one-to-one consultation with a parent or child to resolve a particular problem with the child-parent relationship. It may also involve family consultation in which all the family members work with the social worker in an attempt to improve some aspect of their functioning. Family members may also participate in group counseling with other parents or children experiencing similar problems. The social worker guides the participants as they address the issues relevant to their problems.

In child welfare, the most common outside resources are day-care and homemaker services. Day-care centers provide a stimulating environment for children and relieve parents of the stress created by the child's continual presence in the home. The social worker must know the strengths and limitations of various day-care centers and match children with appropriate resources. Homemaker services help parents learn homemaking skills and reduce the pressures of their caring for the children and the household.

Protective Services

Some children are abused or neglected by one or both parents. Abuse, whether it is physical, sexual, or emotional, is an active mistreatment or exploitation of the child. Neglect is a more passive mistreatment of the child but can be just as damaging. It can take the form of inadequate food and shelter, unwholesome conditions, failure to have the child attend school, or inadequate provision of medical care.

The social worker, as an agent of society, seeks to protect the child without infringing on the rights of the parents. When a referral is received, the social worker must determine if the child is in immediate danger, assess the ability of the parents to resolve the problem, and make a judgment about the risks of working with the family while keeping the child in the home. If the child is removed from the home (with approval of the courts), the social worker continues to work with the family in an effort to eliminate the difficulties that led to the referral. This process may involve individual, family, or group counseling; the provision of support services; or education of family members in the areas of their incompetence.

COMMUNITY AND NEIGHBORHOOD SERVICES

The emphasis of social work on both the person and the environment makes the profession directly concerned with the communities in which people live. Beginning with both the Charity Organization Societies and the Settlement House Movement, social work clearly saw the need to coordinate multiple human services and change the structure and processes of communities to make them more responsive to the needs of people. Many of the social problems that people face (for example, discrimination and unemployment) are at least partially created by the community and not by the individuals affected. Improving the environment is an important factor in improving the quality of life of all people.

In this discussion of community services as a field of social work practice, emphasis is placed on the different practice settings where social workers are employed full-time to help communities improve their functioning. It should be recognized, however, that all social workers have a responsibility as part of their professional commitment to engage in community change activities. Social action might be a responsibility of any social work position or might be conducted as a volunteer activity. Social agencies in almost any practice field occasionally create a position that is defined as a community change or social action job, but the primary settings where social workers focus on community services can be classified as community organization, community planning, and community development. Only about 2 percent of the social workers are engaged in this form of practice on a full-time basis.

Community Organization

A traditional practice area for social work has been working within the network of human services to increase their effectiveness in meeting human needs. This activity involves the collection and analysis of data related to the delivery of services, matching that information with data on population distribution, securing funds to maintain and enhance the quality of services, coordinating the efforts to existing agencies, and educating the general public about these services. The principal agencies in which social workers are employed to do this type of work are community coordinating councils, United Way agencies, and other federations of agencies under the auspices of religious groups such as the Jewish Welfare Federation.

Community Planning

A few social workers with specialized training join physical, economic, and health planners in the long-range planning of communities. This work requires the ability to apply planning technology in order to project the growth and development of communities. The special contribution of the social worker is to analyze the needs for human services as towns, cities, or regions undergo change. These contributions might range from anticipating "boom-town" developments in the energy-impacted areas of Colorado or Wyoming to helping an urban ghetto plan for an increase in human service needs brought about by businesses moving to the suburbs and leaving the central city with an eroding tax base.

Community Development

Social work joins a number of disciplines in giving assistance to people in communities as they seek to improve conditions. This approach is based on a self-help philosophy that encourages members of the community to mobilize their resources in order to study their problems and seek solutions. In rural areas the social worker contributes to this "grass roots" approach by guiding the involved people toward use of a sound process that maximizes the participation of many concerned citizens. The social worker or other professional also serves as a resource for obtaining technical consultation in areas where there is not expertise among the community members. In urban areas this process, sometimes known as an "asphalt roots" approach, is used in helping neighborhoods or special population groups (such as the poor, minorities, or older people) work together to improve the quality of their lives.

CORRECTIONS AND CRIMINAL JUSTICE

The corrections field is founded on the disciplines of law and law enforcement. In the United States there is fear of persons who are deviant—especially those who violate laws. One response has been to control this behavior by punishing and/or taking custody of the lives of people who are repeated offenders. The corrections system has emerged as a highly structured and authoritarian field primarily concerned with controlling the behavior of those who are convicted of law violations.

Social workers often find corrections a difficult field of practice because the authoritarian structure conflicts with many social work values, principles, and techniques. Yet, because the problems faced in this field are basically those of social functioning, the social worker has valuable contributions to make to both the clients and the agencies. Together with other helping disciplines, social work has helped introduce both a treatment and a prevention philosophy into this practice area; however, finding solutions to the many problems that plague the corrections field will require much more work.

The corrections field embraces offenders from all aspects of society—youth and adults, males and females, rich and poor, members of dominant population groups and minorities, and even former White House aides and senators. As indicated in Chapter 11, the poor, especially minorities, however, are very much overrepresented. The social worker's involvement with the criminal justice system can begin at the time of arrest and terminate at the person's release. Some social workers serve as, or work with, juvenile officers in diversionary programs, where they provide crisis intervention or referral services at the time of arrest. These programs divert people from the criminal justice system and into more appropriate community services. Social workers also prepare social histories and make psychosocial assessments of individuals charged with crimes as part of the data a judge uses in making decisions about a case. If the person is placed on probation, a social worker might be the probation officer providing individual, family, or group counseling and helping the convicted person make changes in behavior that will satisfy the terms of probation and prevent additional problems from developing.

Social workers are also found in correctional facilities. In these facilities they provide counseling and serve as a link to the outside world, which encompasses the family, potential employers, and the community service network that will provide support to that person at the time of release. If parole is granted, a social worker might serve as the parole officer or work in a halfway house where the person may live prior to a completely independent re-entry to the community.

FAMILY SERVICES

The strains on the nuclear family have created a varied pattern of family structures. High divorce rates and changing social customs and attitudes related to out-of-wedlock births, single-parent families, child care responsibilities, and sexual preference have presented new perspectives on the family and its function in society. More than 11 percent of today's social workers are actively involved in efforts to understand, interpret, and provide required services as the family experiences this change. In addition to promoting needed programs, the social worker is engaged in three service areas of significance: family counseling, family life education, and family planning.

Family Counseling

Social work employs three approaches to family counseling in an effort to help the family adjust to its changing role and deal with the problems it experiences. The first is *family casework*. This approach emphasizes helping individual members of the family change their behaviors in order to make them more productive contributors to the family. It draws on techniques used in individual casework services that are strongly influenced by psychosocial treatment approaches and a problem-solving orientation.

A second approach is termed *family group work*. Recognizing that the family is a special form of a small group, it incorporates much of the theory of social work practice with groups. This approach emphasizes the process by which the family examines its relationships. The social worker helps family members work together to resolve their problems.

The third approach is *family therapy*. This approach seeks to change the structure of the family to make it more supportive of its members. The family, then, is regarded as a unit that can contribute to the well-being of its individual members and is encouraged to perform this function. As opposed to family casework and family group work, family therapy requires advanced skills and training to prepare properly for this therapeutic activity.

Family Life Education

In recent years an effort has been made to strengthen the family through activities that fall under the label of family life education. This social work practice activity recognizes that all families face certain kinds of stress and seeks to prevent family breakdown by educating the family members to cope with the anticipated problems. The Family Service Association of America (FSAA) has taken an active role in developing family life education programs. FSAA has described the goals of family life education as:

to help group members to understand and anticipate the normal patterns and stresses of family and community living, and thus to improve interpersonal relationships and prevent or reduce situational crises.[11]

Simply stated, family life education provides education about individual and family living. It teaches about interpersonal, family, and sex relationships to help people have more satisfactory and fulfilling lives. Family life education is a preventive approach to human services that has the potential for reaching a large number of people.

Family Planning

Social workers have long been sensitive to the fact that both an unwanted child and the parents often experience problems. Adequately carrying out the responsibilities of raising a child is difficult under the best of circumstances, and an unwanted pregnancy makes it even more difficult. Most social workers contend that each child should have the right to begin life as a wanted person. Helping families to plan the number, spacing, and timing of the births of children to fit with their needs improves the chance of achieving the goal of bearing wanted children.

Family planning does not imply that there should be a minimum or maximum number of children in a family or that any specific birth control method should be used. Rather, from the social work perspective, the family is helped to make decisions about their patterns of reproduction in order to maximize the quality of life for both the child and other family members.

The social worker does not have medical training and cannot replace the important role of physicians and nurses in the physiological aspects of family planning. However, he or she must have a minimal understanding of human reproduction, contraception, and abortion to help families with the decisions they must make. Because the issue of family planning can arise in many counseling situations, social workers in hospitals, public welfare agencies, mental health clinics, family services, health departments, schools, Planned Parenthood clinics, and private practice must be prepared to help clients when the need for family planning decisions arise.

GROUP AND YOUTH SERVICES

Very early in U.S. history a number of social services were developed to provide educational and recreational opportunities for people of all social classes. These services were first aimed at character-building among youth, with organizations such as YMCAs, YWCAs, Boys and Girls Clubs, and the various scouting groups developing. Later, with the growth of settlement houses, programs were broadened to serve other age groups. Although a number of other disciplines also provide staff for these agencies and some agencies have their own career development programs for staff, this field of practice continues to be a small but important area of social work.

Rooted in an institutional philosophy of social welfare, these services seek to enhance the growth and development of all interested participants. Through the use of such activities as crafts, sports, camping, friendship groups, drama, music, informal counseling, and many other forms of group participation, the members are guided toward social development. The role of the social worker might be to administer these agencies, to lead the group process, or to provide individual counseling. In addition, because of their work with youth and older people in identifying the problems and concerns they experience, social workers are in a position to advocate for changes in the factors that contribute to these problems.

With the exception of programs offered through local recreation departments and community education programs, these services are largely concentrated in the private sector of social welfare. Support from churches, United Way funding, foundation gifts, individual memberships, fees for service, and voluntary contributions provide the bulk of the resources for their operation. As opposed to many of the services discussed previously, these programs have developed much more of a middle-class orientation and are, at times, criticized for investing too little of their effort on the more vulnerable parts of the population.

INCOME MAINTENANCE

Although we tend to define poverty in terms of the amount of money available to a person or family, social workers have learned that it is a much more complex and insidious phenomenon. Data reflect that poverty is linked to such factors as health and housing, racism and sexism, old age and youth, single parent status, education and employment, and rural or urban environment. Experience indicates that financial assistance, at least at the levels U.S. society has been willing to make available, will not in itself break the cycle of poverty. The poor are perhaps the most vulnerable population group and are of primary concern to social workers.

Despite the many factors that contribute to poverty, lack of income is an unmet need that brings poor people to the attention of the social worker. A number of government-sponsored and voluntary social provision programs have been developed to provide assistance to, or reduce financial demands on, the poor. The two dominant areas of the income maintenance field are public assistance and social insurance programs, although there are other programs that serve this area of human need.

Public Welfare

From the time of the Charity Organization Societies to the present, social workers have been concerned with financial aid for the poor. The responsibility gradually moved from these private agencies to the states and, with the passage of the Social Security Act in 1935, to combined support at the local, state, and federal levels. Private income maintenance programs have almost disappeared.

Social workers have actively supported the development of adequate income maintenance programs and have led efforts to provide needed services. One major concern, in addition to the low levels of financial assistance, has been the requirement that clients take a degrading means test before they can become eligible for public assistance. All social workers should be familiar with the four basic public assistance programs, since poor people use the services of almost every social agency.

The first public assistance program, *Aid to Families with Dependent Children* (AFDC), provides assistance to children in need through cash grants to the supporting parent or parents—usually the mother. To be eligible, according to the Social Security Act, children must have been deprived of parental care or support because of the death, continued absence from the home, or physical or mental incapacity of a parent. In about one-half of the states children of unemployed fathers are also eligible. These programs are administered by each state with funding from state and federal governments.

The second, the *food stamp program*, is designed to reduce the hunger that is surprisingly prevalent in our wealthy country. Food stamps are available to public assistance recipients and to some other low-income people. The stamps can be traded for groceries at most food markets. Social workers often have administrative responsibilities in food stamp programs, but the eligibility determination and distribution are usually carried out by paraprofessionals.

The third category of public assistance programs is *general assistance*. They are intended to meet temporarily the needs of people not eligible for other public assistance or social insurance programs. They vary widely from state to state because no federal funds are allocated for these programs. In most areas local governments begrudgingly and meagerly support these programs that are largely utilized by able-bodied, unemployed people who have not succeeded in a job market that averages 8–10 percent unemployment.

Hospital and medical care for the poor are provided through the *Medicaid program* in an effort to minimize the financial impact of a serious illness. Medicaid pays the hospital and medical services of persons on welfare as well as the medically indigent. AFDC and Supplemental Security Income recipients, as well as some other poor people, are eligible to receive the benefits of this program. It is administered by the states but has substantial federal funding.

The fourth public assistance program, *Supplemental Security Income* (SSI), is administered by the federal government. This program is intended to provide a national minimum level of income for those people who were once called the "worthy poor" or, in today's rhetoric of the Reagan administration, the "truly needy." The aged, blind, and handicapped are eligible for this program. Most states supplement the federal dollars in order to make the level of support more adequate for the recipients.

Social Insurances

Social provisions that are funded through contributions to a specific program rather than through direct tax revenues are known as social insurance programs. These programs are funded by employee and employer contributions, and the benefits are made available at times when they are most needed. An eligibility test is not required to receive social insurance benefits.

The major social insurance program is *Old Age, Survivors, Disability, and Health Insurance* (OASDHI), better known as Social Security. This program makes benefits available to insured workers when they reach age sixty-five, to dependent spouses of these workers at age sixty-two, and to dependent children under age eighteen. It is intended to replace some of the income lost if a worker dies, becomes disabled, or retires. OASDHI has been under attack because of the manner in which it has been funded. There is much concern that its uncertain fiscal solvency will prevent it from continuing to pay benefits unless supplemental allocations are received from the U.S. Treasury.

Medicare is a federal health insurance program directed at persons over age sixty-five who are vulnerable to serious illnesses that can quickly deplete financial resources and place them permanently in need of public assistance. Medicare pays for hospital care, extended inpatient care, home health services, physicians' fees, and other health related services. If medical costs exceed these benefits, private health insurance or Medicaid can be used to fill the gaps.

Other social insurance programs include *Unemployment Insurance* and *Workman's Compensation Insurance*. The former provides temporary benefits to eligible persons who have lost their jobs, and the latter provides income and medical expenses to people who have been injured on their jobs.

Other Income Maintenance Programs

Cash and in-kind benefits are also available through a variety of private sources in local communities. Local churches and social agencies, such as the Salvation Army and American Red Cross, usually have small amounts of emergency support funds, and a number of other resources usually exist where the poor can obtain help with food, clothing, and shelter. These resources are so indigenous to local areas that local resources must be consulted to learn details. Social workers are familiar with these local sources of help, and frequently they are involved in their provision.

MEDICAL AND HEALTH CARE

Social workers have played a secondary role to physicians in health and medical settings since the early 1900s. With increased understanding that illnesses can be caused or exacerbated by social factors, social work is gaining a more central role in this field. It was the second largest field of practice reported in the NASW Membership Study, with 18.1 percent of the social workers reporting employment in this field.[12] The medical profession has recognized that treating an illness does not necessarily resolve the problems experienced by a patient. Medical problems are often created by emotional and social problems and, at times, cause emotional or social problems. Thus, social workers have been employed in a variety of medical and health care settings.

A primary place for social work practice in this field is in hospitals. In these settings, for example, social workers "attend to social and psychological factors that are either contributing causes of medical ailments or are side effects of a medical condition that must be dealt with to facilitate recovery and prevent occurrences of non-functional dependence."[13] Social workers help to link patients, perhaps with changed levels of functioning due to a medical problem, with their environments by providing individual, group, and family counseling; serving as patient advocates; and working with self-help groups of patients experiencing similar medical or social problems. Social workers also might be engaged in counseling terminally ill patients and their families.

In addition social workers are involved in other health and medical care facilities besides hospitals. They work in public health clinics and private physicians' offices providing counseling and referral services to people who have sought medical treatment related to family planning, prenatal care, child growth and development, venereal disease, and physical disability, for example. They have also taken an active role in health maintenance and disease prevention programs in local communities. With the skyrocketing costs of medical care it is even more important that these efforts be continued by the social work profession.

MENTAL HEALTH AND RETARDATION

Although mental health and mental retardation (or developmental disability as the latter is more currently labeled) are very different conditions, the role of the social worker is similar in each area. Therefore, these practice fields are combined for the purpose of this discussion. Social work has been involved in working with people experiencing both these conditions since the early 1900s and has gradually become a dominant profession in these areas because of the serious problems in social functioning that are frequently caused, or at least increased, by these conditions. It is estimated that more than one-half of all professional mental health personnel are social workers, and one might expect about the same ratio in the area of developmental disability. Furthermore, the 1982 NASW Membership Survey reveals that 40 percent of all social workers are practicing in these two practice fields.[14]

In every type of social agency the social worker will confront problems of emotional disturbance or mental impairment. It is estimated that at any one time 15 percent of the population need mental services,[15] and that 3 percent experience varying degrees of retardation.[16] These problems affect people from all age, religious, and ethnic groups.

Mental retardation refers to those who are developmentally disabled and are impaired in their ability to learn. This may be a mild disability that allows people to function quite normally in most aspects of their lives or a more severe disability that prohibits even minimal functioning. Increasing levels of retardation add to a person's or a family's problems in social functioning and, therefore, require more support from social workers and other helping professionals.

Mental health is defined as "a positive state of mental well-being in which individuals feel basically satisfied with themselves, their roles in life, and relationships with others."[17] The goal of achieving mental health is compatible with the purpose of social work. The absence of mental health, mental illness, takes the form of a wide range of behaviors and is caused by factors ranging from stressful situations to organic problems.

Social workers in the mental health and retardation fields are concerned with caring for the persons experiencing these difficulties, treating those who can make changes or learn to cope with problems in their social functioning, and changing environmental factors to promote better mental health or eliminate social conditions that have a negative impact on people. Some social workers provide these services on an *outpatient* basis in a mental health center, sheltered workshop, or counseling center. They give clinical or therapeutic services to individuals and families, or to clients in small groups. They may also work with a variety of organizations, such as schools or mass media, to attempt to create an environment that is conducive to the healthy growth and development of both clients and the general public.

Other social workers provide services to people on an *inpatient* basis in residential treatment centers, general hospitals, and psychiatric hospitals. These services are given to people of all ages experiencing more severe problems and requiring the more full-time care and structure available at a hospital or other living situation. In addition to providing a variety of treatment activities, these social workers serve as a liaison to that patient's world. A social worker might work to help the patient and family or friends maintain contact while the patient is hospitalized. He or she might also assess the impact of family, friends, employer, school, etc. on the client's situation and offer assistance in helping these significant others change in ways that will benefit the client. Finally, when patients are ready to return to the community, the social worker would become the key professional person helping them to make arrangements for returning to school or work, securing an appropriate living situation, connecting with supportive social service agencies, and developing and maintaining needed social relationships.

SCHOOLS

About 3½ percent of social workers are actively involved with schools either by working with families in other practice settings or by employment within the schools themselves. Because education is compulsory, the schools confront many of the problems of living such as poverty, child abuse, discrimination, developmental disability, and emotional disturbance. These problems impact children and their ability to learn—the primary mission of education—and thus become a concern of school systems.

The traditional approach of social workers in schools has been to counsel the child and confer with the family. They have depended on the cooperation of teachers to make referrals when problems are evident and have had varying degrees of effectiveness depending on the willingness of teachers and school systems to use them as a resource. Problems of truancy, suspected child abuse, inadequate nutrition, substance abuse, parental neglect, and inappropriate behavior are often referred to the social worker.

Recently this practice field has undergone a marked change with the school being approached as a primary setting where social problems should be identified and addressed. Social workers have, under this approach, become more aggressive in their practice activities, serving as a link between school, family, and community. Lela Costin identifies seven primary tasks one can expect to find the social worker performing in the schools today:

1. Facilitate the provision of direct educational and social services and provide direct social casework and group work services to selected pupils.

2. Act as a pupil advocate, focusing upon the urgent needs of selected groups of pupils.

3. Consult with school administrators to jointly identify major problems toward which a planned service approach will be aimed; aid in developing cooperative working relationships with community agencies; and assist in the formulation of school policy that directly affects the welfare of children and young persons.

4. Consult with teachers about techniques for creating a climate in which children are freed and motivated to learn by interpreting social and cultural influences in the lives of pupils, facilitating the use of peers to help a troubled child, or assisting in managing relationships within a classroom.

5. Organize parent and community groups to channel concerns about pupils and school and to improve school and community relations.

6. Develop and maintain liaison between the school and critical fields of social work—child welfare, corrections, mental health, and legal services for the poor. Such liaison facilitates more effective community services for school children and their families, assists with planned change in the community's organizational pattern of social welfare programs and resources, and acts as a catalyst to change the pattern of the social structure.

7. Provide leadership in the coordination of interdisciplinary skills among pupil services personnel, e.g., guidance counselors, psychologists, nurses, and attendance officers.[18]

These tasks clearly match the competencies one would find in the professional social worker.

CONCLUDING COMMENT

For the person considering a career in social work, it is important to have an understanding of the many different fields of practice open to the social worker. It is also important to recognize that the position of social work varies in these different fields; that not only affects the ability of the social worker to provide clients with services, but also influences the manner in which the social worker uses a part of his or her time. However, experience over time has demonstrated that social work has a viable role to perform in many different practice settings.

Two important points made earlier in this book are reinforced by this examination of selected social work practice fields. First, social work is indeed a profession of many faces. The variation in the type of human problems and social change activities in which social workers are involved is extensive. Social work deals with almost every facet of life and almost every element of the population.

Second, social work is unique among the helping professions because of its dual focus on the person and the environment. Social workers help people deal with the world around them in every field of practice. As a consequence, individuals are helped to relate more effectively to families; families are helped to deal with social agencies; social agencies are helped to relate more effectively with communities; and the cycle is completed as communities are helped to be more responsive to the needs of individuals.

The preparation received when obtaining a baccalaureate or master's degree in social work is intended to prepare one with the basic knowledge, values, and skills to engage in social work practice in any of these fields. The ability to transfer these competencies to several different settings gives the social worker considerable flexibility in selecting the setting where he or she will work. However, the social worker will need to acquire more in-depth knowledge about the uniqueness of each new setting and the specialized knowledge and skills that may be used in that particular field.

SUGGESTED READINGS

AGING

Beaver, Marion L. *Human Service Practice with the Elderly.* Englewood Cliffs, N.J.: Prentice-Hall, 1983.

Brody, Elaine M., and Brody, Stanley J. "Aged: Services." *Encyclopedia of Social Work,* edited by Anne Minahan. 18th ed. Silver Spring, Md.: National Association of Social Workers, 1987, Vol. I, pp. 106–126.

Dunkle, Ruth E. "Protective Services for the Aged." *Encyclopedia of Social Work,* edited by Anne Minahan. 18th ed. Silver Spring, Md.: National Association of Social Workers, 1987, Vol. II, pp. 391–396.

Getzel, George S., and Mellor, M. Joanna, eds. *Gerontological Social Work Practice in Long-Term Care.* New York: Haworth, 1983.

BUSINESS AND INDUSTRY

Akabas, Sheila H., and Kurzman, Paul A. *Work, Workers, and Work Organizations.* Englewood Cliffs, N.J.: Prentice-Hall, 1982.

Fabricant, Michael. "The Industrialization of Social Work Practice." *Social Work* 30 (September–October 1985): 389–395.

Googins, Bradley, and Godfrey, Joline. "The Evolution of Occupational Social Work." *Social Work* 30 (September–October 1985): 396–402.

Masi, Dale A. *Human Services in Industry.* Lexington, Mass.: Lexington Books, 1982.

Kurzman, Paul A. "Industrial Social Work (Occupational Social Work)." *Encyclopedia of Social Work*, edited by Anne Minahan. 18th ed. Silver Spring, Md.: National Association of Social Workers, 1987, Vol. I, pp. 899–910.

Wyers, Norman L., and Kaulukukui, Malina. "Social Services in the Workplace: Rhetoric vs. Reality." *Social Work* 29 (March–April 1984): 167–172.

CHILD WELFARE

Faller, Kathleen Coulborn. "Protective Services for Children." *Encyclopedia of Social Work*, edited by Anne Minahan. 18th ed. Silver Spring, Md.: National Association of Social Workers, 1987, Vol. II, pp. 386–391.

Hartman, Ann. *Working with Adoptive Families Beyond Placement.* New York: Child Welfare League of America, 1984.

Horejsi, Charles R. *Foster Family Care: A Handbook for Social Workers and Concerned Citizens.* Springfield, Ill.: Charles C. Thomas, 1979.

Kadushin, Alfred. "Child Welfare Services." *Encyclopedia of Social Work*, edited by Anne Minahan. 18th ed. Silver Spring, Md.: National Association of Social Workers, 1987, Vol. I, pp. 265–275.

Laird, Joan, and Hartman, Ann, eds. *A Handbook of Child Welfare.* New York: Free Press, 1985.

McGowan, Brenda G., and Meexan, William, eds. *Child Welfare: Current Dilemmas, Future Directions.* Itasca, Ill.: F.E. Peacock, 1983.

COMMUNITY AND NEIGHBORHOOD SERVICES

Biegel, David E. "Neighborhoods." *Encyclopedia of Social Work*, edited by Anne Minahan. 18th ed. Silver Spring, Md.: National Association of Social Workers, 1987, Vol. II, pp. 182–197.

Brilliant, Eleanor L. "Community Planning and Community Problem Solving: Past, Present, and Future." *Social Service Review* 60 (December 1986): 568–589.

Gilbert, Neil, and Specht, Harry. "Social Planning and Community Organization." *Encyclopedia of Social Work*, edited by Anne Minahan. 18th ed. Silver Spring, Md.: National Association of Social Workers, 1987, Vol. II, pp. 602–619.

Kramer, Ralph M., and Specht, Harry, eds. *Readings in Community Organization Practice.* 3rd ed. Englewood Cliffs, N.J.: Prentice-Hall, 1983.

Reisch, Michael, and Wenocur, Stanley. "The Future of Community Organization in Social Work: Social Activism and the Politics of Profession Building." *Social Service Review* 60 (March 1986): 70–93.

CORRECTIONS AND CRIMINAL JUSTICE

Ashford, Jose B., Macht, Mary Wirtz, and Mylym, Melissa. "Advocacy by Social Workers in a Public Defender's Office." *Social Work* 32 (May–June 1987): 199–203.

Gottesman, Roberta. *The Child and the Law.* St. Paul, Minn.: West Publishing, 1981.

Longress, John F. "Juvenile Offenders and Delinquency." *Encyclopedia of Social Work*, edited by Anne Minahan. 18th ed. Silver Spring, Md.: National Association of Social Workers, 1987, Vol. II, pp. 21–27.

Netherland, Warren. "Corrections System: Adult." *Encyclopedia of Social Work*, edited by Anne Minahan. 18th ed. Silver Spring, Md.: National Association of Social Workers, 1987, Vol. I, pp. 351–360.

Roberts, Albert R. *Social Work in Juvenile and Criminal Justice Settings*. Springfield, Ill.: Charles C. Thomas, 1983.

FAMILY SERVICES

Erickson, A. Gerald. "Family Services." *Encyclopedia of Social Work*, edited by Anne Minahan. 18th ed. Silver Spring, Md.: National Association of Social Workers, 1987, Vol. I, pp. 589–593.

Jansen, Curtis, and Harris, Oliver. *Family Treatment in Social Work Practice*. Itasca, Ill.: F.E. Peacock, 1980.

Kahn, Alfred J., and Kamerman, Sheila B. *Helping America's Families*. Philadelphia: Temple University Press, 1982.

McGoldrick, Monica, Pierce, J., and Giordano, Joseph, eds. *Ethnicity and Family Therapy*. New York: Guilford Press, 1982.

Munson, Carlton E., ed. *Social Work with Families: Theory and Practice*. New York: Free Press, 1980.

Star, Barbara. "Domestic Violence." *Encyclopedia of Social Work*, edited by Anne Minahan. 18th ed. Silver Spring, Md.: National Association of Social Workers, 1987, Vol. I, pp. 463–476.

GROUP AND YOUTH SERVICES

Feldman, Ronald A. "Youth Service Agencies." *Encyclopedia of Social Work*, edited by Anne Minahan. 18th ed. Silver Spring, Md.: National Association of Social Workers, 1987, Vol. II, pp. 901–907.

Loavenbruck, Grant, and Keys, Paul. "Settlements and Neighborhood Centers." *Encyclopedia of Social Work*, edited by Anne Minahan. 18th ed. Silver Spring, Md.: National Association of Social Workers, 1987, Vol. II, pp. 556–561.

Middleman, Ruth, and Goldberg, Gale. "Social Work Practice with Groups." *Encyclopedia of Social Work*, edited by Anne Minahan. 18th ed. Silver Spring, Md.: National Association of Social Workers, 1987, Vol. II, pp. 714–729.

Reid, Kenneth E. *From Character Building to Social Treatment: The History of Groups in Social Work*. Westport, Conn.: Greenwood Press, 1981.

INCOME MAINTENANCE

Ginsberg, Leon H. *The Practice of Social Work In Public Welfare*. New York: Free Press, 1983.

Teare, Robert J. *Social Work Practice in a Public Welfare Setting: An Empirical Analysis*. New York: Praeger, 1981.

Wyers, Norman L. "Income Maintenance System." *Encyclopedia of Social Work*, edited by Anne Minahan. 18th ed. Silver Spring, Md.: National Association of Social Workers, 1987, Vol. I, pp. 888–898.

Yankey, John. "Public Social Services." *Encyclopedia of Social Work*, edited by Anne Minahan. 18th ed. Silver Spring, Md.: National Association of Social Workers, 1987, Vol. II, pp. 417–426.

MEDICAL AND HEALTH CARE

Kerson, Toba S., ed. *Social Work in Health Settings: Practice in Context.* New York: Longman, 1982.

Leukefeld, Carl G. "Public Health Services." *Encyclopedia of Social Work,* edited by Anne Minahan. 18th ed. Silver Spring, Md.: National Association of Social Workers, 1987, Vol. II, pp. 409–417.

Miller, Rosalind S., and Rehr, Helen, eds. *Social Work Issues in Health Care.* Englewood Cliffs, N.J.: Prentice-Hall, 1983.

Rossen, Salie. "Hospital Social Work." *Encyclopedia of Social Work,* edited by Anne Minahan. 18th ed. Silver Spring, Md.: National Association of Social Workers, 1987, Vol. I, pp. 816–821.

MENTAL HEALTH AND RETARDATION

Biegel, David E., and Naperstek, Arthur J. *Community Support Systems and Mental Health: Practice, Policy, and Research.* New York: Springer, 1982.

Callicutt, James W. "Mental Health Services." *Encyclopedia of Social Work,* edited by Anne Minahan. 18th ed. Silver Spring, Md.: National Association of Social Workers, 1987, Vol. II, pp. 125–135.

Callicutt, James W., and Lecca, P. J., eds. *Social Work and Mental Health.* New York: Free Press, 1983.

Dickerson, Martha Ufford. *Social Work Practice with the Mentally Retarded.* New York: Basic Books, 1981.

McDonald–Wikler, Lynn. "Disabilities: Developmental." *Encyclopedia of Social Work,* edited by Anne Minahan. 18th ed. Silver Spring, Md.: National Association of Social Workers, 1987, Vol. I, pp. 422–434.

SCHOOLS

Constable, Robert T., and Flynn, John P. *School Social Work: Practice and Research Perspectives.* Homewood, Ill.: Dorsey Press, 1982.

Costin, Lela B. "School Social Work." *Encyclopedia of Social Work,* edited by Anne Minahan. 18th ed. Silver Spring, Md.: National Association of Social Workers, 1987, Vol. II, pp. 538–545.

Hancock, Betsy Ledbetter. *School Social Work.* Englewood Cliffs, N.J.: Prentice-Hall, 1982.

Konle, Carolyn. *Social Work Day-to-Day.* New York: Longman, 1982.

McNeely, R. L., and Badami, Mary Kenny. "Interracial Communication in School Social Work." *Social Work* 29 (January–February 1984): 22–27.

Meares, Paul A., Washington, Robert O., and Welsh, Betty L. *Social Work Services in Schools.* Englewood Cliffs, N.J.: Prentice-Hall, 1985.

Radin, Norma, and Welsh, Betty L. "Social Work, Psychology, and Counseling in the Schools." *Social Work* (January–February 1984): 28–34.

ENDNOTES

1. Anne Minahan, ed., *Encyclopedia of Social Work,* 18th ed. (Silver Spring, Md.: National Association of Social Workers, 1987).
2. Ibid., pp. xi–xiii.
3. Bradford W. Sheafor, Charles R. Horejsi, and Gloria A. Horejsi, *Techniques and Guidelines for Social Work Practice* (Boston: Allyn and Bacon, 1988), pp. 199–204.

4. Robert N. Butler and Myrna I. Lewis, *Aging and Mental Health*, 3rd ed. (St. Louis: C.V. Mosby, 1982), pp. 5–17.
5. Lowell E. Jenkins and Alicia S. Cook, "The Rural Hospice: Integrating Helping Systems," *Social Work* 26 (September 1981): 414–416.
6. Philip Poppel, "Social Work Practice in Business and Industry: 1875–1930," *Social Service Review* 55 (June 1981): 257–269.
7. Lou Ann B. Jorgensen, "Social Services in Business and Industry," in Neil Gilbert and Harry Specht, eds., *Handbook for Social Services* (Englewood Cliffs, N.J.: Prentice-Hall, 1981), p. 337.
8. Thomas J. Peters and Robert H. Waterman, Jr., *In Search of Excellence: Lessons from America's Best-Run Companies* (New York: Harper and Row, 1983).
9. Barbara W. Shank and Beth K. Jorve, "Industrial Social Work: A New Arena for the B.S.W.," (Paper presented at the National Symposium of Social Workers, Washington, D.C., 1983), p. 14.
10. National Association of Social Workers, "Membership Survey Shows Practice Shifts," *NASW News* 28 (November 1983): 6–7.
11. National Commission of Family Life Education, "Family Life Programs, Principles, Plans, and Procedures," *Family Coordinator* 17 (July 1968): 211.
12. "NASW Membership Survey," pp. 6–7.
13. Charles Zastrow, *Introduction to Social Welfare Institutions: Social Problems, Services, and Current Issues*, rev. ed. (Homewood, Ill.: Dorsey Press, 1982), p. 331.
14. "NASW Membership Survey," pp. 6–7.
15. Milton G. Thackeray, Rex A. Skidmore, and O. William Farley, *Introduction to Mental Health: Field and Practice* (Englewood Cliffs, N.J.: Prentice-Hall, 1981): 257–269.
16. John B. Turner, ed., *Encyclopedia of Social Work*, 17th issue (Washington, D.C.: National Association of Social Workers, 1977), p. 871.
17. *Introduction to Mental Health*, p. 8.
18. Lela B. Costin, "Social Work in the Schools," in Donald Brieland, Lela B. Costin, and Charles R. Atherton, eds., *Contemporary Social Work and Social Welfare*, 2nd ed., (New York: McGraw-Hill, 1980), p. 247.

CHAPTER 6

Settings for Social Work Practice

Like nursing, teaching, and the clergy, social work practice emerged primarily within organizations and today as in the past most social workers are employed in some form of human service agency. Accreditation standards require that all students complete a substantial learning experience in a social agency, and the profession does not consider social workers ready for independent practice until they have completed a period of supervised work in an agency. Social work is clearly an agency-based profession, as opposed to medicine and law, which are essentially private practice or entrepreneurial professions.

In the last decade, however, social workers began making a shift in this pattern and today an increasing number are employed in settings other than the traditional governmental and nonprofit voluntary social agencies. Many social workers are employed by for-profit organizations such as nursing homes, proprietary hospitals, or even large corporations. They can also be found conducting their own private practices or working in the clinical offices of other professionals.[1] Perhaps more than at any other time in history, social workers must make a choice regarding the type of setting in which to practice.

This chapter identifies the four primary types of organizations where social work practice is conducted and examines special issues the social worker should consider when selecting either agency-based or private practice settings as their place of employment.

CHARACTERISTICS OF PRACTICE SETTINGS

When social programs are created to meet the needs of people, a decision must be made about how the program will be delivered to those in need. Whether the program is a direct benefit such as food stamps or a third-party payment such as Medicare, it must be provided through the auspices of some formal organization. These organizations, or associations, establish the necessary policies and supply the administrative structure to make the program available to recipients. When the organizations employ social workers to provide services or when the professionals have created their own organizations, i.e., private practice, they are described as a practice *setting*.

The type of practice setting in which a social worker is employed partially determines who will be clients and the degree of flexibility possible in the manner in which clients are served. Thus, it is useful to examine the several types of organizations that serve as the settings for social work. Peter Blau and Richard Scott identify four unique types of organizations: mutual benefit, commonweal, service, and business.[2] Social workers can be found in all these forms of organizations, although the commonweal and service agencies are the predominant settings for social workers.

is this misspelled →

Mutual Benefit Organizations

Mutual benefit organizations are created when a group wishes to provide services for its own membership. Churches, labor unions, and civic clubs are examples of this type of organization. Although civic clubs and fraternal organizations such as Rotary, Soroptimist, Kiwanis, and various Masonic organizations support important human services programs ranging from research to sponsorhsip of "Little League" baseball teams, they rarely employ staff and are not considered a setting for social work practice.

Some religious groups have created programs staffed by social workers that are limited to the members of that denomination or faith. However, church sponsored human service agencies that restrict their services to members are only a small part of the social programs supported by religious groups. Most human service programs that are sponsored by religious organizations, e.g., hospitals, children's institutions, homes for the aged, and family counseling agencies serve the whole community and are considered nonprofit voluntary agencies—a different type of organization. Yet, there are some substantial human services provided by denominational groups exclusively for their members. The Jewish welfare system provides an illustration. Reid and Stimpson describe the rationale for limiting these services to members of the faith.

> The Jewish welfare system, like its Catholic counterpart, expanded dramatically in response to mass migration from Europe. Relief societies were created to provide destitute immigrants with financial assistance; settlements were formed to assist them in the task of adjusting to American life.
>
> For the most part Jewish social services developed apart from the synagogue. They were more a response of Jewish communities to the special needs of their members than the work of Jewish religious institutions or rabbis. . . . This is not to say that Jewish welfare activities were completely secular in origin, since their initiators were often religious people acting on religious convictions who often viewed their work, particularly in settlements, as a way of drawing Jews closer to their faith. Another element in this emerging pattern was the cohesive character of Jewish communities, a cohesiveness engendered not only by common religious beliefs but by common ethnic roots and by the anti-Semitic posture of the dominant Protestant culture. The Jews' desire to take care of their own reflected a merging of religious motives and community mindedness.[3]

Also, at the community level, some large churches or synagogues provide "in-house" social services primarily for their own members. These organizations often employ social workers to provide counseling, referral, and youth-oriented services.

Labor unions represent another mutual aid setting where social workers might be found. Although relatively few social workers are employed by labor unions, they have expanded their social services in recent years. Unions historically have been successful in organizing workers who are underpaid and undervalued by management. Women are a large segment of the work force who fit that description making it attractive for labor unions to provide human services that meet the needs of female employees. Thus, it is likely that social work jobs in this setting will increase due to the anticipated growth in the number of employed women.

George Martin indicates that human services offered by labor unions "are characterized by direct service, such as short-term counseling for ills traced to the workplace, and by the employment of full-time social workers on union staffs."[4] Like social workers employed by business and industry, the labor union setting presents an exceptional opportunity to intervene with people at the place they work, and, therefore, improve the likelihood of resolving problems before they reach a crisis. Social workers in these settings typically help union members with such work-related problems as finding child care, dealing with family problems related to work schedules, or addressing stress created by changed family roles when both spouses are employed.

Commonweal Organizations (Public or Governmental Agencies)

Michael Sosin accurately summarizes the emergence of the commonweal or public human service organizations during the past half century and identifies the central role they have played in protecting the poorest members of society:

> Since the New Deal reforms of the 1930s, public bureaucracies have greatly expanded their efforts to ameliorate individual economic distress. Government programs, while perhaps inadequate, now insure many of us against adversity arising from unemployment, illness, or old age. They also provide a financial cushion for many of the most needy families whose members cannot find work. Some have claimed that alternate strategies might have been more effective, but it is clear that the reductions in poverty that have occurred over the last two decades are largely a result of public transfer programs. Many even believe that the gap in the marketplace between the rich and poor is widening and that only governmental programs stand in the way of increasing inequality.[5]

Commonweal organizations are established and funded by the general public with the intent to perform services for the benefit of all people. The mandate is to provide the necessary services to preserve and protect the well-being of all people in the community. These agencies reflect city, county, state, and federal governmental efforts to respond to human needs and are created by law and limited by the provisions established in that law.

Government sponsored human service agencies are the principal type of organization that employs social workers. The 1982 NASW Membership Study found that 45.2 percent of all respondents were employed in this type of social agency[6] and the 1987 NASW Salary Study reported average salaries in public agencies (including military, federal, state, and local organizations) ranging from $29,300 to $32,500.[7]

Most social programs that commonweal agencies offer are created by law-makers in Washington, D.C. or the state capital. These policy makers are usually geographically distant from the clients and service providers alike and, too often, are unfamiliar with the issues that arise when these laws are implemented by local agencies. Social workers often find their practice in government agencies frustrating. There is inherent inflexibility in these settings because laws are difficult to change, budgeting and auditing systems are highly structured, cumbersome civil service or personnel systems are mandated, and coordination among the different governmental levels is difficult. Further, these organizations are subject to political manipulation, and, as we saw when examining the first term of the Reagan administration in Chapter 4, financial support and program development can be significantly influenced by a changing political climate. Except through substantial political action efforts, those who must carry out these programs have limited opportunity to influence their structure and funding.

Although sometimes client fees are required, public agencies are financed almost completely by taxes, and the regular flow of tax money offers some stability to the programs. Legislative bodies are authorized to levy taxes so human needs can be met, and, in times of economic difficulty, when voluntary contributions may be reduced, the legislators have the power to tax and therefore maintain the services. Also, the larger amounts of money potentially available to public agencies allows for experimentation with various methods of service provision. Research and demonstration grants sponsored by government agencies have, in recent years, been the most significant factor in developing new and creative approaches to meeting human needs.

It should be recognized that the commonweal agencies provide services that meet the most basic human needs such as food, clothing, and shelter. It simply is not possible to adequately respond to the fundamental needs of the poor, homeless, retarded, aged, and others through voluntary and for-profit human services. Unless income is redistributed under government auspices and unless tax monies are used to create income maintenance programs, mental hospitals, prisons, and other vital human services, we cannot expect to improve the condition of the most vulnerable members of our society. Public agencies and the social workers they employ are absolutely essential to the success of the social welfare institution.

Service Organizations (Private or Voluntary Agencies)

Private or voluntary social agencies are "nongovernmental, nonprofit organizations formed independently of state mandate"[8] and employ approximately 42 percent of the social workers.[9] Of all employment settings, the private nonprofit sector had the lowest average salary level, i.e., $26,100, reported in the 1987 NASW Salary Study.[10] Private agencies traditionally have depended on voluntary individual and corporate contributions to support their operation. Their sources of funds included gifts and bequests, door-to-door solicitations, membership dues, fees for service, and participation in federated campaigns, such as United Way.

More recently, however, private agencies have begun receiving a substantial share of their funding from governmental allocations. Private agencies receive government funds through contracts to provide specific services, to conduct research and demonstration projects, or to support their operation through revenue sharing allocations. Government agencies have increasingly found this a desirable arrangement because it has allowed them to bypass much of the rigidity of the large bureaucratic organizations in favor of the more flexible private agency structures. It is estimated that federal support now constitutes over 50 percent of the total expenditures in many voluntary human service organizations.[11] Thus, there is an evolving partnership between governmental and voluntary agencies that involves an intermingling of public and private resources making it difficult to clearly distinguish one from the other. Nevertheless, the nonprofit agencies are classified as private or voluntary because they operate with policies established by a governing board made up of volunteers, as opposed to public agencies, which have elected officials who are responsible for making the basic policy decisions.

Private agencies have, in most instances, the advantage of being small and concerned with the provision of services locally. Thus, the board members have the opportunity to become directly exposed to the agency and its method of operation. In other words there is an intimate relationship between governance and service provision that is not usually possible in public agencies.

The boards of voluntary agencies theoretically have considerable flexibility in developing policies to guide the operation of the agency. Yet, that flexibility is increasingly constrained by external forces. For example meeting the standards established by a national organization such as the Child Welfare League of America or the Family Service Association of America may impose some limitations on agency functioning. Likewise, membership in a local United Way may also require the sacrifice of some autonomy. While there are evident benefits to these affiliations, they also reduce agency discretion regarding its program and method of operation. In addition, the relatively heavy dependence on voluntary contributions makes it quite possible that resources could be immediately impacted by changing economic conditions, and, in that event, boards would have little ability to avoid reducing services. Even when there are stable economic conditions, unless a private agency is quite large there is rarely enough new money available in any one year to allow for significant experimentation or change in services. Thus, the voluntary sector, like the public sector, experiences constraints in program innovation.

With the administrative complexity created by the multiple funding sources, volunteer boards experience the difficult task of attempting to balance local needs related to their own mission with the expectations of governmental agencies that contract for services. The frequent absence of both clients and clinical staff from the policy-making role exacerbates these problems.[12] Agency boards, historically composed mostly of people who are influential in the community, have demonstrated that they can be effective in financial planning, public relations, and fund raising, but too often have been unable to become aware of and responsive to client needs.

What is the importance of the voluntary sector in the provision of human services today? Sosin, in summarizing findings from his extensive study of material assistance programs sponsored by nonprofit human services organizations, concludes:

> Though the role of private agencies is limited, it is nevertheless significant. As the evidence suggests, private agencies exist in every community and save many from starvation and homelessness. Often they provide the only source of shelter to hundreds of thousands of people—some the victims of disaster, others facing a sudden loss of income or a change in family circumstances, still other chronically homeless for a number of reasons. Private food programs provide for many who would otherwise go hungry. General programs often cover utility payments, rent, and needs for furniture; side programs cover important health-related expenses; and single-mission agencies provide what they are organized to distribute, whether shoes or shelter. Although public programs may in theory meet the same needs, overlap is only theoretical owing to limited budgets; the private agencies indeed fill needs.[13]

Business Organizations (Entrepreneurial Social Work)

The major business setting where social workers are found is private or proprietary practice. As the most rapidly growing dimension of social work, this setting is characterized by its entrepreneurial nature and by its nonagency structure. Practice in this setting involves the use of a "process in which the values, knowledge, and skills of social work, acquired through sufficient education and experience, are used to deliver services autonomously to clients in exchange for mutually agreed payment."[14]

The term *private practice* is usually used to indicate a practice situation where a direct contract for the provision of clinical service is made between the worker and the clients. *Proprietary practice*, a term sometimes used interchangeably with private practice, refers to nonclinical activities such as consulting, conducting workshops or training programs, or contracting to perform research or other professional services for a fee.[15] Proprietary practice most frequently involves a contract between the social worker and an organization, rather than with individual clients.

Robert Barker has identified ten factors that characterize the private or proprietary practice of social work. He indicates that the practitioner in this setting:

1. has the client (rather than an agency or organization) as the primary obligation;

2. determines who the client will be;

3. determines the techniques to be used;

4. determines practice professionally rather than bureaucratically;

5. receives a fee for service directly from or on behalf of the client;

6. has sufficient education as a social worker;

7. is sufficiently experienced;

8. adheres to social work values and standards;

9. is licensed or certified to engage in private practice if the jurisdiction has such regulations; and

10. is professionally responsible.[16]

The 1987 NASW study of social work salaries indicates that with a $31,100 average salary, self-employed private practitioners were among the highest paid social workers. These data also indicate that the highest one-fourth earned more than $45,000 that year making it the setting with the greatest potential for earning a high income.[17] Barker, writing in the *Encyclopedia of Social Work,* indicates that:

> Private practitioners have always been among the most highly paid of the clinical social work professionals. When they have had the same number of years of training and experience, social workers in private practice have annual incomes and hourly fees about as high as those of other professionals, such as psychologists, lawyers, and accountants. Proprietary social workers have even greater income potential because they are not limited to fees for direct services but can profit from the growth of their organizations. In the early 1980s, the fees charged by private social work practitioners in urban areas ranged from $35 to $70 per hour. Hourly rates for group therapy ranged from $10 to $50 per individual.[18]

Certainly social workers have been rapidly moving into this mode of practice. As reported earlier, the most recent NASW membership study revealed that social workers who consider private practice to be their primary setting increased from 3 percent in 1972 to 12 percent in 1982.[19] Although there are varying estimates of the number of social workers engaged in private practice, the best educated guess is that there are between 10,000 and 30,000 part-time private practitioners and from 4,000 to 10,000 social workers in full-time private practice.[20] In recent years private and proprietary practice has unquestionably become a significant setting for social workers.

Another emerging entrepreneurial setting for social work is in *for-profit organizations*. During the past decade there has been a quiet but substantial transformation in the funding of human service programs. During the past half century a pattern emerged in which legislative bodies allocated funds to the public agencies to provide the services for which they were responsible. Therefore, a relatively large public sector developed. That pattern began to shift through purchase of service agreements and, as indicated previously, voluntary agencies increasingly contracted to provide many of the services the public agencies were obligated to offer. A second, and perhaps even more dramatic, shift known as *privatization* is now occurring. Governmental agencies have begun to invest a substantial amount of their funds in the purchase of service from private organizations that are owned and operated as any other business enterprise.

Because the commodity the for-profit human service organizations deliver is social services, they employ social workers. Data are not available that indicate the number of social workers involved in this practice setting, but the NASW Salary Study does indicate that those who reported in 1987 had an average salary of $29,000 or $1,200 per year more than the average social worker.[21]

Several fields of practice have rapidly increased their reliance on these proprietary organizations to provide human services. For example a national study of child welfare services found that proprietary firms were used as vendors for services by public welfare agencies to a greater degree than either nonprofit or other governmental agencies. The study revealed that government agencies purchased services from for-profit organizations that amounted to 51 percent of all residential treatment, 49 percent of institutional care, and 58 percent of the services provided by group homes. To a lesser but still substantial degree public agencies relied heavily on proprietary organizations to deliver day care and day treatment services.[22]

Rapid expansion of for-profit nursing homes,[23] correctional facilities, and health care organizations is also occurring. Bradford Gray describes this trend in health care:

> With little initial public notice, a vigorous and varied for-profit sector has developed in the predominantly not-for-profit world of medical care. Health services are now being provided by thousands of for-profit organizations that range from large investor-owned hospital and nursing home chains, whose stock has rapidly appreciated on the New York Stock Exchange, to various types of independent medical facilities—such as ambulatory surgery centers, cardiopulmonary testing centers, etc.—owned by local investors who often are also physicians. Sometimes the physician-owners generate revenues for the facilities by referring patients for service.
>
> . . . The exact dimensions of the for-profit sector of providers of health ser-

vices are not known. Rough estimates have put the gross revenues of investor-owned health care industry as high as $40 billion. . . . In 1982 about 10 percent of U.S. hospitals were owned by the for-profit hospital chains, and another 4 percent were managed by those firms. Another 5 percent of U.S. hospitals were independently owned proprietary hospitals.[24]

Why is the privatization of human services occurring at this time? Mimi Abramovitz identifies the Reagan administration's rationale for fostering this dramatic shift in the pattern of funding human services:

> Privatization, or placing public tasks in private hands, is one way the Reagan administration is restructuring the welfare state. Since 1981 it has been part of a broad strategy to cope with the economic crisis, one that includes reduced taxes, domestic program cuts, and the transfer of social welfare responsibility from the federal government to that of the states. The administration's overall plan for promoting economic growth is based on directing larger amounts of capital into the private market and weakening the political power of groups whose social and economic demands have, since the 1930s, politicized the process of income distribution carried out through both government tax and spending programs and the process of trade union collective bargaining.
>
> Privatization channels public dollars into private hands, strengthens the two-class welfare state, and reproduces inequalities that the free market inevitably creates. In trying to serve the needs of both private providers and the poor, the welfare state has failed to modify the market in behalf of social justice, a goal reformers in earlier times had hoped government intervention in the economy would achieve.[25]

Social work, as well as medicine and other professions, is uneasy about the growing amount of for-profit practice. The trend toward the privatization of human services threatens to replace the service orientation of professions with the profit motive. Privatization risks making the bottom line the amount of return to the shareholder rather than the quality of service to the client. When the shareholder is also the professional (as identified by Gray in the previous quotation), serious ethical issues arise that can erode public trust in the professions. The ambivalence of many social workers regarding the growing privatization of human services is captured by Hasenfeld:

> The implications of the trend toward commercialization-privatization for the delivery of human services and quality of care are unclear at the present time. . . .the trend may increase consumer choice and improve efficiency. There is, however, concern that the commercialization of human services will inevitably substitute the profit motive for quality care and concern for the client's welfare. Organizations may select treatment technologies and establish service modalities that enhance their profitability but are not necessarily the most appropriate for or most responsive to the service needs of the population. Moreover, professional autonomy over practice may be seriously eroded as professional decisions become subject to corporate control.

Finally, although the privatization of services increases consumer choice, the major beneficiaries of greater choice would not be the traditional clientele of the welfare state but consumers from middle and working classes to whom social welfare entitlements have been extended in recent years.[26]

ISSUES AFFECTING AGENCY-BASED PRACTICE

More than 85 percent of all experienced social workers and virtually every new social worker is employed in a mutual benefit, public, voluntary, or for-profit human service agency. Thus, when considering possible employment settings, most social workers must examine an agency to determine its relative compatibility with his or her personal and professional interests. The social worker should be knowledgeable about several factors that influence the manner in which a social worker is able to operate within the context of a social agency.

Accommodating Horizontal and Vertical Influences

Although some human service organizations are formed around a single field of practice and offer programs to meet a specific client need, the social workers employed in these agencies recognize they cannot operate in isolation from other agencies. Client needs are not necessarily experienced in the same way as social agencies identify their missions. As a member of the profession with primary responsibility for connecting individual clients, as well as social agencies, with the environment that affects them, social workers must have agency support for their interaction with human service organizations.

At the local level social workers often give leadership to efforts to coordinate the services provided to clients by the full array of social agencies in that community. This coordination requires that interagency networks, or *horizontal affiliations*, are developed among the agencies. The form of these horizontal networks may range from informal discussions among agency representatives regarding human service programs to the formal creation of councils of social agencies or human resources planning organizations that study the local service network, encourage efforts to fill gaps in the services, and facilitate cooperation among the agencies. The ability of a social worker to effectively perform his or her professional tasks is enhanced when there is a strong horizontal interagency network in a community and the social worker's employing agency supports his or her participation in these activities.

Social agencies and social workers are also influenced by *vertical affiliations*, that is, those organizations external to the community that have the authority to at least partially shape the services or operating procedures of a local agency. Voluntary agencies, for example, might affiliate as a chapter or member of a national organization, which can immediately give the agency name recognition, provide the community with some assurance that at least minimum standards acceptable in that practice field are met, make staff development opportunities available through national meetings, and sometimes help secure financial resources. At the same time these agencies give up some local autonomy as they are committed to operate within the guidelines of the national organization. Vertical affiliation with the American Red Cross, Boy or Girl Scouts of America, the YWCA or YMCA, the American Heart Association, the Salvation Army, or the Family Service Association of America are all examples of such affiliations typical of private agencies. Further, many local voluntary agencies must meet state licensing requirements or other state standards if they are vendors of services to public agencies. This also limits their discretion.

Public agencies typically have more direct and formal vertical relationships. A local governmental agency may be implementing programs that have been created and partially funded at the federal level, further defined and partially funded at the state level, and finally modified and also funded by a county commission. Thus, a county social services department, for example, is constrained by requirements imposed by federal, state, and county governments. Although these vertical affiliations add considerably to the complexity of tailoring service programs to local needs, they have the advantage of fostering greater equity in the benefits and services provided to people throughout a region and the nation. Attaining such equity is especially important if the quality of life for all members of the society is to be protected.

Balancing Efficiency and Effectiveness

A fundamental goal of all human service agencies, whether they are public or private, is to use the scarce resources that are available to them to provide the most and the best service possible. To achieve this goal agencies must operate efficiently and effectively. An agency that leans too far in favoring one over the other ultimately creates problems for the social worker employed in that agency.

Efficiency represents the efforts of the agency to achieve the maximum output of services with a minimum input of resources.[27] This goal of efficiency places the emphasis on the quantity of services provided and often attracts most of the attention of lawmakers, governing boards, and the local media. Yet, quantity must be related to quality if an agency is to find a balance that represents the maximum level of service. The qualitative aspects of service are represented in an agency's *effectiveness*, or the degree to which the agency achieves its goals.[28]

The social agency serves as the link between the recipient of service and the community. Martin Wolins has depicted the expectations of client, community, and agency in the following manner:

Client: relieve my distress, impose no conditions which lower my status, assure me help as long as it is needed.

Community: be an expression of our humanitarianism, improve society by returning recipients to productive endeavors, protect us and our institutions against collective and individual unrest.

Agency: serve as a buffer between recipient and community, provide the substance and service to meet needs.[29]

The governance of social agencies has been dominated, in both the public and voluntary sector, by persons who represent the community viewpoint. The persons selected to represent this viewpoint have tended to be the "successful" people who have given leadership to thriving business and industrial enterprises. The secret to that success has been a strong bias toward efficiency; and, although some degree of effectiveness in producing goods was still necessary, low cost-per-unit production was clearly the most valued goal. That orientation is also readily evident in the for-profit human service organizations. Thus, a social worker considering agency employment should carefully examine the agency's effectiveness orientation lest the quality of his or her work be seriously compromised in favor of overemphasis on the community goal of efficiency.

Accommodating the Professional Model

How can efficiency be attained in human service organizations? The successful managers from business and industry transferred the proven tools in their work to the human services. The primary tool was bureaucratic structure. And why not? Bureaucracy had worked to build automobiles and appliances at a fraction of the cost of handmade products. Financial institutions were able to manage the flow of money efficiently with these same principles. Max Weber brought them together into a clear statement of bureaucratic theory. His "ideal-type" description of the characteristics of a bureaucratic organization was intended to reflect a pure, but extreme, statement of the characteristics of a bureaucracy:

1. Division of labor—each person in the organization has a clearly defined and specialized assignment in the organization.

2. Hierarchy—specific lines of authority exist in which every person in the administrative structure is not only responsible for his or her own assignments but is also responsible for the performance of subordinates.

3. Consistent System of Rules—every task in the organization is governed by an explicit set of rules which specify the standards of performance and the relationships among tasks.

4. Spirit of Impersonality—work is to be performed without favoritism or prejudice entering official decisions.

5. Employment Constitutes a Career—persons are employed only on the basis of technical qualifications required by the organization, with rewards provided to encourage loyalty and offer opportunity for a career in that organization.[30]

With some modifications, when applied to the assembly line that produces automobiles in Detroit or toasters in New Jersey, bureaucratic principles led to a high degree of organizational efficiency. This model yielded good results when the product was made from standardized parts. In fact the greater the standardization, the more effective the bureaucratic organization becomes. A person could quickly be trained to perform a very specific function, for example installing a fuel pump as the automobile passes on the assembly line. With a line foreperson to check for quality control and enforce the rules established for efficiency (the worker cannot be on the telephone when the engine is there for a fuel pump), the trainee usually produced a good quality product. Under this system there could be no allowance for the worker's personal problems, nor could he or she be successfully assigned more responsible work simply because of friendship with the boss. Bureaucratic theory assumes that the rewards of seniority, salary increments, and promotion are sufficient to keep the successful employee satisfied with the organization.

As an ideal-type, Weber's characteristics of a bureaucracy draw an extreme picture. These requirements are still present in successful businesses today, but in a considerably modified form. The people-oriented philosophy reflected by Thomas Peters and Robert Waterman in their best selling book, *In Search of Excellence: Lessons from America's Best-Run Companies,*[31] reflect this emerging orientation. Nevertheless, important remnants of the bureaucratic approach are evident in virtually all organizations.

When the leaders of industry attempted to apply these principles to the human service agencies with which they had contact, the social workers and other professionals responsible for providing services found that extensive bureaucratization created problems. The use of bureaucratic principles had the advantages of improving equity for clients and workers, facilitating more efficient operation, and enhancing public support of the agencies. At the same time, for at least two reasons, they were in conflict with the professional model of service provision.

First, in the provision of social services the parts (people) are constantly changing, and the product (human well-being) differs to some degree in each situation. It is simply not realistic to provide narrow technical training, to create highly specialized assignments, or to establish a strict system of rules for a staff that is helping clients or client groups deal with complex personal troubles or public issues. Because social work views special human qualities such as race, ethnicity, gender, and cultural background not only as a reality but also as a desirable feature in human behavior (see Part Four of this book), effective organizations must provide adequate flexibility and autonomy for staff members to be responsive to these individual and cultural differences.[32]

Second, in Chapter 2, we examined the nature of professions and their characteristic methods of accomplishing their work. When the professional model is compared to the bureaucratic model, four inherent areas of conflict emerge. These conflicts have been identified by Richard Scott as: (1) the professional's resistance to bureaucratic rules, (2) the professional's rejection of bureaucratic standards, (3) the professional's resistance to bureaucratic supervision, and (4) the professional's conditional loyalty to the bureaucratic organization.[33] These conflicts are present in varying degrees in any organization where the professional social worker is employed.

Bureaucratic rules present a constant dilemma for professionals. When a division of labor exists, each person provides only a part of the work for the agency. Procedures must then be set up that facilitate interaction among the workers to achieve the goals of the total agency. With bureaucratic rules meetings must be held on time; workers must provide services within the established limits for their discipline; and paperwork must be completed for accountability purposes.

Bureaucratic standards also present difficulties for the professional. Often, the ideals acquired through professional education exceed the limits imposed on professional practice by agency policies and procedures. Agencies operate in the real world and are limited by laws, eligibility requirements, funds, available staff time, and the need to leave a trail of paperwork for accountability purposes. Workers employed in agencies that operate from a residual conception of social welfare are particularly aware of these problems, but such problems can also exist in developmentally oriented programs.

In bureaucratic systems, authority is assigned to a position. Conversely, professional authority is generated from competence as judged by one's peers. It is no wonder that professionals resist *bureaucratic supervision,* which is based on authority derived from a person's place in the organization. A professional is considered competent to perform his or her job without the requirement of someone always reviewing that performance. Because all practice cannot be supervised by direct observation, considerable paperwork is often generated so that supervisors can be aware of the activities of their staff.

Finally, professionals display a *conditional loyalty,* in contrast to a commitment to their organizations. Professionals are prepared with generic competencies that are transferable from one organization to another. A social worker, for example, can move from a welfare department to a juvenile court without additional educational preparation. The basic general skills developed through professional education are applicable with the addition of the specific knowledge required in that particular setting. This additional knowledge can be obtained through reviewing the literature on the subject, through the supervisory process, and through continuing education courses and workshops. People wedded to a bureaucratic organization, however, do not have the same degree of flexibility and can experience job mobility only by moving up in the organization. Support of the organization may be given precedence over personal judgment; for social workers this priority would compromise services to clients.

Succeeding as a Social Worker in an Agency Structure

In many instances it is not sufficient for the social worker merely to be a passive employee who unquestioningly accepts and carries out the rules and regulations of the agency. The organization pressures one to conform. Staff members must perform certain tasks, provide an accounting of the work to a supervisor, complete the appropriate reporting forms, be on the job at the required time, and carry out the programs of the agency as designed by the policy makers and implemented by the administration. Promotions, salary increases, and even continued employment in the agency are often linked to one's conformity to the agency's rules and regulations. The successful agency-based social worker must be smart about organizational issues.

Clearly an employee is obligated to work within the legitimate requirements of his or her employer and a social worker cannot ethically ignore the rules and regulations of the agency. Although it may be personally safe to rigidly conform to agency requirements, most rules and regulations provide some room for flexible interpretation if the workers are creative in their approach. Some regulations, however, may not lend themselves to this flexibility and may, at times, seriously impede the work of the social worker. In this case the social worker should attempt to change these rules. Change, especially in large public agencies, takes considerable time and effort. The social worker who has attempted to bring about such change can identify with the adage, "The change agent must have the time sense of a geologist." With skill, patience, and perseverance, such change can be accomplished, and the attempt should be viewed as a professional responsibility of the social worker. There are times, however, when the social worker fails in an attempt to modify the agency's rules and either must learn to live with the existing regulations or make the decision to seek employment elsewhere.[34]

In addition to attempting to encourage the agency to adapt to his or her practice needs, the social worker must also attempt to adapt his or her practice to the agency. Robert Pruger notes that in addition to their service function, social workers are also bureaucrats—distasteful as this term might be for many social workers—because one of their roles is to implement the policies and procedures of an agency.[35] Maintaining a reasonable balance between the goals of the service provider and those of the bureaucrat is a constant challenge for the social worker. Pruger suggests four tactics that can help the social worker be responsible to the agency and at the same time maximize the ability to provide services to clients.[36]

First, the worker must understand legitimate authority and organizational enforcement. Rules and regulations must be stated in general terms because they must cover an infinite variety of human situations. An important part of professional autonomy is concerned with the interpretation and application of agency regulations. Although clear limits to this discretion may be present, there is usually considerable latitude one can exercise before the agency will enforce disciplinary action. Within the guideline of responsible behavior, the social worker should seek to discover these discretionary limits in order to be of maximum service to the agency's clients.

Second, organizations present many demands that divert worker energy from the primary goal of serving clients. Demands for time in staff meetings, paperwork, evaluation processes, and many more activities are often frustrating for the service-oriented social worker. Moreover, organizations do a poor job of offering the person emotional support or recognition for accomplishment that, if expected by the worker, will surely drain energy from the service tasks. The social worker who builds supportive relationships with other employees can minimize the impact of this potential energy drain.

Third, an employee should seek to develop competencies needed by the organization. Rather than approaching the agency with a minimum personal investment, the social worker should make a special effort to help enhance the functioning of the agency. In addition to continuing professional development related to practice techniques, the social worker should develop needed organizational skills such as grant writing, computer programming, and budget planning. Such positive contributions help create a favorable climate for social work practice.

Finally, the social worker should keep in mind the goals of the agency and not yield unnecessarily to requirements established for administrative convenience. The use of professional judgment is always required, and regulations should constantly be reviewed to determine if they are viable for enhancing the work of the staff and the welfare of clients. Although challenging unproductive regulations may not help the social worker win popularity contests, this action is a valuable contribution to the organization's effectiveness.

In addition to the bureaucrat role required of a direct service provider, agency-based social workers also may assume administrative responsibilities in a human service agency. One important administrative role is that of supervising other social workers and agency staff members. Because they originally adhered to an apprenticeship approach to skill development,[37] social agencies have continued to depend heavily on supervision for monitoring and evaluating the work of practitioners and for helping them upgrade their competence. Increasingly, human service agencies have been emphasizing the educational aspects of supervision, but most have not yet abandoned the supervisory approach in favor of the consultation model that is a more appropriate form of support for professional practice. Consultation is based on seeking advice from the most competent person available and not necessarily from one's immediate supervisor. The effective social work supervisor, however, is able to combine both the supervisor and consultant roles in helping the staff perform the services of the agency. The quality of supervision is one of the most important factors for the new social worker to look for when seeking a social work job.

Other social workers may assume executive or top administrative roles in a human service agency. Some fields of practice have developed career patterns for people in management positions where they receive extensive preparation for these roles. Master's degree programs in education and hospital administration, for example, specifically prepare graduates to administer schools and hospitals. Social agencies have not developed a parallel career line. Some human service organizations have enticed successful clinical social workers to move into administrative positions requiring them to make a transition from the role of service provider to administrator without additional educational preparation.[38] Too often a competent practitioner is converted to a marginal administrator. Other agencies have erred in the direction of seeking persons possessing a master's degree in business administration or in public administration, only to find that they were not appropriately sensitive to the unique organizational requirements for providing human services. This approach, too, has yielded marginal results and argues for social work developing administration specializations in MSW programs that provide a balanced understanding of organizational and professional needs.

The extent to which an agency supports the social worker in providing professional quality services and provides opportunity for career mobility is an important consideration when the new social worker is selecting a setting for employment.

Determining the Status of Social Work

One final factor to consider when selecting a place of employment is the centrality of social work to the mission of that particular setting. The status of social work in an agency influences the manner in which a social worker spends much of his or her time and affects the opportunity of clients to have the full benefit of the perspective that social work brings to the helping situation. When the policies and procedures of the organization are designed to maximize social work services, social workers can most effectively serve their clientele. However, in a practice setting where another discipline is dominant, social workers often spend considerable effort educating members of this discipline about the contributions social work can make to the agency's clientele.

In some practice settings social work is the *primary discipline*. The primary services provided call for social work expertise, most key jobs require social work training, and social workers hold the major administrative jobs. In practice fields (see Chapter 5) such as child welfare, family services, and income maintenance social workers have traditionally been the primary discipline. In these settings other disciplines may be involved to provide specialized expertise or consultation, but the services are organized to maximize the contributions of the social worker.

In other practice settings the social worker is an *equal partner* along with members of one or more other disciplines. The services are organized to maximize interdisciplinary cooperation and a member of any of the disciplines might provide administrative leadership to the agency. The fields of aging, mental health and retardation, community and neighborhood services, and group and youth services are examples of practice fields that are shared by several disciplines.

In still other settings social work might provide supporting services to another profession. As the *secondary discipline* in these agencies social work is, in one sense, a guest of the primary discipline. The agency is organized to allow the primary discipline to work as effectively as possible and the needs of social work or other professions receive lower priority. The role of the social worker in a medical setting illustrates social work as a secondary discipline. Hospitals, one setting for medical practice, are geared to the needs of the physician. Social services are provided at the physician's referral and are organized so they do not compete with the schedule and work of the medical profession. A similar role would be assumed by the social worker in corrections, schools, and industrial settings.

Advantages of Agency-based Practice

Given the complexities of agency practice, why does social work continue to function as an agency-based profession? Why not adopt the private practice model of other successful professions? Most social workers recognize that agency-based practice offers several advantages.

First, it makes the services more visible and, therefore, more accessible to all persons in need. The existence of agencies in a community over time and the attendant publicity about their operation, typically make both their programs and their location familiar to all members of the community. As opposed to nonagency practice that caters to those who can pay the full cost of services, the public and private human service agencies are more likely to have as clients the most vulnerable members of the society. For the social worker committed to serving the part of the population experiencing the most serious social problems, agency practice is the only game in town.

Second, agencies survive because they have received the sanction, or approval, of the community for the services they provide. Clients approach the helping situation with a greater trust in the quality of services they will receive because of the commitment made by the agency and the oversight of its board and administrators. In private practice situations the client must place full trust in the individual practitioner to perform high quality practice.

Third, clients have the benefit of an extra layer of protection against possible misuse of professional authority in social agencies. Clients in any setting are protected by both the professional ethics of the professionals and, in many cases, the legal regulation or licensing of that practice. In agencies, however, they are also protected by the agency's selection of staff and ongoing monitoring of the quality of services.

Fourth, human service agencies tend to have a broad scope and often employ persons from several different professions, which provides clients with ready access to the competencies of multiple professions and gives the worker the opportunity for interdisciplinary practice activities. In addition, as opposed to the more limited service focus found in private practice, agencies typically offer a broad range of services from direct practice to social action. Thus, they provide the social worker with the stimulation of engaging in a range of different practice activities and make it possible to change the focus of one's practice area or move into supervisory or management positions without changing employers.

Fifth, most agencies offer staff development opportunities that stimulate professional growth among workers. Characteristically, social agencies employ a large enough number of staff members that workers do not feel isolated and, in fact, typically carry out programs that contribute to the continued professional growth and development of staff members. The rapidly changing knowledge and skill base of the helping professions makes continuing professional development important to the services the clients receive and adds to the intellectual stimulation of the staff.

Last, agencies have the ability to raise funds from the community, whether from taxes or voluntary contributions, and offer a stable salary to the employees. Agencies do not face the risk of a fluctuating income experienced by persons in private or proprietary practice settings.

ISSUES IN PRIVATE OR PROPRIETARY PRACTICE

The principal option to agency-based practice for the social worker is private or proprietary practice. The remarkable expansion of this setting in the last decade is an important feature of social work today. While social work does not sanction entering private practice immediately upon graduation from professional degree programs, it is useful for all social workers to be aware of the issues that surround this practice setting as they are having a profound influence on the social work profession.

Why is private practice gaining such popularity among social workers? From the vantage point of the social worker, private practice is attractive partially because of the greater opportunity for financial gain but more importantly for more freedom to exercise professional autonomy in the conduct of social work practice. The bureaucratic constraints of many human service agencies have placed such serious restrictions on the ability of social workers to effectively use their professional competencies for the benefit of clients that many have actively sought a different practice setting. In Robert Barker's study of social workers in private practice the respondents identified the opportunity to "get away from the bureaucratic constraints of agency employment" as the primary reason they entered private practice.[39] Other reasons for leaving agency practice, as discovered by Barker, were that private practice offered greater flexibility in hours and practice activities, a desire to remain in direct practice without becoming subordinate to others in an administrative hierarchy, income considerations, a sense of greater challenge, and the opportunity to work with more motivated clients.[40]

Marquis Earl Wallace indicates that a number of historical developments have come together at this time that create a climate that makes private practice attractive to clients.

A growing number of middle-class clients with a variety of personal and interpersonal problems believe that seeking professional consultation is a reasonable step to take. There is less stigma attached to obtaining help today, particularly when it is received from a practitioner who is not a psychiatrist. Moreover, the increasing professionalization of social workers, evidenced by such developments as granting the ACSW by the Academy of Certified

Social Workers, the recent publication of registers of clinical social workers certified for independent practice, legal registration and licensing of social workers, and publicly mandated or privately arranged vendorship, or third-party payments to workers, provides the rationale—and even the means to obtain payment—for private social work services. Finally, within the profession, private practice is not scorned as much as it once was by those who are not private practitioners.[41]

As a nonagency activity, private practice avoids many of the limitations that accrue from practice within a bureaucratic structure but also places greater responsibility on the social worker to practice within the ethical guidelines of the profession. There is no oversight of private practice short of a complaint being filed with a licensing board or the local NASW chapter. NASW has rightfully been concerned about establishing guidelines that will identify for the public those social workers who have the requisite preparation and experience to conduct this autonomous practice.

The Organization of Private Practice

The NASW definition of private practice is sufficiently broad to include social workers providing both private and proprietary practice. Clinical or direct service practice, however, is the dominant approach of private practitioners. In his study of private practice, Wallace found that the average for these social workers was "63 percent of private practice time in individual treatment, 19 percent devoted to work with marital couples, 8 percent to group therapy, 7 percent to family treatment, and 2 percent to joint interviews with clients other than married couples."[42] For the delivery of these clinical services, three organizational approaches are used.

In the first approach the social worker engages in multidisciplinary practice. In this arrangement the social worker participates with members of other disciplines (for example, psychiatry and psychology) to provide a *group practice* that can meet a broad range of client needs. The social worker is an equal partner with the other disciplines and, in fact, is a co-owner of the business.

In the second form of private practice, the social worker provides a *supportive practice* for a member of another profession. For example, some physicians are hiring social workers to help patients deal with personal problems that are related to specific illnesses. The social worker might also provide more general services in the physician's office such as educating expectant parents about child development, counseling families that need help with child rearing practices, or referring people to appropriate community resources for help with problems.

In the third form, social workers are the *sole owners* of their private practice. Sole ownership involves securing office space, hiring staff, advertising services, making contacts to acquire referrals, overseeing the determination and collection of fees, and all other factors related to the management of a small business. Like any other business private practice is a "sink or swim" proposition with no guarantee of income equivalent to expenses. The main problems for full-time private practitioners are generating sufficient referrals to be able to keep the business solvent, handling the business details including securing payment from third-party vendors, obtaining competent consultation, minimizing the inherent isolation and arranging for backup in managing crisis situations, and protecting against their vulnerable position if there should be malpractice charges.[43]

It is estimated that two to three times as many social workers are engaged in part-time as full-time private practice. Many of these social workers are employed by a social agency but maintain a small private practice as well. Patricia Kelley and Paul Alexander identify four groups of social workers who elect to engage in part-time private practice:[44]

- Agency practitioners who welcome the independence and additional income,

- Social workers in supervisory or administrative positions who wish to maintain client contact and clinical skills,

- Educators who wish to have sufficient practice activity to remain sufficiently current with a practice to effectively teach clinical courses, and

- Social workers who are parents of young children and need to control their hours of work.

Part-time private practitioners experience many of the same problems as those in full-time practice. Kelley and Alexander's study of part-time private practitioners indicates that the most serious problems they face in getting a practice started are generating referrals and handling the practical business issues such as locating office space, securing financing, keeping records, etc. Although these matters continue to be problems, they are somewhat transitional and become less consuming once a practice is established. Later, and particularly unique to the person in part-time private practice, time management problems become the most difficult part of maintaining a private practice.[45]

Social workers in proprietary practice provide indirect services such as consultation. Consultation might be provided to another social worker or to a member of another helping profession concerning the handling of case. For example a social worker might consult with a lawyer about a divorce or child custody case. He or she might also be involved in working with a social agency—such as helping a nursing home with budgeting, administrative procedures, or program development.

Another form of indirect private practice involves the training of social workers or members of other disciplines in special skills. The increasing demand for experienced social workers to provide workshops, seminars, or other forms of training is contributing to the growing demand for proprietary practice.

Concerns Related to Private Practice

The private practice approach represents a substantial departure from social work's historical agency orientation. It has not been without controversy in the profession and has experienced problems in becoming accepted and appreciated in the general community. Four issues have emerged concerning this practice mode.

First, social work has maintained somewhat strict standards for private practice. Because private clients do not have the protection of an agency monitoring system to provide protection against incompetence or abuses of the professional monopoly, the profession has been careful to specify more extensive education and experience as minimum preparation for the private practitioner than for the agency-based practitioner. The standards established by NASW call for completion of a master's degree in social work from an accredited school of social work, two years of full-time or 3,000 hours of part-time practice experience, and successfully passing the examination required for membership in the Academy of Certified Social Workers (ACSW). To be listed in both the *National Registry of Health Care Providers in Clinical Social Work* and NASW's *Register of Clinical Social Workers,* a social worker is required to have completed at least two years of full-time, post-master's employment as a social worker.

Second, because many private practitioners work on a part-time basis, some agencies are concerned that private practice will detract from agency practice. They fear the social worker will place self-interest above the needs of the agency. A study of twenty voluntary agencies yielded the following common concerns about private practice:

1. That the worker will not do justice to his agency responsibilities because of the amount of time and energy that may go into private practice.

2. That the worker may take clients from the agency or gain clients in the community who may otherwise have gone to the agency.

3. That the staff person will become more his or her own agent, instead of being an enabler for the agency.

4. That the staff person may not meet the minimum standards set by the National Association of Social Workers for Private Practice.[46]

On the other side of this issue it is argued that private practice offers different professional stimulation than is found in agency practice and also provides a supplemental income to agency salaries that keeps workers satisfied with their agency employment. Some agencies are even encouraging social workers to engage in some part-time private practice by allowing them to use their agency offices in the evenings or by arranging schedules to allow a day off each week for this purpose. Such arrangements, however, are ripe for conflict of interest issues.

Third, some critics have accused private practitioners of "specializing in diseases of the rich" and diverting social work from its mission of serving the most vulnerable members of the society. There is little argument that clinical private practice represents a deviation from social work's philanthropic roots. Barker states, "Undoubtedly, the major dilemma is that private practice services are less accessible to the very people who have historically been social work's traditional clientele—the disadvantaged."[47] Moreover, private practitioners have been accused of failing to perform the social action responsibilities of the profession. Borenzweig's study of agency and private practitioners did not refute that charge but found that agency practitioners were equally guilty of failing to be involved in social action.[48]

Finally, social workers in private practice have faced an uphill battle in gaining public sanction for their activity. Of particular concern to many clinical private practitioners has been the reluctance of health insurance companies and the federal government to recognize social workers as legitimate providers of services that can be reimbursed by insurance programs.

Advantages of Private or Proprietary Practice

There are also arguments in favor of social work's movement toward private and proprietary practice. First, in most human service agencies clients have little opportunity to exercise individual choice in regard to what professionals will provide services. Clients typically cannot select their individual social workers, nor can they fire them if unsatisfied with the services received. Clients exercise considerably more control in a private setting.

Second, from the social worker's perspective, the rules and regulations of agencies place constraints on the worker's ability to conduct a practice in the manner he or she believes would be most effective. Professional autonomy is inherently compromised. For example, agency-based social workers cannot choose their clients; are not completely free to determine the amount and type of service to be given; and are almost always supervised, at times by one who interferes with the professional judgment of the worker.

Third, agency salaries tend to be lower than for the private and proprietary practitioner. Further, as opposed to the market driven income of the private practitioner that is at least theoretically based on competence, agency salaries are based to a greater degree on seniority and position within the agency.

Last, few agencies avoid the pitfalls that plague most bureaucratic organizations in which workers find that a disproportionate share of their time is devoted to meetings and paperwork. The less elaborate mechanisms required for accountability in private practice frees the worker of much of the less people-oriented activity found in agency practice.

For both clients and social workers, there are gains and losses from both agency and private practice. These factors influence the nature and quality of services provided as well as the social worker's satisfaction with his or her employment.

CONCLUDING COMMENT

Social work practice has permeated U.S. society to the extent that it occurs in every type of organization: mutual benefit, governmental, voluntary, and business. Although the roots of social work are in agency-based practice where public concerns for people in need took the form of creating human service agencies, social work now is offered through both agency and private practice modes.

Most social workers continue to be employed in agency settings and they must be able to work effectively within agency structures if they are to maximize their ability to serve clients. Understanding the principles on which agencies are organized and the problems social workers commonly experience in matching their professional orientation with agency requirements is, therefore, important to providing quality services.

An increasing number of social workers have entered private and proprietary practice to avoid some of the problems experienced by the agency-based practitioner and to increase potential income. However, private practice is certainly not trouble-free. Social work is beginning to address the important issues related to ensuring adequate preparation for the responsibilities of independent practice, lessening the quality of agency practice, moving away from the social work mission of focusing services on the poor and other vulnerable population groups, and gaining public sanction and client protection for this relatively new method of service delivery.

It appears at this point in history that the trend in social work is toward an increasing entrepreneurial approach to practice. However, it is clear that many critical social provisions and social services can never be made available in sufficient quantity through the mutual benefit and entrepreneurial human service organizations to meet the needs of the most vulnerable members of this society. Thus, it is reasonable to conclude that social work will continue to be primarily an agency-oriented profession and that social workers must continue to devote attention to means of making these organizations more responsive to the requirements for effective professional practice.

SUGGESTED READINGS

Abramovitz, Mimi. "The Privatization of the Welfare State: A Review." *Social Work* 31 (July–August, 1986): 257–264.

Barker, Robert L. "Private and Proprietary Services." *Encyclopedia of Social Work,* edited by Anne Minahan. 18th ed. Silver Spring, Md.: National Association of Social Workers, 1987, Vol. II, pp. 324–329.

Barker, Robert L. *Social Work in Private Practice: Principles, Issues, Dilemmas.* Washington, D.C.: National Association of Social Workers, 1983.

Blau, Peter M., and Meyer, Marshall W. *Bureaucracy in Modern America.* 2nd ed. New York: Random House, 1975.

Hasenfeld, Yeheskel. "The Changing Context of Human Services Administration." *Social Work* 29 (November–December 1984): 522–529.

Matorin, Susan, Rosenberg, Blanca, Levitt, Marlin, and Rosenblum, Sylvia. "Private Practice in Social Work: Readiness and Opportunity." *Social Casework* 68 (January 1987): 31–37.

Ostrander, Susan A. "Voluntary Social Service Agencies in the United States." *Social Service Review* 59 (September 1985): 435–452.

Sosin, Michael. *Private Benefits: Material Assistance in the Private Sector.* Orlando: Academic Press, 1986.

ENDNOTES

1. B. J. Seymour and Beverly Marston, "Social Work and Optometry: A New Partnership," *Social Work* 29 (November–December 1984): 536–541.
2. Peter M. Blau and Richard Scott, *Formal Organizations: A Comparative Approach* (San Francisco: Chandler, 1962), pp. 40–58.
3. William J. Reid and Peter K. Stimpson, "Sectarian Agencies." Copyright © 1987, National Association of Social Workers. Reprinted with permission from Anne Minahan, ed., *Encyclopedia of Social Work*, Vol. II, p. 548.
4. George T. Martin, Jr., "Union Social Services and Women's Work," *Social Service Review* 59 (March 1985): 62.
5. Michael Sosin, *Private Benefits: Material Assistance in the Private Sector* (Orlando, Fl: Academic Press, 1986), p. 1.
6. National Association of Social Workers, "Membership Survey Shows Practice Shifts," *NASW News* 28 (November 1983): 6–7.
7. National Association of Social Workers, "First-Time Look at Members' Salaries Finds Their Average Income Is $27,800," *NASW News* 33 (January 1988): 18.
8. Susan A. Ostrander, "Voluntary Social Service Agencies in the United States," *Social Service Review* 59 (September 1985): 435–454.
9. "NASW Membership Study," pp. 6–7.
10. "NASW Salary Study," p. 18.
11. Yeheskel Hasenfeld, "The Changing Context of Human Service Administration," *Social Work* 29 (November–December 1984): 526.
12. Bradford W. Sheafor, "The Effect of Board Members on Staff of Community Mental Health Centers: A Study of the Relationship of Their Values to Job Satisfaction," *Journal of Social Welfare* 3 (Spring, 1976): 75–82.
13. Sosin, *Private Benefits*, p. 160.
14. Robert L. Barker, *The Social Work Dictionary* (Silver Spring: Md.: National Association of Social Workers, 1987), p. 125.
15. Robert L. Barker, "Private and Proprietary Services," in Anne Minahan, ed., *Encyclopedia of Social Work*, 18th ed., (Silver Spring, Md.: National Association of Social Workers, 1987), Vol. II, pp. 324–425.
16. Robert L. Barker, *Social Work in Private Practice: Principles, Issues, Dilemmas* (Silver Spring, Md.: National Association of Social Workers, 1983), pp. 20–31.
17. "NASW Salary Study," p. 18.
18. Barker, "Private and Proprietary Services," p. 328.
19. Grant Loavenbruck, "NASW Manpower Survey Finds Increase in Pay for Most Members," *NASW News* 18 (March 1973): 10–11 and "NASW Membership Study," pp. 6–7.
20. Barker, "Private and Proprietary Services," p. 326.
21. "NASW Salary Study," p. 18.
22. Catherine E. Born, "Proprietary Firms and Child Welfare Services: Patterns and Implications," *Child Welfare* 62 (March/April 1983): 112.

23. Mary Adelaide Mendelson, *Tender Loving Greed: How the Incredibly Lucrative Nursing Home "Industry" is Exploiting America's Old People and Defrauding Us All* (New York: Alfred A. Knopf, 1973).

24. Bradford H. Gray, ed., *The New Health Care for Profit: Doctors and Hospitals in a Competitive Environment* (Washington, D.C.: National Academy Press, 1983), pp. 1–2.

25. Mimi Abramovitz, "The Privatization of the Welfare State: A Review," *Social Work* 31 (July–August 1986): 257.

26. Hasenfeld, "The Changing Context," p. 526.

27. Amitai Etzioni, *Modern Organization* (Englewood Cliffs, N.J.: Prentice-Hall, 1964), pp. 8–10.

28. Ibid.

29. Martin Wolins, "Societal Functions of Social Welfare," *New Perspectives* 1 (Fall 1967): 1.

30. Peter M. Blau and Marshall W. Meyer, *Bureaucracy in Modern Society*, 2nd ed., (New York: Random House, 1973), pp. 18–23.

31. Thomas J. Peters and Robert H. Waterman, Jr., *In Search of Excellence: Lessons from America's Best-Run Companies*, (New York: Harper & Row, 1982).

32. James L. Price, *Organizational Effectiveness: An Inventory of Propositions*, (Homewood, Ill.: Richard D. Irwin, 1968), pp. 96–103.

33. W. Richard Scott, "Professionals in Bureaucracies—Areas of Conflict," in Howard M. Vollmer and Donald L. Mills, eds., *Professionalization*, (Englewood Cliffs, N.J.: Prentice-Hall, 1966), pp. 264–275.

34. Kenneth Wooden, *Weeping in the Playtime of Others* (New York: McGraw-Hill, 1976).

35. Robert Pruger, "The Good Bureaucrat," *Social Work* 18 (July 1973): 26–27.

36. Ibid., pp. 28–32.

37. Aase George, "A History of Social Work Field Instruction: Apprenticeship to Instruction," in Bradford W. Sheafor and Lowell E. Jenkins, eds., *Quality Field Instruction in Social Work: Program Development and Maintenance*, (New York: Longman, 1982), pp. 37–59.

38. Raymond Monsor Scurfield, "Clinician to Administrator: Difficult Role Transition?" *Social Work* 26 (November 1981): 495.

39. Robert Barker, "Private Practice Primer for Social Work," *NASW News* 28 (October 1983): 13.

40. Ibid.

41. Marquis Earl Wallace, "Private Practice: A Nationwide Study," *Social Work* 27 (May 1983): 262.

42. Ibid., p. 265.

43. Susan Matorin, Blanca Rosenberg, Marylin Levitt, and Sylvia Rosenblum, "Private Practice in Social Work: Readiness and Opportunity," *Social Casework* 68 (January 1987): 31–37.

44. Patricia Kelley and Paul Alexander, "Part-Time Private Practice: Practical and Ethical Considerations," *Social Work* 30 (May–June 1985): 254.

45. Ibid., p. 255.

46. Janice Proshaska, "Private Practice May Benefit Voluntary Agencies," *Social Casework* 59 (July 1978): 374. Published by the Family Service Association of America.

47. "Private Practice Primer," p. 13.

48. Herman Borenzweig, "Agency vs. Private Practice: Similarities and Differences," *Social Work* 26 (May 1981): 243.

Part Three

The Practice of Social Work

The various activities that a social worker performs in carrying out his or her professional responsibilities constitute the *practice* of social work. In order to carry out the practice of social work effectively, however, the social worker must know *what* he or she is doing, *why* he or she is doing it, and of equal importance, *how* to do it. These three factors translate into the *knowledge* base of social work, the *value* base of social work, and the *skill* base of social work. The knowledge, value, and skill bases of social work provide the core ingredients and foundation of practice that guide the intervention activities of the social worker.

Chapter 7 discusses the basic knowledge a social worker should have. He or she must be well informed about how to help people deal with both their *internal* (psychological) and their *external* (significant others, groups, and neighborhood) environment. A case example provides an opportunity to examine the breadth and depth of knowledge the so-

cial worker needs just to be able to conduct a specific interview with a client.

Chapter 8 examines the value base of social work. The profession of social work is founded upon an adherence to certain values. These values include beliefs that humankind is inherently worthy, that people have the capacity to change, that people have a need to belong, and that all persons have responsibilities to themselves, their fellow human beings, and society. In addition, social workers also believe that society has a responsibility to help those less able to help themselves. Without values, the social work profession would lose its main purpose for being. Social work, in effect, would lose its professional uniqueness.

Chapter 9 focuses on the skill base of social work. In other words, what are the basic skills needed by the social worker as he or she begins to help people? *Skill* is ability to use knowledge effectively and readily in execution or performance. Five basic skills for beginning practice are highlighted, namely, *engagement* skills (that is, how the worker initially connects with people), *observation* skills, *communication* skills, *empathy* skills, and *assessment* skills.

Chapter 10 presents a case study situation in order to demonstrate how the knowledge, value, and skill concepts discussed in Chapters 7, 8, and 9 are put into practice by the social worker. In this case the social worker attempts to help a family that experienced a severe tragedy. As this generalist social worker searches for the roots of the problem, he decides to intervene at a number of levels. The case is intended to provide a basis for integrating the materials in the preceding chapters with special emphasis as it concerns the knowledge, value, and skill base of social work.

CHAPTER 7

The Knowledge Base
of Social Work

To understand the many faces of social work in greater depth, some of the important parts of the field must be isolated for closer scrutiny. The "Working Definition of Social Work Practice,"[1] that separates the knowledge, values, purpose, sanction, and methods or skills of social work, is used as a guide for this task. The first six chapters of this book were concerned with purpose and sanction, which are prerequisites to practice activity. When engaged in practice, the social worker must relate simultaneously to the knowledge, value, and skill aspects of practice. In this way the profession resembles a three-ring circus: social work *skills* are the observable aspect of practice in the center ring, but important contributions are being made by *knowledge* and *values* in the side rings. In this chapter, the knowledge base of social work practice will be examined.

THE KNOWLEDGE BASE

If the social worker is to provide clients with competent service, he or she must be prepared with substantial knowledge. Although "tested" knowledge in the social and behavioral sciences is somewhat limited, the social worker should be familiar with what is available. The social worker should also know and be able to use the many theories and concepts relevant to practice. At a less scientific but equally important level, the social worker must develop individual practice knowledge based on experience in serving clients (*practice wisdom*) and also be sensitive to, and knowledgeable about, oneself—values, beliefs, and intuitions. The effective social worker, then, engages in *knowledge-guided practice*.

Knowledge may be generally defined as the "acquaintance with or theoretical or practical understanding of some branch of science, art, learning, or other area involving study, research, or practice, and the acquisition of skills."[2] All professions draw on a body of knowledge that serves as their basic foundation of practice. The knowledge is usually obtained from more research-oriented disciplines, and in some professions, such as law and medicine, it is accumulated over centuries. In addition to the historical knowledge, any *practitioner* should be aware of the body of knowledge related to his or her special area of practice.

A problem for social work, as well as for many other helping professions, is that a substantial number of social workers seem to have only a limited working conception of how to use knowledge in practice. William E. Gordon suggests that they understand the development of skill much better than they do the pragmatic use of knowledge about a phenomenon in order to affect that phenomenon.[3] If one were to ask a social worker *what* he or she just did and *why* it was done that way, the answer would probably be verbalized with ease. One might say, for example, that an opportunity was created in the interview for Mr. James to cry so that he could vent his feelings. If asked to comment on the knowledge that guided that action, the social worker might describe reliance on a technique that had been observed and subsequently used in practice with good results (practice wisdom). Pursuing the matter further, if this social worker were asked to identify the concepts, propositions, and theory (knowledge base) that guides his or her practice, a reply might be more difficult. Although a major problem is the lack of much verified theory, Harriett Bartlett maintains that the social work profession has not

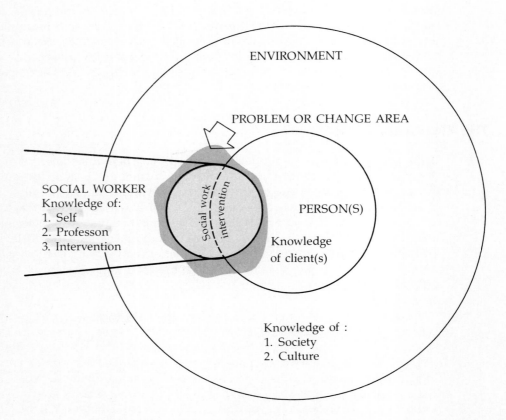

Figure 7–1 *Knowledge components of social work practice*

been accustomed to looking directly and clearly at social work knowledge either as a separate entity or as a guide to practice.[4]

The social worker has been viewed more as a "doer" than as a person engaged in knowledge-guided practice.[5] The low visibility and fragmentation of social work knowledge may also be the result of many social work educators' and staff supervisors' placing greater emphasis on the practitioner's awareness of *feelings* than on awareness of the generalizations on which action rests. The fact that social work has been slow in codifying its knowledge may be another major reason why the profession has only a limited foundation of tested knowledge.[6]

The social worker does not need to possess extensive knowledge in many fields, but it is important to be well versed in subjects related to helping people interact with the environment. Figure 7–1 helps draw some parameters around the specialized knowledge needed by the social worker.

HISTORICAL NOTES

For many years social workers have been attempting to systematize their knowledge. A milestone was the 1917 publication of Mary Richmond's *Social Diagnosis*, the first significant effort toward organizing the knowledge base of one method of social work—social casework. The book systematically set forth an approach to the study and diagnosis of a client's problems and made explicit what have become basic tenets in casework, among them the need to *individualize* each client, the *reciprocity of relationship* between client and social worker, and the client's right to *self-determination*. Richmond established what a social worker ought to know, from the very general to the specific. Commenting on "what is true of everybody," Richmond stated:

> We all have a birthday and a place of birth, and have or had two parents, four grandparents, etc., with all that this implies by way of racial and national characteristics, of family inheritance and tradition, and probably of family environment. Our place of birth (assuming here and elsewhere the conditions of a modern civilization) was a house of some kind, and we have continued to live in this or in a series of other houses ever since. The characteristics of these houses, their neighborhood and atmosphere, have helped to make us what we are.[7]

Contrasting the general "what is true of everybody" to the specific in reference to ethnicity as a factor in working with a client, she commented:

> One of the social worker's difficulties with foreigners is that he does not understand their conventions any more than they do his, a knowledge of their history and of their old world environment is indispensable to the most helpful relations with them.[8]

If Mary Richmond were alive today, she would support contemporary ethnic studies for social work students so they would have the knowledge enabling them to be more effective in helping clients from a variety of ethnic and racial backgrounds.

Another key historical event contributing to the knowledge base of social work was the 1929 Milford Conference, where a number of social work educators and social agency executives met to discuss issues related to social work practice. Porter Lee, a leader of the Milford Conference and director of the New York School of Social Work, promoted the idea that social casework should integrate the insights of psychology, psychiatry, political science, economics, and sociology. His synthesis of ideas from other fields into a new whole helped to formulate the *generic social casework theory* as expressed in the Milford Conference Report.[9] The report attempted to identify the generic components (those having common characteristics) in social casework practice, emphasizing that the *process* (procedure) in social casework and the knowledge base of the social worker should be basically the same for all practice settings.

Initial efforts toward developing a generic component of social work mainly concerned casework, and basic agreement was achieved about the major areas of content in social casework. However, substantial common ground was also discovered in knowledge content lists of casework, group work, and community organization.[10] Seeking a common core curriculum, social work educators proposed a ''Basic Eight'' curriculum to the American Association of Schools of Social Work in 1944.[11] The Basic Eight considered the following areas of particular importance to social work students:

1. Social casework (generic and specialized).
2. Social group work.
3. Community organization.
4. Social research and statistics.
5. Social welfare administration.
6. Public welfare and child welfare.
7. Medical information.
8. Psychiatric information.

The goal of educators in social work during the 1940s was to help students develop competence in three major areas: (1) conceptual and perceptual understanding; (2) skills in methods, procedures, and processes; and (3) personal professional qualities.[12]

As late as 1955 Alfred Kahn criticized the curricula of graduate schools of social work for their emphasis on technical or how-to-do courses. He felt the curriculum structure alone did not clearly indicate what the social work profession considered its knowledge base. After analyzing a group of articles selected at random from social work periodicals, Kahn concluded that social work knowledge was at that time an amalgam of: (1) propositions borrowed from or markedly like those of psychiatry and some branches of psychology; (2) even fewer propositions borrowed from sociology and social anthropology and a scattering from other fields; (3) apparently original propositions about how to do certain things in casework, group work, and community organization; (4) methods, techniques, and attitudes clearly derived from the fields of administration, statistics, and social research; and (5) propositions about how to do things apparently derived from progressive education.[13]

In December 1956 a definition of social work practice was prepared by a task force for the National Association of Social Workers (NASW). "The Working Definition of Social Work Practice" was published in *Social Work* in 1958 and spelled out the constellation of various components found in all professions, such as values, purpose, sanction, knowledge, and method. The particular content and configuration of this constellation in the definition, however, was seen as identifying social work practice and distinguishing it from the practice of other professions.[14] Only the knowledge component of the Working Definition will be considered in this chapter.

The practice of the social worker is seen as typically guided by knowledge of:

1. Human development and behavior characterized by emphasis on the wholeness of the individual and the reciprocal influences of man and his total environment—human, social, economic, and cultural.

2. The psychology of giving and taking help from another person or source outside the individual.

3. Ways in which people communicate with one another and give outer expression to inner feelings, such as words, gestures, and activities.

4. Group process and the effects of groups upon individuals and the reciprocal influence of the individual upon the group.

5. The meaning and effect on the individual, groups, and community of cultural heritage including its religious beliefs, spiritual values, laws, and other social institutions.

6. Relationships, i.e., the interactional processes between individuals, between individual and groups, and between group and group.

7. The community, its internal processes, modes of development and change, its social services and resources.

8. The social services, their structure, organization, and methods.

9. Self, which enables the individual practitioner to be aware of and to take responsibility for his own emotions and attitudes as they affect his professional functions.[15]

As Heraclitus, an ancient Greek philosopher, said, "The same man never washes in the same river twice." Certainly the changeability of people, not to mention the environment, requires flexible application of knowledge. Since scientific knowledge of people is never final or absolute, the social worker is advised to take into account exceptions to existing generalizations and to be aware of, and ready to deal with, the spontaneous and unpredictable in human behavior.[16]

Werner Boehm suggested in 1958 that social work had only fragments of practice theory intermingled with incomplete knowledge of the nature of people, the nature of society, and their relationship. In assuming that social work practice was an art with a foundation of science and values, he perceived three types of knowledge in social work: (1) tested knowledge, (2) hypothetical knowledge that required transformation into tested knowledge, and (3) assumptive knowledge (practice wisdom) that required transformation into hypothetical and then into tested knowledge. The practitioner uses all three types and assumes responsibility for knowing which type of knowledge is being used at any time and what degree of scientific certainty it carries.[17]

In 1959 Alfred Kadushin maintained that the literature detailing what the social worker needs to know, do, and feel was "almost embarrassingly rich."[18] He noted a certain repetitiveness in the materials, with "old friends" appearing many times. Although there were differences among statements regarding the required base of social work knowledge, from one method to another, similarities in the listings may have been due to the *agreement of experts* rather than to a *detailed analysis of practice*. It appeared that there was a plea in the literature to study practice rather than to continue to use expert opinion as a basis for developing knowledge in social work.[19]

Kadushin was able to discern the origins of social work knowledge by building a framework separated into three major areas: social services, social work practice, and human growth and behavior. The *social service* area is concerned with the organization, administration, and operation of social welfare programs and services, the interrelationships of agencies, the historical development of such programs, and the nature of the human needs served by these programs.[20] *Social work practice* concerns the actual process of helping clients, the techniques of helping, the resources for helping, and appropriate attitudes for helping. *Human growth and behavior* is concerned with understanding the client in his or her problem situation, normal and deviant personality development and behavior, and the dynamics of individual and group behavior.[21]

Social work scholars and educators have seen the need become increasingly urgent for the building of additional social work knowledge. In 1962 following several years of discussion, the NASW Commission on Social Work Practice decided to have a "knowledge conference." A task force subsequently did initiate and give some beginning direction to the development of *social work knowledge* as an endeavor to strengthen the knowledge base of the profession.[22] The 117-page conference report was directed to the NASW Commission on Practice. One recommendation of particular interest was:

> That some means be established for systematically collecting and organizing social work knowledge from the three sources so repeatedly emphasized at this conference, that is:

a. Capturing and articulating what is known by practitioners but has not been sufficiently verbalized or communicated to the field at large and is not yet recognized substantively as part of social work's body of knowledge.

b. Deriving clearer and more inclusive description of social work knowledge from social work literature.

c. Supporting efforts to draw relevant knowledge from the social sciences and to develop this relevant knowledge in social work frames of reference.[23]

The conference concluded that the main sources of social work knowledge were the professional literature, relevant concepts from allied fields—especially the social sciences—and the wisdom of practitioners. A consultant at the conference suggested that social work must look more at its own substance for validation, knowledge, and theory-building; and in this process social work findings might contradict some theories in social science, thus demanding new testing by the social sciences.[24]

Merlin Taber and Iris Shapiro conducted a content analysis of 124 social work articles published between 1920 and 1963. They tried to determine the nature and extent of the development of the social work knowledge base. When the data were classified as empirical or verifiable, trends over the forty-year period indicated a slight decrease in the proportion of empirical content, a dramatic increase in references to theories and concepts, and a sharp increase in the amount of verifiable material in each journal studied. Although they concluded that their findings did not show progression toward a "relatively well-confirmed theory," the authors felt there was evidence of much potential for the development of knowledge and for more sophistication in the use of theory and facts.[25]

The search continues for a firm knowledge base in social work. Perhaps the first step in more explicitly identifying the knowledge on which social workers rely is to formulate a clear conception of social work. The knowledge that is essential for social work practice could then be filtered out. Renewed activity to address the problem of identifying a clear concept of social work was stimulated in 1976 by the NASW at a conference on "Conceptual Frameworks for Social Work," held in Madison, Wisconsin, and reported on in a special issue of *Social Work* (September 1977). This effort was followed by the creation of a committee to work toward the development of a "Classification Scheme for Social Work Knowledge." This difficult task was finalized at a meeting in Chicago in May 1979 and resulted in a special second issue of *Social Work* (January 1981) entitled "Conceptual Frameworks II."

An historical review indicates that there remains substantial disagreement as to what specifically constitutes social work knowledge. Mary Burns suggests that social workers must function with a body of knowledge that is at best imprecise, at worst erroneous, and always inadequate and difficult to communicate.[26] The unusually broad boundaries of social work practice significantly contribute to this problem. The boundaries include all that is related to human behavior and could encompass all of society, including a range of conditions from health to pathology and a large selection of skills directed toward improved individual coping, institutional change, social policy and planning, and other areas as social workers enter new arenas of social issues and problems. "In effect," states Carol Meyer, "it would seem that there are hardly any boundaries to the knowledge that is necessary for social workers to have just in order to get through a working day."[27]

KNOWLEDGE THE SOCIAL WORKER NEEDS TODAY

To describe the knowledge base a social worker should have today, a modification of a conceptual formulation developed by Alfred Kadushin is helpful.[28] This formulation identifies five levels of knowledge the social worker must use in the helping process. This knowledge ranges from general knowledge used by the total profession to specific knowledge used in contact with an individual client (see Figure 7–2).

With use of the conceptual framework presented in Figure 7–2, it is possible to examine the knowledge base used by one social worker in a corrections

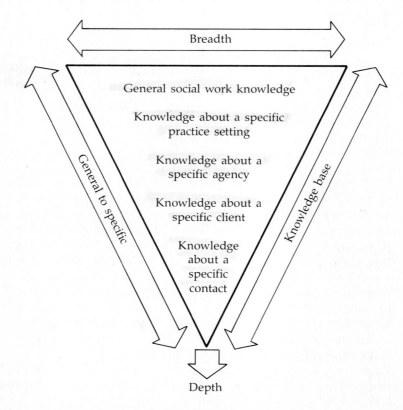

Figure 7–2 Knowledge the social worker needs

setting while working with a particular client. The following case analysis helps to identify the general social work knowledge base, knowledge of a specific practice setting (corrections), knowledge about a specific agency (a twenty-four-hour female juvenile detention facility), knowledge about a specific client (a juvenile female offender), and knowledge about a specific contact (the initial interview).

General Social Work Knowledge

The professionally educated social worker in this case probably obtained his general knowledge base in a social work educational program prior to entering the corrections field. The curriculum content in schools of social work is drawn from the field as well as from other professions and scientific disciplines, to provide students with information constituting *general social work knowledge.* This knowledge is categorized into three broad areas:

1. Social welfare policy and services, including content on social problems; programs and institutions developed to prevent, treat and control problems; movements and forces that have influenced social welfare goals; the impact of social policy; and the role of the social worker in formulating policy.

2. Human behavior and the social environment, including content on human growth and personality development (both normal and abnormal); disease and disability; cultural norms and values; community processes; and other aspects of social functioning of the individual and the group.

3. Methods of social work practice, including methods of direct service— casework, group work, and community organization—and the enabling methods of research and administration.[29]

Knowledge about a Specific Practice Field

This social worker is employed in the *corrections field* and must be acquainted with the goals, philosophy, and functions of the field in society. He needs to know that a function of corrections is punishment of the convicted offender. The types of punishment may be only those allowed by the law: imprisonment (deprivation of the right to liberty), fine (deprivation of property), and death and certain other punishments society in the United States accepts and imposes. The social worker must also be familiar with a common assumption in correctional philosophy, that the penal law and correctional treatment have two purposes: treatment of the offender and protection of the public. Another common assumption is that the treatment of the offender should be *individualized*, that is, appropriate for the particular offender.[30]

The social worker should also be familiar with criminological theories, which may be assembled into three main categories: (1) *biological and constitutional theory,* often called the school of criminal biology, which seeks the mainsprings of deviancy in the inherited physical and mental makeup of

humans; (2) *psychogenic theory*, which traces antisocial character to faulty relationships within the family in the first few years of life; and (3) *sociological
theory*, which maintains that the pressures and pulls of the social environment
produce delinquent and criminal behavior.[31] Some theories, such as those
emphasizing biological factors, date back to the early nineteenth century;
while others, such as that propounded by Richard Cloward and Lloyd Ohlin,
are quite recent. Cloward and Ohlin theorize that boys from urban slums
gravitate to the delinquency subculture when they discover they do not have
access to legitimate avenues of success.[32] Since our social worker is employed
in a specific practice area—probation—he would obviously require more
knowledge of that agency than of the parole or prison systems.

Knowledge about a Specific Agency

The probation department is responsible for probation services for adults and
children as required or authorized by state or local laws. This agency is closely
linked to the court but is not in the judicial branch of government; its services
include the study, treatment, and supervision of probationers. Through this
agency, society tries to provide corrective assistance to the individual in conflict with the law and to protect the community at the same time. Because it
is not socially or economically feasible to imprison all offenders, probation
seeks to rehabilitate persons convicted of crimes by returning them to society
under a period of supervision.

The majority of offenders can be guided into a more constructive life without being removed from family, job, or community. The social worker should
be familiar with the laws governing probation and the services provided by
the probation department. Basic *field service* functions include investigation
to help courts determine the proper sentencing of convicted persons and
supervision of children and adults placed on probation by the courts. In addition to field service, the social worker must be familiar with other service
functions of the department such as: (1) securing suitable living arrangements
for nondelinquent juvenile court wards who are unable to remain in their
own homes, (2) administering temporary detention facilities, and (3) providing *institutional* rehabilitation treatment facilities for juvenile delinquents who
need treatment outside the home.

As can be seen, there are specialized subunits in the probation agency that
require additional knowledge on the part of the social worker. The social
worker in our case example is employed in a twenty-four-hour placement
facility for thirteen- to seventeen-year-old girls. These girls have been made
wards of the juvenile court and have been ordered "suitably placed" in the
institution. The social worker learns that psychotic, drug-addicted, and homosexual girls are not admitted to the institution and that many girls placed
there exhibit behavior or personality disorders.

These disorders, commonly found in juvenile delinquent and adult criminal institutions, may range from those essentially neurotic to behavior bor-
dering on the sociopathic. Given such a range of behavior, the social worker

must have an accurate diagnostic formulation of the ward in order to work out an appropriate treatment plan. In other words the social worker must understand the underlying causes of the behavior problem (symptoms) the girls exhibit such as running away, sex delinquency, incorrigibility, shoplifting, car theft, and assault.

Disruptive Behavior Disorders is a class of disorders described in the American Psychiatric Association's Diagnostic and Statistical Manual of Mental Disorders, commonly known as "DSM III-R," as childhood and adolescent behavior that is socially disruptive and is often more distressing to others than to the persons with the disorders. The subclass of disruptive behavior disorders include *Attention-deficit Hyperactivity Disorder* (ADHD), *Oppositional Defiant Disorder*, and *Conduct Disorder*.

The essential features of ADHD, which begins before age 7, are developmentally inappropriate degrees of inattention, impulsiveness, and hyperactivity. Oppositional Defiant Disorder or Conduct Disorder may develop later in childhood in those with ADHD, and in those who develop Conduct Disorder, a significant number, according to DSM III-R, are found to have Antisocial Personality Disorder in adulthood.[33] In Conduct Disorder the essential feature is a persistent pattern of conduct in which persons violate the basic rights of others and major age-appropriate social norms or rules. This behavior typically presents itself in the home, school, with peers, and in the community. Physical aggression is common and conduct problems are more serious than those seen in Oppositional Defiant Disorder. Early onset of Conduct Disorder in childhood is associated with greater risk of continuation into adolescent and adult life as Antisocial Personality Disorder.

In Oppositional Defiant Disorder there is a pattern of hostile, negative, and defiant behavior without the more serious violations of the basic rights of others that are seen in Conduct Disorder. Persons are more prone to argue, lose their tempers, defy rules, swear, etcetera, rather than physically attack others as is found in Conduct Disorder. Clinicians do not know the course of this disorder, although in many cases it can evolve into Conduct or a Mood Disorder.[34]

The above three Disruptive Behavior Disorders may evolve into adolescent or adult Antisocial Personality Disorder. Conduct Disorder symptoms begin before age 15 and the first symptoms of Conduct Disorder in females who develop Antisocial Personality Disorder usually appear in puberty; in males the Conduct Disorder is generally obvious in childhood. The essential features of this disorder include a history of continual and chronic antisocial behavior in which persons violate the rights of others, persistence into adult life of a pattern of antisocial behavior that began before the age of 15, and failure to sustain good job performance over a period of several years (although this may not be evident in individuals who are self-employed or who have not been in a position to demonstrate this behavior, for example, students or housewives). The antisocial behavior is not due to either severe mental retardation, schizophrenia, or manic episodes.

Lying, stealing, fighting, truancy, and resisting authority are typical early childhood signs. In adolescence unusually early or aggressive sexual behavior, excessive drinking, and use of illicit drugs are frequent. In adulthood these kinds of behavior continue with the addition of the inabilities to sustain consistent work performance, to function as a responsible parent, and to accept social norms with respect to lawful behavior. After age 30 the more flagrant aspects may diminish, particularly sexual promiscuity, fighting, criminality, and vagrancy.

The diagnostic criteria for an Antisocial Personality Disorder (DSM III-R, classification 301.70) include:[35]

A. Current age at least 18.

B. Evidence of Conduct Disorder with onset before age 15, as indicated by a history of *three* or more of the following:

  (1) was often truant
  (2) ran away from home overnight at least twice while living in parental or parental surrogate home (or once without returning)
  (3) often initiated physical fights
  (4) used a weapon in more than one fight
  (5) forced someone into sexual activity with him or her
  (6) was physically cruel to animals
  (7) was physically cruel to other people
  (8) deliberately destroyed others' property (other than by fire-setting)
  (9) deliberately engaged in fire-setting
  (10) often lied (other than to avoid physical or sexual abuse)
  (11) has stolen without confrontation of a victim on more than one occasion (including forgery)
  (12) has stolen with confrontation of a victim (e.g., mugging, purse-snatching, extortion, armed robbery)

C. A pattern of irresponsible and antisocial behavior since the age of 15, as indicated by at least *four* of the following:

  (1) is unable to sustain consistent work behavior, as indicated by any of the following (including similar behavior in academic settings if the person is a student):
    (a) significant unemployment for six months or more within five years when expected to work and work was available
    (b) repeated absences from work unexplained by illness in self or family
    (c) abandonment of several jobs without realistic plans for others
  (2) fails to conform to social norms with respect to lawful behavior, as indicated by repeatedly performing antisocial acts that are grounds for arrest (whether arrested or not), e.g., destroying property, harassing others, stealing, pursuing an illegal occupation
  (3) is irritable and aggressive, as indicated by repeated physical fights or assaults (not required by one's job or to defend someone or oneself), including spouse- or child-beating
  (4) repeatedly fails to honor financial obligations, as indicated by default-

ing on debts or failing to provide child support or support for other dependents on a regular basis

(5) fails to plan ahead, or is impulsive, as indicated by one or both of the following:

(a) traveling from place to place without a prearranged job or clear goal for the period of travel or clear idea about when the travel will terminate

(b) lack of a fixed address for a month or more

(6) has no regard for the truth, as indicated by repeated lying, use of aliases, or "conning" others for personal profit or pleasure

(7) is reckless regarding his or her own or others' personal safety, as indicated by driving while intoxicated, or recurrent speeding

(8) if a parent or guardian, lacks ability to function as a responsible parent, as indicated by one or more of the following:

(a) malnutrition of child

(b) child's illness resulting from lack of minimal hygiene

(c) failure to obtain medical care for a seriously ill child

(d) child's dependence on neighbors or nonresident relatives for food or shelter

(e) failure to arrange for a caretaker for young child when parent is away from home

(f) repeated squandering, on personal items, of money required for household necessities

(9) has never sustained a totally monogamous relationship for more than one year

(10) lacks remorse (feels justified in having hurt, mistreated, or stolen from another)

D. Occurrence of antisocial behavior not exclusively during the course of Schizophrenia or Manic Episodes.

In addition to having a depth of knowledge concerning the major psychiatric diagnostic categories pertaining to delinquent adolescent clientele treated in the institution, the social worker must also become familiar with the physical facilities, policies, and procedures of the program. An Intake Committee composed of a consultant psychiatrist, intake social worker, and school principal meets regularly to discuss:

1. The kind of behavior expected from each girl and ways of dealing with it.

2. The setting of tentative goals for achievement during each girl's stay in the program.

3. Selection of a treatment plan for each girl.

4. The best ways of working with each girl's family.

5. The school program to be followed, whether academic, remedial, or activity.

The social worker must be knowledgeable about treatment plans and resources the institution offers. In this example the agency's treatment plan
falls into three broad categories: individual, group, and family therapy. These
modes of treatment are known as *direct social work practice*, that is, the social
worker works directly with the individual, family, or group. Prior to proceeding with discussions about knowledge of a specific client and about a
specific contact, brief descriptions of family therapy and group and individual
treatment will be offered.

Family Therapy

In considering family therapy, the social worker must recognize that the family is a key factor in the treatment process and that every effort should be
made to involve the family actively in the treatment program. It therefore
becomes important for the social worker to acquire knowledge about family
dynamics and theory.

Family therapy has a sufficiently solid knowledge base to warrant it as a
major mode of treatment. A survey of graduate schools of social work found
that family therapy content was included in the required methods curricula
in 90 percent of the responding schools. Eighty percent of respondents indicated that family therapy was a legitimate area of specialization in the curricula of graduate social work education.[36] Family therapy has many different
therapeutic approaches, each with its own specific theoretical intervention
base. Some family therapy approaches are spontaneous, using interpretations
and uncovering techniques. Other approaches are carefully planned, and the
outcome is documented. Some family therapists are method-oriented and
others are problem-oriented, that is, that they are more eclectic and change
their method based upon the problem. For some the focus can be on expressing emotions or changing family structure.

Depending upon the problem and the family therapist's orientation, the
focus of intervention may be the child in the family (individual), the child
and a parent (dyad), the child and parents (triad), or the child, parents, and
other family members. There are at least three core theories characteristic to
most models of family therapy: *systems theory, family development theory,* and
structural theory. The systems theory views the family as a system of interlocking forces that regulate the ways it and its members operate. The whole
is greater than its parts, and the whole must be known if the parts are to be
understood. Each part contributes to and is affected by the system. Any part
that malfunctions for whatever reason affects the balance or equilibrium of
the total system. An adolescent who acts out stealing a car, for example, might
simply be reacting to stress caused by the impending divorce of his parents;
that is, the system is in a state of disequilibrium.

Family development theory emphasizes the fact that all families are at
various stages of development over time. Families change over the years as
part of a natural process. Family developmental tasks, in large part, parallel
and are intermeshed with individual life tasks. The place of each young per-

son in the family, the meaning this has for the parents and siblings, and the success or difficulty with which the family copes and interacts heavily influence the development of children.[37] In the family life cycle there is a major shift in the hierarchial structure; that is, children shift from being cared for by their parents to being peers of parents to being caretakers of parents in their old age.[38] The family development literature reveals certain common stress points of which the family therapist should be aware. Briefly, they include: (1) marriage, when the young couple must separate from their families and develop new modes of communication and a new emotional alignment; (2) the birth of the first child, an event that creates family developmental problems as emotional alignments are shifted to include the child and parental roles are established; (3) the age when the child first begins to assert his or her autonomy; (4) the entrance of the child into school and related painful feelings of separation, both for the child and the parents; (5) the stormy adolescent years, with their conflict over dependency and independency, self-responsibility and interdependence, intimacy and privacy; (6) the leaving of the last child from home, an event that precipitates the new task of parents having to learn how to relate to one another as middle-aged persons; and (7) old age, with its attendant loss of work and physical and role changes between the parents and their children.[39]

Structural theory is concerned with factors of importance related to the family structure. Family structure can be described in terms of hierarchy based upon power and status. Structural theorists maintain that problems develop when there is a confusion in a hierarchy or a violation of the rules innate in hierarchical organizations.[40] For example, if a father sides consistently with the teenage daughter against the mother, the child is breaching generation lines and so violating the norms and rules of hierarchical structures. This results in stress and problems in the family, between the parents and between the teenage daughter and mother. To intervene effectively, the family therapist conceptualizes the problem family as a system in disequilibrium, looks for developmental phase stressors and structural defects, and then, with the assistance of the family, attempts to correct these problems in order for the family to attain improved psychosocial functioning.

Group Treatment

There appears to be some confusion about the terms *group treatment, group work,* and *group psychotherapy.* Group psychotherapy, in its most traditional form, is a form of treatment in which carefully selected emotionally ill persons are placed in a group, guided by a trained therapist, for the purpose of helping one another effect personality change.[41] It involves an "uncovering" procedure, the achievement of insight into unconscious motivations and other intrapsychic processes. Today there are different types of group psychotherapy, each with its own theoretical base and interventive mode. These include supportive group therapy, analytically oriented group therapy, psychoanalysis of groups, transactional group therapy, and behavioral group therapy.[42] Because all these types of group psychotherapy have as their primary goal being therapeutic or helpful, they are forms of *group treatment*.

Group work is also helpful to people but is not usually referred to as group psychotherapy, since the primary goal is not to uncover unconscious material. Rather, the aim is to help people realize their potential for social functioning. This treatment helps people *through* groups.[43] For example an acting-out, rebellious adolescent may learn to internalize controls by being in a social work group with peers who, through democratic values, processes, and activities, are learning to work together to accomplish goals.

At the institution in our case example, two types of group treatment are offered:

1. Group Work—a group composed of eight to ten girls whose chief focus is on activities that build responsibilities and better relationships between the girls and adults.

2. Group Psychotherapy—a group of six to eight girls, led by a psychiatrist, clinical psychologist, or clinical social worker, whose primary emphasis is psychotherapy.

Individual Treatment

Individual treatment in social work involves the method of casework whereby help is given to individuals case by case, in order to resolve, alleviate, and prevent those problems that undermine the adequacy of their daily life functioning. It is a *method*, meaning the overall sum of procedures, and a *process*, identifying the separate parts and interlocking steps that in the whole constitute a method.[44] The social worker is concerned with the problem and the person who suffers it. Establishing a working relationship between the client and the social worker enhances the therapeutic problem-solving process. From the outset the social worker attempts to involve the client in active work on the problem. Active work involves talking about the problem, explaining possible causes and effects, expressing feelings, exploring wishes in regard to it, expressing reactions to the social worker's inputs about what seems possible, struggling with what to do next, and so on. In short, the client is helped to cope with his or her problem as far as age, mental and physical status, and current situation makes it possible.[45] To accomplish this, the social worker needs to know the client well.

Ethnic, Culturally, and Sensitive Practice

In addition to a social work practitioner having a knowledge base and skills in family, group, and individual treatment, the social worker—in getting to know the client well—must also have some appreciation of the client's ethnic, cultural, and minority status variability in order to optimize therapeutic intervention. Over the last eight years three practice frameworks have evolved to attempt to accomplish this task.

The first framework was introduced by Wynetta Devore and Elfriede G. Schlesinger in 1981 and was referred to as *Ethnic-Sensitive Social Work Practice.* Borrowing from sociological and psychological theories, ethnicity and social class issues were incorporated into social work practice assessment and intervention models. Ethnicity and social class were seen as affecting life's problems and influencing how problems would be resolved. Because of a subordinate, minority group status, social work problem solving was seen as most effective with a micro and macro approach, that is, not only attempting to help the individual and/or the family, but also intervening on the larger societal stressors (e.g., unemployment, poverty) impacting upon the client.[46]

The second framework, which could be called *Cultural Awareness Framework,* advocated by social worker James Green in his 1982 publication *Cultural Awareness in the Human Services,* emphasizes an understanding of each group's cultural background. Special attention is given to the client's definition and understanding of a problem, how *their* language labels and categorizes a problem, what culturally, community-based traditional resources have been utilized in the past dealing with such problems, and the client's cultural prescription for solving the problem.[47]

Being more specific in using a cultural awareness framework in treating black alcoholic families (and black families in general), Mary Lou Politi Ziter advises social workers to consider the following guidelines:[48]

1. Emphasis on the problem-solving process for resolving problems in both the white and black worlds.

2. Appreciation by the family and the practitioner of recurrent behaviors that were functional adaptations when they were originally made for survival and that, although no longer helpful, have been continued through intergenerational identification.

3. A dual perspective in assessment and treatment dictated by biculturalism.

4. The family's control of its recovery and the recognition by members of that control.

5. Emphasis on the larger social system that is necessitated by the victimization of black people in society.

6. Self-assessment by the family of its functioning to check potential bias by the practitioner.

A third conceptual framework developed by Doman Lum in 1986 is called *Ethnic Minority Social Work Practice.* This framework conceptualizes a systematic process-stage approach to minority practice, offers generic principles of practice universal to people of color and supports them with examples from each of the major minority groups (Asians, blacks, Hispanics, American Indians). The framework is based on the notion that there are common themes that pertain to working with people of color; yet, recognizing that each of the major minority groups has its own unique cultural history, socioeconomic problems, and treatment approaches. Lum refers to this emphasis as *cultural commonality* and *cultural specificity*.[49]

Lum defines minority social work practice as:

> . . . the art and science of developing a helping relationship with an individual, family, group, and/or community whose distinctive physical/cultural characteristics and discriminatory experiences require approaches that are sensitive to ethnic and cultural environments. Social work practice relies on a person-to-person human relationship based on personality qualities of warmth, genuineness, and empathy. At the same time, it draws on relevant minority theory from the social sciences that are applicable to social work. The target groups for helping with social problems are minority individuals, families, groups, and communities. But rather than treating people of color as separate entities of concern, social workers need to see ethnic minorities as individuals in collective associations: entities in family and community cohorts. Each minority population has color, language, and behavioral characteristics that distinguish it as a unique group in a multiracial society. Racism, prejudice, and discrimination are often part of the problem complex affecting the minority client. As a result, practice approaches must address the interaction of problems which arise from these ethnic social themes.[50]

The reader can begin to appreciate that not only is there a significant volume of individual, family, and group treatment knowledge that the social worker must learn, but he or she must also be able to integrate this information with ethnic, cultural, and socioeconomic status factors. Chapter 11 of the text, *Social Work with Special Populations*, will go into more depth as it concerns these issues.

Knowledge About a Specific Client

Becoming increasingly specific, the social worker now needs to know something about the delinquent girl assigned to his caseload. The following admissions and intake evaluation report used as an example (with names, dates, and places disguised) is a fairly typical one written by the intake probation officer. The social worker needs this report prior to the first contact with the new probationer to be adequately prepared to provide competent services. The first contact with the social worker does not necessarily signify the time when treatment begins. Actually, treatment may begin at the point of intake, when the agency, through its intake worker, is attempting to establish a cooperative, positive working relationship with the client, to induct the client into the role of "clienthood," and to provide helping interventions appropriate to the intake situation.[51]

LA LLORONA SCHOOL FOR GIRLS
ADMISSIONS AND INTAKE EVALUATION REPORT

Name: Josie Chavez
Age: 15

Josie is a very attractive fifteen-year-old Mexican American, Roman Catholic girl. She is very articulate and is well respected by her peers. She seems to be exceptionally bright and quite manipulative.

The Delinquency

The problem behavior includes: being beyond the control of her parents, truancy, battery, leaving home without permission, runaways, and inhaling glue. She is a ward of the court.

Family Constellation

The family includes the father, age 37; her mother, age 36; a half-sister, age 18; and six full brothers and sisters, ages 13, 12, 11, 10, 7, and 5. Josie is the oldest of the children, and she feels that she is the only child who has "messed up," and said that the others are all doing well. However, the half-sister has been known to the Probation Department for being a runaway and for burglary. When this information was brought to the attention of Josie, she stated that it was such a long time ago and that her half-sister was only 12.

The family lives in a small, crowded, rented home in a poor white community. The father is presently employed as a roofer earning between $200 and $225 per week, of which $250 goes to rent per month. The parents are struggling to keep the family together on his income, and the mother has tried to supplement this income by working. She has not worked in quite some time.

Josie's father was born in California, and her mother in Texas. The half-sister was born out of wedlock, and although Josie's parents have lived together seventeen years, they were married five years ago in Mexico.

The union has been stormy. There have been separations but never for long. Josie suggests that her mother and father are very dependent on each other and have a need to get together again. The mother claims that the trouble is caused by the father's drinking problem.

Last year Josie's mother was having trouble with the father and the girls, so she took the children to Texas. The girls gave her no trouble there, and they seemed happy. They supported themselves, picking potatoes and grapes. They would have liked to remain in Texas, except that they ran out of money. As a result Josie's parents came to Venice to look for work. It was then that the father obtained employment as a roofer through an old friend. The children, in the meanwhile, were in Texas, living with Josie's paternal aunt. The aunt had six children of her own, but Josie liked living there. She feels that her aunt is very much like her and looks like her father. Her cousins did very little in the house, and it was her sisters who did most of the work. When Josie's parents came to pick up the children to take them back to Venice, Josie ran away because she wanted to stay in Texas, and she likes her aunt, who lets her do as she pleases. However, Josie stated that she wanted to go to a fair with some friends, and the friends left her at a park, where she had an appointment to meet a boy friend. She stated that they did nothing but talk and walk around, and then he went home, and she remained in the park. Then she discovered that it was very late, and she was afraid to go home. She fell asleep in the park and then turned herself in to the police. The case was then transferred to the Juvenile Court in Venice. Josie was never happy at home, and she hated school. She didn't like being disciplined by her parents, wouldn't listen to them, annoyed the other family members, and didn't get along with them. Her mother states that Josie could not understand the tremendous financial problems of the family and once became very angry when her mother couldn't buy her gym clothes and on another occasion, when she had a toothache and her mother could not afford to take her to the dentist right away.

Josie's parents state that they want her home, but they feel that they cannot control Josie at home. The father vacillates in his feelings about Josie. They are very confused about the reasons behind Josie's runaways and glue-sniffing and are very unsure of their methods of handling Josie—which alternate between extreme scoldings and sometimes physical punishment and real overprotectiveness. They seem anxious for counseling and appear to be cooperative. They do not want Josie placed with relatives. Josie stated that she likes her grandfather and that he separated from her grandmother when her mother was about fifteen and since has had about five wives. She is quite fond of some of them and very fond of his present wife. She likes this maternal grandfather and says that her maternal grandmother is very much like her own mother. She stated that she hates her grandmother because she makes remarks about her being like her father. Josie stated that she liked school in Texas, even though the school put her back a year because of technicalities related to the transfer.

Court Contact and Some Background on Problem Behavior

Josie first came to the attention of the Juvenile Court two years ago when she was placed under court supervision for battery. She had come to "get" a girl at school, and scratched the registrar, who tried to take her to the office. The probation files show that Josie had been in frequent fights in school and was often truant. While on probation she was again arrested by the police for a second battery. She was counseled and released. Three months later Josie ran away from home and stayed away for nine days. She was to appear in court a week later but her mother had moved all the children to Texas. The father appeared in court, however, and the matter was dismissed. The school reported, on this occasion, that Josie could not stand living in her home where there was so much fighting and noise. Josie's behavior at school had deteriorated, and she showed increasing lack of motivation and was often absent. She remarked that her mother and father were having terrible trouble with each other at home. Her next contact with the law was ten months later when she again ran away from her paternal aunt's home where she was staying. She stated that she was afraid to go home because her parents would not understand why she was out so late and so she turned herself in to the police. She appeared in the Texas Juvenile Court a month later and was declared a ward of the court under Section 601, and the matter was ordered transferred to Venice County (discussed above).

Josie was then released to her parents pending placement. However, Josie ran away again from her home a month later and stayed away until apprehended by her parents a week later at a cousin's home. Josie was found in an intoxicated condition along with five or six other girls, all of whom were quite drunk. The smell on the girls was not of liquor, but of glue. Josie explained that she was late for school in the morning, so she decided not to go and ran away. She had 90 cents in her pocket and decided to visit her friends in a nearby community, and because she wasn't happy at home, she decided to remain away "for good." Josie was detained in Juvenile Hall. At the court hearing a week later, the transfer of wardship from Texas was accepted by Venice County, and an additional petition was filed by the police because of the glue-sniffing, and suitable placement and a clinical study were ordered.

Clinical

Josie was seen by the psychologist, and the report states that she worked fairly well on the tests but seemed quite anxious, showed lack of controls, and although she functioned within the dull-normal range of intelligence (Beta IQ 88), her true potential is well within the bright-normal range and probably as high as superior. Essentially, she is an unhappy, depressed, immature, hedonistic youngster, whose sexual and self-identity are confused. She sees herself as bad, worthless, and guilty, and relatively impotent in terms of succeeding at anything in the world. The diagnostic impression: antisocial personality in formation.

The report states that she needs a highly structured, limit-setting situation in which she can begin to develop controls and psychotherapy to help her work through her deep feelings of rejection and hostility. Adequate stable female and male identification models are essential to her further development, particularly if her delinquent-like orientation is to be changed. She desperately needs socially acceptable success experiences (academics, peer group activities, etc.) if she is to internalize healthy values. Her personality and intellectual potentials are very rich but must be tapped before she solidifies an antisocial character structure.

Cottage Report

The cottage report describes Josie as being generally quiet and cooperative. She follows instructions, although she is occasionally slow in doing so. She is constantly being called on "too close" physical contact with other girls. When questioned, Josie was very vague and maintained that she is not involved in "chic-vot" (homosexual behavior). When confronted with staff's opinion that she was, she did not become hostile but merely denied it. When specific instances were mentioned, she said she was perhaps too much of a close friend and that she was by habit an affectionate person. She said she might consider curbing her physical contacting but that this was her "pride and joy." Josie is generally polite to staff, although she reacts violently on being called on physical contacting, expressing this by dirty looks and under-the-breath remarks. She admits she is very distrusting of staff but gives no reasons for this. She usually becomes very nervous when talking to staff. Josie appears to enjoy being seductive with everyone. She complies with instructions and appears to want people to think well of her, but she excuses her inappropriate behavior through rationalizations.

School Report

Josie is in the B–8 with academic deficiencies. She will complete the A–8 in summer school and enter the ninth grade in September. Her cumulative record indicates that she has always been an underachiever. The school report for Josie is generally negative at this point. Her behavior ranges from excessive talking, open hostility, and writing on desks to showing open dislike for conformers or responsive students. Josie's best class is physical education, where she is earning a B. In her other classes, she is doing just enough to get by. She has been observed to sit with her back to the teacher, and, thus far, she has not really been reported to have any special interests in school. She gets along well with "acting-out" peers but can be easily irritated by the conformers. Josie plans to complete high school only. She is interested in nursing as a vocation.

Medical Report

The physician requested that a thorough urological checkup be made. At age 8 Josie had suffered severe kidney infection that required hospitalization. There have been recurrences of this problem. Josie also suffers from severe menstrual cramps and has blacked out on occasion.

Intake Evaluation and Treatment Recommendation

At the intake evaluation Josie appeared guarded, aloof, and evasive. As usual, her dress was exceptionally neat and her skirt pleated. She had taken pains to arrange her hair very neatly. Josie warmed up momentarily upon hearing herself described as a very beautiful child. She appeared to respond better whenever she was gently wheedled into dribbling out the information as she saw it. Her sum total seemed the same, but it was a matter of how the conclusions were reached. Josie disagreed with many of the statements that appeared in her court report.

The majority of the staff felt that the prognosis for Josie was poor. Josie's intake probation officer felt that Josie was "workable" through peer-group pressure. Mrs. Garcia, a staff person who had worked very closely with Mexicans in Mexico for eleven years, felt that Josie was innately very Mexican and could be worked with on a warm one-to-one basis and especially through peer pressure. She suggested that Josie be assigned to Mr. Lopez, a social worker on the staff, who was of similar ethnic background. Because of this ethnic factor it was felt that Mr. Lopez would have an advantage in hastening a therapeutic working relationship with Josie and at the same time provide her with a consistent, warm, parental-authority figure that she desperately needed. The staff agreed and assigned the case to Mr. Lopez.

Knowledge about a Specific Contact

The social worker, Mr. Lopez, carefully studied Josie's file and was prepared for their first meeting, sometimes referred to as the *initial interview*. From knowledge obtained through literature and practice, he knew the first interview was very important in establishing a beginning working relationship with the client. He knew girls like Josie harbored much anger toward authority figures, especially men, and frequently tried to challenge, manipulate, and test adults to see if they could make them lose their temper. Success in this regard would confirm their feelings that adults could not be trusted, which, in turn, would create more anxiety. Josie's history revealed assaultive behavior (fight) as well as running-away (flight) behavior. Mr. Lopez's knowledge of therapeutic skills would take these factors into account in order to provide Josie the opportunity to establish a relationship. He set aside a period of time ranging from fifteen minutes to one hour for Josie, the length of the session depending upon the amount of anxiety, anger, or emotional needs Josie would express during the interview. Mr. Lopez called Josie's cottage and asked that she be sent over to visit him. The following is the acutal interview (names disguised) as reported by Mr. Lopez:

> Josie knocked on the door and I asked her to come into my office. She avoided looking at me and plopped herself into a chair by my desk. After a few moments of silence, she glared at me.
>
> "I'm Mr. Lopez, your new probation officer."
>
> "I know," she said, "you're a 'long-term' probation officer and keep your girls here a long time."
>
> "In part that might be true," I said. "Sometimes the girls are ready to go home in five or six months, and some are not ready until thirteen or fourteen months. It depends on the girl and her family."
>
> "Well, I don't want to see my parents. I *hate* them! They're always fighting."
>
> I didn't say anything as I felt she was trying to see how I would react to her not wanting to see her parents. Furthermore, it would have been premature for me to enter into this sensitive area without the necessary foundation of a good relationship with Josie. After another moment of silence, Josie became anxious and said:
>
> "Just *how* long do I have to stay in this fucking place?"

"I don't know, Josie. A lot depends on how hard you try to help yourself."

"What do you mean? Just be a kiss-ass in school and do everything *you* tell me?"

"No. For one thing, I noticed that you were very angry at your parents. At some point, when *you* think you are ready, *we'll* invite them for a conference to see what is going on between you and your parents."

"I never want to see them again!" Josie screamed.

She began to get angrier and glared at me. She grabbed an ashtray and said:

"I'm going to throw this at you, you bastard!"

I calmly told her that if she would strike me, she would be hurting me and herself because she would be in even more trouble and she would probably be placed in a more confining institution—the state school. In a gentle, supportive manner, I then handed her a box of Kleenex and told her to throw it at the door. She put down the ashtray and hurled the box at the door very hard. She left her seat and picked it up again and threw it against the door several times while cussing. Tears began to run down her cheeks. She sat down sobbing with her face in her hands. I got another box of Kleenex from my desk and leaned over and offered her some Kleenex to blow her nose. It was a tangible gesture of help.

"Josie," I said, in a soft empathetic voice, "I *know* this is very painful for you. But I think you've made a *great* start."

She looked at me rather puzzled and asked sarcastically why I thought it was a "*great* start." I told her that she had shown judgment and control by not hurting me or herself and that this gave me a lot of confidence in her emotional strength.

"It proved to me that when you want to, you can make the right decisions!"

She seemed more controlled, pensive, and had stopped crying.

"Can I go now?" she asked.

I said she could leave if she wanted to. She stood up and as she was walking out she asked:

"When can I see you again?"

"Tomorrow, or the next day," I said, "or next week, or the week after that. Whenever you say, as long as it's never more than an hour a day. In other words, let's work *together* on these things whenever *you* feel you want to."

"Can I see you tomorrow?"

"Yes, at 11:00 A.M."

"Goodbye 'Long Term,'" she said, smiling as she walked toward her cottage.

This was a brief, but very intense, powerful interview. It was an *initial interview* with a purpose—establishing a beginning relationship with an angry adolescent female probationer. A knowledge base from numerous sources prepared the social worker for that one interview. Knowledge alone, without the *skill*, however, would have accomplished little. Mr. Lopez is a skilled social worker whose practice is guided by a solid knowledge base.

CONCLUDING COMMENT

The effective social worker must engage in knowledge-guided practice. He or she must be well versed in subjects related to helping people interact with the environment. The social worker's knowledge base includes knowledge of self, of the profession, of practice intervention modalities, and of the behavior of individuals, groups, the community, and society. It seems impossible for a social worker to master all the knowledge that can apply to social work practice. Because of this seeming impossibility, a conceptual framework was developed to demonstrate how the knowledge a social worker needs can be reduced to a manageable level. The paradigm highlights a guideline reflecting breadth and depth and ranging from the general to the specific. A case example was applied to a specific practice setting in a specific agency with a specific client in a specific initial interview.

SUGGESTED READINGS

Baer, Betty L., and Federico, Ronald. *Educating the Baccalaureate Social Worker* Vol. I. Boston: Ballinger, 1978, pp. 186–223.

Bartlett, Harriett. *The Common Base of Social Work Practice.* New York: National Association of Social Workers, 1970.

Bartlett, Harriett. "The Place and Use of Knowledge in Social Work Practice." *Social Work* 9 (July 1964): 36–46.

Burns, Mary E. "Paths to Knowledge: Some Prospects and Problems." *Journal of Education for Social Work* 1 (Spring 1965): 13–17.

Goldstein, Eda G. "Knowledge Base of Clinical Social Work." *Social Work* 25 (May 1980): 173–177.

Gordon, William E. "Knowledge and Value: Their Distinction and Relationship in Clarifying Social Work Practice." *Social Work* 10 (July 1965): 32–39.

Green, James W. *Cultural Awareness in the Human Services.* Englewood Cliffs, N.J.: Prentice-Hall, 1982.

Kadushin, Alfred. "The Knowledge Base of Social Work." *Issues in American Social Work*, edited by Alfred J. Kahn. New York: Columbia University Press, 1959, pp. 39–79.

Kahn, Alfred J. "The Nature of Social Work Knowledge," *New Directions in Social Work*, edited by Cora Kasius. New York: Harper, 1954, pp. 194–214.

Lum, Doman. *Social Work Practice and People of Color.* Monterey, Calif.: Brooks/Cole Publishing Co., 1986, p. 66.

Main, Marjorie White. "Restructuring Social Work Education: Knowledge, Curriculum, Instruction." *Journal of Education for Social Work* 7 (Spring 1971): 31–38.

National Association of Social Workers. *Building Social Work Knowledge: Report of a Conference.* New York: The Association, 1964.

Pollack, Otto. "Contributions of Sociological and Psychological Theory to Casework Practice." *Journal of Education for Social Work* 4 (Spring 1968): 49–54.

Taber, Merlin, and Shapiro, Iris. "Social Work and Its Knowledge Base: A Content Analysis of the Periodical Literature." *Social Work* 10 (October 1965): 100–106.

Warren, Roland L. "Application of Social Science Knowledge to the Community Organization Field." *Journal of Education for Social Work* 3 (Spring 1967): 60–72.

Willer, Judith. *The Social Determination of Knowledge.* Englewood Cliffs, N.J.: Prentice-Hall, 1971.

ENDNOTES

1. Harriett M. Bartlett, "Toward Clarification and Improvement of Social Work Practice," *Social Work* 3 (April 1958): 5–7.
2. *Webster's Third New International Dictionary* (Springfield, Mass.: G. & C. Merriam, 1966), p. 1252.
3. William E. Gordon, "Toward a Social Work Frame of Reference," *Journal of Education for Social Work* 1 (Fall 1965): 23.
4. Harriett M. Bartlett, "The Place and Use of Knowledge in Social Work Practice," *Social Work* 9 (July 1964): 36.
5. Alfred J. Kahn, "The Nature of Social Work Knowledge," in Cora Kasius, ed., *New Directions in Social Work* (New York: Harper, 1954), p. 195.
6. Harry L. Lurie, ed., *Encyclopedia of Social Work,* 15th issue (New York: National Association of Social Workers, 1965), p. 757.
7. Mary E. Richmond, *Social Diagnosis* (New York: Free Press, 1965), pp. 375–377.
8. Ibid., p. 73.
9. Robert Morris, ed., *Encyclopedia of Social Work,* 16th issue (New York: National Association of Social Workers, 1971), p. 752. For further information, see also *The Milford Conference Reports: Social Casework, Generic and Specific* (New York: American Association of Social Workers, 1929).
10. Kahn, "Social Work Knowledge," p. 196.
11. Ibid. For further information, see also *American Association of Schools of Social Work, Recommendations and Report of the Work of the Curriculum Committee January 1943–January 1944* (New York: The Association, 1944).
12. Walter A. Friedlander, *Introduction to Social Welfare* (New York: Prentice-Hall, 1955), p. 626.
13. Kahn, "Social Work Knowledge," p. 197.
14. Copyright © 1962, National Association of Social Workers, Inc. Reprinted with permission from Harriett M. Bartlett, "Toward Clarification and Improvement of Social Work Practice," *Social Work* 3 (April 1958): 3–9. See also William E. Gordon, "A Critique of the Working Definition," *Social Work* 7 (October 1962): 3–13.
15. Bartlett, "Clarification of Social Work Practice," pp. 6–7.
16. Ibid.
17. Werner W. Boehm, "The Nature of Social Work," *Social Work* 3 (April 1958): 11.
18. Alfred Kadushin, "The Knowledge Base of Social Work," in Alfred J. Kahn, ed., *Issues in American Social Work* (New York: Columbia University Press, 1959), p. 39.
19. Ibid., p. 42.
20. Ibid.
21. Ibid., p. 43.
22. *Building Social Work Knowledge, Report of a Conference* (New York: National Association of Social Workers, 1964), p. vi.
23. Ibid., p. 111.
24. Ibid., p. 114.
25. Merlin Taber and Iris Shapiro, "Social Work and Its Knowledge Base: A Content Analysis of the Periodical Literature," *Social Work* 10 (October 1965): 106.
26. Mary Burns, "Paths to Knowledge: Some Prospects and Problems," *Journal of Education for Social Work* 1 (Spring 1965): 13.

27. Carol H. Meyer, *Social Work Practice: A Response to the Urban Crisis* (New York: Free Press, 1970), p. 27.
28. Kadushin, "Knowledge Base of Social Work," p. 44.
29. Harry L. Lurie, *Encyclopedia of Social Work*, pp. 280–281.
30. Sol Rubin, "Loss and Curtailment of Rights," in Leon Radzinowicz and Marvin E. Wolfgang, eds., *Crime and Justice*, Vol. 3 (New York: Basic Books, 1971), p. 25.
31. Walter C. Reckless, "A New Theory of Delinquency and Crime," in Ruth Shonle Cavan, ed., *Readings in Juvenile Delinquency* (New York: Lippincott, 1969), p. 165.
32. Richard A. Cloward and Lloyd E. Ohlin, *Delinquency and Opportunity* (Glencoe, Ill.: Free Press, 1960).
33. *DSM III-R—Diagnostic and Statistical Manual of Mental Disorders*, 3rd ed. (Washington, D.C.: American Psychiatric Association, 1987), p. 51. Reprinted with permission from the *Diagnostic and Statistical Manual of Mental Disorders*, Revised. Copyright 1987 American Psychiatric Association.
34. Ibid., pp. 53–57.
35. Ibid., pp. 344–346.
36. Max Siporin, "Marriage and Family Therapy in Social Work," *Social Casework* 61 (January 1980), pp. 11–21.
37. Francis H. Scherz, "Family Services: Family Therapy," in Robert Morris, ed., *Encyclopedia of Social Work* 16th issue, Vol. 1 (New York: National Association of Social Work, 1971), p. 402.
38. Jay Haley, "Family Therapy," in Alfred M. Freedman, Harold I. Kaplan, and Benjamin J. Sadock, eds., *Comprehensive Textbook of Psychiatry II*, 2nd ed. (Baltimore: Williams and Wilkins Co., 1975), p. 1,883.
39. Scherz, "Family Services," p. 400.
40. Haley, "Family Therapy," p. 1,883.
41. Benjamin J. Sadock, "Group Psychotherapy," *Comprehensive Textbook*, p. 1,850.
42. Ibid., p. 1,852.
48. Emanuel Tropp, "Social Group Work: The Developmental Approach," *Encyclopedia of Social Work*, p. 1,251.
44. Helen Harris Perlman, "Social Casework," in Neil Gilbert and Harry Specht, eds., *Handbook of the Social Services* (Englewood Cliffs: Prentice-Hall, 1981), pp. 434–451.
45. Ibid., p. 441.
46. Wynetta Devore, and Elfrieda G. Schlesinger, *Ethnic-Sensitive Social Work Practice* (St. Louis: C.V. Mosby Co., 1981).
47. James W. Green, *Cultural Awareness in the Human Services* (Englewood Cliffs: N.J.: Prentice-Hall, 1982).
48. Mary Lou Politi Ziter, "Culturally Sensitive Treatment of Black Alcoholic Families," *Social Work*, Vol. 32, No. 2, March–April 1987, p. 132.
49. Doman Lum, *Social Work Practice and People of Color* (Monterey, Calif.: Brooks/Cole Publishing Co., 1986), p. 66.
50. Ibid., p. 3.
51. Max Siporin, *Introduction to Social Work Practice* (New York: Macmillan, 1975), pp. 193–194.

CHAPTER 8

The Value Base
of Social Work

If clients are to be helped to resolve social problems or enhance their levels of social functioning, social workers must bring the best knowledge available to bear on the situation. Knowledge, however, must be applied within the context of a judgment about what is good, proper, just, and humane. In other words the use of knowledge must be conditioned by value considerations. A vivid illustration is the fact that through sheer knowledge the United States has built a nuclear arsenal that is capable of destroying life in all parts of the world. Because of the belief that life itself is precious, however, restraint has been used in the deployment of these weapons.

Values are the essential tools for selecting knowledge that is consistent with our beliefs about what we should be doing and how we should be doing it.[1] We could reduce the number of children on the AFDC rolls by sterilizing all recipients, but social work's value of protecting individual choice prohibits such action. We could reduce homelessness by forcing homeless people into hospitals or prisons, but that is contrary to social work's commitment to helping people develop the ability to help themselves. We could perhaps even reduce the spread of AIDS by publishing the names of known AIDS carriers who use human services, but that would violate the social worker's commitment to protecting the confidential nature of information gained in helping relationships. The social worker, then, must engage in value-guided as well as knowledge-guided practice.

THE NATURE OF VALUES

As opposed to knowledge, which explains what is, values express what ought to be. Milton Rokeach more precisely defines values as "a type of belief, centrally located in one's total belief system, about how one ought or ought not to behave, or about some end-state of existence worth or not worth attaining."[2] In short, values guide our thinking about how we should behave and what we want to accomplish.

Values, however, are much more than emotional reactions to situations or doing what feels right. Values are the fundamental criteria that lead us to thoughtful decisions. There is growing evidence that in most cases people act on the basis of their values. Lynn Kahle thoroughly reviewed the research

on the relationship between values and action and concluded that "both laboratory and survey studies have shown that values do indeed lead to commensurate behaviors."[3]

It is important to recognize that people do not always behave in a manner
consistent with their values. Values guide decisions but do not dictate choices.
People can and do make decisions contrary to their values. Such decisions
might be made when other factors are given priority ("I know that I shouldn't
have done that, but when will I ever get another chance like that?"), the
person acts on emotion ("I was just so angry I hit her without thinking"),
or when one fails to adequately think through and understand the value
issues in a situation ("It just didn't occur to me that my quitting school would
make my parents think that they have failed").

At other times a person may be forced to choose among values that are in
conflict with one another. Who can avoid wrestling with a *value conflict* when
confronted by a person on the street asking for a dollar to buy something to
eat? We may value responding to people in need, but we may equally value
encouraging people to use the organized system for receiving financial assistance that does not put the person into the degrading position of panhan-
dling. The resultant decision represents a *value choice*.

Each person values a variety of things in life. Differences in the strength
with which one holds any particular value and the priority a particular value
will have among the whole constellation of that person's values, i.e., the
person's *value system*, is a part of what makes individuals unique. For example,
most people value having sufficient income to live comfortably, giving service
to others in need, and feeling secure in their relationships with loved ones.
For some, generating income is the driving force in their lives. For others,
giving service or maintaining relationships dominates their value system. Still
others will attempt to maintain some balance among these values.

Dealing with values is particularly difficult for at least three reasons. First,
values are such a central part of each person's thought processes that we
often are not consciously aware of them and therefore are unable to identify
their influence on our decisions. The social worker should constantly be alert
to values in practice situations as these values may subtly influence the
thoughts, feelings, attitudes, and behaviors of both the clients and the social
worker.

Second, addressing values in the abstract may be quite different from approaching them in a real-life situation. Having the ability to identify and
resolve value conflicts is an important skill for every person. We may feel
that we have a pretty good understanding of the priorities in our own value
system only to find that when applied to the realities of a series of actual
events, these priorities are altered. Similarly, the social worker must recognize
that clients may not act on the basis of value choices made in an interview
when they are confronted with the unique situations that arise in the course
of their daily lives.

Finally, values are problematic because of their dynamic quality. Priorities
in our value system and the intensity with which we may hold a particular

value can change over time. When we do not accomplish what we value, we can change our values or change our behaviors. In fact, we do both. Thus, various events, experiences, and even new information can lead us to adapt our system of values to more closely fit our reality.

THE PLACE OF VALUES IN SOCIAL WORK

Helping people to be clear about their individual values, i.e., *values clarification*,[4] and facilitating their understanding of how the particular set of values they hold influences their goals and decisions, is an important aspect of social work practice. At times clients also must be assisted in recognizing and understanding the values of others. Taking into consideration the values of family members, friends, employers, teachers, or others in that person's environment may be prerequisite to making appropriate and workable decisions. The matter becomes more complicated when social work practice involves more than one person, as it is likely that each will have a somewhat different value system. In that case the social worker may need to help resolve issues that stem from differences in values.

Further, the social worker must be concerned with his or her own values and control for their inappropriate intrusion into practice situations. Value choices that may be viable personally for the social worker may not coincide with the needs, wants, priorities, or realities the client experiences. Ultimately, the client must live with the decisions that are made and they should be consistent with his or her own value system—not the value system of the social worker.

People are attracted to particular helping professions because they perceive that the work they do will be consistent with their personal values, and, therefore, the job will be satisfying. The way a profession views its role in society, the client groups it serves, the knowledge it selects as the basis for its practice, its requirements for ethical practice behavior, etcetera are all influenced by the profession's values. It is evident that a profession's values exert a significant influence on professional practice and the person considering a career in any helping profession should carefully examine the value base of this profession.

Agency values and the values of the larger society also affect social work practice. Since professions receive their sanction from the society in general and their communities in particular, professionals are constrained from too much departure from the values held by the general public. The result is an inherent conservatism or pressure toward maintenance of the existing social structure. Charles Frankel notes that "professional knowledge cannot be deployed and a professional ethic cannot be successfully followed unless certain basic institutions of our society—schools, courts, hospitals, welfare arrangements—are reasonably stable and reasonably insulated from the grosser pressures of the political environment. In these respects, too, a professional code carries an implicit commitment to the *status quo*."[5]

With social work practice focused at the interface between person and environment, the social worker must be aware of several sets of values at the same time. This awareness should center on the client's values, but the social worker must also attend to the values of the social work profession, the employing agency, the community, and the larger society. Frankel identifies the complexity the social worker faces when attempting to be sensitive to the several sets of values that may influence a practice situation:

> Undoubtedly, the tension between community sentiments and professional values is particularly acute in social work. The nature of the profession itself is such that the choices the professional worker must make between his professional values and the broader social values are more difficult and ambiguous. Social work's purpose is to guide and reinforce people's efforts to find and use their own powers. Unlike law or medicine, the social worker does not do the job for his client. In the end, the purpose is that the client should do the job. Thus, as a professional, the social worker has to make a special effort to enter into the perspectives and values of the nonprofessional.[6]

It is no wonder that social work has perhaps devoted more attention to values than has any other helping profession. Harold McPheeters and Robert Ryan criticize other human service professions for having given limited attention to the whole matter of values and attitudes, on the assumption that they are "value-free" professions—when, in fact, every behavior is influenced by some value orientation.[7] Although social work has not developed a sufficiently clear and adequately tested statement of its core values, it has been consistent throughout its development that values constitute a central dimension of practice. As early as the 1920s, for example, a series of meetings (commonly referred to as the Milford Conference) were held in an effort to identify the commonalities in social work practice. The report of these meetings concluded that a philosophy of practice is required for the social worker and that there must be continued effort to identify and clarify the important value issues. The summary of the thinking of the Milford Conference participants was the following:

> The social caseworker has need of a thought-out system of social values not only to clarify his general purpose and orient him in relation to theories of social progress, but also to guide him in every professional contact. Such practical questions as the following illustrate the need of a philosophy:
>
> What are the client's rights as an individual?
>
> Under what circumstances is it good to try to maintain a family as such unbroken?
>
> Under what circumstances is it good to try to break up a family? (i.e., What values are involved for individual, group, society?)
>
> Is coercion justified in any case?

How far and when is individual dependency a public responsibility, how far and when a private responsibility?

How far should social environment be altered in the interest of the sick or unadjusted person?

In what circumstances, if any, should the client's confidence be violated by the social case worker?[8]

SOCIAL VALUES IN AMERICAN SOCIETY

Values differ from needs. The latter refers to the basic biological or psychological urges of people, while values reflect what people want to get out of life and how this should be accomplished. Chapter 4, "Understanding the Social Welfare Institution," identified basic human needs, i.e., survival, safety, belongingness, esteem, and self-actualization and indicated that social institutions are fostered to help people meet these needs. The choice of what needs a society will attempt to meet depends on what it values. Thus, as a society's values change through time, so will the social needs it attempts to meet.

Shepard Clough suggests the single most uniform characteristic of all cultures is that they have basic values about what the "people want to get out of life, such as entry into heaven, freedom from want, the achieving of some masterpiece, control over their physical environment, and harmony in relation with their fellow beings."[9] He notes that the most predominant feature of Western society is the central place of the individual, i.e., the society exists to help individuals lead satisfying and productive lives. The individual is the "masterpiece" of Western culture.

Like other parts of Western culture the values that guide choices in U.S. society also center on the individual. The dominant social values in the United States have their roots in at least four different sources, all of which are concerned with the responsibilities of the individual toward self and society and/or the society's responsibility to the individual.

1. The Judeo–Christian doctrine with its concept of the integral worth of humans and their responsibilities for their neighbors;

2. The democratic ideals that emphasize the equality of all people and a person's right to "life, liberty, and the pursuit of happiness";

3. The Puritan ethic, which says that character is all, circumstances nothing, that the moral person is the one who works and is independent, and that pleasure is sinful;

4. The tenets of Social Darwinism, which emphasize that the fittest survive and the weak perish in a natural evolutionary process that produces the strong individual and society.[10]

It is evident that much of the disagreement in the United States over the provision of human services results from value conflicts inherent in the U.S. public's value system. Naomi Brill points out that:

> Even the casual reader will see that a dichotomy exists within this value system. We hold that all men are equal, but he who does not work is less equal. . . . We hold that the individual life has worth, but that only the fit should survive. We believe that we are responsible for each other, but he who is dependent upon another for his living is of lesser worth.[11]

In carrying out the commitments of the social welfare institution to respond to human needs, the social worker becomes an intermediary between people in need and society's value judgments about what needs are to be met. As one cynic phrased it, the social worker stands "between the demanding recipient and the grudging donor." Therefore, the social worker must be particularly knowledgeable about the values that are dominant in U.S. society.

What is the constellation of values held by the U.S. population? Recognizing the importance of values, one is surprised that relatively little solid research has been conducted to determine the dominant values held by the U.S. public. In 1983 a study was published that begins to remedy this problem. The study, *Social Values and Social Change: Adaptation to Life in America*,[12] drew on interviews with a carefully selected sample of noninstitutionalized adults selected from throughout the forty-eight contiguous states. Building on prior efforts of Milton Rokeach and others[13] in isolating the dominant values in U.S. society, this study asked 2,264 respondents to judge which was the *most important* among eight fundamental values commonly held by the people of the United States. Recognizing the limitations of any attempt to represent the viewpoint of a nation based on a small sample of its population, one nevertheless finds it instructive to note the percentage of respondents who rated the following values as most important in their lives.

21.1%   *Self-respect:* looking within oneself for satisfaction in regard to achieving goals or taking pride in having done the "honorable or just thing."

20.6%   *Security:* achieving a sense of freedom from danger or risk, i.e., achieving economic and existential security or feeling personally safe about being able to live comfortably in the future.

16.2%   *Warm relationships with others;* appreciating the significance of friendships or companionship in one's life. This value reflects more than just sociability; it also represents the importance of establishing and maintaining nurturing relationships.

11.4%   *Sense of accomplishment:* believing that the activities one sets out to complete are successfully done. The emphasis in this value is on the person feeling successful.

9.6%   *Self-fulfillment:* feeling that the accomplishments in one's life are personally satisfying or rewarding—that one's efforts are worthwhile. The person selecting this value feels good about what he or she has done or is doing.

8.8%   *Being well respected:* having others admire the manner in which a person acts or the status one has achieved. The well respected person is held in high esteem and looked up to by others.

7.9%   *Sense of belonging:* satisfying the need to be personally accepted by others and become a meaningful part of a group or collection of people. The person gains support from the group.

4.5%   *Fun-enjoyment-excitment:* wishing for an exciting, stimulating, active life that includes enjoyable and pleasurable activities.

Note that the preceding descriptions of the individual values were not reported in the study. The authors of this book derived these statements from the information reported in the study design and analysis of responses. The statements are included to give the reader a general understanding of intended meaning of each value item.

When one is taking a global view of the most important values of the U.S. public, it is evident that the individual or personal orientation of Western culture also dominates the fundamental attitudes about what their goals in life should be and how these goals should be accomplished. The two values viewed as most important by the people interviewed in this study reflect the desire to feel good about oneself and feel personally secure for the future. These values reflect the self-oriented priorities in U.S. society. The interpersonal-oriented values, i.e., warm relationships, being well respected, and having a sense of belonging, were rated as most important by less than one-third of the respondents.

Although social workers provide a number of services that can help people accomplish self-oriented goals and are responsible for the delivery of social provisions that help people attain at least minimal levels of security, social workers' primary work centers on interpersonal behaviors. The value system of the U.S. public evident from these data perhaps helps one to understand the low priority given to many human service programs.

DOMINANT VALUES IN SELECTED POPULATION GROUPS

Since people vary in the values they consider most important, it is useful to identify value differences associated with various population groups—particularly those that are frequently the recipients of human services. Drawn from data reported in *Social Values and Social Change*, the value responses of selected population groups are summarized. The subtitle of the study, "Adaptation to Life in America," reveals an important point to recognize when one is drawing conclusions from these data. People adapt their value preferences to fit the reality of their lives. They do not place high priority on values they do not think they can realize.[14]

To highlight areas where a particular segment of the population reflected somewhat different value preferences from the total group of respondents, Tables 8–1 through 8–5 were prepared. When a particular category of respondent differed from the total by 15 percent or more (or 20 percent or more in the case of age) a plus (+) or minus (−) was recorded on the table indicating whether the respondents in that category were substantially above or below the norm.

Gender

As Table 8-1 indicates, men and women were similar in their selection of values regarding self-respect, security, self-fulfillment, and being respected. The differences confirmed the popular viewpoint that men tend to be more self-oriented and women more other-oriented. Women substantially exceed men in selecting warm relationships with others (18.5 percent to 13.1 percent) and sense of belonging (9.6 percent to 5.6 percent) as the most important values. Men, on the other hand, identified a sense of accomplishment or success (14.3 percent to 9.2 percent) and fun/enjoyment/excitement (6.9 percent to 2.7 percent) as the dominant value in their lives more frequently than women. Using warm relationships and sense of belonging to reflect interpersonal values, women exceed men 28.1 percent to 18.7 percent. At the same time more than twice as many men as women selected the self-oriented values of accomplishment and fun/enjoyment/excitement (23.9 percent to 11.9 percent).[15]

The influence that having a family has on a person's outlook is revealed by examining the responses of those respondents who had children. Men with children tended to differ from those without children in several areas. Those with children placed the values of self-respect and security considerably

TABLE 8–1 PRIMARY VALUES (15 PERCENT OR MORE FROM AVERAGE) BY GENDER

	MALE	FEMALE
Self-respect		
Security		
Warm relationships with others	−	+
Sense of accomplishment	+	−
Self-fulfillment		
Being well respected		
Sense of belonging	−	+
Fun/excitement/enjoyment	+	−

higher than those without, while the latter group emphasized warm relationships with friends, self-fulfillment, and fun/enjoyment/excitement to a much greater degree. Similarly, women with children tended to value self-respect, security, and being well respected more than their counterparts who did not have children. Women without children gave much greater emphasis to the values of accomplishment, self-fulfillment, and fun/enjoyment/excitement than those who did have children.[16]

Age

The data suggest there is considerable similarity among men and women in various age groups. Table 8–2 represents the comparative data on three selected age groups: the youngest, oldest, and one middle-age group. When compared to the norms of all persons of their sex, the middle-age women differed from the men in that age group only in placing higher value on security and lower value on accomplishment. Older women were also less inclined to look for fun/enjoyment/excitement from life. Older men differed from older women by placing less value on warm relationships and having a sense of belonging but placed greater value on being respected. With these six exceptions, men and women in the three selected age groups deviated from overall average of their genders in exactly the same way.

   Examination of the data for all age groups reveals that until a person reaches the late-20s or early-30s, self-respect and security do not take the dominant place in one's value system that they do later on. For both young adult males and females, warm relationships with friends, a sense of accomplishment, self-fulfillment, and fun/enjoyment/excitement are the dominant values. The substantial differences in this young adult group from the total

TABLE 8–2 PRIMARY VALUES (20 PERCENT OR MORE FROM AVERAGE) BY AGE AND GENDER

	YOUNG ADULT (21–24)	MIDDLE AGE (45–49)	OLDER (70 & OVER)
Self-respect	−	+	
Security	−	+ (f)	+
Warm relationships with others	+		− (m)
Sense of accomplishment	+	− (f)	−
Self-fulfillment	+	−	−
Being well respected	−		+ (m)
Sense of belonging	−		− (m)
Fun/excitement/enjoyment	+	−	− (f)

Note: the designation for females (f) and males (m) identifies values where only persons of that gender deviated from the norm.

population is seen in the fact that they differ substantially from the norm on every value. To reflect the extent of this difference, it is instructive to analyze the two most dominant values: self-respect and security. For the sample as a whole, 41.3 percent of all women and 42.2 percent of the men selected one of these values as the most important. For the young adults, only 23.5 percent of the women and 20.6 percent of the men chose one of these as most important in their lives.[17]

For the 45–49 age group the importance of warm relationships with friends and companions, as well as giving priority to fun/enjoyment/excitement, was substantially lower than for the young adults. Achieving self-respect and security (for women) were much more prominent in their value systems. Achieving self-respect was identified as the most important value for 31.5 percent of the men and 32.6 percent of the women in this age group compared to 21.7 percent and 20.6 percent, respectively, for the total population. For women in this age group achieving a sense of security was valued highly. More than one-fourth (26.1 percent) of the middle-age women identified security as their number one value, while only one-fifth of all women considered this the most important.[18]

For the respondents age 70 and over, the desire for security, warm relationships with others, and being respected dominate the responses. The responses from those persons in the sample who were retired were similar. Nearly 65 percent of the retired persons in the sample listed one of these three values as most important to them.[19]

Race and Ethnicity

Some value differences existed among the white, black, and Hispanic respondents. Due to the predominance of white people in the United States and, therefore, in the sample, one would not expect that Table 8–3 would reflect areas where the white respondents were substantially different from the total sample. White and black respondents were similar in their selection of self-respect as their most important value (21.1 percent and 21.3 percent, respectively), but only 16.3 percent of the Hispanic respondents identified this as the most important value. At the same time a much higher percent of Hispanic respondents (14.3 percent) selected being respected by others than did the white (8.5 percent) or black (10.2 percent) persons who were interviewed.[20]

Perhaps the most dramatic and telling difference among any population groups in the study is in the value placed on security by minority group members. The white respondents selected this value as their first priority 18.8 percent of the time, while the black and Hispanic persons interviewed chose security as the most important value, 33.6 percent and 30.6 percent, respectively. Kahle concludes that "black and Hispanic respondents worry far more about basic security than do their white counterparts." It is also of note that black and Hispanic respondents were considerably less likely than whites to value self-fulfillment (5.3 percent and 6.1 percent compared to 10.2 percent) and a sense of belonging (4.5 percent and 4.1 percent compared to 8.5 per-

TABLE 8–3 PRIMARY VALUES (15 PERCENT OR MORE FROM AVERAGE) BY RACE AND ETHNICITY

	WHITE	BLACK	HISPANIC
Self-respect			−
Security		+	+
Warm relationships with others		−	
Sense of accomplishment			−
Self-fulfillment		−	−
Being well respected			+
Sense of belonging		−	−
Fun/excitement/enjoyment		−	

cent).[21] The effects of discrimination would appear to be reflected in these differences. Life is more insecure for blacks and Hispanics and they often do not feel that they are fully accepted into the dominant society and therefore lack a sense of belonging. Their value preferences are adapted to that reality.

Educational Level

Educational level, too, appears to affect one's value system. In Table 8–4 it is evident that persons with a grade school education are most concerned with security and being respected by others. More than 45 percent of the respondents at this level selected one of these two values as most important to them. The persons with a high school education were similar to the total group in all values except sense of belonging, which 11 percent considered the most important, compared to 6.8 percent of the grade school and 4 percent of the college graduates. The college educated respondents reflected consid-

TABLE 8–4 PRIMARY VALUES (15 PERCENT OR MORE FROM AVERAGE) BY EDUCATIONAL LEVEL

	GRADE SCHOOL	HIGH SCHOOL	COLLEGE
Self-respect			
Security	+		−
Warm relationships with others			
Sense of accomplishment	−		+
Self-fulfillment	−		+
Being well respected	+		−
Sense of belonging	−	+	−
Fun/excitement/enjoyment			+

erably less concern with security (15.0 percent), being well respected (2.9 percent), and having a sense of belonging. College educated persons exceeded the other groups in their value of a sense of accomplishment (15.7 percent), self-fulfillment (15.2 percent), and their desire for fun/enjoyment/excitement (5.7 percent).[22]

Income Level

While income is associated with gender, age, race or ethnicity, and educational level, the data from this study reflect some rather clear value differences among the low-, middle-, and upper-income groups. As Table 8–5 indicates, people at the lowest end of the income scale were much more likely to value security (26.7 percent) than those in the middle-income group selected for analysis and those in the highest-income group. They also placed substantially more emphasis on being well respected by others (16.2 percent). The respondents from the middle-income group placed greater priority on having a sense of belonging to a group. The highest-income group considered their own self-respect and experiencing a sense of accomplishment their most important values, while having warm friendships and being respected were of lesser importance.[23]

It is evident from the above data that people differ in their values and these differences are affected by one's experience in society. Depending on where one is in the life cycle, whether he or she is employed, or even if one has children, for example, the priorities among values will differ. Victims of the "isms," e.g., ageism, sexism, or racism, reflect a particularly significant difference in values from the parts of the society that do not experience this discrimination. Those most likely to experience discrimination consistently place higher value on having security in their lives. When the members of a society fail to adequately protect against their fears about the future, these groups turn to a greater degree to intrapersonal values such as gaining respect from others, belonging, and having warm relationships with friends and companions.

TABLE 8–5 PRIMARY VALUES (15 PERCENT OR MORE FROM AVERAGE) BY INCOME LEVEL

	LOWEST	MIDDLE	HIGHEST
Self-respect		−	+
Security	+		
Warm relationships with others		+	−
Sense of accomplishment	−		+
Self-fulfillment	−		
Being well respected	+		−
Sense of belonging	−		
Fun/excitement/enjoyment			

TABLE 8–6 PRIMARY VALUES OF PROFESSIONALS AND TOTAL SAMPLE

	PROFESSIONALS	TOTAL SAMPLE
Self-respect	24.9%	21.1%
Security	11.8	20.6
Warm relationships with others	17.1	16.2
Sense of accomplishment	18.4	11.4
Self-fulfillment	16.7	9.6
Being well respected	2.9	8.8
Sense of belonging	4.5	7.9
Fun/excitement/enjoyment	3.7	4.5

One final population group analyzed in Kahle's study of values is of interest to the social worker. The data make it clear that there are distinct differences in values among different groups of occupations. The professional category (see Table 8–6), which includes social work as well as other professions, valued security, being well respected, and experiencing a sense of belonging much less than did other groups. At the same time they were substantially more likely to indicate that having a sense of accomplishment and fulfillment were the things they valued most.[24] The data support the inference that professionals consider achieving personal satisfaction from their work the central feature in their experience and that status issues such as income, being respected, and sensing acceptance from a group are of lesser importance.

VALUES HELD BY SOCIAL WORKERS

We have seen that the social worker must relate to the values of both the client or client group and the society. In order to avoid imposing personal values on the client or making inappropriate judgments about a client's values, the social worker must have a clear understanding of his or her own personal values. In addition the social worker must be fully aware of, and guided by, the fundamental values of the social work profession.

What, then, are the values commonly held by social workers? The International Federation of Social Workers, an organization comprising fifty-six professional membership associations including the National Association of Social Workers (NASW), has devoted considerable effort to identifying values and ethical behaviors appropriate for all social workers. Although social work is significantly affected by the culture in which its practice occurs, the International Federation of Social Workers has been successful at transcending the cultural differences of the many nations to develop a code of ethical behavior applicable to the whole of social work practice. The preamble of that Code concisely summarizes the most fundamental values of this profession:

Social work originates from humanitarian ideals and democratic philosophy and has universal application to meet human needs arising from personal-societal interactions and to develop human potential. Professional social workers are dedicated to service for the welfare and self-realization of human beings; to the disciplined use of scientific knowledge regarding human and societal behavior; to the development of resources to meet individual, group, national and international needs and aspirations; and to the achievement of social justice.[25]

As a part of NASW's effort to establish a classification scheme for the different practice levels (see Chapter 3, "Entry to the Social Work Profession"), the committee developing this scheme found it useful to identify the basic values that are central to social work practice at any level. As a result ten values were identified in the guidelines for the classification of social work practice.[26] When this report was adopted by the Board of Directors, the following values statements became an NASW sanctioned expression of the basic U.S. social work values.

1. *Commitment to the primary importance of the individual in society.* In this value statement social work reaffirms its commitment to the most basic cultural value in Western society—the primacy of the individual. In his classic work entitled *Basic Values of Western Civilization*, Clough identifies the significance of this value choice:

> In spite of a certain amount of intracultural difference on this issue in the West, the predominant "ideal" value holds that the end of man on this earth is man. The very foundation of the credo of the West is that the chief goal of man is for him to realize ever more fully the total complex of our cultural values. The basic purpose of man in the West is neither to honor a deity or deities, nor to be the servant of any small group, nor to sacrifice the individual for the advancement of some social institution such as the national state. Ours is a humanistic view. The masterpiece of man is "better man," living in a "better society," partaking of a "fuller" life, and producing and enjoying more of what we consider to be the "finer" things of human existence.[27]

Social work accepts the position that the individual is the center of practice and that every person is of inherent worth because of his or her humanness. "The primary activity of the social worker is to help people change; it is not intended to punish or condemn. Therefore, it is necessary to accept clients as valued people simply because of their humanity and to avoid making judgments of worth based on personal or dominant societal values."[28] The social worker need not approve of what a person does but must value that person as an important member of society. Each client should be treated with dignity.[29]

Commitment to the centrality of the individual has also led social workers to recognize that each person is unique and that practice activities must be tailored to that person's or group's uniqueness. Such individualization permits the worker to determine where and how to intervene in each helping situation while, at the same time, communicating respect for the people being served.

2. *Commitment to social change to meet socially recognized needs.* Giving primacy to the individual does not minimize the commitment of the social worker to achieve social change. Rather, it suggests that the social worker recognizes that the outcome of change activities in the larger society must ultimately benefit individuals.

As discussed in Chapter 4, social work evolved as the primary profession responsible for helping society fulfill its commitment to meet the social needs of people, i.e., to operationalize the social welfare institution. The obligation of social work is not only to deliver social provisions and social services to people in need, but also value serving as instruments of social change as a means of allowing each person to realize his or her fullest potential.[30]

Social workers, then, are committed to the belief that the society has a responsibility to provide resources and services to help people avoid such problems as hunger, insufficient education, discrimination, illness without care, and inadequate housing. While social workers accept the primacy of the individual, they also hold the society responsible for meeting social needs. Social workers serve both the person and the environment in responding to social needs.

3. *Commitment to social justice and the economic, physical, and mental well-being of all in society.* The obligation of social workers is to attempt to improve the quality of all people's lives. Social workers believe that social justice must be achieved if each person is to have the opportunity to develop his or her unique potential and, therefore, make his or her maximum contribution to the society. Thus, social workers believe that each person should have the right to participate in molding the social institutions and the decision-making processes in U.S. society so that the programs, policies, and procedures are responsive to the needs and conditions of all.

Of course, when needs are competing in a diverse society and when resources are limited, choices must be made. Every person cannot have all needs met. When they are making choices, the values held by social workers emphasize the importance of responding to the needs of the most vulnerable members of the society. Typically, these vulnerable people are children, the aged, minority group members, the handicapped, women, and others who have been victims of institutionalized discrimination. Social workers are committed to assuring that social justice is achieved for these persons individually and as a population group.

4. *Respect and appreciation for individual and group differences.* Social workers recognize that there are common needs, goals, aspirations, and wants that are held by all people. In some ways we are all alike. However, social workers also recognize that in other ways each individual's life experience and capacities make him or her different from others.[31] Where some may fear differences or resist working with people who are not like themselves, social

workers value and respect uniqueness. They believe that the quality of life is enriched by different cultural patterns, different beliefs, and different forms of activity. As opposed to efforts to assimilate persons who are in some way different from the general population, social workers value a pluralistic society that can accommodate a range of beliefs, behaviors, languages, and customs.

The title of this book, *Social Work: A Profession of Many Faces*, is intended to suggest that social work not only includes people of many backgrounds performing a wide variety of human services but that social workers also provide services to people from virtually all backgrounds and walks of life. The chapters in Part Four, "Special Populations and Concerns in Social Work," elaborate on some of these differences and their impact on social work practice.

5. *Commitment to developing clients' ability to help themselves*. If clients are to change their social conditions, their actions that contributed to the conditions must ultimately change. Unlike medicine where an injection may solve a patient's problem, social change requires that the people affected become personally engaged in the change process and actively work to create the desired change. Underpinning social work practice, then, must be the social worker's belief that each person has an inherent capacity and drive that can result in desirable change.

Social workers do not view people as static or unchanging, nor is anyone assumed to be unable to engage in activities that may produce a more satisfying and rewarding life. Rather, social workers view people as adaptable. Although there are conditions that some people face that cannot be changed, the people themselves or the world around them can be helped to adapt to these conditions. For example, the terminally ill patient cannot be made well, the blind child cannot be made to see, or the severely retarded person cannot be made self-sustaining. Yet, in each case the person involved can be helped to adjust to these conditions and the person's environment can be adapted to more adequately accommodate special needs.

Within the individual's or group's capacities, the social worker places high value on helping people take responsibility for their own decisions and actions. Writing more than a quarter century ago, Isidor Chein clearly captured the essence of this value:

> [Man is viewed] as an active, responsible agent . . . a being who actively does something with regard to some of the things that happen to him; a being who, for instance, tries to increase the likelihood that some things will happen and to decrease the likelihood that other things will happen; a being who tries to generate circumstances that are compatible with the execution of his intentions; a being who will try to inject harmony where he finds disharmony or will sometimes seek to generate disharmony; a being who seeks to shape his environment rather than passively permit himself to be shaped by the latter; a being, in short, who insists on injecting himself into the casual process of the world around him. If man is said to respond to his environment, the word response is to be taken in the sense that it has an active dialogue rather than a sense of an automatic consequence.[32]

6. *Willingness to transmit knowledge and skills to others.* Since the social worker cannot change the client, perhaps the most important function performed by the social worker in helping clients accomplish the change they desire is to effectively guide the change process. A significant part of this guidance involves helping clients understand the situation they experience from both a personal perspective and the perspectives of others as well as helping them develop the skills to resolve their problems.

Effective helping avoids making clients dependent on the helpers and prepares them to address other issues that arise in their lives. Thus, it is important that social workers assist clients to identify their strengths that can be mobilized for solving the immediate problem and to help them learn how to use these strengths in solving problems that may arise in the future.

A second application of this value concerns the commitment of professionals to share knowledge with colleagues. Knowledge or skills developed by a social worker are not to be kept secret or limited to clients who work only with that social worker. Rather, the social worker is obligated to transmit this information to other social workers so that they might bring the best knowledge and skill possible to their clients.

7. *Willingness to keep personal feelings and needs separate from professional relationships.* It is important that the social worker recognize that the focus of practice must be maintained on the client—not the social worker. Because social workers care about the people they work with, it is easy to become overidentified with clients' lives or even to develop personal relationships with them. If that happens, the client loses the benefit of an objective helper, the social worker can be placed in a compromising position, and the quality of the helping process is diminished because the relationship has changed from professional to personal.

As opposed to the many personal relationships that each person has throughout life, professional relationships require that a degree of professional objectivity be maintained. If a social worker becomes too closely identified with the client, the ability to stand back from the situation and view it from a neutral position is minimized. Sheafor, Horejsi, and Horejsi identify the importance of maintaining an appropriate degree of personal distance from clients:

> By the time most clients come into contact with a professional helper, they have usually attempted to resolve the situation themselves—by either personally working through the situation or getting assistance from family, friends, or other natural helpers. Often, these helping efforts are thwarted by high levels of emotion that preclude clear understanding and response to the situation. As opposed to the natural helper, the professional adds a new dimension to the client or client group by operating with a degree of emotional neutrality.
>
> Maintaining this neutrality without appearing unconcerned or uncaring is a delicate balancing act for the social worker The worker who becomes too identified with the client's situation can lose perspective and objectivity.[33]

8. *Respect for the confidentiality of relationships with clients.* Although it is rare that the social worker can guarantee "absolute confidentiality" to a client, social work values achieving the maximum possible protection of information received in working with clients.[34] The very nature of a helping relationship suggests that there is sensitive information that must be shared between the person being helped and the helper. For example, the social worker must learn the reasons a client has been fired from a job, why a developmentally disabled patient has failed in a community group home placement, what keeps a homeless person from being able to secure resources to pay rent, why an alcoholic has not been able to stop drinking, or the reasons a couple involved in marriage counseling has not been able to solve problems without fighting, etcetera. In each case some information typically passes between client and worker that could potentially be emotionally or economically damaging if it is inappropriately revealed to other parties. Social workers consider it of critical importance to respect the privacy of this communication.

9. *Willingness to persist in efforts on behalf of clients despite frustration.* The situations that require social work intervention typically did not develop quickly and usually cannot be resolved readily. Recognizing the frustration that social workers experience when change is slow to occur, they have come to value tenacity in addressing both individual problems and the problems that affect groups of people, organizations, communities, and the society in general.

When providing direct services, a social worker may become frustrated with a client who at a given time is unable or unwilling to engage in activities that the social worker believes would improve the situation. Or, when advocating on behalf of a client with another agency to provide needed services, the social worker may also experience frustration when the client is denied service or is placed on a waiting list. Advocacy for classes of clients or in relation to broad social issues can also prove quite frustrating. If delay tactics or the length of the change process is extended, the social worker may understandably become discouraged. Social workers must be persistent.

10. *Commitment to a high standard of personal and professional conduct.* The final value on the NASW list directs the worker to use the highest ethical standards in his or her practice. It suggests that the worker must conduct professional activities in a manner that protects the interests of the public, the agency, the clients, and the social worker.

This value has been operationalized in the form of the social work Code of Ethics, which is perhaps the single most important unifying element among social workers. Loewenberg and Dolgoff identify the following four functions served by the Code of Ethics:

1. Provide practitioners with guidance when faced by practice dilemmas that include ethical issues.

2. Provide clients and prospective clients who have no way of assessing a professional's integrity and competence with protection against incompetence and charlatanism.

3. Regulate the behavior of practitioners and their relations with clients, colleagues, practitioners from other professions, employer (if employed), and the community.

4. Provide supervisors, consultants, and other professionals with a basis for appraising and evaluating practitioner activities.[35]

To join NASW the social worker must sign a statement agreeing to abide by the ethical standards contained in the Code of Ethics. Negative sanctions against a member may be applied if the Code is violated. To protect against misuse of negative sanctions, NASW has created an elaborate procedure for hearing grievances at both the local or chapter and national levels. The 1987 Annual Report of NASW activities reports the following actions:

> In fiscal year 1987, NASW chapter committees on inquiry adjudicated 70 cases. The National Committee on Inquiry (NCOI), mandated by association bylaws, ruled on 52 cases, including appeals and reviews. The NASW board's Executive Committee, authorized to hear appeals of cases acted upon by NCOI and make final disposition, ruled on 10 appeals, imposed 16 sanctions, and removed 6 previously enforced sanctions.[36]

It is evident that social work does not take its Code of Ethics lightly and that every social worker should be thoroughly familiar with its contents (see Box 8–1). It is not only the basis on which negative sanctions might be imposed against a social worker by NASW, but more importantly, it provides a very helpful guide to practice that protects the interests of clients, agencies, the profession, and the communities in which social workers practice.

A CASE ILLUSTRATION: THE BRANDON CASE

R. Huws Jones, a prominent British social work educator, once stated that "A man's values are like his kidneys; he rarely knows he has any until they are upset."[37] For most social workers engaged in practice, the more theoretical or abstract discussion of values is not a daily event. It is only when value dilemmas or ethical issues are experienced in working with clients that these matters take on their fullest significance.

However, social workers regularly must address practical matters of values and ethics in their daily practice activities. M. C. Hokenstad notes that "half of professional decision making requires ethical rather than scientific judgment. . . . Such judgment requires the capability to make moral precepts operational in specific situations and calls for tolerance of ambiguity in some cases and the ability to resolve conflicts between principles in others."[38] It is through consideration of a case example describing a social worker in action that the reader may be able to extend his or her more applied understanding of social work values.

In her book *Never Too Old*, Esther Twente presented an excellent case illustration of a social worker providing service to an aged widower who was

BOX 8–1 THE NASW CODE OF ETHICS

Preamble

This code is intended to serve as a guide to the everyday conduct of members of the social work profession and as a basis for the adjudication of issues in ethics when the conduct of social workers is alleged to deviate from the standards expressed or implied in this code. It represents standards of ethical behavior for social workers in professional relationships with those served, with colleagues, with employers, with other individuals and professions, and with the community and society as a whole. It also embodies standards of ethical behavior governing individual conduct to the extent that such conduct is associated with an individual's status and identity as a social worker.

This code is based on the fundamental values of the social work profession that include the worth, dignity, and uniqueness of all persons as well as their rights and opportunities. It is also based on the nature of social work, which fosters conditions that promote these values.

In subscribing to and abiding by this code, the social worker is expected to view ethical responsibility in as inclusive a context as each situation demands and within which ethical judgment is required. The social worker is expected to take into consideration all the principles in this code that have a bearing upon any situation in which ethical judgment is to be exercised and professional intervention or conduct is planned. The course of action that the social worker chooses is expected to be consistent with the spirit as well as the letter of this code.

In itself, this code does not represent a set of rules that will prescribe all the behaviors of social workers in all the complexities of professional life. Rather, it offers general principles to guide conduct, and the judicious appraisal of conduct, in situations that have ethical implications. It provides the basis for making judgments about ethical actions before and after they occur. Frequently, the particular situation determines the ethical principles that apply and the manner of their application. In such cases, not only the particular ethical principles are taken into immediate consideration, but also the entire code and its spirit. Specific applications of ethical principles must be judged within the context in which they are being considered. Ethical behavior in a given situation must satisfy not only the judgment of the individual social worker, but also the judgment of an unbiased jury of professional peers.

This code should not be used as an instrument to deprive any social worker of the opportunity or freedom to practice with complete professional integrity; nor should any disciplinary action be taken on the basis of this code without maximum provision for safeguarding the rights of the social worker affected.

The ethical behavior of social workers results not from edict, but from a personal commitment of the individual. This code is offered to affirm the will and zeal of all social workers to be ethical and to act ethically in all that they do as social workers.

The following codified ethical principles should guide social workers in the various roles and relationships and at the various levels of responsibility in which they function professionally. These principles also serve as a basis for the adjudication by the National Association of Social Workers of issues in ethics.

In subscribing to this code, social workers are required to cooperate in its implementation and abide by any disciplinary rulings based on it. They should also take adequate measures to discourage, prevent, expose, and correct the unethical conduct of colleagues. Finally, social workers should be equally ready to defend and assist colleagues unjustly charged with unethical conduct.

I. The Social Worker's Conduct and Comportment as a Social Worker

A. Propriety—The social worker should maintain high standards of personal conduct in the capacity or identity as social worker.
   1. The private conduct of the social worker is a personal matter to the same degree as is any other person's, except when such conduct compromises the fulfillment of professional responsibilities.
   2. The social worker should not participate in, condone, or be associated with dishonesty, fraud, deceit, or misrepresentation.
   3. The social worker should distinguish clearly between statements and actions made as a private individual and as a representative of the social work profession or an organization or group.
B. Competence and Professional Development—The social worker should strive to become and remain proficient in professional practice and the performance of professional functions.
   1. The social worker should accept responsibility or employment only on the basis of existing competence or the intention to acquire the necessary competence.
   2. The social worker should not misrepresent professional qualifications, education, experience, or affiliations.
C. Service—The social worker should regard as primary the service obligation of the social work profession.
   1. The social worker should retain ultimate responsibility for the quality and extent of the service that that individual assumes, assigns, or performs.
   2. The social worker should act to prevent practices that are inhumane or discriminatory against any person or group of persons.
D. Integrity—The social worker should act in accordance with the highest standards of professional integrity and impartiality.
   1. The social worker should be alert to and resist the influences and pressures that interfere with the exercise of professonal discretion and impartial judgment required for the performance of professional functions.
   2. The social worker should not exploit professional relationships for personal gain.
E. Scholarship and Research—The social worker engaged in study and research should be guided by the conventions of scholarly inquiry.
   1. The social worker engaged in research should consider carefully its possible consequences for human beings.

2. The social worker engaged in research should ascertain that the consent of participants in the research is voluntary and informed, without any implied deprivation or penalty for refusal to participate, and with due regard for participants' privacy and dignity.
3. The social worker engaged in research should protect participants from unwarranted physical or mental discomfort, distress, harm, danger, or deprivation.
4. The social worker who engages in the evaluation of services or cases should discuss them only for professional purposes and only with persons directly and professionally concerned with them.
5. Information obtained about participants in research should be treated as confidential.
6. The social worker should take credit only for work actually done in connection with scholarly and research endeavors and credit contributions made by others.

II. The Social Worker's Ethical Responsibility to Clients

F. Primacy of Clients' Interests—The social worker's primary responsibility is to clients.
   1. The social worker should serve clients with devotion, loyalty, determination, and the maximum application of professional skill and competence.
   2. The social worker should not exploit relationships with clients for personal advantage or solicit the clients of one's agency for private practice.
   3. The social worker should not practice, condone, facilitate, or collaborate with any form of discrimination on the basis of race, color, sex, sexual orientation, age, religion, national origin, marital status, political belief, mental or physical handicap, or any other preference or personal characteristic, condition, or status.
   4. The social worker should avoid relationships or commitments that conflict with the interests of clients.
   5. The social worker should under no circumstances engage in sexual activities with clients.
   6. The social worker should provide clients with accurate and complete information regarding the extent and nature of the services available to them.
   7. The social worker should apprise clients of their risks, rights, opportunities, and obligations associated with social service to them.
   8. The social worker should seek advice and counsel of colleagues and supervisors whenever such consultation is in the best interest of clients.
   9. The social worker should terminate service to clients, and professional relationships with them, when such service and relationships are no longer required or no longer serve the clients' needs or interests.
   10. The social worker should withdraw services precipitously only under unusual circumstances, giving careful consideration to all fac-

tors in the situation and taking care to minimize possible adverse effects.

11. The social worker who anticipates the termination or interruption of service to clients should notify clients promptly and seek the transfer, referral, or continuation of service in relation to the clients' needs and preferences.

G. Rights and Prerogatives of Clients—The social worker should make every effort to foster maximum self-determination on the part of clients.

1. When the social worker must act on behalf of a client who has been adjudged legally incompetent, the social worker should safeguard the interests and rights of that client.

2. When another individual has been legally authorized to act in behalf of a client, the social worker should deal with that person always with the client's best interest in mind.

3. The social worker should not engage in any action that violates or diminishes the civil or legal rights of clients.

H. Confidentiality and Privacy—The social worker should respect the privacy of clients and hold in confidence all information obtained in the course of professional service.

1. The social worker should share with others confidences revealed by clients, without their consent, only for compelling professional reasons.

2. The social worker should inform clients fully about the limits of confidentiality in a given situation, the purposes for which information is obtained, and how it may be used.

3. The social worker should afford clients reasonable access to any official social work records concerning them.

4. When providing clients with access to records, the social worker should take due care to protect the confidences of others contained in those records.

5. The social worker should obtain informed consent of clients before taping, recording, or permitting third party observation of their activities.

I. Fees—When setting fees, the social worker should ensure that they are fair, reasonable, considerate, and commensurate with the service performed and with due regard for the clients' ability to pay.

1. The social worker should not divide a fee or accept or give anything of value for receiving or making a referral.

III. The Social Worker's Ethical Responsibility to Colleagues

J. Respect, Fairness, and Courtesy—The social worker should treat colleagues with respect, courtesy, fairness, and good faith.

1. The social worker should cooperate with colleagues to promote professional interests and concerns.

2. The social worker should respect confidences shared by colleagues in the course of their professional relationships and transactions.

3. The social worker should create and maintain conditions of practice that facilitate ethical and competent professional performance by colleagues.

4. The social worker should treat with respect, and represent accurately and fairly, the qualifications, views, and findings of colleagues and use appropriate channels to express judgments on these matters.

5. The social worker who replaces or is replaced by a colleague in professional practice should act with consideration for the interest, character, and reputation of that colleague.

6. The social worker should not exploit a dispute between a colleague and employers to obtain a position or otherwise advance the social worker's interest.

7. The social worker should seek arbitration or mediation when conflicts with colleagues require resolution for compelling professional reasons.

8. The social worker should extend to colleagues of other professions the same respect and cooperation that is extended to social work colleagues.

9. The social worker who serves as an employer, supervisor, or mentor to colleagues should make orderly and explicit arrangements regarding the conditions of their continuing professional relationship.

10. The social worker who has the responsibility for employing and evaluating the performance of other staff members should fulfill such responsibility in a fair, considerate, and equitable manner, on the basis of clearly enunciated criteria.

11. The social worker who has the responsibility for evaluating the performance of employees, supervisees, or students should share evaluations with them.

K. Dealing with Colleagues' Clients—The social worker has the responsibility to relate to the clients of colleagues with full professional consideration.

1. The social worker should not solicit the clients of colleagues.

2. The social worker should not assume professional responsibility for the clients of another agency or a colleague without appropriate communication with that agency or colleague.

3. The social worker who serves the clients of colleagues during a temporary absence or emergency should serve those clients with the same consideration as that afforded any client.

IV. The Social Worker's Ethical Responsibility to Employers and Employing Organizations

L. Commitment to Employing Organization—The social worker should adhere to commitments made to the employing organization.

1. The social worker should work to improve the employing agency's policies and procedures and the efficiency and effectiveness of its services.

2. The social worker should not accept employment or arrange student field placements in an organization which is currently under public sanction by NASW for violating personnel standards or imposing limitations on or penalties for professional actions on behalf of clients.

3. The social worker should act to prevent and eliminate discrimination in the employing organization's work assignments and its employment policies and practice.
4. The social worker should use with scrupulous regard, and only for the purpose for which they are intended, the resources of the employing organization.

V. The Social Worker's Ethical Responsibility to the Social Work Profession

M. Maintaining the Integrity of the Profession—The social worker should uphold and advance the values, ethics, knowledge, and mission of the profession.
1. The social worker should protect and enhance the dignity and integrity of the profession and should be responsible and vigorous in discussion and criticism of the profession.
2. The social worker should take action through appropriate channels against unethical conduct by any other member of the profession.
3. The social worker should act to prevent the unauthorized and unqualified practice of social work.
4. The social worker should make no misrepresentation in advertising as to qualifications, competence, service, or results to be achieved.
N. Community Service—The social worker should assist the profession in making social services available to the general public.
1. The social worker should contribute time and professional expertise to activities that promote respect for the utility, the integrity, and the competence of the social work profession.
2. The social worker should support the formulation, development, enactment, and implementation of social policies of concern to the profession.
O. Development of Knowledge—The social worker should take responsibility for identifying, developing, and fully utilizing knowledge for professional practice.
1. The social worker should base practice upon recognized knowledge relevant to social work.
2. The social worker should critically examine, and keep current with, emerging knowledge relevant to social work.
3. The social worker should contribute to the knowledge base of social work and share research knowledge and practice wisdom with colleagues.

VI. The Social Worker's Ethical Responsibility to Society

P. Promoting the General Welfare—The social worker should promote the general welfare of society.
1. The social worker should act to prevent and eliminate discrimination against any person or group on the basis of race, color, sex, sexual orientation, age, religion, national origin, marital status, political belief, mental or physical handicap, or any other preference or personal characteristic, condition, or status.

2. The social worker should act to ensure that all persons have access to the resources, services and opportunities which they require.
3. The social worker should act to expand choice and opportunity for all persons, with special regard for disadvantaged or oppressed groups and persons.
4. The social worker should promote conditions that encourage respect for the diversity of cultures which constitute American society.
5. The social worker should provide appropriate professional services in public emergencies.
6. The social worker should advocate changes in policy and legislation to improve social conditions and to promote social justice.
7. The social worker should encourage informed participation by the public in shaping social policies and institutions.

Source: Copyright © 1980, National Association of Social Workers, Inc. Reprinted with permission from *NASW News* 25, No. 1 (January 1980): 24–25.

lustration of a social worker providing service to an aged widower who was unsuccessfully attempting to establish a new life with his son and his son's family.[39] In the following excerpt from this case, some values issues become evident.

When Miss Jones visits Mr. Brandon, Sr., he at first seems determined not to enter into any kind of a discussion. He answers with a curt "no" or "yes" or "hmmm." Some reference to an old chair in which he sits brings forth the comment that it belonged to "mom and me." It was bought secondhand when they "set up housekeeping."

"How long ago was that?" asks Miss Jones.

"Fifty-one years last February," Mr. Brandon is struggling with tears.

"It must be hard to go on without her," comments Miss Jones quietly. Mr. Brandon nods. There is a sob. Miss Jones rises, walks to the bedtable and looks closely at a photograph. "Is this she?"

"Yes," Miss Jones sits down again. There is a silence. "There never was a better wife or mother than she." Miss Jones nods sympathetically. "Is the other picture on the table of your granddaughter?" she asks. "There seems to be a resemblance."

"There is," responds Mr. Brandon, and for the first time his face lights up. "She is like my wife, Peggy is. Sometimes she comes into my room and asks me questions. All kinds of fool questions. She'll say, 'Grandpa, how did you meet grandma?' or 'What did you do when you took her out?' or 'Did you and grandma dance at parties?' And when I'll say, 'Yes, but not the kind of dances you kids dance,' she'll get up and do some funny turns and say, 'Was it like this, Grandpa?' I tell her, 'No. We waltzed and sometimes I jigged.' 'Show me, Grandpa,' she says. And I get up, but these stiff hips of mine won't move like they ought to." Then he becomes silent again.

The gentle probing of Miss Jones in this part of the case allows her to understand some of the things that Mr. Brandon values, such as the satisfaction from the warm relationship he had with his wife and the joy he gets from his granddaughter. The social worker reflects her value of the worth of Mr. Brandon and treats him with dignity by listening carefully and showing interest in his experiences and feelings. He is important not because of his charm or good looks, but because of his humanness. The case continues.

"You aren't very happy here, are you?"

The next comments come like the rush of water through a broken dam. "No, I'm not happy. How can I be? I am just an old man in everybody's way. Oh, perhaps that is not quite true of Peggy. She likes to visit me, I think. But she has many friends. You know how popular young girls are. Tom is a good son. He works hard, and sometimes he comes in to talk to me. But I can tell he would rather read about sports or look at TV."

"How about Tom Junior?" prods Miss Jones.

"Oh, young Tom is like all young fellers. He is so busy going off on hikes and playing ball and the likes, he doesn't know I exist. I have his room. That should not be. The boy needs his own room to keep things like rocks and frogs and snakes." Again, there is that impish expression. Now there can be no mistaking it. "Margaret doesn't like them things in the house, and she's put her foot down about bringing them alive into the basement. She says she has to do the washing down there and she doesn't want the critters around her feet."

"You don't get along too well with Margaret," said Miss Jones.

"Oh, Margaret's all right. She is just too persnickity. When I first came I said, 'Now, Margaret, you let me do the dishes.' She said it would be hard for me to get them clean because I don't see so well. Well, I washed them, and then I saw her wash them over again. I don't see so bad, but I could see what she did." Then, after a short pause, "I am just in the way. I am an old farmer, and I am what I am. Margaret doesn't like the way I eat. When they had fancy company, she said to me, 'Grandpa, would you prefer to eat in your own room? I can fix your dinner on the card table.' I knew the score. She just didn't want me."

In this passage Mr. Brandon reflects his loss of a sense of self-respect. He views himself as an unimportant old man who doesn't suit the tastes of his daughter-in-law and is a burden for the rest of the family. Like many older people, he feels that he is of little use in a society that values work and productivity. While his life may have been fulfilling before and there was a real sense of achievement when he was managing the farm, life was hollow for Mr. Brandon now. Miss Jones communicates genuine concern about his well-being and seeks to understand the roots of the problem. The story goes on:

After a while Miss Jones asks him if he knows anyone in town besides Tom and his family. "No, all of my friends are out in the country, what is left of them. I can't go out there and they can't come in. Too far."

"And how about church?" asks Miss Jones.

"Mom and I always went to the Methodist Church. Tom and Margaret go to the Christian. Disciples of Christ, they call it. That was Margaret's church. Tom had to be 'ducked' before he could belong." Mr. Brandon does not want to be baptized again. "Once is enough." And he doesn't know anybody. So he stays at home and listens to the radio. Anyhow, his stiff hips can't do those steps very well. "Did you ever like fishing or hunting?" asks Miss Jones. "No, you know, where we lived there was no water for miles around. And as to hunting, there are jackrabbits and prairie dogs, but I was never one to shoot except to protect the crops."

"When you and your wife had company on Sunday afternoons, what did you men do?" Miss Jones continues her questions.

"Oh, we talked politics and things like that, and looked at crops; and sometimes we played horseshoe," replies Mr. Brandon. "Horseshoe was fun, then, but with these hips, it's out of the question." "How about Sunday afternoons in the winter?" Miss Jones is not giving up.

"Well, we played checkers and dominoes and sometimes Flinch."

"Did you enjoy that?" asks Miss Jones.

"Yes." His face brightens. "Hank Brown and I used to play checkers. We played to win. Maggie, that was my wife, and Elizabeth, Hank's wife, had to remind us that the stock had to be fed and we had to go home."

"Would you care to play checkers now, that is, if there were someone to play with you?"

"No. Anyhow, there's nobody to play with."

"There is a Center on Elm Street and retired men get together for checkers and cards. They seem to have fun."

Here Miss Jones moves the conversation to understand better the uniqueness of Mr. Brandon. Although he faces problems experienced by other old people, Mr. Brandon is a unique individual with his own interests and abilities. Miss Jones responds to his need to belong and searches for interests that match community resources which would provide him with an opportunity to make new friends. She knows that men in Mr. Brandon's age group especially need to have warm relationships with a group of friends. Miss Jones reflects the belief that people can change in a new environment and that Mr. Brandon could once again enter the mainstream of life. She is persistent and does not let his despair frustrate her efforts to help find a solution.

Mr. Brandon shakes his head. "I've heard about the Center but it does not appeal to me. Anyhow, I won't be in town very long. I overheard Tom and Margaret discuss me. They want me to go into a home." He seems resigned.

"And do you want to go?" Miss Jones keeps on digging.

"Hell, no. But what can an old man like me do? I don't want to stay where I am not wanted. Not me."

"I am not sure that you are not wanted," says Miss Jones. "Why don't you talk it over with Tom and Margaret and tell them how you feel?"

"I couldn't do that," says Mr. Brandon. "Anyhow, what's the use? I shouldn't have blabbered so much to you. I wasn't going to, and then I went and did it anyhow."

"Do you want me to talk to Tom and Margaret and perhaps with Peggy and young Tom present, too?" asks Miss Jones.

"What would Peggy and Young Tom have to do with it?" He is almost shouting. "They are not responsible for me. Not them young kids."

"No, they aren't, but they are a part of the family and they know whether they want you to stay or to leave. I think Peggy, especially, would hate to see you go to a home."

"Well, I'm going and that is that." Mr. Brandon is trembling. "Like I told you, I am not going to be in anybody's way."

"Do you want me to tell you about the homes nearby?" asks Miss Jones.

The answer sounds something like assent. Miss Jones lists the four different kinds of institutions in the county and briefly describes each one. Mr. Brandon is silent. After a while he says, "You sure know about all these things, don't you?"

"It's my business to know," says Miss Jones.

There is another pause. This time it is a long one. "Does Tom know about all of this, I mean all of these homes?"

"Yes," replies Miss Jones, "I told them when they came in to see me."

"And they want me to go?"

"Only Tom and Margaret and Peggy and Tom Junior can answer that," says Miss Jones. "I do think they would like to see you happier than you have been here."

"Well, I would be! A damn sight happier!" Then, in quite another voice, "Can family visit you in those places? I mean, can young kids come too?"

"Yes, they can, especially during visiting hours."

"What do you have to do with all of this?" he then asks.

"Really very little, Mr. Brandon. We do give information when it is wanted and needed, and sometimes we help with the finances. Most of all we are interested in trying to help families find the best solutions in situations like yours. Tom and Margaret told us they were concerned about you. They know you are lonely and unhappy. They thought a home might be a solution and they asked for information."

"Did they also ask you to come and talk with me?" Mr. Brandon is shouting again.

"Yes, but they understood that I would not try to persuade you to go to a home or do anything else you don't want to do. I think this is up to you and your family."

"And that includes Peggy and Tom Junior?"

"To me it would seem so."

Soon after that, Mr. Brandon comments, "Well, I've got something to think about."

We find Miss Jones reflecting the social work value of helping the clients help themselves. She recognizes that people must be permitted to determine what is best for them and take responsibility for these decisions. Miss Jones is also aware that Mr. Brandon said some things he would not want her to report back to Tom and Margaret. She reinforces the confidentiality of their conversation by asking if he wants her to talk with the family about his views. Yet, she refuses to be drawn into the role of an interpreter for the family and, instead, helps them come together to talk about the problems and possible solutions. The final decision, however, is left to them. Although frustrated at times, she continues to pursue working with the family until a satisfactory solution is achieved.

CONCLUDING COMMENT

One cannot understand social work without being sensitive to values. Values represent a highly individual and personal view that must be constantly examined during practice.

The social worker must be aware of the value system of the client or client group and the values held by society that impinge upon the client. Research reported in the chapter identifies the dominant values in U.S. society that form the context in which social programs are formulated and social workers and their clients engage in the helping process. These values, however, are not held equally by all people and client groups can be expected to vary in the intensity with which they hold particular values.

The social worker must be especially cognizant of his or her personal values, lest they intrude into the helping process. Certainly it would be unrealistic to expect, or even desire, that the helping process occur in a value-free environment. Yet the social worker must attempt to avoid imposing personal values inappropriately on the client or client groups. In order to practice social work, one must be prepared to accept and understand people who hold values that are different from their own.

The social worker also must be guided by the values of the social work profession—including the Code of Ethics. These particular values are not held exclusively by social workers. Other professions hold many of them. There is growing evidence that people involved in the helping professions hold values that are somewhat different from other groups in the population.[40] Although the research is inconclusive at this time, it appears that social workers may reflect some differing values from the other helping professions, particularly those that support social work's dual focus on person and society.

One study, for example, revealed that the social values of teachers and social workers were significantly different.[41] More study of social work values and their relationship to those of other helping professions is needed.

In many ways values or beliefs about how things ought to be or how people ought to behave are the cornerstone of social work. It does not take long in many practice situations to recognize that the knowledge available may be insufficient to guide practice. Moreover, skills required to be helpful to clients in a specific situation may exceed the competence of the worker. In such an event the social worker who falls back on the values of the social work profession cannot go far wrong in guiding the helping process. Thus, in addition to serving as guidelines for the selection of knowledge and skills for practice, social work values serve as a safety valve for client protection.

SUGGESTED READINGS

Baier, Kurt, and Rescher, Nichols. *Values and the Future.* New York: Free Press, 1969.

Clough, Shepard B. *Basic Values of Western Civilization.* New York: Columbia University Press, 1960.

Goldstein, Howard. "The Neglected Moral Link in Social Work Practice." *Social Work* 32 (May–June 1987): 179–180.

Gordon, William E. "Knowledge and Value: Their Distinction and Relationship in Clarifying Social Work Practice." *Social Work* 10 (July 1965): 32–39.

Kahle, Lynn R., ed. *Social Values and Social Change: Adaptation to Life in America.* New York: Praeger, 1983.

Leiby, James. "Moral Foundations of Social Welfare and Social Work: A Historical View." *Social Work* 30 (July–August 1985): 323–330.

Levy, Charles S. *Social Work Ethics.* New York: Human Services Press, 1976.

Loewenberg, Frank and Dolgoff, Ralph. *Ethical Decisions for Social Work Practice*, 3rd ed., Itasca, Ill.: F.E. Peacock, 1988.

Reamer, Frederic G. "Ethics Committees in Social Work." *Social Work* 32 (May–June 1987): 188–192.

Reamer, Frederic G. *Ethical Dilemmas in Social Service.* New York: Columbia University Press, 1982.

Rokeach, Milton. *The Nature of Human Values.* New York: Free Press, 1973.

Rokeach, Milton. *Understanding Human Values: Individual and Societal.* New York: Free Press, 1979.

Timms, Noel. *Social Work Values: An Inquiry.* London: Routledge & Kegan Paul, 1983.

Walsh, Joseph A. "Burnout and Values in the Social Service Profession." *Social Casework* 68 (May 1987): 279–283.

Wells, Carolyn Cressy, with Masch, M. Kathleen. *Social Work Ethics Day to Day: Guidelines for Professional Practice.* New York: Longman, 1986.

ENDNOTES

1. Charles S. Levy, *Social Work Ethics* (New York: Human Services Press, 1976), p. 14.
2. Robin M. Williams, Jr., *American Society: A Sociological Interpretation*, 3d ed. (New York: Alfred A. Knopf, 1970), p. 440.
3. Lynn R. Kahle & Susan Goff Timmer, "A Theory and a Method for Studying

Values," in *Social Values and Social Change: Adaptation to Life in America*, Lynn R. Kahle, ed. (Praeger Publishers, New York, a division of Greenwood Press, Inc., 1983), p. 52. Copyright © 1983 by Praeger Publishers. Used with permission.

4. Gordon M. Hart, *Values Clarification for Counselors: How Counselors, Social Workers, Psychologists, and Other Human Service Workers Can Use Available Techniques* (Springfield, Ill.: Thomas, 1978) and Sidney B. Simon, Leland W. Howe, and Howard Kindenbaum, *Values Clarification: A Handbook of Practical Strategies for Teachers and Students*, rev. ed. (New York: Hart, 1978).

5. Charles Frankel, "Social Values and Professional Values," *Journal of Education for Social Work* 5 (Spring 1969): 31–32.

6. Ibid., p. 35.

7. Harold L. McPheeters and Robert M. Ryan, *A Core of Competence for Baccalaureate Social Welfare and Curricular Implications* (Atlanta: Southern Regional Education Board, 1971), pp. 74–75.

8. American Association of Social Workers, *Social Case Work: Generic and Specific: A Report of the Milford Conference*, reprinted, (Washington, D.C.: National Association of Social Workers, 1974), p. 28.

9. Shepard B. Clough, *Basic Values of Western Civilization*, (New York: Columbia University Press, 1960), p. 5.

10. Naomi I. Brill, *Working With People: The Helping Process* (Philadelphia: Lippincott, 1973), p. 11.

11. Ibid., p. 12.

12. Kahle, *Social Values and Social Change*.

13. Milton Rokeach, *The Nature of Human Values* (New York: Free Press, 1973) and Milton Rokeach, *Understanding Human Values: Individual and Societal* (New York: Free Press, 1979).

14. Lynn R. Kahle & Susan Goff Timmer, "A Theory and a Method for Studying Values," in *Social Values and Social Change: Adaptation to Life in America*, Lynn R. Kahle, ed. (Praeger Publishers, New York, a division of Greenwood Press, Inc., 1983), pp. 47–51. Copyright © 1983 by Praeger Publishers. Used with permission.

15. Susan Goff Timmer and Lynn R. Kahle, "Birthright Demographic Correlates of Values," in *Social Values and Social Change: Adaptation to Life in America*, Lynn R. Kahle, ed. (Praeger Publishers, New York, a division of Greenwood Press, Inc., 1983), p. 76. Copyright © 1983 by Praeger Publishers. Used with permission.

16. Debra C. Eisert, "Marriage and Parenting," in *Social Values and Social Change: Adaptation to Life in America*, Lynn R. Kahle, ed. (Praeger Publishers, New York, a division of Greenwood Press, Inc., 1983), pp. 149–150. Copyright © 1983 by Praeger Publishers. Used with permission.

17. Susan Goff Timmer and Lynn R. Kahle, "Birthright Demographic Correlates of Values," in *Social Values and Social Change: Adaptation to Life in America*, Lynn R. Kahle, ed. (Praeger Publishers, New York, a division of Greenwood Press, Inc., 1983), pp. 84–85. Copyright © 1983 by Praeger Publishers. Used with permission.

18. Susan Goff Timmer and Lynn R. Kahle, "Birthright Demographic Correlates of Values," in *Social Values and Social Change: Adaptation to Life in America*, Lynn R. Kahle, ed. (Praeger Publishers, New York, a division of Greenwood Press, Inc., 1983), pp. 84–85. Copyright © 1983 by Praeger Publishers. Used with permission.

19. Kathleen J. Pottick, "Work and Leisure," in *Social Values and Social Change: Adaptation to Life in America*, Lynn R. Kahle, ed. (Praeger Publishers, New York, a division of Greenwood Press, Inc., 1983), p. 120. Copyright © 1983 by Praeger Publishers. Used with permission.

20. Susan Goff Timmer and Lynn R. Kahle, "Birthright Demographic Correlates of Values," in *Social Values and Social Change: Adaptation to Life in America*, Lynn R. Kahle, ed. (Praeger Publishers, New York, a division of Greenwood Press, Inc., 1983), p. 94. Copyright © 1983 by Praeger Publishers. Used with permission.

21. Susan Goff Timmer and Lynn R. Kahle, "Birthright Demographic Correlates of Values," in *Social Values and Social Change: Adaptation to Life in America*, Lynn R. Kahle, ed. (Praeger Publishers, New York, a division of Greenwood Press, Inc., 1983), pp. 94–95. Copyright © 1983 by Praeger Publishers. Used with permission.
22. Susan Goff Timmer and Lynn R. Kahle, "Ascribed and Attained Demographic Correlates of Values," in *Social Values and Social Change: Adaptation to Life in America*, Lynn R. Kahle, ed. (Praeger Publishers, New York, a division of Greenwood Press, Inc., 1983), p. 106. Copyright © 1983 by Praeger Publishers. Used with permission.
23. Susan Goff Timmer and Lynn R. Kahle, "Ascribed and Attained Demographic Correlates of Values," in *Social Values and Social Change: Adaptation to Life in America*, Lynn R. Kahle, ed. (Praeger Publishers, New York, a division of Greenwood Press, Inc., 1983), p. 108. Copyright © 1983 by Praeger Publishers. Used with permission.
24. Susan Goff Timmer and Lynn R. Kahle, "Ascribed and Attained Demographic Correlates of Values," in *Social Values and Social Change: Adaptation to Life in America*, Lynn R. Kahle, ed. (Praeger Publishers, New York, a division of Greenwood Press, Inc., 1983), p. 110. Copyright © 1983 by Praeger Publishers. Used with permission.
25. Chauncy A. Alexander, "An International Code of Ethics for the Professional Social Worker" (Washington, D.C.: National Association of Social Workers, 1975), p. 2 (mimeographed).
26. National Association of Social Workers, *NASW Standards for the Classification of Social Work Practice, Policy Statement 4*, Silver Spring, Md: NASW, September 1981: p. 18.
27. Clough, *Basic Values of Western Society*, p. 15.
28. Bradford W. Sheafor, Charles R. Horejsi, and Gloria A. Horejsi, *Techniques and Guidelines for Social Work Practice* (Boston, Allyn and Bacon, 1988) p. 59.
29. Allen F. Klein, *Effective Groupwork: An Introduction to Principle and Method* (New York: Association Press, 1972), p. 23.
30. Ruth Elizabeth Smalley, *Theory for Social Work Practice* (New York: Columbia University Press, 1967), p. 1.
31. Harriett M. Bartlett, Toward Clarification and Improvement of Social Work Practice," *Social Work* 3 (April 1958): 5–8.
32. Isidor Chein, "The Image of Man," *Journal of Social Issues* 18 (October 1962: 2–3.
33. Sheafor, Horejsi, and Horejsi, *Techniques and Guidelines*, p. 56.
34. Suanna J. Wilson, *Confidentiality in Social Work: Issues and Principles* (New York: Free Press, 1978), pp. 2–4.
35. Frank Loewenberg and Ralph Dolgoff, *Ethical Decisions for Social Work Practice*, 2nd ed. (Itasca, Ill.: F.E. Peacock, 1985): 21.
36. *Annual Report, 1987,* Silver Spring, Md.: National Association of Social Workers, 1987), p. 16.
37. R. Huws Jones, "Social Values and Social Work Education," in Katherine A. Kendall, (ed.), *Social Work Values in an Age of Discontent* (New York: Council on Social Work Education, 1970).
38. M. C. "Terry" Hokenstad, "Teaching Practitioners Ethical Judgment," *NASW News* 32 (October 1987): 4.
39. Esther E. Twente, *Never Too Old: The Aged in Community Life* (San Francisco: Jossey–Bass, 1970), pp. 151–158.
40. Bradford W. Sheafor, "The Effects of Board Members on Staff of Community Mental Health Centers: A Study of the Relationship of Their Values to Job Satisfaction," *Journal of Social Welfare* 3 (Spring 1976): 75–82 and Arthur W. Combs et al., *Florida Studies in the Helping Professions*, University of Florida Social Science Monograph 37 (Gainesville: University of Florida Press, 1969).
41. Henry J. Meyer, Eugene Likwak, and Donald Warren, "Occupational and Class Differences in Social Values: A Comparison of Teachers and Social Workers," *Sociology of Education* 41 (Summer 1968): 263–281.

CHAPTER

9

The Skill Base
of Social Work

Among the many definitions of social work are several that appropriately describe social work as both an art and a science. Certainly there is an artful part of social work practice that relates to the natural abilities and personality traits of the social worker. Inherent ability is especially apparent in the skills of some social workers. Undoubtedly, some people possess special qualities that make them good natural helpers. However, many skills required for practice have a knowledge base and can be learned. The social worker's batting average is, of course, improved when he or she demonstrates both natural abilities and professionally developed skills.

To be effective the social worker must have the capacity to use a wide repertoire of techniques. The skill of social work requires both the appropriate selection of techniques for a particular situation and the ability to use the techniques effectively. Selection of particular techniques must be based on a conscious effort to use the best available knowledge and to screen that knowledge carefully to be sure it is compatible with social work values. In a sense values become a filter between the available knowledge and the skills used by the social worker in providing services. Once appropriate knowledge and values have been given full consideration, the practice skill of the social worker comes into play (see Figure 9–1).

THE NATURE OF SKILL

When one has an opportunity to observe a social worker in practice, his or her skill is readily apparent. *Skill* may be defined as the "ability to use knowledge effectively and readily in execution or performance."[1] The term is used somewhat differently in other fields. In industry a person is regarded as skilled when he or she is qualified to carry out trade or craft work involving knowledge, judgment, accuracy, and manual deftness, usually acquired through extensive training. In *motor* or *manual skills*, the overt action forms an essential part of the activity. Psychologists use the concept of *mental skills*, in which the overt actions play a more incidental part, giving expression to a skill rather than forming an essential part of it.[2] In social work, on the other hand, overt actions are rarely observed as part of the mental skills of the social

243

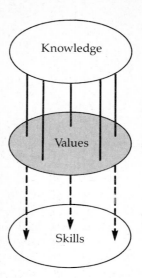

Figure 9–1 *Factors underpinning social work skill*

worker in a helping role, except, for example, when a worker uses recreational activities in working with a group.

A major distinction between professional and nonprofessional occupations is the possession of skill and knowledge generally not available to the public. Many nonprofessional occupations involve skill—in many cases greater than that of professions. A major distinction between the two, however, rests on a *body of knowledge* organized into a system that can be called a body of theory. The acquisition of skill in professions, therefore, depends on the mastery of the underlying body of theory, which, in turn, demands education and training of a high order.[3]

Unlike many professionals, the social worker does not bring many tangible resources to the helping situation. The social worker brings a body of knowledge, a set of values, and a repertoire of skills from which the most promising helping approach or intervention is selected. Unlike the physician, for example, who can administer medication that will "cure" the patient's illness, the social worker can only help the client or clients improve their social functioning. Central to this task is the development and maintenance of a mutually trusting, satisfying, and productive relationship between client(s) and social worker. Some professionals offer their skills "to" the client, but the social worker uses skills "with" the client. As Figure 9–2 suggests, the successful helping process not only requires the skill of the social worker but also the skill of the client in using the available help and in changing his or her social functioning.

SKILL IN SOCIAL WORK

Werner Boehm suggests that professional skill is expressed in the activities

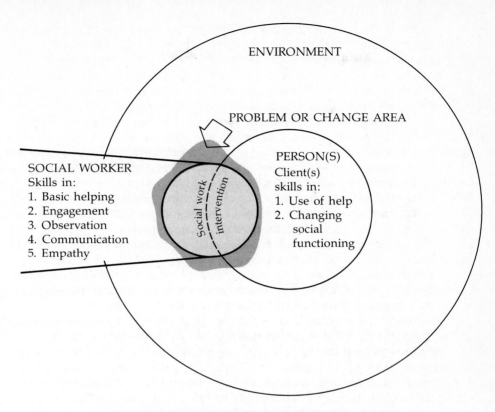

Figure 9–2 *Skill elements in social work practice*

of the social worker. It constitutes the social worker's artistic creation resulting from three internal processes: (1) conscious selection of knowledge pertinent to the professional task at hand, (2) fusion of this knowledge with social work values, and (3) expression of this synthesis in *professionally relevant activity*.[4] What constitutes professionally relevant activity, however, does not seem explicit and allows room for subjective interpretation. As Boehm states:

> Social work should and does adopt what may often be unpopular positions. In the light of its own selection and interpretation of certain values which other sections of society may view differently, social work may also serve as the conscience of society.[5]

Demonstrating social work skills in a professionally relevant activity seems to leave determination of that activity with the agency and the social work profession. The implication is that the social worker's activity needs to be "sanctioned." But would not the sanction of the client also be of paramount importance? In this view the social worker would be using skills in *client-relevant activity;* the activity would be determined by client needs. Yet, agency and social work sanction do not have to be a condition of intervention if the activity takes place independent of the agency and the profession. For example a social worker in private practice who treats a police brutality victim in emotional crisis and who then helps similar victims organize in the community to protest against such police practices is using social work skills to help people in need who sanction this intervention. This intervention may or may not be sanctioned by the profession, but it is still social work practice.

Given the foregoing discussion, we propose the following definition of social work skill. *Social work skill is the social worker's capacity to set in motion, in a relationship with the client (individual, group, community), guided psychosocial interventive processes of change based on social work values and knowledge in a specific situation relevant to the client. The change that begins to occur as the result of this skilled intervention is effected with the greatest degree of consideration for the client and by the use of the strengths and capacity of the client.*

The social worker's skill is expressed within the framework of one or more social work methods. As an orderly, systematic mode of procedure common to a discipline, practice, or range of disciplines and practices, the term *method* in social work traditionally encompasses social casework, social group work, and community organization, but increasingly relates to a generic practice method.[6] The social work method is the responsible, conscious, skilled, disciplined use of self in a relationship with an individual or group. It includes systematic observation and assessment of the client and formulation of an appropriate plan of action. Implicit in this process, according to William Gordon, is a continuing evaluation of the nature of the relationship between the social worker and the client and of its effect on both the participant individual or group and the social worker.

TECHNIQUES AND SOCIAL WORK SKILLS

Techniques, that is, instruments or specific procedures and operations used in a given discipline, are incorporated in the use of the social work method. Gordon lists some of the techniques that may be applied in different combinations by social workers: support, clarification, information giving, interpretation, development of insight, differentiation of the social worker from the individual or group, identification with agency function, creation and use of structure, use of activities and projects, provision of positive experiences, teaching, stimulation of group interaction, limit setting, utilization of available social resources, effecting change in immediate environmental forces operating upon the individual or groups, and synthesis.[7]

Competence in social work practice lies in developing skill in the use of the social work method and its techniques. Skill entails the ability to help a particular client or clients in such a way that they clearly understand the social worker's role and intention and are able to participate in the process of solving their problems or enhancing their social functioning. In further defining social work skills, Gordon adds:

Setting the stage, the strict observation of confidentiality, encouragement, stimulation or participation, empathy, and objectivity are means of facilitating communication. The individual social worker always makes his *own* creative contribution in the application of social work method to any setting or activity.[8]

THE SKILL-LEARNING PROCESS

It is impossible for any one social worker to learn all skills of practice. Social casework, for example, has a distinct repertoire of skills, based on either the "functional approach," the "problem-solving approach," or the "psychosocial approach" to intervention.[9] The social group worker is also faced with a wide range of skills to learn depending on which interventive mode is selected for practice. There are, for example, the "developmental approach," the "interactionist approach," and the "preventive and rehabilitative approach."[10] In community organization the crucial elements of practice and the field's boundaries and content are very much in flux.[11] Several problem-solving models are difficult to define because of overlap in purpose and method among the various community organization, development, and planning approaches.[12] Because of the lack of definition, learning community organization practice skills is therefore even more difficult than learning the skills of casework and group work.

Social work's many faces cover a wide variety of social phenomena and practice interventions, each requiring special skills. It should be pointed out that although certain aspects of practice call for specialization, there are still many skills more generic in nature. Harriet Bartlett maintains that the idea of a *common base*—one whose elements are applied together in practice but that vary according to the particular characteristics of the practice—brings together the concepts of generic and specific, of basic and specialized.[13]

Setting aside for a moment the social worker's task of learning generic and specialized skills for practice, we turn to the more basic issue of *how* the social worker learns a particular skill. It is not difficult, for example, to tell a social work student or worker to develop skills in interviewing. However, simply assigning a book on interviewing skills will not guarantee that the necessary skills will be learned.

An adult who sets out to acquire a new skill usually begins with a communicable program of instruction. Another person communicates or demonstrates what the learner is supposed to do. But just having the written or oral strategy is not enough to acquire certain skills. For example almost no one—including physicists, engineers, and bicycle manufacturers—can communicate how to keep your balance when you ride a bicycle. "Turn your handle bars in the direction you are falling," the teacher says, and the student accepts blindly, not quite understanding then or later why this method works. Some teachers may not impart any instructions at all but run alongside the bicycle, holding it up until the learner gets the feel and the idea. Skills, particularly mental skills, are uniquely taught and learned. Given verbal and written instructions about skills, when forming a plan (even an inefficient plan) to guide their actions, people find for themselves the essential elements of the skill. Finding these elements is basically a test of the adequacy of the strategy. Once a strategy has been developed, alternative modes of action become possible. The person now understands the specific job he or she has to do and has acquired the necessary skill to get it done.[14]

Techniques, which are refinements of skill, should not be rigid, particularly as they pertain to mental skills applied in helping human beings:

> There are so many knotty problems with which they (caseworkers) deal, so many stubbornly closed doors that will not yield to their opening devices, that they look eagerly for some keys, be they words or actions, which will prove to be open-sesames. *But the more individualized and creative a process is, the more skill eludes being captured* and held in the small snares of prefabricated kinds of behavior, and the paradox is that the less susceptible skill is to being caught, and mastered by ready-made formulas, the more anxiously are formulas sought. "What should I say when . . . ?" "What does one do if . . . ?" "How do you get a client to . . . ?" These are the questions caseworkers typically bring to supervisors, to psychiatric consultants, or to their peers, seeking for *the* manner, *the* word, that will break the impasse.[15]

Thus, we view social work practice as a science—that is, the systematic application of knowledge and skill in effecting a desired result, combined with the art each social worker develops in the unique selection and application of appropriate techniques and skills. From practice experience every social worker develops special ways of saying and doing what his or her knowledge and values determine will most effectively achieve the client's goals.

BASIC SKILLS FOR BEGINNING PRACTICE

Social workers in the human services must have at their disposal a wide repertoire of knowledge, skills, techniques, and strategies to attain goals with people. In application of knowledge and skills, values are inseparable from any step in the process, for without values the social worker may be a technician rather than a value-directed human services professional.[16]

Built on a foundation of knowledge and values, the element of skill in social work has two preliminary applications: to select the method or methods to use (or not use) and to act accordingly.[17] An experienced practitioner knows, for example, that it is rarely helpful—and often counter-productive—to encourage a grossly psychotic individual to elaborate on his or her hallucinations. Instead, the skillful social worker will carefully direct the patient to a more realistic level of functioning by asking the patient simple, clear, concrete questions. The skillful, appropriate selection and application of a method in this case appears rather uncomplicated; but a great deal of preparation is needed.

There is a gradation of skill attainment from a low to a high level of sophistication among social work practitioners. The advanced social worker is expected to have more interventive skills than a beginning social worker. But what are the appropriate skill expectations of the social work student? Traditionally, social service agencies serving as field placements have provided the major opportunity for skill learning, and in many educational programs field experience coincides with a practice course. Effective and efficient learning is likely when classroom and field faculty work together in identifying common objectives and in integrating learning activities.

Frank Loewenberg and Ralph Dolgoff maintain, however, that students should develop elementary skills, such as interviewing, *before* they come to the field-work placement agency.[18] They provide several ideas and suggestions as to what should be included in basic skills for beginning practice. This section, with various modifications, relies upon their contributions. The following skill areas, with accompanying key concepts, will be highlighted as recommended basic skills for beginning practice: (1) basic helping skills; (2) engagement skills; (3) observation skills; (4) communication skills; (5) empathy skills; and (6) social work assessment skills. Each person learns and applies helping skills in his or her own way. Skills mechanically learned and applied will be perceived by clients as false and superficial and will only interfere with the helping process.

Basic Helping Skills

Helping people is a planned, purposeful process that involves a helping worker. The student needs to develop perceptive skills in order to look at familiar things with new eyes to identify people who need help and conditions that need changing. For example the neighborhood bully whom everyone dislikes may be acting out feelings of inadequacy in response to brutal treatment by his or her parents. The task is to look for the cause of the behavior.

Helping people is a purposeful response to individual needs, group and community requirements, and societal conditions. The helper's relationship with the person receiving help varies and depends on the problem or condition; the helping strategy selected; characteristics of the individual, family, or group asking for help; and characteristics of other elements of the system.

The helper-receiver relationship need not always be a direct relationship. For example the bed-wetting problem of a five-year-old might be resolved in a specific case by helping the parents feel less anxious about being parents rather than by focusing only on the child.

Developing relationships is an essential helping skill. For a helper to have a positive effect on another person, a good relationship is fundamental. In the process of helping people, social workers must develop working relationships within a bureaucratic organization, with other bureaucratic organizations, and with other professional helpers.

Using oneself appropriately and purposefully is an important skill. Social workers have to work both independently and as members of a team. A related factor is understanding the meaning of supervision and consultation and using that assistance effectively. The skill to organize one's work effectively benefits the client both directly and indirectly.

Some basic principles in the helping process are accepting others as they are, treating people as individuals, maintaining one's own integrity, respecting a person's right to self-determination, and working with people at *their* pace.

In developing one's basic helping skills, one must continue to learn. Opportunities for further education must be cultivated. Professional journals, books, institutes, and workshops can be rich sources of learning. And, in addition to learning from colleagues, one can learn from clients.

Engagement Skills

The process of effectively involving individuals, families, or groups in a helping situation requires the purposeful use of self. In attempting to achieve this, the goals, purposes, role, and position of the worker must be made explicit to the person needing help. Likewise, the goals, purposes, role, and position of the person needing help have to be made clear. For example, a wife asking a family services worker to make her alcoholic husband "behave" must understand that the worker can only invite the husband to join a discussion of her concerns. He, in turn, might share his concerns about his wife. The worker's role then might assume a more supportive, neutral, facilitative, conciliatory posture, depending upon the new merged goals and purposes evolving from discussions.

Role and status factors impinge on the helping process. Engagement skills have to consider stratification factors, knowledge of subcultures, deviant groups, reference groups, ethnic minority groups, and differing value systems and life styles. Ignoring these factors can make it difficult to establish working relationships with people from these groups. If, for example, a worker were to try to impose a heterosexual value system on a gay client who is attempting to work through separation feelings after abandonment by his lover, it would probably not be too long before the client would disengage himself from the helping relationship.

Context and structure affect the engagement process. Factors such as the time, setting, and structure of the interview may enhance or impede the engagement process. The time and setting should be chosen for the convenience of the person being helped. Distractions and inconveniences should be minimized to afford worker and client maximum attention and concentration. The availability of the worker may also affect the engagement process. If it is difficult to contact the worker, the engagement process suffers.

There are specific phases in the engagement process. Usually, it is fairly easy to establish a working relationship with persons who initiated the contact for help. They are often precise in defining their problems and are motivated to work on them. When the contact is initiated by the social agency or by a third party such as the church or police, it is usually more difficult to establish a good working relationship, since these people may not want help. In such cases, the engagement process is enhanced when the worker is able to establish clearly what his or her role and responsibilities will be. The client's rights, responsibilities, and options should also be spelled out. Once the initial working relationship is established and client resistance is at a minimum, the engagement process may be strengthened and the potential contribution of the worker becomes more obvious to the client. It is in this middle phase that the worker can more efficiently and effectively help individuals, families, and groups identify and define problem areas and can develop and implement intervention action strategies. The ending phase of the engagement process is concerned with the delicate process of termination. Depending on the nature and depth of the relationship between the worker and the individual, family, or group, careful planning of the termination process can result in a positive separation.

Elimination of the negatives helps the engagement process. Workers with punitive and judgmental attitudes have difficulty establishing a helpful relationship with clients. Scolding a client who is late for an appointment may only evoke resentment. Criticizing a welfare mother because she occasionally goes to night clubs rather than to church will likewise place the client on the defensive and will make it difficult for her to trust the worker. Holding unrealistic expectations for clients may initially motivate and excite them; but, when they are unable to achieve these goals, frustration, guilt, and even anger toward the worker may result. Subsequent attempts to engage the client in other efforts may prove fruitless. Unwarranted promises by the worker may also contribute to the client's frustration and may make the engagement process more difficult. In short eliminating the negatives and striving to be open, honest, nonjudgmental, realistic, and dependable will enhance the engagement process. Basic guidelines include patience, understanding, and acceptance of different values and life styles.

Observation Skills

People see only what they are socially conditioned to look for. During the conditioning process, a person absorbs countless biases—conscious and unconscious. In learning observation skills, therefore, a fundamental goal is for social workers to become more aware of the particular biases that color their perception of others. Of course, it is doubtful that pure, objective perception is possible.

Observation is more than just "seeing." Obviously, the worker observes what the client says. The worker should also note what the client does *not* say, such as significant gaps in a story. For example, a married man in the first few sessions may talk about how frustrated he feels on the job. His not mentioning significant people in his life, such as his family, is important to note. The worker should also notice physical appearance, that is, bodily tensions, flushing, perspiration, trembling, excitability, and looks of dejection, because these factors supplement—and at times may even contradict—an impression given by the client's words. The mother who smilingly complains that her acting-out teenage son is "growing up to be just like his father" may not be aware of her ambivalent feelings about her son. Observation of the client's physical behavior can often provide clues to deeper motivations.

An observation involves a choice of what to see. The worker must continually decide what should be observed, because it is never possible to observe everything. In family therapy, for example, if the worker observes only the verbose mother who is attempting to dominate and control the family with her talking, the result may be that the mother also dominates the social worker. However, if the worker observes the other family members and then shares his or her observations with the family that some members appeared angry, bored, or "turned off" by the mother's talking, this statement will immediately encourage responses that will confirm or reject the initial observations. In this respect, the helper's observation is not passive but always goal-directed.

The observer's presence influences the person or behavior observed. Even the most passive observer will affect the individual or group being observed. If, for example, a client is told that she is going to be observed through a two-way mirror during an interview, her behavior will be affected in some way. A worker's raised eyebrow or skeptical look in response to an exaggeration by the client may cause the client to become angry, threatened, or embarrassed. Such subtle but powerful confrontations by the observer can best take place after a good relationship has been established, when the worker knows the client well and has sufficient basis for questioning certain information. The observer has to be conscious that his or her reactions do not necessarily lead the client into discussing approved client behavior.

Communication Skills

Communication—that is, the exchange of information between people—is the basic ingredient in helping people. It is the social worker's chief tool. The client has to be able to tell the worker what is troubling him or her, and the worker has to let the client know he or she understands what is said. Through the reciprocal process of communication and understanding, the client is then in the best position to transform new information into new behavior.

An individual or group can accept a communication only when the communication is understood. If the communication is not understood, it will be disregarded. The most obvious example is a client who communicates in a different language from the worker's. Interpreters improve the situation somewhat, but injecting a third party increases the chances for distortion. Communication should also be compatible with the client's life style and general interests. Often, words used by one group of people are not understood by another. For example, a worker might comment, "It apparently was a traumatic episode that caused you some anxiety." The client might reply, "Oh, no, man. I was scared shitless and uptight!" The worker should use clear, nontechnical words: "You were probably scared and nervous."

Nonverbal behavior can also be significant communication. A handshake, facial expression, mode of eye contact, bodily posture, yawning, and other nonverbal behavior can communicate valuable information about the client to the skilled observer. These behaviors often communicate feelings that the client is unable to say in words. Emotional pain may render one speechless. Tears may communicate pain, in which case the worker can respond empathetically: "I guess it hurts you so much that it's hard to talk about it." In family treatment, children often sit by their favorite parent; increased social distance in seating arrangements may indicate the less preferred members of the family. The distance and postures that clients assume in their interviews with the worker also indicate the amount of acceptance or rejection they feel toward the worker.

Interviewing involves listening, interpreting, and questioning. Annette Garrett once said that interviewing is an art and that everyone engages in interviewing. While the social worker is interviewing a client, the client is also interviewing the worker! The social worker, however, is a professional interviewer whose skilled technique is accompanied by theoretical knowledge, appropriate values, and by conscious study of his or her own practice. "The obvious fact about interviewing," states Garrett, "is that it involves communication between two people. It might be called professional conversation."[19]

Listening is a fundamental task of interviewing. A good interviewer is a good listener. A good listener does not merely listen passively but is sincerely interested in, and concentrating on, what is being said. Occasional brief, relevant comments or questions give the client the feeling that the listener wants to and does understand to a great degree what the client is trying to say. Listening to silences may occasionally be embarrassing, but one should not be too quick to fill them with comments or further questions. Silences must be respected because the client may be searching for words to communicate something difficult or painful. The listener must be sensitive to the client's needs and feelings and must recognize when so many areas are being opened up that neither the interviewer nor the client can handle them all at once.

The process of *interpretation* should be continuous in communication between the social worker and the individual or group. In achieving as fully as possible an understanding of the client's problem, the worker has to interpret constantly the meanings (conscious and unconscious) of the client's behavior and words. The social worker should, in effect, develop a "third ear" tuned to deeper interpretations of what the client is saying. Initially, the worker should make interpretations only for herself or himself, not for the client. These initial interpretations are hypotheses to be tested and either rejected or retained, pending further confirmation. "Flexibility, the ability to change our hypothesis with the appearance of new evidence," notes Garrett, "is a trait well worth cultivating."[20]

Generally, interpreting case material for clients is not as productive as helping clients to arrive at their own interpretations and conclusions at their own place. On occasion the worker can, however, help the client make connections. In order to do this, at least three conditions have to exist: (1) a good working relationship, (2) good timing, and (3) indications that the material is already near a level of awareness or consciousness. The following case, involving incest between a father and his oldest daughter, age fourteen, highlights these three factors. The daughter, who is being seen individually, is not in the interview. It is the third interview with the father and mother.

Father: My wife is very hard to live with. She's always nagging that I'm always laying around the house doing nothing.

Mother: That's true. He had his auto accident three years ago, and I know he'll never regain the complete use of his leg—but he can at least do some things around the house. He's like one of the kids. I constantly have to yell at all of them.

Father: Yep! That's true (laughing).

Worker: That must have been quite a responsibility you assumed following your husband's accident. Were there ever times when you yelled at or scolded Tricia (fourteen-year-old daughter) and your husband?

Mother: Yes. Many times. Why, they used to sneak off together in the car and he would buy her things. It made me jealous. When they'd get back, I'd really scold them!

Father: See what I mean? She really can be a bitch. You can't blame me for wanting to get out of the house.

Worker: It sounds as if your husband *adopted* or was *placed* in the role of a peer or boyfriend to Tricia since the accident.

Father: (Smiling.)

Mother: I guess I was behaving like a mother to him, too. I really think that's what happened. Maybe I pushed him into it.

Father: (Father didn't say anything but looked at mother very seriously and in thought.)

Questioning is another component in communication that is an important skill for social workers to develop. What you ask is what you get! Accusatory, tricky, abrupt, interrogation-type questions are counterproductive in social work interviews because they place the client on the defensive. The manner and tone in which questions are asked will often determine whether or not the question will be answered. Again, good timing, appropriateness, and a good relationship with the client enhance the questioning process.

Usually, questions that are leading and open-ended are more productive than questions that can be answered with a simple yes or no. Open-ended questions stimulate the client to elaborate on the story. Questions should evolve smoothly and not interrupt the comfortable pace of the client. Charging ahead of the client with questions may result in confusion for the client and in valuable information missed for the worker. Garrett suggests that a good general rule is to ask questions for only two purposes: to obtain needed information or to direct the client's conversation from fruitless to fruitful channels.[21]

Empathy Skills

The term *empathy* has been defined as the "imaginative projection of one's own consciousness into another being."[22] Empathy may be viewed as both a cognitive and affective process and as a complex skill containing three components: (1) the ability to distinguish among and label the thoughts and feelings of another, (2) the ability to take mentally the role of another, as in role-taking, and (3) the ability to become emotionally responsive to another's feelings.[23] The ability to empathize enhances the helping relationship between the social worker and the client.

The social worker must be willing to enter into the emotional experience of the client. The verbal and nonverbal feeling cues that manifest themselves in the client's internal state are perceived by the social worker in an open, receptive, passive manner. Thomas Keefe states:

> Clients evoke physiological and emotional responses in the worker. When unfettered by complex cognitive processes, such as premature diagnosing, the worker sorts his or her own unique responses to the client from the feelings shared with the client. The worker than provides accurate verbal feedback to the client regarding his or her understanding and feelings. These several behaviors, feelings and thoughts comprise empathy.[24]

For example, Mr. Bolton, an elderly man in his mid-seventies who lives alone, who suffers from high blood pressure, and who was recently robbed by three young men, tells the social worker about his fear of leaving his apartment. He feels very depressed and lonely. After listening intently and empathetically to Mr. Bolton's story, the social worker says:

> It must be very, very difficult to be somewhat limited because of your high blood pressure, getting older, and then being assaulted and robbed. I can really understand how you feel and why you are afraid to leave your apartment. It is the only place you feel safe. However, isolating yourself can contribute to your feelings of loneliness. We've got to figure out how you can leave your apartment safely and begin to reach out and establish new social relationships.

The social worker, in effect, placed himself emotionally and psychologically in Mr. Bolton's situation and felt the physical security of the apartment but also its confining and socially isolating aspects. Even though the social worker did not change Mr. Bolton's situation, the fact that he verbalized what Mr.

Bolton was feeling made the elderly man feel that at least one person in the world understood what he was experiencing. Mr. Bolton did not feel he was alone—he felt supported. Furthermore the worker's statement, *"We've* got to figure out how you can leave your apartment safely," reinforced Mr. Bolton's feelings that he indeed was not alone and that *together* they would find a solution to the problem.

Research has demonstrated that when suffering and dilemma is sensed by another person, it is perceived as empathic by the client.[25] Because of this empathy, the client will share more about himself or herself. This additional disclosure of feelings and personal discussion by the client builds more trust into the client/social worker relationship and facilitates problem solving in the treatment process.[26] Moreover, being empathetic makes the social worker more cognizant of the client and his or her social context.

Social Work Assessment Skills

Having developed the basics of helping, engagement, observation, communication, and empathy skills, the next task is to develop basic social work assessment skills in order to have a conceptual framework for helping people with their difficulties. In its purest form assessment is simply the basis for a plan of action. In social work it is the assessment of the person-in-environment complex out of which develops a plan for intervention. It includes those activities in the selection and interpretation of information relevant to treatment. The goal is to define the areas for intervention and delineate the types of intervention strategies and treatment goals.[27]

Marjorie Monkman and Paula Allen–Meares present a social work assessment model called TIE (the *T*ransactions between *I*ndividuals and *E*nvironments). This framework, developed by Marjorie Monkman, maps the domain of social work assessment, intervention, and outcome. This framework also has other uses in outcome research and for organizing values, knowledge, and skills in practice settings. Using an ecological perspective, the "TIE Framework" centers on the transactions and interface between persons and the environment. In theory the worker can be more effective in the intervention when he or she has assessed fully each side of the interface between person and environment.[28]

On the *person* side of the interface, the social worker focuses on the coping behaviors (cognitive, behavioral, affective) of the person, which include: (1) *surviving;* (2) *affiliating;* and (3) *growing and achieving.* Surviving–coping behaviors are defined by Monkman and Allen–Meares as those behaviors that enable the person to obtain and use resources and make it possible to continue life or activity. Affiliating–coping behaviors are the behaviors that enable the person to relate to other persons and institutions in the environment satisfactorily, that is, the capacity to develop and maintain close personal relationships as well as relate to resources and structures (institutions). Growing-and-achieving coping behaviors are the behaviors that enable the person to pursue intellectual and social activities valuable to the self as well as others.[29]

On the environment side of the interface of the framework is the "Quality of Impinging Environments." This is defined as those positive and negative qualities and characteristics of the situation with which the person (client) is in direct contact. The three major components of this environment include: (1) *resources* (people, organizations, or institutions that can be helpful); (2) *expectations* (roles, tasks); and (3) *laws and policies* (binding customs, rules, policies governing individual behaviors).

The task of the social worker, then, is to help people and their environment form a better match so that persons can live a more enriched and productive life, hence, also improving the environment. In short the social worker intervenes with the goal of bringing about a more positive outcome for both the person and the environment. The following case provided by the authors will serve as an example for incorporating the "TIE" assessment framework.

CASE ILLUSTRATION

Mark, an only child, is a bright, fourteen-year-old middle-class Anglo youngster residing in an affluent West coast suburban area. He was referred to a community drug treatment program by the school because he was caught using cocaine with a few male peers on two occasions. His parents had been divorced three years and had joint custody of Mark. Although the parents were only a few miles from each other, Mark "bounced" back and forth living with his parents depending upon each of his parents' business and social commitments. Mark admitted using cocaine about three times per week and getting "loaded" on marijuana, "coke" and alcohol on weekends. He began experimenting with marijuana at age 11 when his parents were divorcing. Six months later, his maternal grandmother, who often took care of him on weekends, suddenly died of a heart attack.

Mark's parents were college graduates. His father, a realtor and former 1960s "flower child," admitted that he on occasion would smoke marijuana in his son's presence. The mother, a department store manager, divorced the father because he had been involved in several affairs over most of the years they had been married. The parents tended to minimize Mark's drug use but they did acknowledge that his school performance had been deteriorating for a few years.

The focus of the TIE Framework begins by identifying the critical players and elements in the case: Mark, the mother, the father, the deceased grandmother, *and* the transactions between and among them and the environment. The drug treatment social worker begins with Mark since he is having the most difficulty functioning. There are certain questions that the worker has to ask to assist in the assessment, outlined as follows:

Mark's Transactions

What are the transactions between and among Mark and his mother, Mark and his father, Mark and his late grandmother? What are Mark's transactions with the school, peers at school, peers at home, and drug life style? What are his transactions with the drug program? What are his social and recreational resources and expectations?

Mother's Transactions

What are the transactions between and among the mother and Mark, the mother and the father, the mother and the late grandmother? What are the transactions between the mother and her employment, social life (new relationship?), and relatives? What are her psychosocial strengths and housing, recreational, and economic resources? Does her current life style and structure involve a place for Mark? What are her expectations concerning Mark?

Father's Transactions

What are the transactions between and among the father and Mark, the father and mother, the father and late grandmother? What are the transactions between the father and his employment, social life (new relationship?), and relatives? What are his psychosocial strengths and housing, recreational, and economic resources? Does the father's life style and structure permit a place for Mark? What are the father's expectations concerning Mark?

Late Grandmother's Transactions

What were the transactions between and among the grandmother and Mark, his mother and father? What emotional and economic resources did she provide Mark and the parents? Did the grandmother's life style and structure provide a place for Mark? What were her expectations concerning Mark?

Even though the grandmother was not living, her loss was still having a significant emotional impact upon Mark's life. Among life's most stressful, critical life events for adolescents, is the loss of a parent through death, secondly, losing a parent through divorce. In Mark's case he lost his parents through divorce and six months later he lost his grandmother—indeed two very traumatic life events.

The following TIE Framework (Table 9–1) presented by Monkman and Allen–Meares, assists in the identification of critical elements, the focus of the change efforts, and the areas in which the results of the change efforts are found.[30]

The TIE Framework reveals that a significant amount of positive change occurred in Mark's case. Other cases may exhibit more or less change. Sometimes negative trends can be seen, which then call for different, more effective intervention strategies. Changes that are often related as change in one category may affect change in others. For example, as Mark vented his unresolved feelings about his grandmother, he felt less depressed, hence, had less need for drugs. His health improved and he went out for sports. As he

TABLE 9–1 TIE ASSESSMENT AND EVALUATION OUTCOME FRAMEWORK

COPING BEHAVIORS	QUALITY OF IMPINGING ENVIRONMENT
Surviving	*Resources Informal*
Assessment: Mark's school work is poor. He has a substance abuse problem.	*Assessment:* Housing is inconsistent for Mark. Receives minimal affection and care from his parents.
Outcome: Mark is in a drug treatment program. School work is improving.	*Outcome:* The parents are providing Mark more consistent housing and involving him more in their lives.
Affiliating	*Societal*
Assessment: Mark's relationship to his parents is strained—Mark still misses the grandmother.	*Assessment:* Drug treatment and tutoring program is needed for Mark. Family therapy is indicated.
Outcome: Mark's relationship with his parents is improving. He is working through his loss of the grandmother.	*Outcome:* Mark is attending a drug treatment program and receiving tutoring. Mark and his parents are in family therapy.
Information and Skills	*Formal*
Assessment: The parents did not know where to obtain family therapy or a tutor for Mark.	*Assessment:* Some local business firms provide recreational outings for youths.
Outcome: The parents learned about family therapy services from the drug program. At the parents' request, the school obtained a tutor for Mark.	*Outcome:* Mark is participating regularly in business-sponsored recreational activities. He is developing new, positive friends.
Growth and Achievement	*Expectations*
Assessment: Mark has poor academic achievement and frequent truancy. His health has deteriorated due to late evening life style and drugs.	*Assessment:* Neither parent wanted to assume responsibility for Mark.

TABLE 9–1 (*continued*)

Outcome:	*Outcome:*
Mark has stopped drugs. Has gone out for the cross-country team. With tutoring, grades are improving. Is working as a boxboy on weekends.	Both parents have now given Mark priority in their lives. Parents are giving Mark much more attention and assisting him with some of his homework.
Coping Pattern	***Policies and Procedures***
Assessment:	*Assessment:*
Mark's behavioral pattern toward school was irresponsible, as was his life with illegal drugs. Drugs were in part dulling his psychological pain related to parental rejection and the loss of the grandmother.	The school had the option of sending Mark to juvenile court for his substance abuse and truancy.
Outcome:	*Outcome:*
Mark is planning to graduate from high school and go to junior college. He is coping better with the loss of the grandmother. Feels less angry toward parents.	School policies permitted a diversion program referral for Mark's drug problem. The school decided to allow Mark to improve his school performance.

was feeling psychologically better, he had much less need to use drugs, which improved his health; this motivated him to do better in school. Soon, he was "drug free."

METHODS ENHANCING THE DEVELOPMENT OF SOCIAL WORK SKILLS

As a means of increasing social work skills and providing guides and controls to the activity of the social worker, Gordon suggests the employment of case recording, supervision, case conferences, review and evaluation, and consultation.[31] Since increasing skill and providing controls are processes of different orders, each with a specific goal, only components related to the development of social work skill will be discussed here. Methods used in social work that have as a primary goal the enhancement and development of social work skills are *case recording, supervision,* and *consultation.* These methods may be used at any level of social work practice, from work with individuals to community organization activity.

Case Recording

The expectation that the helping process will be carefully recorded has been an important part of the social work profession for many years. Although recording might also be accomplished through an audio recorder or video tape recorder and perhaps be utilized even more effectively than *written* documents, these methods tend to be the exception rather than the rule in student field placements. This section will therefore concern only written process recording. Case recording can be laborious, frustrating, and time consuming.[32] Some agency administrators argue that the freeing of time previously used for recording permits social workers to devote their energies to direct service, research, advancement of professional knowledge, and skill development.[33] Although this view has merit—particularly in the case of experienced, skilled social workers—case recording, and particularly process recording, remains a valuable tool for developing skills in the social work student. *Process recording* has been defined as the written description of the dynamic interaction that has taken place in an interview. This description should contain factual information, student observations, and an account of both the client's and the student's activity.[34]

Process recording is a tool in developing skills that encourages the student or practitioner to rethink each interview with the awareness that the experiences of interaction with the client must be made explicit for the supervisor to provide maximum assistance. The written report also allows the supervisor to evaluate rather quickly a student's ability to respond to a client's feelings as well as the extent to which the student can integrate knowledge and theory from reading, practice experience, and the classroom.[35]

Margaret Dwyer and Martha Urbanowski maintain that although *unstructured* process recording may be useful in early stages of learning, it gradually diminishes in value. As a means of retaining the value of process recording as a tool for learning, they suggest introducing *structure* into it. They offer an operational framework the social worker can adapt to his or her own particular needs and rate of development. Having been tested over a considerable period of time, the framework includes six parts:

1. *Purpose of interview.* The social worker should formulate a statement of purpose that is clear, concise, and specific.

2. *Observations.* The social worker should state general impressions of the physical and emotional climate at the outset of the interview and its impact on the client.

3. *Content.* One section of the recording should be devoted to the actual description of the interview, its length, depending upon the person's stage of development, and learning patterns. The content section should include:
   a. A description of how the interview began.
   b. Pertinent factual information and responses to it by both the client and student.

    c. A description of the feeling content of the interview on the part of both student and client.

    d. Notes on the client's preparation for the next interview and on how the interview ended.

4. *Impressions.* This part should include impressions based on facts. This process gradually develops into diagnostic thinking as one begins to integrate course content and to gain understanding of the interaction between oneself and the client.

5. *Worker's role.* This section highlights activity in the interview and reflects use of social work skills and techniques one has acquired.

6. *Plan.* The worker should make a brief statement of plans for the next interview and record thoughts about some long-range goals for this client.[36]

Dwyer and Urbanowski point out that people differ in their readiness to become more selective in recording the content of an interview. Because each social worker is unique in life experiences, exposure to social work, personal talents, and cultural background, instruction in process recording must be tailored to individual needs. They also add that the ability to risk oneself in recording is largely dependent on one's relationship with the supervisor.[37]

Supervision

In social work, *supervision* has been defined as an "administrative process designed to improve services to clients through development of skill in the employment of agency-structured processes."[38] Traditionally, two major functions in supervision are recognized: an administrative function and a teaching function. Only the teaching function in supervision will be discussed here.

The teaching function of supervision can generally be divided into five areas: (1) social work philosophy and the history and policies of the agency; (2) self-awareness; (3) available resources in the agency and community; (4) the priorities of case service and management of time; and (5) social work knowledge, techniques, and skills.[39] The emphasis in this chapter will be on the fifth area.

Kenneth Watson describes six different models of supervision in social work: tutorial, case consultation, supervisory group, peer-group supervision, tandem supervision, and team model. He claims that social work has vacillated between a tutorial model that needlessly restricts competent social workers and abandonment of this model for some type of group method that might do the supervisory job more efficiently.[40] In elaborating the strengths and weaknesses of each model, Watson states that the tutorial model is the most useful approach for students or inexperienced workers. The teaching-learning component is important in this model because both parties assume responsibility for its success.[41]

The teaching role in social work supervision has blended psychoanalytic theory with educational principles. Lucille Austin cites the following educational principles that have evolved in supervisory teaching in social work:

1. The importance of understanding the needs and capacities of the individuals who are learning must be recognized.

2. The subject matter to be learned and the student's way of learning must be related to each other.

3. The subject matter to be taught must be generalized from significant specific facts in the case (or group of cases) and must be presented in meaningful ways with some orderly progression in intellectual and emotional demands on the learner.

4. The task of mastering a substantial body of knowledge from other disciplines, the sciences of human relations, and from the growing body of social work knowledge and social work demands that a high degree of disciplined use of the intellect be brought to bear in learning.

5. Learning about people in order to help them is a highly charged emotional situation that can be a spur to learning but can also be a source of conflict.

6. A student learns best from a teacher he or she likes.

7. Self-awareness is essential to understanding others.[42]

The supervisor-student (or -worker) relationship is seen as a primary factor in learning. This relationship is viewed as a means to an end, not an end in itself. Becoming too dependent is discouraged and other sources of learning are encouraged. In addition to process recording, the discussion method has been the method of choice in supervisory teaching, according to Austin, because it allows for participation by the learner, who must develop his or her own ideas. Assuming a positive relationship exists between supervisor and student, the supervisor can take a more active role in helping the student develop specific skills. The kind of role depends, however, on the teaching style of the supervisor and the scope of his or her imagination. One supervisor discovered, for example, that by using a color chart, students increased their skill in perceiving different client defense mechanisms in interviews. The students were asked to underline their process recordings in a color to show the different defense mechanisms used by their clients: red was used for denial, orange for resistance, yellow for projection, and so forth. Defense mechanisms dominating a particular interview were thus easily discovered. In addition, because several interviews were reviewed, the students could see changes taking place over time. As a result of this teaching technique, the supervisor found that much time was saved and much anger and frustration were avoided. "At the same time, however," stated the supervisor, "the student was still 'forced' into thinking, which is a significant ingredient of any teaching endeavor."[43]

Consultation

Consultation in social work is a method of problem solving that involves a time-limited, purposeful, contractual relationship between a knowledgeable expert (the consultant) and a less knowledgeable practitioner (the social worker or student). According to Lydia Rapoport, consultation

> involves a process concerned with problem definition and problem solution for the purpose of strengthening the consultee in his designated professional role functioning by increasing his knowledge and skills, modifying his attitudes and behavior to solve specific work problems or more generally to enhance his work performance for the ultimate benefit of the clientele he serves.[44]

A consultant is usually invited by an agency to provide a specific consultation service. The content may be focussed on client casework problems, development of policy, administrative problems, or program planning. When the focus is an individual client problem, supervisory staff should also be actively involved, since the entry of a consultant into an agency often creates anxiety and insecurity, particularly among training staff and supervisors. Because consultation approximates the functions of supervision and training, care must be taken not to undermine staff roles, status, and responsibility.[45]

For example the consultant process in a *client-centered* case presentation involves mutual interaction of consultant and consultee to solve a problem. The consultee (social worker or student) selects a case about which there is concern. The consultant carefully listens to all details of the case, emphasizing areas where the consultee is experiencing anxiety, psychological "blocks," or limited skills. These factors, usually unknown to the consultee, frequently impede progress with the case. On occasion, merely discussing a case with an objective outsider leads to insight about the problem. When the consultee is not aware of a problem limiting movement in the case, the consultant may skillfully point out what the issues are in such a way that the consultee does not feel threatened or anxious. The consultant's goals are to help clients indirectly by helping those persons (consultees) who are trying to help clients. Also, by participating in consultation, the consultee gains more self-awareness and develops additional skills in social work practice.

CONCLUDING COMMENT

Social work skill is defined as the social worker's capacity to set in motion with a client interventive processes of change based on social work values and knowledge in a situation relevant to the client. Competence in social work practice lies in developing skill in the use of social work methods and social work techniques for intervention into problem situations.

The dynamic process in learning skills is complex and difficult to communicate. Mental skills are uniquely taught and learned. Given written and oral instructions about skills and given time, individuals may develop the skill themselves when they form a plan to guide their actions; yet they will fully maximize these skills only with experience. By viewing social work practice as an art, each practitioner will develop a configuration of techniques and skills that reflects his or her own style.

Six areas and related key concepts were highlighted as recommended basic skills for beginning social work practice: *basic helping skills, engagement skills, observation skills, communication skills, empathy skills*, and *social work assessment skills.* The new worker needs to develop perceptive skills in order to look at familiar things with new eyes to identify people who need help and conditions that need to be changed. In developing engagement skills, the process of effectively involving individuals, families, or groups in a helping situation requires the purposeful use of self. Factors such as the time, setting, and structure of the interview may enhance or impede the engagement process. The engagement process includes beginning, middle, and ending phases. In learning observation skills, social workers must become aware of particular biases that distort their perception of others. Observation is more than just seeing; the observer chooses what to see. Equally important are communication skills. Clients can accept a communication only when they understand it. Various suggestions, supported by brief case examples, were provided for developing skill in some components of communication (listening, interpreting, and questioning). Empathy is both a cognitive and an affective process, a complex skill that can be learned in order to help people. The ability to enter into the emotional experience of the client enhances the therapeutic relationship. Developing assessment skills helps the social worker develop plans for intervention.

As a means of developing and enhancing social work skills, process recording, supervision, and consultation are frequently used. *Process recording* encourages the student to rethink each helping experience in detail. It also allows the supervisor to evaluate quickly a social worker's ability to respond to a client's feeling.

In *supervision*, the supervisor-supervisee relationship is one of the primary factors in learning. In addition to process recording, the *discussion method* is most useful in supervisory teaching because it allows participation of the learner, who must generate his or her own ideas.

Consultation is a method of problem solving that involves a time-limited, purposeful, contractual relationship between a knowledgeable expert (the consultant) and a less knowledgeable practitioner (the consultee). Upon presentation of a problem case, the consultant carefully listens to details of the case and tactfully helps the consultee identify factors impeding progress. The purpose of the consultation is to strengthen the consultee's skill in the helping process for the benefit of the clients being served.

SUGGESTED READINGS

Bartlett, Harriett M. *The Common Base of Social Work Practice.* New York: National Association of Social Workers, 1970.

Bisno, Herbert. "A Theoretical Framework for Teaching Social Work Methods and Skills." *Undergraduate Social Work Education for Practice: A Report on Curriculum Content and Issues,* edited by Lester J. Glick. Vol. I. Washington, D.C.: U.S. Government Printing Office, 1971.

Caplan, Gerald. *The Theory and Practice of Mental Health Consultation.* New York: Basic Books, 1970.

Chea, Mary Wong. "Research on Recording." *Social Casework* 53 (March 1972): 177–180.

Crawford, Blaine. "Use of Color Charts in Supervision." *Social Casework* 52 (April 1971): 220–222.

Dwyer, Margaret, and Urbanowski, Martha. "Student Process Recording: A Plea for Structure." *Social Casework* 46 (May 1965): 283–286.

Garrett, Annette. *Interviewing: Its Principles and Methods.* New York: Family Service Association of America, 1972.

Gartner, Alan, and Riessman, Frank. "New Training for New Services." *Social Work* 17 (November 1972): 55–63.

Getzel, George S., Goldberg, Jack R., and Salmon, Robert. "Supervising in Groups as a Model for Today." *Social Casework* 52 (March 1971): 154–163.

Heraud, Brian J. *Sociology and Social Work.* New York: Pergamon Press, 1970.

Kadushin, Alfred. *Consultation in Social Work* 2nd ed. New York: Columbia University Press, 1985.

Kadushin, Alfred. "Supervisor-Supervisee: A Survey." *Social Work* 19 (May 1974): 288–297.

Legge, David, ed. *Skills.* Baltimore: Penguin Books, 1970.

Loewenberg, Frank, and Dolgoff, Ralph. *Teaching of Practice Skills in Undergraduate Programs in Social Welfare and Other Helping Services.* New York: Council on Social Work Education, 1971.

Lusby, Sarah T., and Rudney, Bernice D. "One Agency's Solution to the Recording Problem." *Social Casework* 54 (December 1973): 586–590.

Monkman, Marjorie, and Allen–Meares, Paula. "The TIE Framework: A Conceptual Map for Social Work Assessment," *Areté,* Vol. 10, No. 1, Spring 1985, The University of South Carolina, p. 42. Also see Marjorie Monkman, "A National Study of Outcome Objectives in Social Work Practice: Person and Environment," unpublished paper, University of Illinois, Urbana Illinois.

Murdaugh, Jessica. "Student Supervision Unbound." *Social Work* 19 (March 1974): 131–132.

Perlman, Helen Harris. *Social Casework: A Problem-Solving Process.* Chicago: University of Chicago Press, 1957.

Pierson, Arthur. "Social Work Techniques with the Poor." *Social Casework* 51 (October 1970): 481–485.

Rapoport, Lydia, ed. *Consultation in Social Work Practice.* New York: National Association of Social Workers, 1971.

Rose, Sheldon D. "Students View Their Supervision: A Scale Analysis." *Social Work* 10 (April 1965): 90–96.

Stringer, Lorene A. "Consultation: Some Expectations, Principles and Skills." *Social Work* 6 (July 1961): 85–90.

Taylor, Alice L. "Case Recording: An Administrative Responsibility." *Social Casework* 34 (June 1953): 240–246.

ENDNOTES

1. *Webster's Third New International Dictionary* (Springfield, Mass.: G. & C. Merriam, 1966). p. 2133.
2. A. T. Welford, "On the Nature of Skill," in David Legge, ed., *Skills* (Baltimore: Penguin Books, 1970), pp. 21–22.

3. Brian J. Heraud, *Sociology and Social Work* (New York: Pergamon Press, 1970), p. 223.
4. Werner W. Boehm, "The Nature of Social Work," *Social Work* 3 (April 1958): 11.
5. Ibid.
6. William E. Gordon, "A Critique of the Working Definition," *Social Work* 7 (October 1962): 7.
7. Ibid., p. 8.
8. Ibid. Italics (ours) call attention to the fact that the way a social worker applies skills is a unique phenomenon, an "artistic creation."
9. See Ruth Smalley, "Social Casework: The Functional Approach"; Helen Harris Perlman, "Social Casework: The Problem-Solving Approach"; and Florence Hollis, "Social Casework: The Psychological Approach," in Robert Morris, ed., *Encyclopedia of Social Work,* 16th issue (New York: National Association of Social Workers, 1971), pp. 1195–1225.
10. See Emanuel Tropp, "Social Group Work: The Developmental Approach"; William Schwartz, "Social Group Work: The Interactionist Approach"; and Charles D. Garvin and Paul H. Glasser, "Social Group Work: The Preventive and Rehabilitative Approach," in *Encyclopedia of Social Work,* pp. 1246–1272.
11. Robert Perlman, "Social Planning and Community Organization: Approaches," in Robert Morris, op. cit., p. 1338.
12. See Ibid., p. 1339: Robert Perlman and Arnold Gurin, *Community Organization and Social Planning* (New York: John Wiley, 1972), pp. 52–89; Alfred J. Kahn, *Theory and Practice of Social Planning* (New York: Russell Sage Foundation, 1969), pp. 60–129; and Bradford W. Sheafor, "The Community Adjustment Process from a System Perspective," *Journal of Social Welfare* 1 (April 1974): 37–44.
13. Harriett M. Bartlett, *The Common Base of Social Work Practice* (New York: National Association of Social Workers, 1970), p. 195.
14. Legge, *Skills,* pp. 237–248.
15. Helen Harris Perlman, *Social Casework: A Problem-Solving Process* (Chicago: University of Chicago Press, 1957), pp. 157–158 (emphasis ours).
16. Frank Loewenberg and Ralph Dolgoff, *Teaching of Practice Skills in Undergraduate Programs in Social Welfare and Other Helping Services* (New York: Council on Social Work Education, 1971), p. 6.
17. Herbert Bisno, "A Theoretical Framework for Teaching Social Work Methods and Skills," in Lester J. Glick, ed., *Undergraduate Social Work Education for Practice: A Report on Curriculum Content and Issues,* Vol. I (Washington, D.C.: U.S. Government Printing Office, 1971), p. 248.
18. Loewenberg and Dolgoff, *Teaching of Practice Skills,* pp. 60–67.
19. Annette Garrett, *Interviewing: Its Principles and Methods* (New York: Family Service Association of America, 1972), p. 5. Ms. Garrett's book, first published in 1942, has been translated into nineteen foreign languages. A true classic in the social work literature, it is an unparalleled resource for learning about interviewing.
20. Ibid., p. 61.
21. Ibid., p. 48.
22. *Webster's New Collegiate Dictionary* (Springfield, Mass.: G. & C. Merriam Co., Publishers, 1950), p. 269.
23. Norma D. Feshbach, "Empathy in Children: Some Theoretical and Empirical Considerations," *Counseling Psychologist,* 5 (1975): 25–30.
24. Thomas Keefe, "Empathy Skill and Critical Consciousness," *Social Casework* 61 (September 1980): 388–389. Reprinted with permission of the Family Service Association of America.
25. Wilbur Wright, "Counselor Dogmatism, Willingness to Disclose and Client's Empathy Ratings," *Journal of Counseling Psychology* 22 (September 1975): 390–394.
26. Tamar Plitt Halpern, "Degree of Client Disclosure as a Function of Past Disclosure, Counselor Disclosure, and Counselor Facilitativeness," *Journal of Counseling* 24 (January 1977): 41–47.

27. Srinika Jayaratne and Rona Levy, *Empirical Clinical Practice* (New York: Columbia Press, 1979), p. 17.
28. Marjorie Monkman and Paula Allen–Meares, "The TIE Framework: A Conceptual Map for Social Work Assessment," *Aretê*, Vol. 10, No. 1, Spring 1985, The University of South Carolina, p. 42. Also see Marjorie Monkman, "A National Study of Outcome Objectives in Social Work Practice: Person and Environment," unpublished paper, School of Social Work, University of Illinois, Urbana Illinois.
29. Ibid, p. 42.
30. Ibid, p. 47–48.
31. Gordon, "A Critique of the Working Profession," p. 7.
32. Sarah T. Lusby and Bernice D. Rudney, "One Agency's Solution to the Recording Problem," *Social Casework* 54 (December 1973): 586.
33. Mary Wong Chea, "Research on Recording," *Social Casework* 53 (March 1972): 178.
34. Margaret Dwyer and Martha Urbanowski, "Student Process Recording: A Plea for Structure," *Social Casework* 46 (May 1965): 283. Reprinted with permission of the Family Service Association of America. This section is based upon their unique contribution.
35. Ibid.
36. Ibid., pp. 285–286.
37. Ibid.
38. Sidney S. Eisenberg, *Supervision in the Changing Field of Social Work* (Philadelphia: Jewish Family Service of Philadelphia and the University of Pennsylvania School of Social Work, 1956), p. 51, as quoted in Charles S. Levy, "The Ethics of Supervision," *Social Work* 18 (March 1973): 14.
39. Kenneth W. Watson, "Differential Supervision," *Social Work* 18 (November 1973): 81.
40. Ibid., p. 87.
41. Ibid., p. 83.
42. Lucille N. Austin, "Supervision in Social Work," in Russell H. Kurtz, ed., *Social Work Year Book 1960*, (New York: National Association of Social Workers, 1960), p. 582.
43. Blaine Crawford, "Use of Color Charts in Supervision," *Social Casework* 52 (April 1971): 220–222.
44. Lydia Rapaport, "Consultation in Social Work," in *Encyclopedia of Social Work*, p. 157.
45. Ibid., p. 158.

CHAPTER 10

The Social Worker
in Action

For the social worker the reward is helping clients restore or enhance their social functioning or creating societal conditions favorable to good social functioning. He or she brings to the practice knowledge, values, and skills acquired through preparation and experience as a social worker, plus life experience and innate helping abilities. The way the fundamentals of social work are employed is therefore related to the unique style of each social worker, whose individuality becomes evident through this style. We can best observe this individuality by viewing the social worker in practice activity.

The following case description is one means of observing the work of one social worker involved in helping a family respond to a tragic fire (direct service intervention). The worker also serves as a catalyst in mobilizing a community to address several problems in the social service delivery system that became dramatically evident because of the fire (indirect service intervention). Although social workers are not always active at so many practice levels, the example helps illustrate the many faces of social work.

THE BAEZ FAMILY FIRE*

While driving to work one crisp winter morning, Allen Sutton thought about the peaceful pace of life in Rock Creek. As he passed groups of children walking to school or engaged in lively discussions while they waited for school buses, Allen found the carefree children and quiet neighborhoods somewhat incongruous with the pain and suffering he frequently encountered in his work as a social worker in the Evergreen County Department of Social Welfare.

"Even though we have our problems here, Rock Creek is a good place to raise a family," he mumbled to himself, wishing he had found time for another cup of coffee before starting for work. Most people in Rock Creek undoubtedly would have agreed with Allen's sentiments. Although the town

* The theme for this case is used by permission from the University of Kansas and the University of Kansas School of Social Welfare, Copyright © 1946, University of Kansas.

of 50,000 people was only forty miles from the many cultural and economic resources of Smog City, the state capital, it functioned as a small, self-contained community. The schools were good; the hospitals seemed adequate; a new library was under construction; the people were friendly; and most had enough income to live comfortably.

Turning onto one of the more heavily traveled streets leading to the central business district where his office was located, Allen put on the car radio, hoping a little rock music would substitute for that second cup of coffee. As the radio warmed up, Allen realized that he was going to catch the morning news before any music would be played.

"Station WROK from Rock Creek presents the local news," a familiar voice blared. The voice was that of Harvey McGill, a popular newscaster, disc jockey, and occasional handball partner of Allen's.

"This morning only one news item seems important to this reporter," Harvey began, "and I will change our usual format to insert my own editorial comment in relation to this story."

"This must be important," thought Allen, as he abandoned his impulse to push another button in search of music from one of the Smog City stations.

Harvey continued, "Last night Rock Creek was struck by a tragedy. A flash fire in the home of the David Baez family at 234½ North Pine has killed Mr. Baez and his seven-month-old daughter, Wendy. Mrs. Karen Baez and three other children, who were in the home at the time, were seriously burned and are now being treated at Rock Creek Memorial Hospital.

"The house at 234½ North Pine was once a garage, but when the Baez family moved to Rock Creek one year ago, they could find no adequate housing they could afford. Thus, Mr. Baez worked out an agreement with the owner to convert the garage to a residence in exchange for reduced rent. Baez completed the work last summer, and the family considered it home.

"Baez had been an employee of the Rock Creek Cement Block Company up until three months ago, when a broken leg prevented him from continuing that job. In recent months he had been unemployed.

"The fire began at ten o'clock last night when Baez was filling the gasoline stoves used to heat the house. As he poured the fluid into one of the stoves, there was an explosion, followed by the fire, which gutted the house and burned the people inside.

"After this commercial announcement," Harvey inserted, "I will share with you my personal experiences and reactions to this tragedy."

Allen mentally tuned out the commercial as his thoughts moved to the day David Baez had been in his office seeking financial assistance for his family. It was about six months ago that the case had been assigned to Allen for evaluation of the family's financial needs. Mr. Baez was reluctant to apply for assistance, saying he always thought it was a man's job to provide for his family and he guessed he had failed because there just wasn't enough money for food, clothes, transportation, and housing for a family of six.

When calculating the eligibility of the Baezes for financial assistance, Allen found that Mr. Baez worked full-time at the cement block company as a laborer earning slightly more than minimum wage, around $800 per month, and, with the work he was doing to convert the garage, there was no time to take a "moonlight" job— even if one had been available.

David Baez had also listed his monthly expenses at the time. Deductions from his paycheck (Social Security, health insurance, and so on) amounted to $100. His rent was $250; utilities, especially the high cost of fuel oil to heat the poorly insulated garage, averaged $60; shoes and clothing for a growing family required around $50; car payments and fuel to get to work and meet the usual family transportation needs cost $100; and even with no serious illnesses, medical and dental bills averaged $50. This left almost $200 per month to pay the skyrocketing cost of food for a family of six.

The Baezes were not eligible for financial assistance even though Allen was sympathetic with the very real need for more money, but they did qualify for food stamps, which allowed them to stretch the food money a little farther.

Although Allen knew he had given them all the assistance permitted, he suddenly felt angry, guilty, and distressed that a plea for help had been rejected and had contributed to this tragedy and that he had not tried harder to fight the system when he knew the need was real. "Am I getting hardened to human suffering?" he asked himself as the traffic light changed to green, and he continued toward his office.

Because the Baez family was still part of his case load, Allen knew he would carry major responsibility in helping the surviving members of the family recover from this tragedy. He knew he would have to work out his own guilt if he was to be of maximum help to Mrs. Baez and the children.

The return of Harvey McGill's voice to the radio brought Allen's attention back to the present. "Last night the police monitor at WROK brought news of the fire at 234½ North Pine, and I immediately went to the scene of the tragedy that took the lives of two members of the David Baez family and has left the other four members seriously burned. The remainder of this broadcast will recount my own experiences from the time I reached the scene.

"I was one of the first to arrive at the burning house, where I found that the two ambulances in Rock Creek were insufficient to transport all the burn victims to the hospital. A neighbor and I took one of the children in my car to the emergency room. This badly burned and frightened ten-year-old girl was inconsolable even by the warm and loving neighbor who accompanied us to the hospital.

"The scene at the hospital was indescribable. The one physician on duty made a heroic effort to help the burned and dying members of the Baez family, but there was some delay until additional physicians arrived at the hospital, making this effort less than effective. The small emergency room was inadequate to care for so many people at one time, and the situation was at best chaotic. I stayed on at the hospital until three A.M., doing what I could or what they asked me to do.

"The hospital also was so crowded with patients that most of the surviving family members had to be placed in the halls. The severely burned children were crying and sobbing. We knew the father and the baby were not going to live, and we were fearful for the life of the mother, Karen Baez.

"I saw nurses who daily work with death and suffering crying, and, believe me, I was near to crying myself. It was horrible.

"When I went home a little after three in the morning and tried to sleep, I found it impossible to put the situation out of my head. I got up and took a couple of stiff drinks, but no matter how I tried, I couldn't erase the picture of those badly burned children.

"Also, I kept reminding myself that there had been six people living in that converted garage and that it was miraculous any of them still lived.

"This morning I was up at six o'clock, having enjoyed little or no sleep. I came down to the station and was unable to concentrate on preparing my usual news broadcast. All I could think about was the Baez family and their tragedy. I kept saying to myself: 'Now see here, McGill, you are a veteran reporter. You have seen death and suffering many times. Why are you letting this one get you down?' But no matter how I have tried, it continues to bother me.

"Several questions are running through my mind at this moment:

Can we blame David Baez for not providing more adequate and safe housing for his family?

Is his employer to blame for not paying him more adequately for his labor?

Should our minimum-wage law be revised to ensure that every person who works full time can support his or her family at a sufficient level to provide good and safe housing?

What happened to the enforcement of our building code requirements?

Why was welfare money not made available to ensure that this family had safe housing?

How many more families are there in Rock Creek who risk their lives in unsafe housing each day?

Why doesn't Rock Creek have more adequate ambulance service and emergency room preparedness, and the hospital capacity to take care of such emergencies?

Did the fact that the Baezes are a minority family have anything to do with their situation?

Who will pay the hospital, medical, and funeral expenses this family will face?

How can the people of this community help the surviving members of the Baez family reconstruct their lives?

Who is responsible for this tragedy???

"I will close with this thought: may our complacency disturb us profoundly today."

Allen Sutton turned off the radio as he drove into the parking lot beside his office and thought how lucky Rock Creek was to have a newscaster with the insight of Harvey McGill. Once inside he found the police had already notified the agency that help would be needed for the Baezes, and their case file was waiting on Allen's desk. His already crowded schedule would have to be cancelled to respond to the immediate crisis of the Baez family.

Direct Service Intervention

Allen Sutton knew there were several direct service intervention procedures that he had to institute to help the Baez family. He organized the tasks into three levels of descending immediacy.

First-level tasks:

1. Visit Mrs. Baez in the hospital to help her develop plans for the funeral of her husband and baby daughter.

2. Help Mrs. Baez and her three remaining children deal with grief through supportive counseling.

3. Contact the extended family to help secure their involvement in helping the Baez family.

Second-level tasks:

1. Explore the availability of public housing for the Baez family and try to get them first priority on the waiting list.

2. Alert the Red Cross and Salvation Army of the impending need for clothing and furniture for the Baez family.

3. Arrange for home tutoring for the three Baez children, ages ten, nine, and six, if they are unable to attend school because of injuries.

Third-level tasks:

1. Begin processing public assistance grant for additional medical expenses and financial aid.

2. Arrange for health insurance and Social Security benefit payments to the Baez family.

The first-level tasks seemed to Allen to be the most delicate, since they dealt directly with the emotions of the family. These tasks would call upon Allen's experience, knowledge, and therapeutic skill in dealing with a family in crisis. Allen recalled that crisis can occur at any point in a person's life and that some people react to a greater degree than others to the emotional hazards inherent in certain events. A *crisis* is the *emotional state*, the reaction of the individual or family to the hazardous situation, not the hazardous situation per se. A hazardous event calls for a solution new to the individual or family in relation to life experience.[1]

There are three broad types of crisis situations that may enrich or endanger personality functioning: (1) those that are "biologically tinged," such as adolescence or menopause, and therefore may be anticipated by all people as part of the life cycle; (2) those that are "environmentally tinged," such as a change of job or retirement, and hence are somewhat less inevitable but are usually anticipated; (3) those that are "adventitious," such as disasters, floods, and fire, which are attributable to chance and cannot be anticipated.[2]

Allen had learned that during the crisis period an individual is in a state of acute anxiety. Feelings of helplessness and maybe also hopelessness abound, in particular, if the individual fears he or she is headed in the wrong direction. In this situation, ego patterns are more likely to be open to influence and correction. As defenses are lowered during this temporary period of disequilibrium, the client is usually more accessible to therapeutic influence than prior to the crisis or following establishment of a new equilibrium with its accompanying defense patterns.[3] In this period of upset, there are emotional signs such as tension, anxiety, shame, guilt, or hostility. Old conflicts that may or may not have been satisfactorily resolved in the past may be reactivated because the stresses of a crisis may be viewed as a threat, either to instinctual needs or to one's sense of integrity, a loss involving either a person or a feeling of acute deprivation, or a challenge.[4] Each of these states usually has a typical characteristic accompanying the emotional effect. If the crisis situation is primarily experienced as a threat, for example, it will be accompanied by a great deal of anxiety. If the crisis is experienced primarily as a loss, it will involve depression and mourning. If viewed as a challenge, it will be accompanied by some anxiety or drive for problem solving.[5]

Allen knew Mrs. Baez and the children would be experiencing depression and mourning because of the loss of Mr. Baez and the baby. A certain amount of "grief work" would have to be undertaken with Mrs. Baez and the children in helping them deal with the crisis. Some of the usual tasks in this "grief work," as pointed out by Erich Lindemann, include disconnecting the survivors from psychological bondage to the deceased (they must "bury the dead") by allowing the normal misery of mourning, which may include feelings of somatic distress, weakness, preoccupation with the image of the deceased, and temporary feelings of unreality and guilt; helping the survivors readapt to the environment in which the loved one is missing; and helping them form new social relationships.[6]

Allen had to work quickly, knowing that the state of upset is limited in time. The acute phase of a crisis does not go on indefinitely because somehow the individual or family pushes toward reestablishing itself and achieving a new equilibrium. The new equilibrium, however, may be either healthy or pathological. The natural history of the crisis, with its built-in time limits, therefore suggests that the practitioner must intervene during this acute period if he or she is going to influence the outcome in a brief or economical manner.[7]

As he drove to the hospital, Allen had mixed feelings about approaching the Baez family. He wondered if he could still rely on the crisis intervention knowledge and skills he had learned five years earlier as a social work student at the Smog City Suicide Prevention Center. There were no mental health facilities in Rock Creek other than "old Dr. Reters," a psychiatrist who promised Allen he would see Mrs. Baez once she was out of the hospital if she needed psychiatric treatment. It might be too late then—they needed help now! Even if there were good mental health services available, it might be best for Allen to work with Mrs. Baez if they could develop a good relationship.

At the hospital Allen was told by Dr. Grebb, the staff physician, that he could not speak to Mrs. Baez or the children, as all were under heavy sedation. Mrs. Baez and two of the children were now off the critical list, but their conditions were listed as serious. Danny Baez, age six, was still listed as critical. Dr. Grebb said they had not told Mrs. Baez about her husband's or baby daughter's death so that she would not feel worse. When Allen explained to Dr. Grebb the importance of Mrs. Baez's knowing the true facts of her family to avoid a serious regression or depression, Dr. Grebb agreed to allow him to begin the necessary "grief work" in two days. At that time Mrs. Baez would be on lower doses of medicine and capable of carrying on a conversation.

Two days later Allen visited Mrs. Baez at the hospital. She had second-and-third-degree burns on the upper part of her body. Her arms were the most seriously burned as the result of carrying and protecting her children from the flames. She already seemed quite depressed in response to the severe traumatic assault on her body. She commented that Allen was the first non-hospital person that had visited her. She inquired if her husband and Wendy were doing better and if Allen had seen them. Allen gently informed Mrs. Baez that they had died as a result of the fire. Mrs. Baez stared in disbelief and angrily accused Allen of lying, stating that the nurses had said her husband and Wendy were improving. Allen again told Mrs. Baez that they had passed away. Mrs. Baez began sobbing deeply and then started swearing at the nurses, accusing them of being deceitful. After some moments of crying, Mrs. Baez inquired about the status of her other three children, and Allen told her that two of them had been taken off the critical list and that Danny was beginning to show definite signs of improvement. Mrs. Baez made gestures of wanting to get up, desperately pleading, "I've got to go to them. I've got to go to them." She could hardly move and again began sobbing, stating that she was no good to anyone and that it would have been better if she had died in the fire. Allen commented that although she could not yet be of physical help to the family, certain things required her immediate decisions. She sensed these pertained to arrangements for the funeral of her husband and daughter. She told Allen to go ahead and contact a funeral home and make all the arrangements. She would sign the necessary papers. Noting that

Mrs. Baez was tiring emotionally, Allen asked her if he could contact a clergyman who could see her in the evening. She stated that she was a Roman Catholic and that she had found Father Gallagher very helpful when her father had passed away the year before. She thanked Allen for being thoughtful and apologized for having been angry with him. He said he understood what she was going through and that quite likely the children were experiencing similar feelings. Again Mrs. Baez began to weep, and Allen asked if he had her permission to seek approval from Dr. Grebb for her to speak to the children on the telephone. Mrs. Baez smiled and nodded yes.

The following day Dr. Grebb gave approval for the Baez children to speak to their mother on the telephone. They also did not know of the deaths of their father and sister. When Allen gave Mrs. Baez the news, she didn't know if she would be strong enough to speak to her children. Allen pointed out how strong she had been the day before and said today she might even be stronger. He urged her to call them and said they needed to know the truth and have her reassurance that she would take care of them. She should indicate to her children that she was maintaining control and that they would be together as soon as their medical conditions permitted.

Allen also suggested Mrs. Baez listen to what her children had to say about the event, and if they were silent, that she encourage them to talk. Silence would only lead to increased fears and anxieties. Following Allen's suggestions, Mrs. Baez spoke to the two youngest children, who seemed extremely happy to hear from their mother. She seemed pained as six-year-old Danny cried because he wanted her to see him right away. She promised she would call him three or four times a day, at least for a week or so. Nine-year-old Emma wasn't burned as seriously as had initially been thought, and she told her mother about the new friends she was making in her ward. Emma said she was now walking around and would soon be visiting her mother. Mrs. Baez smiled. Donna, the ten-year-old, was the only one to inquire about her father and Wendy. Mrs. Baez calmly told Donna what had happened to her father and sister. Donna began to cry, and Mrs. Baez's tears ran down her cheeks as she covered the phone. After a minute or so, Mrs. Baez told Donna that it was now up to both of them to try to keep the family together. Donna responded well to this suggestion, according to Mrs. Baez. Mrs. Baez felt better when Allen promised her he would visit the children to keep up their morale.

Allen told Mrs. Baez he had already contacted her sister, as she had suggested, and that she had assumed the responsibility of notifying all the relatives and family friends about the funeral. The funeral was going to be on Saturday (two days hence), and Mrs. Baez cried as she said she wanted to go. Both Mrs. Baez and Allen spoke to Dr. Grebb about this possibility, but the doctor said it would be medically impossible for her even to leave her bed for at least another five to seven days. Allen tried to comfort Mrs. Baez and suggested that perhaps some of her relatives could be invited to visit her following the funeral. She only wanted her mother, sister, in-laws, and

Father Gallagher to visit her. Allen took responsibility for making these arrangements.

Two weeks after the funeral Allen obtained public housing for the Baez family. Mrs. Baez decided to remain in Rock Creek because many people had been so helpful, particularly Maria Bowen, a neighbor who had been taking care of Emma, who had been released from the hospital the previous week. Food supplies, clothing, and furniture were now available at the Red Cross and Salvation Army and would be delivered when needed. Donna was the only child who would not be able to return to school immediately and would require home tutoring for at least six to eight weeks. When contacted by Allen, the school agreed to provide this service.

Allen processed all necessary documents to obtain Social Security, medical benefits, and public assistance for the Baez family. These benefits would begin within thirty days of Mrs. Baez's release from the hospital.

After four weeks Mrs. Baez was making excellent medical progress. Allen arranged temporary homemaker services as she was still unable to use her hands because of heavy gauze bandages. More important, however, Mrs. Baez had now regained her emotional confidence, and, although saddened by the loss of her husband and daughter, she felt she could manage and make a new life for herself and the children. As she left the hospital with her two children, she thanked Allen for all his help and particularly for "forcing" her to face what had to be done.

Indirect Service Intervention

It was apparent to Allen Sutton that many problems that dramatically came to the attention of the community through the Baez tragedy had existed for a long time and certainly needed correcting. He knew that other families in this and other communities were vulnerable to similar tragedies. He understood, too, that the best time to seek resolution of these problems was now when the community had tangible evidence of the impact of these problems on its residents.

As the central helping person in the community involved with the Baez family, Allen felt it was his responsibility to serve as a catalyst for helping Rock Creek initiate plans to prevent additional tragedies. His social work education had prepared him to engage in this type of practice, sometimes called *primary prevention,* and, although most of his work was at the direct service level, he was prepared to offer his leadership in community activities that would indirectly benefit the people of his town.

Although several problems in the service delivery system were apparent, Allen limited his consideration to three. First, he believed he could work productively with the board of the Evergreen County Department of Social Welfare to seek reconsideration of the policies denying financial assistance to a family in such obvious need of additional income. Second, he felt he might encourage several groups in the community to consider supporting a bill before the U.S. Congress to increase the minimum wage. Finally, he believed the community was ready to examine its ambulance service and the adequacy of the emergency room and bed space at Rock Creek Memorial Hospital. Knowing that he had only limited time to work on these issues, Allen was forced to select one of them for his primary attention and give only minimal attention to the others.

Eligibility for Financial Assistance   It was almost a daily experience for Allen to hear criticism of the public assistance program and its requirements. On one side, many people in Rock Creek complained to Allen, when they learned he was a social worker, that too many people were on welfare who could support themselves if they really wanted to exert an effort. On the other side, client groups, such as the Welfare Rights Organization, complained that many people in great need were not eligible for financial aid and that, when people *were* eligible, payments were so low it was almost impossible to make ends meet. Some people on both sides seemed to hold Allen responsible for the policies legislated by the U.S. Congress, adopted by the state welfare department in Smog City, and ultimately carried out by the social worker in Rock Creek—even though Allen, too, was sometimes frustrated by these policies.

One policy that seemed especially damaging was the maximum income requirement for financial assistance. Allen's knowledge of how this policy was established enabled him to know that the state welfare department, within the constraints of federal and state legislation, established the eligibility requirements that had prohibited David Baez from receiving financial assistance, even though his need was obvious. Moreover, because his values were contradicted when he had to refuse service and/or financial assistance to persons he believed were in need of help (thus knowing that their opportunity to develop their fullest potential would be reduced), Allen was motivated to change these policies.

It was evident to Allen that the personal tragedy of the Baez family might be turned into a vehicle to change the eligibility requirements for receiving financial assistance. However, the Baez fire was essentially an issue of local concern and probably would have little impact at the state or federal level. Thus, Allen reluctantly decided to make only a nominal effort to act on this problem at the county level.

With the encouragement of Leonard Amos, director of the Evergreen County Department of Social Welfare, Allen prepared a report on the Baez family, pointing out their serious need even though they were ineligible for financial assistance. This report was presented to the board of the Evergreen County Department of Social Welfare, with copies sent to the state board of social welfare in Smog City. The report concluded with a call for immediate review of the eligibility requirements for public assistance.

Minimum-Wage Legislation   The fact that a person could work full-time at the minimum-wage level and still would not be able to support his or her family adequately was also evident in the case of the Baez family. Again, the public concern over the failure to have adequate legislation for preventing such problems made the time ripe to help the public understand the inadequacies of the existing minimum-wage law.

Because minimum wage is established by federal legislation, Allen knew the tragedy in Rock Creek would have little direct impact on Congress. However, he believed the general community understanding of the problem, which this case would highlight, might influence Congressman Jim Corbin from the Fifth District to support bill H.R. 676, pending before the U.S. House of Representatives. Bill H.R. 676 would increase the minimum wage, which would have meant important increased earnings for David Baez.

Allen again decided on a simple approach to this problem. When Mrs. Baez was well enough, he told her of his desire to visit civic clubs in Rock Creek to discuss the plight of the Baez family prior to the fire and to urge members to express their views to Congressman Corbin.

"If you think this will help other folks, Mr. Sutton," Karen Baez replied, "then please don't hesitate to use our situation as an example. I sure hope no one else has to go through the kind of experience we had." With her willingness to be identified and thus to personalize the problem for the citizens of Rock Creek, Allen arranged speaking engagements with the Chamber of Commerce, the League of Women Voters, the National Association of Social Workers, the Young Democrats, the G.I. Forum, and the Rotary and Kiwanis Clubs during the next month. Although he did not always receive enthusiastic support, Allen felt the issue had received a good hearing in the community.

When Allen later contacted Congressman Corbin's office, he learned there had been a large number of letters supporting H.R. 676 and that Corbin had decided to support the bill.

Emergency Preparedness Allen decided to concentrate his community change activities on encouraging the people of Rock Creek to improve the emergency preparedness of the hospital. This was a problem that could be solved locally, and Allen Sutton believed he might serve effectively as a catalyst for change.

Allen recognized his values placed a premium on community services that provide the best health care possible for each person. "If people are going to be free enough to make the most of their talents," he thought, "they have got to feel that adequate health services are available when needed—especially in an emergency. It is frightening to everyone in town, including me, to think that people may have died because there was inadequate preparation for emergencies at Rock Creek Hospital." Allen also believed it was the responsibility of the community to see that adequate services are provided.

As Allen analyzed the problem, he concluded that Rock Creek had grown rapidly over the past few years and that the hospital had not grown proportionally. Thus, the facilities were overcrowded and inadequate to meet the needs of the population—especially when an emergency placed a sudden demand on the already overtaxed facilities. Clearly, a problem existed, but the hospital's board of directors had not acted to expand the facilities.

Allen's decision was to act to force the hospital board to expand the hospital facilities. In a preliminary examination of this problem, Allen identified four parts. First, the hospital had not made plans to have enough physicians available either at the hospital or on call to respond quickly in such an emergency. Second, there were not enough ambulances, and there was no backup plan. Third, the hospital's emergency room seemed incapable of handling an emergency requiring service to more than two persons at a time. Finally, the general bed capacity of the hospital appeared taxed to the maximum, with little leeway to respond to a rapid influx of new patients.

Allen was aware that he had few data to support his preliminary conclusions that these were significant problems. His next task, then, was to put together a group of people who could study the problem more completely and could actively seek change if it was warranted.

Harvey McGill would be a critical person to involve. He was concerned about the problem and had firsthand experience with the impact of the tragedy on the lives of the Baez family. Furthermore, he was a member of the community's press and could help with public education if needed.

Allen also knew that it would be necessary to involve Dr. Mark Blakeslee, medical director of the hospital, and Ernest Padilla, the hospital administrator. Both had extensive knowledge of the hospital's current operations and its plans for future development. Their technical knowledge would be valuable in defining the problem and in seeking change.

Since Allen anticipated that this activity might lead to a hospital bond issue, Mayor Henrietta Schutz and Mildred Katz, president of the League of Women Voters, also seemed important people to involve. In addition, Allen believed it would be essential to include Lowell O'Hanlon, chairman of the board of the First National Bank of Rock Creek. Mr. O'Hanlon had the reputation of being the most influential person in town, and he could use his power to block change or could be a moving force to create change.

To stimulate consideration of this problem, Allen decided to call all these people together to examine the issue of emergency preparedness and to consider planning action to alleviate the problem. Allen asked Harvey McGill to serve as chairman of this planning group, and Harvey readily agreed, saying, "This thing has been gnawing at me, but I haven't known how to go about attacking the problem."

Harvey invited the others to a meeting to discuss the problem, and all agreed to attend except Lowell O'Hanlon, who expressed interest but would be out of town for three weeks. However, he agreed to have Sheila Siple, executive vice-president of the bank, take his place on the committee.

Allen and Harvey carefully planned the first meeting to allow for full discussion of the problems Allen had identified as well as other issues the members wanted to raise. They discussed the issues fully and pinpointed additional data they would need to understand the problems. The responsibility for collecting data was divided among the members, with Ernest Padilla carrying major responsibility for collecting data about hospital use and national guidelines for emergency preparedness.

At the next meeting these data were discussed, and alternative solutions were considered. First, Dr. Blakeslee agreed to ask the County Medical Society to develop a plan for assuring that medical coverage be available to meet emergency situations at all times. The committee agreed that if the medical society accepted that responsibility, the committee would have only a watchdog role on the issue. Later, this did occur, and a suitable plan of on-duty medical service was developed.

Second, Mayor Schutz reported it would not be economically feasible for the city to maintain more extensive ambulance service, since the present service was not used to its capacity and was already losing money. She suggested, however, that the city might enter into an agreement with Shadow Mountain, a town twenty miles away, to serve one another in a backup capacity for emergency ambulance service. Mayor Schutz and Ernest Padilla prepared a recommendation to the city commission, which subsequently negotiated such an agreement with the Shadow Mountain ambulance service.

Last, the problems of the inadequate emergency room facilities and overcrowded hospital rooms were related to rapid population growth in Rock Creek and the hospital's failure to keep up with that growth. It was evident that a substantial building program would be necessary to correct the problem.

Allen helped the committee think through its goals at this stage of the process. All members believed that each person in the community should have health care available at all times. They also agreed they should work together to stimulate action to improve the physical structure of the hospital to accommodate this need. However, members disagreed on financing plans. One argument was for a forty-year bond issue, while another called for a special tax and increased patient fees. Although Ms. Siple argued that users of the service should carry the burden of the cost and called for the quick payoff of any building debts, the argument for spreading the cost over an extended period of time to all citizens who depend on the hospital for medical care was finally accepted. Ms. Siple reluctantly agreed to support the plan.

The committee next examined the range of strategies that might encourage the hospital board, the body that could decide on this issue, to begin action to improve the hospital facilities. The process would involve a thorough study of health care resources in the area, a project to design and estimate the costs of a new building, a bond issue election by the public, and, ultimately, construction of the new facilities. The planning committee sought a strategy that would help the hospital board assume responsibility for this activity.

"Perhaps I can be of help in thinking about alternative strategies," Allen noted, "by sharing with you a description of several change strategies." Allen then went to a blackboard and drew the following chart.[8]

Perception of Change	Response	Intervention
Rearrangement of resources	Consensus	Collaboration
Redistribution of resources	Difference	Campaign
Change in status relationships	Dissensus	Contest or disruption
Reconstruction of entire system	Insurrection	Violence

Allen noted, "There is no evidence that the members of the hospital board are opposed to this action. Dr. Blakeslee and Mr. Padilla are closely associated with them and have said that they did not act sooner because there was no public expression of concern and that the members needed Mr. Padilla to make the hospital run as efficiently as possible to get maximum use of the existing space."

"Initially," Allen continued, "I see the only demand on the board being to rearrange their resources by diverting staff time into planning. Thus, I would expect a *consensual* situation with the board and suggest a strategy that would allow for a *collaborative* relationship." After some discussion, the other members of the committee agreed with this assessment and turned their attention to means of implementing this strategy.

Again, they agreed their action should be based on an educational approach. They decided to incorporate their findings and recommendations into a report that would be submitted to the hospital board along with a request for an opportunity to present their view at the next meeting of the board.

Dr. Blakeslee, Mr. Padilla, and Allen Sutton wrote the report and submitted it to the board. When they met with the board, Harvey McGill made a moving statement based on his observations of the Baez family tragedy. Mayor Schutz discussed the citizen's dependence on the hospital for medical care and the importance of the adequacy of this service not only for those now living in Rock Creek but also as a prerequisite for future growth and development of the community. Ms. Katz and Ms. Siple expressed their support of the recommendations. Both indicated that if a more thorough study supported the conclusions this committee had reached, the board could count on them to work diligently to gain support for a bond issue to improve the hospital facilities.

Adam Davis, the chairman of the hospital board, expressed appreciation for the work and interest of the committee and indicated that the members would study the material and take action as soon as possible.

At the next meeting, the hospital board voted to *accept the recommendation* and begin a thorough study of expansion of the hospital facilities. The hospital's administrative staff was instructed to plan its activity in a manner that would free time for such study and planning. As administrator of the hospital, Mr. Padilla enthusiastically assumed this new assignment.

Although considerable work remained to be completed, Allen felt gratified that he had helped stimulate Rock Creek to address this problem. "You know," he thought to himself as he drove home from the meeting, "this town can solve many of its problems if we can just find the right way to tackle them."

CONCLUDING COMMENT

The tragic experience of the Baez family provided a skilled social worker with the opportunities to be of professional assistance to a family in crisis and to serve as a community-organizing catalyst regarding several problems in the human service delivery system. This detailed case provides a helpful means of putting flesh on the bones of social work as described in earlier chapters. It is possible to identify many of the concepts discussed previously in terms of this situation and thus to achieve greater appreciation of their meaning.

The competent social worker must be prepared to engage in a wide range of tasks to serve the clients of a social agency effectively. The social worker with a more limited approach might have stopped with providing personal counseling and securing the tangible resources of food, shelter, and clothing for Mrs. Baez. These actions would have achieved the *social work objective* (Figure 1–1) of helping the family *restore its capacity for social functioning*. Important as those services were to Mrs. Baez, Allen Sutton's generalist perspective led him to extend his work on this case to helping the community *create more favorable conditions for social functioning* by preventing similar problems for other families in the future.

Allen assumed a *direct service* crisis intervention role by helping Mrs. Baez confront the painful realities of her life situation. He was able to mobilize her inner psychological strengths that had been temporarily shattered. In part, he did this by meeting some of her dependency needs through assuming responsibilities that Mrs. Baez was not emotionally or physically capable of undertaking for herself, such as making arrangements for the funeral. The social worker was also able to call on Mrs. Baez's emotional strengths of independence by placing her in a role of meeting the dependency needs of her children. Allen Sutton's skillful intervention in helping the family maintain communication ties during the critical stages of the crisis no doubt helped the family remain together. By making sure that the family would have food, shelter, clothing, and money upon their return to the community, the social worker made its adjustment less difficult.

The social worker's *indirect service* intervention role is an example of primary prevention work. That is, the Baez family experience highlighted several conditions that could endanger other unknowing victims. Prevention of similar tragedies, therefore, was the indirect service goal of Allen Sutton.

After giving priority to several problems in the social service delivery system, Allen organized support among key individuals, which led to the preparation of a report calling for an immediate review of the eligibility requirements for public assistance. He interested numerous community groups in a bill that would increase the minimum wage. Strong local support for this measure secured the endorsement of the community's congressman. With regard to the community's poor medical emergency preparedness, the social worker drew on his community change process skills to organize a task force to address this problem. The task force effectively presented its findings to the hospital board, which voted to begin a thorough study of the expansion needs of the hospital.

Allen Sutton was employed by a *social agency*—the Evergreen County Department of Social Welfare. Its primary task was provision of financial assistance to persons in need. The agency served as a vehicle for the *social welfare institution;* it attempted to resolve problems in the area of *economic conditions*. Yet Allen's work quickly led to service in the area of *interpersonal competence* when he helped Mrs. Baez and her children deal with the emotional problems related to the deaths of Mr. Baez and Wendy. It also led him into the *health care* arena in the community.

At all points the social worker was dealing with problems at the *interface between person and environment*. By extending support and encouragement, Allen helped Mrs. Baez interact helpfully with her children when she informed them of the deaths of their father and sister. Although he did most of his work with Karen Baez, Allen always focused his practice on the remaining members of the family so as to keep them together as a family. As shown in Figure 10–1, the person or client in this case was the Baez family. Even the memories of the departed father and baby were viewed as important factors in Allen's work with the family. However, Allen did not view the situation as one in which the transactions were initiated only on behalf of a single case. He also recognized that changes were needed in some aspects of the community to make it more responsive to residents' needs. Whether concerned with minimum-wage legislation, public welfare eligibility requirements, or the hospital's emergency preparedness, Allen's perspective made it possible to relate these environmental factors to their impact on the lives of people. He was able to maintain a dual focus on person and environment.

Identifying and assessing the resources available to help in resolving problems are important tasks for the social worker. These resources may be friends, family, social agencies, social programs, or other people who can help in improving other resources. As Figure 10–1 illustrates, a large number of resources are involved in almost every helping situation. The social worker must have considerable knowledge and skill to work effectively with this wide range of resources.

Allen Sutton had the *sanction of the community* to move into this helping situation, partly because of his own unique qualities, partly because of the authority of his position in the Evergreen County Department of Social Welfare, and partly because he was identified as a professional social worker. As a social worker he was able to develop quickly a positive relationship with Mrs. Baez. She knew Allen, as a responsible professional, was there to serve her interests and would not attempt to take advantage of her vulnerable situation. Similarly, because of the historical development of social work as a profession concerned with social change, it was not viewed as inappropriate

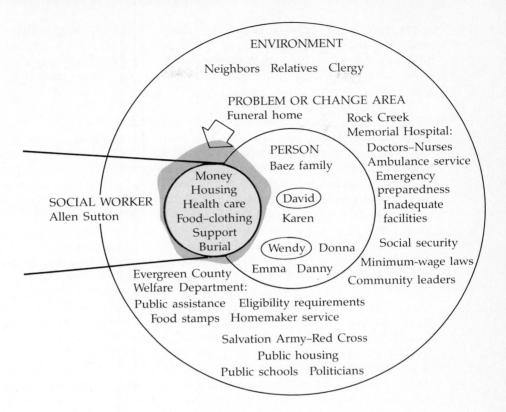

Figure 10–1 *Assessment of the Baez family's problems and resources*

for Allen to assume the role of catalyst for improving community social services. The sanction of this activity for social work in turn provided Allen with the sanction to serve as a social change agent.

It was, of course, essential that Allen had adequate education and experience to provide the services required in this case. Allen entered social work as an undergraduate student and completed a BSW degree. After two years of practice in the Evergreen County Department of Social Welfare, he entered graduate school. Allen had recently completed his MSW degree and returned to the department. He found that his undergraduate educational experience, which provided him with a generalist perspective, had enabled him to identify a number of ways to respond helpfully to this situation and to initiate his practice with some skill. He was also appreciative of the specialized skills in crisis intervention and community problem-solving that he had developed in his MSW program. Certainly Mrs. Baez and the city of Rock Creek benefited from Allen Sutton's good preparedness for social work practice.

Allen's work in the Baez case clearly reflected the *values* held by the social work profession. For instance, he treated Mrs. Baez as a person of worth who needed assistance in this situation. He supported and encouraged her efforts to handle this very difficult situation and always allowed her to make the decisions that would affect her life. Similarly, he helped Rock Creek fulfill its potential of providing needed services for its residents through encouraging appropriate persons in the community to make the final decisions.

Considerable *knowledge* was required to support Allen's actions. He had to have a good general knowledge of his profession, his community, different ethnic groups, and human behavior. He knew the resources available through the social agency he represented and not only used them fully but also attempted to improve them where they were deficient. He acquired knowledge of the Baez family and their needs and strengths. Allen's assessment of the situation allowed him to select appropriate intervention strategies. Specific knowledge of helping processes for serving both Mrs. Baez and the community underpinned Allen's actions at each point of intervention into the case. Consistent with the NASW Definition of Social Work (Figure 1–1), he used knowledge of "human development and behavior; of social, economic, and cultural institutions; and of the interaction of all of these factors."

Finally, the *skill* with which Allen Sutton functioned was essential to success. He skillfully selected and carried out helping techniques through such activities as interviewing Mrs. Baez, creating and working with a task force on problems of the hospital, and speaking before civic groups to promote minimum-wage legislation. In fact, he engaged in virtually the whole range of service-giving activities identified in the NASW Definition of Social Work: "helping people obtain tangible services; counseling and psychotherapy with individuals, families, and groups; helping communities or groups provide or improve social and health services; and participating in relevant legislative processes."

When one examines the practice of a social worker in even a single case, the complexities of social work practice become evident. Multiply this example by the many cases a social worker serves and the multitude of practice settings where social workers are employed, and it becomes readily apparent that social work is a profession of many faces.

SUGGESTED READINGS

Caplan, Gerald. *Principles of Preventive Psychiatry.* New York: Basic Books, 1964.

Cummings, John, and Cummings, Elaine. *Ego and Milieu.* New York: Atherton, 1962.

Lindemann, Erich. "The Meaning of Crisis in Individuals and Family Living." *Teachers College Record* 57 (February 1965): 310–315.

Parad, Howard J. "Crisis Intervention," in *Encyclopedia of Social Work,* edited by Robert Morris. 16th issue. Vol. I. New York: National Association of Social Workers, 1971.

Rapoport, Lydia. "Crisis-Oriented Short-Term Casework." *Social Service Review* 41 (March 1967): 31–43.

Selby, Lola G. "Social Work and Crisis Theory." *Social Work Papers* 10 (1963): 3–23.

Sheafor, Bradford W."The Community Adjustment Process from a System Perspective." *Journal of Social Welfare* 1 (April 1973): 37–44.

Specht, Harry. "Disruptive Tactics." *Social Work* 14 (April 1969): 372–386.

ENDNOTES

1. Lola G. Selby, "Social Work and Crisis Theory," *Social Work Papers* 10 (1963): 3.
2. See John Cummings and Elaine Cummings, *Ego and Milieu* (New York: Atherton Press, 1962), as cited by Howard J. Parad. "Crisis Intervention," in Robert Morris, ed., *Encyclopedia of Social Work*, 16th issue, Vol. 1 (New York: National Association of Social Workers, 1971), pp. 196–202.
3. See Gerald Caplan, *Principles of Preventive Psychiatry* (New York: Basic Books, 1964); Erich Lindemann, "The Meaning of Crisis in Individuals and Family Living," *Teachers College Record* 57 (February 1963), as cited by Howard J. Parad. "Crisis Intervention," pp. 198–199.
4. Lydia Rapoport, "Crisis-Oriented Short-Term Casework," *Social Service Review* 41 (March 1967): 35.
5. Ibid., p. 37.
6. As cited by Howard J. Parad, "Crisis Intervention," p. 198.
7. Rapoport, "Crisis-Oriented Casework," p. 37.
8. Harry Specht, "Disruptive Tactics," *Social Work* 14 (April 1969): 372–380.

Part Four

Special Populations and Concerns in Social Work

Part One provided an overview of social work: its domain of practice, its emergence, and entry into the profession. Part Two examined social welfare institutions, fields of social work practice, and agency and private practice in social work. Part Three dealt with the knowledge, value, and skill requirements of the social worker. The prospective social worker may now feel that all that is needed to enter the "waiting arms" of the community is superhuman energy and altruism. However, much like the new physician, who discovers with frustration that his or her impoverished patients cannot afford the medications prescribed, or the rookie policeman or policewoman who wishes to fight crime in the poor community only to become the most hated person in the neighborhood, the social worker may become discouraged in the effort to help people with their problems.

To avoid such discouragement, the student has to be prepared with additional knowledge, values, and skills.

The purposes of Part Four, therefore, are (1) to expose the potential social work practitioner to various ideological concerns and issues that may be confronted in poor communities, particularly in ethnic minority communities throughout the United States; (2) to help the student distinguish the impact of various forces at work in poor communities, such as social welfare, social services, social agency bureaucracies, social workers, sexism, racism, ageism, and class discrimination; and (3) to help students develop a perception of the knowledge and skills needed for working in specific minority communities and understand better the cultural and value systems found in some ethnic communities.

It was stated in Chapter 4 that *social welfare* represents society's formal effort—independent of the family and private enterprise—to maintain or improve the economic conditions, health care, or interpersonal competence of some or all parts of the population. *So-*

cial agencies, such as welfare and probation departments, are organizations established to carry out the social welfare functions in a specific region of a state. Briefly restated, *social work* was seen as the professional activity of helping individuals, groups, or communities enhance or restore their capacity for social functioning and for creating societal conditions favorable to that goal. Social workers are persons employed by social agencies to carry out professional social work activities within the framework of policies, rules, ethics, and regulations of social welfare, the social agency, and the social work profession.

These distinctions must constantly be kept in mind when one is reading the following chapters because social work and social workers are often blamed for conditions that are neither of their making nor within their control. Nevertheless, some of these critical voices have already had an impressive impact on minority communities and among social workers.

A brief comment before each chapter in Part Four introduces the highlights and main issues in the chapter. When possible, areas involving skill, values, and knowledge pertinent to social work are pointed out.

Chapter 11, "Social Work with Special Populations," is a chapter developed by Armando Morales to serve both as an informational and demographic needs assessment and conceptual foundation for Part Four. A definition of special populations is provided, which includes persons such as women, the elderly, and minorities who have unique needs. The new, emerging special population groups include the growing "homeless" people of the United States and persons suffering from and dying from AIDS. For centu-

ries the world has feared the poor reminding many in society that "there, but for the grace of God, go I." AIDS victims today are seen in many ways as history's dreaded "lepers" of society with occasional cries for quarantine of this population. All these special populations share a second-class status in society and suffer the consequences of sexism, ageism, racism, homophobia, and classism. An ecosystems model is developed to assist social workers in assessing the psychosocial needs of special populations.

Chapter 12 deals with the issue of sexism. Sexism is a contemporary term that appears in few dictionaries. It pertains to the feelings of superiority by one sex toward the other. Julia B. Rauch, in "Gender as a Factor in Practice," sees sexism to be deeply entrenched in U.S. society and affecting social work in myriad ways. She argues that the social work profession needs to understand clearly the impact sexism has on both clients and practitioners, and to make a stronger commitment to nonsexist practice.

In Chapter 13, "Medical and Psychiatric Needs of the Homeless—A Preliminary Response" by Robert W. Surber, Eleanor Dwyer, Katherine J. Ryan, Stephen M. Goldfinger, and John T. Kelly, these practitioners report on their fine micro to macro-level intervention work with a large San Francisco homeless population. They were able to develop a community outreach model that operated in eight community shelters and hotels. Their comprehensive, multidisciplinary approach addressed basic social, living, psychiatric, and medical needs of homeless people.

In Chapter 14, "Attitudes Toward Elderly Clients," Jordan I. Kosberg and Audrey P. Harris state that as the number of persons over age sixty-five in the United States continues to increase, more and more social workers will be employed in work directly or indirectly related to older persons. The authors' survey of the literature revealed that both professional and nonprofessional caregivers harbored various negative attitudes toward elderly persons. They believe that social workers who possess these negative perceptions toward elderly clients will have impaired effectiveness with these clients. The authors add that ageism (discrimination against people because they are old) is at times expressed more strongly in the United States than racism and sexism.

Chapter 15, "Practice in Rural America: The Appalachian Experience," by Bradford W. Sheafor and Robert G. Lewis is a new, original addition to the fifth edition of *Social Work: A Profession of Many Faces*. Readers of previous editions and practitioners in the field cry out for more exposure in the literature of a neglected special population in the United States, the rural poor. A case example is the millions of poor people in need of social services in rural Appalachia. They often have the same needs and problems as urban clients, but additionally because they are so isolated, rural people encounter numerous barriers in the delivery of services. These populations have been ignored for many years and it is the intention of the authors that in some way social work practitioners will develop an interest in serving this population.

Chapter 16, "Urban Gang Violence: A Psychosocial Crisis" was written for the fifth edition by Armando Morales, a former gang group worker, probation officer, and currently a state parole mental health consultant. Inner city areas in many parts of the nation are in crisis with violence and homicide reaching astounding rates resulting in thousands of young males being killed each year. The quality of life for these victims and family survivors should definitely become a health and mental health concern and once again, a priority practice area for social work. Social work historically has a body of knowledge dealing with gangs in the 1930s, 1940s, and 1950s, and an appeal is made to update and upgrade the profession's micro and macro practice intervention skills to deal with this growing problem.

Chapter 17, "The Juvenile Justice System and Minorities," by Armando Morales, Yvonne Ferguson, and Paul R. Munford, discusses the various components of the juvenile justice system (police, probation, courts, and institutions) as well as the failure of this system to provide equal treatment to minority juveniles. An in-depth case study of minorities in detention reflects an almshouse-like standard of care. Serious behavioral and psychiatric problems, including psychosis, did not result in psychiatric referrals by custody staff. Social work values mandate that quality-care standards be maintained for dependent populations such as children.

Ethnic and racial minorities have been and continue to be over-represented among the underclass. A racist might state, for example, that black minorities are over-represented among the poor because they are somehow inherently or biologically inferior to whites who generally continue to have a significantly higher standard of living. Either minorities are inferior (a racist perspective), or white racism has prevented their natural equality with whites from asserting itself during their more than 100 to 300 years in the United States. Those who deny that overt racism and institutional subordination are essentially responsible for the current lower status of minorities are implying that minorities are biologically or inherently inferior.

Chapter 18, "The Impact of Macro Systems on Puerto Rican Families," by Emelicia Mizio, highlights the importance of understanding the cultural heritage of Puerto Ricans and the degree of each family's identification with Puerto Rican or Anglo culture. Mizio suggests the Puerto Rican family has to be permitted to utilize its own strength, draw upon its humanitarian values, and support its kin and the Puerto Rican community at large.

Chapter 19, "Social Work with Native Americans," by Ronald G. Lewis and Man Keung Ho, cautions social workers that to serve American Indians effectively, they must understand their distinctive characteristics and vary their techniques accordingly. The authors attribute social workers' lack of success in helping Native Americans to several causes: lack of understanding of the culture, retention of stereotyped images of Native Americans, and the use of standard techniques and approaches. The concept of social work intervention may be consistent with much of white culture, they state, but it diametrically opposes the Native American's cultural concept of *noninterference*. Social workers are given suggestions regarding client-worker relations, family counseling, and group and community work.

In Chapter 20, "Practice with Asian Americans," author Man Keung Ho has written a "state-of-the-art" original, new chapter to replace his classic piece published in 1976 and making its first appearance in this text in 1977. Dr. Ho provides excellent demographic and cultural information that assists the

reader in distinguishing the great heterogeneity found in the Asian American population (Chinese, Filipino, Japanese, Korean, Vietnamese, Cambodian, Samoan, and Guamanian). He describes therapy models developed by different Asian cultures such as "Morita therapy," "Maikan therapy," and "Ho'oponopono" (Hawaiian family therapy). Without having knowledge of these therapies, social work practitioners may unknowingly cause problems for themselves or the Asian clients they are attempting to help.

Chapter 21, "Social Work with Mexican Americans," an original chapter by Armando Morales and Ramon Salcido, points out that the Mexican American population is a very heterogeneous one and one of the most diverse groups in the United States. Much like the American Indian population, it is one of the oldest groups in the United States, and because of continuing migration, it is also one of the newest. Mexican Americans number about 11.7 million, and some experts estimate the number is closer to 15 million when Mexicans without documentation are included. The median age is 23.5 compared to 31.9 for the overall population. Whereas 11 percent of the general population is over sixty-five years old, only 4 percent of Mexican Americans are in this age group. This dramatic emphasis on youth translates into different human service needs compared to the general population. Their general state of political powerlessness makes it difficult for Mexican Americans to persuade human service institutions to become more responsive to their needs.

Morales and Salcido show that Mexican Americans do have mental health needs and do avail themselves of direct services when Mexican Americans are provided services at minimum cost, in their primary language, and near their homes. The authors offer practice suggestions that have implications for macro social work in the barrio.

Chapter 22, "Social Work with Afro-Americans," by Barbara Bryant Solomon, helps social workers understand this large population. Afro-Americans, numbering 25 million persons in the United States, are a very heterogeneous group, with more than half residing in central cities throughout the United States. The author maintains that racism and discrimination, rather than the pro-

cess of urbanization, contribute to the creation of an underclass among some Afro-Americans.

Solomon encourages social workers to learn to know Afro-Americans better by becoming actively involved in the educational, political, and cultural life of blacks. In helping Afro-Americans, Solomon suggests the intervention strategy of empowerment, which encourages the social worker to engage in activities with clients that will help reduce this psychosocial powerlessness caused by society.

Social Work with Special Populations

Armando Morales

PREFATORY COMMENT

"Social Work with Special Populations" is a chapter developed to serve both as an informational and demographic needs assessment profile and conceptual framework for Part Four. Special population members such as women, children, the elderly, and minorities continue to share a second-class status in the United States. In recent times economic forces and a frightening virus have produced two new, growing special population groups, respectively the homeless and AIDS (acquired immune deficiency syndrome) victims, who also suffer social stigma and are generally denied the kinds of economic resources and medical treatment and research they need to function in society in a more humane, comfortable manner.

The practice skills of social workers are being challenged by special population groups and in beginning to meet this challenge, the author presents an evolving ecosystems model that assists the social worker in obtaining a comprehensive analysis of a specific case. The author also provides micro to macro intervention suggestions.

The concept of human diversity appears in the literature from time to time and refers to persons who are perceived as members of diverse groups such as women, the elderly, and racial and ethnic minorities. Some recipients of the label, however, reject the label and do not feel they should be perceived as "diverse" persons, or as members of "diverse groups" in U.S. society. Although the intent of the concept is positive as a means of assisting practitioners in the helping profession develop skills in recognizing and accepting differences in needs, communication, relationship and life styles, the term ironically seems to create divisiveness. Inherent in the word diverse is a divisive rather than an integrative quality.

Beginning with the first edition of this volume in 1977, the authors preferred to substitute the term special populations. In the definition of special, according to Webster's Third New International Dictionary, there is something "additional to the regular." In the context of human behavior, all humans have certain universal needs, but in addition to these needs, some people have special needs beyond what might normally already be applicable or available to others. Within this conceptual definition, special populations such as the elderly, the homeless, children, women, AIDS victims, and minorities, bring unique needs and circumstances that must be recognized when the social worker serves these persons. A year after the authors began using the term "special populations," the President's Commission on Mental Health produced their definition, which was similar, defining special populations as:

> *Americans who are characterized by (1) uniqueness and diversity in terms of race, ethnic origin, sex, and physical status and (2) by de facto second class status in American Society.*[1]

The President's Commission added that special population groups are both at times overrepresented in the statistics on mental health or inappropriately served by the current mental health system in the United States. Women, for example, are overrepresented in the mental health system and suffer the stresses of second-class status. Children, minorities, and the elderly are very underserved in human service systems based upon their needs, and also suffer the psychosocial consequences of second-class status. Citing what it referred to as a well-documented national scandal, the President's Commission reported that, whereas middle-class nonminority children with behavior problems receive appropriate mental health services in voluntary clinical settings, minority children are more likely to be processed by the police and the juvenile courts for the same behavioral problems.[2] *Those persons being tracked into the juvenile and adult criminal justice systems may also be included in the definition of a special population, in which there is a severe overrepresentation of minorities. This will be discussed in greater detail in Chapter 17.*

SOCIETALLY INDUCED STRESSORS AFFECTING SPECIAL POPULATIONS

In attempting to help persons who may be from the special populations groups as previously defined, the social worker needs to understand what forces are at work to keep these groups in a disadvantaged, second-class status position in society. The biopsychosocial experience of living as a second-class-status person is quite stressful, often resulting in non-health-related premature death (accidents, suicide, homicide), poor physical and mental health, chronic substance abuse, and repeated voluntary and involuntary institutionalization. The "forces" or stressors that keep many special population members from realizing their full potential to contribute to society include sexism, homophobia, ageism, racism, and class discrimination. These factors are also directly correlated with and contribute to poverty.

Are women and minorities overrepresented among the poor because they are in some way inherently or biologically inferior to men and whites? Either women and minorities are inferior—women biologically and emotionally inferior to men, minorities biologically inferior to whites, a sexist and racist perspective—or sexism and racism have restricted women and minorities from functioning to their optimal capacity. The crippling effects of sexism and racism are being expressed through the structural fabric of U.S. society. Those who deny the existence of sexism and racism are in effect implying that women and minorities *are* biologically and inherently inferior. Beyond identifying sexism, racism, and ageism as factors that contribute to the poverty of special populations, one must also understand the *functions* these factors fulfill in U.S. society, hence, their persistence. Sexism and ageism, like racism, provide definite benefits to those who dominate. These factors yield significant psychological, political, and economic advantages to the predominantly white middle and upper classes in U.S. society.[3] For example, men of all classes generally have a psychological need to feel superior to women. Whites representing all socioeconomic levels generally have a psychological need to feel superior to minorities. Younger persons of all ethnic-racial groups and classes generally are threatened by the aging process and have a need to feel superior to, and ignore and discriminate against the elderly. Those receiving the benefits will fight very hard to maintain their advantaged, superior position. Perhaps it is the economic benefits derived from discrimination against women, minorities, and the elderly that function most strongly and effectively to perpetuate this massive U.S. problem that keeps many living in a state of poverty.

The origin of these discriminatory attitudes may be traced to England in the 18th century, as reflected in the political economy writings of Adam Smith and Thomas Malthus. England was in the midst of an industrial revolution that found the government catering to the interests of big business. The poor were economically exploited and further impoverished, but this did not seem to concern the middle class as they had developed the rationale of *laissez-faire*—the doctrine of free enterprise unrestricted by government intervention. Out of unrestricted competition, in theory, the strong would survive and society would benefit—a "trickle down" theory of the 18th century. In *The Wealth of Nations*, Adam Smith argued that one of the roles of government was the defense of the rich against the poor. He saw public assistance for the poor as an artificial and "evil" arrangement in which the poor consumed money that could have been used for wages. "Unearned subsistence" (welfare), according to Smith, simply furthered human misery.[4]

Malthus, in his *Essay on Population*, believed populations would always outrun food supply. War, pestilence, and famine were therefore seen by Malthus as positive checks on the growth of populations. These theories were absorbed into Social Darwinism as advocated by Englishman Herbert Spencer (1820–1903). Extending lower life biological theories to humans, he originated the concept of "survival of the fittest." Spencer opposed all state welfare assistance to the poor because he felt they were unfit and should be eliminated. He stated:

> The whole effort of nature is to get rid of such, to clear the world of them, and make room for the better. If they are sufficiently complete to live, they do live. If they are not sufficiently complete to live, they die, and it is best they should die.[5]

Spencer's doctrines had significant impact upon U.S. thought and many of his ideas were adopted.[6]

In the Social Darwinistic militant stage, society is organized chiefly for survival, bristling with military weapons, training its people for warfare, relying more on an autocratic state, submerging the individual, and imposing a vast amount of compulsory cooperation.[7] In pointing out the U.S.'s priorities, NASW reported in 1970 that over 66 percent of the U.S. annual budget of $200 billion went for military purposes, with 34 percent for all other governmental expenditures including health, education, welfare, agriculture, national resources, pollution, post offices, roads, and foreign relations. More specifically, the United States was spending $480 per person for war and $14 per person for health.[8] An upward trend in military spending began in 1979 before President Reagan took office, but since then there has been a rapid increase, from $176 billion to $254 billion in 1985. This represents the most sustained military buildup in the nation's history![9] It is clear that U.S. priority is in military spending rather than human services programs. Special populations will be the hardest hit, resulting in greater poverty.

According to Gloria Powell and Rodney Powell, poverty is the most severely disabling condition in childhood, handicapping 9 million white children and 6 million minority group children in the United States. The Powells point out that White House Conferences on Children held each decade over the last seventy years have been laudable in their ideals but short on action and accomplishment, particularly for minorities.[10] There has been a significant drop in infant mortality in the United States during the twentieth century, but the mortality rate for minority infants is triple that for white infants. The maternal mortality rate is four times higher for minority mothers than for white mothers. Another disturbing fact is that the combined perinatal and maternal mortality rates have actually increased for minorities relative to whites. In considering the five leading causes of death through ages 1 to 14 (accidents, congenital malformations, malignant diseases, influenza, and pneumonia), the rates for minority children have been consistently higher (often twice as high) than for white children over the last forty years.[11] Poverty is indeed a stressor that can and *does* kill. Policymakers during the twentieth century, representing the world's richest and most powerful country, have had the data and recommendations in their hands to reduce the suffering among poor children but have chosen to spend money on other priorities. It is a penalty to be born poor, according to DeLone, and to be born to parents with little education; these penalties are even greater for minority children.[12]

THE SPECIAL POPULATIONS

Based upon the definition of special populations established by the President's Commission on Mental Health, children, women, the elderly, and minorities could be included. Each suffers the effects of a second-class status in society. Since infants and children have already been commented upon, the following discussion will involve mainly women, the elderly, minorities, AIDS patients (physical status), and the homeless, which includes many special population members.

Women

Considering that females number 51.4 percent of the population in the United States, they are by far the largest special population group. Among females whites comprise 92.5 million, blacks 13.7 million, Hispanics 7.3 million, and "other races" 2.8 million. The median age for white women is 32.9, compared to 26.1 for blacks and 23.8 for Hispanics. Black and Hispanic women have a much higher fertility rate (ages 15 to 24 years), 540 per 1000 and 475 per 1000, respectively, compared to white women, 262 per 1000. Sixty-nine percent of white women are high school graduates compared to 52 percent for blacks and 43 percent for Hispanics. The percent of women over 16 in the labor force in 1980 was 53 percent for black women, 49.9 percent for Hispanics and 49 percent for whites. The median income in 1982 for female householders with no husband present was $13,496 for white women, $7,458 for black women and $7,436 for Hispanic women. Women living below the poverty level in 1982 includes 39.3 percent of black females, 31.3 percent of Hispanics and 13.2 percent of whites.[13] The 1980 Census revealed that of 11,114,000 families who were living in poverty and headed by a female, the rate was 65 percent for Hispanics, 64.8 percent for blacks, and 41.6 percent for whites.[14]

Even though white women have a higher educational and income level than minority women, the fact is that sexism functions to keep *all* women economically below men! The income allocation falls in this order: (1) white men, (2) black men, (3) white women, and (4) black women.[15] If Hispanic women were to be included in the above, they would be alongside black women. In addition to sexism, however, minority women carry the additional burden of racism. Sexism and racism result in an overrepresentation of women in the lower class and in poverty since income is closely associated with the type of employment women are able to obtain. Sexual inequality compounded by racism results in lower wages for women.[16]

Women share not only the debilitating effects of economic exploitation and inequality, but also the traumatic experience of physical and sexual abuse. Although it is generally believed that wife abuse primarily occurs among the poor, current research indicates that this is not true. There is a certain universality of wife abuse that cuts across ethnic, racial, and socioeconomic class boundaries.[17] Approximately 50 percent of *all* adult women, according to Lenore Walker, will be battered at some time in their lives and it is estimated that 24 million women have been beaten at least once by men they live with in an intimate relationship.[18] A national sample of U.S. families revealed that up to 60 percent of all marriages contain some violence.[19] Domestic violence, if not checked, may escalate in frequency and intensity and result in homicide. One quarter of all homicides in the nation involve close family members and in over half of these one spouse killed the other, with wives being the victim in 52 percent of the cases and the perpetrator in 49 percent of the cases.[20] In California approximately one-third of all female homicide victims were killed by their husbands.[21] In Kansas City spousal homicides accounted for 40 percent of all homicides in one year and in 50 percent of these cases police had been called five times or more within a two-year period prior to the murder.[22] Like poverty, sexism in its most advanced form can kill and, like poverty, there are many warning signs prior to the actual event.

Rape is another major form of sexist abuse that, according to the Federal Bureau of Investigation statistics, is reported once every ten minutes in the United States.[23] Gail Abarbanel states that not every rape is reported and that there is a ratio of 1 to 3.5 between victims who do report the crime and those who do not. She adds that with a population of over 100 million females in the nation it is reasonable to assume that at least 250,000 of these women will be raped in a year. If the rate were to remain constant, the likelihood that a female will be raped at some time during her life is one in 15![24] In addition to physical injury, the rape victim is injured psychologically. She is terrorized by her total loss of control, an assault on her integrity, sense of security, and personal identity. Rape produces acute post-traumatic stress disorder symptoms that may become chronic without prompt intervention. It causes a social disruption in her life, her primary relationship, and that of her family.[25]

Although physical and sexual abuse of women by men are both sexist acts, not only do the underlying causes share similar dynamics, but also differences. One predominant theory of wife abuse argues that it occurs because of the sexist structure and traditions of Western society. The norms and values in U.S. society define women as unequal and subordinate to men. These sexist norms and values permeate the entire society and are accepted by the majority of persons in society. The oppressive economic structure that constrains women's opportunities and the legal traditions (e.g., women not permitted to vote until 1920, 144 years after men) which confirm a second-class status for women are evidence of the sexist structure of the United States. Responding to this clear message that they are the ruling sex and acting out their various frustrations, men batter women![26] A second major contrasting theory is proposed by Richard Gelles, who maintains that all family violence is a behavior that is learned in the family of origin. He sees the family as society's primary socializing institution—teaching norms, values, and techniques of violence. He adds that family violence is a response to stress that originates in the social structure of Western society and sees the stresses of poverty, unemployment, and unmet role expectations leading to frustration and ultimately to violence. Gelles believes because structural stresses affect the lower classes to a greater extent, family violence will also occur there more frequently.[27] Previously quoted data concerning the prevalence of female physical abuse do not support this theory.

Theoretical explanations concerning sexual abuse of women have victim precipitation as a core concept; that is, that women's behavior is claimed to cause assaults. Freud's libido and unconscious motivation theories explain rape as the result of conscious and unconscious sexual desires of women, or as emanating from the rapist's feelings of penis inadequacy and castration anxiety rooted in their anxious relations with mothers, wives, and girl-friends.[28] Some theorists see "situational contingencies" as being a cause of rape with culture and social structure establishing the preconditions for rape. Again, the victim is blamed for dressing too seductively, going to singles bars, hitchhiking, or going out alone at night.[29]

Another theory based on gender-role socialization explains the cause of female sexual assault as males learning that masculinity means domination and that rape is the ultimate act of man's domination over women. The male is stereotypically seen as a natural sexual predator.[30] Within the theoretical context of a radical feminist perspective, according to Margaret L. Andersen and Claire Renzetti, the sexual assault of women by men is a political-economic phenomenon related to women's lack of political and economic autonomy.[31] Drawing on cross-cultural data, Peggy Reeves Sanday demonstrates that male violence against women is not universal; rather, it is related to the social inequality of women and the interpersonal violence in a society.[32] Considering the severe inequality women suffer in the United States coupled with the fact that the United States ranks *first* in violence among the seventeen Western democracies, it should not be surprising to observe the magnitude of physical and sexual abuse directed at women.[33] A sexist, violent country places this special population at great risk; this should be a top priority for social work. More specific data on spousal homicide appears in Chapter 16.

The Elderly

Large numbers of people over sixty-five in the United States are a fairly recent phenomenon. Persons over sixty-five numbered only 3.1 million in 1900 (4 percent); today they number more than 25 million persons, or 11.2 percent of the population. Estimates are that by the year 2000 they will number more than 31 million (12.2 percent) and by 2030 they will number 55 million (18.3 percent). These projections are based on the assumption that there will be no major biomedical breakthroughs that significantly extend the life expectancy of the middle-aged and elderly. Not only will there be a proportionately larger elderly population in the future, but the median age of the elderly will be higher. For example in 1980 40 percent of elderly persons were seventy-five years of age or older. By the year 2000 49 percent of the aged will be over seventy-five.[34]

The elderly are the most vulnerable special population group with respect to physical health, mental health, income, and housing status. They are often victimized and suffer the stresses of ageism, class discrimination, sexism, poverty, and racism. The income levels of the elderly are substantially less than those of younger persons and the incidence of poverty is significantly higher.[35] Many aged poor become poor only after reaching old age, losing half to two-thirds of their total income from loss of wages and retirement.[36] Women outnumber men among the elderly population, numbering approximately 60 percent of the total. Elderly women as a group are poorer than elderly men, and less often employed. The black elderly profile (median family income $5,177 compared to $8,676 for whites) caps a lifetime of limited economic rewards, as earnings for blacks of all ages are below the levels of their white peers.[37] Elderly Hispanics also have much higher rates of poverty than their white counterparts.[38] The minority elderly are at higher risk than whites as a result of their pervasive poverty; this is compounded by problems of access to services because of institutional racism barriers, even more so for those Hispanics who speak primarily Spanish. Normally, Title XX funds of the Social Security Act flow to states depending upon need indicators such as the percentage of a state's poor elderly population and percent of minority elderly population. Tragically, however, the greater the percentage of elderly minorities in a state's population, the larger the corresponding decrease in the elderly poor's share of Title XX funds has been.[39]

Only 5 percent of the elderly reside in nursing homes and other long-term institutions. Almost 76 percent of elderly men lived with their wives and 7 percent with children or other relatives. Women were far worse off; only 38 percent lived with their husbands and another 19 percent lived with their children or other relatives. The likelihood of living alone increases significantly with age at the same time that the aging process increases the need to be functionally dependent.[40]

The health problems of the elderly are quite different than those of younger persons. Whereas accidents are the leading cause of death among persons under forty-five, accidents are only the seventh leading cause of death in the elderly. The leading killers of older persons are heart disease, cancer, and stroke. The likelihood of dying from stroke, influenza, pneumonia, and arteriosclerosis all increase significantly as persons live to be sixty-five and older. A national health survey of the elderly found that 90 percent of persons over sixty-five had at least one chronic condition and many had multiple chronic illnesses. The most commonly reported chronic health conditions were arthritis at 44 percent, hypertension at 39 percent, hearing loss at 28 percent, and heart ailments at 27 percent.[41] Because of their poor health status the elderly account for a third more physician visits than the population as a whole and they use three times as many hospital days.[42] The rates of psychosis and organic mental disorders rise with advancing age. There is a high reported correlation between physical and mental illness, and the linkage is highest between physical and organic mental impairment.[43]

In a profit-making capitalist system, the nonproductive elderly are simply "dead weight" and are often treated as such. Government will provide them with as little resources as it can, in order to invest more in defense or other more profitable projects. One is reminded of Dr. Eileen M. Gardner, an appointee to the Reagan administration's Department of Education, who, in testimony before the Senate Appropriations Committee's Health and Human Services subcommittee, stated that handicapped children were draining badly needed resources from the normal school population. The Secretary of Education asked for her resignation.[44] The U.S. population, according to Robert Butler, suffers from a personal and institutionalized prejudice against the elderly, which he attributes to a primitive dread of aging.[45] That was written eleven years ago. This may be even more so in today's age of narcissism, beautiful bodies, and the worshiping of the young. Perhaps ageism and its persistence has at its core thanatophobia—the fear of death! It is ironic that people in the United States worship youth and are looking desperately for ways to prolong life, while at the same time largely neglecting the elderly, those whose lives have been made longer.

In addition to institutional neglect increasing numbers of the elderly are suffering physical abuse. Ira Reiss reports that 4 percent of the elderly population (one million persons) are abused by their children, and the abuse increases as the numbers of elderly grow.[46] The types of abuse include physical assault, verbal harrassment, malnutrition, theft or financial mismanagement, unreasonable confinement, over-sedation, sexual abuse, threats, withholding of medication or aids required (false teeth, glasses, hearing aids), neglect, humiliation, and violation of legal rights. The victim is usually over seventy-five with significant physical or mental impairment.[47] Much more research is needed to understand the incidence and prevalence of a significant and growing social problem among the elderly.

It should come as no surprise, then, that the elderly lead the nation in suicide. In 1980 the suicide rate for fifteen- to twenty-four-year-olds was 11.9 percent per 100,000 and 17.7 percent for persons over sixty-five. This pattern has existed since 1900. Women are a low risk group for suicide at all ages—especially in old age—while men are generally a high risk group and especially in old age.[48] Whereas the elderly comprised 11.3 percent of the population in 1980, they accounted for 16.9 percent of the suicides. White males are at highest risk for suicide, as are those persons over seventy-five. Other high risk elderly groups include the widowed, those who have experienced recent losses, those with chronic physical pain, and those who have undergone status changes such as retirement with loss of income status, roles, and independence. In contrast minority group suicide peaks in young adulthood and declines significantly in old age.[49] It appears that whites (mostly males) kill themselves when they become old and have lost their income, status, role, and independence, and minorities (mostly males) more often kill themselves at a young age in their losing struggle to obtain income, status, role, and independence. To be more succinct, racism kills some minorities on the way up and ageism kills some whites on the way down.

Minorities

Next to women the second-largest population group in the United States are the ethnic-racial minorities—sometimes referred to as "third-world" people. This group, numbering over 40 million people, excludes white ethnics, who have an even higher educational and income status than Anglo-American Protestants.[50] Minorities will be well represented in any special populations group but in *addition* to suffering the same stresses of sexism, AIDS, homelessness, ageism, poverty, and class discrimination, their condition is compounded by racism.[51] Racism is the assumption and belief of inherent, biological racial superiority or the purity and superiority of certain races and consequent discrimination against other races. Racism is any attitude, action, or institutional structure (institutional racism) that subordinates a person or group because of color. While "race" and "color" refer to two different types of human characteristics, in the United States it is the visibility of skin color and other physical traits associated with particular skin colors that marks specific persons as targets for subordination by members of the white majority.[52] This can be seen clearly in Chapter 23 in which Section 287.1 (c) of the Operating Instructions of the U.S. Immigration and Naturalization Service is cited, identifying "foreign cultural characteristics" as one of the "articulable factors" or reasons officers may use to stop and question a person suspected of not being legally in the United States. No doubt the officers must have internalized consciously and unconsciously subjective criteria as to who appears "foreign" and who does not. Those who are not considered "white" by whites include ethnic-racial groups such as blacks, Chinese, Vietnamese, Mexican Americans, Cubans, Puerto Ricans, Central and South Americans, Japanese, and American Indians. Some minority group members are actually Caucasian or "white" (e.g., Mexican Americans) and may even want to be identified as such, but they will still be rejected by whites unless they are able to "pass" on the basis of fair skin and light-colored hair and eyes.[53] The following discussion will focus on the larger minority groups in the United States such as American Indians, Asian Americans, blacks, and Hispanics. A framework highlighting each group's demographic profile, health and mental status, and special social problem areas will be utilized. Chapters 18 through 22 will deal more specifically with social work practice intervention strategies concerning each of these minority groups.

On April 26, 1985, Mae Chee Castillo, a seventy-two-year-old volunteer aide Navajo woman, was publicly honored in person at the White House by President Ronald Reagan for having rescued ten children from a burning bus. Instead of verbalizing her appreciation for the recognition being offered to her by the President, she told the President her people needed schools, hospitals, housing for the elderly, and other facilities. She added:

> We need to continue the current level of economic benefits such as Social Security since many, many Native American elderly depend on this support for their only source of income. We need funds for these services that I have mentioned because, in Indian country, there is little or no private sector. I ask for your support, Mr. President.[54]

The President replied:

> Most of those things that you were talking about here, those problems come under what we have called the safety net and which we intend to continue and, even in our battles to lower the deficit, these things will not be done away with or reduced.[55]

The old Navajo woman tried to give a White House aide a woven basket and rug for the President but it was rejected as she was ushered out "very quickly."[56] Those few moments of interaction between two elderly people symbolize the history of the relationship between American Indians and whites in positions of power. Responding to poverty and powerlessness imposed by whites, the American Indian practically has to beg for mercy and justice and even offers gifts of peace, kindness, and good faith. And, as has been the traditional response for well over a hundred years, both the request for help and the gifts (and American Indians) are rejected!

Due to changing definitions of the term "American Indian" by the U.S. Bureau of the Census, it is difficult to obtain an accurate appraisal of the size of the Indian population in the United States. When American Indians, Alaskan Natives, and Aleuts are included, Indians numbered 827,000 persons in 1975, a 51 percent increase over the 1960 Census.[57] American Indians may be found in most states although their highest concentration is in California, Oklahoma, Arizona, New Mexico, and North Carolina. Within the last ten years, the American Indian population in California has tripled. American Indians are a very heterogeneous group comprised of approximately 481 tribal groups, many with unique norms, culture, and language. Half of all American Indians belong to nine tribes with the largest tribal group being the Navajo, numbering 140,000.[58] About half of all Indians live in urban areas and the other half reside in rural areas or reservations. Urban Indians are generally older than rural or reservation Indians. In Utah, for example, median Indian age is 15.6 compared to 26.4 in New York.[59]

American Indians, like persons of Mexican descent, are different from other minority groups in that they were *not* immigrants. The immigrants were the Anglo-Americans, who conquered the Indians on their land. Furthermore, Indians, like Mexican Americans, fought several battles with the U.S. Army before finally being defeated. Anglo-American resentment toward Indians goes back many years and is expressed both overtly and in subtle, destructive ways. For example in the late eighteenth century California Indians numbered about 250,000. By 1900 California's Indian population was down to 10,000 due to "peaceful" attrition by European civilization and its attendant diseases, dehumanizing and decimating conditions, warfare, slave-like treatment, and genocide by whites.[60]

Racism toward Indians has been expressed in the lack of a comprehensive, progressive federal policy over a period of many years, a lack that has severely hampered the Indians' ability to move forward in the United States. Their health is very poor, educational achievement dismal, and many live in extreme poverty, both on and off the reservations. Although Indians governed themselves for centuries until the "white man" invaded their territories, they were not permitted to vote until 1924 when they were declared citizens of the United States. In 1934 the Indian Reorganization Act was passed, which permitted tribal self-government.[61] Another landmark occurred in 1955 when the Indian Health Service was established under the U.S. Public Health Service rather than the Bureau of Indian Affairs. The Indian Civil Rights Act, which was passed in 1968, required due process in tribal courts and right to legal counsel, but no appropriations were provided to exercise these rights. In 1975 the Indian Self Determination and Education Act (P.L. 93–638) was passed, which permitted tribes to contract with the Bureau of Indian Affairs and the Indian Health Services for services, with funding from these sources. Another very important piece of legislation and tragically, very late, was the passage of the Indian Child Welfare Act in 1978. It established minimum standards for state custody proceedings affecting Indian children, with the jurisdiction of child welfare matters returned to the tribes. Funds ($5.5 million) were appropriated by Congress in 1979 for services to strengthen families and serve children.[62] This represents a little over $5 for each American Indian in the United States. A greater commitment is needed in order to make any significant impact. The Indian Child Welfare Act, however, establishes the legal foundation that will permit Indians to have greater authority in attempting to keep and enhance the lives of children *in* the tribal environment. It also provides Indians a unique opportunity to try to maintain their culture.[63]

During one historical period all school-age American Indian children were required to attend federal boarding schools. Even today, according to Evelyn Blanchard and Russel Barsh, it is difficult to find an Indian whose parent, grandparent or other close relative has not attended boarding school.[64] A 1977 survey by the Association on American Indian Affairs reported that 25 to 35 percent of all Indian children are separated from their families and placed in foster homes, adoptive homes, or institutions.[65] Such practices can only have the result of destroying the family unit. Byler concludes that federal assimilation policies cause the Indian family to break up, with a loss of self-esteem in the parents, cultural disorientation in the children, and loss of identity resulting in school failure, suicide, alcohol abuse, and alcoholism.[66]

Alcoholism is a significant problem in the American Indian community and stereotypes have been created about the Indians' attraction to alcohol. The alcohol abuse is simply a symptom of the inhuman social conditions (historical and contemporary) in which the Indian has been forced to live. Child abuse and neglect exist in the Indian community, where alcohol plays a role in about half the cases, as it does in most child abuse. Some Indian parents themselves have suffered abuse and neglect in their lives, according to Anne Metcalf, but the grandparents should not be blamed. Rather, it is the disruption in Indian families caused by Anglo-American institutions that is the underlying cause. As Anglo institutions encroached more and more on Indian family life, the effects on Indian children became more and more disruptive.[67]

The term "Asian Americans" commonly refers to Chinese, Koreans, Japanese, Vietnamese, Thais, and Pacific Islands persons (Hawaiians, Guamanians, Filipinos, and Samoans). Asian Americans, hereafter referred to as Asians, are, like Indians and Hispanics, a very heterogeneous group, each with its own unique language, history, culture, religion, and appearance. They share immigration and assimilation stresses, historical and current economic exploitation, and suffer the consequences of racism.[68] Largely drawn by the U.S. demand for manual labor, Asians immigrated to the United States during several different periods, with the greatest number of Chinese arriving between 1850 and 1882; the Japanese from 1880 to 1924; and most Filipinos in the 1920s and again in the mid-1960s. Various discriminatory laws and legislation controlling the flow of Asian immigrants—at times restricting admission of Asian women—created a severe sex imbalance that led to serious personal, social, and community life consequences for many Asian immigrant males. For over 100 years, Kenji Murase states, Asian Americans have been the victims of "humiliating, repressive, and vicious acts of racism."[69] Murase documents numerous examples of legislative racism directed at Asians, a few of which will be highlighted, such as California's 1850 Foreign Miners' Tax directed at Chinese miners, the 1882 federal law prohibiting Chinese from becoming naturalized, the massacre and lynching of Chinese in Wyoming (1885) and Idaho (1888), segregated schools for Chinese and Japanese in California (1860, 1906); prohibition against racial intermarriage in California (1906); and the anti-alien land law prohibiting property purchases in California (1913).[70] One of the most brutal acts of U.S. racism directed specifically at Asian Americans occurred in 1942 when President Franklin D. Roosevelt, who held the racist belief "once a Jap always a Jap," signed an order forcibly uprooting more than 110,000 innocent Japanese Americans in three West coast states and placing them in so-called "relocation centers." They were in fact concentration camps, as opposed to genocide camps in Hitler's Germany. The Japanese Americans, both were alien and citizens, young and old, rich and poor, were sent to ten concentration camps to live in barracks surrounded by barbed wire, with armed guards, in largely barren areas in the interior of the United States, from California to Arkansas.[71] The Japanese Americans suffered poverty, deprivation, loss of property, and were left with lifetime emotional scars.[72] According to Lindbergh Sata, the imprisonment experience caused a cultural erosion of established roles and functions within the family unit, while the establishment of English as a primary mode of communication both emancipated and deprived Japanese Americans of the stabilizing influence of family life.[73] Their culture was raped. Today, forty-six years after their U.S. concentration-camp experience, many emotionally traumatic residues continue to exist for Japanese Americans.

One of the newest Asian immigrant groups to enter the United States, the Vietnamese, present a host of very serious cultural, economic, and psychosocial problems requiring immediate, comprehensive intervention. Vietnamese came to the United States in two separate groups at two different times. The first group was comprised of about 20,000 students, permanent residents, and war brides, prior to the fall of Saigon in April, 1975. The second group consisted of over 140,000 adults and children who fled their homeland during and after the fall of Saigon. In their struggle to escape from Vietnam, many died on their way to the United States. Daniel D. Le states succinctly that for the Vietnamese refugee, all the forces of disaster such as war, death, injury, loss of home, possessions, and family memorabilia, are joined with the crushing losses of country, culture, language, tradition, and history, "endlessly inflicting painful memories down to the lowest trivia of life."[74]

The current mental health problems and needs of the Vietnamese are many. Like other minority groups in the United States, they are confronted with white racism, a foreign culture, a confusing and complicated economic, social, and political system, and ignorance about their rights and obligations. Perhaps the greatest handicap is language, the tool they require in order to negotiate on the most basic level. At best Vietnamese refugees symbolize the United States's painful, ambivalent sacrifice in a "no win" war and at worst, Vietnamese will be scapegoats, blamed for that war and the loss of thousands of U.S. soldiers.

Unemployment among Vietnamese is high due to the unavailability of jobs and to language barriers; many Vietnamese veterans were trained only for war and are without vocational skills. They feel frustrated, resentful, and angry, feelings that are often turned inward, resulting in depression. Vietnamese women feel even more isolated and alienated from U.S. society and cannot even communicate with their English-speaking neighbors. They have large families, suffer poverty, and reside in high-crime areas in the cities. Their children also suffer severe psychological problems related to their experiences and psychosocial development level. Many are still experiencing war-related, post-traumatic stress disorder symptoms; some are suffering culture shock manifested in various speech problems, and many adolescents are experiencing a severe identity crisis. All these problems are exacerbated by an unstable home situation governed by parents who are also experiencing major emotional difficulties.[75] In short the mental health situation of Vietnamese is critical and, according to Le, "may soon become disastrous."[76] He calls for immediate, positive intervention. Will the future of the Vietnamese parallel that of blacks who lost their African culture and language, yet were and are still barred from entering the U.S. mainstream? The Vietnamese, like other political war refugees such as Central Americans, present a real challenge to the social work profession.

Blacks, sometimes referred to as Afro-Americans (not of Hispanic origin), constitute the largest minority group in the nation with a population numbering 25.3 million persons. Fifty-four percent live in the South but 76 percent of all Afro-Americans live in cities, with 57 percent residing in the central city.[77] The median family income gap between Afro-Americans and whites continues to grow, with Afro-Americans in 1980 earning a median income of $12,674 compared to $21,904 for whites. The number of poor Afro-American families was as high in 1980 as in 1970, while the number of poor white families decreased.[78] Like other minorities, Afro-Americans are a very heterogeneous group, with the majority being productive members of society. However, their overrepresentation among the poor as the result of institutional racism in U.S. society, places many of them under severe stress, creating an affected and at-risk, highly vulnerable group. They remain far behind whites in almost every social, health, and economic measurement.

Blacks have been the most brutalized minority group in the United States ever since their transport to the North American continent as slaves 350 years ago. Andrew Billingsley once noted that black families have shown an amazing ability to survive in the face of impossible conditions.[79] The centuries-old African tradition based on ritual, custom, and law of maintaining family ties wherever and whenever possible, has survived an enormous traumatization as "subhuman" slaves whose family members were sold as market commodities.[80] Today approximately two-thirds of Afro-American families are nuclear, comprised of mother, father, and children. They are economically heterogeneous with about 40 percent of Afro-American families in the middle class, 10 percent in the upper class, and about 50 percent in the lower class. Twenty-five percent of the lower class are classified as "non-working poor" and it is this group that receives the most attention from the media, the academic community, law enforcement and social work, and reinforces white prejudice, racism, and discrimination toward blacks.[81] The vast majority of Afro-Americans have experienced the effects of white racism in one form or another, whether overt or covert. For example, according to the National Center for Health Statistics, black babies born in Detroit today are dying at twice the national rate, 22.1 per 1,000 live births compared to 10.6. Low birth weight is the primary cause of death. This is caused in turn by social and economic problems such as the poor maternal diet, inadequate education about the need for prenatal care, lack of access to proper care, smoking, alcohol, and drug abuse. A city health official remarked, "Infant mortality is the medical expression of a social problem. The problem is poverty—poverty of resources."[82]

Based upon their actual mental health needs, blacks underutilize mental health services. Those that have entered the mental health system face discrimination and tend to be treated less often as outpatients, more often with drugs, less often with one-to-one modalities, and drop out earlier in the treatment process. Many blacks who go to mental health agencies have been referred by agents of social control. Barbara Solomon maintains that Afro-Americans experience the same mental health problems as those occurring in all groups in U.S. society, such as schizophrenia, depression, adjustment reactions, and so on. However, the *cause* of those problems may be different. Feelings related to self-esteem and powerlessness may play a greater etiological role with Afro-Americans than with whites experiencing the same problems, according to Solomon. Some problems such as dysfunctional male-female relationships may be unique to Afro-Americans, created by a combination of the slavery experience, subsequent employment practices, the current feminist movement, and the ratio of Afro-American men to women.[83]

Large-scale wars such as the Second World War, the Korean War, the Vietnam War, in conjunction with a contemporary volunteer U.S. army comprised of 50 percent minorities, a continuing overrepresentation of Afro-Americans in juvenile and adult detention facilities, high homicide and suicide rates, and police homicides of blacks, have significantly reduced the availability and ratio of young black males in relationship to black females. For example Lawrence Sherman points out that there is an extremely disproportionate number of police "executions" of blacks without trial. National official statistics revealed that in 1975, blacks comprised 46 percent of people killed by police while constituting only 11.5 percent of the population! The national death rate from police homicide of black males over ten years of age in a recent ten-year period was ten times higher than the rate for white males.[84] Hispanic males are also at high risk with respect to police homicide; in Chicago, for example, a death rate of 4.5 per 100,000 compared to 2.67 per 100,000 for blacks and .34 per 100,000 for whites. The killing of blacks and Hispanics by police was far out of proportion to their felony crime rate.[85] The discussion of the incarceration of Afro-Americans will be combined with that of Hispanics, following a demographic description of the Hispanic population.

In 1970 there were nine million Hispanics in the United States; by March 1987 the Bureau of the Census reported 18.7 million Hispanics. In 1987 Hispanics of Mexican descent numbered 11.7 million (62 percent), Puerto Ricans 2.2 million, Central and South Americans 2.1 million, Cubans 1 million, and other Hispanics 1.5 million. Not included in these population figures were an estimated six million undocumented aliens, mostly from Mexico.[86] Demographers predict that by 1990 Hispanics will be the nation's largest minority, half the population in California, a third in Texas, and the majority population in three states by the year 2000.[87] Over 50 percent of all Hispanics reside in California (31 percent) and Texas (20 percent), followed by New York (11 percent), Florida (6 percent), Illinois (4 percent), Arizona, Colorado, and New Mexico (9 percent), and the remainder of the United States (18 percent). Additional, detailed demographic data concerning Hispanics are presented in Chapters 18 and 21. Hispanics are (1) largely urban dwellers with 84 percent residing in metropolitan areas, (2) a youthful population, with a median age of 23.5 years vs. 31.9 for the overall population, (3) low educational achievement with 58 percent of Hispanics being high school graduates vs. 88 percent for non-Hispanics, and (4) generally poor with a median income of $16,399 vs. $23,907 for non-Hispanics.

Perhaps the most significant aspect of Hispanic cultural heritage is the Spanish language, as over 80 percent of Hispanics report Spanish as their primary language.[88] Many Hispanics suffer the effects of poverty to a much greater extent than the general population. Low income, unemployment, underemployment, and undereducation, discrimination, racism, prejudice, poor housing and cultural-linguistic barriers, according to the President's Commission on Mental Health, have been compounded by the low quality and quantity of mental health services available to Hispanics. These conditions have placed undue stress on Hispanics with serious consequences as evidenced by the increased prevalence of alcoholism and substance abuse,[89] juvenile delinquency and gangs,[90] and an overrepresentation of adults in jails and prisons.[91] This will be discussed in more detail in Chapters 16 and 17.

The largest minority groups in the United States, Afro-Americans and Hispanics are an increasingly high-risk group as their numbers continue to escalate dramatically in all aspects of the juvenile and adult criminal justice system. Currently, on any given day there are approximately 2.4 million persons under public correctional supervision in the United States. (Jails, 210,000; prisons, 412,000; adult parole, 220,400; adult probation, 1,118,100; juvenile detention, 12,300; juvenile training school, 25,000; juvenile camps and ranches, 4,860; juvenile probation, 328,900; juvenile parole, 53,300.) There are 622,000 incarcerated adults and 42,300 juveniles housed in public juvenile correctional facilities. About seven million jail bookings occur per year. By the end of 1983 the U.S. Bureau of Justice Statistics reported 438,830 adults confined in state and federal prisons, indicating that the nation's prison population had doubled during the last decade and had become the largest in U.S. history.[92] Ninety-six percent of this total population were males and 48 percent were black, far exceeding their proportion in the general population. The statistics for Hispanic males were not consistently available, yet experts believe prison incarceration rates for Hispanics are higher than for white males.[93]

The state and federal prison incarceration rate has been steadily increasing over the last sixty years, from seventy-nine per 100,000 persons in 1925 to ninety-eight per 100,000 in 1945, to 108 per 100,000 in 1965, to 111 per 100,000 in 1975, and 179 per 100,000 in 1983. The U.S. Government Accounting Office projects that by 1990, the U.S. prison population will be 566,170, an all-time incarceration rate of 227 per 100,000.[94] States have identified four factors related to prison population growth. The first is demographic, as certain age, sex, and racial-ethnic groups in the general population have higher arrest rates and imprisonment than others. A self-fulfilling prophecy is often at work in that poor minorities are *believed* to be more criminal and are under greater police surveillance, hence more likely to be arrested (see Chapters 16, 17, and 23). Given the increasing numbers of minorities in the nation and their low median age, the percent of minorities in prison is going to become greater.

Crime rates are the second factor related to incarceration rates, but this is a widely debated issue with no clear answers. Historically there is an inverse relationship between crime rates and incarceration; that is, as crime rates increase, fewer persons fall under correctional supervision. On the other hand the prison population grows as crime rates decline.[95]

A third factor, which is really more of a theory, suggests that imprisonment is strongly related to economic conditions, more specifically to rates of unemployment and poverty levels. Those supporting this view cite the high rate of unemployment among minority youth and the disproportionate number of incarcerated minorities. This view is strongly challenged by James Austin and Barry Krisberg who point out from 1978 to 1983 the unemployment rate increased dramatically for minorities, yet the crime rate held steady and later even declined while the prison population increased during the same period.[96]

The final factor related to imprisonment rates concerns changes in criminal justice policies, such as determinate sentences, mandatory sentencing legislation, and increasing penalties and prison terms—in short, "get tough" approaches. The general public, police, and legislators want to "crack down" hard on crime but, as will be seen, they are very selective as to whom they decide to punish more severely—usually it is minorities.

Rarely do social scientists examine prejudice, racism, and class discrimination in the criminal justice system (police, prosecutors, judges, correctional facilities, probation, parole) as factors that may play a significant role in determining who is incarcerated. For example, the U.S. Department of Justice funded the "SHODI" (Serious Habitual Offenders—Drug Involved) program to identify "serious" offenders and ensure they receive "stiff" sentences. Almost 25 percent of "SHODIs" had never appeared in court (no convictions) and in one city 83 percent of SHODIs were minority youths (see Chapter 23 for a detailed discussion of the SHODI program). In comparing a middle-class white and lower-class Hispanic community of similar size and very similar juvenile crime rates in Los Angeles, Hispanic youths were twenty-three times more likely to be arrested for loitering offenses compared to non-Hispanic white youths (see Chapter 17).

The policies and attitudes toward juvenile crime and minorities differ from state to state. In a selection of four large states with large urban areas and large minority populations, the collective attitudes of policy makers are dramatically transformed into incarceration rates shown in Table 11–1.[97] California does not have juvenile delinquents ten times more criminal than New York. Rather, the incarceration rates reflect the *attitudes* of the criminal justice system. California has 10 percent of the nation's 10–19 year-old juvenile population, yet 30 percent of the nation's juvenile detention admissions occurred in California (138,000 out of 451,000 detentions).[98] California is #1 in this regard.

California Attorney General John Van de Kamp reported that juvenile crime had dropped by 41.2 percent between 1974 and 1983, but that the number of youths committed to local and state detention centers had increased by 11 percent.[99] In California in 1983 the percentage of non-Hispanic white juveniles ages 10 to 19 was 61.1 percent; Hispanic, 24 percent; black, 9.6 percent; and other, 5.3 percent. Non-Hispanic white juveniles were involved in 44 percent (50,000 offenses) of felony arrests that year compared to 27.6 percent (31,000 offenses) for Hispanics and 25.3 percent (28,500 of-

TABLE 11–1 JUVENILE INCARCERATION RATES OF SELECTED STATES

STATE	MAJOR CITY	ADMISSION TO DETENTION	ADMISSION TO TRAINING SCHOOL
New York	New York (42% minority)	455/100,000	38/100,000
Illinois	Chicago (57% minority)	871/100,000	114/100,000
Michigan	Detroit (67% minority)	1300/100,000	53/100,000
California	Los Angeles (52% minority)	4400/100,000	447/100,000

fenses) for blacks. Thirty-three percent of non-Hispanic white arrests were for violent offenses, compared to 27 percent for Hispanics and 36 percent for blacks.[100] It is interesting to note that even though non-Hispanic whites committed the most felonies (44 percent), the percentage committed (first commitment) to the California Youth Authority was 27.7 percent, a −16.3 percent drop. On the other hand there was a 4.5 percent increase of CYA commitments of Hispanics (up to 32.1 percent) based upon their percentage of felonies (27.6 percent), and a significant 13 percent increase of CYA commitments for blacks (up to 38.1 percent) in light of their felony percentage (25.3 percent). Since blacks and non-Hispanic whites had similar felony offense rates, one would have expected similar first time CYA commitments. The CYA institution juvenile inmate population reflects the same ethnic-racial percentages as first-time commitments, 73 percent minorities and 27 percent non-Hispanic whites.[101] It is obvious that the *public* juvenile justice system resists the penetration of white youths while easily admitting minority youths in disproportionate numbers. However, the *private* juvenile justice system (private, non-government-administered training schools, ranches, camps, halfway houses, group homes) resists the penetration of minorities and admits 65 percent to 70 percent whites, but only 25 percent blacks and 7 percent Hispanics.[102] The third system to which juvenile delinquents may be tracked is called the "hidden" juvenile justice system, located in private psychiatric hospitals, with a 95 percent population of affluent white adolescents. This is discussed in Chapter 23. A triple standard of justice, therefore, exists for acting-out juveniles.

Commenting on a similar discriminatory phenomenon in the adult criminal justice system, Joan Petersilia states:

> Critics of the criminal justice system view the arrest and imprisonment of blacks and other minorities as evidence of racial discrimination. Although the laws governing the system contain no racial bias, these critics claim that where the system allows discretion to criminal justice officials in handling offenders, discrimination can, and often does, enter in. They argue that blacks, for example, who make up 12 percent of the national population, could not possibly commit 48 percent of the crimes—but that is exactly what their arrest and imprisonment rates imply.[103]

Significant sentencing disparities exist between crime rates and imprisonment. For example blacks account for 30 percent of the arrests for larceny in the nation, yet are 51 percent of those imprisoned for larceny. Petersilia concludes that a great deal of discretion by all aspects of the criminal justice system leads to discrimination. Petersilia further adds that an astonishing 51 percent of black males residing in large cities are arrested at least once during their lives for an index crime (murder, rape, robbery, assault, burglary, larceny/theft, auto theft, and arson), compared to only 14 percent of white males. Blacks are six times (18 percent to 3 percent) more likely than whites to serve time in a correctional facility either as juveniles or adults.[104] A similar pattern seems to be emerging for Hispanics. Since half of black males and also a very significant number of Hispanic males are coming to the attention of the juvenile and adult criminal justice system, it would seem mandatory that social workers know something about the interactional dynamics of these systems with minorities in order to make an accurate assessment of the client(s) and be more effective. An additional law enforcement stressor affecting Hispanics involves contact with the patrol officers of the U.S. Immigration and Naturalization Service. A detailed account of the psychiatric symptoms produced by INS interrogations among Hispanics *suspected* of being undocumented, is reported in Chapter 23 in the section called "Class Action Social Work and Prevention."

Normally, when one migrates from one country to another, a certain amount of immigration and acculturation stress will be experienced by the migrant. The degree of the stress, however, will in part be related to the economic and social resources available to the migrant, how similar or different the new culture is, and the perception and receptiveness of the immigrant by the new country. For example, the United States will be much more receptive toward a Russian communist ballerina who is defecting to the United States to escape what she considers an oppressive Soviet government than toward a Guatemalan who entered the United States illegally to escape Central American right-wing death squads. Politics and racism, therefore, will affect the nurturing or negative reaction the United States will have toward the new immigrant. Many Hispanics legally and illegally entering the United States as political or economic refugees *are* experiencing migration and acculturation stress, and have a fear of being apprehended and deported by INS officials, with possible execution upon return home, or assassination in the United States by compatriots of a rival political party, or abrupt removal from wives and children.

It is estimated that undocumented persons residing in the United States entering from the Canadian and Mexican borders range from two to ten million.[105] The majority appear to be economic refugees. In recent years, however, greater numbers of political refugees—mostly from Central America—are entering the United States. The Legal Aid Office of the Archdiocese of San Salvador reported that during the first ten months of 1983, 4113 civilians were killed by the security forces, the army, and right wing death squads. Sixty-seven were killed by guerrillas.[106] Guatemalan refugees report that the army's anti-guerrilla campaign in rural Guatemala has resulted in genocide, kidnappings, burning of residences, and torture.[107] The U.S. government usually resists acknowledging that many apprehended, undocumented Hispanics are political refugees, perhaps due in part to the fact that the United States supports some of the Central and South American right-wing political groups. Those documented and undocumented Hispanics suffering migration and acculturation stress (including culture shock), fear of apprehension, and post-traumatic stress disorders related to war, civil conflict, and torture, require psychotherapeutic intervention yet find it difficult to obtain these services due to a lack of financial or insurance resources to pay for them. They are also handicapped by their legal status and by the scarcity of bilingual-

TABLE 11–2 MENTAL HEALTH DISCIPLINE BY ETHNICITY IN LOS ANGELES COUNTY* (LA COUNTY POPULATION: 7.5 MILLION; HISPANICS: 2.5 MILLION (33%)

DISCIPLINE	TOTAL	HISPANICS	% HISPANICS
Child Psychiatrists	61	1	2%
Psychiatric Nurses	46	3	7%
Ph.D. Psychologists	153	5	3%
Nurses, R.N.	226	9	4%
Psychiatrists	233	11	5%
MSWs	451	44	10%

* Data taken from Floyd H. Martinez, "Mental Health Manpower Survey for Los Angeles County Department of Mental Health," September, 1983, p. 4. The survey included all Short–Doyle and Short–Doyle Medi-Cal providers in the county, representing 3959 employees of mental health facilities.

bicultural mental health practitioners. Consider the Los Angeles mental health manpower situation, for example, where Hispanics number 2.5 million persons or 33 percent of the population. The number of bilingual-bicultural mental health practitioners is shown in Table 11–2. Regardless of legal or economic status, Spanish-speaking Hispanics find it difficult to obtain bilingual therapists since approximately 75 percent of mental health practitioners are English-speaking, non-Hispanic whites and the majority of Hispanics are Spanish-speaking. The situation is also difficult for other minorities, and Los Angeles now has a population comprised of 54 percent minorities. This presents a real challenge to federal, state, and local mental health planners and professional schools.

The Homeless

The economic gap between the "haves" and the "have nots" is at the widest point since government began monitoring this factor over forty years ago. J. Larry Brown points out that the last time unemployment was at current levels, the United States had 24 million people living in poverty in 1977. Today the rate is 2 percent higher with 32 million people living in poverty. In 1985 the media reported that 20 million U.S. persons were going hungry and the problem was getting worse. A year later in May 1986, President Ronald Reagan defended his administration stating that hungry people were simply too ignorant to know where to obtain food.[108] Brown issues a warning stating:

> America has changed greatly during this decade. We are a nation that has millions more who are hungry. Millions more who are without homes in which to raise families. Millions more who are poor. We are a country where economic disparity has reached a record high. America is at a crossroads.[109]

One of the symptoms of poverty is people not having the financial resources to obtain housing. In 1984 the U.S. Department of Housing and Urban Development described the homeless as belonging to three major categories: (1) those who encountered economic problems such as unemployment; (2) the chronically disabled; and (3) those with personal crises (divorce, domestic violence, health problems).[110] In these categories may be found people evicted from their residences due to no funds, former state hospital patients, substance abusers, runaway youths, the unemployed, and families. Twenty percent of the nation's homeless are comprised of homeless families.[111]

The people described above in HUD's three categories could be called the "old homeless" population but a "new homeless," more heterogeneous group is emerging in the late 1980s comprised of even more families, young people, minorities, and women. A survey of the homeless in thirteen U.S. cities by the U.S. Conference of Mayors revealed the following ethnic pattern: 51.9 percent black; 33.3 percent non-Hispanic white; and 14.8 percent Hispanic, Native, and Asian Americans. Another survey covering sixteen cities involving 42,539 cases showed that 51 percent of clients receiving services were minority (blacks, 40 percent; Hispanics, 11 percent). In three large cities, New York, St. Louis, and Los Angeles, 65 percent of the homeless were racial, ethnic minorities. In Chicago 69 percent of survey homeless respondents were minority.[112] A significantly greater number (75 percent) of minority group homeless were permanent residents of the districts they were interviewed in compared to non-Hispanic white homeless persons (60 percent). It appears that homelessness for minorities may be related more to economic factors than non-Hispanic white homeless persons. For example in Ohio black respondents were less likely than non-Hispanic whites to have had income from earnings in "the last month," and nearly 20 percent never had a job. The conclusion was that blacks suffered more than whites from unemployment even when blacks had more education and better preparation for employment.[113] It would appear that in addition to racism and economic hardship, immigration stress, being non-English-speaking and having illegal status would be contributing factors to homelessness in Hispanic groups.

Richard J. First et al. point out that social work as a profession has a critical role, yet to be played, in designing, documenting, and testing policy approaches to alleviating minority group homelessness. He adds that some are simply unemployed, some are mentally ill, and others are not or have never been linked to traditional social support systems.[114]

Zeroing in on the psychiatric aspects of the homeless, Lillian Gelberg and associates studied 529 homeless adults who had used in-patient and outpatient mental health services. They found that many of the homeless subjects had an overwhelming set of social, mental health, criminal, alcohol, and drug problems. The greatest number of problems was found in those homeless who had a previous psychiatric hospitalization.[115] The findings reported in these various studies indicate that the homeless population is rather heterogeneous with diverse needs, hence, requires different psychosocial strategies of intervention.

AIDS Patients

Persons diagnosed with AIDS (acquired immune deficiency syndrome) eventually die of this disease. A cure has not yet been found. According to the U.S. Center for Disease Control with six years of studying 54,723 AIDS cases, there are only three ways the disease is transmitted in the United States: through blood contamination, sexual contact, and birth to an infected mother.[116] More than 81,000 AIDS cases had been reported by 133 countries to the World Health Organization by February 1988, twice the number that had been reported the year before. The United States had the most cases with a little over 54,000, up from 31,000 cases the year before.[117] The likelihood of suicide among AIDS patients far exceeds that of persons suffering from other major illnesses, including cancer. The risk of suicide among U.S. men with AIDS is 66 times higher than in the general population.

A new AIDS study (March 1988) in Los Angeles County predicts that as many as 340,000 people in the country will be infected by the AIDS virus by 1991, with 16,000 to 23,000 of those infected actually dying. The latest health department statistics reported that there had been 4354 confirmed cases of AIDS as of January 31, 1987, which included 2722 who died of the virus. The persons considered at highest risk are homosexual males and intravenous drug users.[118] Hispanics, who comprise 7 percent of the U.S. population, represent nearly 14 percent of the 54,000 AIDS cases in the United States. Hispanics also have a high representation of heroin addicts.

The medical treatment aspect of AIDS is hopeless, as a cure is yet to be found. The psychiatric and clinical intervention aspects with persons suffering from AIDS are also very difficult for the patient as well as for the therapist. It is usually very difficult to work with people who have a terminal illness. It becomes even more difficult when working with patients who are stigmatized by the public *and* by many mental health professionals. Some hospitals are beginning to set up support groups for staff who work with AIDS patients.[119]

Psychiatrist Francisco Fernandez states that both anxiety disorders and depression are prevalent in AIDS patients and usually these disorders can be treated with psychiatric medications along with psychotherapy. But subtle to more serious organic mental disturbances accompanying AIDS (found in 80 percent of cases) make medication treatment complicated because of central-nervous-system side effects such as Parkinsonism, hypotension, sedation, and confusion. Fernandez adds that few AIDS patients respond even moderately to antidepressant medication.[120]

B. A. Navia, B. D. Jordan, and R. W. Price found in their study of AIDS patients that 66 percent suffered from progressive dementia with apathy, social withdrawal, and emotional blunting being the most common initial behavioral symptoms.[121] Stephen Buckingham and Wilfred Van Gorp identified specific social work intervention strategies when they were working with AIDS patients with related dementia. Treatment intervention assistance can be in the following areas:[122]

1. Problem solving with everyday concerns and difficulties.
2. Estate planning.
3. Decreasing the level of hypochondriacal preoccupation.
4. Guidance in designing adequate structure and limits for activities of daily living.
5. Assisting with family conflict.

The AIDS problem certainly is a challenge for the medical and mental health professions. AIDS patients and their helpers are currently overwhelmed by this problem. It was included as a special population issue as it is increasingly becoming a greater societal concern. Social workers need to learn more about this topic.

We seem to have a better treatment prognosis with other special population groups. A comprehensive, conceptual ecosystems model may assist in developing intervention approaches in working with special populations.

ECOSYSTEMS MODEL

The practice of social work involves a focus on the interaction between the person (or couple, family, group, organization, community, or larger societal structure) and the environment. The social work intervention focus might be directed at the person, environment, or both. The goal of the social worker is to enhance and restore the psychosocial functioning of persons or to change noxious social conditions that impede the mutually beneficial interaction between persons and their environment.

It was seen that the interaction between special population groups and their respective environments involves social, economic, and political factors, physical and mental health, and noxious forces such as ageism, sexism, racism, and class discrimination, all exerting various effects on the lives of special population members. In identifying special population needs in order to provide services, the social worker should seek to understand both their feelings and attitudes about these factors and noxious forces and the impact they exert. The social worker then attempts to meet social work goals to "enhance and restore social functioning and to improve social conditions."[123]

Carol Meyer maintains that for many years social work has been offering its well honed methods only to those who could use them instead of first finding out what was needed and then selecting the practice method from its interventive repertoire or inventing new methods. She believes the current social work methods framework maintains social work's denial of what had to be done with regard to broader social problems. She therefore suggests an ecosystems orientation to practice that involves the application of ecology (the study of the relationship between organisms and their environment) and general systems theory to professional tasks. This ecosystems perspective, according to Meyer, allows

> . . . social workers to look at psychological phenomena, account for complex variables, assess the dynamic interplay of these variables, draw conceptual boundaries around the unit of attention or the case, and then generate ideas for interventions. At this point methodology enters in; for in any particular case—meaning a particular individual, family, group, institutional unit, or geographical area—any number of practice interventions might be needed.[124]

This ecosystems model of practice would help to promote social workers' understanding of the psychosocial problems experienced by special populations, the incidence, prevalence, intensity and harmfulness of sexism, ageism, racism, and class discrimination, and the social environments (enhancing as well as noxious) in which special populations struggle to survive.

Urie Bronfenbrenner originally developed an ecological model in 1977 utilizing four factors, such as individual, family, social structural and sociocultural, affecting human development.[125] Bonnie Carlson in 1984 then adapted this model to the problem area of domestic violence. The model conceptualizes ecological space comprised of four different levels or systems, each of which is nested within the next.[126] This ecological framework, which can be called an ecosystems model, may be a helpful tool in analyzing from a micro to macro perspective the various factors impacting special population members. In addition to the minor modifications of two items—"sociocultural" to culture, and "social structural" to environmental-structural—as a means of more crisply delineating cultural from social or environmental-structural factors, the authors added a fifth-level factor for analysis, the historical.[127] Historical factors are particularly important for special populations as the historical origins of sexism, ageism, and racism, for example, continue to function today to "lock in" these groups in U.S. society. The ecosystems model is presented in Figure 11–1.

First, at the *individual level*, the focus is on the biopsychological endowment each person possesses, including their personality strengths, level of psychosocial development, cognition, perception, problem solving skills, emotional temperament, habit formation, and communication and language skills. Additionally, it is important to be knowledgeable about the person's attitudes, values, cultural beliefs, life style, skills, and abilities; their view of the world and how they respond to and cope with physical and psychological stress and problems. This only represents the highlights of factors at the individual level; the list is by no means exhaustive. The same, brief format will be seen in the other levels of analysis.

Second, at the *family level*, the focus is on the nature of family life style, culture, organization, family, division of labor, sex role structure, and interactional dynamics. Within a cultural context each family is unique. It is there-

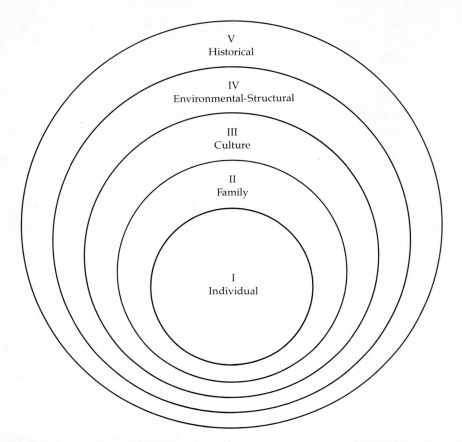

Figure 11–1 *Ecosystems Model for Analysis of Psychosocial Factors Impacting on Special Populations*

fore important to know its values, beliefs, emotional support capacity, affective style, tradition, rituals, overall strengths and vulnerabilities, and how it manages internal or external stress. The nature and quality of the spousal relationship and the depth of connectedness to children and extended family are other areas requiring examination.

Third, in civilizations cultures have evolved for survival purposes. Each culture develops behavioral responses influenced by the environment, historical and social processes incorporating specific structures such as language, food, kinship styles, religion, communications, norms, beliefs, and values. At the *cultural level* of the ecosystems model, therefore, the focus should be on understanding the cultural values, belief systems, and societal norms of the host culture, and in the case of minorities, their original culture. There may exist a conflict of cultures that in advanced form, may result in mental-emotional impairment due to culture shock. The enhancing, nurturing aspects of the culture(s) should be noted as well as noxious elements such as sexism, ageism, and racism.

The fourth level of analysis involves *environmental-structural* factors and the positive or negative impact they have on special populations. Environmental-structural theories postulate that many of the problems of affected oppressed groups, such as special populations, are caused by the economic and social structure of U.S. society. Women, for example, are not poorer as a group than men because of biological or cultural inferiority. Rather, sexism is a U.S. male cultural value that is expressed and reinforced through the structure of economic, political, educational, and other social institutions. Ryan states that when U.S. white society looks at the poorly educated minority group child in the ghetto or *barrio* school, blame is placed upon the parents (no books in the home), the child (impulse-ridden, nonverbal), minority culture (no value on education), or their socioeconomic status (i.e., they are socially and economically deprived and don't know any better). In pursuing this logic, Ryan adds, no one remembers to ask questions about the collapsing buildings, old, torn textbooks, insensitive teachers, the relentless segregation, callous administrators—in short, the environmental structure imposed upon the person with its accompanying negative consequences.[128]

The fifth and final level of the ecosystems model concerns positive and noxious factors in the *historical experience* of the special population member(s). The historical roots and experience of female subordination by males, for example, will affect the nature and quality of the women's interaction with all agencies and their representatives. The male social worker may not be aware of his unconscious sexist behavior—the result of decades of conditioning—as he attempts to "help" female clients with their problems. Years of minority group oppression and exploitation, at times including genocide, lynching, and "police executions without trial," have left deep scars in minority group members and will affect the way they relate to human service agency representatives. Some elderly whites may recall very positive historical experiences recalling how supportive and encouraging U.S. social institutions had been, only to become depressed and discouraged when abandoned by the government. In addition to knowing about the U.S. historical experience, it is also of value to know the historical experience of immigrants and the countries they came from.

To illustrate how the ecosystems model might work, the following case example is presented:

José is a small, frail-looking 14-year-old Spanish-speaking only youngster brought into the community mental health center by his mother because he began to yell, cry, and scream and threw himself under a table at a public laundromat. The Anglo-American psychiatrist who saw José was able to speak some Spanish. José told the doctor that he was at the laundromat with his mother the day before and that he had seen a police car slowly pass by the laundromat. He insisted the police officer on the passenger side of the car pointed his machine gun at the laundromat. At that time, fearing for his life he threw himself under one of the tables and began screaming.

The mother confirmed that a police car had passed the laundromat but stated that the officers merely passed and did not expose any firearms. Other symptoms José was exhibiting were fear to go to school (where he was failing), fear of leaving the house, nightmares (people trying to kill him), insomnia, fear of being arrested by immigration officials and deported, depression, agitation, and increasingly becoming more suspicious of people and irratable, especially at his mother, stepfather, and siblings. This progressively deteriorating behavior had been going on for about six months. The doctor concluded that José was at times incoherent, delusional, was having visual hallucinations, and was displaying behavior that was at times disorganized. This clinical picture was consistent with DSM III 298.80, Brief Reactive Psychosis. He was prescribed anti-psychotic medication. He continued in treatment for two weeks but his symptoms did not subside. The medication was not having any effect.

An Hispanic bilingual-bicultural mental health consultant was asked to see José and his mother and make an assessment and treatment recommendation. José was born in "Muy Lejos," a rural, agricultural village in El Salvador. His parents were both farm laborers as were his grandparents. He was raised in a very traditional, religious, rural culture where sex roles, division of labor, and respect for the elderly, extended family and authority figures were valued. When José was six, his father was suspected of being a guerrilla and was killed by right-wing government forces. Sensing her life was also in danger, José's mother left him with his grandparents and came to the United States without documents in order to obtain employment and then send for José and other relatives. José felt abandoned and cried on the phone whenever his mother was able to call him, which was once every three or four months. Frequently, José would have to join other villagers and escape into the hills, sometimes for several months. José saw many killings, including decapitated bodies placed in the village by the right-wing forces to intimidate villagers.

In the meantime the mother struggled for several years as a low-paid domestic and began to live with a documented Hispanic male. They had two children, two and four years younger than José. Finally, the mother was able to save enough money to send for José. He was brought to the United States by a secret, underground system some six months previously. Initially he was happy to be reunited with his mother, but then the previously discussed symptoms began to surface.

José presents a difficult, complex case although in no way is his situation unique. Rather than presenting one clearly identified specific problem for the mental health practitioner to treat, as is often the case with many middle-class clients, José brings at least five major problems. They have to be prioritized in terms of severity and treated in a sequential manner. First of all José is suffering acute post-traumatic stress disorder symptoms that have to be treated, including appropriately prescribed medication that will reduce his anxiety and fear, and permit him to sleep. Second, he is experiencing culture shock, having abruptly left an agrarian environment and then being placed in the central cities area of Los Angeles. He doesn't understand the language or the requirements of school. He is being chased by urban gangs. Third, he is experiencing separation pain, having left his loving grandparents, who were really his substitute parents. It is also painful to separate from relatives, friends, and one's country, never knowing if one will return. Fourth, he harbors a significant amount of unresolved anger toward his mother, who he believes abandoned him at a critical point in his life. These unresolved issues are intensified at his current psychosocial developmental level of adolescence. Finally, young José is confronted with a reconstituted family. He has to learn to deal with a stepfather who is taking the place of his beloved father. He also has to learn to live with a ten- and twelve-year-old step-sister and step-brother. In short he is a complete outsider in *all* respects.

Following the treatment of the psychiatric symptoms, José then will have to work on cultural shock issues, separation anxiety, and unresolved matters related to his mother. At the appropriate time family therapy should also be initiated to help them function more positively as a family unit. The social worker may also have to help José resolve school and community stress problems and link him up with community social-recreation programs.

In working with special population groups once a sound knowledge base is established through the use of a conceptual tool such as the ecosystems model, the social worker has to intervene at both micro and macro intervention levels. In cases such as that of José, a detailed biological-psychological-sociological, cultural, and historical assessment has to be made in order to know what is needed and more important, what has to be done. The case highlighted more micro intervention strategies than macro. Macro intervention approaches would have utilized the helping concepts of client advocacy, empowerment, social action, networking, and class action social work, which involves collaboration with the legal profession on behalf of oppressed, disadvantaged special populations. These approaches are spelled out in detail in Chapter 23. Part Four explores further various interventions with special populations.

CONCLUDING COMMENT

Special populations are persons such as women, the elderly, AIDS patients, the homeless, and minorities, who have unique needs and circumstances that must be recognized when the social worker attempts to provide services to these persons. Not only are special population members unique because of their sex, age, race, or ethnicity, but they also share a second-class status in U.S. society. They are indeed a high-risk group because of their status in society.

The crippling effects of sexism, ageism, homophobia, and racism as expressed through the structural fabric of U.S. society, were analyzed not only as to their intensity and prevalence, but also with respect to the basic causes and functions of these stresses. Understanding the historical origin of these attitudes assists the social worker in understanding their expression as modern dynamics.

An examination of overall trends and demographics involving special population problems and needs shows that matters are becoming worse, especially given the attitudes of the Reagan administration toward human services programs. The income gap between men and women continues to widen, AIDS has made its appearance, the elderly are finding a greater economic and health struggle as they get older, there are more homeless, and minorities, especially blacks and Hispanics, are being directed into the juvenile and adult criminal justice system in even greater and more disproportionate numbers.

The practice skills of the social work profession are being challenged as never before by special populations needs. An ecosystems model adapted from other theorists was presented to assist the social worker in obtaining a comprehensive analysis of a special populations case. A case was presented to demonstrate how a mistaken diagnosis can occur unless all factors concerning the individual, his or her family and culture, the environmental structural context in which the person lives, and the historical experience are considered. Suggestions for micro and macro level interventions were presented.

Perhaps Anne Minahan, then Editor of *Social Work,* says it best in reminding social workers about their professional values and commitment to help oppressed people:

> Social workers can help people cope with their situations and increase their competence, but the very nature of the problems that oppressed people face are linked to the discrimination and exploitation they face in their environment. Social workers can work to make organizations and societal institutions responsive. Social workers can help people obtain resources. Social workers can work to influence social and environmental policy. Social workers pursue all these activities in social service organizations, in schools, in health and mental health facilities, in criminal justice institutions, in services designed for people with special problems or age characteristics, and in different geographic areas. In all these activities, social workers must value and respond humanely and helpfully to diverse populations and help others to do the same.[129]

SUGGESTED READINGS

Allen, C., and Brotman, H., eds. *Chartbook on Aging in America.* Washington, D.C.: White House Conference on Aging, 1981.

The Annals of the American Academy of Political and Social Science, entire issue, "Our Crowded Prisons," 478 (March 1985).

Bass, Barbara Ann, Wyatt, Gail Elizabeth, and Powell, Gloria Johnson, eds. *The Afro American Family: Assessment, Treatment and Research Issues.* New York: Grune & Stratton, 1982.

Becerra, Rosina M., Karno, Marvin, and Escobar, Javier I., eds. *Mental Health and Hispanic Americans: Clinical Perspectives.* New York: Grune & Stratton, 1982.

Billingsley, Andrew. *Black Families in White America.* Englewood Cliffs, N.J.: Prentice-Hall, 1968.

Buckingham, Stephen L., and Van Gorp, Wilfred G. "Essential Knowledge about AIDS Dementia." *Social Work,* Vol. 33, No. 2, March–April 1988, pp. 112–115.

Daniels, Roger, and Kitano, Harry H. L. *American Racism: Exploration of the Nature of Prejudice.* Englewood Cliffs, N.J.: Prentice-Hall, 1970.

Deloria, Vine, Jr. "Native Americans: The American Indian Today." *The Annals of the American Academy of Political and Social Science* 454 (March 1981): pp. 139–149.

First, Richard J., Roth, Dee, and Arewa, Bobbie Darden. "Homelessness: Understanding the Dimensions of the Problem for Minorities," *Social Work,* Vol. 33, No. 2, March–April, 1988, p. 120.

Gelberg, Lillian, Linn, Lawrence S., and Leake, Barbara D. "Mental Health, Alcohol and Drug Abuse, and Criminal History Among Homeless Adults," *The American Journal of Psychiatry,* Vol. 145, No. 2, February 1988, pp. 191–196.

Graham, Hugh Davis, and Gurr, Ted Robert. *Violence in America: Historical and Comparative Perspectives.* New York: Bantam Books, 1969.

McIntosh, John L. "Suicide Among the Elderly: Levels and Trends." *American Journal of Orthopsychiatry* 55 (April 1985): 288–293.

Mahaffey, Maryann. "Sexism in Social Work." *Social Work* 2 (November 1976): 419.

Martin, Del. *Battered Wives.* New York: Pocket Books, 1977.

Morales, Armando. "The Collective Preconscious and Racism." *Social Casework* 52 (May 1971): 285–293.

Morales, Armando. "Social Work with Third World People." *Social Work* 26 (January 1981): 45–51.

Morales, Armando. "Substance Abuse and Mexican American Youth: An Overview." *Journal of Drug Issues* 14 (Spring 1984): 297–311.

Murase, Kenji. "Minorities: Asian Americans." *Encyclopedia of Social Work Seventeenth Issue,* Vol. 2, edited by John B. Turner. Washington, D.C.: National Association of Social Workers, 1977, pp. 953–960.

Powell, Gloria Johnson, Yamamoto, Joe, Romero, Annelisa, and Morales, Armando, eds. *The Psychosocial Development of Minority Group Children.* New York: Brunner/Mazel, Inc., 1983.

President's Commission on Mental Health. *Mental Health in America: 1978,* Vol. III. Washington, D.C.: U.S. Government Printing Office, 1978.

Sherman, Lawrence W. "Execution Without Trial: Police Homicide and the Constitution." *Vanderbilt Law Review* 33 (January 1980): 71–100.

Social Work. Special Issue on Women. 21 (November 1976).

Solomon, Barbara Bryant. "Is it Sex, Race or Class?" *Social Work* 21 (November 1976): 421–426.

Valentich, Mary, and Gripton, James. "Ideological Perspectives on the Sexual Assault of Women." *Social Service Review* 58 (September 1984): 448–461.

Vladeck, Bruce C., and Firman, James P. "The Aging of the Population and Health Services." *The Annals of the American Academy of Political and Social Science* 468 (July 1983): 132–148.

Walker, Lenore E. *The Battered Woman.* New York: Harper and Row, 1979.

ENDNOTES

1. President's Commission on Mental Health, *Mental Health in America: 1978,* Vol. III (Washington, D.C.: U.S. Government Printing Office, 1978), p. 731.
2. President's Commission on Mental Health, Vol. III, Appendix, 1978, p. 646.
3. The U.S. Commission on Civil Rights, *Racism in America and How to Combat It* (Washington, D.C.: U.S. Government Printing Office, 1970) p. 19.

4. Blanch D. Coll, *Perspectives in Public Welfare* (Washington, D.C.: U.S. Department of Health, Education and Welfare, 1969), p. 9.
5. Richard Hofstadter, *Social Darwinism in American Thought* (Boston: Beacon Press, 1944), p. 41.
6. Ibid., p. 50.
7. Ibid., p. 42.
8. "The Crisis is Mounting," Special Report, National Association of Social Workers, Los Angeles Area Chapter, 1970.
9. *U.S. News and World Report,* April 15, 1985, p. 25.
10. Gloria Johnson Powell and Rodney N. Powell, "Epilogue: Poverty—the Greatest and Severest Handicapping Condition in Childhood," in Gloria Johnson Powell, Joe Yamamoto, Annelisa Romero, and Armando Morales (eds.), *The Psychosocial Development of Minority Group Children* (New York: Brunner/Mazel, Inc., 1983), p. 579.
11. Ibid., p. 577.
12. R. H. DeLone, *Small Futures: Children, Inequality and the Limits of Liberal Reform* (New York: Harcourt, Brace, Jovanovich, 1979), p. 4.
13. Carmen De Navas and Edward Fernandez, "Condition of Hispanic Women Today," U.S. Department of Commerce, Bureau of the Census, July 27, 1984.
14. U.S. Department of Commerce, Bureau of the Census, *Current Population Reports,* Series p. 60, No. 127, "Money, Income and Poverty Status of Families and Persons in the United States: 1980 (Advance Data from the March, 1981 Current Population Survey)," (August, 1981), Tables 16 and 18.
15. Maryann Maheffey, "Sexism in Social Work," *Social Work 2* (November 1976): 419.
16. Barbara Bryant Solomon, "Is it Sex, Race or Class?" *Social Work* 21 (November 1976): 420.
17. Del Martin, *Battered Wives* (New York: Pocket Books, 1977), pp. 10–42.
18. Lenore E. Walker, *The Battered Woman* (New York: Harper and Row, 1979).
19. Murray A. Straus, "Social Stress and Marital Violence in a National Sample of American Families," *Annals of New York Academy of Sciences* 347 (1980): 229–250.
20. Anna F. Kuhl, "A Preliminary Profile of Abusing Men," a paper presented at the Annual Meeting of the Academy for Criminal Justice Sciences, Philadelphia, Pennsylvania, 1980.
21. Commission on Crime Control and Violence Prevention, *Ounces of Prevention: Toward an Understanding of the Causes of Violence,* 1982 Final Report to the People of California, monograph, Sacramento, California, p. 33.
22. Del Martin, *Battered Wives,* p. 14.
23. Clarence Kelley, *Uniform Crime Reports for the United States* (Washington, D.C.: U.S. Government Printing Office, 1974).
24. Gail Abarbanel, "Helping Victims of Rape," *Social Work* 21 (November 1976): 478.
25. Ibid.
26. Roger Petersen, "Social Class, Social Learning, and Wife Abuse," *Social Service Review* 54 (September 1980): 399.
27. Richard J. Gelles, *The Violent Home* (Beverly Hills, Calif.: Sage Publications, Inc., 1972), pp. 183–190.
28. Mary Valentich and James Gripton, "Ideological Perspectives on the Sexual Assault of Women," *Social Service Review* 58 (September 1984): 451.
29. Lorne Gibson, Rick Linden, and Stuart Johnson, "A Situational Theory of Rape," *Canadian Journal of Criminology* 22 (1980): 51–65.
30. Susan Brownmiller, *Against Our Will* (New York: Simon and Schuster, 1975).
31. Margaret L. Andersen and Claire Renzetti, "Rape Crisis, Counseling and the Culture of Individualism," *Contemporary Crisis* 4 (1980): 331–332.
32. Peggy Reeves Sanday, *Female Power and Male Dominance: On the Origins of Sexual Inequality* (Cambridge: Cambridge University Press, 1981).

33. Hugh Davis Graham and Ted Robert Gurr, *Violence in America: Historical and Comparative Perspectives* (New York: Bantam Books, 1969), p. 799.
34. Bruce C. Vladeck and James P. Firman, "The Aging of the Population and Health Services," *The Annals of the American Academy of Political and Social Science* 468 (July 1983): 133.
35. Ibid., p. 137.
36. Elaine M. Brody, "Aging," in John B. Turner, ed., *Encyclopedia of Social Work Seventeenth Issue*, Vol. I (Washington, D.C.: National Association of Social Workers, 1977), p. 57.
37. Lawrence S. Root and John E. Tropman, "Income Sources of the Elderly," *Social Service Review* 58 (September 1984): 390, 393.
38. C. Allen and H. Brotman, eds. *Chartbook on Aging in America* (Washington, D.C.: White House Conference on Aging, 1981), p. 57.
39. Gary M. Nelson, "How States Distribute Title XX Funds to the Elderly Poor," *Social Work Research and Abstracts* 19 (Summer 1983): 5, 7.
40. Vladeck and Firman, p. 138.
41. Allen and Brotman, pp. 78–80.
42. Allen and Brotman, p. 17.
43. Brody, p. 57.
44. *Los Angeles Times*, April 21, 1985, Part IV, p. 5.
45. Robert N. Butler, "Geriatric Medicine," *New York State Journal of Medicine* 77 (August 1977): 1471.
46. Ira Reiss, *Family Systems in America*, Third Edition (New York: Holt, Rinehart and Winston, 1980).
47. R. Douglass, "A Study of Maltreatment of the Elderly and Other Vulnerable Adults," Institute of Gerontology and School of Public Health (University of Michigan, Ann Arbor, 1980).
48. John L. McIntosh, "Suicide Among the Elderly: Levels and Trends," *American Journal of Orthopsychiatry* 55 (April 1985): 289.
49. Ibid., p. 291.
50. Armando Morales, "Social Work with Third World People," *Social Work* 26 (January 1981): 45.
51. Armando Morales, "The Collective Preconscious and Racism," *Social Casework* 52 (May 1971): 285–293.
52. *Racism in America*, p. 5.
53. Ibid.
54. *Los Angeles Times*, April 27, 1985, Part I, p. 12.
55. Ibid.
56. Ibid.
57. J. S. Passel, "Provisional Evaluation of the 1970 Census Count of American Indians," *Demography* 13 (1976): 397–409.
58. U.S. Department of Health, Education and Welfare, Office of Health Research, Statistics and Technology, *Health United States: 1979*, No. 80–1232 (Washington D.C.: U.S. Government Printing Office, 1980); also see Armando Morales, "Social Work with Third World People," p. 45.
59. Vine Deloria, Jr., "Native Americans: The American Indian Today," *The Annals of the American Academy of Political and Social Science* 454 (March 1981): 140, 141.
60. Roger Daniels and Harry H. L. Kitano, *American Racism: Exploration of the Nature of Prejudice* (Englewood Cliffs, N.J.: Prentice-Hall, 1970), pp. 29–33.
61. Vine Deloria, Jr., p. 146.
62. Ronald S. Fischler, "Protecting American Indian Children," *Social Work* 25 (September 1980): 342, 347.
63. Evelyn Lance Blanchard and Russel Lawrence Barsh, "What is Best for Tribal Children? A Response to Fischler," *Social Work* 25 (September 1980): 350, 354.
64. Ibid., p. 352.

65. James Abourezk, "The Role of the Federal Government: A Congressional View," in Steven Unger, ed., *The Destruction of American Indian Families* (New York: Association on American Indian Affairs, 1977), p. 12.
66. William Byler, "The Destruction of American Indian Families," in Steven Unger, ed., *The Destruction of American Indian Families*, p. 1.
67. Anne Metcalf, *A Model for Treatment in a Native American Family Service Center* (Seattle: School of Social Work, University of Washington, 1978), pp. 4–6.
68. Kenji Murase, "Minorities: Asian Americans," in John B. Turner, ed., *Encyclopedia of Social Work Seventeenth Issue*, Vol. 2 (Washington, D.C.: National Association of Social Workers, 1977), p. 953.
69. Ibid.
70. Ibid.
71. Roger Daniels and Harry Kitano, p. 62.
72. Gloria Johnson Powell, Joe Yamamoto, Annelisa Romero, and Armando Morales, eds., *The Psychosocial Development of Minority Group Children*, p. 240.
73. Lindbergh S. Sata, "Mental Health Issues of Japanese-American Children," in Gloria Johnson Powell et al., p. 366.
74. Daniel D. Le, "Mental Health and Vietnamese Children," in Gloria Johnson Powell et al., p. 373.
75. Ibid., p. 378, 379.
76. Ibid., p. 383.
77. "Blacks and Hispanics in the United States," Data Track 6 (Washington, D.C. American Council of Life Insurance, 1979), p. 5.
78. U.S. Bureau of the Census, *Current Population Reports Characteristics of Populations Below Poverty Line*, Series P-60, No. 130 (Washington, D.C.: U.S. Government Printing Office, 1979).
79. Andrew Billingsley, *Black Families in White America.* (Englewood Cliffs, N.J.: Prentice-Hall, 1968), p. 71.
80. Barbara Ann Bass, Gail Elizabeth Wyatt, and Gloria Johnson Powell, eds., *The Afro American Family: Assessment, Treatment and Research Issues* (New York: Grune and Stratton, 1982), p. 10.
81. Ibid., pp. 10, 11.
82. *Los Angeles Times*, April 28, 1985, Part I, p. 4.
83. Barbara Bryant Solomon, "The Delivery of Mental Health Services to Afro American Individuals and Families: Translating Theory into Practice," in Barbara Ann Bass, et al., *The Afro American Family: Assessment, Treatment and Research Issues*, pp. 165, 166.
84. Lawrence W. Sherman, "Execution Without Trial: Police Homicide and the Constitution," *Vanderbilt Law Review* 33 (January 1980): 95, 96.
85. Armando Morales, "Police Deadly Force: Government-Sanctioned Execution of Hispanics," Paper presented at National Council of La Raza Symposium on Crime and Justice for Hispanics, Racine, Wisconsin, June 28–30, 1979, p. 6.
86. "The Hispanic Population in the United States: March 1986 and 1987 (Advance Report)," U.S. Department of Commerce, *Bureau of the Census*, Series P-20, No. 416, issued August 1987, p. 5.
87. *Business Week*, June 23, 1980, p. 86.
88. "Report of the Special Populations Subpanel on Mental Health of Hispanic Americans," *The President's Commission on Mental Health, Volume III, Appendix* (Washington, D.C.: U.S. Government Printing Office, 1978), p. 905.
89. Armando Morales, "Substance Abuse and Mexican American Youth: An Overview," *Journal of Drug Issues* 14 (Spring 1984): 297–311.
90. Armando Morales, "The Mexican American Gang Member: Evaluation and Treatment," in Rosina M. Becerra, Marvin Karno, and Javier I. Escobar, eds., *Mental Health and Hispanic Americans: Clinical Perspectives* (New York: Grune & Stratton, 1982), pp. 139–155.

91. Armando Morales, "Institutional Racism in Mental Health and Criminal Justice," *Social Casework* 59 (July 1978): 387–395.
92. *Prisoners in 1983*, Bureau of Justice Statistics Bulletin (Washington, D.C.: Department of Justice, BJS, 1984), App. A.
93. James Austin and Barry Krisberg, "Incarceration in the United States: The Extent and Future of the Problem," *The Annals of the American Academy of Political and Social Science* 478 (March 1985): 24.
94. *Federal, District of Columbia, and States Future Prison and Correctional Institution Populations and Capacities, GAO/GGD-84-56* (Gaithersburg, Md.: Government Accounting Office, 1984).
95. Austin and Krisberg, p. 25.
96. Ibid., p. 26.
97. Barry Krisberg and Ira Schwartz, "Rethinking Juvenile Justice," *Crime and Delinquency* (July 1983): 346–349.
98. Ibid., p. 351.
99. *Sacramento Chronicle,* September 26, 1984, p. 1.
100. "Arrests in California and First Commitments to the Youth Authority by Race/Ethnicity," Department of the Youth Authority, State of California, February 1985, p. 7; also see "Ethnic Groups in Correctional Facilities, 1983," statistics, California Youth Authority, #586IHY-1, 1983.
101. "A Comparison of Characteristics of Youth Authority Wards in Institutions and on Parole, 1974–1983," November 1983, Department of the Youth Authority, State of California, p. 9.
102. "United States Private Juvenile Correctional Facilities 1-Day Counts, 1983," U.S. Bureau of the Census, Children in Custody Series.
103. Joan Petersilia, "Racial Disparities in the Criminal Justice System," June 1983, Rand Corporation, Santa Monica, Calif., pp. v, xii.
104. Lawrence A. Greenfeld, "Measuring the Application and Use of Punishment," National Institute of Justice, Washington, D.C., November 1981.
105. Tom Morganthau, "Closing the Door," *Newsweek,* June 25, 1984, p. 19.
106. Ed Griffin, "Reagan Runs into the Religious Left," *In These Times,* April 11–17, 1984, p. 11.
107. "Social Work in the Sanctuary Movement for Central American Refugees," *Social Work* 30 (February 1985): 74, 75.
108. J. Larry Brown, "Domestic Hunger is No Accident," *Social Work,* March–April 1988, Vol. 33, No. 2, p. 99.
109. Ibid, p. 100.
110. "A Report to the Secretary on the Homeless and Emergency Shelters," U.S. Department of Housing and Urban Development, Office of Policy Development and Research, May 1984.
111. Ellen L. Bassuk, Lenore Rubin, and Alison S. Lauriat, "Characteristics of Sheltered Homeless Families," *American Journal of Public Health,* September 1986, pp. 1097–1101.
112. Richard J. First, Dee Roth, and Bobbie Darden Arewa, "Homelessness: Understanding the Dimensions of the Problem for Minorities," *Social Work,* Vol. 33, No. 2, March–April, 1988, p. 120.
113. Ibid., p. 122.
114. Ibid., p. 123.
115. Lillian Gelberg, Lawrence S. Linn, and Barbara D. Leake, "Mental Health, Alcohol and Drug Use, and Criminal History Among Homeless Adults," *The American Journal of Psychiatry,* Vol. 145, No. 2, February 1988, pp. 191–196.
116. *Los Angeles Times,* Part II, Friday, March 4, 1988, p. 8.
117. Ibid.
118. *Los Angeles Times,* Part I, Saturday, March 19, 1988, p. 30.
119. Kathleen Moriarty and Teddye Clayton, "Highlights of the 39th Institute on Hos-

pital and Community Psychiatry," *Hospital and Community Psychiatry*, Vol. 39, No. 2, February 1988, p. 131.

120. Ibid.

121. B. A. Navia, B. D. Jordan, and R. W. Price, "The AIDS Dementia Complex: Clinical Features," *Annals of Neurology*, Vol. 19, June 1986, pp. 517–524.

122. Stephen L. Buckingham and Wilfred G. Van Gorp, "Essential Knowledge about AIDS Dementia," *Social Work*, Vol. 33, No. 2, March–April 1988, pp. 112–115.

123. Armando Morales, "Social Work with Third World People," p. 46.

124. Carol H. Meyer, "What Directions for Direct Practice?" *Social Work* 24 (July 1979): 271.

125. Urie Bronfenbrenner, "Toward an Experimental Ecology of Human Development," *American Psychologist* 32 (1977): 513–551.

126. Bonnie E. Carlson, "Causes and Maintenance of Domestic Violence: an Ecological Analysis," *Social Service Review* 58 (December 1984): 569–587.

127. Nick Vaca, "The Mexican American in the Social Sciences," Part II, *El Grito* IV (Fall 1970): 17–15.

128. William Ryan, *Blaming the Victim* (New York: Pantheon Books, 1971), p. 4.

129. Anne Minahan, "Social Workers and Oppressed People," *Social Work* 26 (May 1981): 184.

Gender as a Factor
in Practice

Julia B. Rauch

PREFATORY COMMENT

Julia B. Rauch sees sexism as deeply entrenched in U.S. society and affecting social work in myriad ways. She argues that the social work profession needs to understand clearly the impact sexism has on clients, practitioners, and itself and to make a stronger commitment to nonsexist practice. Sexism pertains to the feelings of superiority by one sex toward the other. Usually these sexist attitudes are attributed to men.

The article highlights four issues involving women and social work practice: (1) preparation for practice, (2) the predominance of women clients, (3) relationships between clients and workers, and (4) racism and sexism in social work. Rauch states that social work education does not adequately prepare students for nonsexist practice. For example stereotypic notions of women are perpetuated in the social sciences by authors such as Parsons, Lidz, and Erikson. This knowledge has been incorporated into the social work curricula. The author believes that if the initiative for nonsexist education does not come from within social work faculties, change in curricula may prove to be a function of external pressure.

Rauch sees a variety of factors producing a predominance of women as social work clients. Three of these factors are: (1) that the service delivery system is skewed toward women, (2) that society has a different attitude toward dependence for men compared to women, and (3) that poor men—particularly if they are not white—are punished for their poverty by being shunted into the correctional system, whereas women are tracked into the welfare and social service system.

In analyzing relationships between clients and workers, Rauch raises some intriguing points based on gender of clients and social workers. Her experience has led her to believe that some male clients who have female workers tend to feel uncomfortable with the reversal of status and may respond by attempting to sexualize the relationship, by "cutting up" the worker, or by relating to her as a mother figure. Racial and ethnic factors may also affect the client-worker relationship. Working-class white males may tend to react differently to black male workers, black female workers, and white female workers.

Rauch views sexism and racism in the United States as being inextricably linked. Both sustain economic exploitation and both are divisive. Rauch cautions that in combating sexism the profession must keep clearly in mind the ways in which class and racial differences affect the implementation of social policy. One example she cites concerns sterilization: among middle-class women sterilization is a method of birth control: for poor women it can become a means of oppression, that is, an involuntary alternative.

Social work is generally described as a woman's profession. The majority of social workers are women. In sociological terms, social work is a sex-typed occupation. According to Merton,

> Occupations can be described as sex-typed when a very large majority of those in them are of one sex and when there is an associated normative expectation that this is as it should be.[1]

Perceived as an extension of the feminine role, social work is viewed as involving expressive and person-oriented tasks that differ from the instrumental and object-oriented tasks of "men's work." The valued capacities of social workers lie in the affective realm: the ideal social worker, like the ideal woman, is selfless, nurturant, empathic, warm.

Social work is a woman's profession in another sense. The majority of social work clients are women. About three-fourths of all persons receiving income from public assistance and welfare payments are women.[2] As mothers, to whom society delegates primary responsibility for child rearing, women are primary users of child welfare services. They utilize mental health services more than men and are the major consumers of services for the aged. They are the primary clients of family planning, pregnancy counseling, and abortion services. Other agencies, such as rape crisis centers and shelters for battered wives, are intended specifically for women.

Paradoxically, social work has only slowly recognized that gender is a factor in practice. As recently as September 1974, a special issue of *Social Work*, "Looking Forward: Social Work into the 80's," failed to identify women as one of the specific client groups about which social work should be concerned. Examining articles published in *Social Work* over an eight-year period, Schwartz discovered that authors ignored gender and that unisex labels, such as "the poor" or "the worker" were common.[3] At the time this article was written, there was no anthology that examined sexism in practice comparable to *Dynamics of Racism in Social Work Practice*, nor an overview of research on sexism similar to *Race, Research, and Reason*.[4] Practice texts virtually ignore the topic. In his book on interviewing, Kadushin summarized findings of an extensive literature of class and ethnic differences, but he was forced to report that "the effect of sex of participants on the social work interview has not been studied."[5]

FERMENT IN OTHER FIELDS

Social work's lack of activity with regard to women's issues contrasts with the ferment in other fields. A women's caucus succeeded in establishing the

Psychology of Women Quarterly as an official publication of the American Psychological Association. In medicine, the treatment of women is being sharply challenged: another new periodical, *Journal of Women and Health,* manifests this concern. Law and the courts have been, of course, major arenas of the women's movement, with the struggle often led by members of a new breed of feminist lawyers; and a women lawyer's group, the National Conference on Women and the Law, sponsors a yearly conference on legal issues related to women.

In the academic disciplines, women's caucuses are proliferating along with scholarly articles, special issues of journals, and monographs focused on women's topics. The agitation has been so great that women's studies has emerged as a discipline in its own right, and the National Women's Studies Association was founded in January 1977. A new scholarly journal, *Signs: Journal of Women in Culture and Society,* exemplifies the intellectually rich, innovative work now being done in the new discipline. Topics covered in this journal include father-daughter incest, widowhood, economics of women's volunteer work, occupational segregation, discrimination and poverty among women who head families, anorexia nervosa, family backgrounds of skid-row women, and the politics of the welfare mother's movement. Other new journals include *Sex Roles* and *Women's Studies.*

Women's studies are challenging dominant theoretical orientations. Psychoanalytic theory, long a major foundation of social work practice, has been charged with sexism, with lacking an empirical basis for major theoretical concepts related to women, with failure to take into account the impact of social institutions on behavior, and with encouraging women to adapt to oppressive conditions. Functionalism, the dominant thrust in sociology in the United States, has been charged with justifying the suppression of women and with inadequate analysis of their position in this society.[6] Referring to psychiatry, Seiden points out that increasing the knowledge about women and beginning the revision of theory will have an effect on practice.[7] However, social work is not building on women's studies. The literature dealing with sex and sexism as factors in social work practice is scant and of varying quality.

Why has social work not been more actively concerned with this area? Paradoxically, the numerical dominance of female social workers may contribute to this lack of activity. Unlike women in male-dominated occupations, female social workers are not an isolated minority, and they may be less conscious of themselves as a distinct group and less aware of sexism directed against them. Adams suggested that female social workers are in a "compassion trap"—their commitment to the ideal of service fosters their exploitation, to the detriment of themselves, their clients, and the profession.[8] Women who opt for social work may differ from women who pursue careers that are sex-typed for men—the female psychologist, physician, sociologist, lawyer, or political scientist may be more assertive and more ready than her sister social worker to combat the status quo. The profession's commitment to the eradication of poverty and racism may be deflecting attention from women's issues. Some people stereotype women's liberation as a movement on behalf of well-educated and privileged women with insubstantial griev-ances—forgetting that welfare rights is also a women's issue. The predom-inance of male social work authors may also contribute to the lack of attention paid in the literature to sex and sexism as factors in practice.[9]

Whatever the reasons for the lagging interest, sensitivity to women's issues within the profession is finally increasing. New services for women, such as shelters for battered women and abortion counseling, are proliferating. Al-though often founded by volunteers rather than by social workers, these services are drawing attention to women's problems and testing new forms of practice. The National Association of Social Workers is committed to ex-tending women's civil, human and economic rights.[10] Since 1970 articles ex-ploring the sex of workers and clients as a factor in practice and describing alternative services for women have been published more frequently. The special issue of *Social Work* on women, published in November 1976, was particularly welcome.

Women's status within the profession has been carefully examined—at least in the literature. It has been well documented that female social workers are tracked into casework positions, receive lower salaries than their male colleagues, and are less likely to advance professionally.[11] Other frequently discussed dilemmas confronting female professionals include dilution of their commitment to a career by role conflict, interruption of their careers, multiple family responsibilities, subordination of married women's careers to that of their husbands, and even the "motive to fail."

However, other issues involving women and social work practice have been neglected. Four such issues are discussed in this article: (1) preparation for practice, (2) the predominance of female clients, (3) relationships between clients and workers, and (4) racism and sexism in social work.

PREPARATION FOR PRACTICE

Social work education is not as yet adequately preparing students for non-sexist practice. Stereotypic notions of women are perpetuated in the social sciences, which are the foundation of social work practice. For example, Par-sons differentiates the expressive functions of women and the instrumental functions of men, holding that the stability of family systems depends on the complementarity of roles.[12] Lidz views parental deviance from role differ-entiation as emotionally unhealthy for children. The importance he attaches to the two-parent family leads him to blame black "matriarchy" for the "pa-thology" of black communities.[13] Erikson unabashedly states that "anatomy is destiny," asserting that women's passive behavior is a biologically deter-mined consequence of reproductive and lacteal functions.[14] In a widely used book on the family, a startling example of sexism is a description of father-daughter incest as the result of daughters acting out their oedipal wishes![15]

Unfortunately, sexist information from the social sciences has been incorporated into social work curricula.[16] Social work faculty have also committed sins of omission. For instance, units on the profession seldom incorporate such topics as the status of women in the profession, conflicts confronting professional women, the behavior of women in organizations, or the impact sex-typing women's roles has on the profession. As previously noted, practice texts virtually ignore gender as a factor in practice.

Gaps in knowledge, where social scientists have ignored important topics about women in society, are also a problem. For example, work is typically defined as paid employment, and scant attention has been paid to the domestic labor of the majority of adult women. The effects on children of the father's absence have been written about extensively; the effects of the mother's presence and the multiple stresses on mothers who head families have been given short shrift. There is a dearth of knowledge about women's psychosexual development. One review found that homosexual men were studied three times more often than lesbians, an interesting indication of male bias.[17]

Tasks facing social work education, therefore, include eliminating sexist content while providing students with the skills necessary to recognize sexism in any guise, including the scientific. Another major task is to find an appropriate, nonsexist theoretical framework. Loewenstein has suggested that power relations among people is a unifying concept that can be used to integrate the topics of racism and sexism into the human behavior sequence.[18]

In addition to developing a nonsexist curriculum, social work educators need to examine their own practice with students. In a study of graduate students, Brager and Michael found that the tracking of men into community organization and women into casework began during training.[19] Self-selection was a factor, but so was differential recruitment. One worker described her experience as follows:

> During my admissions interview I was convinced by my interviewer that community organization was an inappropriate and impractical choice for a white, middle class, married woman. I was informed that I would have to work nights in dangerous neighborhoods and that even if I completed the program that I would have difficulty in getting a C.O. (community organizer's) job. She added that I was "jumping the gun," that C.O. was really for Black men, and that group work was an excellent compromise.[20]

Sex-role stereotypes most likely influence educators' expectations of students and the guidance they offer. These stereotypes may have permeated social work education in unrecognized ways. For example to what extent is the less frequent and less rigorous use of research and statistics a concession to the widely held belief that women are inept in mathematics and science? Is the emphasis on feelings a response to the needs of clients or to the conviction that women's greatest asset is their empathy?

As gatekeepers of the profession, social work educators are responsible for preparing students for nonsexist practice, but obstacles to change exist. Faced with diminishing resources, social work programs may be unable to allot the time and other resources necessary for reeducating faculty and instituting systematic curriculum review. At the time this article was written, there was no bibliography on women and social work to help faculty locate teaching materials. These, however, are practical problems: encouraging interested and informed faculty to teach electives dealing with women and practice is a feasible way of introducing this content. The greatest obstacle to change may prove to be a lack of strong commitment among faculty members to the elimination of sexism in their programs.

As a group, male educators benefit directly from institutional sexism. They are represented on faculties in numbers disproportionate to their numbers in the profession: they receive higher salaries than their female colleagues; they fill deanships disproportionately. It is conceivable, therefore, that female faculty and their supporters will find themselves in adversary relationships with other faculty members over equalization of salaries and other controversial issues. Being a social worker is not proof against sexism, and some male professors are overtly sexist, acting in seductive, condescending, or exploitive ways toward female students and colleagues.

To what extent will the initiative for change come from within social work faculties? Some nonsexist educators may choose, for a variety of reasons, to give only passive support to efforts for change. Some female faculty members, perhaps because of the "compassion trap"—their selfless commitment to serving others—are indifferent to women's issues. The degree and rapidity with which nonsexist theory and content is incorporated into social work curricula may prove to be a function of the amount of external pressure brought to bear on the faculty of social work educational programs.

FEMALE CLIENTS

Why are more women than men social work clients? One reason is that women outnumber men in the United States. Another is self-selection: most women in this country are socialized to accept "weakness" and dependence with more ease than men. The role of client is compatible with behaviors expected of women but is not congruent with men's expectations of themselves.

No doubt a variety of other factors interact to produce this predominance of women as clients. For example, to some degree the service delivery system is skewed toward women and discriminates against men. As female volunteers created social services during the late nineteenth and early twentieth centuries, they established agencies that used their "feminine" skills and that served clients with whom they felt comfortable—the widow with children rather than the prostitute, the aged sick man rather than the convict.[21] The spawning of new services today by the women's movement indicates the role that sponsors' interests and needs play in founding new voluntary services. There has not been an equivalent explosion of new services for men.

Another factor that may be skewing the delivery system is society's attitude toward dependence in men and women. Even though the number of women in paid employment is increasing, the value that a woman should depend on a male breadwinner is deeply ingrained, making material and emotional dependence more acceptable in women than in men. In the nineteenth century, the philanthropists and their agencies, such as the Charity Organization Societies, accepted the widow with children compassionately; but even during economic depressions, they scorned the unemployed man as an unworthy malingerer, undeserving of aid. These attitudes persist; although women are allowed to receive financial help, public assistance discriminates against women who have a "man in the house" who does not support them. Some people contend that in this way the program encourages men to leave their families and weakens family life. Further, poor men, particularly if they are not white, are punished for their poverty by being shunted into the correctional system, whereas their partners are thrown onto welfare and into the social service system. This differential treatment of men and women indicates the degree to which sex-role stereotyping permeates social institutions.

Although it is difficult to document, it is also likely that female clients predominate because the incidence of psychosocial problems is higher among women than among men. Poverty, for example, is a woman's problem. Some women are poor because their male partners are poor; others are poor in their own right. Women are an exploited group. Only a relatively few women are able to obtain well-paying, interesting, fulfilling work; most are concentrated in the lower-paying, lower-status jobs. Working women earn less than men, and the gap in earnings is widening. In 1960 the median income of women employed full time the year round was 61 percent of that received by their male counterparts; in 1975, this figure had fallen to 57 percent. Women's unemployment rate is higher than men's, and it, too, is becoming worse.[22] Social security provisions discriminate against widows; benefits received by women who have worked are lower than those received by retired men.[23] The number of poor households headed by women is increasing. In March 1968, 5.3 million female-headed households were classified by the government as poor; five years later, the number had increased to 6.6 million.[24] In the face of such statistics, it is not surprising that almost three-fourths of public assistance and social welfare recipients are women.[25] One economic simulation found that some women can earn more from Aid to Families with Dependent Children than they can from working.[26] Although black, Spanish-speaking, and other minority-group women are hit hardest by economic exploitation and poverty, indigence among women knows no racial boundaries.

Poverty is not, however, the only reason women become social work clients. Women of all classes confront problems in living—their difficulties are truly biopsychosocial. Consider the following problems resulting from women's reproductive functions: teenage and unwanted pregnancies, postpartum depression, and sexual dysfunction; the need, resulting from the concentration of parenting functions in women's hands, for services for mothers who abuse or neglect their children and for the mothers of emotionally dis-

turbed, learning-disabled, mentally retarded, blind, or otherwise handicapped children; women's vulnerability to wife abuse and rape; the limitations of the wife-mother role and the "empty nest" syndrome; the practical
and emotional stresses for women of separation or divorce and the difficulties
of raising children alone; and the norm that women marry older men, which,
in combination with women's longer life expectancy, leads to widowhood
and the stresses of bereavement, loss of the role of wife, and loneliness.

Differences in available coping resources may also contribute to differences
in the utilization of social services by men and women. Both role socialization
and the structure of adults' daily lives foster such differences. Except for those
who are retired or victims of unemployment, most men work, and their time
and activities, as well as their interaction with other adults, are structured.
This is not the case with the housewife-mother. Gove and Tudor suggest that
housewives' social isolation and lack of external structure are two factors that
contribute to the higher incidence of mental illness among women.[27] Mostow
and Newberry found that depressed women employed outside the home
recover more quickly than housewives, and Lopata found that widows who
are lonely differ from those who are not in both their life situation and their
personal coping mechanisms.[28] Such traits as submissiveness, passivity, and
dependence are poor equipment for coping maturely with problems in living.
One characteristic of a sample of middle-aged females who abused medication
was their subordination within authoritarian marriages.[29]

Self-selection, skewing of the service delivery system, higher incidence of
psychosocial problems, and less adequate coping resources are only four of
the factors that may interact to account for the predominance of female social
work clients. Each has implications for practice. To develop more effective
intervention strategies, the profession needs to develop a clearer compre-
hension of these and other dynamics of women's greater utilization of social
work services.

CLIENTS AND WORKERS

How do social workers perceive female clients? Efforts have been made to
determine the extent to which members of the helping professions hold stereotyped perceptions of women. A landmark study found that clinicians' judgments of the healthy mature adult female paralleled stereotypic role differences.[30] The extent to which stereotyping occurs, however, remains unclear.
Subsequent studies have had equivocal results, and some have had methodological shortcomings.[31] It is also questionable whether survey responses
predict behavior accurately. Research that will study actual behavior, using
videotaping or other more relevant methods, is needed to determine the
extent of sex-role stereotyping.

Furthermore, studies of sex-role stereotyping have confused normative ideals and stereotypes; they have also naively assumed that there is a single stereotype of women. The ideal American woman is said to be youthful and beautiful and obtain fulfillment from her maternal and wifely functions. She is warm, empathic, sensitive, emotional, graceful, and compliant. A bestseller delineates her virtues in the following perfectly serious description:

> A "Domestic Goddess" is a woman who is a good homemaker. She keeps a clean, orderly home, has well-behaved children, cooks delicious meals and is successful in her overall career in the home. But, the term "Goddess," implies something more than these domestic achievements. It relates to the woman herself, indicating a glory which she has added to the home. . . . The Domestic Goddess serves faithfully as the understanding wife, the devoted mother and the successful homemaker. . . . She gives a *warmth* to her household. It is she who makes a *house* a home, filling it with understanding, love and happiness.[32]

This social ideal, toward which countless women strive, is counterbalanced by ideas of what women are really like. In this area, negative images are pervasive. The "bitch," for example, is a dominant theme in American literature.[33] Judging from television commercials, women are mindless and narcissistic. Pejorative terms such as "dumb blond" pepper the language, and the words used to describe black women are particularly denigrating.[34]

Evidence for the existence of a single, general stereotype of women is weak. Clifton, McGrath, and Wick suggest five categories of stereotypes: housewife, "bunny sex object," club woman, career woman, and woman athlete.[35] However, these categories do not take into account the interaction of class, ethnic, and racial stereotypes with sex stereotypes, a shamefully neglected aspect of current research. For example, two common stereotypes are the black matriarch and the Jewish American Princess. Researchers have also neglected the class background, ethnicity, race, and sex of the perceiver. For example, stereotypes of white woman held by black and white men probably differ.

The crucial issue is whether and how stereotypes affect practitioners' assessments of clients, recommendations for intervention, and behavior in interaction with clients. Miller's study of practitioners' judgments of case analogues, in which only sex was varied, found that the practitioners saw passivity as less of a problem for women than for men and that their recommendations for treatment varied according to the client's sex.[36] A study of referrals to a child guidance clinic found that reasons for referral varied according to the sex of the clients and also supported the hypothesis that children are rated as more disturbed when they do not conform to sex-role expectations.[37]

The effect of stereotyped expectations on practitioners' behavior is doubtlessly subtle and profound. When one researcher viewed a tape of an interview he had conducted with a woman who was having conflicts about her family responsibilities and career aspirations, he discovered that he averted his eyes when she made positive, career-oriented remarks. In contrast, he nodded and was otherwise encouraging when she spoke of fulfilling family responsibilities.[38]

The practitioners' own sex-role socialization and style will also affect his or her approach to clients. Sex-role socialization is certainly one factor in the selection of casework by women and of community organization and administration by men. Even with method held constant, however, it is possible that male and female practitioners behave differently and in ways that may not be the most responsive to client's needs. The profession's traditional emphasis on casework—a focus that troubles those who believe that clients' needs would be better served by an activist, instrumental stance—may be related to the predominance of white middle-class women in the profession. In this area, too, one would expect an interaction with racial and ethnic factors. For example, the style of black female practitioners may differ from that of white women or black men.

How do clients react to female workers, and what is the nature of the interaction between them? Clients' reactions to a worker's pregnancy have been discussed elsewhere, and some authors have suggested that it is advantageous to female clients to assign them to female workers.[39] However, relatively little attention has been paid to specific technical problems confronting the female practitioner. For example, it is the author's personal experience as a caseworker, reinforced by informal discussion with others, that male clients who have female workers tend to feel uncomfortable with the reversal of status. Some respond by attempting to sexualize the relationship, others by "cutting up" the worker, and others by relating to her as a mother figure. In this area, too, racial and ethnic background are factors. For example, working-class white males may tend to react differently to black male workers, black female workers, and white female workers.

Although the focus of the limited literature has been on casework, gender is a factor in all types of practice. Carlock and Martin suggest that the behaviors, perceptions, and emotional experiences of group members vary in same-sex and mixed-sex groups.[40] The sex of the group leader undoubtedly also affects group process and outcome. Consider, for example, a group of adolescent girls led by a man or by a woman. It is likely that the problems encountered when attempting to organize women differ from those met when organizing men.

Social work relationships are complex interactions affected by class, race, ethnicity, organizational setting, and gender. Aside from efforts to determine the extent of practitioners' sex-role stereotyping, gender as a variable in relationships between clients and workers has not been sufficiently studied and is little understood. Taping of sessions for use in behavioral study of gender as a factor in practice should be encouraged. Individual practitioners, of course, should strive to be conscious of ways in which sex-role stereotypes affect their expectations of clients, their behavior toward clients, and clients' reactions to them.

RACISM AND SEXISM

The white middle-class bias of feminist writings is striking. For example, one of their major concerns is women's traditional role as housewife and the denial to women of the option of a career outside the home. This understanding of women is historically false and simply inapplicable to black, immigrant, and other working-class women. The more scholarly literature in women's studies also tends toward bias, for example, in its concerns with the career choices of college women, with women in the professions, or with the motive to fail. Although fine material on black women has been published, the tendency is to discuss "American women" as if all were white, college-educated, suburban housewives or assistant college professors.[41] A similar bias appears in social work writings about women and practice. For example, one description of feminist therapy was based on the author's experience as a private practitioner, and her clients were chiefly young, white, depressed women who already had a feminist outlook.[42] Whether such an experience can foster development of practice models suitable to other types of female clients is open to question. Although it is difficult to document, it is safe to assert that minority-group women are disproportionately represented in social work's clientele.

Social work must be sensitive to the implications of a racist society for women's issues. In the United States, sexism and racism are inextricably linked. Both sustain economic exploitation and both are divisive. King contends that there is little hope for an effective interracial alliance capable of obtaining equal benefits for black and white women.[43] She argues that sex-role differences between black and white women make it inappropriate to apply the definition of the American woman's traditional status to the black woman's predicament as a guide for action. She also argues that the racial dichotomy in the United States cuts so deeply that the women's movement will make concessions to the racism of white housewives and other potential supporters. In effect, she is predicting that history will repeat itself. In the early part of this century, supporters of women's suffrage acquiesced to both racism and nativism, using anti-black and anti-immigrant arguments to buttress their case.[44] King's prediction is sobering; but unless there is a marked shift in the country, her assessment may well prove to be accurate.

In combating sexism, the profession needs to keep clearly in mind the ways in which class and racial differences affect the implementation of social policy. For example, acceptance of sterilization, which for middle-class women is a widening of options for birth control, can become a means of oppression for poor women by opening the door to involuntary sterilization. Part-time work, also hailed by some as providing more options for women, can intensify the exploitation of working-class and white-collar women. Part-time work provides employers with eager low-paid workers who resist unionization and for whom benefits need not be provided. Without an economy of full employment, affirmative action for women may work to the advantage of white women and to the disadvantage of minority men and women. For example, white women, who are more likely to have the resources to obtain college and professional education, are likely to have an advantage when competing in the job market.

Social workers are more equipped than other groups to be sensitive to the existence of racism and are committed to its eradication. In the struggle against sexism, social workers should seek to build an effective interracial alliance to obtain equal benefits for all.

Sexism is deeply entrenched in this society and affects social work in myriad ways. Social work needs to understand clearly the impact sexism has on clients, practitioners, and the profession and to make a stronger commitment to nonsexist practice.

ENDNOTES

1. Robert K. Merton, quoted in Cynthia Fuchs Epstein, *Woman's Place: Options and Limits in Professional Careers* (Berkeley, Calif.: University of California Press, 1970), p. 152.
2. U.S. Commission on Civil Rights. *Women and Poverty, Staff Report* (Washington, D.C.: U.S. Government Printing Office, 1974), p. 53.
3. Mary C. Schwartz, "Importance of Sex of Worker and Client," *Social Work* 19 (March 1974): 177–186.
4. James Goodman, ed., *Dynamics of Racism in Social Work Practice* (Washington, D.C.: National Association of Social Workers, 1972); and Roger Miller, ed., *Race, Research, and Reason: Social Work Perspectives* (New York: National Association of Social Workers, 1969).
5. Alfred Kadushin, *The Social Work Interview* (New York: Columbia University Press, 1972), p. 242.
6. See, for example, Phyllis Chesler, *Women and Madness* (New York: Doubleday & Co., 1972); Naomi Weisstein, "Psychology Constructs the Female," in Vivian Gornick and Barbara K. Moran, eds., *Women in Sexist Society: Studies in Power and Powerlessness* (New York: Basic Books, 1971), pp. 133–143; Carol Ehrlich, "The Male Sociologist's Burden: The Place of Women in Marriage and Family Texts," *Journal of Marriage and the Family* 33 (August 1971): 409–416; Lynn H. Lofland, "The 'Thereness' of Women: A Selective Review of Urban Sociology," in Marcia Millman and Rosbeth Moss, eds., *Another Voice: Feminist Perspectives on Social Life and Social Science* (Garden City, N.Y.: Anchor Books, 1975), pp. 144–170; and Dean D. Knudsen, "The Declining Status of Women: Popular Myths and the Failure of Functionalist Thought," *Social Forces* 48 (December 1969): 183–192.
7. Anne M. Seiden, "Overview: Research on the Psychology of Women. I. Gender Differences and Sexual and Reproductive Life," and "II. Women in Families, Work and Psychotherapy," *American Journal of Psychiatry* 133 (September and October 1976): 995–1007, 1111–1133.
8. Margaret Adams, "The Compassion Trap," in Gornick and Moran, eds., op. cit., pp. 410–415.
9. Aaron Rosenblatt et al., "Predominance of Male Authors in Social Work Publications," *Social Casework* 51 (July 1970): 421–430.
10. "Policy on Women's Issues," *NASW News* 22 (July 1977): 40.
11. Janet Saltzman Chafetz, "Women in Social Work," *Social Work* 17 (September 1972): 12–18; Cynthia Fuchs Epstein, "Encountering the Male Establishment: Sex-

Status Limits on Women's Careers in the Professions," *American Journal of Sociology* 75 (May 1970): 965–982; Epstein, "Women's Place"; David Fanshel, "Status Differentials: Men and Women in Social Work, *Social Work* 21 (November 1976): 448–454; Ketayun Gould and Bok–Lim C. Kim, "Salary Inequalities between Men and Women in Schools of Social Work: Myth or Reality?" *Journal of Education for Social Work* 12 (Winter 1976): 50–55; Dorothy C. Herberg, "A Study of Work Participation by Graduate Female Social Workers: Some Implications for Professional Social Work Training," *Journal of Education for Social Work* 9 (Fall 1973): 16–23; Edward Gross, "Plus ça Change . . . The Sexual Structure of Occupations over Time," *Social Problems* 16 (Fall 1968): 198–220; Richard L. Simpson and Ida Harper Simpson, "Women and Bureaucracy in the Semi-Professions," in Amitai Etzioni, ed., *The Semi-Professions and Their Organization* (New York: The Free Press, 1969), pp. 196–266; Bernard C. Scotch, "Sex Status in Social Work: Grist for Women's Liberation," *Social Work* 16 (July 1971): 5–11; Alfred M. Stamm, "NASW Membership: Characteristics, Development and Salaries," *Personnel Information* 12 (May 1969): 1, 45; and Martha Williams, Liz Ho, and Lucy Field, "Career Patterns: More Grist for Women's Liberation," *Social Work* 19 (July 1974): 463–466.

12. Talcott Parsons and Robert F. Bales, *Family, Socialization and Interaction Process* (New York: The Free Press, 1955).

13. Theodore Lidz, *The Person: His Development through the Life Cycle* (New York: Basic Books, 1968), pp. 45–69.

14. Erik H. Erikson, "Inner and Outer Space: Reflections on Womanhood," *Daedalus* 9 (Spring 1964): 585–606.

15. Irving Kaufman, Alice L. Peck, and Consuelo K. Tagiuri, "The Family Constellation and Overt Incestuous Relations between Father and Daughter," in Norman W. Bell and Ezra F. Vogel, eds., *A Modern Introduction to the Family* (New York: The Free Press, 1968), pp. 599–609.

16. Mary Schwartz, "Sexism in the Social Work Curriculum," *Journal of Education for Social Work* 9 (Fall 1973): 65–70.

17. S. F. Morin, "An Annotated Bibliography of Research on Lesbianism and Male Homosexuality (1967–1974)," cited in Reesa M. Vaughter, "Review Essay: Psychology," *Signs: Journal of Women in Culture and Society* 2 (Autumn 1976): 132.

18. Sophie F. Loewenstein, "Integrating Content on Feminism and Racism into the Social Work Curriculum," *Journal of Educational for Social Work* 12 (Winter 1976): 91–96.

19. George Brager and John A. Michael, "The Sex Distribution in Social Work: Causes and Consequences," *Social Casework* 50 (December 1969): 595–601.

20. Joanne Fischer Wolf, "Sexism and Social Work," p. 2. Paper presented at the 101st Annual Forum, National Conference on Social Welfare, Cincinnati, Ohio, May 1974. (Mimeographed.)

21. See Julia B. Rauch, "Women in Social Work: Friendly Visitors in Philadelphia, 1880," *Social Service Review* 49 (June 1975): 241–259.

22. Women's Bureau, U.S. Department of Labor, Employment Standards Administration, *1975 Handbook on Women Workers*, Bulletin 297 (Washington, D.C.: U.S. Government Printing Office, 1975), p. 91; U.S. Bureau of the Census, "A Statistical Portrait of Women in the U.S.," *Current Population Reports: Special Studies*, Series P–23, No. 58 (Washington, D.C.: U.S. Government Printing Office, 1976), p. 45; and U.S. Commission on Civil Rights, op. cit., p. 5.

23. Dalmer Hoskins and Lenore E. Bixby, *Women and Social Security: Law and Policy in Five Countries*. Research Report No. 42 (Washington, D.C.: Social Security Administration, U.S. Department of Health, Education & Welfare), pp. 73–95. See also Linda Rosenman, "Inequities in Income Security," *Social Work* 21 (November 1976): 472–477.

24. U.S. Commission on Civil Rights, op. cit., p. 5.

25. U.S. Bureau of the Census, op. cit., p. 1.
26. Isabel Sawhill, "Discrimination and Poverty among Women Who Head Families," *Signs: Journal of Women in Culture and Society* 1 (Spring 1976): special supplement, pp. 201–212.
27. Walter R. Gove and Jeanette F. Tudor, "Adult Sex Roles and Mental Illness," in Joan Huber, ed., *Changing Women in a Changing Society* (Chicago: University of Chicago Press, 1973), pp. 50–73.
28. E. Mostow and P. Newberry, "Work Role and Depression in Women: A Comparison of Workers and Housewives in Treatment," *American Journal of Orthopsychiatry* 45 (July 1975): 538–548; Helena Z. Lopata, "Loneliness: Forms and Components," *Social Problems* 17 (Fall 1969): 248–262; Lopata, "The Social Involvement of American Widows," *American Behavioral Scientist* 14 (September–October 1970): 41–58.
29. Robert D. Borgman, "Medication Abuse by Middle-Aged Women," *Social Casework* 54 (November 1973): 526–532.
30. Inge K. Broverman et al., "Sex-Role Stereotypes and Clinical Judgments of Mental Health," *Journal of Consulting and Clinical Psychology* 34 (February 1970): 1–7.
31. Inge K. Broverman et al., "Sex-Role Stereotypes: A Current Appraisal," *Journal of Social Issues* 28 (April 1972): 59–70; Gloria Cowan, "Therapist Judgments of Clients: Sex-Role Problems," *Psychology of Women Quarterly* 1 (Winter 1976): 115–124; Beverly Gomes and Stephen I. Abramowitz, "Sex-Related Patient and Therapist Effects on Clinical Judgment," *Sex Roles* 2 (March 1976): 1–13; Joel Fischer et al., "Are Social Workers Sexists?" *Social Work* 21 (November 1976): 428–433; Linda Hall Harris and Margaret Exner Lucas, "Sex-Role Stereotyping," *Social Work* 21 (September 1976): 390–395; and Caree Rosen Brown and Marilyn Levitt Hellinger, "Therapists' Attitudes toward Women," *Social Work* 20 (July 1975): 266–270.
32. Helen B. Andelin, *Fascinating Womanhood* (Santa Barbara, Calif.: Pacific Press, 1965), p. 220.
33. Judith Gustafson, "Stereotypes of Women in American Literature: Will the Real Great American Bitch Please Stand Up," in Betty E. Chamj, ed., *Image, Myth and Beyond: American Women and American Studies*, vol. 2 (Pittsburg, Pa.: Know, 1972), pp. 253–274.
34. Patricia Bell Scott, "The English Language and Black Womanhood: A Low Blow at Self-Esteem," *Journal of Afro-American Issues* 2 (Summer 1974): 218–226.
35. A. Kay Clifton, Diane McGrath, and Bonnie Wick, "Stereotypes of Woman: A Single Category?" *Sex Roles* 2 (June 1976): 135–145.
36. Donna Miller, "The Influence of the Patient's Sex on Clinical Judgment," *Smith College Studies in Social Work* 44 (February 1974): 89–100.
37. John A. Feinblatt and Alice R. Gold, "Sex Roles and the Psychiatric Referral Process," *Sex Roles* 2 (June 1976): 109–122.
38. Personal conversation with Allen Ivey, Professor, School of Education, University of Massachusetts at Amherst, June 1977.
39. Carol Nadelson et al., "The Pregnant Therapist," *American Journal of Psychiatry* 131 (October 1974): 1107–1111; Mary C. Schwartz, "Casework Implications of a Worker's Pregnancy," *Social Casework* 56 (January 1975): 27–34; Maureen M. Underwood and Edwin D. Underwood, "Clinical Observations of a Pregnant Therapist," *Social Work* 21 (November 1976): 512–514; Charlotte Krause, "The Femininity Complex and Women Therapists," *Journal of Marriage and the Family* 33 (August 1971): 476–482; Marjorie D. Mosko, "Feminist Theory and Casework Practice," in Bernard Ross and S. K. Khinduka, eds., *Social Work in Practice* (Washington, D.C.: National Association of Social Workers, 1976), pp. 181–190.
40. Charlene J. Carlock and Patricia Yancey Martin, "Sex Composition and the Intensive Group Experience," *Social Work* 22 (January 1977): 27–33.
41. See, for example, Toni Cade, ed., *The Black Woman: An Anthology* (New York: New

American Library, 1970): Joyce A. Ladner, *Tomorrow's Tomorrow: The Black Woman* (Garden City, N.Y.: Anchor Books, 1972); and Gerda Lerner, ed., *Black Women in White America: A Documentary History* (New York: Vintage Press, 1973).

42. Mosko, op. cit.
43. Mae C. King, "Oppression and Power: The Unique Status of the Black Woman in the American Political System," *Social Science Quarterly* 56 (June 1975): 116–128.
44. See Aileen S. Kraditor, *The Ideas of the Woman Suffrage Movement, 1890–1920* (Garden City, N.Y.: Anchor Press, 1971).

CHAPTER 13

Medical and Psychiatric Needs of the Homeless— A Preliminary Response

Robert W. Surber, Eleanor Dwyer, Katherine J. Ryan, Stephen M. Goldfinger, and John T. Kelly

PREFATORY COMMENT

Robert W. Surber, et al., maintain that the homeless represent the failure of human services in the United States. The homeless people have, first of all, the problem of no housing, and secondly, whatever problems caused them to be without housing.

These authors specifically focused their research on the medical and psychiatric needs of a homeless population in San Francisco—an area in which its findings corroborated information in other parts of the country. The most common medical problems affecting the homeless were hypertension and other arteriosclerotic cardiovascular illnesses, trauma, scabies and lice, overexposure to the elements, nutritional deficiencies, and peripheral vascular diseases such as cellulitis and leg ulcers. The most frequent psychiatric problems uncovered among the homeless were schizophrenia, major affective disorders, substance abuse, and severe personality disorders.

These authors developed a micro to macro-level intervention program operating in eight sites (community shelters and hotels) that addressed basic living, medical, psychiatric, and social needs. Two multidisciplinary teams, each composed of a physician, a nurse, social worker, licensed psychiatric technician, and two graduate-level social work interns, provided the various direct and indirect services, including advocacy at the agency and political level. Such a creative, beginning intervention effort is the greatest challenge facing the social work profession in an era of increasing bureaucratic specialization, increasing fees, and indifference to the poor.

Homeless individuals suffer from multiple needs in many spheres. In addition to a lack of adequate shelter, they frequently have difficulty obtaining adequate food and clothing. Also, homeless people face the problems that caused or contributed to their homelessness, and from other problems that result from being homeless.

This article describes an effort to understand and respond to the medical and psychiatric needs of the homeless. San Francisco began organizing a service delivery system for its homeless people in October 1982 when a group of agencies that serve this population met to coordinate services. Mayor Diane Feinstein appointed a task force to advise her on issues involving the homeless, and out of the task force grew a working group of service providers, known as the Shelter Providers Coalition. The Shelter Providers Coalition has a broad membership, including representatives from agencies as diverse as the Social Security Administration, the Veterans Administration Hospital, veterans' and welfare rights groups, the mayor's office, all city shelters, San Francisco General Hospital (SFGH), San Francisco Community Mental Health Services, and the San Francisco Department of Public Health.

MEDICAL AND PSYCHIATRIC NEEDS

Little is known about the medical problems facing America's homeless population. Research at St. Vincent's Hospital in New York reveals the wide range of illnesses the homeless experience.[1] Not surprisingly, these include the most common illnesses that affect the general population, such as hypertension, other arteriosclerotic cardiovascular illnesses, and major infections. Other illnesses appear with far greater prevalence among homeless people, and have serious consequences when the illnesses remain untreated, as they often do. These include trauma, infestations such as scabies and lice, problems arising from exposure, nutritional and vitamin deficiencies, and peripheral vascular diseases such as cellulitis and leg ulcers.

Many of these conditions are relatively simple to treat and are treated routinely on an outpatient basis in their early stages. Yet because the homeless often are unable for economic reasons, or unwilling because of fear or alienation, to obtain health care, the diseases can in their advanced stages be accompanied by extreme morbidity and mortality. For example, the prevalence of tuberculosis in the United States is .0123 percent, or 12.3 cases per 100,000 persons per year.[2] In comparison, 8.5 percent of the residents of one shelter in New York have active tuberculosis, a rate nearly 700 times greater than the national average.[3]

No problem of homelessness has received as much concern and publicity as the problem of homeless mentally ill persons, perhaps because of their high visibility and disturbing public behavior. This group's history can be traced more easily. In 1959, 559,000 chronically mentally ill individuals were in state hospitals.[4] Today, there are fewer than 130,000 individuals in these institutions. The community mental health movement was intended to provide care for these former state hospital inmates in the community. However, because of lack of funds, unclear priorities, and inadequate technology, these individuals frequently do not receive care and treatment and often are forced to fend for themselves on the streets.

Since 1980, a large number of studies have been done to determine the nature and extent of psychiatric disability among the homeless. Despite diverse study populations in various locations, the results are dramatically similar. Bassuk, who studied 78 shelter residents in the Boston area, found that 40 percent had major mental disorders.[5] Arce and his coworkers, who observed 193 individuals in a city-run shelter in Philadelphia in 1981, also found a 40-percent prevalence of major mental illness.[6] Other studies, which used evaluations of current mental status or a history of use of psychiatric services, yielded essentially similar figures for Baltimore, Ohio, and New York City.[7] In virtually all of the studies that note diagnosis, schizophrenia is the most frequently encountered disorder, usually followed by major affective disorders, problems with substance abuse, and severe personality disorders.

Several studies have focused on the prevalence of homelessness among those requesting treatment in psychiatric emergency services. Lipton, Sabatini, and Katz reported on 100 consecutive homeless patients who received emergency psychiatric care at Bellevue Hospital in New York City. Seventy-two percent had a diagnosis of schizophrenia, and approximately 40 percent had concomitant alcohol or drug abuse.[8] Chafetz and Goldfinger found that 46 percent of the patients at the Psychiatric Emergency Service at San Francisco General Hospital were, or recently had been, without housing.[9]

MEDICAL AND PSYCHIATRIC SERVICE USE

Homeless individuals suffer from a large number of severe medical and psychiatric illnesses and the frequency with which these illnesses occur is far greater than for those who are not homeless. Most studies surveyed shelter populations in an attempt to establish the prevalence of various illnesses. To assess the overall need for medical and psychiatric services and to plan relevant and acceptable services, it was necessary in San Francisco to understand how the homeless population uses existing medical and mental health services. Additionally, by examining the use of the most expensive source of acute medical care, the authors felt that some light could be shed on the severity and prevalence of acute illness in this population, and some evidence gathered of the extraordinary cost of this group to society in terms of disability, human suffering, and health care dollars. To accomplish these goals, the San Francisco Department of Public Health completed two independent but corroborative studies.

UTILIZATION STUDY

Researchers for the utilization survey interviewed 170 homeless persons to explore the extent to which they use medical and psychiatric services. Information on substance abuse history also was gathered.

A team of four interviewers conducted the survey at three shelters and one food line. The interviewers obtained verbal consent from each respondent and the right to refuse was honored. A standardized questionnaire was used and anonymity was maintained. Those persons who appeared intoxicated or incoherent were not approached, because the responses required a self-report of current and past medical and psychiatric service use.

Of the 170 respondents, 147 were male and 23 were female. The ages of the interviewees ranged from 15 to 70. Approximately 20 percent of the men approached refused to participate in the survey, and almost 50 percent of the women refused. In general, the men were cooperative and friendly and the women were noticeably more fearful, suspicious and hostile. This pattern held true regardless of whether the interviewer was male or female.

The results indicated a high utilization of medical services. More than 75 percent of those surveyed reported receiving medical services during the past year and of these, more than 80 percent did so during the previous three months. This rate of service use may be no different than in the general population. However, 30 percent of those utilizing medical services reported being hospitalized in an inpatient setting and 76 percent were treated in emergency rooms.

The results also suggest a high incidence of mental illness among the sample. Slightly more than one third reported previous psychiatric hospitalizations. Twenty-two percent reported receiving mental health services in the past 12 months.

Almost 60 percent reported problems with alcohol, drug abuse, or both. Two-thirds of the respondents who reported drug and alcohol problems indicated that their substance abuse is chronic.

INPATIENT STUDY

The inpatient study was designed to identify the specific illnesses that affect homeless people and to quantify their use of inpatient services. SFGH is responsible for treating the medically indigent in San Francisco and, therefore, is the facility that predominantly provides treatment of acute illness to the homeless. Researchers reviewed the charts of homeless patients admitted to the medical/surgical and psychiatric services of the hospital.

Researchers identified homeless persons admitted to SFGH by reviewing the financial screening records for all 4,436 admissions from January to March 31, 1983. The criterion for inclusion in the study was an address listed as "streets," "transient," or "no local address"; 318 patients were identified and 285 of the medical records were reviewed. Of the 285 homeless patients in the sample, 78 percent were male and 21.4 percent were female. The sample population ranged in age from under 20 to over 80.

The diagnosis of the homeless patients admitted for medical or surgical services described a broad spectrum of problems. The most frequent diagnosis was cellulitis, which accounted for 24 percent of the admissions. Trauma (such as stab wounds and major fractures); respiratory problems (pneumonia or chronic obstructive pulmonary disease and tuberculosis); and alcohol- and drug-related problems together accounted for 51 percent of the admissions. The remainder of the patients had other problems including congestive heart failure, stroke, hypothermia, burns, dehydration, gangrene, sepsis, and cardiac arrest.

The diagnosis of the homeless patients admitted to the psychiatric services also were varied. The most frequent diagnosis was schizohrenia, which accounted for 36 percent of the admissions; affective disorders accounted for 24 percent. Given the psychological trauma of homelessness itself, a high prevalence of depression and other affective disorders could be expected in this population. Other diagnostic categories for admission included all other psychoses, substance abuse disorders, and personality disorders. Substance abuse disorders probably are underrepresented because of MediCal (California's Medicaid program) regulations, which discourage the use of these diagnoses in acute psychiatric settings. The range and distribution of diagnoses do not differ significantly from that of the overall inpatient psychiatric population, except that schizophrenia appears to be overrepresented.

Homeless patients admitted for either service remained considerably longer than other patients—18 percent longer for medical/surgical services and 23 percent longer for psychiatric services. Many of the patients in the sample were hospitalized repeatedly at SFGH. Fifty-one percent of the homeless patients admitted to medical/surgical services had been hospitalized previously at SFGH, and 39 percent of the psychiatric patients were readmitted between March 1983 and May 1984.

It is reasonable to assume a certain amount of validity in these results because they are consonant with findings elsewhere in the country, and because the findings from two different information sources corroborate each other. The results suggest several considerations for program planning for this population.

PROGRAM DESIGN AND IMPLEMENTATION

Because homeless people suffer from a wide variety of medical and psychiatric illnesses, and the prevalence of illness so severe as to require hospitalization is quite high, treatment efforts must respond to the whole gamut of medical and psychiatric problems and must be integrated with the full spectrum of treatment resources. Because a large percentage of individuals in the shelters were unwilling or unable to participate in a brief interview, the incidence of mental illness probably was underreported. Whether this assumption is correct or not, it is clear that a number of homeless people are suspicious, fearful, and likely to be uncooperative. Thus, programs to serve them not only have to be highly accessible, but also must develop strategies to gain trust and engage the clients. Programs designed to respond to the health needs of the population also must respond to the problems and sequelae of substance abuse.

Considerable resources are devoted to providing health care to homeless people, but these resources may not be spent effectively or efficiently. Homeless people often were hospitalized for conditions such as cellulitis that should be able to be managed in an outpatient setting, and homeless patients remained hospitalized longer than patients who had housing. In addition, the homeless reported utilizing emergency rooms frequently. Although this probably results in part from the fact that they wait until a problem becomes acute before seeking treatment, it also may be because emergency rooms are readily accessible at all times and, therefore, are used frequently in noncrisis situations. Not only is emergency room care more expensive than traditional outpatient care, it generally is not a very effective way to obtain routine medical treatment. Services designed to provide early detection and intervention should prevent considerable suffering, and could reduce reliance on expensive acute care. The savings could be directed into more preventive and maintenance programs.

Two principles have guided the implementation of the program. First, the program must be fully integrated into the programs of the homeless shelters and into the service system of the San Francisco Department of Public Health, which is charged with providing medical and mental health care to the indigent. Second, health is a function of overall well-being and the program must be comprehensive by responding to basic living needs and social needs, as well as to medical and psychiatric needs.

The program operates in eight sites—five shelters and three hotels—that provide temporary residence for approximately 500 homeless individuals at any time. Two multidisciplinary teams work in four sites each, and each is composed of a quarter-time physician supervisor, a nurse practitioner, a professional social worker, a licensed psychiatric technician, and two graduate-level social work interns. The teams rotate through all of the sites and provide a wide array of medical and psychiatric treatments and referrals, and social service interventions. Team members refer clients to each other for services. In addition to providing all direct service, the teams assess the overall scope of the problems and issues they face in meeting the needs of this population.

The process of determining and implementing the functions of the program was difficult and lengthy. Some of the problems encountered are described for the benefit of those who are developing similar programs. For instance, several hurdles had to be overcome in the first months of operation. Staff turnover initially was quite high, as optimistic expectations of the program's effects met the apparently overwhelming needs of the clients. Team members' unrealistic expectations of each other also led to considerable frustration and even to anger. For instance, a nurse felt that a social worker should be able to find clients jobs or housing, and the social worker expected quick remission of longstanding medical problems as a result of efforts of the medical staff. These problems were addressed in team meetings in which more appropriate expectations for each member and the overall effort could be worked out. In addition, the teams required training in issues such as gaining access to available resources, self-defense, psychiatric medications, and acquired immune deficiency syndrome. The effort also was useful in helping the team operate as a collaborative and integrated whole, rather than as a conglomerate of individual efforts.

Once the initial problems began to be resolved, the program was able to broaden its focus and reach out to the needier clients in the shelters. When the clinics began to operate, the healthier and more able clients lined up for care. Although these individuals had legitimate needs for service, there remained those—such as the elderly gentleman who was too frail to stand in line, or the young woman who was too withdrawn to be aware of the line—who had perhaps an even greater need for service. The teams began working to identify and attempt to serve those with the least capacity to help themselves.

The teams then began to experience great frustration with established medical and mental health services. Because the homeless population has widespread and severe health problems, and because the teams had limited resources, the program was designed to provide only minimal direct treatment and social service interventions. The program planned to refer clients to other community medical and mental health clinics and facilities, and supportive social services. However, it was difficult to make these referrals.

The existing service system was functioning at or beyond capacity and was not able to accept large numbers of new referrals. Some clinics had waiting lists of six to eight weeks and were not able to treat those with immediate needs.

More disconcerting was the fact that most programs, by design or by default, excluded the homeless population. For example, medical clinics were not eager to serve people who smelled bad or were lice-infested, and in many subtle and overt ways made homeless people feel unwelcome. Mental health programs served only those who could make and keep regularly scheduled appointments and refused to see anyone who smelled of alcohol. Substance abuse services served only those who were able to remain completely abstinent. Even a minor relapse resulted in immediate dismissal from many programs. Substance abuse services also refused to serve anyone who used psychotropic medications for mental illness. County public assistance requirements, such as possessing certain types of identification or making recipients search extensively for jobs, kept many from obtaining or maintaining an income with which they might obtain housing.

These problems led program staff to make networking with other agencies a central focus of the program. Staff spent a considerable portion of their time advocating on behalf of specific clients, educating other programs on the needs of homeless people, and suggesting ways the programs could better serve this population. Change has not come easily and program staff have had to be persistent and assertive. To integrate the program's services with inpatient care, program staff have been assigned to work part time in SFGH.

Working at the program level often has been insufficient, because the staff of other agencies have not always had the authority or resources to make necessary changes. Political advocacy has been required, and program staff have joined other representatives in the Shelter Providers Coalition and other community groups to lobby for broader changes in the service system. The coalition has developed a proposal for sweeping changes in the City's General Assistance Ordinance, which would make this entitlement much more accessible to the homeless and to the mentally disabled, and new city funding has been made available for a residential hotel to house homeless people with AIDS.

The professional social workers' role has become very broad in this program. Approximately 30 percent of each social worker's time is spent working with individuals, both helping clients obtain concrete services, such as public assistance, more permanent housing, and eyeglasses, and providing clinical services, such as helping clients understand and cope with mental illness, face the loss of health from chronic and debilitating illnesses, or accept the need to deal with an alcohol or drug problem.

Another 30 percent of each social worker's time is spent in group work. Although groups provide a way to serve more clients, novel ways have had to be developed to get the shelter residents to participate. For instance, one social worker calls one of her groups the "self-help committee." The committee focuses on practical issues by helping clients identify their goals (for example, obtaining housing and a job or stopping drug use) and team with another group member who has a similar goal so that they can support each other. Another group, called the "Monday night invitational," is a more traditional therapy group.

Approximately 30 percent of the social workers' time is spent in advocacy both at the agency level at at the political level. The remaining 10 percent of the time is devoted to continuing needs assessment.

FURTHER STRATEGIES

It is appropriate and consistent with social work philosophy to begin where the client is by meeting homeless people's immediate needs for shelter and care. But even a good system of shelters and care within those shelters is insufficient. Providing temporary housing for some number of those in need and decent services for those who are fortunate enough to get into that temporary housing is unsatisfactory. The issue of homelessness itself must be addressed.

Homelessness, and the fact that it apparently is a growing problem, represents the failure of human services in this country. Homeless people, by definition, have multiple problems (specifically, the problem of no housing, and whatever problems caused them to be without housing). In order to deal with homelessness, a human service system must be developed that is responsive to people with multiple needs and assures access to low-income, permanent housing.

Although a complex and expensive human service network has been developed for the poor and needy in this country in the past half-century, this has been done by establishing large, monolithic bureaucracies that respond to one kind of problem. For instance, there is a system to provide medical and psychiatric treatment, separate systems for financial entitlements, another to provide housing, another for vocational rehabilitation, and so on. Services such as these not only are fragmented and uncoordinated, but they also frequently have competing and contradicting mandates, policies, and procedures that make comprehensive care for homeless individuals with multiple problems impossible. As a result, those homeless individuals who need help the most are denied access to care and services.

Lack of coordination and integration of service mandates is a result of policy decisions at all levels of government and all levels of the service delivery system. The program described in this article requires a considerable amount of its resources to network and advocate on behalf of its homeless clients with other local programs. This is essential in order for its clients to receive necessary services. The social work profession as a whole should work to change the policies and practices required by legislation and regulations at all levels of government to assure that those with multiple problems receive the services they need. The integration of the human service network is the greatest challenge that the social work profession faces.

An inadequate and perhaps diminishing stock of low income housing is another cause of homelessness. Although it is necessary to take immediate steps to advocate on behalf of homeless clients and support them with the services they need to enable them to make use of the existing housing resources, the fact remains that there is not enough low-income housing. As long as this condition exists, the most needy and most vulnerable will be pushed out of the housing market and onto the streets. It therefore is essential that the social work profession become much more active in real estate issues. Social workers, among other things, could advocate to keep lower-income housing resources. For example, social workers could oppose conversion of single-room-occupancy hotels to tourist hotels. In addition, they could advocate for development of specialized residential programming, such as group homes and residential treatment facilities; and advocate for financing and building of low-income housing by both the public and private sectors. If basic necessity of housing is unmet, serving the needs of homeless clients will continue to be an uphill battle.

ENDNOTES

1. P. W. Brickner et al., eds., *Health Care of Homeless People* (New York: Springer Publishing Co., 1985).
2. M. Iseman, "Tuberculosis: An Overview," in Brickner et al., eds., *Health Care of Homeless People*, pp. 151–154.
3. J. McAdam et al., "Tuberculosis in the SRO/Homeless Population," in Brickner et al., eds., *Health Care of Homeless People*, pp. 155–175.
4. H. H. Goldman, N. H. Adams, and C. A. Taube, "Deinstitutionalization: The Data Demythologized," *Hospital & Community Psychiatry*, 34 (1983), pp. 129–134.
5. E. L. Bassuk, "Addressing the Needs of the Homeless," *Boston Globe Magazine*, November 6, 1983, pp. 12, 60, *ff*.
6. A. A. Arce et al., "A Psychiatric Profile of Street People Admitted to an Emergency Shelter," *Hospital & Community Psychiatry*, 34 (1983), pp. 812–817.
7. P. J. Fischer and W. R. Breakey, "Homelessness and Mental Health: An Overview," *International Journal of Mental Health*, 14 (1985–1986), pp. 6–41; D. Roth et al., *Homeless in Ohio: A Study of People in Need* (Ohio Department of Mental Health, Office of Program Evaluation and Research, 1985); and S. Crystal, S. Ladner, and R. Towber, "Multiple Impairment Patterns in the Mentally Ill Homeless," *International Journal of Mental Health*, 14 (1985–1986), pp. 61–73.
8. F. R. Lipton, A. Sabatini, and S. E. Katz, "Down and Out in the City: The Homeless Mentally Ill," *Hospital and Community Psychiatry*, 34 (1983), pp. 817–821.
9. L. Chafetz and S. Goldfinger, "Residential Instability in a Psychiatric Emergency Service," *Psychiatric Quarterly*, 56 (1984), pp. 20–34.

CHAPTER 14

Attitudes Toward Elderly Clients

Jordan I. Kosberg and
Audrey P. Harris

PREFATORY COMMENT

According to Jordan Kosberg and Audrey Harris, as the number of persons over age sixty-five in the United States continues to increase, more and more social workers will be employed in work directly or indirectly related to older persons. From 1950 to 1980, the sixty-five and older group more than doubled to over 25 million persons (11.3 percent of the total population) and by the year 2000, the sixty-five and older population will be more than 35 million and represent 13.1 percent of the nation's population. The authors' survey of the literature revealed that both professional and nonprofessional caregivers harbored various negative attitudes toward elderly persons. They believe social workers who possess these negative perceptions toward elderly clients will have their effectiveness with these clients impaired.

Kosberg and Harris state that ageism—discrimination against people because they are old—is a product of society that emphasizes attractiveness, productivity, youth, and activity. At times ageism is expressed even more strongly in U.S. society than are racism and sexism. Ageism is observable in the general reluctance among professionals to work with elderly clients; in the limited resources provided for the elderly; and in the distinctions made in referrals, diagnosis, and treatment on the basis of the age of the clients.

On the premise that all social work professionals who work with the elderly should have appropriate and positive attitudes toward them, the authors introduce four mechanisms to help accomplish this task: formal education, short-term training, staff screening, and social change. The authors feel the gerontological material in courses, which is reinforced by field placements, is uneven in many schools of social work. They call for all schools to make gerontology and geriatrics courses mandatory. Such a requirement, they believe, would result in greater interest by future professionals in work with the elderly.

Although the authors offer no real conclusive research evidence from the literature that short-term training or other in-service programs actually change staff attitudes, they nevertheless recommend this method as one mechanism for attempting to change attitudes. They hope that the profession's understanding of the impact of these programs on attitudes will increase over time.

As for the third mechanism Kosberg and Harris view a careful screening process for new employees as an interim safeguard to be used by those responsible for hiring staff or for training professionals who will work with elderly clients.

As for the final mechanism, social change, the authors see a need for advocacy efforts that challenge widespread ageism and ageist values. They want to see a stop to social work services that emphasize helping the elderly to adjust to their station in life rather than to change their situation. They call for a greater emphasis on social change at the local level of the agency and at the national level as well through lobbying efforts on Capitol Hill.

In 1974, 11 percent of the population in the United States was over 65 years of age, and it was estimated that this proportion had almost tripled since 1900 and could grow to almost 20 percent in the next century.[1] In all likelihood, therefore, professionals such as nurses, physicians, dentists, psychologists, and lawyers will become increasingly involved with elderly clients, and this will certainly be true for social workers as well. Future projections indicate that the number of individuals 60 years of age and older will increase by 31 percent by the year 2000, when 43 percent of those over 65 will be 75 years or older.[2] Members of this latter age group often become economically, socially, and psychologically dependent on their families, society, and community resources and frequently require increased health care and social services.

Unquestionably, the need for health services and general social services on the part of the growing number of elderly individuals in this country has been a major factor in the expansion of these areas and has increased the likelihood that more and more social workers will be employed in work directly or indirectly related to older persons. In the past decade, one-tenth of all new social work jobs were created by the expansion taking place in the field of health services, which grew at 3 times the rate of the general economy.[3] Moreover, in a period of 8 years, the number of social workers employed in the mental health field more than doubled.[4] Anticipated increases in funding suggest that the field of health care will continue to be an area of potential growth for social work employment.[5]

PROFESSIONAL ATTITUDES

Ideally, those who work with older clients do so out of concern for the elderly and their problems. However, the jobs professionals take are often a function of what is available to them in the job market. Thus, at present and in the future, social workers involved with the elderly may have been trained to work with other age groups and, indeed, may prefer to work with them. What concerns the authors is not so much that certain social workers are dealing with clients other than those of their choice but that these professionals may hold negative and stereotypical attitudes toward the elderly individuals they are to assist.

Values are among the important factors that determine behavior. Part of the social worker's education involves exposure to the values on which the profession is based, which include a positive orientation toward the client, who is to be respected, individualized, and treated with dignity. Like everyone else, however, social workers hold certain biases and prejudices toward various individuals and groups, and these individual predispositions may affect the outcome of intervention and the type of treatment provided.

Nevertheless, social work education and training generally emphasize methods, procedures, ethics, and technical skills; less attention is paid to attitudes. Moreover, the need for rapport and positive relationships between clients and those working in such professions as medicine, nursing, social work, and psychology is especially great. Positive attitudes toward clients are the foundation of social work practice. Although it is believed social workers will increasingly be involved with older clients, research findings unfortunately indicate that social workers and others who provide social services and health care often hold negative attitudes toward the elderly in general and older clients in particular. This has been found to be true within institutional as well as community settings.

FINDINGS ON ATTITUDES

A survey of research findings will indicate that the attitudes of both professional and nonprofessional care-givers toward elderly clients are not necessarily positive. The survey is not meant to be a definitive or exhaustive review but a representative sampling of studies on attitudes toward the elderly.

Kahana and Coe studied professional staff in a home for elderly and encountered negative attitudes toward the residents.[6] They concluded that this was attributable to the professionals' view of the elderly as being difficult to work with and to their concern about the residents' manageability. The influence of the attitudes of professional staff on residents was highlighted in this study by the researchers' observation that "staff expectations and attitudes may contribute to the depersonalizing process of institutionalization even when staff evaluations of residents are generally positive."[7]

Dealing with the same kind of setting, Wolk and Wolk explored the attitudes of social service workers, psychologists, and nurses working in a home for the elderly.[8] They concluded that positive attitudes were held by nurses in general, that younger professionals held less negative attitudes than older professionals did, and that the attitudes of those who chose to work with the elderly were the least negative of the individuals surveyed in the home. They thus confirmed the relationship between desire to work with an elderly population and positive attitudes toward such a population.

Similarly, the senior author, Cohen, and Mendlovitz studied the attitudes of supervisory staff in a home for the elderly and explored the staff's perceptions of elderly people, humanistic values, the care and service to be provided in the home, and the home itself.[9] The researchers found that the social work supervisors surveyed held more positive attitudes than the registered

nurses, whose perceptions, in turn, were more positive than those of supervisors who were nonprofessionals. Although formal education was associated with positive attitudes, chronological age and time employed in the
facility were not.

In another study dealing with professionals and nursing homes, the senior
author found that social workers were infrequently involved with homes because they viewed such institutions negatively, regarded proprietary settings
as inappropriate, perceived elderly clients as too much of a challenge and
change as too difficult to achieve, and felt that the elderly reminded them of
their own mortality.[10]

Investigators of attitudes in settings other than the nursing home have
recorded similar findings. Troll and Schlossberg studied the bias of members
of the helping professions such as vocational rehabilitation counselors, adult
educators, and psychologists against elderly individuals and found that no
group was free of bias and that men were more biased than women.[11] The
researchers concluded that the age and special training of the individuals
surveyed were unrelated to their attitudes, and they speculated that biased
attitudes could be reflected in on-the-job performance.

Cyrus–Lutz and Gaitz studied psychiatrists' attitudes toward the elderly
and found that the individuals in their sample were bored with, impatient
with, and resentful of many elderly clients.[12] Many of the psychiatrists felt
inadequate in regard to treating older people. However, the researchers indicated that "the extent to which a psychiatrist's personal values directly affect
his choice of patients and the quality of his involvement with them (was not)
determined by (the) study."[13]

In another study, Kastenbaum found psychotherapists reluctant to work
with the elderly and concluded that they calculated an elderly person would
not live "long enough" to "pay back" their investment of time and effort.[14]

In a study conducted in a large general hospital, it was found that
psychologists held biases against the elderly and were less likely to refer
older persons than persons of other ages for appropriate psychological consultation. The researchers concluded that referring physicians were "less
sensitive" to the complaints of elderly individuals requiring referrals and
believed "that older people were less likely to profit from psychological
intervention."[15]

Conte, Plutchik, and Weiner attempted to identify the qualities that contributed to the success of certain aides and orderlies working with institutionalized elderly individuals.[16] They found that staff members who were
rated as "successful" by their supervisors were patient, accepting, flexible,
tolerant, and respectful and more often failed to support negative stereotypes
of elderly people than staff who were less successful.

In a report on the attitudes of caseworkers toward elderly clients, Burger
assumed that a worker's attitude would influence his or her ability to provide
care effectively.[17] Findings indicated that although the attitudes surveyed
were basically more positive than negative, workers who were over 30 and
had some graduate education expressed the most positive responses. Positive

attitudes were not associated with level of employment or experience. Both caseworkers and aides believed the characteristics of their elderly clients rather than something in themselves acted as barriers to communication.

Although Burger found that workers over the age of 30 had more positive attitudes than younger workers toward the elderly, Lowry and his associates found that the younger workers they surveyed had the most positive attitudes, followed by older workers, and then middle-aged workers.[18] They measured the cognitive and affective attitudes of social workers and nurses toward aging and the elderly and hypothesized that a relationship existed between the attitudes held by these two professional groups and the morale of their clients. Such a relationship was found. This study decidedly confirms the assumption that the attitudes of professionals affect their clients, or at least the morale of their clients.

Thorson, Whatly, and Hancock studied the attitudes toward the elderly of students, registered nurses, social workers, and homemaker–home health aides engaged in delivering services to elderly individuals.[19] The researchers found that negative attitudes increased with the age of the individual being surveyed and that a positive relationship existed between attitudes and years of education completed.

Although the differences in the methodologies, samples, and measurements used in the studies prevent definitive conclusions from being drawn about the characteristics of individuals that accompany negative and positive attitudes toward the elderly, it is apparent that attitudes toward elderly clients vary among professionals. Like other professional and nonprofessional care-givers, social workers have negative attitudes toward elderly clients, and it may be assumed that these negative perceptions can impair their effectiveness with these clients. Indeed, several of the studies found that needed referrals and intervention were not always carried out because of the biases held by some professionals against the elderly. If the reasons behind the negative attitudes of many care-givers were understood, it might be possible to change the attitudes of professionals already in practice and to instill positive attitudes toward elderly clients in prospective practitioners. The authors will therefore explore these reasons in an attempt to help influence professional attitudes toward elderly in individuals.

AGEISM IN SOCIETY

In a society such as the United States, which emphasizes attractiveness, productivity, youth, and activity, the elderly are not valued. Rather, elderly people in this country increasingly find themselves without roles and functions as a result of the following factors: social policies such as the institution of work disincentives, low social security benefits, and mandatory retirement; social changes such as those taking place in the family and the greater mobility seen among individuals; and the process of aging, which is characterized by physiological change and often the onset of greater health problems. Negative attitudes and ageism have followed, and they have been described in the following way by Butler and Lewis:

> Ageism can be seen as a process of systematic stereotyping of and discrimination against people because they are old, just as racism and sexism accomplish this with skin color and gender. Old people are categorized as senile, rigid in thought and manner, old-fashioned in morality and skills. . . . Ageism allows the younger generations to see older people as different from themselves; thus they subtly cease to identify with their elders as human beings.[20]

Although attitudes toward the elderly are changing for the better, they are changing slowly. It is within this societal context of a prevailingly negative view of elderly individuals that social workers develop their values and orientations and the profession of social work is practiced. Not surprisingly then ageism is observable in the general reluctance among professionals to work with elderly clients, in the limited resources available for the elderly, and in the distinctions made in referrals, diagnoses, and treatment on the basis of the chronological age of clients.

WORKING WITH THE ELDERLY

One explanation offered for prejudice against the elderly among professionals is that work with older clients may be perceived as representing the antithesis of social work practice.[21] That is, social workers are dedicated to and have been trained to effect the improvement or restoration of their clients' ability to function, but they may view the elderly individual as being incapable of responding to treatment. Workers should instead recognize that age and illness may impede improvement of function and that such improvement may come about more slowly, less dramatically, and with more difficulty in the elderly than in younger clients.

Related to this issue is the fact that some social workers are goal oriented and need to see tangible results from their professional interventions. Others are inner-directed and can gain satisfaction from less obvious indicators. In general, however, a social worker's expectations should be adjusted to the characteristics of the particular client served. In regard to the elderly these expectations should not include the anticipation of instant and dramatic change but of a modification in behavior, condition, and functioning. Professional practice with the ill, the handicapped, the old, and the dying demands a maturity and a humanism consistent with what the profession values most highly.

Another explanation for the seeming lack of attraction felt by many workers for the elderly client is their perception that the effects of professional intervention with such a client may be short-lived and that work with the elderly is an inefficient use of professional talents and personnel. Crane has reported that many physicians evaluate patients for treatment in terms of the psychosocial aspects of their illness and the possibility of their resuming their former social roles. Moreover, a relatively high percentage of physicians surveyed admitted that they withheld treatment on the basis of such evaluations.[22] Is it possible that social workers make similar decisions regarding the withholding of treatment?

Furthermore, since work with the elderly often involves exposure to serious illness and death, it may be unattractive to many workers because it reminds them of their own mortality. Although the professional literature and the media have begun to emphasize the importance of work in the areas of death and dying, some professionals may dread working with the elderly. It is interesting to note that workers frequently have negative feelings about institutional settings for elderly people but often refer older clients to such settings. While doing so, they may communicate their unfavorable attitudes to clients and their families and to institutional staff. The myth that those living in institutions cannot be helped results in an unfortunate self-fulfilling prophecy. In addition, professionals are influenced by the belief that those working within institutions for the elderly are less competent than their colleagues who work in other settings.

The attitudes of workers toward the elderly may also be influenced by experiential factors. An unfortunate personal experience with an older person in the past may determine an enduring attitude on the part of an individual. In addition, unrecognized idiosyncratic, latent, and unresolved personal problems may be triggered by contact with elderly clients and result in negative attitudes toward them.

Ultimately, if social workers perceive elderly clients negatively, it may be because they come into contact with what is, in a sense, a biased sample. In general, helping profesionals come into contact with older individuals who are ill, poor, dependent, or confused. Although recently graduated professionals frequently begin practice with high ideals, a firm commitment to provide care, and positive expectations for clients' improvement, their colleagues may ridicule their "idealism" and instill in them a more "realistic" perception of the ability of elderly clients to be helped. This may especially be true when the clients involved are ill, poor, or minority group members.

To sum up, the origin and persistence of attitudes, both positive and negative, are related to a multiplicity of factors. Differences in attitudes toward the elderly among social work professionals may be traced to personal, professional, and societal sources. Given the premise that all social work professionals who work with the elderly should have positive and appropriate attitudes, what mechanisms can be set in motion to assure that they do? The authors will discuss four such mechanisms that in their opinion warrant the profession's consideration: formal education, short-term training, staff screening, and social change.

Formal Education

All too often, required core courses in the social work curriculum that deal with human growth and development virtually ignore the development of the individual beyond adolescence. The study of adulthood and the years leading to old age is frequently dealt with as secondary in importance to the exploration of the adolescent years and contributes little to the student's understanding of life-cycle changes or the process of maturation.

Moreover, schools of social work vary greatly in regard to the amount of gerontological material covered in their course offerings and the field placements they make available to students. Several schools have course concentrations and specialized centers relating to work with the elderly, but others have attempted to include material concerning the later part of the life cycle in their courses on human development. Too frequently, however, material relating to later adulthood is squeezed in at a course's conclusion.

All schools of social work would therefore do well to institute required courses in social gerontology.[23] Mandatory courses in gerontology or geriatrics would stimulate the interest of future professionals in academic practice, sensitize all students to the characteristics and needs of the elderly, and explore the personal attitudes of students toward older individuals. Such a recommendation is, of course, predicated on the belief that education can change attitudes.

Education and Attitudes

Can education actually affect attitudes? Cicchetti and his colleagues studied the attitudes of medical students toward the elderly before and after exposure to a course in social medicine that focused on older people.[24] Attitudes remained negative in both the control and experimental groups, and the authors pointed out that their findings were consistent with those of other studies. They drew the following conclusion:

> The results suggest that the negative findings reported in other investigations of attitude change can probably not be understood on the basis of methodological deficiencies alone. Moreover, if the findings of this study are generalizable, then medical schools may have much to accomplish in order to cope with society's ever-increasing geriatric problem.[25]

Other studies of medical students' attitudes, such as that done by Spence and Faigenbaum, found that the students' prejudice regarding the elderly was stronger than their racial prejudice.[26] Would studies conducted with social work students reveal similar findings?

Apparently, nursing students may often have prejudiced attitudes toward older people. In a report on long-term care, the American Nurses Association recommended that "basic and graduate educational programs for registered nurses need to emphasize gerontology and geriatric nursing care, not only in the classroom but in clinical facilities."[27] Steinbaum also recognized the need for nursing students to change their stereotypical beliefs about older people and designed a course in which students came in contact with healthy older people.[28] She found that significant positive changes did occur in the attitudes of the students and that an increased number of them indicated a preference for working with the elderly. Although such finding are encouraging, they do not help answer the questions of whether attitudes change, and if so, for how long.

In contrast to the contradictory findings in regard to education's effect on attitudes, Biehler has stated that attempts to teach pupils attitudes and values appear to produce results. He has also suggested that pupils' attitudes are influenced by teachers who have certain qualities but that the pedagogical methods used by teachers have little effect in this regard.[29]

Although some of the findings described challenge Biehler's optimism, the authors nevertheless believe that future social work practitioners, planners, and administrators should at least be exposed to material dealing with gerontology and geriatrics in their courses if they have not taken specialized courses in these areas. Schools should also coordinate students' field work placements with the content of their courses. If students worked with the elderly while they were learning about them, their field placement would reinforce their classwork.

Short-Term Training

Various efforts have focused on changing the attitudes of professional social workers who deal with the elderly. In general these efforts have attempted to increase the workers' knowledge of and sensitivity to the special needs of elderly individuals, and they have frequently taken place in the form of workshops at the state, regional, and local level. For example the National Association of Social Workers recently conducted Project Provide, a training program for social workers and their designees working in facilities providing long-term care. The project was funded by the U.S. Department of Health, Education, and Welfare, and approximately 2,700 persons participated in it.[30] Although the program was considered a success in terms of the number of people who participated and the increase in interest expressed about the elderly, it is not known whether the changes in attitudes that were presumed to take place were real and long lasting. Indeed, as Hickey and his associates have pointed out, "without systematic, evaluative data, the possibility exists that programs meant to improve attitudes may in fact be confirming negative attitudes and stereotypes."[31]

Other efforts to influence professional attitudes have taken place within schools of social work, some of which have instituted continuing education programs as well as seminars in working with the elderly. Again, although it is generally assumed that such programs are effective in modifying attitudes, empirical findings regarding them may not be whole-heartedly endorsed by research methodologists who question the value-laden measurements of benefits received from workshops, classes, and seminars.

In addition, in-service training for professional social workers that takes place within their agencies has been an especially popular method of attempting to change attitudes. As is true with other such attempts, research evaluating these efforts has been generally lacking. Nevertheless, a recent study of the impact of in-service training on the attitudes of health care staff concluded that the content and the form of training activities had different effects on participants.[32]

Various other studies have raised doubts about the effectiveness of in-service programs in changing attitudes. For example, when the senior author,

Cohen, and Mendlovitz surveyed the attitudes of staff in a home for the elderly in which periodic in-service training programs were held, they encountered negative attitudes among staff members both before and after training.[33] Length of time employed in the facility was found to be unrelated to attitudes, and the researchers concluded that the training had little impact on the attitudes of the staff. When a follow-up study including volunteers and board members of the same institution was carried out, similar findings emerged.[34]

Staff Screening

The negative findings of the studies just described raise certain disturbing questions. If, despite being exposed to in-service training over the years, supervisors and staff who have worked in a facility for some time do not have more positive attitudes than more recent employees, the issue of better screening for new employees becomes much more important than previously realized. As the administrator of the facility studied indicated, "While it is possible to train employees for performance of technical duties, changing attitudes is clearly a more difficult task."[35]

Schools of social work, professional organizations, and agencies have an obligation to assure society that their members possess the appropriate attitudes as well as the appropriate professional credentials for carrying out their responsibilities. A growing body of literature deals with the importance of certain characteristics that professionals should possess, such as empathy, warmth, genuineness, and self-awareness, and the existence of these characteristics in a care-giver is generally thought to be related to the effectiveness of the treatment he or she provides. Positive attitudes toward the elderly are necessary in the professionals who work with them, and the attitudes of these workers should be assessed at some point.

It is too soon to conclude that formal education, in-service training, and staff development efforts are not as effective as had been assumed in changing the attitudes of professionals toward the elderly. Education and training programs should continue, for the profession's understanding of their impact on attitudes will increase over time. However, until more is known, a careful screening process for new employees is certainly needed as an interim safeguard to be used by those responsible for hiring staff or for training professionals who will work with elderly clients.

Social Change

Schools of social work do not function in isolation from society at large. It may therefore be said that the content of social work curricula and courses dealing with the elderly reflects values and attitudes prevalent in society. There is, then, a need for advocacy efforts that challenge currently widespread ageist values. Although undertaking such a challenge is a lengthy and formidable task, schools of social work and the profession should nevertheless initiate this kind of effort. By alerting as many students as possible to ageism and to myths and stereotypes regarding old age, the profession may assure the sensitization of future professionals to the characteristics, strengths, and needs of the elderly.

Social change can also be effected by the actions of professional social workers. Social policy is, at once, a reflection of general attitudes toward the elderly and the determinant of opportunities for elderly individuals. The profession can focus on the effects of ageism as evinced in the limited resources and alternatives available to older persons, which preclude their self-determination; the overuse of institutions that deny the possibility of independent living for elderly individuals; the prevalence of adverse conditions within institutions for the elderly, which help deprive them of their individuality and self-respect; and the biased treatment of the elderly by professionals, which affords older persons what is at best second-class citizenship.

The social work profession should also focus on the causes of negative values and practices that perpetuate a dependent role for the elderly. Specifically, older people should be provided with greater opportunities and assistance for the attainment of economic security, with a variety of available vocational and leisure activities, and with more accessible and affordable health care based on the philosophy that care is a right for all and not a privilege of the younger or wealthier members of society. Overall, if the elderly were allowed to be independent, active, involved, and healthy, society's perceptions of them would change.

In summary both the causes and the effects of ageism must be dealt with, and the social work profession must help usher in these changes. In addition, it is obliged to make certain that those of its members who work with the elderly are, at the very least, offering them the same care and treatment available to younger clients. Social workers have tended to assist older people to accept and adjust to adverse social conditions. As the senior author has pointed out elsewhere,

> We have treated the elderly where we have found them and provided them with traditional casework and groupwork services. The emphasis has been on helping them adjust to their station in life, rather than attempting to change their situation.[36]

This tendency should be eliminated. Social workers should initiate a greater emphasis on social change at the local level of the agency and at the national level as well through lobbying efforts on Capitol Hill.

Social workers will increasingly be directly or indirectly involved with the elderly, yet the attitudes of professionals toward older people have generally been found to be less than positive. As Maldonado has stated, certain myths about the elderly have "blinded both social scientists who formulate theories and the practitioners who provide social services."[37] It is thus important that the attitudes of professionals be assessed for work with elderly individuals, along with their technical skills and knowledge. In describing the gap that exists between social work training and practice, Brody has indicated that "discrepancies appear in outmoded and inappropriate attitudes towards the aged."[38]

In addition to exploring research findings on professionals' attitudes toward the elderly, this article discussed the role of formal education, short-term training, and social change in altering attitudes. Evaluative studies of the effect of these elements on attitudes have resulted in findings that are, at best, inconclusive. Often, empirical research has not been undertaken at all. Some findings have indicated that formal education and in-service training may not be able to reverse personal and social forces helping to create and sustain negative attitudes toward the elderly. The question then becomes whether careful screening can be initiated to assure that care-givers hold appropriate attitudes. Until further knowledge of effective methodology for changing attitudes is developed, the authors advocate the meticulous screening at the entry level of professionals who will work with the elderly.

This article has not intended to denigrate the importance of formal social work education in gerontology or of in-service training and staff development for those already in the field. It has attempted to point out that such efforts do not ipso facto guarantee attitudinal changes along with the development of knowledge and skills. Above all social work must seek change in societal and professional attitudes toward the elderly. From change should follow more effective and equitable care and treatment.

ENDNOTES

1. Frederick R. Eisele, ed., *Political Consequences of Aging: The Annals of the American Academy of Political and Social Sciences* 415 (September 1974): iv.
2. Donald G. Fowles, "U.S. 60+ Population May Rise 31% to 41 Million by Year 2000," *Aging*, Nos. 248–249 (June and July 1975): 14–16; and U.S. Bureau of the Census, *Some Demographic Aspects of Aging in the United States*, "Current Population Reports," Series No. 43 (Washington, D.C.: U.S. Government Printing Office, 1973), p. 1.
3. Nora Piore, "Health as a Social Problem: Economic and Social Consequences of Illness," in *Encyclopedia of Social Work*, vol. 1 (New York: National Association of Social Workers, 1971), p. 498.
4. Milton Wittman, "Social Work Manpower for the Health Services," *American Journal of Public Health* 64 (April 1974): 371.
5. *NASW News* 20 (March 1975): 8.
6. Eva Kahana and Rodney M. Coe, "Self and Staff Conceptions of Institutionalized Aged," *Gerontologist* 9, Part I (Winter 1969): 264–267.
7. Ibid., p. 267.
8. Robert L. Wolk and Rochelle B. Wolk, "Professional Workers' Attitudes Toward the Aged," *Journal of the American Geriatrics Society* 19 (July 1971): 624–639.
9. Jordan I. Kosberg, Stephen Z. Cohen, and Al Mendlovitz, "Comparison of Supervisors' Attitudes in a Home for the Aged," *Gerontologist* 12, Part I (Autumn 1972): 241–245.
10. Jordan I. Kosberg, "The Nursing Home: A Social Work Paradox," *Social Work* 18 (March 1973): 104–110.
11. Lillian E. Troll and Nancy Schlossberg, "A Preliminary Investigation of 'Age Bias' in the Helping Professions," Paper presented before the 23rd Annual Meeting of the Gerontological Society, Toronto, Ontario, Canada. October 1970. (Mimeographed.)
12. Catherine Cyrus–Lutz and Charles M. Gaitz, "Psychiatrists' Attitudes Toward the Aged and Aging," *Gerontologist* 12, Part I (Summer 1972): 163–167.
13. Ibid., p. 167.

14. Robert Kastenbaum, "The Reluctant Therapist," *Geriatrics* 18 (April 1933): 296–301.
15. Arlene B. Ginsburg and Steven G. Goldstein, "Age Bias in Referral for Psychological Consultation," *Journal of Gerontology* 29 (July 1974): 410–415.
16. H. R. Conte, R. Plutchik, and M. B. Weiner, "Qualities Characteristic of Successful Workers with Aged Persons," Paper presented before the 27th Annual Meeting of the Gerontological Society, Portland, Oregon, October 1974. (Mimeographed.)
17. G. Burger, "Casework Differences in Attitudes Toward the Aged," Paper presented before the 25th Annual Meeting of the Gerontological Society. San Juan, Puerto Rico, December 1972. (Mimeographed.)
18. Louis Lowry et al. "Attitudes of Nurses and Social Workers Toward Aging and Their Relationship to Life Satisfaction of Patients and Clients," Paper presented before the 27th Annual Meeting of the Gerontological Society, Portland, Oregon, October 1974. (Mimeographed.)
19. James A. Thorson, Lynda Whatly, and Karen Hancock, "Attitudes Toward the Aged as a Function of Age and Education," *Gerontologist* 14 (Autumn 1974): 316–318.
20. Robert N. Butler and Myra I. Lewis, *Aging and Mental Health: Positive Psychosocial Approaches* (St. Louis, Mo.: C.V. Mosby, 1973), p. ix.
21. See Jordan I. Kosberg, "Social Work with Geriatric Patients and Their Families: Past Neglect and Present Responsibilities," in Elizabeth R. Drichard et al., *The Family and Death: Social Work Perspectives* (New York: Columbia University Press, 1977), pp. 155–168.
22. See Diana Crane, "Decisions to Treat Critically Ill Patients: A Comparison of Social Versus the Medical Consideration," *Millbank Memorial Fund Quarterly: Health and Society* 53 (Winter 1975): 1–33.
23. See Jordan I. Kosberg, "A Social Problems Approach to Gerontology in Social Work Education," *Journal of Social Work Education* 12 (Winter 1976): 78–84.
24. Domenic Cicchetti et al., "Effects of a Social Medicine Course on the Attitudes of Medical Students Toward the Elderly: A Controlled Study," *Journal of Gerontology* 28 (July 1973): 370–373.
25. Ibid., p. 373.
26. See, for example, Donald L. Spence and Elliott M. Faigenbaum, "Medical Students' Attitudes Toward the Geriatric Patient," *Journal of the American Geriatrics Society* 16 (September 1968): 976–983.
27. *Nursing and Long-Term Care: Toward Quality Care for the Aging* (Kansas City, Mo.: American Nurses Association, 1975), p. xvii.
28. Barbara H. Steinbaum, "Effects of Selected Learning Experiences on the Attitudes of Nursing Students Toward the Aged," Paper presented before the 26th Annual Meeting of the Gerontological Society, Miami Beach, Florida, November 1973. (Mimeographed.)
29. Robert F. Biehler, *Psychology Applied to Teaching* (Boston: Houghton Mifflin Co., 1971).
30. *NASW NEWS* 21 (October 1975): 6.
31. Tom Hickey et al., "Attitudes Toward Aging as a Function of In-Service Training and Practitioner Age," *Journal of Gerontology* 13 (November 1976): 681–686.
32. Ibid.
33. Kosberg, Cohen, and Mendlovitz, op. cit.
34. Jordan I. Kosberg and Joanna F. Gorman, "Perceptions toward the Care of Institutionalized Aged," *Gerontologist* 90 (Winter 1975): 398–403.
35. Kosberg, Cohen, and Mendlovitz, op. cit., p. 245.
36. Kosberg, "A Social Problems Approach to Gerontology in Social Work Education," p. 79.
37. David Maldonado, Jr., "The Chicano Aged," *Social Work* 20 (May 1975): 213–216.
38. Elaine M. Brody, "Serving the Aged: Educational Need as Viewed by Practice," *Social Work* 15 (October 1970): 42.

CHAPTER 15

Practice in Rural Areas: The Appalachian Experience

Bradford W. Sheafor and
Robert G. Lewis

PREFATORY COMMENT

This chapter highlighting social work practice in the rural United States is a scholarly work prepared for the fifth edition by Bradford W. Sheafor and Robert G. Lewis. Indeed, the many faces of social work also finds the profession visiting the many faces of the United States—in this case, a neglected part of it. The rural poor, especially in Appalachia, who number in the tens of millions, have on the one hand, the same health, mental health, and socioeconomic problems that confront the urban poor, but on the other hand, they are confronted with limited services and impractical systems of delivery caused by geographic and social isolation.

Another unique characteristic of the rural Appalachian population is that it has a traditional, family-oriented culture that also values the extended family and cohesiveness in the immediate community. Family reputations have been developed over generations. Outsiders are suspect, especially those who claim they want to help families and the community. Sheafor and Lewis offer excellent micro and macro practice case examples and suggestions about how to work with this special population group.

The commitment of social workers to the betterment of the most vulnerable members of society has led them to focus their attention on the personal characteristics of people, e.g., age, gender, sexual preference, and race or ethnic background. When these attributes are associated with the dominant social problems of the day such as poverty, crime, mental illness, and homelessness, they become key variables in the development of social programs and approaches to service delivery. Social work's uniqueness among the helping professions, however, lies in its simultaneous attention to both people and their environment. It is surprising, then, that much of the social work research and most of the positions taken on social policy issues by the social work profession do not adequately address important environmental factors that relate to these problems.[1] Virtually all the social programs and most of the practice approaches formulated by social workers assume that they will be used in the location where these problems are most visible, i.e., the urban United States. The special needs of the residents of rural areas have for the most part been ignored and the rural U.S. population has become a new "special population" that requires the attention of social workers.

In recent years the rural United States has undergone dramatic change that has profoundly affected the basic social institutions of rural life. The rise of corporate farming and timber harvesting, the depletion of mineral reserves and the discovery of new energy sources in isolated areas, substantial fluctuations in the farm economy, the often rapid expansion and contraction of ski, fishing, and other recreation oriented areas, and the confiscation of rural towns to serve as "bedroom communities" for urban dwellers has dramatically changed rural life. Pamela Landon and Marvin Feit contend that most rural communities today are in the process of a major transition from one form of community to another.[2]

For many years the problems of poverty, poor health care, and lack of adequate housing have been more prevalent in rural than in metropolitan areas.[3] The rapid changes that have more recently affected the rural economy and rural communities have exacerbated these and other social problems. For example farming and ranching families experience unusually high levels of stress as a result of the "farm crisis" in the South or Midwest. A boom and bust phenomenon resulting from the changing demand for U.S. produced energy sources has created severe hardships in mining towns of the West and Appalachia. In all parts of the country the arrival of new people with different backgrounds and different expectations for the communities have often brought with them a new set of problems, yet their very presence has disrupted the established decision-making processes, making it more difficult to resolve them.

If social workers are to respond to the special needs that are prevalent among the rural U.S. population, appropriate knowledge and practice competencies will be required. Social workers in rural areas should be aware that like other special population groups, rural people have much in common. They share a dependence on the land and they tend to be more religious than urban dwellers. They also tend to be more independent and conservative in their attitudes about social problems and resisting of government interventions to resolve them. In addition, in most communities rural people also have the common experience of living in an environment that is undergoing such rapid social change that the existing social institutions cannot adequately adapt. The ensuing social problems require human service programs and interventive techniques tailored to the special needs of that population.

When dealing with any special population group, the social worker should be cautious in making assumptions based on a single characteristic, e.g., race, gender, rural, or urban residence. Individual attributes or unique circumstances may far outweigh any generalizations that can be made about the total group. In fact, it is useful for the social worker to consider the generalizations regarding all the special populations in Part Four of this book as only background information for making tentative hypotheses that must be confirmed or rejected in individual situations. In relation to rural social work practice this hypothesis testing should not only be applied to individuals but should also be followed in relation to different regions of the country where important variations occur. While commonalities exist in characteristics of the people and the social problems experienced in the rural United States, the nature of these problems may be substantially different, for example, in the rural Southwest from those in rural New England.

This chapter presents an overview of the changing rural United States and the social problems that social workers must address today. In addition, it examines both the micro and macro level practice activities that characterize social work in these areas. To illustrate the unique dimensions of rural social work practice in one geographic area of the United States, Appalachia has been selected as a case example. Appalachia includes all the state of West Virginia and parts of twelve other states extending 1300 miles from New York to Mississippi. Although more than one-half the Appalachian population is considered rural, it is useful to note that this region includes several large urban centers. Appalachia and rural are not synonymous. Further, there are distinct cultural variations among the subregions of Appalachia. Yet, rural Appalachia has developed a somewhat unique culture and becomes a useful case example for illustrating adaptations required for effective social work practice.

Characteristics of the Rural United States

Rural life has played a gradually diminishing role in U.S. society. Until the twentieth century, the United States was primarily rural and its social institutions were organized around rural life. As the open lands to the West were settled and the frontier closed, as the Industrial Revolution increasingly required large numbers of people in concentrated geographic areas in order to manufacture needed products, and as the rapid population increase in the United States ballooned the size of its cities, rural life dropped from the mainstream of public interest and the rural population became second-class citizens. The emphasis of evolving social policies in the United States became urban living and the rural areas were largely neglected in the formulation of social programs and the allocation of resources.

The ability to address the social problems of rural people is partially hampered by the difficulty in finding a satisfactory definition of what is "rural." In the early periods of U.S. history, the isolation rural people experienced contributed to developing a social life that centered around towns or trade centers where goods were bought and sold or traded, churches were located, and schools organized. These communities became the focal point of interpersonal interaction and thus definitions of *rural* tended to be based on the number of people located in a geographic area.

The U.S. Bureau of the Census traditionally classified only those sparsely populated areas with 2500 people or less as "rural." Communities were subsequently excluded from rural identification because they had gained population, yet many maintained most of the important characteristics of rural life. Beginning in 1980 census data reported on the rural United States include all the population *except* those living in "a central city or core, together with contiguous and closely settled territory, that combined have a total population of 50,000."[4] The U.S. Bureau of the Census moved from viewing rural as small and isolated areas to considering all nonmetropolitan areas as rural. To many experts on the rural United States, that definition has gone too far toward including larger communities that reflect patterns of interaction and attitudes that are significantly different from those traditionally found in rural life.

The recognition that population size as a single descriptor does not adequately define rural life suggests the importance of using more sophisticated conceptions. Richard DuBord helpfully suggests that in addition to their relationship to an urban center, rural communities can be characterized by the fact that they are primarily dependent on occupations that are tied to the land and with people who typically have a common set of somewhat conservative attitudes about life.[5] Gretchen Waltman, too, notes that ". . . the word rural means more than a numerical population limit. It connotes a way of and an outlook on life characterized by a closeness to nature, slower pace of living, and a somewhat conservative life-style that values tradition, independence and self-reliance, and privacy."[6]

Recognizing the importance of these additional variables when one is attempting to understand rural people as a special population, the authors of this chapter provide an overview of the land, economy, people, and communities of the rural United States. Understanding these four characteristics of the rural United States is essential background information for the rural social worker as well as the urban social worker who works with people who have recently migrated from rural areas.

The Land   Rural life is directly linked to the land and to nature. The primary land uses in rural areas have been for agriculture, mining and energy development, timber, fishing, recreation, and absorbing urban sprawl. The urban population has depended on farmers and ranchers to provide their food supplies. They have also expected rural communities to incorporate the often dramatically different population groups that may suddenly arrive to set up oil rigs, to extract minerals from the land, or to fish or ski during relatively short periods of the year. Similarly, rural people are expected to give up farmland to housing developments and to integrate the new residents into their social structures.

One byproduct of the dependence on the land and nature for earning a living involves always living with a degree of risk. A wet planting or harvest season, an early frost, a hailstorm, a forest fire, the presence of pollutants in a lake, a mine shaft cave-in, or even the price of a barrel of oil in the Middle East can dramatically affect life for the rural population. For these reasons, religion[7] and fatalism are inherent parts of rural culture and a certain amount of emotional stress is ever-present in rural life.

The Economy   The rural economy is intertwined with the land. Changing employment patterns in agriculture and the "extractive" occupations affect the rural economy, as do changes in land use patterns. For example the primary rural occupations, agriculture and the retail trades that support agriculture, are currently experiencing rapid change due to mechanization and the large capital investment and amount of land required to profitably maintain a commercial farm or ranch. Rodefeld summarizes trends in farm ownership that have occurred during the last half-century and have dramatically affected life in many rural communities:

> The last four decades have produced extensive changes in farm ownership, management, and labor, which may continue into the future. Since the mid-1930s, many new mechanical, biological, chemical, and cultural practices have been adopted by farmers. Yields of many crops and production efficiency of many types of livestock have doubled and, in some cases, tripled. In forty years, total farm production doubled, while the total hours of farm work were reduced by three-quarters. Simultaneously, the number of farms and farmers fell by more than two-thirds.[8]

What happens to these displaced farmers? Social workers must be concerned about whether they have the necessary skills to compete in an urban employment market and, if not, what other options may be available to them.

Similarly, reports of boom and bust conditions in mining towns in the Rocky Mountain West[9] and virtually every other rural area of the United States document dramatic changes in ownership, management, and demand for differing occupational skills. Inevitably, these changes impact the employment patterns, the economy of the rural communities, and the qualify of life.

While the social structures in rural communities were once able to accommodate the gradual changes that occurred, the rapid development of corporate agriculture, changing national and international price structures, enhanced transportation systems surrounding metropolitan areas, and expanding or contracting tourism have variously strained the economic institutions in the rural United States. Major events such as the "farm crisis" and the "energy crisis," or less obvious trends such as changing tourist tastes or new land use patterns, can substantially change the economy of a rural area.

The People   Who are the people that inhabit the rural United States? The U.S. Bureau of the Census reports that 59.5 million people or 24.2 percent of the population in the United States live in rural areas.[10] People typically select rural life because their livelihood is bound to the land, they prefer what they consider the qualitative aspects of rural living over residing in urban areas, or they are trapped by a lack of resources and skills or family situations that require their presence. For whatever reasons, a substantial number of people have elected to reside in rural areas.

Rural areas are characterized by population characteristics that differ from urban areas. Data from the 1980 Census reveal the comparisons reported in

Table 15–1. It is evident from these data that rural people are more likely than their urban counterparts to be male, married, disabled, unemployed, and poor. They also live in larger households with fewer breadwinners to support them. At the same time they are less likely to be members of a minority group (except for Native Americans), are typically less educated, are less likely to be part of the labor force (particularly the females), and are more seldom foreign-born than would be found in the the urban population.

Emilia Martinez–Brawley underscores the excessive amount of poverty in rural America by noting that "although only 25 percent of the total population lives in nonmetropolitan areas, about 40 percent of the 27 million poor concentrate in these areas."[11] Despite the smaller number of racial and ethnic minorities in rural areas, they experience a disproportionate amount of poverty. Martinez–Brawley also makes this point clearly by noting that "most of the 85 counties in which up to half the population lives in poverty are located in Appalachia, the Ozarks, and in areas of the Southern Coastal Plain, the Southwest, and the Northern Plains. In these counties at least 40 percent of the population is black, Hispanic, or American Indian."[12]

Historically, rural people have been exceptionally family oriented. The demands of farm life required that all able family members help with preparing and tilling the land, planting and harvesting the crops, and maintaining the equipment and farm. The extended family, therefore, was an important part of rural life and there was usually some meaningful work that could be done by people of all ages—even those with physical and intellectual handicaps. Rural culture was family centered.

The reality of rural family life today is that economic conditions have forced millions of families to leave agriculture and the characteristics of rural families are now much more similar to urban families. Rural families now include their share of single-parent families, dual-employment families, and families living in poverty. They, too, experience rising rates of substance abuse, divorce, family violence, and adolescent pregnancies.[13] Despite these similarities to urban families, the culture of rural life continues to maintain the family as a central social institution and many social activities and social programs are designed around the family.

Religion plays a particularly important part in the lives of rural people. Studies of rural and urban populations indicate that rural people are more religiously oriented than their urban counterparts. Diana Meystedt summarizes the findings of several such studies.

> In comparison to urban populations, rural people are more likely to rate themselves as "very" or "fairly" religious and to a greater extent feel that religion can answer "all or most of today's problems." In other dimensions, such as Bible reading, they also exceed urbanites; rural people are resisting the nationwide downward trend in church attendance. Nearly 75 percent of persons in rural areas profess "a great deal" or "quite a lot" of respect for and confidence in the church and organized religion.[14]

In addition to worship, instruction, and other activities of religious expres-

TABLE 15–1 Population Characteristics of Urban and Rural Residents, 1980

CHARACTERISTICS	URBAN	RURAL
Age Distribution		
Under 18 years	27.1%	31.0%
18–64 years	61.5	58.1
65 years and older	11.4	10.0
Median age of Males	30.0 years	30.2 years
Median age of Females	31.4	31.6
Families and Households		
Average persons per family	3.25	3.24
Average persons per family 65 and over	.25	.32
Average persons per household	2.68	2.95
Married persons		
Males	60.0%	67.7%
Females	54.5	66.4
Median family income (1979)	$20,653	$17,995
Per capita income (1979)	7,645	6,332
Families living in poverty	9.2%	10.6%
Persons living in poverty	12.1	13.2
Educational Levels (Persons 25 Years and Over)		
Less than high school graduates	16.4%	28.6%
High school graduates	66.5	60.4
Four or more years of college	18.1	11.0
Racial and Ethnic Distribution		
White	71.4%	29.6%
Puerto Rican	97.0	3.0
Native American	53.9	46.1
Asian American	93.1	6.9
Mexican American	87.7	12.3
Black (Afro-American)	85.3	14.7
Percent Foreign-born (Persons 14 and Over)	7.7%	2.0%
Employment Patterns		
Males (age 16 and over) in the labor force	75.7%	73.7%
Females (age 16 and over) in the labor force	51.4	45.5
Nonworkers per 100 workers	108	130
Unemployed	6.4%	7.0%
Work disability (ages 16–64)		
Males	8.5%	10.6%
Females	7.8	8.6

Source: U.S. Bureau of the Census, *1980 Census of the Population: Characteristics of the Population*, Vol. 1, Part 1, Washington, D.C.: U.S. Department of Commerce, 1983: Tables 1, 18, 37, 40, 72, 73, 106, and 109.

sion, the churches have a central place in rural life because of the various social functions such as dinners, group meetings, and youth activities they sponsor.

The more conservative political positions held by the people of rural America are documented by Norval Glenn and Lester Hill in their analysis of a series of Gallup Polls conducted in the mid-1970s. These data indicate that people living in communities of less than 50,000 population differed from people living in large communities on many political and social issues. For example they tended to be more opposed to abortion, premarital sex, the Equal Rights Amendment, female presidential candidates, amnesty for draft evaders, the registration of firearms, and restablishing diplomatic ties with Cuba than persons living in urban areas.[15]

The people of rural areas, then, differ from the urban population in the central role played by the family and religion in their lives. Further, they tend to be more conservative politically than their urban counterparts and often elect to suffer from social problems rather than seek help from human service agencies or professional caregivers. The rural population has an especially strong dedication to the earth and the land[16] making foreclosures or the necessity for an elderly person to sell the farm and move to a town or nursing home, for example, an event that has significant emotional, as well as economic, implications.

Finally, rural culture places great value on friendships, interpersonal communication, and helping acquaintances in need. The pace of life tends to be slower than in urban areas, there is time for more leisurely interpersonal interactions, and perhaps the strongest natural helping networks in the United States exist in rural communities.[17] At the same time, sparse population creates high visibility making it difficult for a person or family to maintain the level of privacy that urban people expect. One's family history colors the perception of the individual, few matters remain secret for any length of time, and gossip serves as an effective social control mechanism. Rural people, then, reflect a mix of attitudes that can best be characterized as "conservative, provincial, traditional, primary relationships, informal decision-making process, sense of independence and self-reliance, wholesome, simple, natural, and folksy."[18]

The Communities   Rural America cannot be fully appreciated without recognizing the importance of communities in enhancing the quality of life for the people. Rural towns serve as important centers of business, trade, education, religion, and interpersonal interaction. The relative isolation experienced by many rural people makes community activities especially important. These activities tend to center around schools (and especially school sports), churches, retail stores, and outlets where necessary equipment or products grown and produced are bought and sold, e.g., the local Coop, grain elevator, or farm implement store.

Several types of rural communities can be identified—including the farm/ranch trade center, the mining/energy/timber company town, the tourist center, and the bedroom community for metropolitan areas. Each type of community faces unique problems, but all are undergoing rapid transition and experience difficulty in maintaining appropriate decision-making structures that can address these problems. Rural towns have traditionally exercised a considerable degree of internal control and have been tenacious in maintaining the power to decide community issues. That power was usually located in a few influential, but accessible members of the community. Increasingly, community issues have been decided by the often "invisible" representatives of corporations that control the economy of rural towns and by state and national governmental bodies that construct guidelines or make decisions that affect the schools, roads, and other public programs. Local control in rural communities has clearly been diminished.[19]

The development of extensive highway systems has reduced the geographic isolation of rural inhabitants. Increasingly, trade is conducted in urban centers some distance from the rural community, which erodes the ability of local merchants to succeed in business and for the community to perform its traditional role as the center of economic and social activity. The pressure to "buy local" takes on great significance in rural communities.

Social Welfare in Rural Areas

An extensive array of human services have emerged in recent years. Access to these services in times of need has become an expectation of every person in the United States—rich or poor, majority or minority, urban or rural. Advancing technology has increased the complexity of providing these services and has encouraged the professions that deliver them to become more and more specialized. At the same time the major programs developed to respond to the social welfare needs of the U.S. population have characteristically been designed in an urban mode where it is assumed that people can readily see helping professionals in their offices. For persons residing in rural areas where the population is insufficient to support even a limited number of highly specialized full-time human service providers, that service delivery approach restricts the ability of rural people to obtain professional help.

Several barriers are present when professional services are required by the inhabitants of rural areas. Cultural factors such as a sense of independence and self-reliance discourage needy people from seeking help. In addition the financial burden and travel requirement too often is placed on the person needing the service. It is costly and time consuming for recipients of services to travel great distances to reach the providers and, given the high poverty rates, many simply do not receive needed services. Their health and social problems go unattended—or friends and family, i.e., natural helpers, address the matter as best they can.

Services are typically provided through governmental agencies on a county or regional basis by public welfare departments, community mental health centers, the criminal justice system, nursing homes, hospitals and public health care agencies, and schools. The private or voluntary services are more

limited in scope and often depend on individual volunteers and local organizations such as churches, fraternal groups, and youth oriented programs
(e.g., 4-H and scouting). The "farm crisis" has eroded both the tax base and
the voluntary contributions in many rural states making it increasingly difficult for either the private agencies or state and local governments that fund
more than 35 percent of these services[20] to supplement the expenses borne
by low-income individuals.

Within the rural areas the social problems that must be addressed are
relatively similar. Leona Bachrach, when speaking about mental health problems, notes that "although every rural community is admittedly unique—
with its own problems, its own patterns of caring for those in need, and its
own special resources—there is substantial evidence in the literature that a
common set of problems generally characterizes the delivery of mental health
services in most rural portions of the nation."[21]

One exception is the community experiencing rapid change in number and
composition of residents. The increase in social problems in one boom town,
for example, illustrates the dramatic impact of rapid change. Bachrach cites
the following example:

> In one Colorado boom town the population increased by 43 percent between
> 1973 and 1976. Over the same time period there were parallel—but strikingly
> disproportionate—increases in selected reported social problems for that
> community: respectively, a 130 percent increase in reported child neglect
> and abuse, a 222 percent increase in crimes against property, a 352 percent
> increase in family disturbances, a 623 percent increase in substance abuse,
> and a dramatic 900 percent in crimes against persons.[22]

A second exception is the rural town that is becoming a "bedroom" community to an urban area. Often an idealized view of rural life attracts the
urban family that hopes the wholesome environment will solve their problems. The middle- and upper-class family that has its primary employment
in an urban area often will commute many miles each day in order to raise
their children in a rural community. More often than not, they simply transfer
their problems to an area that is even less equipped to deal with them than
was the urban center.[23] William Farley, et al., report one case example.

> A superintendent of a rural school district recently commented on the effects
> of a large, ten-acre per home site, raw land development within the bound-
> aries of his school district. He said that families in this tract area represent
> 5 percent of the school population, require 15 percent of bussing funds,
> represent 85 percent of school attendance problems, and require more than
> half of the pupil personnel resources.[24]

It is evident some social problems are experienced more intensely in rural
areas, but the most significant difference between urban and rural human
services is in the approaches required to deliver the services to rural people.
Louise Johnson concludes from her review of the rural social work literature

that "when considering the distinctive attributes of social work in nonmetropolitan America, the major difference seems to be in the service delivery
system."[25] The solutions to problems in service delivery lie in taking the
programs to the people and in adopting practice approaches that are appropriate to rural communities. Innovative delivery mechanisms such as "circuit
riding" professionals, mobile human service agencies, and maintaining one
day or evening per week office hours in rural schools or churches are examples
of efforts to develop more appropriate means of serving rural populations.

Implications for Social Work Practice in Rural Areas

Given the uniqueness of rural life and the particular problems experienced
in delivering human services, the social worker in a rural area must also have
special competencies. The social worker frequently is the only (or one of a
very few) professional in the community. Wide-ranging knowledge and skill
is required in order to respond to the needs of the people. Specialization is
a luxury that sparsely populated rural areas simply cannot support. This "all
purpose" social worker must be innovative, resourceful, self-motivating, and
able to function with minimal supervision.

Employing agencies must also recognize that rural practice requires more
than transporting urban social workers to rural areas. They must select and/
or prepare their staff members for the uniqueness of rural practice. Rural
social workers cannot work exclusively at either practice extreme—i.e.,
"deep-dish" therapy or social policy analysis.[26] Rather, their skills must be
focused on the middle range of social work activities. They are most likely
to be involved in generalized counseling with individuals and families, building support networks and accessing natural helpers to aid people in need,
and facilitating the efforts of the communities to engage in self-help efforts
to prevent or resolve their problems.

The practice model most generally accepted as appropriate for rural practice
is labeled "generalist."[27] While the generalist model has been explicated more
clearly in the social work literature in recent years, the concept has been
present in social work from its very beginning. Mary Richmond, in her Preface
to *Social Diagnosis*, stated:

> Fifteen years ago, I began to take notes, gather illustrations, and even draft
> a few chapters for a book on Social Work in Families. In it I hoped to pass
> on to the younger people coming into the charity organization field an ex-
> planation of the methods that their seniors had found useful. It soon became
> apparent, however, that no methods or aims were peculiarly and solely
> adapted to the treatment of the families that found their way to a charity
> organization society; that, in essentials, the methods and aims of social case
> work were or should be the same in every type of service, whether the
> subject was a homeless paralytic, the neglected boy of drunken parents, or
> the widowed mother of small children. Some procedures, of course, were
> peculiar to one group of cases and some to another, according to the special

social disability under treatment. But the things that most needed to be said about case work were the things that were common to all.[28]

A generalist perspective requires that the social worker approach practice without a methodological bias about what services to provide. That is, the social worker does not predetermine that the service to be given in a specific helping situation will involve behavior modification, family therapy, group work, community advocacy, or some other method of service. Rather, the generalist social worker has the competence to assess the client (individual, family, organization, community) needs and bring appropriate helping approaches to bear on the matter. As summarized in the *Encyclopedia of Social Work*, "Generalist practice requires that the social worker examine the various facets of a situation that needs intervention and apply the knowledge, values, and skills either to initiate service or to secure appropriate specialized expertise. Thus generalist practice involves both the capacity to take a wide view of the practice situation and the necessary abilities to intervene at multiple levels and in a range of situations."[29]

Mona Schatz and Lowell Jenkins conducted an extensive research project in an attempt to further clarify the generalist concept. Their research methodology used the Delphi technique in which a panel of experts were asked through several rounds of questionnaires to help refine thinking about the generalist concept. Their work resulted in 85 percent of the experts agreeing with the following summary statement about generalist social work:

Generalist social work can be defined as a perspective for viewing social work practice that is organized predominantly through the knowledge base of eco-social systems, organizational and human behavior theories but not constrained by any one theory, method or level of system intervention.

Generalist social work practice uses the generic foundation of social work and incorporates a problem-solving multi-level assessment and methodology in social and cultural contexts to meet the needs of client system(s) and match clients and resources for the aim of improved social functioning and person–environment optimum fit.[30]

The conclusions from the Schatz and Jenkins research indicate that the leading scholars on this topic do not view the generalist approach as a method with an attached body of knowledge and skills, but rather it is a perspective on practice that adjusts to the situation presented for help. It is client-centered in that it fits practice to the client rather than attempting to fit the client to a particular practice approach. This perspective directs the social worker to consider possible interventions at both the micro and macro levels and to selectively draw from a range of knowledge and skills for intervention. The respondents to the study agreed that to approach practice from the generalist perspective, it is necessary for the social worker to have the ability to analyze and synthesize information that can be derived from a liberal education and a research orientation. Further, they also conclude that the generalist social worker should have mastered the generic elements of the social work profession (e.g., the ethics, principles, sources of sanction, change process, etc.) and should be guided by such ideals as humanism, normalization, and empowerment.[31]

The social worker practicing from a generalist perspective in rural areas might be viewed as a "utility" worker. Like the utility infielder on a baseball team, he or she must be prepared to enter virtually any practice situation with at least the beginning competence to intervene at both the micro and at the macro practice levels.

Micro Practice in Rural Areas At the micro or direct-practice level, rural social workers provide face-to-face services to clients as would any other social worker. However, the social worker must be especially alert to the fact that because of the strong value placed on self-reliance, rural clients may be resistant to counseling services and reluctant to accept tangible assistance, i.e., social provisions. When combined with the traditional dependence on friends, family, or other natural helpers, the professional helper is truly a "resource of last resort" and the problems presented tend to be severe. The intake and engagement phase of the helping process is one of the most critical parts of practice with rural people. It is critical that the social worker reflect empathy, warmth, and genuineness in the helping relationship.[32] At the same time, due to the high visibility of people and the likelihood of interaction between worker and client in other activities in rural communities, it is essential that the client understands the special nature of professional relationships and that the social worker provides protections to maximize confidentiality regarding the practice activity.[33]

The generalist worker must be prepared to offer a wide range of services, but must also be cautious not to slip into the trap of believing that he or she has the tools to solve all problems. There are times when specialized service is in the best interest of the client and referral to existing services within the community or in urban areas is essential. The task of becoming knowledgeable about the available resources in the region for the many problems the rural social worker confronts is an onerous, but essential activity. Once appropriate resources are identified, considerable care and skill is required to complete a successful referral. While many people view referral as a relatively simple task, it is actually a very complex procedure. Studies indicate that many attempted referrals end in failure.[34]

Another direct practice activity that is compatible with the orientation of rural people involves engaging clients in self-help groups and supporting the use of natural helping networks that can meet their less complicated needs. This activity is especially important both because the culture supports caregiving by friends and families and because professional service providers have limited time to devote to any single practice situation. The challenge for the social worker is to determine which situations are appropriate for this type of intervention and to mobilize the appropriate natural helpers to perform this service.

Macro Practice in Rural Areas While all social workers are expected to engage in both direct and indirect service activity, the rural worker is much more likely to devote a substantial part of his or her time to indirect or macro practice activity. The central place of community life in rural areas suggests the importance of providing community-centered, rather than problem or case-centered services.

Existing social organizations such as churches, schools, and local government agencies are important resources for collaboration by the rural social worker.[35] To effectively use these resources to solve or prevent social problems in the community, the worker must be skilled at needs assessment, social policy analysis, small town politics, and be able to work intimately with the community leadership. It is important for the worker to be able to accurately assess the local decision-making structure and to effectively interpret the needs of the residents to these people. The opportunity for face-to-face contact to influence these decision makers, or even becoming one of the key decision makers is especially possible once the social worker is well-established in a rural community.

Efforts to advocate for client services need not stop with the local community. The rural social worker has a particularly good opportunity to interpret the community's needs and to lobby directly with county and state legislators who represent that district. To work at these levels, the social worker needs to be competent in program and practice research, social policy development, community planning activities, and influencing the legislative process.[36]

Social work practice in rural areas, then, requires knowledge of the special issues that face rural people, a generalist perspective for practice, and skills for working with people at both the micro and macro levels. Regional differences, too, affect practice in various parts of the United States. The Appalachian region illustrates a rural area with some unique characteristics and needs.

Rural Social Work Practice in Appalachia

The Appalachian region has been recognized as a unique and distinctive part of the United States for more than a century. However, the term "Appalachia" was rarely used until the early 1960s. Prior to that time the terms most frequently used in the literature about Appalachians were mountaineers, highlanders, Southern mountain people, and mountain people. These terms continue to be used by many contemporary Appalachian writers.

The names given to Appalachians reflect the most significant characteristic that contributes to a common identity for the people of this region—the Appalachian mountain chain that extends from Maine to Georgia. These mountains have shaped the lives of the people in this region.

The mountainous topography creates conditions of difficult accessibility, limits the amount of level buildable land, and increases flood dangers. The general north-south orientation of the Appalachian mountains tends to make for difficult east-west access across the mountains and divides the region into a number of north-south valleys.[37]

Appalachia is a much misunderstood region of the United States and has experienced enormous negative publicity and stereotyping by the mass media. While the Appalachian people have resented the "hillbilly" image that too often was associated with this publicity, they have also benefited from the national attention focused on the region that resulted in three massive economic development projects. The first occurred in the 1930s. In the midst of the "Great Depression" and a media blitz regarding the extensive poverty in Appalachia at that time, Congress created the Tennessee Valley Authority (TVA), which was the most massive federal project to that date intended to help a large section of the country become economically viable. The construction of hydroelectric dams resulted in flood control, improved navigation, and affordable electricity to the Tennessee Valley.

Again in the 1960s the publicity that surrounded President Lyndon Johnson's "War on Poverty" focused much of its attention on Appalachia. Problems of extreme poverty in the region and all the associated implications, such as poor health, illiteracy, substandard housing, etc., were presented in the media as the way of life in Appalachia and helped to gain public support for the programs incorporated in the Economic Opportunity Act of 1964. It should be recognized, however, that although serious social problems existed (and continue to exist) throughout the region, there was also a large middle-class whose income, values, educational levels, and lifestyles were very similar to those found throughout mainstream United States.

In an effort to "correct" the apparent economic ills of Appalachia, Congress passed the Appalachian Regional Redevelopment Act and created the Appalachian Regional Commission (ARC) in 1965. Hundreds of federal programs funded through the Economic Opportunity Act and the Appalachian Regional Redevelopment Act were implemented during the 1960s and 1970s. Although duplication and lack of coordination hampered the effectiveness of these efforts, much was accomplished. More than $5 billion has been spent by the Appalachian Regional Commission since its inception, with most aimed at improving the infrastructure and making the region more viable economically. Approximately 1700 miles of new highways were built through funding from the Commission and new vocational-technical schools, hospitals, clinics, airports, and public service systems were built to place the region in a more competitive position in the national marketplace.

The results of these projects were substantial, but not enough to bring Appalachia to national averages of income and literacy, for example. *U.S. News and World Report* examined the situation in 1984 and concluded that "Today, after 5 billion dollars of federal spending, . . . the region known as Appalachia is, indeed, filled with public works projects—but its residents remain among the poorest in the nation."[38] In relation to educational levels between 1970 and 1980 the adult population with at least a high school education increased from 43.8 percent to 57.4 percent and by 1990 it is expected that there will be a 46 percent increase in college graduates over 1980. Nevertheless, 30 percent of the Appalachians remain functionally illiterate compared to 20 percent of the U.S. population.[39]

Some sections of the region, especially those areas that are dependent on the coal mining and associated industries, continue to experience extremely high rates of unemployment, poverty, poor health, illiteracy, and other social problems. Although Appalachia is now closer to the national averages in terms of education, health care, income, etc., than before these federal programs were initiated, the region is still somewhat below the rest of the country in most important indicators of social well-being. Presently, the funding for the Appalachian Regional Commission has been severely reduced and continued progress in the region's economic development is likely to proceed at a slower pace.

If social workers who serve rural Appalachians are to maximize their effectiveness, it is imperative that they have an appreciation for the unique background of these people. Social workers employed in rural Appalachia, and especially those who are not of Appalachian background, require this insight. Also, high unemployment in rural areas has forced rural people into urban centers in Appalachia such as Birmingham, Alabama and Pittsburgh, Pennsylvania where urban social workers may contact them. Finally, between 1940 and 1970 more than 3.1 million Appalachians moved out of that region[40] with many receiving services from social workers in cities such in Nashville, Atlanta, Detroit, and Chicago. Thus, an understanding of the rural Appalachian land, economy, people, and communities is important for a large number of social workers.

The Land As can be readily seen in the map of the eastern United States (Figure 15–1) Appalachia is a large geographical area. Although its boundaries have been redefined several times since the 1920s, the current definition used by the Appalachian Regional Commission is generally accepted and includes 194,871 square miles[41]—an area comparable in size to Central America.

For purposes of differentiating parts of the region for more specific analysis, the ARC has defined three subregions—the northern, central, and southern subregions. Initially the Highlands Area (i.e., all parts of Appalachia with an altitude of 1000 ft or more above sea level) was considered a fourth subregion, but later was incorporated into the other three. The most populous and urbanized subregion, Northern Appalachia, includes the Appalachian portion of New York, Pennsylvania, Ohio, Maryland, and all except the nine southern counties of West Virginia. The subregion that is smallest, most rural, and experiences the most poverty is Central Appalachia, which includes all Appalachian Kentucky, the northwestern counties of Appalachian Tennessee, the seven coal producing counties in the southwestern tip of Virginia, and the remaining nine counties of West Virginia. Finally, Southern Appalachia extends from the highlands of Virginia to the margins of the Mississippi coastal plains. It includes the Appalachian portions of Alabama, Georgia,

Figure 15–1 *Appalachia and the Appalachian Subregions*

Mississippi, North Carolina, South Carolina, the eastern counties in Tennessee, and fourteen counties in Virginia. This subregion is characterized by a modern industrial base and is experiencing industrial diversification and expansion.[42]

In contemporary rural Appalachia, the uses of land and the close relationship between the people and the land is similar to other parts of the rural United States. Yet notable differences exist. Although the steep mountain slopes and narrow valleys, which are prone to flooding, have prohibited extensive commercial agricultural development, the land is central to the way of life for Appalachian people. The extractive industries (especially coal mining and gas production), timber harvesting, and tourism and recreation dominate the Appalachian economy. Each depends on the land and is subject to the risks of depleted resources and changing demand and fluctuating price structures throughout the world.

The difficulties of travel in the rugged terrain made it hard to reach markets to trade goods, which forced the family farm to be a self-contained socioeconomic unit. The result was extreme isolation for rural Appalachian people. Not only did the mountains isolate the people from the outside world, but they also isolated them from one another. Thus, the family farm was the primary social unit in early Appalachian life. While agriculture in contemporary rural Appalachia has experienced the recent "farm crisis" as severely as other parts of the rural United States, the impact has been primarily on individual rather than corporate farmers.

Family farms are considerably smaller in acreage than farms in the Midwest and other agricultural areas, a problem that has been compounded as each generation has fewer acres to subdivide among the heirs. Consequently, there are many part-time farmers whose primary employment is in another occupation in a nearby town or city. "The land has been the worker-farmer's insurance against hard times at the mill, and the mill or factory has been supplement to hard times on the land."[43] Some part-time farmers live and work during the week in cities outside the region and return to work the family farm on weekends placing strain on family life.

The federal government, having acquired more than fourteen million acres of timber land by 1970, became the largest single landholder in Appalachia. Much of this land is now federal parks and forests, which has increased tourism and recreation in the region. However, the problems associated with the tourist industry, such as seasonal employment and relatively low wages, undermine a stable economic base for local residents.

The extraction of minerals from beneath the land draws many corporations into the life of Appalachia. Coal mining is the primary extractive industry and extends throughout the central and much of the northern subregions, but the mining of iron ore, aluminum, and other metals is extensive. Unfortunately, few local people own mineral rights or mineral land. According to the Appalachian Land Ownership Study, "ownership of land and minerals in rural Appalachia is concentrated among a few absentee and corporate owners, resulting in little land actually being available to local people."[44] More specifically, this analysis of landownership in eighty counties located in six states revealed some startling ownership patterns:

- A combination of absentee landholders, corporations, government agencies, and just 1 percent of the local population control at least 53 percent of the land surface in the eighty counties studied.

- Contrary to expectations that absentee ownership would predominate only in the coal counties of central Appalachia, the study found a high level of absentee ownership throughout all the counties studied.

- Mineral rights are greatly underassessed for property tax purposes and the large corporate and absentee owners go relatively tax-free while citizens face a paucity of needed services despite the presence of considerable taxable property wealth in their counties.

- Through absentee ownership, the wealth derived from the land and mineral resources is drained from the region and, with the ownership concentrated in the hands of a few primarily corporate owners, external forces dominate local economic development. One result has been a failure to diversify economically, establishing a condition ripe for a boom or bust economy.[45]

Rural Appalachia is also experiencing an influx of middle-class and wealthy urbanite landowners who do not become permanent residents. Many have purchased homes in ski and other resort areas but reside there only one season of the year or commute to their Appalachian residence on occasional weekends. These homeowners utilize the land, but contribute little back to the improvement of the economy or quality of community life.

As John Otto notes, "the expansion of federal forests, the introduction of strip mining, and the migration of marginal farmers contributed to the demise of mountain agriculture. For example the harvested cropland in the Appalachian mountains of Kentucky, West Virginia, and Tennessee plummeted from 600,000 acres in 1939 to only 35,000 in 1974."[46] Today a large proportion of the land is owned and operated by outsiders and the rural Appalachians feel that they have little control over their destiny. The corporations and absentee landowners are politically powerful and have been able to control decisions that affect their industries and, of course, the earnings of their stockholders. As a result tax and regulatory laws have not adequately addressed critical problems such as mine safety, Black Lung Disease, unemployment, water pollution, destruction of the surface land, and other harmful factors associated with these industries.

External ownership, then, has created a condition where important income generated by the region does not return to the local economy and, therefore, does not compensate for the resources taken from the land and does not help to alleviate the social and health problems they have created. John Gaventa concludes:

> The point is this: the wealth produced within Appalachia has not come back to develop Appalachia. Rather, it has been reinvested by the transnational owners of our region into other regions, industries, countries without regard or commitment to the communities from which the wealth came.[47]

The Economy   The economic history of Appalachia is intertwined with the land and its outside ownership. First came the timber barons who purchased hundreds of thousands of acres of prime virgin timber at only a fraction of its true value. Next came the large corporations that bought mineral rights and land at prices that were substantially below their real value. Then the railroads were built with government subsidies in order to have a means to transport timber, coal, and other extracted natural resources to national markets and to departure points for international markets. Finally, the tourism and recreation industry emerged as another central part of the economy.

The problems of outside land ownership are most pronounced in the rural areas that have been exploited by extractive industries. Harry Caudill effectively brought this issue to public attention when writing *Night Comes to the Cumberlands*.

> We have seen that the mountaineer sold his great trees for a consideration little more than nominal, but if his timber brought him a small financial reward, his minerals were virtually given away. The going price in the early years was fifty cents per acre . . . and a seam of coal five feet thick produced a minimum of five thousand tons per acre! Where more than one seam was mined, a single acre sometimes yielded fifteen or twenty thousand tons! . . . For this vast mineral wealth the mountaineer in most instances received a single half-dollar.[48]

Since the mining company had no need for the land after it was mined, many purchased the mineral rights but not the surface land. The agent of the company entering into such contracts was usually an educated, sophisticated person, who was dealing primarily with illiterate mountaineers. As a result, the language in these instruments of conveyance, later known as "broad-form" deeds, was constructed to benefit the mining companies at the expense of the landowners. In some instances families lost their gardens, yards, and even their houses, so the company could extract the minerals underneath. Caudill, again, highlights the discriminatory nature of these demands.

> The broad-form deeds passed to the coal companies title to all coal, oil, and gas and all 'mineral and metallic substances and all combinations of the same.' They authorized the grantees to excavate for the minerals, to build roads and structures on the land and to use the surface for any purpose 'convenient or necessary' to the company and its successors in title.[49]

Chronic economic problems have persisted due to the lack of a diversified industrial economy. Although improvements have been realized in some areas during the past twenty years, the region has suffered historically from boom and bust periods associated with the extractive industries. As the price of oil changed on the international market or as modernized mining methods in coal production reduced the required labor force, poverty increased in Appalachia because there have not been viable alternative sources of employment.

The decline of employment in the coal industry has been devastating to areas that were overly dependent on coal mining and some areas of Pennsylvania and West Virginia had the problem compounded by the major reductions in the steel industry. Where the economy was not diversified, there were few options for the workers laid off by a mining or steel company. Their choices were unemployment or moving out of Appalachia to an urban center where manufacturing jobs might be found. The result, as described by Gaventa, has been to eliminate many of the gains made through the substantial economic and social development programs of the 1960s and 1970s.

For many of the regions's people, however, the first five years of the 1980s have seen the erosion of whatever gains had been made and an increasing gap between the region and affluent America:

- Since 1970, despite 20 years of economic development activity, almost two-thirds of the counties in the region have actually declined economically, related to the rest of the region.

- At the end of 1985, four-fifths of the region's counties had an official unemployment rate higher than the national rate of 6.7%.[50]

Areas that experience economic decline must attract other industries if they are to recover. The skills required for mining or working in the steel industry do not readily transfer to many other jobs except in manufacturing. Attracting large manufactures, however, requires building expensive modern highways and other transportation systems to move the goods produced to the markets. In most areas the economy cannot support building the costly roads and highways that are needed.

All rural Appalachia should not be viewed as economically depressed and under the control of multinational conglomerates. Although the economic situation in the coalfields and steel industry is rather dismal, other areas are economically healthy and closely resemble the affluence found in mainstream United States. One example is the southern subregion, which has a variety of geographical features including the Piedmont and the Coastal Plains areas that are in a good location to serve large national markets. The recent industrial development in these areas has involved the utilization of modern technology and innovations not practical for some of the older industrial areas.

The People   The 20,418,800 people residing in Appalachia make up approximately 9 percent of the population of the United States.[51] Although hundreds of small towns and some ciities (e.g., Pittsburgh, Pennsylvania; Roanoke, Virginia; Chattanooga, Tennessee; and Birmingham, Alabama) dot the landscape, 52 percent of the region's population is rural. Thus, Appalachia contains double the national average for rural population.[52] Although the region has experienced considerable out-migration from people who once lived in rural areas and many Appalachians have moved from rural to urban centers to find employment, the region's rural population remained at more than one-half of the total.[53]

The majority of the people are of Anglo-Saxon extraction and are descendants of several generations of Appalachians. Consequently, the region has a small foreign-born and minority population. It also has a black population, mostly concentrated in urban areas, of 1.6 million people or 8 percent of its total.[54]

Contrary to some portrayals of the region and its people, there is enormous social, economic, and cultural diversity throughout the region, which contradicts the popular perception of a single homogeneous culture. Instead, it should be recognized that numerous subcultures exist. Even the most rural families today are increasingly less isolated and insulated from the outside world than in the past. They are made aware of mainstream culture through regular exposure to the mass media, especially television. Also, today's money-oriented society, as opposed to the former trade-oriented economy, makes it necessary for people to interface with social systems and institutions in mainstream Appalachia. Lewis accurately characterizes rural people as being bicultural, since most learn and practice both mainstream and mountain culture simultaneously.[55] This bicultural perspective is also observable to some degree among middle-class urban Appalachians, since most have roots in the rural areas.

The mass media has provided the people of the United States with regular doses of distorted images of the region and its people. More stereotypes are centered around a few perceived character or behavioral traits such as laziness, ignorance, uncleanliness, immorality, violence, and passivity. Television programs that have been the most stereotypical include *The Beverly Hillbillies, Green Acres,* and *Gomer Pyle.* Currently *Hee Haw* is perhaps the biggest offender. Comic strips like "Snuffy Smith" and "L'il Abner" have also contributed their share of mythical descriptions of Appalachian life. Among the many movies that have stereotyped the people, few can surpass *Deliverance.* Stereotypes usually have some basis in fact, but accuracy is soon lost through distortion and exaggeration, which is then generalized to include a whole region, race, or class of people. For example, those outside the region, whose only information about Appalachia is from movies, television, and the print media tend to rely on the stereotypes as true representations of the population.

The prevalent cultural values that are ascribed to Appalachians had their origins in the early frontier-agrarian society. These values include strong family ties, individualism and self-reliance, traditionalism, fatalism, and religious fundamentalism. They are an outgrowth of the harsh realities of survival in the rugged mountains and hollows of the eighteenth, nineteenth, and early part of the twentieth centuries. Families were self-contained social units, with each household living its own life independently of other families in the hollow. Family members were dependent upon one another for survival, and opportunities for activities outside the nuclear and extended family were severely restricted. Until fairly recently three-generation households were not unusual and much of the out-migration during the past three decades included moving the nuclear family, as well as some of the extended family members. Today that is no longer the usual family constellation. Now the typical rural Appalachian family, as in the urban United States, is the nuclear family consisting of husband, wife, and dependent children. Also, it is now much less common for adult children to remain in the same locality as their parents because most must relocate in order to find employment.

Even with the out-migration of rural Appalachian families (a trend, incidentally, that has now been reversed), the attachment to extended family members has not been lost. Visiting and other social relationships are regular occurrences among distant relatives such as second and third cousins and great-aunts and uncles. Even migrated families maintain frequent contacts with family members "back home." Many make weekend trips several times each year for this purpose. Family members nearby and from great distances gather quickly when there is serious illness or a death in the family. Naturally, family relationships have changed as Appalachia has changed, but there is strong evidence that rural Appalachian families continue to be among the closest knit families in the United States.

Another characteristic of the people in the rural areas of Appalachia is the importance of the family surname. Individuals are evaluated and even judged to a large extent on the reputation of their family, which may be considered more important than a person's accomplishments or the lack thereof. This is an advantage to some and a detriment to others. A person whose family is held in low esteem may not be able to overcome the stigma, even through educational achievement and material success. On the other hand, a person from one of the "good" families generally maintains a positive status, even if little is achieved on his or her own merits.

Individualism and self-reliance were traits necessary for survival on the frontier, and they served the frontier family well. However, the ability to exercise these traits is increasingly restricted in today's expanding industrial economy. Loyal Jones notes that, "the mountaineer withdrew from the doings of society, and it passed him by. With the changing of the economy, this free man became a captive of circumstances. But the belief in independence and self-reliance is still there, whether or not the mountaineer is truly independent and self-reliant."[56]

Traditionalism has characterized the rural Appalachian for generations. It was easier and safer to hold on to the "old ways" than to adapt to a changing society. That characteristic, too, may be passing and many Appalachians have demonstrated their desire and capacity to be progressive and participate in the emerging industrial economy. For example, something more than passive resignation to the declining regional economy would have prevented the massive out-migration of people in search of a better life.

Fatalism is intertwined with religion and is internalized primarily by the poor and oppressed. It is viewed as being an adjustive or survival technique of the powerless. For those who endure deprivation and hardships on a daily basis, it is comforting to have something to sustain them. The black Delta sharecropper, the white mountain tenant farmer, and the chronically unemployed and dispossessed with good reason believe that their living conditions will never improve and are comforted by this religious fatalism. One hears statements in rural Appalachia like, "This is God's will," "God will not put more on you than you can take," and "Blessed are the poor. . . ." Present life is devalued with the expectation of receiving their rewards in Heaven.

The nationwide return to religion at the turn of the nineteenth century, known as the "Great Revival," had a profound impact on Appalachia. The Great Revival introduced a very personal and conversion-oriented theology into the region. "Mountain preaching was now seen as good if it was exhortative and brought one to conversion. Along with the new ideology and way of preaching, this revival introduced the camp meeting, song schools, gospel songs, shaped-note singing, mourners' pit, and an emotional religious setting. . . ."[57]

Initially, the mountaineers were Presbyterians, Episcopalians, and other formally organized denominations with educated clergy. For the most part these denominations did not meet the needs of an uneducated congregation and many locally autonomous sects emerged with their own home-grown clergy.[58] Today there is a mixed pattern of traditional religious groups and local sects. Most rural Appalachians, however, adhere to fundamentalism that includes a belief in the literal interpretation of the Bible and results in the selection of churches that reflect this view.

Non-denominational local sects are especially prevalent among the poor. Many of the churches are crudely built small structures that bear the name of the community or the person, usually the pastor, on whose land they are located. Services are typically conducted three or four times per week and last from three to five hours. Services have a highly emotional tone, and such rituals as faith healing are not uncommon. Rural Appalachia has almost no Jewish synagogues and few Roman Catholic churches. Although modernistic Protestant churches and religious practices are a part of urban Appalachia, they are not common in the rural areas.

According to Richard Humphrey, religion appears to be the social institution that has resisted change more than any other.[59] Therefore, it is incumbent upon social workers as well as other service providers to know and to respect the people's religion. One cannot understand the Appalachian without first understanding his or her religion, because religious beliefs and practices permeate every facet of life.

Additional strong values among Appalachians are neighborliness and hospitality, personalism, love of place, modesty and being one's self, sense of beauty, sense of humor, and patriotism. Jones views the values of Appalachians primarily as being positive, but also recognizes that some of the values are counterproductive.

> Our fatalistic religious attitudes often cause us to adopt a "What will be, will be" approach to social problems. Our "Original Sin" orientation inhibits us from trying to change the nature or practices of people. Our individualism keeps us from getting involved, from creating a sense of community and cooperation and causes us to shy away from those who want to involve us in social causes. Our love of place, sometimes, keeps us in places where there is no hope of creating decent lives.[60]

The Communities The typical rural communities in Appalachia are small towns and even smaller villages and hamlets. The changing economy has created distressed conditions for many towns that traditionally have been dependent on agriculture and coal mining. Many formerly vibrant towns have become little more than "ghost towns." In the 1950s the coal camps and company owned towns began to decline and most had disappeared by the end of the following decade. Dilapidated company houses were either dismantled by the company or abandoned. Houses that were in good condition or could be repaired were sold, generally to retirees who could afford the purchase price of a few hundred dollars.

The more moderate size towns, especially those accessible by interstates and other major highways, have experienced industrial growth that created a more healthy economy. At the same time small towns that previously served as trade centers for people who lived in isolated areas were adversely affected by the expanded highway system that allowed people to make their purchases in larger trade centers. Many middle-class Appalachians take periodic shopping trips to urban areas or shopping centers that have emerged on the fringes even though the centers may be as far as fifty to one hundred miles away. This trend has changed the "local flavor" of businesses in rural Appalachia. Many small grocery stores and general merchandise stores that used to be scattered through the remote areas no longer exist. The few business establishments in the small "crossroads" communities are primarily self-service establishments serving a motoring clientele. The discontinuance of many post offices in very small localities has also affected the role of the community as a gathering place for people in the area. The social activities of "loafing" and chatting with neighbors in the stores or post office has practically ceased and the important role of communities as social centers has diminished.

School consolidation has also affected community life. Many rural parents feel intimidated by contact with the larger consolidated schools and find that it does not represent a meaningful place for social interaction because it includes people that have not traditionally engaged in face-to-face interaction. Many of the rural children, too, do not adjust to the large consolidated schools because of perceived social and cultural inferiorities as measured against the more affluent "town kids" that frequently are enrolled in the consolidated schools. Consequently, neither the parents nor children involve themselves in school related activities, and the school drop-out rate, already high, increases as the school performs a less important role in Appalachian life. However, churches and church centered social events continue to be important in rural communities. Churches and the institution of religion have been, perhaps, the most stable institutions in rural Appalachia and continue to perform a central social, as well as religious, function.

Unlike many other rural areas Appalachia has not spawned "bedroom communities" to absorb urban sprawl. Even the northern subregion, which is relatively close to major population centers, is not in daily commuting distance to urban centers due to transportation difficulties created by the mountainous terrain.

In sum, traditionally the daily activities of rural families took place in the community of their residence. With few exceptions, people worked, shopped, worshipped, and attended school within walking distance or a short commuting distance from home. This changed with the abandonment of family farms, the disappearance of coal camps, school consolidation, and opportunities for greater mobility. Now many workers commute many miles each day to reach their jobs, shop outside their local community, and the children commute by school bus or other means to a consolidated school. These societal changes have lessened the Appalachian's sense of community identity and cohesiveness. The decreasing isolation and the increasing interaction and communication with mainstream society is causing many rural communities to lose their central role in the lives of the people.

Social Welfare in Rural Appalachia

Social welfare in rural Appalachia includes restrictive service delivery modes and other barriers to effective human service provision that are identified with the rural United States. The major differences lie in the severity of the communities' inability to finance adequate services and outreach efforts, as well as the reluctance of many potential recipients to seek out and utilize services that are available. As the Manpower Education and Training Project Rural Task Force of the Southern Regional Educational Board points out:

> Problems of rural areas tend to be more like problems of underdeveloped countries; that is, basic public services and necessities are lacking. Services related to sustaining life will have priority (i.e., food, shelter, health, transportation, etc.) over social services focused on the quality of life.[61]

This characterization of rural problems and services does not apply universally, but it accurately reflects the deprivation experienced in rural Appalachia.

Not only do the localities not have a tax base sufficient to support even a limited number of highly specialized full-time human service providers, but they are also often unable to either recruit or support an adequate number of service providers with minimum qualifications. For example, positions designed for social workers are often held by persons whose educational background is not in social work and their clients too often do not receive an adequate quality of service. This is not unique to Appalachia, but in vast areas of the region it is virtually impossible to recruit professionals who are not native to the localities and few such qualified natives are available.

Cultural factors such as independence and self-reliance may influence Appalachians more than any other group of people. The kinship group generally does what it can to take care of its own, and outside help is usually sought only as a last resort. Therefore, social agencies are constantly dealing with crisis situations. In addition the isolation in the region causes enormous transportation problems for consumers of services. Although this is generally the situation throughout rural America, much of Appalachia is especially hampered by travel requirements. Many recipients must depend on neighbors or other individuals for transportation, and even nominal costs place an additional burden on extremely limited budgets. Also, out-migration consisting mostly of the young and healthy has left many areas with a disproportionate share of elderly, for whom travel may be virtually an impossibility.

An alternative is to take the services to the clients. Service delivery in a few settings is primarily through home visits, and the travel time required of service creates a costly and inefficient system for the agencies and workers. Travel time often exceeds the time available for professional contacts with recipients of service.

The public welfare department is the major service agency and generally the only source of financial assistance, except for those eligible for Supplemental Security Income (SSI). Mental health centers have been slow in locating in the more rural areas, and many have only a satellite center staffed part-time as an extension of an urban mental health agency. Also, the staff of the rural center frequently does not include the parent agency's most qualified staff members. Contract services between public and private agencies in rural areas are extremely limited because of the scarcity of private agencies.

Nursing homes and hospitals are generally overburdened with indigent patients. Support services, which would enable many of these patients to remain in their own homes or with relatives, seldom exist. The problems of the aged are magnified in Appalachia because of the vulnerability of an enormously large aged population.

Limited private or voluntary services are provided by churches and other benevolent groups on a selective basis. One frequently hears the statement that "God helps those who help themselves," so those organizations working through God may tend to provide assistance only to those who are considered to be "deserving." This problem is compounded by the fact that rural Appalachians are reluctant to contribute to "worthy causes" that have unknown beneficiaries. However, on a personal level, individuals and small groups are known to be liberal in sharing their resources with others.

The attitudes of Appalachians toward social welfare are heavily influenced by cultural beliefs in the importance of independence and self-reliance, as well as religious fatalism. However, this view was modified during the major economic downturns that resulted in massive unemployment. Harry Caudill observed this in the Eastern Kentucky coalfields in the 1950s and early 1960s. The rapid decline in the coal industry created special hardships for the middle-age unemployed miner, who was less likely to find employment outside the industry and less able and willing to leave the area. Therefore, the only way for the family to survive was to qualify for public assistance based on the disability of the wage earner. Many became "symptom hunters" in order to convince physicians they were "sick enough to draw." They complained of a wide range of ailments, and many could point to scars on arms, legs, and chest—mementos of old mining accidents—to support their claims. Above all they complained of having "bad nerves."[62] Roger Nooe discovered similar behavior among mental patients in rural Appalachia:

> The client may have taken a sick role in relating to his environment through either self-labelling or the influence of environmental forces. A good example of this negative environmental influence is the unemployed coal miner who

finds that being mentally ill may enable maintaining some dignity and justify welfare for family support. Thus, illness serves as a rationale for a social situation in which the independent, self-reliant rural individual finds himself.[63]

One social worker reports that when employed in a county welfare department in the late 1950s and early 1960s in Appalachian Virginia, it was not uncommon to find written after an applicant's medical diagnosis by the local psychiatrist—"coal miner's syndrome." This was generally interpreted to constitute disability because of the debilitating emotional and physical effects of long-term unemployment and allowed the miner to have a medical reason for receiving a social provision.

The solutions to service delivery problems in Appalachia approximate those considered desirable for other rural areas. "Circuit riding" has been a mainstay of public welfare departments. These circuit riders conduct initial as well as follow-up services in locations other than the main offices. Due to funding limitations and the occasional need for technical diagnostic equipment, it is not feasible for all human service providers to make home visits, and serious attention should be given to the establishment of mobile as well as permanent substations of social agencies. Some agencies have been innovative in scheduling nontraditional office hours, but there is an increasing need for more flexibility in this regard. The problems of transportation cannot be seriously reduced without changes in policies and many are concerned that funding for these programs might create additional burdens for these localities.

Micro Social Work Practice in Rural Appalachia Most professional service providers in rural Appalachia serve lower-class or working-class consumers whose cultural values are different from their own. It is imperative that the professional helpers understand and appreciate the client's culture as being different—not deficient—and develop innovative service approaches and tools that are appropriate for this population. Although his remarks were not directed specifically toward Appalachians, Alfred Kudushin accurately captured this perspective:

> A knowledge of the client's cultural milieu is necessary in understanding the client as well as in helping in problem solving. A client who may appear to be withdrawn and excessively passive may be only reflecting the norms of his group. Advice and suggestions which may seem eminently serviceable in the interviewer's group context may be inappropriate and inapplicable in the interviewee's cultural situation.

> Good interviewing in a contact with a client who differs from the interviewer in some significant characteristics requires more than a knowledge of the culture and life-style of the interviewee. It also requires an adaptation of interview techniques—pace of interview, activity level, choice of appropriate vocabulary, modification of nonverbal approaches—to be in tune with the needs of the interviewee.[64]

The rural Appalachian places great value on personal relationships and is dismayed by persons he perceives to be cold, methodical, or indifferent. During the first contact with the human service agency, the Appalachian can be expected to be cautious, suspicious, and highly anxious. It is essential that the worker demonstrate empathy, unconditional acceptance, and a warm personal regard for the client. Otherwise, the person is likely to withdraw from the situation regardless of the severity of need. Although the professional relationship is essential in social work practice regardless of the clientele served, it will take more effort and time to develop this with the Appalachian client, especially if the worker is viewed as an outsider. This point is forcefully illustrated by John Fetterman when he notes that "The mountaineer would like to have one person—one day—come into his hollow and show some signs of approval of the way he has lived over the decades, and the way he wants to live forever, and not try to change him without first knowing him."[65]

The Appalachian client is not impressed by professional qualifications and credentials and is unlikely to inquire about such matters. However, "who" the worker is as a person is likely to be of great concern. For example, the belief in God, friendliness, and a familiar name or location will expedite the client–worker relationship. Most will continue seeing a professional they like, even if the person is not fully competent. An elderly Appalachian woman nearly died recently from improper care by her physician. After being rushed to the city hospital where she survived, she returned to her "regular" doctor for follow-up treatment. Her rationale was that she thought he was a nice person because he talked to her, was friendly, and had a nice family that attended church regularly. She did not consider returning to the physician who saved her life.

The use of language and communication skills are important considerations. The rural uneducated Appalachian has a very limited vocabulary and usually a slow pattern of speech. Communication may be deliberate, passive, and unexpressive and there may be difficulty in responding to open-ended questions until one feels comfortable with the social worker. The use of localisms, colloquialisms, etcetera may be unique to this particular subculture and the social worker should be prepared to seek clarification when necessary. For example, one client of a native Appalachian social worker, expressed concern about her son-in-law, indicating several times that he had a "white liver." Further probing by the social worker revealed that she considered the son-in-law to be oversexed. Since language is not always understood even by native social workers, it can present especially difficult communication problems for the outsider.

It is very difficult for the rural Appalachian to understand the need for the many forms and extensive documentation that may be required when receiving services. Immediate results are expected and there is likely to be little patience with long-term goals. The following remarks by a client illustrate this viewpoint:

Why, I went in there for help and they didn't say 'Ha!' or nothin'. They just stuck this paper under my nose, told me to fill it out (didn't even give me a pencil). When I'd done that, they begun asking me sech questions about my ma and pa and me. I got mad and left. I ain't no dog. I'm one of God's children. Why did they treat me that way? That's what they always do. You go for help and instead you fill out forms or answer dumb questions. All they have to do is eyeball ya and say, 'What's the trouble' or 'Can I help ya?' O Lord, we would surely tell them if'n they had a mind to listen.[66]

The millions of Appalachians who have migrated to the non-Appalachian cities are counted statistically as urbanites. Many experience upward mobility and become assimilated into the mainstream of city culture. However, tens of thousands could be described more accurately as "urban mountaineers" and many interface with the social welfare system. Therefore, service providers need to understand and relate to these individuals in a manner that is sensitive to their cultural differences.

The generalist perspective is critical to the social worker serving Appalachian people and he or she must be especially skilled in making appropriate referrals for specialized services. An important role is to serve as a broker in assisting with arrangements and advocating on behalf of clients. The client is usually fearful of entering into another unknown situation when referrals are made, and the social worker should be especially careful to "pave the way" by helping with logistical factors such as transportation and scheduling appointments. The worker also needs to prepare the client carefully to utilize the services and provide as much information as possible in order to reduce the anxiety. When possible the social worker should consider the use of the natural helping networks of the community. This resource is especially important because of the underdevelopment of human services and the people's preference for being in an environment with family and friends.

The essence of micro practice with rural Appalachians was succinctly captured by Humphrey:

> If agency workers are to help maintain people they must understand what their clients' words and actions are actually trying to convey to them. It is then that services may be offered in ways people can accept. Their place, their families and their religion all are parts of a very intricate culture which must be respected and taken seriously. The social worker must first come to know the person before he or she can help him.[67]

Macro Social Work Practice in Rural Appalachia Since rural communities rarely have full-time social work specialists at the macro level, the generalist's efforts to effect change at the group and community levels is crucial. The task of involving poor Appalachians in activity that might improve their conditions is especially difficult. Much of the social life of the rural Appalachian centers around reference groups that provide comfort and security, but also discourage them from engaging in change efforts. Weller recognizes this problem:

> Let everyone who works in the Appalachian South take cognizance of the

> power of these reference groups, which stand at the very center of the moun-
> taineer's life. To step out of the group would mean loss of identity. To stand
> out in the group or to try to change the group from within is practically
> impossible, for one would quickly be ostracized. Any outsider who tries to
> change the reference group is very likely to find himself rejected by it.[68]

Although many changes have been realized through group efforts, the impetus and leadership have generally been provided by persons not strongly
entrenched in the reference groups. For example, the organization of the
United Mine Workers Union in the 1930s was a very successful endeavor,
but much outside leadership was utilized.

In order to facilitate change at the community level the social worker must
become an accepted member of the community. The "circuit rider," who lives
elsewhere and comes into the community periodically to fulfill his or her
professional role is doomed to failure at the macro practice level. The same
holds true for the "outsider" who comes into the community for a temporary
prescribed period of time in an effort to affect community change. This was
demonstrated forcefully by the "War on Poverty" programs that brought
thousands of "saviors" from outside the region. They were community action
program workers, VISTA volunteers, Appalachian volunteers, and others
whose motives were benevolent but whose actions reflected considerable na-
ivete. The local power structure and established social agencies were often
ignored, thus ostracizing potentially strong allies.

The social worker involved in community change in rural Appalachia faces
a dilemma. The community power structure may, at times, be the target of
change, yet the support of these influential community members is imperative
if one is to be successful in achieving desired change. The worker must be
patient as community changes are likely to evolve over a long period of time.
People often hold steadfastly to established community values and institutions, and are not amenable to rapid change. Social action approaches and
techniques found to be effective in urban areas must be evaluated carefully
for their appropriate use in the rural context. For example efforts to mobilize
a segment of the community to boycott business establishments or to withhold
rent from "slumlords" may prove disastrous in small, tight-knit communities.
Individuals may be willing to protest on a person-to-person basis, but are not
likely to participate in collective organized efforts. Their sense of powerlessness, fear of retribution, and reluctance to become involved in either small
or large group efforts generally preclude aggressive social action as an effective means to change communities and organizations in rural Appalachia.

To be successful at community change, then, social structures and organizations that are indigenous to the people must be utilized to the fullest,
and the worker must have a thorough knowledge of the power structures
and invisible influences that facilitate decision making. Local governing bodies are powerful, and many have real or implied obligations to outside corporate owners. Therefore, the social worker must constantly walk the thin
line of garnering political support for needed changes while maintaining a

productive relationship with the power structure. Some very sensitive areas relate to health and environmental concerns where this balance is difficult to maintain. For example occupational hazards and industrial pollution generally cannot be dealt with effectively at the local level because of the locality's overdependence on the particular industry. However, changes that take place at the state and national levels relieve the localities of possible blame and retribution. It is essential for the social worker, then, to develop and maintain close relationships with area legislators at all levels with the goal and ability to influence legislative processes for community improvements.

CONCLUDING COMMENT

Changes in rural areas have placed nearly one-fourth of the population of the United States into a category of special population that requires some adaptations to social work practice. A new practice specialization based on the generalist perspective is emerging, which is helping to address the uniqueness of practice in rural America.[69] The definition of rural social work included in the *The Social Work Dictionary* captures the essential elements that make this specialization unique. Rural practice is defined as:

> Social work practice oriented to helping people who have unique problems and needs arising out of living in agricultural or sparsely populated areas or small towns. These people face most of the same problems and needs as do urban clients; in addition, however, they often encounter difficulties because of limited services and "resource systems," less acceptance of any variations from the social norms prevalent in the area, and fewer educational and economic opportunities.[70]

It is important that social workers who intend to practice in rural areas recognize that it is not sufficient to simply transfer an urban perspective to a rural environment. Effective rural social work requires understanding the specific culture (e.g., Appalachian culture), rural people, and the unique role rural communities play in the lives of the people. It involves working with both clients and communities that is, perhaps, best served by the generalist practice perspective. And it involves a tolerance for professional isolation, a more conservative political climate, a resistance to professional services, and a dependence on natural helping systems.

When entering a rural community, the social worker should be prepared for the fact that he or she will be viewed as an outsider. While perhaps extreme, it is said that one is not accepted into a rural community until a family member is buried there. One must earn a place through evidence of a willingness to behave within the community norms such as working hard, not displaying wealth, supporting local establishments, attending church and school functions, and, above all, being friendly.

Due to the isolation professionals experience in rural practice, the employing agencies must make special efforts to help the social workers regularly experience professional stimulation and development through conference and workshop attendance. In addition innovative approaches such as televised staff development programming and teleconference consultation services are needed to support rural practice.

The uniquenesses identified in this description of rural Appalachia and their influence on social work practice with this population help one to appreciate the importance of adapting to the special characteristics of the people being served. All Appalachians are not alike and, to an even greater degree, all rural people are not alike. Yet, there are many similar issues that rural social workers need to address. The National Association of Social Workers' public policy statement on "Social Work in Rural Areas" points out some actions that should be taken to address these issues:

- Social work should play an important role as advocate for the empowerment of people in rural areas.

- The profession must influence the public policies of the federal, state, and local governments that affect the development and reorientation of the service delivery systems in rural areas.

- NASW must support rural social work educators in their attempt to incorporate rural content into the curricula of schools of social work, within the context of the present or future accreditation requirements of the Council on Social Work Education.

- Social work should continue to work for appropriate and broadly based legislation and regulations on health care, transportation, employment, and housing for rural America.

- Social work must develop further expertise in and become more involved in issues related to the ownership and retention of land.

- Moreover, the profession must refine its position vis-à-vis rural development, taking into account social issues and the survival of rural life-styles as well as those of economic growth. Thus, it is incumbent on the profession to have appropriate knowledge of the diverse needs, norms, and values of rural men and women.[71]

SUGGESTED READINGS

Arnow, Harriette Simpson. *The Dollmaker.* Lexington: University Press of Kentucky, 1985.

Caudill, Harry M. *Night Comes to the Cumberlands: A Biography of a Depressed Area.* Boston: Little, Brown and Co., 1963.

Coles, Robert. *Migrants, Share Croppers, Mountaineers: Volume II of Children in Crisis.* Boston: Little, Brown and Co., 1971.

Dillman, Don A. and Hobbs, Daryl J., eds. *Rural Society in the U.S.: Issues for the 1980s.* Boulder, Co.: Westview, 1982.

Ergood, Bruce and Kuhre, Bruce E., eds. *Appalachia: Social Context Past and Present,* 2nd ed. Dubuque, Ia.: Kendall/Hunt, 1983.

Farley, O. William, Griffiths, Kenneth A., Skidmore, Rex A., and Thackeray, Milton
  G. *Rural Social Work Practice.* New York: Free Press, 1982.
Gaventa, John. *Power and Powerlessness: Quiescence and Rebellion in the Appalachian Valley.*
  Urbana: University of Illinois Press, 1980.
Ginsberg, Leon H., ed. *Social Work in Rural Communities.* New York: Council on Social
  Work Education, 1976.
Johnson, H. Wayne. *Rural Human Services.* Itasca, Ill.: F.E. Peacock, 1980.
Kahn, Kathy. *Hillbilly Women.* Garden City, N.Y.: Doubleday, 1973.
Looff, David H. *Appalachia's Children: The Challenge of Mental Health.* Lexington: Uni-
  versity Press of Kentucky, 1971.
Martinez–Brawley, Emilia E. "Rural Social Work" in Anne Minahan, ed., *Encyclopedia
  of Social Work,* 18th ed. Silver Spring, Md.: National Association of Social Workers,
  1987, Vol. 2, pp. 521–537.
Martinez–Brawley, Emilia E. *Seven Decades of Rural Social Work.* New York: Praeger,
  1980.
Moon, William Least Heat. *Blue Highways: A Journey Into America.* New York: Fawcett
  Crest, 1982.
Philliber, William W., McCoy, Clyde B., and Dillingham, Harry C., eds. *The Invisible
  Minority: Urban Appalachians.* Lexington: University Press of Kentucky, 1981.
Rodefeld, Richard D., Flora, Jan, Voth, Donald, Fujimoto, Isao, and Converse, Jim,
  eds. *Change in Rural America: Causes, Consequences, and Alternatives.* St. Louis: C.V.
  Mosby, 1978.
Turner, William H., and Cabbell, Edward J., eds. *Blacks in Appalachia.* Lexington: Uni-
  versity Press of Kentucky, 1985.
Waltman, Gretchen H., "Main Street Revisited: Social Work Practice in Rural Areas."
  Social Casework 66, October, 1986:446–474.
Watkins, Julie M., and Watkins, Dennis A. *Social Policy and the Rural Setting.* New
  York: Springer, 1984.
Whisnant, David E. *Modernizing the Mountaineer.* Boone, N.C.: Appalachian Consor-
  tium Press, 1980.

ENDNOTES

1. Copyright © 1985, National Association of Social Workers, Inc. Reprinted with
   permission from *Compilation of Public Social Policy Statements.*
2. Pamela S. Landon and Marvin D. Feit, "Is Your Rural the Same as My Rural? A
   Framework for Individualizing the Rural Community." (Paper presented at the
   Eighth Annual National Institute on Social Work in Rural Areas, Cheney, Washington, July 25, 1983, p. 3).
3. *Compilation of Public Social Policy Statements,* p. 182.
4. U.S. Bureau of the Census, *Statistical Abstracts of the U.S., 1987* (107th edition)
   Washington, D.C., pp. 3–4.
5. Richard A. DuBord, "The Rural Minority in an Urban Society: Content for Social
   Work Education," University of Utah. Unpublished Paper, 1979, p. 9, cited in O.
   William Farley, Kenneth A. Griffiths, Rex A. Skidmore, and Milton G. Thackeray,
   Rural Social Work Practice. (New York: Free Press, 1982), pp. 6–7.
6. Gretchen H. Waltman, "Main Street Revisited: Social Work Practice in Rural
   Areas," *Social Casework* 66 (October 1986): p. 467.
7. Diana M. Meystedt, "Religion and the Rural Population: Implications for Social
   Work," *Social Casework* 64 (April 1984): 219–226.
8. Richard D. Rodefeld, "Who Will Own and Operate America's Farms?" in Don A.
   Dillman and Daryl J. Hobbs, eds., *Rural Society in the U.S.: Issues for the 1980s*
   (Boulder, Col.: Westview, 1978), p. 328.

9. Judith A. Davenport and Joseph Davenport, III, eds., *Boom Towns and Human Services* (Laramie, Wyo.: University of Wyoming, 1979); Joseph Davenport, III, and Judith A. Davenport, eds., *The Boom Town: Problems and Promises in the Energy Vortex* (Laramie: University of Wyoming, 1980); and Julie M. Uhlmann and Judith K. Olson, *Planning for Rural Human Services: The Western Energy–Impact Experience* (Laramie: Human Services Consulting Associates, 1983).
10. *Statistical Abstracts, 1987*, p. 22.
11. Emilia Martinez–Brawley, "Rural Social Work," in Anne Minahan, ed., *Encyclopedia of Social Work*, 18th ed. (Silver Spring, Md.: National Association of Social Workers, 1987), Vol. 2, p. 523.
12. Ibid.
13. Raymond T. Coward and William M. Smith, Jr., "Families in Rural Society," in Dillman and Hobbs, *Rural Society in the U.S.*, pp. 77–78.
14. Meystedt, "Religion and the Rural Population," pp. 219–220.
15. Norval D. Glenn and Lester Hill, Jr., "Rural–Urban Differences in Attitudes and Behavior in the United States," in Richard D. Rodefeld, Jan Flora, Donald Voth, Isao Fujimoto, and Jim Converse, eds., *Change in Rural America: Causes, Consequences, and Alternatives* (St. Louis: C.V. Mosby, 1978), p. 356.
16. Clarke Chambers, "Myths of Rural America," in H. Wayne Johnson, ed., *Rural Human Services: A Book of Readings* (Itasca, Ill. F.E. Peacock, 1980), p. 173.
17. Alice H. Collins and Diane L. Pancoast, *Natural Helping Networks: A Strategy for Intervention* (Washington, D.C.: National Association of Social Workers, 1976) and James K. Whittaker and James Garbarino, *Social Support Networks: Informal Helping in the Human Services* (New York: Aldine de Gruyter, 1983).
18. DuBord, "Rural Minority in an Urban Society," p. 9.
19. Donald R. Field and Robert M. Dimit, "Population Change in South Dakota Small Towns and Cities, 1949–1960," in Rodefeld, *Change in Rural America*, pp. 309–310.
20. *Statistical Abstracts, 1987*, p. 341.
21. Leona L. Bachrach, "A Sociological Perspective," in L. Ralph Jones and Richard R. Parlour, *Psychiatric Services for Underserved Rural Populations* (New York: Brunner/Mazel, 1985), p. 6.
22. Ibid., p. 10.
23. Judy Strasser, "The Land Is No Escape," in Rodefeld, *Change in Rural America*, pp. 316–321.
24. Farley, *Rural Social Work Practice*, p. 231.
25. Louise C. Johnson, "Human Service Delivery Patterns in Nonmetropolitan Communities," in H. Wayne Johnson, *Rural Human Services*, p. 65.
26. Karen Vice Irey, "The Social Work Generalist In a Rural Context: An Ecological Perspective," *Journal of Education for Social Work* 15 (Fall 1980): 36–42.
27. Waltman, "Main Street Revisited," p. 472 and Emilia E. Martinez–Brawley, "Beyond Cracker-Barrel Images: The Rural Social Work Specialty," *Social Casework* 66 (February 1986): 103–106.
28. Mary E. Richmond, *Social Diagnosis* (New York: Russell Sage Foundation, 1917), p. 5.
29. Bradford W. Sheafor and Pamela S. Landon, "Generalist Perspective," in Anne Minahan, ed., *Encyclopedia of Social Work*, 18th ed. (Silver Spring, Md., National Association of Social Workers, 1987), Vol. 1, p. 664.
30. Mona Struhsaker Schatz and Lowell E. Jenkins, "Social Work in a Generalist Perspective: Undergraduate and Graduate Education." (Unpublished manuscript, Colorado State University, 1987, pp. 18–19.)
31. Ibid., pp. 19–24.
32. Joel Fischer, *Effective Casework Practice: An Eclectic Approach* (New York: McGraw-Hill, 1978), p. 191.
33. Barbara Lou Fenby, "Social Work in a Rural Setting," *Social Work* 23 (March 1978): 162–163.

34. Bradford W. Sheafor, Charles R. Horejsi, and Gloria A. Horejsi, *Techniques and Guidelines for Social Work Practice,* (Boston: Allyn and Bacon, 1988), pp. 199–203.
35. Irey, "The Generalist in the Rural Context," pp. 36–38.
36. Sheafor, Horejsi, and Horejsi, *Techniques and Guidelines,* pp. 472–497.
37. "Why Study Appalachia?" in Bruce Ergood and Bruce E. Kuhre, eds., *Appalachia: Social Context Past and Present,* 2nd ed., Dubuque, Iowa: Kendall/Hunt, 1983), p. 6.
38. "In Appalachia, Proud Faces Mask Troubled Times," *U.S. News and World Report* (September 10, 1984): 75.
39. "Appalachia: The Economic Outlook Through the Eighties," *Appalachia* 17 (November–December 1983): 3.
40. Clyde B. McCoy, and James S. Brown, "Appalachian Migration to Midwestern Cities," in William W. Philliber and Clyde B. McCoy, eds., with Harry C. Dillingham, *The Invisible Minority: Urban Appalachians,* (Lexington, Ky.: The University Press of Kentucky, 1981), pp. 35–39.
41. "The New Appalachian Subregions and their Development Strategies," reprinted with permission from *Appalachia,* Journal of the Appalachian Regional Commission, Vol. 8, No.1 (August–September) 1974, pp. 10–27.
42. Ibid., p. 27.
43. John Gaventa, "Poverty of Abundance Revisited," *Appalachian Journal* 14 (Fall 1987): 27.
44. Appalachian Land Ownership Task Force, "Alliance Releases Land Ownership Study Findings: Land Task Force Urges Community Response," in Ergood and Kuhre, *Appalachia: Social Context Past and Present,* p. 173.
45. Ibid.
46. John Solomon Otto, "Reconsidering the Southern 'Hillbilly': Appalachia and the Ozarks," *Appalachian Journal* 12 (Summer 1985): 329.
47. Gaventa, "Poverty of Abundance Revisited," p. 31.
48. Harry M. Caudill, *Night Comes to the Cumberlands: A Biography of a Depressed Area* (Boston: Little, Brown, 1963), p. 75.
49. Ibid.
50. Gaventa, "Poverty of Abundance Revisited," pp. 24–25.
51. Jerome Pickard, "Appalachian Population Growth Slows," *Appalachia* 18 (September–December 1984): 20.
52. Ibid.
53. Appalachian Regional Commission, "Appalachia: The Economic Outlook Through the Eighties," *Appalachia* 17 (November–December 1983): 5.
54. Wilber Hayden, Jr., "Blacks: An Invisible Institution in Appalachia?" (Paper presented at the Eighth Annual Appalachian Studies Conference, Berea, Kentucky, March 30, 1985), p. 2.
55. Helen Lewis, "Fatalism or the Coal Industry?" in Frank S. Riddel, ed., *Appalachia: Its People, Heritage, and Problems* (Dubuque, Iowa: Kendall/Hunt, 1974), pp. 224–225.
56. Loyal Jones, "Appalachian Values" (Reprinted from *Twigs* magazine, Fall 1973, Vol. X, No. 1, p. 85.)
57. Richard A. Humphrey, "Religion in Appalachia: Implications for Social Work Practice," *Journal of Humanics* 8 (December 1980): 6.
58. Jones (Reprinted from *Twigs* magazine, Fall 1973, Vol. X, No. 1, p. 83.)
59. Humphrey, "Religion in Appalachia," p. 4.
60. Jones (Reprinted from *Twigs* magazine, Fall 1973, Vol. X, No. 1, p. 93.)
61. Southern Regional Education Board, Manpower Education and Training Project Rural Task Force, "Educational Assumptions for Rural Social Work," in Leon H. Ginsberg, ed., *Social Work in Rural Communities* (New York: Council on Social Work Education, 1976), p. 41.
62. Caudill, *Night Comes to the Cumberlands,* pp. 279–281.

63. Roger M. Nooe, "A Clinical Model for Rural Practice," in Ronald K. Green and Stephen A. Webster, eds., *Social Work in Rural Areas: Preparation and Practice* (Knoxville: University of Tennessee School of Social Work, 1977), p. 355.

64. Alfred Kadushin, *The Social Work Interview* (New York: Columbia University Press, 1983), pp. 303–304.

65. John Fetterman, *Stinking Creek* (New York: E.P. Dutton, 1967), p. 33.

66. Humphrey, "Religion in Appalachia," p. 16.

67. Ibid, p. 17.

68. Jack E. Weller, *Yesterday's People* (Lexington: The University Press of Kentucky, 1965), p. 59.

69. Martinez–Brawley, "Beyond Cracker-Barrel Images," pp. 101–107.

70. Copyright © 1987, National Association of Social Workers, Inc. Reprinted with permission from *The Social Work Dictionary* ed. by Robert L. Barker, p. 142.

71. *Compilation of Public Social Policy Statements*, pp. 186–187.

CHAPTER 16

Urban Gang Violence: A Psychosocial Crisis

Armando Morales

PREFATORY COMMENT

The philosophical spirit of this textbook (originally published in 1977) is to provide readers timely, relevant, scholarly material not only to reflect social work's past and current status concerning particular problem areas, but also to shed light on new *problem areas requiring the profession's attention. To maintain this spirit, the authors decided to include a chapter dealing with an urban psychosocial crisis that is resulting in the premature death of thousands of adolescent and young adults across the nation as the result of gang homicide.*

Violent urban gangs, therefore, are in social work's practice environment contributing to social disorganization and dysfunction. Youth gangs and their violent behavior are a symptom of the community telling the world that their needs are not being met by the family, neighborhood, and various social institutions and *the social work profession. These youths have the same rights to service as other clients. In addition to highlighting epidemiological data about homicide in general as well as it involves gangs, social work intervention strategies are suggested for work with individual gang members, families, gang groups, and the community.*

The Editor-in-Chief of *Social Work* maintains that violence in the United States has become one of the most pervasive issues of our time and that U.S. ambivalence on violence is historic.[1] The profession of social work increasingly in recent years has been focusing on some aspects of the violence problem, primarily in domestic violence (family, spousal, and child abuse) and suicide. The most recent issue of the *Encyclopedia of Social Work*, for example, devotes entire chapters to these topics.[2]

Including all ages suicide is the tenth leading cause of death in the United States and is viewed as a public health concern. Because of its person-in-situation perspective and the presence from time to time of suicidal clients in mental health and social service agencies, the profession of social work has also adopted this high-risk population as one of its practice tasks.

A comparable leading cause of death in the United States is homicide, which historically has been a matter of concern for law enforcement, criminologists, sociologists, and more recently, the health profession. *Homicide* is defined as death due to injuries purposefully inflicted by another person or persons, not including deaths caused by law enforcement officers or legal execution by the federal or state government. Aside from occasional, brief epidemiological (incidence and prevalence rates) data related to forensic populations, suicide, or domestic violence, this subject is by and large ignored in the social work literature. As is the case with suicide clientele many social workers deal daily with people suffering the effects of social, psychological, economic, and political oppression and dehumanization, who eventually become homicide perpetrators or victims. June Gary Hopps argues that social workers are in the best position to articulate the relationship of micro to macro psychosocial forces to violence and contribute recommendations for positive change. Offering a challenge to social work, Hopps asks: "If we in the social work profession don't, who will?"[4] This chapter will attempt to provide an in-depth look at one dimension of the problem, specifically, urban youth gang violence and homicide.

During the Great Depression in the late 1920s and 1930s in urban areas such as Chicago, social workers armed with social group work skills were deployed from settlement houses to work directly with youth gangs. Social workers also made their presence known as gang group workers in Los Angeles following massive violent confrontations between U.S. servicemen and Hispanic gang youths in the early 1940s. These intergroup conflict situations were called the "Zoot Suit Riots." Working with gangs in various parts of the country continued to be an area of practice interest for social work in the 1950s and into the 1960s with the federally funded Office of Economic Opportunity teen post programs. In those early days, noted Gertrude Wilson, social work was painfully aware of the deprivation of people and never lost sight of the fact that institutional change was a prerequisite to the actual relief of suffering.[5]

Since the 1960s there has been a growing public apathy toward the poor in the United States, particularly the immense needs of inner city youth. Group work, anchored in social work's longstanding values of social reform and concern for oppressed people dwindled as a practice interest increasingly replaced by a shift to the clinical, intrapsychic functioning of individuals and families.[6] Jerry R. Fox points out that the quality of life in U.S. cities has continued to decline and that social workers have paid little attention to the urban youth gang, symptomatic about what is feared most concerning the consequences of human and environmental neglect.[7] Fox's 1985 social work article dealing with urban youth gangs is only the second article to date appearing in a social work journal since June 1984, perhaps confirming that gangs are no longer a social work practice interest.[8] The "gang" label has a negative connotation and has been applied to what is generally considered a unique lower-class phenomenon. Rarely are middle-class adolescent groups referred to as gangs, irrespective of the similarity of their criminal behavior to their lower-economic-class counterparts. For example, the white, middle-class youths involved in the killing of a black in 1986 at Howard Beach in New York were not referred to as a "gang." The author therefore, proposes the following definition:[9]

A *gang* is a peer group of persons in a lower, middle, or upper-class community who participate in activities that are either harmful to themselves and/or others in society.

Urban gangs are viewed as a growing health and mental health crisis; their anti-social behavior is resulting in thousands of homicides and assaults each year and their involvement with drugs, both as consumers as well as dealers, is causing untold human destruction in central city communities, particularly as it concerns poor families. Last year at a public hearing conducted by the California State Task Force on Youth Gang Violence, a victimized parent who lost two sons stated:[10]

> When I lost my second son I was depressed and in shock. I couldn't believe that this happened to me, not twice. After this, I thought I was the only mother who had lost two sons. Since then, I have met other mothers who have lost a couple of sons to gang violence.

Gangs are not a unique U.S. phenomenon, as most countries have gangs. In Japan they are called "Mambos," in Germany, "Halbstarke," in Italy, "Vitelloni," in South Africa, "Tsotsio," in France, "Blousons Noir," and in England, "Teddys."[11]

The History of Gangs

There is no doubt that gangs have been with us since the beginning of civilization, but the concept of gangs was first reported in the literature by a former gang member, St. Augustine (A.D. 354–430), over 1600 years ago. His father was described as a pagan who lived a "loose life" and his mother, whom he loved greatly, was a pious Christian who had difficulty controlling St. Augustine during his adolescent years. In his book *Confessions*, he demonstrates an astute understanding of the psychology of adolescent gangs with his discovery that committing a crime in the company of others further enhances the gratifications derived from it. Through his autobiographical psychoanalytical method, he discovers that actions are determined by more than a single motive, stating:[12]

> I loved then in it also the company of the accomplices with whom I did it . . . for had I then loved the pears I stole and wished to enjoy them I might have done it alone, had the bare commission of the theft sufficed to attain my pleasure; nor needed I have inflamed the itching of my desires by the excitement of accomplices. But since my pleasure was not in those pears, it was in the offense itself, which the company of fellow-sinners occasioned.

The first youth gangs in the United States made their appearance in the national turf-oriented atmosphere of "manifest destiny" (the rationale justifying the forceful take-over of the Mexican-owned great Southwest) in the mid-1800s. These gangs did much more than steal pears from neighbors and were first seen in Philadelphia in the 1840s. They evolved from volunteer fire companies. Volunteer fire companies provided status and recognition to young, white, lower-class adult males who were competitive with other companies in trying to be first in extinguishing a fire. The intense competition at times developed into physical conflict and even killing when a company extinguished a fire in the rival company's "turf." The tough firemen—the Super Bowl heroes of that era—were the idols of neighborhood adolescents who looked upon them with awe. These "groupies," who likewise identified with the company's turf, also engaged in physical fights with rival fire company youth groups. These early gangs had names such as the "Rats," the "Bouncers," and the "Skinners." With graffiti they defaced walls, fences, and buildings, similar to what gangs do today in urban areas. The Philadelphia *Public Ledger* on August 13, 1846, described them as being "armed to the teeth with slug shots, pistols, and knives." The biggest provocation to violence was the intrusion of rival gangs into their turf.[13]

During this pre–Civil War period, intense conflict was also seen in New York among white adolescent and young adult gangs forcibly attempting to establish dominance over a particular neighborhood. Herbert Asbury writes in *The Gangs of New York*:[14]

> The greatest gang conflicts of the early nineteenth century were fought by these groups (the Bowery Boys and the Dead Rabbits) . . . sometimes the battles raged for two or three days without cessation, while the streets of the gang area were barricaded with carts and paving stones, and the gangsters blazed away at each other with musket and pistol, or engaged in close work with knives, brickbats, bludgeons, teeth, and fists.

Police were reluctant to and did not intervene during this gang conflict, which at times lasted two or three days. Gangs comprised of latency age children, eight to twelve years of age such as the "Little Plug Uglies" or the "Little Daybreak Boys," were almost as ferocious as the older gang members whose name they adopted and crimes they tried hard to imitate. Such intense, prolonged conflict is not seen today among gangs. Rather, one of the most frequent violent gang crimes committed today is the "drive-by" shooting made possible by automobiles. A gang will seek out a home, vehicles, or "hangouts" of a rival gang and, using an assortment of weapons, including automatics, drive by and shoot randomly. As in the nineteenth century, there are instances in which innocent people are accidentally wounded and/or killed. Police officer Julio Perrera, of Fresno, California, commenting on citizens being victimized by gangs, stated:[15]

> We had a recent murder where an innocent woman and her 3-year-old were killed during a drug deal. The juveniles that pulled the trigger will do time in the Youth Authority until they're 25 years old, then they'll be back on the streets again.

It would be difficult to document whether the nineteenth century gangs were more lethal than contemporary urban gangs as homicide statistics were not uniformly recorded at that time.

The Prevalence of Gangs

It is possible, however, to compare the volume of gangs in the early 1900s with the volume of gangs in some cities today. The most comprehensive study of gangs was undertaken by Frederick M. Thrasher in Chicago between 1919 and 1927. In his book *The Gang: A Study of 1,313 Gangs in Chicago*, he found that the 1313 gangs comprised various ethnic and racial groups, which included Polish, Italian, Irish, Anglo-American, Jewish, Slavic, Bohemian, German, Swedish, Lithuanian, Chinese, black, and Mexican youths. Three hundred and fifty-one of these gangs contained "mixed nationalities" but the other 962 gangs comprised a single ethnic or racial group. The Polish, numbering 16.4 percent of the population, had the most gangs, 148, followed by the Italian, 99, Irish, 75, and black, 63. Membership in gangs and conflict between gangs was related more to turf rather than to racial or nationality factors. A "fair-minded," thirteen-year-old Lithuanian gang leader once remarked:[16]

> I never ask what nationality he is. A Jew or nigger can be a pal of mine if he's a good fellow.

It is interesting to note that by and large, the *white* ethnics described above have faced fewer barriers in the road to assimilation when compared to the Asians, blacks, and Hispanics, who still have gangs in Chicago sixty-nine years later.

As far as can be determined, to date there has not been a solid, data-based gathering of information comparable to Thrasher's classic work, as to the numbers of gangs currently in large cities. It is generally agreed that the County of Los Angeles has the most youth gangs in the nation, with estimates ranging from 300 gangs with 30,000 members to 500 gangs, with 50,000 members.[17] Even the larger figures fall significantly short of Chicago's 1313 gangs in the 1920s. In that period Chicago had approximately 65 gangs per 100,000 population compared to 7 gangs per 100,000 for Los Angeles in 1987. In other words Chicago had a ratio of gangs per population nine times greater than Los Angeles! In Los Angeles, where minorities represent 54 percent of the population, with Hispanics being the largest minority group, at 2.4 million, two-thirds of all gangs are composed of Hispanics, followed by blacks, non-Hispanic whites, and Asians.

Theories of Gangs

Five theoretical perspectives concerning gangs will be examined. The first theory is similar to Frederick Thrasher's classic description of gangs in the 1920s in which gangs are seen as a natural progression from, and the consequence of, a youth's search for excitement in a frustrating and limiting environment. They are usually a result of a general breakdown of social controls, and characterized by persons with few social ties, such as immigrants, the mentally ill, and the destitute, and a corresponding lack of parental control over the young.[18]

A second causal factor has been proposed by anthropologist Walter Miller who studied lower-class gangs in Boston. He describes gang members as males who usually were reared in a female-dominated household and consequently, in adolescence, the gang, he says, "provided the first real opportunity to learn essential aspects of the male role in the context of peers facing similar problems of sex role identification."[19] This theory does not account for the fact that even though 68 percent of black and 67 percent of Hispanic poor families were headed by a woman, according to a 1983 U.S. Commission on Civil Rights report, approximately 95 percent of the youths were *not* gang members or delinquents.[20]

A third perspective is suggested by social scientists such as Albert Cohen, Richard Cloward, and Lloyd Ohlin. They maintain that the gang is the collective solution of young, lower-class males placed in a situation of stress, where opportunities for the attainment of wealth and/or status through legitimate channels are blocked. In response the gang develops a subculture or "contra-culture." The gang, therefore, must be explained in terms of social conditions in which lower-class youths are placed by the dominant society.[21] This would account for the continued existence of minority group gangs in Chicago since 1918 and the general absence of white ethnic gangs. In other words minority youth are far more likely to be "blocked out" from having equal access to resources in society. However, this theory does not explain the growing number of white, middle-class gangs in some parts of the country, which will be discussed later.

A fourth perspective is advanced by David Matza who challenges the "blocked out" subculture theory, stating that it explains too much delinquency. He believes that gangs exist because adolescents are in a state of suspension between childhood and adulthood; hence, they spend most of their time with peers and are anxious about both their identity as males and their acceptance by the peer group (gang). They conform to the norms of the gang because not to do so would threaten their status.[22] This theory is limited in explaining the continued involvement of some adult and middle-aged *veterano* (veteran) gang members found in some Hispanic *barrios*, who are responsible family providers, yet occasionally participate in some gang activities.

All the above theories have merit and are applicable in many instances as gangs are very complex and cannot be explained by one theory. The author proposes a fifth theoretical perspective concerning the family. In a study of East Los Angeles Hispanic gang and non-gang probation juvenile camp graduates, the author found that gang members, significantly more often than non-gang members, came from families exhibiting more family breakdown, greater poverty, poorer housing, more alcoholism, drug addiction, and major chronic illness, and more family members involved with law enforcement and correctional agencies.[23] In the face of these overwhelming problems, the youngster turns to the gang as a *surrogate family*. Here, the gang member receives affection, understanding, recognition, loyalty, and emotional and physical protection. In this respect the gang is psychologically adaptive rather than maladaptive. It would not appear to be a coincidence that one of the largest Hispanic gangs in California is called "Nuestra Familia (Our Family)." Hispanic gang members call themselves "homeboys" or "homegirls," again labels consistent with a family and home orientation. Black gang members often refer to themselves as "brothers" or "sisters." Indeed, close friends *can* be good medicine. Many gang members will often die or kill rival gang members for their gang or turf in the neighborhood. When this occurs, membership then becomes maladaptive. Adding to this powerful group cohesion of Hispanic gangs that have existed in Chicago, El Paso, and East Los Angeles *barrios* for almost seventy years—as have those socioeconomic conditions that produced them—is the reinforcement of the gang culture and tradition by older brothers, uncles, fathers, and even grandfathers.[24] One also finds increasing evidence of Hispanic female gangs, estimated at 10 percent (about twenty to thirty gangs) in Los Angeles. This is significantly more than the five female gangs Thrasher found in his 1313 gangs. White middle-class family breakdown may also be one of the factors accounting for an increase in non-Hispanic white adolescent gangs.

Types of Gangs

Youth gangs can be analyzed from the standpoint of their primary function, orientation or activity, organizational structure, age, ethnicity, race, and sex. Most social scientists investigating gangs today would agree that there are at least three types of gangs: the *criminal*, the *conflict*, and the *retreatist gang*. The author suggests that a fourth type of gang is emerging in recent years, which could be called the *cult/occult gang*.

The *criminal gang* has as its primary goal material gain through criminal activities. Material success is obtained through the theft of property from premises or persons, extortion, fencing, and obtaining and selling illegal substances such as drugs. In the 1920s Thrasher discovered that some of the wealthiest youth gangs—which he called "beer gangs"—were involved in the illegal liquor business during Prohibition.[25] Today gangs are making their money in drugs.

At an NAACP-sponsored conference on gang problems in Los Angeles in 1987 authorities reported that black street gangs controlled at least one hundred "rock houses" (rock cocaine) and that thousands of gang members were eager to cash in on a nationwide cocaine epidemic. According to police gang members were now selling rock cocaine in Phoenix, Arizona, Portland, Oregon, Denver, Colorado, Las Vegas, Nevada, and Shreveport, Louisiana. Gwen Cordova, a community person, commented:[26]

When a kid can make $3,000 a week selling drugs, why would he take a job at McDonald's for $3.50 an hour? In a capitalistic society they're taught to go after the best deal, and unfortunately, they do.

The majority of criminal gangs in Los Angeles are black, and as Raymond Johnson of the NAACP warned:[27]

The Black gangs at this point in time are more organized and they are making the money. Eventually, the other gangs (Hispanic and Asian) are going to learn the technique and they will be doing the same thing.

Asian gangs are similar to other racial/ethnic gangs, as they grew out of a need to protect their communities. However, according to authorities, contemporary Asian gangs are more the criminal type, as they are more concerned with generating profits from illegal activities (extortion, gambling, prostitution) within their communities rather than protecting their territory, or "turf." The newest Asian gangs are composed of Korean and Vietnamese youth.[28]

The *conflict gang* is very turf-oriented and will engage in violent battle with individuals or rival groups that invade their neighborhood, or commit acts that they consider insulting or degrading. Respect is highly valued and defended. Hispanic gangs, in most cities, are highly represented among conflict gangs. Their mores, values, rituals, and codes are highly consistent in various neighborhoods and cities throughout the nation and have existed in some areas for almost seventy years. As Father Terrance A. Sweeney learned in his work with conflict gangs:[29]

The Code of the *Barrio* means watching out for your neighborhood. This entails protecting your homeboys (and family) and the area designated as your 'neighborhood.' The Code demands absolute loyalty; every gang member must be willing to die for his *neighborhood* (homeboys and turf)."

Of the 300 to 500 gangs in Los Angeles, approximately two-thirds are Hispanic (200 to 332 gangs) and most of these are conflict-type gangs. Currently, in Chicago, where Irving A. Spergel identified fifty-five conflict gangs, thirty-three were Hispanic, fifteen were black, and seven were non-Hispanic white.[30]

The predominant feature of the *retreatist gang* is in the pursuit of getting "loaded" or "high" on alcohol, marijuana, heroin, acid, cocaine, or other drug substances. Retreatism is seen by Cloward and Ohlin as an isolated adaptation, characterized by a breakdown in relationships with other persons. The drug user has a need to become affiliated with other retreatist users to secure access to a steady supply of drugs.[31] What distinguishes the criminal gang involved in drugs from the retreatist gang is that the former is primarily involved with drugs for financial profit. The retreatist gangs' involvement with drugs is primarily for consumption.

The fourth type of adolescent delinquent group is the *cult/occult gang*.[32] "Cult" pertains to a system of worshiping the Devil or evil. "Occult" means keeping something hidden or secret, or a belief in mysterious or supernatural powers. Not all cult-occultic Devil or evil worship groups are involved in criminal activity or ritualistic crime. The Ku Klux Klan, for example, may be seen as a cult group and in some chapters, in spite of their hate rhetoric, are law abiding, whereas other chapters have committed criminal acts. The Charles Manson Family is perhaps one of the better known cult-occultic criminal groups. Some of the occultic groups place a great deal of emphasis on sexuality and violence, believing that by sexually violating a virgin or innocent child, they have defiled Christianity. One occultic group called "OTO" (Ordo Templi Orientis) had eleven members convicted of felony child abuse in Riverside County in California.[33]

The majority of occultic groups, whether criminal or law abiding, are composed of adults. However, some juvenile groups are becoming interested in some of these satanic and black magic practices, and are using them for their own gratification of sadistic, sexual, and antisocial behavior. Their knowledge and application of rigid, ritualistic occultic practices, however, is often haphazard. Los Angeles has perhaps the largest number of these adolescent cult/occultic-type gangs, numbering about thirty-two gangs.[34] These gangs are composed predominantly of white, non-Hispanic middle-class youths and a few middle-class Hispanics. They are not turf-oriented like conflict gangs, but are found in several middle-class locations. These gangs call themselves "Stoners," such as the "Alhambra Stoners," or the "Whittier Stoners." Stoners from one location are allied with Stoners of other locations. They originally named themselves after the "Rolling Stones," and valued "getting stoned."

Their philosophy is based on "Do what you will. The end is soon; live for today." "Heavy Metal" music is very popular with Stoners and among their heroes are Aleister Crowley, leading occultist in the United States in the early 1900s, who advocated violation of every moral law from sexual perversion to homicide, as well as Adolf Hitler and Charles Manson. Some of the self-destructive activities in which Stoners participate, in addition to substance abuse, include sadism and masochism, and suicide. Their antisocial crimes are violence for violence's sake, ritual rape, ritual child abuse, and ritual homicide. Some examples of the graffiti of these groups are "666" (Biblical sign of the beast), "KKK," "FTW" (Fuck the World), and "SWP" (Supreme White People). Law enforcement officials are becoming more concerned about the growth of white middle-class Stoner-type gangs. The author suggests that these cult-occult gangs are a symptom of psychologically deteriorating middle-class Anglo white families. Economic pressures often force both parents to spend many hours working and away from their children. In treating Stoners coming out of juvenile correctional institutions, the author has observed some of them to be quite emotionally disturbed, having been raised in families that physically abused them as children, or having had a parent or sibling with severe mental illness.

Age Levels

The age levels of gang members are fairly consistent among the four types of gangs and seem to be related to maturational and natural developmental stages of growth. Thrasher in the 1920s described four general "gang-age types" as follows:[35]

"Gang child"	6–12 years (child)
"Gang boy"	11–17 (early adolescent)
"Gang boy"	15–25 (later adolescent)
"Gang man"	21–50 (adult)

In contemporary conflict and criminal gangs, a similar natural age-group phenomena may be observed, however, with more specific age categories required by the gang. Small gangs may range in size from ten to twenty members, but in larger gangs with 200–300 members, the age categories are more obvious as follows:[36]

"Pee Wees"	8–12 years
"Tinys"	12–14 years
"Dukes"	14–16 years
"Cutdowns"	16–18 years (or major name of the gang)
"Veteranos"	18–20 years
"Locos"	mixed ages (the "crazies")

Girls' gangs will adopt similar age categories and gang names. For example the "Cloverettes" will be from "Clover," where the "Clover Street" gang is found. Female adolescent gangs either assume a subordinate, supportive role to male gangs or will be completely independent from the male gangs and, for defensive purposes, even engage in violent confrontations with male gang members from their own neighborhood. Female gang members have been known to murder male gang members and rival female gang members.

The age levels of retreatist and cult/occult-type gangs are less formal and female participation is minimal. The cult/occult gang age categories are more consistent with school grade levels, such as fifth and sixth grade, junior high, and high school. Older adolescent and young adult members, predominantly male, are often found in juvenile and adult correctional facilities.

Homicide as a Health–Mental Health Concern

In 1984 the Secretary of Health and Human Services issued an annual report in which it was noted that the health and longevity of the U.S. population have continued to improve but the prospect for living a healthy and full life was not shared equally by many minorities; for example, there is a gap of more than five years in life expectancy between blacks and whites. The Secretary called attention to the historical and persistent burden of disability, disease, and death experienced by minorities. One specific health area in which minorities had "excess deaths" was homicide.[37] Homicide as a health issue is the eleventh leading cause of death (suicide is tenth) for all ages and races combined. According to a 1986 report of the Secretary's Task Force on Black and Minority Health, homicides in 1983 accounted for more than 19,000 deaths per year in the United States, a rate of eight homicides per 100,000 population. This is seven to eight times higher than any other industrialized European nation.[38]

The health professions are in the trenches when it comes to homicide and persons injured by the violent behavior of others. In addition to the unmeasurable emotional costs suffered by victims and survivors, the health costs of violence now amount to over 7 percent of national health care expenditures. Additionally, financial costs such as property damage, insurance payments, and in foregone earnings, results in 2.3 percent of the Gross National Product.[39] At one hospital, "one month's worth" of violence-related injuries, that is, inpatient medical care for nine randomly selected victims (three gunshot victims, three stabbing victims, three assault victims) cost $655,595. A yearly projected cost would be $7.9 million at one hospital.[40]

Etiology of Homicide

The United States has the highest rate of homicide of any developed country in the world, with blacks, Hispanics, and Native Americans generally having even higher rates than the already high national average.[41] Excluding minorities from these homicide rates would not alter this nation's negative distinction. It is *not* that United States citizens are naturally born more violent than persons in other countries; rather, U.S. citizens are being raised in a social and cultural environment that encourages and conditions people to be more violent.[42] There is not *one* single factor as a cause of violence and homicide; instead, this complex, biopsychosocial problem can be seen as having several independent and interrelated causes, ranging from micro (individual) to macro (societal) etiological factors. These factors can be arranged from micro to macro level causes into three major categories: (1) biological causes; (2) developmental–psychological causes; and (3) sociocultural environmental causes.

Biological Causes A significant amount of controversy exists in attempting to link biological factors to violence. At best it can be said that *some* biological factors such as genetic conditions, hormonal imbalance, brain disease, and brain chemistry dysfunction may predispose *some* individuals toward violence under a certain set of circumstances. One cannot predict who will be violent with any high degree of accuracy but only that given certain biological predisposition factors, the *potential* for violence exists.[43]

A growing body of brain chemistry research with animals and humans has been able to demonstrate that pharmacologic modulation of neurotransmitter systems and electrical stimulation of regions of the brain produces marked alterations in aggressive and violent behavior. Such treatment has been found to be successful in the treatment of some institutionalized psychiatric patients and forensic prisoners.[44] It is reported that even the most adamant proponents of the biological perspective maintain that social factors are by far the most significant determinants of violent behavior.[45]

Chemicals such as food additives, environmental pollutants, toxic metals, and vitamin deficiencies or imbalances have been known to trigger violent behavior or aggravate pre-existing tendencies toward violence in *some* people. Poor nutrition and/or substance abuse by a mother during pregnancy can negatively affect the fetus, causing low birth weight, premature birth, mental retardation, or abnormal brain development, conditions that are related to an increased probability of violent behavior by the parent or child. Depressant drugs, such as barbiturates and alcohol, are highly conducive to violence. Alcohol use is associated with up to two-thirds of all violent situations. Drugs and violence often depend upon the interaction of factors such as the type of drug substance and dosage, the personality of the user, user expectations of the drug experience, and the environmental situational context.[46]

The major physiological factor related to homicide concerns age and gender. Almost 90 percent of homicide victims are males, mostly killed by other males. The majority of homicide victims and perpetrators are older juveniles, young adults, and adults up to 35 years of age.[47]

Psychological/Developmental Causes In theory, a positive birth experience characterized by a gentle, loving and nontraumatic experience in every respect, increases the likelihood of healthy, emotional, cognitive, and behavioral child development and hence, a nonviolent person. However, there is no *direct* link known to exist between the birth experience and violent behavior.[48] The quality of parenting, early childhood development, and experience may determine the nature of subsequent social relations. Many juvenile and adult violent criminal offenders had a history of childhood physical abuse (including corporal punishment) and neglect by their parents. These factors can lead to poor self-esteem, a negative or criminal self-image and feelings of distrust, frustration, and powerlessness—feelings not uncommon among violent offenders.[49]

Unlike other health problems homicide is the outcome of psychological thinking processes that result in conscious efforts to cause harm to another person. Although there are many psychological and psychiatric theories to explain violence and homicide, there is broad agreement, according to the Secretary's Task Force on Black and Minority Health, that persons who commit homicide and other violent crimes fall into a number of modal groups as follows:[50]

1. Normal, socialized persons exposed to extremely provocative or frustrating situations or circumstances, at times coupled with inhibition-lowering drugs or alcohol.

2. Persons committed to a violent life style with supporting attitudes and values.

3. Persons whose inhibitions against violence are impaired by functional (e.g., paranoia) or organic pathology (e.g., abnormal brain chemistry).

4. Overcontrolled persons whose violence stems from excessive, inflexible inhibitions against the expression of normal aggressive behavior.

5. Persons who are highly prone toward aggression or anger resulting from frustration, revenge, jealousy, and oppression.

6. Persons who engage in violence as a means to achieving goals other than injuring the victim, such as robbers.

Sociocultural Environmental Causes In analyzing the causes of citizen violence and homicide in the world's most violent nation, the social, cultural, and environmental context and values structure in which it occurs must be examined. A nation founded on violence and preoccupied with power and past and present oppression of Native Americans and other minorities, women, and the poor—respectively consistent with the values of institutional racism, sexism, and class discrimination—occurring within the powerfully violent modeling context of wars, the advocacy and practice of capital punishment, and an obsession with the possession and use of firearms, all contribute to the creation of a violent citizenry. There is evidence of an association between war and individual violence as a society at war is teaching its members that such behavior is acceptable under certain circumstances. Warring nations are more likely to experience increases in homicide rates than nations not involved in war. The nation's homicide rate more than doubled (4.5 per 100,000 in 1963 to 9.3 in 1973) during the Vietnam War years. Researchers found the fact of war as the most plausible explanation and the most influential variable in the causal equation.[51] Vietnam veterans, especially combat veterans, are more likely than non-veterans to be violence-prone and evidence more social, psychological, and substance abuse problems than non-veterans.[52]

Like war, capital punishment may have a negative effect upon the public. One study concluded that publicized executions by the state, instead of deterring further violence, may incite imitative execution-like behavior in society.[53]

Of the homicides committed in the country, about three-fourths involve handguns. Whereas some industrialized nations permit their citizens to possess shotguns, rifles, and other hunting weapons, only the United States allows its citizens relatively unlimited access to and ownership of guns. The U.S. gun homicide rate is on an average fifty times higher than England, Germany, and Japan! It is estimated that the number of firearms in private hands nationwide is 120 million. A firearm kept in the home is six times more likely to be used against a family member, accidentally or otherwise, than against an intruder.[54]

The U.S. media also plays a significant role in modeling and influencing young minds. Children spend more time watching television than any other single activity and by the age of 18, the average person has witnessed over

18,000 homicides on television. Sixty percent of prime-time TV programs contain violent solutions to conflict situations, with cartoons being among the most violent programs. Research findings do not support the notion that television violence has a cathartic effect on the viewer. In fact children who watch TV violence are much less likely than those who do not, to stop other children from hurting one another.[55]

The ultimate sexist act by a male is the homicide of a female during a rape. One of every ten female homicide victims in the United States is killed during a rape or other sexual attack. Rape victims claim that the fear of being killed is a major reason for submitting to rape. As with other violent crimes rape victims are more likely to be assaulted by a member of their own ethnic or racial group, and like their victims, the perpetrators are mainly from the younger age groups, with up to 70 percent being under twenty years of age. The high volume of rape in the United States results from sociocultural roots as well as individual psychological factors. Experts believe the existence of rape is associated with sexist culturally sanctioned and institutionalized values, attitudes, and sex-role norms.[56]

Contributing the most to the high rates of homicide and violence are the social factors pertaining to low socioeconomic status and institutional racism. *Institutional racism* may be defined as institutional behavior on a conscious, unconscious, or pre-conscious level that treats members of different ethnic and racial groups inequitably and differently from the majority.[57] High black homicide rates often have focused on greater poverty in the black population as the most important contributing factor. When socioeconomic status is taken into account, racial differences in homicide rates disappear and are not significant. Poverty, therefore, unequivocally increases the risk of homicide.[58]

High minority group homicides can also be attributed to the psychological scars caused by racism, particularly among the poor. The psychological harm expresses itself in feelings of low self-esteem, self-hatred, and rage, that at times transforms itself to violence against others.[59]

In further analyzing the relationship between institutional racism and economic factors, of the total work force, over twice as many blacks (13 percent) are unemployed compared to non-Hispanic white males (6 percent), with Hispanics at 8 percent. Blacks as a group, in addition to being twice as likely to be unemployed, are more than three times as likely to be living below the poverty level. Rates of homicide and violent behavior are highest among young black, poverty-stricken males who live in urban ghettos and are unemployed, untrained, and subjected to racism, hence, hindered from achieving success.[60]

Federal data revealed that black and Hispanic males in addition to experiencing more unemployment and underemployment than whites, were more likely to be overeducated for the jobs they held (37 percent for blacks, 19 percent for Hispanics, 23 percent for whites), and more likely to receive inequitable pay for comparable work (19 percent for blacks, 18.9 percent for Hispanics, and 13.8 percent for whites).[61] Noting the connection between institutional racism and economic factors, the California Commission on

Crime Control and Violence Prevention in its public report to the people stated:[62]

> High crime rates among some minority groups, particularly Black and Hispanic, may be due to the relegation of a substantial number of their members to a permanent underclass. Members of the underclass are denied participation in mainstream American life—economically and politically. This condition fosters alienation, deprivation and powerlessness, which in turn may lead to a negative form of adaptation whereby members of these groups react with violence.

This observation appears to be applicable to minority community gangs that find themselves "blocked out" from the mainstream society. In response they develop their own contra-culture and in a reaction-formation way to a state of powerlessness, they become overly powerful, i.e., violent!

Homicide Rates

Contributing to the health status "gap" between whites and minorities was the remarkably high rates of homicide among certain minority populations—particularly among blacks and Hispanics. These minority groups were six to nine times more likely than non-Hispanic whites to die from homicide. Including all ethnic and racial groups, the highest risk of homicide involves young males, most often killed by friends or acquaintances employing firearms (usually handguns) during the course of an argument.

This pattern is manifested most clearly among black homicide victims. During a fourteen-year period from 1970 to 1983 in every region of the United States for both sexes and every age category, blacks were many more times more likely than non-Hispanic whites or persons from other ethnic/racial groups to die from homicide.[63] Whereas in 1983 homicide for non-Hispanic whites fifteen to twenty-four years of age was the third leading cause of death (with accidents #1, and suicide #2) and the fourth leading cause of death in the twenty-five to thirty-four years of age category (accidents #1, suicide #2, and cancer #3), among blacks it was *the* leading cause of death for both age categories.[64]

Approximately 60 percent of all Hispanics in the United States reside in the Southwestern states of Arizona, California, Colorado, New Mexico, and Texas. A Center for Disease Control study in this geographical area, including the years of 1976 through 1980, revealed that the Hispanic homicide rate was almost three times higher than non-Hispanic whites, specifically 21.6 per 100,000 to 7.7 per 100,000. The national rate in 1979 was 10.2 per 100,000. Hispanic males had a higher homicide rate than non-Hispanic whites for every age group studied. The most dramatic difference occurred among males in the twenty to twenty-four years of age category, the age category in which most homicides appeared for both groups. Here, non-Hispanic white males had a rate of 18.5 per 100,000 compared to Hispanic males with a rate of 83.3 per 100,000.[65]

The Indian Health Service (IHS) reporting on approximately 888,000 Native Americans (American Indians and Alaska Natives) residing in twenty-eight reservation states, revealed that overall, death rates from homicides, suicides, and unintentional injuries were higher among Native Americans than among the United States population as a whole. These deaths occur most often to male teenagers and young adults and because Native Americans are a relatively youthful population with 33 percent of its members under fifteen years of age, the IHS believed that violent behavior for Native Americans was likely to remain high for the foreseeable future.[66] In 1974 the Native American homicide rate stood at 30.1 per 100,000, almost three times that of the general population. By 1980 the rate had declined to 18.1 compared to 10.8 for the general population, i.e., still 70 percent higher.[67]

The homicide rates may be even higher for Native Americans in more urban areas compared to reservations. For example homicides in Bernalillo County, New Mexico, which includes Albuquerque, covering the five-year period from 1978 to 1982, revealed that in the 15 to 19, 20 to 24, and 25 to 29 age categories, Native Americans had a rate of 50.4, 50.4, and 68.2 per 100,000 respectively. This was significantly higher than the rate for non-Hispanic whites in the same age categories, which was 5.8, 15.7, and 16.9 per 100,000 population.[68]

Homicide rates for Asian Americans residing in the United States are difficult to calculate because: (1) their population is very small; (2) they appear to suffer very few homicides, even far less than non-Hispanic whites; and (3) the few Asian American homicides that occur are often listed in the race/ethnic category of "other." For example, in a ten-year study of 4950 homicides in Los Angeles City from 1970 to 1979, 47.4 percent of victims were black, 27.1 percent were non-Hispanic white, 22.9 percent were Hispanic, and 2.6 percent were "other race/ethnic groups."[69] During the study period Asian Americans numbered from 100,000 to 700,000 persons. The little data that are available concerning Asian American homicides reveal that Asian Americans in Los Angeles are far more likely to be killed by a stranger with a handgun in a crime-related circumstance compared to other ethnic-racial groups.[70] When a person is killed as the byproduct of a crime such as a robbery or burglary, it is referred to as a *felony* homicide. A person killing another person where the primary intent is to cause harm, such as a spouse killing a spouse as the result of an argument, would be called a *criminal* homicide. Of 157,003 homicides occurring in the United States for the period 1976 to 1983, approximately two-thirds were *criminal* homicides.[71]

Relationship of Victim to Assailant

National homicide data for the 1976 through 1983 period reveal that black homicide victims knew their assailant in 59.8 percent of the cases compared to "whites" (48.4 percent) and "other races" (48.8 percent). It is not clear in which category Hispanics were included, "white" or "other races." Among black male victims, the assailant was known in 58.3 percent of the cases and in over three-fourths of these homicides, the perpetrator was an acquaintance and not a family member. Among black female victims, however, the assailant was known in 65.8 percent of the cases, and in 43.8 percent of these, the assailant was a family member. Twenty-eight percent of black female victims were killed by family members compared to 13.3 percent of black male victims. The pattern of a larger proportion of female than male victims being killed by family members was also present among whites and persons of other races, 31.9 percent and 28.7 percent, respectively. Among white males and males of other races, the perpetrator was a family member in 12.1 percent and 11.4 percent of the cases.[72]

The national data do not make clear the role of gangs in homicides, that is, the percentages of persons in each ethnic and racial group killed by gang perpetrators. These data are, however, beginning to be documented by some states that provide clear information about the seriousness of the problem in urban areas. The Illinois Criminal Justice Information Authority had been collecting lethal violence data over a seventeen-year period (1965–1981) for Chicago. Females were found to have a lower risk of victimization than males, and females were far less prone to commit homicide whatever their race or ethnic background. More black wives killed their husbands than black husbands killed their wives. Homicide by wives or girlfriends constituted 13 percent of black male victims as compared to 5 percent of white males and 2 percent of Hispanic males being killed by women from their ethnic group. White males committed homicide less than blacks or Hispanics but when white males killed, the victim was three times more likely to be a female as compared to blacks. Hispanic females are much less likely to be involved in a homicide, either as a victim or offender, than are members of any other group.[73] The study revealed that violence against women, young children, and the elderly was very rare in the Hispanic population. Rape homicide as an example, was virtually unknown among Hispanics as no rape homicide was attributed to Hispanic offenders during the entire seventeen-year period.[74]

Lower homicide rates in Hispanic families have also been found in California, perhaps indicating a traditional Hispanic cultural norm in which the family is valued and protected. This might represent the positive aspects of *machismo* (strong, responsible, family-oriented, protective husband and father) as opposed to the negative *macho* (irresponsible, drinking, womanizer who physically abuses his wife and children). Table 16–1 represents 2453 homicides in California in 1985 by known relationship of victim to offender by the race or ethnic group of the victim. In Table 16–1, it is seen that black victims are more likely to be a friend or acquaintance (60.8 percent) to the offender than the non-Hispanic whites (51.1 percent) or Hispanic victims (54.2 percent). Non-Hispanic white victims, however, were significantly more likely to be the spouse, parent, or child of the perpetrator (19.7 percent) than either the black (7.5 percent) or Hispanic (6.4 percent) victims. Does the fact that non-Hispanic white family members are three times more likely than

TABLE 16–1 Relationship of Victim to Offender Distributed by Race/Ethnic Group of Victim

	FRIEND ACQUAINTANCE	SPOUSE/ PARENT CHILD	STRANGER	GANG MEMBER	ALL OTHER
White (not Hisp.)	51.1%	19.7%	23.7%	1.4%	4.1%
Black	60.8	7.5	16.8	11.6	3.3
Hispanic	54.2	6.4	21.5	14.1	3.8

Hispanics and 2.6 times more likely than blacks to be killed by a family member reflect serious problems in Anglo-American culture or is it a symptom of psychologically deteriorating middle-class Anglo-American families?

Marvin Wolgang suggests that culturally learned patterns of behavior account for violence differences between racial groups; that blacks have learned to use violence in more situations, thus having higher homicide rates. According to this view, non-Hispanic whites have not internalized this learning, hence, have lower homicide rates.[76] Can it be said that non-Hispanic families have "learned" to use more violence *within* the family compared to Hispanic and black families? The author, in comparing two predominantly Hispanic communities with two predominantly non-Hispanic white middle-class communities in Los Angeles, found that the two Hispanic communities had significantly lower rates of homicide (4.2 and 6.1/100,000) compared to the two non-Hispanic white communities (9.4 and 22.8/100,000). What appeared to account for this dramatic difference was the fact that the two Hispanic areas were *middle-class* communities. The two non-Hispanic white communities surpassed the two Hispanic communities in *five* of the "Seven Major Crimes" category (homicide, forcible rape, burglary, larceny, auto theft). The results were not definitive in the two remaining major crime categories with the two Hispanic communities having aggravated assault rates of 535 and 381/100,000, compared to 563 and 263/100,000 for the non-Hispanic communities. Robbery was the final major crime category with the Hispanic communities having a rate of 261 and 188/100,000 compared to 414 and 257/100,000 for the two white communities.[77] Socioeconomic factors, therefore, appear to play a significant role in Hispanic violence and major crime!

Non-Hispanic white and Hispanic victims had comparable percentages of being killed as strangers, 23.7 to 21.5 percent, respectively. Surprisingly, blacks were less likely to be killed as strangers (11.6 percent) than either non-Hispanic whites or Hispanics. Hispanic and black victims were far more likely, however, than non-Hispanic whites to be gang members, 14.1 and 11.6 percent, respectively, compared to non-Hispanic whites, 1.4 percent. In other words Hispanic homicide victims were ten times more likely to be gang members—and black victims eight times more likely—than non-Hispanic whites. Being a young black or Hispanic male gang member, therefore, places a person at very high risk for becoming a homicide victim. More male gang members were killed (10.5 percent) than female gang members (1.6 percent).[78]

This pattern is also seen in other large urban areas such as Chicago, which reported in its seventeen-year study of 12,872 homicides, that 25 percent of murders of teen-agers *in general* involved "multiple offenders," that is, a group attack. The risk of a gang-related homicide for Hispanics, however, was much higher than for non-Hispanic whites or blacks, whatever their age. More than half of murdered Hispanic youths were killed in gang-related altercations, and the trend was reportedly increasing,[79] as it is in Los Angeles. The Chicago Police Department defines a *gang-related homicide* as any homicide in which the motive for the killing was related to gang activity.[80] The California homicide data do not define "gang-related homicide." There does not appear to be a uniformity in criteria in reporting this information. Perhaps these decisions are made at the local law enforcement level. For more accurate reporting concerning "gang-related homicides," states will have to develop standard definitions and criteria within and among states.

Large U.S. cities have comparable high homicide rates per 100,000 population. For example, in 1981, Philadelphia had a rate of 22, New York City 26, Chicago 29, Los Angeles 29, Houston 39, and Detroit 42.[81] The more one focuses in depth in a specific area, the more one learns about what specific populations are at higher risk for homicide. Consider Table 16–2, which reports homicide rates from a national level to specific ethnic/racial communities with gangs:[82]

TABLE 16–2 1983 Homicide Rates per 100,000
Population: U.S., California, and Los Angeles Gang Rates

United States	8.0
California	10.5
Los Angeles	26.8
East L.A. Barrio (Hispanic area)	25.4
77th Street Precinct (black area)	46
Los Angeles Gangs[A] (300 gangs, 30,000 members, 200 homicides)	666
Los Angeles Gangs[B] (500 gangs, 50,000 members, 300 homicides)	600

A: Low estimate
B: High estimate

In Table 16–2, it is seen that the East Los Angeles *barrio* in the city had a homicide rate three times higher than the nation but comparable to Los Angeles. The black community in the city's 77th Street police precinct had a rate almost six times higher than the nation and almost twice the rate of the city. These figures become even more dramatic when gang homicides are analyzed since the greatest number of gangs are found in poor, minority communities. Accepting law enforcement's estimate that there are 300 to 500 gangs with 30,000 to 50,000 members that have committed 200 to 300 homicides per year, one might be misled by thinking—in taking the lower figure—that 300 gangs committing 200 homicides averages out to less than one homicide per gang per year.

However, since those who are more likely to be killed are *in* that 30,000 to 50,000 at-risk population, then the homicides rates per population are astounding, e.g., 200 homicides in a gang population of 30,000 = 666/100,000;

or 300 homicides in a gang population of 50,000 = 600/100,000. In the City of Los Angeles in 1986, 24 percent (187) of 777 homicides were committed by gangs.[83] The Los Angeles County figure was similar with 60 gang homicides (23 percent) out of a total of 260 homicides for FY 1985–1986. The vast majority of those killed by gangs were either gang members or involved in gang-related activities.[84] The Sheriff of Los Angeles County, Sherman Block, reported that in 1987, gang-related homicides increased to 387.[85]

The magnitude of the urban gang homicide crisis perhaps can best be measured more accurately by the potential years of life lost annually in addition to the high-risk rates of 600/100,000. The number of years of potential life lost (YPLL) is measured by subtracting the age of death from the age sixty-five.[86] Assuming that the 300 gang members averaged twenty years of age at the time of death and normally would have been expected to live up to the age of sixty-five, each victim, therefore, lost forty-five years of potential life, i.e., 45 years × 300 victims = 13,500 years of potential life lost! Poor minority communities, therefore, are losing one of their most valuable resources, their youth.

Gang Intervention Approaches

For over a century our society has developed different approaches in dealing with gangs, usually related more to the economic, emotional, and political climate of the time rather than to the comprehensive needs of the gang and its host community as symptoms of societal psychosocial and political neglect. For example one weekend evening in January 1988 in the white, very affluent Westwood Village adjacent to the UCLA campus, a spontaneous, very brief shooting conflict between rival gang members visiting the "Village" left one innocent female bystander dead. Local citizens were shocked to experience what is not an unusual "quality of life" experience in poor, minority communities. Overnight police patrols in Westwood were *tripled* while screams of racism came from the poor communities charging that for years they had been asking for more police only to be told by law enforcement officials that their limited budgets prohibited this.[87] Prompted by the Westwood homicide, the L.A. City Council voted to expand its police force by 150 officers at a cost of $9 million.[88]

Two weeks later in the inner city of Los Angeles, seven minority persons were shot (two died) in three separate "drive-by" shootings termed "probable" gang-related.[89] A "declaration of war" against gang mentality developed in the frustrated, five-member governing body of the County of Los Angeles, known as the Board of Supervisors. Suggestions were made to use the National Guard against gangs and urged the federal government to "declare war" on countries that support international narcotics trade that feeds gangs. The Board voted to provide $1.5 million to expand the Sheriff's Department anti-gang program and place more deputies on patrol—a total increase of seventy-five officers.[90] Obviously, the approach to the problem was force and efforts to suppress the symptom, which *is* needed. However, how, and *when* will the underlying causes be addressed, and who will do it?

It had been twenty-three years earlier when angry, frustrated government officials literally sent in the National Guard and law enforcement to suppress the "Watts Riots" of August 1965 in the black community in Los Angeles that left thirty-four persons dead and over $40 million in property damage. "Watts," which triggered hundreds of riots in 150 cities across the nation, with six occurring in the East Los Angeles Hispanic community in 1970–71,[91] indeed was a symptom of racism and societal neglect. The McCone Commission was appointed by the governor in 1965 to investigate the causes of "Watts." Almost twenty years after "Watts," the McCone report and recommendations were "revisited" in 1985 producing the following findings:[92]

> Virtually all presenters agreed that many problems remain unresolved and that a great deal remains to be done. Representatives of civil rights and community organizations testified that South Central Los Angeles is a low government priority: they felt there was, and is, a lack of commitment in governmental leadership and more generally a failure to initiate planning, strategy or solutions to problems and issues cited in the McCone Commission report . . . the overall conclusion of those testifying was that conditions are as bad, or worse, in South Central Los Angeles today as they were 19 years ago. As one speaker testified: 'a basic problem in South Central Los Angeles in 1984, as it was in 1965, is poverty—grinding, unending, and debilitating for all whom it touches.'

In response to racism and societal neglect, "Watts" anger was externalized and expressed through its youth and young adults against "whitey" with slogans of "Burn, baby, burn!" During the six 1970–71 Hispanic community riots, which covered a period of twenty months, there were no juvenile homicides. Anger was projected onto police and white businesses in the *barrio*.[93] With a few exceptions in which innocent bystanders are killed, the epidemic gang violence of the 1980s by and large represents a fratricidal-like behavior, i.e., "homeboy" killing "homeboy," a "brother killing a brother." The homicidal anger and frustration is being internalized by gangs into the community and directed at one's own people, more specifically, at one's own image. Homicide is the flip side of suicide. Many persons who kill others eventually kill themselves.

Different gang intervention approaches may have varied effects upon the gangs but most of the interventions are surface, short-term, symptom-oriented remedial measures that at times may be of some benefit to society (increasing arrests of gang members) or the gang (the provision of social-recreational programs). The following represents some of society's responses in attempting to solve the gang problem.

1. *The Law Enforcement–Institutionalization Approach.* The "send in the military," "get tough," "lock them up" approach previously described as a gov-

ernmental response to the gang problem is not atypical. The public *does* have
to be protected and violence suspects have to be arrested and have their day
in court and if convicted, incarcerated if the seriousness of the case warrants
this disposition. The gang is seen as something evil and, hence, something
that has to be destroyed. The gang will often be harassed and intimidated
by the police, the intent being to discourage the gang members from asso-
ciating. The vast majority of gang youth are *not* violent but they are *all* seen
as violent and frequently non-gang minority youth are caught up in the police
enforcement dragnet. They will be frequently arrested for even minor offenses
until there are sufficient arrests to warrant institutionalization. For example
a week after Los Angeles city and county officials decided to declare war on
gangs and curtail gang violence, *200* additional officers were assigned to patrol
gang areas. Between 6:30 P.M. on a Friday to 3:00 A.M. on Saturday (8½ hours),
the special task force arrested 121 gang member suspects on charges ranging
from curfew violations to narcotics possession. Fifty-eight cars were im-
pounded, 213 traffic citations were issued, twenty grams of cocaine, twelve
grams of marijuana, and eight handguns were seized. In spite of this impressive law enforcement suppression effort, two young men were killed and
three others were wounded in gang-related shootings during this time period!
No arrests were made related to the shootings.[94] Police officers are in a very
difficult position and find themselves in a dilemma. On one hand society
expects them to solve the gang problem while not providing resources to
address the underlying social causes. If law enforcement admits that more
police will *not* solve the problem, they may not receive additional resources.
Police officers once again, as was the case with urban riots, find themselves
in a "damned if you do or don't" position. They are assigned by the political
power structure to sit on the lid of the TNT barrel.

A special effort is usually made by police, parole, and probation officers,
to rid the gang of its "leader," the theory here being that if one takes away
the leader of the gang, the gang in its confusion will dissolve. These tactics
are rarely, if ever, successful and could be even considered counterproductive
as the youngster's path toward criminalization is accelerated. (See Chapters
11 and 17.)

Gang youth are frequently placed in juvenile detention facilities for their
gang behavior. This delinquent behavior usually involves "joy-riding," curfew violation, alcohol and drug abuse, and misdemeanor and felony assault
offenses. Gang youths respond very well to the requirements of the institution
and a study revealed that they held the highest positions of authority in
various probation camps. They were experts at group process and soon were
running the institution. Following graduation from the institution, however,
most gang members (75 percent) became recidivists within three months.
There was rarely any carry-over of what they had learned in the institution
and secondly, they returned to the same oppressive conditions that were a
major cause of their initial downfall.[95] The institutionalization "solution" becomes a revolving door leading to more youths being incarcerated. As was

seen in Chapter 11, California leads the nation with this approach and it is not working. Sixteen- and seventeen-year-old murderers are usually handled in adult court and if convicted, like adults, are sent to state prison.

2. *The Community Organization Approach. Community organization* is a macro level practice activity in which practitioners working within the network of human service agencies attempt to increase their effectiveness in meeting the needs of an identified population. In theory a community organization approach involves: (1) the definition of the problem; (2) a needs assessment in relationship to the problem; (3) recommending resources addressing the needs of the problem to various private and public agencies and influential citizens and politicians; and (4) obtaining and applying resources to the population in need, hence, eliminating the problem.[96]

Following the 1965 "Watts Riots" for example, the McCone Commission in its investigation into problem areas related to the causes of the riots, developed recommendations concerning police–community relations, welfare and social services, employment, health, housing, transportation, and education. In its nineteen-year follow-up inquiry into the status of the McCone Commission recommendations, the City and County Human Relations Commissions found that the greatest improvement had been made in the public transportation system and in the health area where a major hospital and postgraduate medical school were built *in* the community seven years later. Police–community relations had improved with an increase of black officers, but numbers of officers and their deployment became an issue of considerable discontent, especially as it concerned crimes against property and gang violence. Problems related to welfare and social services, and employment remained "critical" with housing continuing to be one of the "most critical" problems. Education problems were seen as "growing worse" as evidenced by greater racial isolation of blacks, overcrowding, overabundance of substitute teachers, chronic shortage of math and science teachers, and poor student academic achievement levels in comparison to other parts of the city.[97] Although the community was very satisfied with its new 480-bed hospital, the 1985 "McCone Revisited" testimony revealed that 83 percent of the patients using the hospital were there for the treatment of trauma wounds, primarily caused by handguns. Most of these violence and homicide victims were young black males.[98] The report did not make it clear if they were gang-related homicides but if one considers the numerous gangs in that community, it is quite likely that they were.

After studying the causes of hundreds of riots in 150 cities across the United States in the mid-1960s, the U.S. Riot Commission issued its findings known as the "Kerner Report" stating:[99]

> The record before this Commission reveals that the causes of recent racial disorders are imbedded in a massive tangle of issues and circumstances— social, economic, political, and psychological—which arise out of the historical pattern of Negro-White relations in America . . . White racism is essentially responsible for the explosive mixture which has been accumulating

in our cities since the end of World War II . . . The ghettos too often mean men and women without jobs, families without men, and schools where children are processed instead of educated, until they return to the street—to crime, narcotics, to dependency on welfare, and to bitterness and resentment against society in general and White society in particular.

Similar findings were seen in a report commissioned by the Congress of Mexican American Unity and the Chicano Moratorium Committee as the causes of the Hispanic community riots in 1970–71 in East Los Angeles.[100]

Frederick Thrasher did not attribute the existence of 1313 gangs in Chicago in the 1920s to white racism—since the great majority of those gangs *were* "white" (not Hispanic). However, he cited similar underlying causes as found in the McCone and Kerner Commission reports, i.e., failure of social institutions to function efficiently in the youngster's experience as indicated by disintegration of the family, "inefficiency of schools," political indifference, low wages, unemployment, and lack of recreational opportunities. Thrasher added:[101]

> The gang functions with reference to these conditions in two ways: It offers a substitute for what society fails to give; and it provides a relief from suppression and distasteful behavior. It fills a gap and affords an escape . . . Thus the gang, itself a natural and spontaneous type of organization arising through conflict, is a symptom of disorganization in the larger framework. These conclusions, suggested by the present study, seem amply verified by data from other cities in the United States and in other countries.

Thrasher, therefore, concluded that the gang was a function of specific conditions, and "it does not tend to appear in the absence of these conditions."[102] Perhaps the core problem is societal discrimination toward the *poor*, which in turn, is compounded by ethnic and racial prejudice and *racism*. The "conditions" nevertheless, continue to exist as do gangs in these communities; that, being the bottom line. In *addition* to the chronic gang problem, spontaneous minority communal riots make their appearance every ten or twenty years or so when frustrations peak, e.g., 1920s, 1940s, 1960s, and 1970s. As was the case with riots, broadly based "Blue Ribbon" committees and commissions have to be appointed to make comprehensive inquiries into the gang problem, with society being prepared to make a commitment to allocate resources to the problem. The government has on occasion appointed committees such as California's State Task Force on Youth Gang Violence to investigate gang problems. These bodies, however, are usually organized by and are well represented by criminal justice professionals, who understandably view the problem mainly from a law enforcement perspective; hence, they produce law enforcement-type recommendations such as increasing incarceration penalties for gang members, improving the effectiveness of prosecuting attorneys in handling gang cases, adding gang training in criminal justice classes, and obtaining increased federal funding for witness protection programs. The State Task Force report did not address any of the underlying social and economic causes of the gang, which was consistent with its man-dated goal, to:[103]

> . . . recommend statewide policy, and legislative and budget priorities to the Governor and California State Legislature to combat youth gangs and youth gang violence.

In 1972, a Los Angeles County Department of Community Services reported that community organization efforts be made to attack the basic social and economic problems that were seen as the underlying reasons for the existence of gangs. Nothing additional with regard to the community organization approach was offered—in short, nothing happened.[104]

3. *The Social-Recreational Approach.* This traditional approach views the gang as being unhappy adolescents who lack social and recreational outlets. Attempts are made by social–recreational agencies to give the gang a positive identity as a result of their hard work in planning and having dances and other social–recreational activities. Through various fund raising efforts, they eventually are able to purchase lettered jackets for themselves. This approach simply utilizes group processes to transform group values and behaviors. Frederick Thrasher cites examples of how in the 1920s, they were able to transform violent, destructive youth gangs into Boy Scout Troops.[105] The group cohesion is maintained but its activities are redirected.

On the other hand there is a theory that gang–group cohesiveness and delinquency are related, that factors increasing gang cohesiveness (of which worker emphasis on group programming is one) will lead to increased gang recruitment and delinquency. This conclusion suggests that the gang group worker approach should be severely modified or abandoned.[106]

The main problem with both of these approaches is that they are superficial in that they do not deal with the *basic* causes of the gang. As soon as one rides the current wave and calms the symptom, another wave composed of younger brothers and sisters is on the horizon.

Competitive sports is another social–recreational approach, as some believe that the underlying force in the gang is aggression.[107] It would seem logical, therefore, to channel the aggression into more positive outlets, such as boxing. Some gang youth prefer boxing over what they consider to be less masculine team sports such as baseball, basketball, and football. The main drawback with this approach is the same as with the previous approach, that is, that it temporarily only deals with the symptom. It also communicates to the youngster that this may be all he will ever be good for, to beat someone or be beaten. Sports may be a way to at least initially gain the youngster's interest while other more solid, promising career opportunities are worked out.

Other social–recreation gang intervention approaches involve a host of modest programs designed to impact on some aspects of the gang problem.

For example there may be neighborhood meetings to educate parents about gangs or anti-gang curriculum taught to elementary-age children in the schools. Some programs focus on gang youth with regard to vocational/employment training and provide consultation to schools concerning gang problems occurring on the school grounds. Teaching gang youths about art and music and developing these skills through mural painting and performing in musical groups is still another approach. Some gang members are organized into supervised groups and paid for removing graffiti from walls in their neighborhoods. All these programs have some value, but are small in number, underfunded, and, like other programs, do not address the underlying causes of the problem.

4.   *The Spiritual Approach.*   Some religious groups representing various denominations have attempted to win over gang members in order to spiritually "rehabilitate" them. One such group having much success is called "Victory Outreach," which has attracted some Hispanic gang members in Los Angeles. Victory Outreach was founded by Sonny Aguizoni, a former addict, who began the group in 1967 in East Los Angeles. The main function of Victory Outreach has been to bring the teachings of Jesus directly to drug addicts and gang members who are caught up in an "immoral" life. Many gang youth have joined this new "Born Again Christian" movement and have become *barrio* missionaries for Christ.[108] Beginning with only one chapel and a handful of members, it has grown to at least twelve chapels and an estimated 5,000 members throughout the Southwest. While no actual statistics exist to show its success rate in working with gangs and addicts, Victory Outreach has established a definite presence in some *barrios*. With many years of experience in working with gang members, the author has found that when there is a major *structural* change in their lives such as entering into a marital relationship, having a child, obtaining a steady job, re-enrolling and attending school or becoming a "Born Again Christian," they seem to abandon the gang.

5.   *The Street Worker–Counselor Approach.*   This intervention strategy, next to law enforcement gang suppression programs, is a traditional approach to reduce gang violence.[109] The "street workers" or "street counselors" as they sometimes are called, are often former gang members and serve as a go-between for gangs and other community agencies and organizations. Following the "Philadelphia Plan" model, which was effective in reducing gang homicides in Philadelphia in the late 1970s, street counselors armed with "beepers" follow a crisis mode of intervention and immediately defuse potential violent confrontations between gangs by reducing rumors, anger, and, at times, calling the police. They often attempt to persuade warring gangs to sign "peace treaties." The primary goal of this approach is violence reduction; hence, it is symptom-centered and not oriented toward addressing the basic causes of the gang.

6.   *The Sociopolitical Approach.*   Gangs are an extremely cohesive unit and

members have a dedication to one another that often surpasses their loyalty to their families. Such powerful cohesion, which gang members need for survival in a hostile, insensitive environment, can be enhanced, transformed, and directed toward efforts that will improve their community. This may be called the "sociopolitical approach."[110] The gang is politicized by the community's political activists, intellectuals, and respected, responsible former veteran gang members. They are helped to develop an even greater pride in themselves that extends beyond their cherished turf. Gang members gradually would become aware of the absence of community representatives on various boards of agencies that are supposed to serve them. Through political pressure they would eventually assume positions of authority in various agencies and have a direct hand in improving their community. This effort begins to change a youth's negative life style. By developing political consciousness, they do not have to feel powerless when faced with an insensitive welfare, health, law enforcement and political system. The gang members will engage in political activism, resulting in positive social change for their communities.

There is a precedence for this approach. In the Woodlawn area of Chicago in the late 1960s, the Blackstone Rangers, a black gang numbering 1800 members, were responsible for a 25 percent reduction in crime in their community. This gang was successful in signing treaties with other gangs and, in so doing, helped to prevent riots in their area. As a result of this accomplishment they were soon thereafter courted by political forces. Of equal if not greater importance is the fact that members of this gang developed an awareness of their power base that they could use to positive ends; in turn, they were able to organize businesses and obtain grants for projects that benefited the community. They were able to accomplish these objectives even in the face of an unremitting policy of harassment by a task force of the Chicago Police Department.[111]

A similar phenomenon occurred in numerous *barrios* throughout the Southwest in the late 1960s and early 1970s. Numerous Hispanic gang members joined an organization called the Brown Berets. They politicized their communities, protected them from what they perceived as police harassment and in some *barrios*, established "free clinics." As Matthew Dumont once said, "The line between destructive and constructive activism is much finer than the line between activism itself and passivity."[112] Few would disagree that a crucial element of mental health is a sense of environmental mastery, a feeling that some part of the environment, however small, is subject to the control and manipulation of the individual. This approach does not destroy the gang, but rather changes and redirects its activities and energies toward doing something about its environment. It begins to attack the basic cause of the gang. As it participates in political activities, it is no longer participating in activities that are harmful to the gang and/or others in the community. It, therefore, no longer can be defined as a "gang." While in the 1920s gang group cohesion was maintained as the gang was transformed into a Boy Scout troop, in the late 1980s and 1990s, group cohesion may have to be used as an intervention approach on a selective basis to transform some gangs into a positive, political group.

IMPLICATIONS FOR SOCIAL WORK

Of all the major helping professions, it would appear that social work is best suited from a values, knowledge, and skills perspective to once again attempt to develop intervention strategies concerning one of the most serious psychosocial problems confronting many of the U.S.'s cities today—gangs! It was seen in Chapter 1 that social work is the professional activity of helping individuals, groups, or communities enhance or restore their capacity for social functioning and creating conditions favorable to that goal. Gangs as a focus for practice find the social worker helping individuals, groups, families, and the community, i.e., micro to macro level intervention.

The Individual and the Family

In addition to theories about gangs to explain crime and violence, there are also theories to explain individual crime and violence. Is the gang member, for example, participating in delinquent activities simply as a means of conforming to a subcultural group norm and in this sense is he or she a "healthy" individual? Or is the gang member primarily acting out his or her individual psychopathology through the gang? In many cases these factors may be related. Based upon thirty years of work with gang members as a gang group worker, probation officer, and mental health therapist, the author has found that the vast majority of gang members are not mentally disturbed. It is quite probable that the percent of mentally disturbed gang members is comparable to the general population. If the social worker believes the gang member is relatively "healthy," then a group intervention approach to modify the delinquent gang behavior will be indicated. If, however, the gang member is diagnostically psychotic, neurotic, or has a personality disorder or an adjustment reaction to adolescence, then an individual intervention approach appropriate to the problem is indicated along with involvement of the family as needed or as much as *they* will permit. Although not identifying a specific diagnostic label, Adelaide M. Johnson advocates an approach using both an individual psychotherapy and a community treatment approach for gang members. Johnson states:[113]

> The sociologist, in his enthusiasm for a therapeutic attack on a gang area, should not overlook those delinquents who have internal conflicts not susceptible to the techniques of therapy drawn from the community. It is necessary, therefore, diagnostically and therapeutically, that the sociologist and psychiatrist work together very closely.

S. Berman sees the juvenile's antisocial behavior becoming more manifest as the youngster gets older, especially when he or she is confronted with the demands for social adaptation in school. Then the well-known symptoms of truancy, defiance of teachers, stealing, fire-setting, untruthfulness, irresponsibility, staying away from home, and fighting with other juveniles is observed. Berman suggests that treatment should involve the participation of the parents, especially the mother, for whom the juvenile holds intense hostility due to toilet training difficulties. Psychotherapy requires active and direct collaboration on the part of the therapist. The juvenile is seen as reacting to the therapist with hostile, destructive behavior. Only gradually is it possible for the juvenile to trust the egosyntonic support of the therapist. Berman adds that the correction of distorted object relations and the establishment of new identifications for the child can occur only when the therapist is neither seductive nor rejecting. It requires a benevolent, objective, incorruptible relationship in which the juvenile gradually feels he or she has support and understanding of the therapist.[114]

The following case seen by the author is an example of an adolescent gang member experiencing family, sexual, and gang problems.

"Bluto," a large, 200-pound, fifteen-year-old male gang member, was referred to the mental health agency by the probation department for child molestation. He scored 67 on a WISC IQ test. Initial efforts to involve his parents in family therapy produced few results due to the father's chronic alcoholism. The father came to the only two family sessions red-faced and intoxicated and passively smiled during the mother's and the worker's conversation. "Bluto," also very quiet, was embarrassed by his father's behavior and was intimidated by his mother's articulate skills and aggressive manner. The father did not seem concerned about Bluto's behavior nor his own alcoholism and rejected the suggestion of a referral to an alcoholism treatment program. In several ways the parents were contributing to Bluto's feelings of inadequacy expressed in his interest in little girls and overcompensated for in his participation in aggressive gang activities. He was involved in many fights. The intervention approaches with him were multiple and included some basic sex education sessions with a book, role playing, psychodrama, and socialization, the social worker being a positive role model and assisting him in developing verbal and physical coping skills. The treatment approach was supportive and mild to moderately insight-oriented. Bluto felt very proud when the social worker went to his church to witness his First Communion ceremony and was particularly happy when the social worker watched him play basketball in an organized league on a few occasions. Therapist after hours efforts were sanctioned by the agency but were not financially reimbursable.

Bluto's participation in treatment sessions was excellent, as out of a total of thirty-five weekly sessions, he had only one cancellation and two "no shows." He was dismissed from probation after his tenth session. He did not have any more arrests and after nine months he left his gang. He played varsity football and graduated from high school.

Ideally, efforts should be made to involve the family in the treatment of the adolescent, especially in the case of latency-age or early-adolescent young-sters. In Bluto's case, however, because of the seriousness of the parents' problems, the social worker made a decision to focus more on Bluto to help him develop his strengths and understanding of the stresses going on in his life and his negative ways of coping that were threatening his life (gang fights) and bringing him to the attention of the authorities (sexual behavior). If the agency had had a social group work program, a worker would have been assigned to begin working with Bluto's gang if the gang did not have a worker.

The Group

In the case of Bluto, he was the primary social work practice unit of attention. In social group work, the unit of attention is primarily the group. The group worker requires a knowledge of: group structure and processes, intervention approaches, individual members, group goals, nature of intragroup inter-action, and needs, interests, and values of the members. The group worker also understands his or her role in the group, his or her minimal control over the group, and the group's right to self-determination. The group is seen as a microcosm in which positive gains made by the group through group pro-cess can produce growth and change in the individual, the group and com-munity through the group's social action, even in the larger environment.[115]

Jerry R. Fox points out that social work *can* adapt its social group work practice methodology to serve urban gang members and their community through the "detached worker" or gang group worker, engaged directly with the gang and supported through community-based agencies. Working with gangs requires that the social worker spend a significant amount of time in the client's (gang's) immediate environment rather than in the agency, hence the term "detached" or "street worker." The author, having worked with gangs, agrees with Fox when he states that: (1) even though gangs have the same needs and rights to services as others, prejudice and distorted fear of inner-city minority group youth gangs prohibits many competent social work-ers from entering these communities; (2) most gang members are surprisingly receptive to a helping relationship and are usually quite willing to permit the worker to engage the gang as a group within the purposes of social work practice; and (3) the social worker can help urban youth gangs to change from being a destructive force to being a constructive contributor to the community while maintaining the gang's right to self-determination.[116]

One of the tasks of the worker is to assist the gang in obtaining resources in pursuit of their goals. In working toward this, the worker has an oppor-tunity not only to help the gang obtain needed resources, but in the process also modify the negative image of the gang held by the community. This is illustrated in the following case:[117]

> Gang members expressed boredom and frustration about the lack of athletic facilities in the neighborhood. Consequently, one of their favorite activities was harassing employees and destroying property at a nearby hospital.

With the Gang's consent, the worker approached the hospital's administration to suggest that part of the hospital's large paved parking lot be equipped with backboards and basketball court markings. The administration agreed to try this in the hope that it would reduce harassment from the gang. The worker arranged a meeting between several gang members and the hospital superintendent of buildings and grounds for a semi-formal presentation of the court to the gang. There was an immediate cessation of trouble from the gang, and the members expressed great satisfaction with the new facility.

In the above case, the group worker, while adopting an advocate and enabler role, was able to create positive change in the gang *and* the institution, which was helpful to both parties. The gang, through observing their group worker, learned there were ways of accomplishing goals in life other than through the use of intimidation and violence.

The Community

The gang is, in the final analysis, a product and symptom of the community indicating that some of the needs of youth are not being met by the family, neighborhood, and traditional community institutions such as the police, school, and religious and recreational institutions. To meet its needs the gang creates its own institution—the gang. In pursuit of its needs the gang often functions in delinquent ways, subjecting community members to anti-social acts, including homicide. Their negative behavior contributes to social dysfunction and disorganization in the community.[118]

In developing a social work community intervention model with regard to gangs, Irving A. Spergel recommends dealing with the problem at two levels, the larger structural and the local institutional. Attention has to be given to the major underlying social, economic, cultural, political, and legal conditions that contribute to the gang problem—such conditions evolving at the national and international level. Spergel believes national level problems that affect gang violence such as housing segregation, unemployment, immigrant flow, and access to handguns, can be modified through appropriate public policies.[119]

In addition to addressing the need for social policy changes at the national level, attention also has to be focused on the local community institutional and program level. Institutional problems such as weak local community organization, unsystematic police strategies, restrictive youth agency membership age policies, and lack of young adult bridging mechanisms will require intervention. Weak community organization is one of the contributing factors for the existence of gangs, and therefore, has to be strengthened, according to Spergel. As part of the structure of the community the components of social controls (law enforcement) and social opportunities (resources and services) have to be analyzed. There needs to be a *balance* between law enforcement control and provision of resources, according to Spergel. Too much law enforcement emphasis with resulting imprisonment leads to increased criminal behavior of gang members, and too much "do-goodism" can result in exploitation and manipulation of resources by gangs, resulting in increased criminal behavior. Spergel believes if the community is more effectively organized, including the presence of adequate social control and social service provision, the violent gang as a transitional institution may no longer be necessary. Spergel offers a gang violence intervention operational model with five objectives, stated in brief form as follows:[120]

1. Foremost is mediation of gang disputes and tensions that contribute to intergang violence. The objective is achieved through a process of crisis counseling and intergroup communication in the course of patrol and surveillance of the community during times when violent gang disputes are likely to erupt.

2. Mobilization of community groups and organizations to restrain gang violence, such as block clubs, local improvement organizations, mother's groups, and church groups, who would intervene directly through patrols, marches, and closer communication with the police.

3. Assistance to various neighborhood groups and organizations to better target and utilize their resources concerning the needs of gang youth for education, training, jobs, family counseling, drug rehabilitation, and other services.

4. Prevention of gang violence and improved social adaptation of male gang members between thirteen and sixteen years referred to counseling by police for incipient violent gang activity.

5. Coordinated participation of key organizations, community groups, and justice system agencies in the development and evaluation of special programs focusing on gang violence reduction.

Spergel sees these five objectives as being interrelated. Appropriate staff time and resources have to be allocated in order for the model to be effective. An essential ingredient is also the involvement of "grass roots" people, indigenous community workers, professional social workers, and graduate students. The creation of a "community council," "advisory board" or "town hall" group comprised of members representing all concerned agencies, community people, gang members, and politicians, would then improve communication and strengthen the organization of the community.

CONCLUDING COMMENT

Violent, delinquent gangs have been part of the U.S. scene since at least 1842. It may very well be that gangs have never been more violent than they are today, with homicides at an unbelievable rate of 600 per 100,000 in that specific population in some urban areas. Gangs have always been primarily a law enforcement problem area; the 1920s–1960s have shown some group work and community organization practice interest from the social work profession.

However, beginning in the 1970s and 1980s, the profession has been steadily moving away from criminal justice populations, gangs, and the urban social problems of poor minorities and has increasingly taken a path toward private practice and industrial social work while becoming more "clinical" with a predominantly middle-class clientele.

The values, knowledge, and skills base of the social work profession places it in a unique position compared to other helping professions to seriously address the growing urban gang psychosocial crisis. For example the profession has a historical knowledge base concerning group work with gangs and an impressive theory and practice foundation relating to community organization. Additionally, the profession's clinical skills have advanced significantly since the 1940s and in specialized cases such as "Bluto" the social workers can be effective in treating gang members.

Jerry R. Fox's impressive work with gangs reminds the profession that not only are gangs still present in the late 1980s, but also the presence of social group work skills. A community gang intervention model developed by Irving Spergel provides the social work community organizer a framework for practice that could reduce gang violence in a given community.

Urban gang violence is indeed a psychosocial crisis that will not go away. It *is* a challenge to the profession and an opportunity to demonstrate that it is a unique micro to macro practice discipline and *can* do some things that other helping professions cannot. Social work's values tell us that we have no choice but to help those most in need.

SUGGESTED READINGS

Fox, Jerry R. "Mission Impossible? Social Work Practice with Black Urban Youth Gangs." *Social Work* (January–February 1985) Vol. 30, pp. 25–31.

Hopps, June Gary. "Violence—A Personal and Societal Challenge." *Social Work* (November–December 1987) Vol. 32, No. 6, pp. 467–468.

Middleman, Ruth R., and Goldberg, Gale. "Social Work Practice with Groups." *Encyclopedia of Social Work* 18th ed. Vol. II Silver Spring, Md.: National Association of Social Workers, 1987, pp. 714–729.

Morales, Armando. "The Mexican American Gang Member: Evaluation and Treatment," in Rosina M. Becerra, Marvin Karno, and Javier Escobar, eds., *Mental Health and Hispanic Americans: Clinical Perspectives*. New York: Grune and Stratton, Inc., 1982.

Report of the Secretary's Task Force on Black and Minority Health, Vol. 5, U.S. Department of Health and Human Services, January 1986.

Spergel, Irving A. "Violent Gangs in Chicago: In Search of Social Policy." *Social Service Review*, (June 1984) Vol. 58, No. 2, pp. 199–226.

Thrasher, Frederick M. *The Gang: A Study of 1313 Gangs in Chicago*. Chicago: The University of Chicago Press, 1963.

ENDNOTES

1. June Gary Hopps, "Violence—A Personal and Societal Challenge," *Social Work*, (November–December 1987) Vol. 32, No. 6, pp. 467–468.

2. See E. Milling Kinard, "Child Abuse and Neglect," pp. 223–231; Barbara Star, "Domestic Violence," pp. 463–476, Vol. I, and Andre M. Ivanoff, "Suicide," pp. 737–748, in *Encyclopedia of Social Work*, 18th ed., Vol. II (Silver Spring, Md.: National Association of Social Workers, 1987).

3. Ivanoff, p. 744.

4. Hopps, p. 468.

5. Gertrude Wilson, "From Practice to Theory: A Personalized History," in Robert Roberts and Helen Northen, eds., *Theories of Social Work with Groups* (New York: Columbia University Press, 1976), p. 11.

6. Ruth R. Middleman and Gale Goldberg, "Social Work Practice with Groups," *Encyclopedia of Social Work*, 18th ed., Volume II (Silver Spring, Md.: National Association of Social Workers, 1987), p. 715.

7. Jerry R. Fox, "Mission Impossible? Social Work Practice with Black Urban Youth Gangs," Copyright © 1985, National Association of Social Workers, Inc. Reprinted with permission from *Social Work*, Vol. 30, (January–February) p. 25.

8. The other article was written by Irving A. Spergel, "Violent Gangs in Chicago: In Search of Social Policy," *Social Service Review* (June 1984) Vol. 58, No. 2, pp. 199–226.

9. Armando Morales, "The Need for Nontraditional Mental Health Programs in the Barrio," in J. Manuel Casas and Susan E. Keefe, eds., *Family and Mental Health in the Mexican-American Community* (Los Angeles, Calif.: UCLA Spanish-Speaking Mental Health Research Center 1978), Monograph No. 7, p. 133.

10. *State Task Force on Youth Gang Violence*, Final Report, California Council on Criminal Justice, January 1986, p. 4.

11. F. J. O'Hagan, "Gang Characteristics—An Empirical Survey," in *Journal of Child Psychology and Psychiatry*, Vol. 17, 1976, pp. 305–314.

12. Saint Augustine, *Confessions* (New York: The Modern Library, 1949), p. 34.

13. A. Davis and M. Haller, eds., *The People of Philadelphia* (Temple University Press, 1973), p. 78.

14. H. Asbury, *The Gangs of New York: An Informal History of the Underworld* (New York: Alfred A. Knopf, 1927), p. 29.

15. *State Task Force*, p. 30.

16. F. M. Thrasher, *The Gang: A Study of 1,313 Gangs in Chicago* (Chicago: The University of Chicago Press, 1963), p. 151.

17. *State Task Force*, p. viii.

18. Thrasher, pp. 31–35.

19. W. B. Miller, "Lower Class Culture as a Generating Milieu of Gang Delinquency," *Journal of Social Issues* 14 (1958):5–19.

20. *Los Angeles Times*, Part I, April 12, 1983, p. 6.

21. See A. K. Cohen, *Delinquent Boys: The Culture of the Gang* (Glencoe, Ill.: The Free Press, 1955); and R. A. Cloward and L. E. Ohlin, *Delinquency and Opportunity* (New York: The Free Press, 1960).

22. D. Matza, *Delinquency and Drift* (New York: Wiley, 1964).

23. Armando Morales, "A Study of Recidivism of Mexican-American Junior Forestry Camp Graduates. (Unpublished master's thesis, School of Social Work, University of Southern California, 1963.)

24. A. Morales, "The Mexican-American Gang Member: Evaluation and Treatment," in R. Becerra, M. Karno, and J. Escobar, eds., *Mental Health and Hispanic Americans: Clinical Perspectives* (New York: Grune and Stratton, 1982), p. 153.

25. Thrasher, p. 117.

26. *Los Angeles Times*, Part I, November 17, 1986, p. 18.

27. *Los Angeles Times*, Part I, January 11, 1987, p. 23.

28. *Report on Youth Gang Violence in California*, The Attorney General's Youth Gang Task Force, June 1981, pp. 16–20.

29. T. A. Sweeney, *Streets of Anger: Streets of Hope* (Glendale, Calif.: Great Western Publishing, 1980), p. 86.

30. I. A. Spergel, "Violent Gangs in Chicago: In Search of Social Policy," *Social Service Review*, Vol. 58 (June 1984) p. 206.
31. Cloward and Ohlin, p. 178.
32. *State Task Force*, p. 8.
33. T. Kerfoot, "Crime and the Occult," *Peace Officers Association of Los Angeles County*, October 1985, p. 23.
34. M. Poirier, "Street Gangs of Los Angeles County." (Unpublished pamphlet, 1982.)
35. Thrasher, p. 60.
36. Morales (1982), p. 156.
37. Report of the Secretary's Task Force on Black and Minority Health, Vol. 5, U.S. Department of Health and Human Services. (January 1986), p. v.
38. *Report of the Secretary*, p. 5.
39. E. Muñoz, "Economic Costs of Trauma, United States, 1982," *Journal of Trauma*, Vol. 24, No. 3, 1984.
40. Burnet B. Sumner, Elizabeth R. Mintz, and Patricia L. Brown, "Interviewing Persons Hospitalized with Interpersonal Violence-Related Injuries: A Pilot Study," in *Report of the Secretary*, pp. 305–306.
41. *Report of the Secretary*. p. 29.
42. "Ounces of Prevention: Toward an Understanding of the Causes of Violence," *1982 Final Report to the People of California*, Commission on Crime Control and Violence Prevention, State of California, p. 1.
43. *1982 Final Report to the People of California*, pp. 81–82.
44. Burr Eichelman, "Toward a Rational Pharmacotherapy for Aggressive and Violent Behavior," *Hospital and Community Psychiatry*, Vol. 39, No. 1, (January 1988) p. 31.
45. *1982 Final Report to the People of California*, p. 82.
46. *1982 Final Report to the People of California*, p. 11.
47. *Report of the Secretary*, p. 32.
48. *1982 Final Report to the People of California*, p. 13.
49. *1982 Final Report to the People of California*, p. 6.
50. *Report of the Secretary*, pp. 29, 31.
51. Irwin L. Kutash, Samuel B. Kutash, and Louis B. Schlesinger, eds., *Violence: Perspective on Murder and Aggression* (San Francisco, Calif.: Jossey–Bass, 1978), pp. 219–232.
52. *1982 Final Report to the People of California*, p. 137.
53. *1982 Final Report to the People of California*, p. 138.
54. *1982 Final Report to the People of California*, pp. 139–140.
55. Ronald S. Prabman and Margaret H. Thomas, "Children's Imitation of Aggressive and Pro-Social Behavior when Viewing Alone and in Pairs," *Journal of Communication*, Vol. 27, No. 3, 1977, pp. 199–205.
56. *1982 Final Report to the People of California*, pp. 109–133.
57. Armando Morales, "Institutional Racism in Mental Health and Criminal Justice," *Social Casework* (July 1978) p. 387.
58. Centers for Disease Control, Homicide Surveillance: High-Risk Racial and Ethnic Groups—Blacks and Hispanics, 1970–1983, Atlanta: Centers for Disease Control, November, 1986, p. 7.
59. Alvin Poussaint, "Black-on-Black Homicide: A Psychological–Political Perspective," *Victimology*, Vol. 8, 1983, pp. 161–169.
60. *1982 Final Report to the People of California*, p. 51–52.
61. U.S. Commission on Civil Rights. *Unemployment and Underemployment Among Blacks, Hispanics and Women*. Clearinghouse Publication 74, November 1982.
62. *1982 Final Report to the People of California*, p. 53.
63. Centers for Disease Control, Homicide Surveillance: High-Risk Racial and Ethnic Groups—Blacks and Hispanics, 1970 to 1983, Atlanta: Centers for Disease Control, November 1986, p. 7.

64. Centers for Disease Control, pp. 14–15.
65. Centers for Disease Control, p. 16.
66. Listening Post 5: No. 1, February 1984. A Periodical of the Mental Health Programs, Indian Health Service.
67. Indian Health Service, Chart Book Series: June 1984.
68. Cynthia Leyba, "Homicide in Bernalillo County: 1978–1982." (Paper commissioned by the Research Conference on Violence and Homicide in Hispanic Communities, University of California, Los Angeles, September 14 and 15, 1987, Table 6, p. 14.)
69. University of California, Los Angeles, Centers for Disease Control: The Epidemiology of Homicide in the City of Los Angeles, 1970–1979, Department of Health and Human Services, Public Health Service, Centers for Disease Control, August 1985, p. 18.
70. Fred Loya, Philip Garcia, John D. Sullivan, Luis A. Vargas, Nancy Allen, and James A. Mercy, "Conditional Risks of Types of Homicide Among Anglo, Hispanic, Black and Asian Victims in Los Angeles, 1970–1979," in *Report of the Secretary*, p. 123.
71. Centers for Disease Control, p. 5.
72. Centers for Disease Control, p. 5.
73. Carolyn Rebecca Block, "Lethal Violence in Chicago Over Seventeen Years: Homicides Known to the Police, 1965–1981, Illinois Criminal Justice Information Authority, July 1985, p. 68.
74. Carolyn Rebecca Block, p. iv.
75. "Homicide in California, 1985," Department of Justice, Bureau of Criminal Statistics and Special Services, State of California, 1985, p. 67.
76. Marvin E. Wolfgang and Franco Ferracuti, *The Subculture of Violence: Towards an Integrated Theory in Criminology* (Beverly Hills, Calif.: Sage Publications, 1982).
77. Armando Morales, "Hispanic Gang Violence and Homicide." (Paper commissioned by the Research Conference on Violence and Homicide in Hispanic Communities, sponsored by the Office of Minority Health, Department of Health and Human Services, the National Institute of Mental Health and the U.S. Centers for Disease Control, University of California, Los Angeles, September 14–15, 1987, p. 30.)
78. *Homicide in California, 1985*, p. 17.
79. Carolyn Rebecca Block, p. 69.
80. Carolyn Rebecca Block, "Specification of Patterns Over Time in Chicago Homicide: Increases and Decreases, 1965–1981," Illinois Criminal Justice Information Authority, October 1985, p. 16.
81. Carolyn Rebecca Block, "Specification of Patterns Over Time in Chicago Homicide: Increases and Decreases, 1965–1981," Illinois Criminal Justice Information Authority, October 1985, p. 87.
82. Sources: *Homicide in California, 1985*; "Statistical Digest, 1983," Automated Information Division, Los Angeles Police Department; *State Task Force on Youth Gang Violence*, Final Report, California Council on Criminal Justice, January 1986.
83. "Statistical Digest, 1986," Automated Information Division, Los Angeles Police Department.
84. "Fiscal Year 1985–86 Statistical Summary," Los Angeles County Sheriff's Department.
85. *Los Angeles Times*, Part II, Wednesday, February 24, 1988, p. 1.
86. Centers for Disease Control, p. 3.
87. *Los Angeles Times*, Metro, Part II, Saturday, February 6, 1988, p. 9.
88. *Los Angeles Times*, Metro, Part II, Wednesday, February 10, 1988, p. 1.
89. *Los Angeles Times*, Metro, Part II, Sunday, February 14, 1988, p. 1.
90. *Los Angeles Times*, Metro, Part II, Wednesday, February 24, 1988, p. 1.
91. Armando Morales, *Ando Sangrando: I am Bleeding: A Study of Mexican American Police Conflict* (La Puente, Calif.: Perspectiva Publications, 1972), pp. 91–122.

92. "McCone Revisited: A Focus on Solutions to Continuing Problems in South Central Los Angeles," a Joint Report by the Los Angeles County Commission on Human Relations, and the Los Angeles City Human Relations Commission, January 1985, p. 2.

93. Armando Morales, *Ando Sangrando.*

94. *Los Angeles Times*, Metro, Part II, Sunday, February 28, 1988, p. 2.

95. Armando Morales, "A Study of Recidivism of Mexican American Gang and Non-Gang Forestry Camp Graduates," (Unpublished master's thesis, School of Social Work, University of Southern California, 1963.)

96. See Thomas M. Meenaghan, "Macro Practice: Current Trends and Issues," in *Encyclopedia of Social Work*, 18th ed., Vol. II (Silver Spring, Md.: National Association of Social Workers, 1987), pp. 82–89; and Armando Morales and Bradford W. Sheafor, *Social Work: A Profession of Many Faces*, 4th ed. (Boston, Mass.: Allyn and Bacon, 1986), pp. 131–132.

97. "McCone Revisited," pp. 4–14.

98. "McCone Revisited," p. 7.

99. *Report of the National Advisory Commission on Civil Disorders*, (New York: Bantam Books, 1968), p. 206.

100. Armando Morales, *Ando Sangrando*, pp. 91–122.

101. Frederick M. Thrasher, *The Gang*, p. 33.

102. Frederick M. Thrasher, p. 35.

103. *State Task Force on Youth Gang Violence*, Final Report, California Council on Criminal Justice, January 1986, p. viii.

104. "A Program to Combat Gang Problems in Los Angeles County," Los Angeles County Department of Community Services, November 1972, p. 5.

105. Frederick M. Thrasher, p. 353.

106. Malcolm W. Klein, *Street Gangs and Street Workers* (Englewood Cliffs, N.J.: Prentice-Hall, Inc., 1971).

107. Jerome Singer, *The Control of Aggression and Violence* (New York: Academic Press, 1971).

108. "Victory Outreach Friendship Station," Newsletter, 1978.

109. "Early Gang Intervention," Transfer of Knowledge Workshop, Department of the Youth Authority, Office of Criminal Justice Planning, February 1985, p. 9.

110. Armando Morales, "The Need for Non-Traditional Programs in the *Barrio*," pp. 133–141.

111. Matthew P. Dumont, *The Absurd Healer*, (New York: The Viking Press, 1968), p. 151.

112. Matthew P. Dumont, p. 151.

113. Adelaide M. Johnson, "Juvenile Delinquency," in Silvano Arieti, ed., *American Handbook of Psychiatry* (New York: Basic Books, 1959), p. 854.

114. S. Berman, "Antisocial Character Disorder," in Ruth S. Cavan, ed., *Readings in Juvenile Delinquency*, 2nd ed., (New York: J.B. Lippincott, 1969), pp. 147–157.

115. Ruth R. Middleman and Gale Goldberg, "Social Work Practice with Groups," *Encyclopedia of Social Work*, pp. 718–719.

116. Jerry R. Fox, pp. 26–27.

117. Jerry R. Fox, p. 29.

118. Jerry R. Fox, p. 26.

119. Irving A. Spergel, p. 220.

120. Irving A. Spergel, pp. 221–222.

CHAPTER 17

The Juvenile Justice
System and Minorities

Armando Morales,
Yvonne Ferguson, and Paul R. Munford

PREFATORY COMMENT

This chapter was included to show how the juvenile justice system (police, probation, the juvenile court, placement institutions) affects minority youths. The authors, Armando Morales, a social worker, Yvonne Ferguson, a child psychiatrist and Paul R. Munford, a psychologist, maintain that minority juveniles are not receiving equal treatment before the law and that they are over-represented in correctional institutions. An analysis of minorities in juvenile hall detention reveals an almshouse-like standard of care for juveniles with serious behavioral and psychiatric problems. As an alternative to institutional care for minority offenders, these authors suggest social and community and behavioral intervention types of programs.

The "Juvenile Justice System" refers to official structures, agencies and institutions with which juveniles may become involved, including the Juvenile Court, law enforcement agencies, detention facilities, the probation department, correctional institutions and after-care programs. This system is guided by a complex interplay of laws, heritage and current cultural and political forces. Its resultant functions reveal major philosophical and programmatic contradictions. For example, the juvenile court is ostensibly a benevolent setting functioning to help the child; however, children now have to be protected by attorneys in court given common due process violations. The goal of punishing the child is rarely stated as the philosophical rationale regarding the purpose of the Juvenile Court, yet this seems to be the clear intention of many individuals in the general public and among many judges and law enforcement personnel. In some instances, these intentions are also present in the law. For example, in discussing Juvenile Court Law, the California Welfare and Institutions Code (Section 502a) states that "the purpose of this chapter is . . . to impose on the minor a sense of responsibility for his own acts."

From: Gloria Johnson Powell, Joe Yamamoto, Annelisa Romero, Armando Morales (Eds.), *The Psychosocial Development of Minority Group Children* (New York: Brunner/Mazel, Inc., 1983).

Even a liberal such as Senator Edward Kennedy shares such views regarding what should be a goal of the juvenile justice system. In a 1978 speech to the International Association of Chiefs of Police, he advocated "significant punishment" for juvenile offenders (*L.A. Times*, 1978b).

Currently, one finds three trends in the handling of youths in the juvenile criminal justice system: (1) more lenient dispositions—often non-court— of those youngsters (sometimes called status offenders) who commit crimes which, had they been committed by adults, would not have been considered crimes (truants, runaways, incorrigibles); (2) the effort to shift the treatment of status offenders from courts and probation programs to community social agencies; and (3) harsher treatment of juvenile offenders who commit serious crimes. The literature does not make it clear, however, whether or not minority youth are receiving equal treatment in the juvenile justice system as to arrests, diversion opportunities (out-of-court, probation, and institution handling) and punishment. Some authors, such as Sarri and Vinter, would argue that minority youth are *not* receiving equal treatment. For example, a National Assessment of Juvenile Corrections (NAJC) study of 42 randomly selected correctional programs involving 922 youths ranging in age from 8 to 24 revealed that more than half (55 percent) of institutionalized youth were minority (mostly Blacks, 32.2 percent), with whites representing 45 percent. For juvenile delinquents referred to community residential programs, the opposite was found to be true with whites comprising almost 54 percent of those in community programs and minorities 46 percent. This finding is even more dramatic considering that the minority population in the United States is only 15 percent. Sarri and Vinter (1976) therefore concluded that:

> . . . these findings clearly indicate that juvenile correctional programs disproportionately represent minority populations. Overall, however, we have no information showing that minority youth are more delinquent than whites, either in terms of self-reported frequency or in engagement in a variety of delinquent behaviors, or in terms of the offenses for which they were committed.

It would appear that subtle, institutional racism dynamics in the juvenile justice system would be one factor to be considered in the overrepresentation of minority youth. In this respect, minority children are at far greater risk than white children of being permanently emotionally scarred by their experiences with the juvenile justice system. Additionally, the impact of their arrests and court records will handicap them further in future employment in a society with an increasing paucity of job opportunities for inner-city minority youth. Meager employment opportunities will further lock them into a life of continued poverty and possibly also criminality.

This chapter will examine more closely the minority youth experiences in the juvenile justice system in the Los Angeles area where the total minority poulation reached 51 percent in 1980. These experiences might be shared by minority youth in other parts of the country. Following a few historical comments concerning the juvenile justice system, the components of the system (police, probation, juvenile court, and institutions) will be discussed in greater detail.

HISTORICAL OVERVIEW

A review of selected philosophical treatises on children's rights by Worsfold (1974) serves to highlight parallel milestones in the history of the juvenile justice system. In the 17th century, Thomas Hobbes espoused the paternalistic view that children were cared for solely because they were capable of serving their fathers who held absolute authority over their offspring's life and well-being. John Locke later emphasized the elements of children's "natural rights" which included freedom from anything which might ever injure or affront them, the safeguard of which rested solely on the benevolence of parents. Still later in the 19th century, John Stuart Mill pronounced society's absolute authority over children, excluding them from any right to free choice because of their inability to decide what is in their own best interest.

Embracing these themes of ideological development, medieval society for all practical purposes regarded children as little adults, as, for example, manifested by their dress and titles, if aristocratic, with many attendant adult responsibilities once they became verbal and motorically developed enough to not require adult supervision. The psychosexual period called adolescence was virtually ignored in order to provide necessary labor to a society which was inching its way out of an agrarian order and to condense life scripts into the much shorter life span of that period. At the turn of the century, the large demand for cheap and free labor necessitated by the Industrial Revolution heralded the era of social reform in regard to the rights of children—particularly children of the poor who were being exploited in factories and incarcerated with adults in almshouses, asylums, and prisons. Juvenile reformatories in the United States numbered sixty-five by 1900 (Polier, 1974).

In 1909 the White House convened a Conference on the Care of Dependent Children organized by the leaders of the Setttlement House Movement such as social workers Jane Addams and Lillian Wald, and the National Child Labor Committee. This was the first of such conferences held each decade thereafter which brought together concerned professionals, parents, and political agitators for child advocacy. Congress created the Children's Bureau with its focus on infant and maternal mortality and health, funding it a controversial $25,000 (Beck, 1973). As a result of these collective efforts, several states passed statutes establishing juvenile courts in which delinquent children were to be handled separately and differently from adult violators of the law. The practice of placing youth on probation and assigning probation officers was initiated as an alternative to sentencing and dismissal of the case (Kanner, 1972).

These reforms ushered in the child guidance movement of the 1920s, led by Thom in Boston. With the opening of demonstration clinics in several New

England cities staffed by interdisciplinary professional teams, the field of psychiatry officially recognized the unique problems and needs of persons under 18 years of age. Gradually, foster home placement organizations and the field of special education arose, providing yet additional services to juvenile courts (Kanner, 1972).

Currently, within the juvenile justice system there is wide variation in policies and practices from state to state and within states. This should not preclude the determination of a set of policy and operational standards which would ultimately permit optimal reintegration of youth into society where guilt is judged. In cases where guilt is not found, such standards should ensure that innocent youth are not traumatized by society's mistakes.

THE POLICE

Juvenile delinquency, crime, violence, and police policy and practices have a strong effect on children growing up in minority communities. The Joint Commission on Mental Health of Children (1969) recommended that the nature of this effect and its relationship to mental health be more closely examined. The majority of Hispanic *barrio* and Black ghetto residents resent police surveillance. The feeling is even more intense among minority youth (Wertham and Piliavin, 1975). As soon as a patrolman begins to interrogate these youngsters, they often feel their moral identity is being challenged because of their dress, hair style, skin color and presence in the community itself. Often this is true. It is not uncommon, for example, for police to *believe* it to be a fact that minorities commit more crimes than whites even when actual statistics may reveal the contrary (Morales, 1975). These stereotypic beliefs will often lead to a greater saturation of police in the minority community. Such saturation will produce a larger number of arrests and no doubt inhibit some kind of criminal activity, but according to criminologist Gilbert Geis (1962), "it is the police activity and not the behavior of the group itself which is conditioning the crime rates for the group as these eventually appear in the printed statistics." This phenomenon leads to what Robert K. Merton called a "self-fulfilling prophecy."

Los Angeles has numerous juvenile gangs, comprised of Hispanics, Blacks, Whites, Asian-Americans. The majority, however, are Hispanic and Black. A major police agency in Los Angeles has developed a "Street Gangs" manual to "assist the field officer in understanding and dealing with the gang phenomenon." It is filled with racist stereotypes of Black and Hispanic youth in terms of clothing, nicknames and lifestyles common in inner-city minority communities. In the 16-page manual, *only one sentence is devoted to Anglo gangs!* The officer is psychologically conditioned to seek out Black and Hispanic youth who conform to the manual's criteria as to who is supposed to be a gang member. The fact is that over 95 percent of minority youth are not gang members, yet may meet the stereotypic criteria in the manual. Furthermore, intentionally or not, the manual in effect is asking officers to ignore white gangs by not providing them with any specific information about white gangs. The following are some instructions in the manual as to an Hispanic gang member's appearance (Street Gangs, 1980):

Watch Cap—The cap ("Beany") is worn by the member primarily in the winter but may be worn in the summer. It is pulled down to cover the ears, with a small roll at the bottom. It is blue in color and made of a knit material.

Bandana—The bandana or "moco rag" is worn just over the forehead and tied in the back.

Hat—The "stingy" brim is favored by the gang member but recently the baseball cap is being utilized.

Shirts—The Pendleton shirt has long been a favorite of the gang member.

T-Shirt—The round or V-neck T-shirt is worn during the summer.

Blue Jeans—also known as "counties," are highly starched, baggy, and rolled in small rolls at the cuff and slit up the side.

Shoes—Shoes may range from tennis shoes to french-toed shoes. If the shoes are leather they will be highly shined.

The manual described the Black gang member's appearance as follows:

Headgear—Black gang members wear "stingy" brims, leather "pork-pies," and floppy-type hats, with jewelry attached. Some will wear handkerchiefs.

Jackets—The bomber- and tanker-type are preferred.

Shirts—The black gang member likes to wear the black T-shirt rather than the white T-shirt.

Pants—The pants are usually jeans with rolled-up cuffs. Suspenders are commonly worn with the pants.

Shoes—The shoes range from canvas Crocker Sacks to shiny leather shoes.

Miscellaneous—Black gang members may wear earrings and carry a cane or umbrella (walking type). Many carry handkerchiefs, railroad-type (blue or red), hanging from the rear pocket.

With regard to the type of vehicles Black and Hispanic gang members drive, the manual informs officers that they favor Chevrolets of the mid-1960s era, which are "lowered and may have a very small chrome or vinyl covered steering wheel, fur on the dashboard and chrome or mag wheels" (p. 11). Car clubs in minority communities, therefore, may be perceived by police as being gang-oriented. The manual also familiarizes officers with nicknames gang members have, such as "Angel," "Blackie," "Huero," "Junior," "Pee Wee," "Porky," "Cowboy," "Turkey," and "Mando," the latter being a nickname of one of the authors. Considering that the vast majority of minority youth are not gang members, these very common nicknames would be more prevalent in the general minority population. The manual concludes with the statement that the police are taking a "proactive" rather than a "reactive" stance, and that they are attempting "to identify the gang members before they commit a crime, thus removing the anonymity factor. (p. 15)" Such a policing strategy would not appear to be consistent with a basic American judicial tenet of "innocent until proven guilty."

A proactive rather than a reactive law enforcement stance is not an uncommon police deployment strategy, sometimes referred to as "aggressive preventive patrol." The President's Commission on Law Enforcement and the Administration of Justice found that police spend half of their time on preventive patrol, but that no police chief can obtain even a rough estimate of how much crime is thereby prevented (President's Commission, 1967). Although it might be difficult to measure the crime prevention outcomes of police patrol, it would be possible to measure what James Q. Wilson calls "Police-Invoked Order Maintenance," that is, police-initiated intervention. This was discussed in the previous chapter.

The "proactive" patrol, "aggressive preventive patrol," or "police-invoked order maintenance"—all representing police initiated intervention—also may have negative consequences for minority juveniles. There is no denying that gang violence exists in the inner cities, but often public and police beliefs surpass the actual facts. For example, the major newspaper in Southern California, the *Los Angeles Times*, reported that there had been "160 gang-related deaths in East Los Angeles last year (1979)." East Los Angeles is a predominantly Hispanic community. The statistical facts are that there were only a total of 20 gang-related deaths in East Los Angeles for the year in question (Friendship, 1978).

During the early part of 1979, a gang film about East Los Angeles called "Boulevard Nights" was shown. Based upon the belief that gang members were as dangerous as the press had led people to believe, the L.A. County Sheriff's Department increased its patrol of Whittier Boulevard—a popular social area for Hispanic youth—four times the usual number. The result was that arrests for the weekend quadrupled, with 391 arrests being made, five for assault and the rest for minor offenses such as loitering (*L.A. Times*, 1979a). This is a clear example of police behavior inflating the crime rate in a specific community.

One may argue that only in some special circumstances, such as the showing of a gang film, will there be a need to increase police-initiated patrol intervention. The point is that the probabilities of a juvenile being arrested by the police is more a function of where that person lives rather than of his or her behavior. Consider the following selected arrests involving juveniles in a lower-class predominantly Hispanic community, and a middle-class predominantly white community in Los Angeles County (Statistical Summary, 1974–75) [in Table 17–1].

From [these] arrests, it is seen that proportionately because of the smaller white population, there is more crime in the white community for grand theft, burglary, and especially petty theft. These are not police-invoked order main-

TABLE 17-1

COMMUNITY	SQ. MI.	POPULATION	ANNUAL JUVENILE ARRESTS				
			GRAND THEFT	BURGLARY	PETTY THEFT	LOITERING	
Predominantly Hispanic	8.36	102,358	13	131	49	483	
Predominantly white	9.55	81,630	11	121	208	21	

tenance types of offenses since the police became involved *after* the offenses had been committed. However, loitering offenses are police-invoked order maintenance type of offenses as the police are initiating the contact with the juvenile. In other words, because the police believe that minorities generally commit more crime than whites, with their belief reinforced by field deployment and patrol policies which supposedly describe minority gang members in terms of clothing, nicknames and lifestyles, Hispanic youth would appear to be 23 times more likely to be arrested for loitering offenses as compared to whites. Such discriminatory practices, which are supposed to be crime preventive in nature, actually increase crime statistics in the minority community, generate the need for more police manpower based upon an increase in "crime," contribute to a juvenile's arrest record, and prematurely introduce minority youth into the juvenile justice system. As the minority juvenile's arrest record increases, it makes it more difficult for him or her, in comparison to white youngsters, to qualify for more lenient juvenile diversion (away from the juvenile justice system) processing by police.

Pursuant to Sections 224 (a) (3) and 527 of the Juvenile Justice and Delinquency Prevention Act of 1974, and Sections 301 and 451 of the Omnibus Crime Control Act of 1968 as amended, the purpose of diversion programs is to divert juveniles from involvement with the traditional juvenile justice system at the critical points of penetration, and to determine the significance of providing effective and coordinated services to some of those youth diverted. Various dispositional alternatives may be available to juvenile justice system officials at the various points where a youth is in contact with the system. These alternatives might range from counsel and release by police to participation in a community-based public or private residential program by direction of the juvenile court prior to adjudication. *Diversion* as a concept would appear to hold promise for minority youth who are overrepresented in the juvenile justice system. Police cooperation, however, would be paramount in order for this to become a reality.

In a study of 35 police departments with diversion programs, Klein and his colleagues (1976) found that police motives for diversion are often not what is commonly implied by the term "diversion." Factors which led to referral away from the system included shorter prior arrest records (two priors or less), a preference for younger offenders over older ones, and the officer's estimation that the youth was not likely to be rearrested. "Thus," Klein concluded, "the composite picture of the more referable offender seems to be of the young, minor offender with little or no record, who is unlikely to be rearrested in any case" (page 107–108).

Klein and colleagues cite the case of one rather large police agency which specifically lists cases for which diversion may not be employed. Cases may not be diverted and referred if they involve the following (page 108):

1. felony offenses resulting in death or serious injury;
2. known gang members;
3. more than two prior arrests;

4. offenders already on probation or parole;

5. crimes against police officers, school personnel (teachers, administrators, or any other regular employee), or employees of the recreation department;

6. offenses that disrupt school or recreation department activities or destroy property of school and recreation departments;

7. use or possession of a deadly weapon;

8. offenders judged physically dangerous to the public because of a mental or physical deficiency, disorder, or abnormality;

9. escapees from probation institutions;

10. selected Vehicle Code violations, primarily hit-and-run, auto theft and driving under the influence of or in possession of drugs, liquor, or weapons;

11. a prior arrest with a referral to a treatment agency.

Klein concludes that the dominant trend in diversion has been to ignore the more serious cases while diverting and referring those less in need but more likely to yield positive results, since the less serious cases seldom recidivate. It would also seem that minority youth would have less of a chance to be diverted due to the increased likelihood of their having more than two arrests and being labeled (often erroneously) a gang member.

A recent study revealed that the Los Angeles diversion situation leaves much to be desired and is similar to the findings of Klein and associates. Lipsey and Johnston (1979) report:

> Diversion has considerable *potential* for reducing the volume of referrals to probation—law enforcement diversions are equivalent to about 20% of the number of juveniles they refer to probation. The projects of the Regional Diversion Program,* however, do not appear to be receiving a significant number of cases that otherwise would have been sent for probation processing. Instead, most law diversions are made from among those juveniles who otherwise would have received counsel-and-release dispositions (page II).

The authors of the report recommended an increase of diversion referrals of cases involving more serious juvenile offenders. The report did not make it clear, however, the impact diversion programs were having upon minority youth. Rarely, if ever, were minorities mentioned in the 104-page report. If the general conclusion is that the police are diverting those juveniles who otherwise would have received counsel-and-release dispositions anyway, it could also be concluded that the number of minority youth being referred to the probation department, i.e., into the juvenile justice system, remains relatively unchanged.

---

*The Los Angeles County Regional Diversion Program is comprised of thirteen projects with a combined annual budget of 4.5 million dollars.

PROBATION

Juveniles are referred to probation by the police, schools, welfare departments, and parents. The probation department may undertake an investigation of the case and close it at intake, which results in no further action, or file a petition to the Juvenile Court, where a formal presentation is made of information surrounding the alleged offense. This procedure is similar to a criminal petition for an adult. The Court may order detention of the youth in a juvenile institution or, as an alternative, refer the youngster to probation supervision which permits the juvenile to remain in the community. A youngster on probation typically receives supervision and casework services. A deputy probation officer usually provides these services to the extent of his/her training, caseload, and department organization permits. In addition, the deputy probation officer also makes referrals to a variety of educational, health, vocational, social welfare, mental health, and legal agencies.

Supervision of the minor is a major function of the deputy probation officer. Since the youth has been declared a ward of the Court for a specified period of time, it is the deputy probation officer's responsibility to supervise the ward to ensure that he or she is following the requirements of probation. The following general conditions are usually applicable to all probationers: regular school attendance or steady employment; maintaining periodic contacts with the deputy probation officer, abiding by curfew regulations, avoiding contacts with other delinquent youths, complying with parental directions and obeying the law. In addition, specific requirements can be stipulated relative to the nature of the offense committed and the history of the probationer. These include financial or other forms of restitution to victims, avoiding specific individuals or situations deleterious to the probationer and seeking and participating in psychotherapeutic treatment or other rehabilitation procedures such as special educational or training programs. Another major task of the deputy probation officer is to provide casework services. These include the provision of individual and group counseling, functioning as a liaison between the home and school, providing parent counseling and making referrals for their probationers to other agencies, institutions and health care providers.

Finally, the deputy probation officer makes periodic reports to the Court on their probationers' adherence to the conditions of probation or commission of new offenses. On these occasions, the officer may recommend the Court to terminate probation, continue probation or commit the youth to an institution. Although the final decision is the Court's, it usually concurs with the probation officer's recommendation.

The projected ethnic composition for Los Angeles County for 1980 was estimated to be 44.4 percent white, 28.8 percent Hispanic, and 21.5 percent Black. Presumably the remaining percentage of 5.3 percent is comprised of Asian-Americans, American Indians and "others" (*L.A. Times*, 1978a). the total number of juveniles referred to the Los Angeles County Probation Department in 1976 was 54,767. Of these, 23,341 (42.6 percent) were White;

TABLE 17–2 Six Most Frequent Probation Referral Offenses By Ethnicity and Race

WHITE			HISPANIC			BLACK			ASIAN AMERICAN			AMERICAN INDIAN		
	#	%		#	%		#	%		#	%		#	%
Burglary	(4234)	44	Burglary	(1876)	20	Burglary	(3395)	35	Burglary	(12)	1	Burglary	(31)	.3
Poss. Marij.	(2699)	51	Poss. Marij.	(1052)	20	Petty Theft	(1653)	35	Petty Theft	(9)	0	Transient	(15)	1
Petty Theft	(2033)	43	Auto Theft/ Joy Riding	(1045)	32	Poss. Marij.	(1417)	27	Auto Theft/ Joy Riding	(7)	.2	Glue Sniffing	(15)	1
Transient	(1468)	67	Petty Theft	(969)	20	Robbery	(1288)	60	Poss. Marij.	(7)	.1	Battery	(14)	.7
Man-slaughter	(1053)	41	Curfew	(814)	33	Auto Theft/ Joy Riding	(966)	29	Man-slaughter	(4)	0	Petty Theft	(14)	0
Drunk	(1030)	50	Drunk	(801)	50	Assault w/ Deadly Wpn	(792)	41	Curfew	(4)	.2	Poss. Marij.	(12)	.2
									Runaway	(4)	0	Drunk	(28)	1

14,154 (25.8 percent) were Hispanic; 15,860 (29 percent) were Black; 94 (.2 percent) were Asian-American; 219 (.4 percent) were American Indian; and 1099 (2 percent) were "other" (Probation, 1978). Since the probation department figures were from 1976, it is apparent that there was an overrepresentation of Hispanics and Blacks in probation referrals and conversely, an underrepresentation of whites, Asian-Americans and American Indians. Table 17–2 reports the six most frequent offenses for which the various ethnic/racial groups were referred to probation.

From the data presented in Table 17–2, it is seen that the first three most common offenses for whites and minorities were similar, that is, burglary, petty theft, and the possession of marijuana. From the standpoint of dangerousness to others in the remaining offenses, Whites were the most dangerous group as they had committed 41 percent (1053) of all manslaughter offenses, as compared to 31 percent for Blacks and 21 percent for Hispanics. White juveniles committed 24 homicides, Blacks 60, and Hispanics 41. Since seriousness of offense is an important factor in referring juveniles into the juvenile justice system, one would expect whites to be very well represented in juvenile hall. They are not, as will be seen in the following discussion of minorities detained in Juvenile Hall awaiting a court disposition of their case.

MINORITIES IN JUVENILE HALL DETENTION

A case study program evaluation involves data collection on a unique, uncontrolled population for purposes of recommending improvements in the delivery system for evaluating the effectiveness of service programs (Fink and Kosecoff, 1978). Of such a nature is this case study of a typical, large, urban juvenile detention facility for youth awaiting adjudication and placement for the alleged commitment of "602" offenses, that is, offenses which, if committed by adults, would constitute a crime, according to the California Penal Code. The study, undertaken by one of the authors, a child psychiatrist for the Western Center on Law and Poverty, Inc., in Los Angeles, California, was submitted as expert testimony in a 1975 class-action suit, Manney vs. Cabell et al., filed in the United States District Court. The suit was filed on behalf of Dwight Manney and all other male juveniles being held in detention at that time and previously, charging the Central Juvenile Hall administration and Los Angeles County officials with the abridgment of the youths' civil rights. Some of the civil rights in question were those guaranteed by the Eighth Amendment which prohibits "cruel and unusual punishments," including mental and psychological anguish; the right to due process and equal protection of the laws; and rights provided by the First Amendment—freedom of privacy and speech.

Two purposes of the study were to make recommendations for improvements in the existing detention program at the Los Angeles County Probation Department Central Juvenile Hall, hereafter referred to as CJH, and to evaluate its effectiveness from the perspective of its delivery of mental health services. The population consisted of the staff (administrative as well as on-line staff counselors) and male residents, ranging in age from 12 to 17. On-line counselors at CJH are probation officers hired by the Los Angeles County Probation Department through the civil service process. The following means of data collection were used: observations of the physical facility, observation of staff-resident and resident-resident interactions, interviews of staff and residents who were available for questioning, archive review of available documents from CJH and the Los Angeles County Department of Public Social Services, including a review of two hundred medical and behavioral charts of residents. The focus of the study was the evaluation of the psychological milieu at CJH and its effects, particularly on the alleged first-time offender.

Although the stated philosophy of CJH, according to administrators, was indeed the optimal reintegration of youthful offenders, in fact it was the "unspoken philosophy" perceived as being operational at CJH which determined policy and practice at the institution. Some of the effects of this philosophy were explored. First there was a presumed "guilt-until-proven-otherwise" attitude which pervaded the administrative and on-line staff thinking throughout the facility. Secondly, approximately 80 to 85 percent of the resident population were Black, with Whites and Hispanic youth making up the remainder. As was seen earlier in this chapter and documented by other investigators, minority youth are more likely to be subjected to discriminatory apprehension practices by police prior to detention which would account for the ethnically disproportionate ratio observed. These two features of practice taken together might make it difficult for personnel to draw other than the conclusion that minorities must have the upper hand on delinquency. Once a youth reached the facility, the Intake Detention Control (IDC) became the critical point of entry where far-reaching decisions appeared to be made on rather arbitrary bases by non-professionally trained personnel. Not only did personnel in IDC determine whether a juvenile was to be detained, but they also employed unproven criteria for classifying youth according to their "releasibility." Characteristics such as age, size, previous arrests and detention records and family histories, constituted subjective indices for making judgments as to youths' escape risk.

Following processing by IDC, unit assignments appeared to be made on the basis of capricious criteria—in some cases involving ethnicity or race. For example, there was a Spanish-speaking only unit; on others, it was physical size. Once a youth was processed within the system and assigned to a unit, the guiding principle in terms of how staff were to interact with the youth appeared to be related to institutional needs such as behavior control and management of large numbers of boys—this, in direct contradiction to the commitment to rehabilitate and fulfill the role of *parens patriae*. In many instances the CJH system exhibited elements existing primarily to meet the needs of the staff, not of the youth who resided there. This was evident in the restrictive, negatively phrased language of rules. For example, youth were forbidden to talk during meals or mass movements. "Horseplay" was forbidden. Attendance to physiological needs such as the satisfaction of one's thirst or the elimination of one's bladder or bowels was forbidden except at prescribed times.

One of the greatest obstacles to juvenile rehabilitation is seen when no attempt is made to pre-screen counselor applicants who may have personality factors as violence-proneness, problems with authority, and sadistic tendencies. Under these circumstances, detention centers with such hiring practices may become the stage for some disturbed personnel who may unconsciously trigger acting-out among the juveniles. In this regard the lack of an effective grievance procedure for juvenile residents prevented the discovery of abusive conduct on the part of staff and encouraged the tacit approval of such behavior as a routine part of institutional life. All animals tend to adapt and become sophisticated with experience, and humans are no exception. Unfortunately, it is the newcomer, the first-time alleged offender, who pays the greatest emotional toll in this type of setting. After the initial shock of confinement to a new residential system, he is likely to experience the conflict of succumbing to feared retaliation if he does not conform or of forfeiting some of his identity if he does. In such a youthful population, one would expect to find the usual adolescent turmoil and chaos exacerbated by this type of stressful environment. It would be difficult, if not impossible, for a first offender or innocent juvenile to pass through such an environment emotionally unscathed.

The physical milieu of the facility may be as traumatic as the emotional atmosphere at CJH. The oldest buildings, which were more than fifty years old, were laid out on a campus model set around a main recreation field. There were a total of ten units housed in five buildings on the "602" side, which had a bed capacity of 328. One of these (Unit I) was the infirmary. There was a multidenominational chapel, a school, one dining hall, two basketball courts, a gymnasium, and a baseball diamond. Although the large fields gave the impression of spaciousness, the amount of time spent outside (two 45-minute recreation periods a day) meant that most of the juveniles' day was spent indoors. The interiors of most units were lacking any aesthetic qualities. Dark or dingy colors, with a few exceptions, cast a forlorness throughout the units. In some, paint was peeling, collections of dust could be seen in the corners of the rooms, and the amount of daylight entering through the windows was considerably less than optimal.

The rooms, as they were called, looked like cells. They were small, allowing for a single bed with a non-spring mattress; usually a metal desk with an attached swing-out stool; a wash basin; and in some rooms, a urinal. On unit "EF," there were no urinals in the rooms. Estimated room size was 8' × 10' × 6'. There was a dim ceiling light which appeared to be inadequate for nighttime reading. Each door had a small 1' × 1½' window, usually without safety glass but with iron bars on the outside. The only means of communication once the doors were locked was yelling or banging—ironically, the very reasons why some youth were sent to the intensive care unit.*

---

* "ICU" for short was Unit XY which served the dual purpose of providing isolation as punishment and the purported observation of severely disturbed youth such as psychotic or suicidal individuals.

There was no evidence of any resident individuality or creativity in any of the rooms expressed through the presence of posters or personal items such as pictures or radios. At night when the doors were locked and the lights turned off, the ensuing nine or ten hours of relative sensory deprivation with entrapment would be sufficient to precipitate an acute psychotic episode in a normal sleep-deprived youth such as an anxious first-timer or in an emotionally unstable one. The mechanism of this phenomenon is as follows: With decreased stimulation, conflicts from past experiences begin to surface to the consciousness but have no means for expression, as talking or noise-making at this time was forbidden. Furthermore, this is the time when staff are least available. Most units had only one evening staff member for 40 boys. Indeed, counseling youth at this most appropriate time, which is statistically when most suicide attempts, hallucinations, disturbing thoughts and dreams occur, would tend to interfere with other duties of the staff such as charting or college "homework." Despite their age and superficial sophistication, these youth *do* experience anxiety about being separated from their families, which tends to be exaggerated and intensified under such conditions (Crewe, 1973).

All units had a day room for approximately every 20 occupants, which had a television, several straight-backed metal chairs, and occasionally a ping-pong table. This was the room where any counseling, outside of one's individual room, usually took place as well, if it occurred at all. It was not possible to find a relatively quiet atmosphere in this or any other room on a unit. No units had any facilities for privacy other than individual residents' rooms. There were no treatment or consultation rooms on the residential units. The lack of privacy in some units even extended to residents' use of the toilet. On Unit "M and N," large glass windows on two sides of the bathroom afforded more than ample opportunity for observation by anyone, an interior design feature which can contribute to paranoid ideation in persons so disposed.

Among some youths interviewed, the physical conditions most disturbing were the cold, unsavory meals which often were not served in sufficient proportions; the cockroaches, which crawled under some of the residents' bodies at night; and the mice which ran around the rooms. A meal cart was observed which contained food overcooked to the extent that its exact nature was indeterminable. Some youths stated the taste of the food was so bad they refused to eat it and drank only the milk.

In summary, this "almshouse" standard of care constituted basically a custodial milieu. The counselor's primary responsibilities consisted of supervising the juveniles in carrying out personal hygiene activities, procuring meals, attending scheduled events, and bedding down for the night. Hence, the misnomer of "counselor." Anything which interfered with these responsibilities was considered obstructive and the desire for counseling itself tended to fall into that category if it was not requested at a convenient time or if it was solicited through attention-getting behavior rather than verbally.

The adequacy of the school program was not investigated as it was not felt by the plaintiffs to constitute a civil rights abridgment. During hours which were scheduled as school time (8:30 A.M.–11:30 A.M. and 1:00 P.M.–3:00 P.M.) many youths were observed lying around in their units, some sleeping, others looking bored. When inquiry was made regarding their absence from school, the explanation given was that some were messengers, an elite group of youth who escorted other youth to appointments and performed special duties which conflicted with school attendance several times a week. These youths were therefore being kept out of school for the convenience of the institution. Other youth were awaiting testing, medical appointments or court hearings.

Recreation was theoretically scheduled for 2½ hours per day but an average individual juvenile spent at most two 45-minute sessions in recreational activities. On Unit "XY," one of these sessions was spent outdoors. Outside recreation consisted of volleyball, football, baseball and relay races. All recreation was of a competitive nature and in actuality encouraged only the athletically proficient. Thus smaller, less motorically adept youth became socially ostracized and often the target for cruel namecalling and jokes by peers. There were no individualized recreational programs nor was there any opportunity for a youth to participate in recreation at times other than those scheduled. No therapeutic use of recreational facilities, such as the displacement of aggressive impulses onto a punching bag rather than a person, was observed. Recreation time was sometimes withheld from youth as a disciplinary measure.

Even less individual flexibility was permitted during meal times. In the classic American family setting this is a time of coming together of all the members and sharing of the fruits of parental labor. In some families it may have religious significance as well. It is ideally a relaxed time when events of the day are exchanged by different members of the family and important issues are discussed. No such significance appeared to apply in the dining hall and pantries at CJH. Here again the theme of control was dominant. Serving and eating were accomplished in 30 minutes per shift. Talking was prohibited. Food at best symbolized satisfaction of physiologic hunger but had to be competed for as there was never enough to go around. Frustration during dining, therefore, often was a set-up for fights. One youth stated that handwashing before meals was not allowed. In Unit "XY," youth were even deprived of the non-verbal experience of eating with other youth as they had to eat solitarily in their rooms.

Though counselors reported that youth were permitted many kinds of activities during what "free time" existed between activities, this time was observed to be spent either watching television or just sitting. Juveniles were noted to look bored and lethargic. Few engaged in activities requiring participation by two or more, such as ping pong. Rarely could music be heard on a unit. According to the residents interviewed, "free time" had to accommodate institutional work details. These consisted of garbage collection, serving meals, mopping floors, laundry work, and other maintenance responsibilities. On some units, this free labor formed the foundation of elementary merit systems. In some cases, basic accommodations such as toilet and shower activities had to be earned by performance of these tasks. Refusal to carry out one's work detail could result in an "F" grade or transfer to ICU, both of which carry negative influence in Court disposition hearings. Were it not for the free labor extracted from these youths, the County would have had to hire personnel to perform these maintenance functions.

No occupational therapy program existed at CJH. Not only could leisure time be used constructively through tapping undeveloped avocational talents of youth, but important assessments could be made about the juveniles' perceptual and motor skills by occupational therapists trained to design and execute individualized programs for each of the residents. Job training could be one aspect of such programs.

The above description of daily activities is the operational schema when there are no kinks in the system; but what if a youngster did not want to go to school or do his work detail or get out of bed? In a family or small institutional setting there would be some flexibility in the expectation for performance of various responsibilities. The perception of most staff interviewed was that one or two youths' refusal to comply with institutional expectations for the day would negatively influence every other youth's participation. To avert this end, strict compliance was always demanded rather than seeking an individual's motivation for refusing to comply and in some instances allowing it where appropriate, e.g., illness or emotional upset. Lacking sophisticated behavioral skills, however, staff often resorted to various punitive measures such as those described above in order to enforce rigid adherence to routine.

Personal hygiene activities such as showering and use of the toilet as well as the opportunity of drinking water or moving to or from another location had become highly ritualized and regimented events for the convenience of the staff. If a youth found himself with the urge to urinate after "head call," then he either had to suppress that urge until morning or urinate out of his window. Whenever unit movement was called for, such as in going to the school, the dining hall, or to recreational activities, the residents were required to do so in a militaristic fashion—marching double-file with hands in their pockets and without talking. Even the terminology employed in such an activity illustrates the point—"movement control." This was felt to be one of the most anti-therapeutic, depersonalizing aspects of the entire milieu. Individuality and creativity, powerful adolescent needs, were extinguished whenever they surfaced, as manifested in the restrictions against individualized dressing, certain hair styles, roughhousing, certain language, and the like (Kahn and Piockowski, 1974). One youth was transferred to ICU because of wearing his clothes in an "unusual manner," namely with his T-shirt sleeves rolled up and his sweatshirt tied around his neck. Another youth was sent to ICU for not combing out his braids before going to school (braids are an acceptable male hairstyle in the Black subculture). Any behavior which deviated from a fantasied norm in the minds of staff—and this differed from person to person—was considered unacceptable and a target for alteration. Consequently, individual expressions of emotional release such as singing, laughing, graffiti-writing, and "horseplay," became punishable behaviors.

Often it was difficult to trace an individual resident's stay at CJH chronologically because of what appeared to be an inordinately large number of transfers between the Los Angeles County detention facility and other outlying facilities. Therefore, an attempt was made to roughly assess an "average" number of transfers for a given period of time for a given youth. An audit of some 75 randomly selected charts revealed transfers ranging on the order of four to six a month for many youths. These transfers were for various reasons—medical evaluations or treatment, disciplinary actions, court hearings, and placements; however, the effect of these moves was to create a sense of instability, a lack of esprit de corps, and a rationalization for not effecting any kind of treatment program. It was argued by some staff that the residents did not remain on a unit long enough to carry out treatment. The time required for these transfers varied but often a resident's whole day was spent in waiting and/or actual travel time. Valuable school and potential treatment time was lost, youth became bored, uncomfortable, and exerienced a sense of confusion, lack of time and spatial orientation, and frustration. In addition, valuable staff time was wasted in supervision of these transfers. Such adverse effects, as well as the expense involved, could easily have been prevented by availing each facility of such satellite services as medical facilities and courtrooms.

Transfers to ICU and downgrading (issuing "F" grades) as two forms of discipline have been mentioned; however, the concept of discipline in general deserves discussion. One staff person commented that if he had his way he would make CJH "tougher" so that youth would not want to come back. This philosophy unfortunately has prevailed among some lawmakers, correctional personnel, and society in general for some time. Most staff had very few psychologically sound behavioral skills which they exercised for altering "negative behavior" on the part of juveniles. "Negative behavior," for example, talking after lights went off, was arbitrarily defined and tended to reflect individual staff persons' personal attitudes rather than being based on sound psychological principles. Since staff were outnumbered, they most frequently used the mechanism of verbal threats to elicit compliance. When this failed, as most normal adolescents will eventually challenge threats, then staff sometimes resorted to room restrictions, downgrading or the withdrawal of "privileges." Such practices could be very effective means of shaping behavior if used properly; however, even on the so-called merit or point-system living units which subscribed to behavior modification principles, no consistently well-planned and practiced behavioral programs were observed. When these more benign strategies failed, some staff, feeling frustrated and impotent, would resort to rather regressed means of control—name-calling (an infraction when used by the juveniles). Some youth even reported instances of physical abuse by staff. These two measures were reported to be frequently exercised by certain staff according to juveniles interviewed. Ultimately a youth might be transferred to ICU (Intensive Care Unit), otherwise known as Unit XY (or to the youth as "lock-up") for rules infractions. A log documenting the reason for each transfer was kept. Behaviorally speaking, most inconsequential behavior, i.e., behavior resulting in no harm to persons or property but primarily attention-seeking in nature, can be reduced in frequency or extinguished altogether by ignoring it; however, many instances of behavior that would fall into this category were dealt with by transferring the youth to ICU. According to staff, disciplinary transfers should have never lasted longer than 24 hours; however, youths reported being there up to a week in some cases.

Unit XY itself merits mention, for being there was by definition restrictive and punitive. It was the maximum security unit, surrounded by a high wall that segregated its residents from the rest of CJH population. It had two wings, an "X" wing for "hard-core" offenders, or youth alleged to have committed serious offenses such as those against persons, and a "Y" wing for disciplinary problem youth from other units or other facilities. As mentioned previously, recreation was more restricted—no intramural activities took place with other units, for XY residents had their own small field which was approximately the length and width of the unit itself. The grass on this field was remarkably unworn. There was no collective eating and the youth attended school on the unit. For having allegedly committed a serious offense, therefore, a youth could be sent directly to XY before his adjudication hearing and be deprived of many of the "relative freedoms" experienced by his peers in other units. Unit XY also served as an observation unit for the more seriously disturbed youth, as was the case of Unit J. In particular, youth who had attempted suicide were sent to XY for "their own protection." Therefore, it might be expected to be the unit with the most psychologically sophisticated personnel and its residents might be expected to receive the most intensive psychiatric care. Unfortunately, this was not the case. Psychiatric treatment for these disturbed youth was not routine, but rather obtained at the discretion of the counselors in this unit who possessed no particular behavioral science skills and who often felt the disturbed behavior was a manifestation of the youth's "just being bad," manipulating, or wanting attention.

There were gross examples of behavioral problems which in adolescents often indicate depression, hyperkinesis, mental retardation and learning disorders, and even psychosis, which did not result in psychiatric referrals. Such problems often required exhaustive use of staff and even resulted in the youth or others being injured as a result of the problem. Some serious disturbances lasted for months or the duration of the youth's stay. Another glaringly overlooked psychiatric disorder was that of drug dependency. In none of such cases reviewed could instances of psychiatric referrals for the drug dependency itself be found although often extensive medical workups had been performed.

Psychiatric consultations reviewed were of varying quality. Most initial consultations appeared to reflect a 30- to 60-minute session spent with the youth. Rarely was this stated. The type of report on the charts was usually a court-ordered report and since court-ordered psychiatric reports need not include all information obtained by a consultant and because they are written for lay persons, it was not always clear just how thorough such evaluations had been. The most glaring variability was in diagnoses. From the reports it was often difficult to determine the basis for a particular diagnosis, with different consultants appearing to employ their own unique criteria rather than universal standards, as found in the Amerian Psychiatric Association Diagnostic and Statistical Manual (DSM III). A most disturbing phenomena, given the present state of the art in psychiatry, was the prediction of violence and the labeling of certain youth as potential murderers by psychiatrists and psychologists. It is generally agreed upon by colleagues in this field that because of infrequent commission of violence, particularly murder, by a given individual, and because murderers fall into many different diagnostic categories, including essentially normal persons, behavioral scientists are not equipped to make such predictions (Sendi and Blomgren, 1975). Furthermore, to do so can be extremely dangerous since, once someone receives the label of potential murderer, a self-fulfilling prophecy is often set in motion. Often mental health professionals unwittingly become tools of social control when they impose subjective definitions of behavior and use arbitrary criteria which ensure certain predictable social consequences (Miller, 1971).

The second phase of treatment is the actual therapy which is usually delivered primarily by psychiatrists, clinical social workers and psychologists. In a setting such as CJH where other staff have more frequent contact with the residents, mental health professionals may prescribe certain therapeutic milieus or interventions which can be carried out by non-mental health personnel. As far as could be determined from the charts, post-evaluation therapy at CJH consisted of medication. Only rarely did the same therapist see the youth in subsequent follow-up sessions, so that continuity of care for the most part did not exist. Body restraints, a medical tool, were used, as far as could be determined, by non-medical personnel, *without* a physician's order.

Family therapy, a modality which is being used with increasing efficacy for adolescents, was recommended in only one consultation which was reviewed. Of all the youth interviewed, only one was scheduled to receive this form of therapy, which is no longer conducted at CJH. Where individual therapy was recommended, it often was not clear who would carry it out and whether it was to take place at CJH, in a placement facility, or after release. When intensive individual therapy in an inpatient setting was recommended, it was not effected if Unit III (psychiatric unit) of Los Angeles County–USC Medical Center had no beds available.

Comprehensive psychiatric care should include some form of follow-up or a built-in assessment and maintenance of the efficacy of interventions. This is made difficult at CJH because of the mobility of this population. Often follow-up can be effected by a mere phone call and not necessarily by a medically trained person, although where medication was the intervention a physician should assess its efficacy over time. This phase of treatment becomes extremely important in such a population as the one at CJH where psychiatric intervention was not sought by the youth or family itself. Home visits by the probation officer, social worker, or public health nurse, or calls to placement facilities to ascertain the status of the presenting problem and to insure continuity of care, are critical in this age of cost-effectiveness, dwindling resources and ever-increasing demand for those resources. Without such follow-up, valuable assessment and treatment time and energy may be for naught.

Of the various indirect psychiatric services in a program such as the one at CJH, charting also becomes critical. It assumes systematic, uniform recording of events in an unbiased, objective, scientifically observant fashion by staff on all shifts. Charting must be legible, it must leave nothing to the imagination, and entries should be based on reliable information. Such was not the case in charts which were reviewed.

First, there were two sets of charts for residents: (1) a medical chart which remained in the infirmary and (2) a behavioral chart which remained on the unit. This was an extremely cumbersome system, although it raised an important issue—that of confidentiality. Ideally, non-medical personnel should not have access to medical records without proper consent; however, there must be some communication between medical personnel and on-line staff who work with the youth daily. To deliver comprehensive medical care, medical personnel should be aware of the day-to-day behaviors of a resident and, conversely, counselors need to be aware of certain medical problems which may affect youths' on-the-unit behavior. The impression formed was that such an exchange of information did not take place in either direction, at least not in any systematic fashion. Evidence in the charts revealed that there was no indication of implementation of many of the psychiatric consultants' recommendations. Similarly, a familiarity with a patient's daily behavior was not conveyed in many of the psychiatric consultations. The apparent lack of training in charting skills by the staff was evidenced by contradictory entries by different staff regarding the same event. For instance, one staff member graded a youth's behavior with an "A" for being exceptional, while another staff member commented on the youth's behavior as "rapidly deteriorating" and deserving an "F." Colloquial expressions were used without explanation. A behavior was described as "a bit loose" without any elaboration. Even pseudo-objective jargon such as "negative behavior" as a reason for being downgraded is not sufficiently defined for someone else to understand its meaning. The negative orientation of many staff towards behavior was reflected in the manner in which entries are phrased: "No problems today," rather than recording positive, healthy examples of behavior. Even forms, which are presumed to be an effort to bring some uniformity to charting, are vague. Such a form was the *Special Incident Report* form under the section "classification of incident," which contained a checklist of various generic types of incidents without requiring further explanation.

The juvenile population at Central Juvenile Hall, by virtue of its age and sex, is at risk for having emotional and psychological problems—many of which have social, familial, and economic components—such as depression, drug abuse, and academic failure, to name but a few (Glueck and Glueck, 1962). Often these problems are related to the nature of the offenses the youths are *alleged* to have committed, as in the example of the commission of burglary to maintain a drug habit. The necessity for comprehensive psychiatric treatment by the most competent practitioners speaks for itself. What was found at CJH was the following situation: the population was one with a high incidence of problems for which some form of treatment exists and *almost one half of detained youths subsequently were released at court detention hearings because their petitions were not sustained (found not guilty)!** The question arose, then, of whether such a facility at CJH was in fact necessary. Certainly, the large number of beds observed at the time were not needed, for many youth should never have been detained in the first place and many whose petitions were sustained had committed the less serious types of crimes— victimless crimes, e.g., curfew violations, or running away from placement, or crimes against property. For this group of offenders, diversion-type community-based programs such as drug rehabilitation programs, individual, group and family programs, employment and job training programs, special education, foster homes and the like are necessary and preferable to institutions to meet the particular needs of the individual youth (Nelson, Wolff and Batalden, 1975).

SOCIAL AND COMMUNITY AND BEHAVIORAL INTERVENTION PROGRAMS

Within the general framework of the casework method, the predominant approach to delinquency has been based on the medical model of treatment which has produced disappointing results (Schwitzgebel, 1972). Traditional psychiatric approaches have had even more dismal results with minority group clients because of the wide acceptance of the hypothesis that "difference equals deficiency." Hence, minority patients have been assessed as more pathological than they actually are. This misperception, as well as preconceived notions regarding their response to certain treatment modalities, has led to referrals to inappropriate services (Mayo, 1974). As a consequence, minority clients have not received even the benefits that are possible from traditional interventions. To remedy these and other shortcomings, alternative approaches to the rehabilitation of delinquents have emerged. Generally, they can be classified under the headings of social and community interventions and behavioral interventions. Both show promise for providing more effective rehabilitation outcomes than the traditional model because they are highly adaptable to the particular needs and values of the ethnic and cultural groups to which they are addressed.

*In March, 1976, according to CJH and Los Padrinos IDC Monthly Statistics, of 1122 boys accepted for temporary custody, 551 were released.

The Crenshaw Community Day Center (CCDC), a social and community intervention-type program funded by the Los Angeles County Probation Department and the State of California Youth Authority, serves 30 Black adolescents who have been adjudged wards of the Juvenile Court. The youths reside in their own homes and attend classes at the Center which is located in their neighborhood. The offenses which have resulted in their probationary status range from relatively minor delinquent acts such as curfew violations and truancy to more serious offenses such as assault and robbery. Although the degree of delinquent sophistication varies, as well as the socioeconomic status of their families, the youths all share the common problems of school failure resulting from chronic truancy, learning disabilities, and behavioral disorders. The program is located in the facilities of a community YMCA where the youths receive individualized attention to overcome their school learning difficulties and behavioral problems. Once this occurs, they are mainstreamed back into their neighborhood schools.

The program is staffed by Los Angeles County probation officers, Los Angeles City continuation high school teachers, and graduate students and faculty from the Department of Special Education of the University of Southern California. Thus, it draws on a wide range of expertise in education, adolescent development and rehabilitation of juvenile offenders. Through weekly staff meetings, the combined agencies provide input into educational programs and policies and casework problems. Furthermore, the youngsters have daily contact with their probation officer who is a resident member of the Center. Thus a climate of trust and mutual cooperation is fostered between probation officers and probationers.

The academic program centers around the concept of individualized instruction and providing each student the opportunity to learn various subjects at his or her own pace. Upon entering the program, the student is educationally assessed and placed at the appropriate level of difficulty of subject matter which corresponds with that required for a regular high school graduation. The daily school program applies social learning principles in the form of a token economy system. Points are used as reinforcers for school attendance, academic achievement, and appropriate social behavior. Social praise is paired with delivery of these points with the expectation that eventually the youths will function effectively with only social reinforcement. The points, however, are redeemable for free time, snacks, and even money. Thus, for the first time, tangible motivation for achievement and appropriate social interactions are experienced by many youths who have heretofore viewed school as nothing but a series of repeated failures.

Frequent parent conferences are held to apprise parents of their child's progress. The topics discussed include learning problems and other difficulties the youth may have in successfully completing a period of probation. The Center's staff interacts with parents in a style designed to alter their misconceptions of school and probation personnel as nothing more than disciplinarians. A positive experience between the Center staff and parents is generally achieved by reinforcing with praise the progress made by their children. This also helps to promote the parents' increased use of positive statements in the home.

The results of the Crenshaw Community Day Center program have been good. There have been fewer arrests of CCDC students following their enrollment in this program as compared to their pre-enrollment experience. Also, there have been fewer arrests of CCDC minors than similar minors supervised on a regular probation caseload in the same area. School attendance increased for CCDC minors once they entered the program. As a consequence, academic achievement has been educationally significant in that for each month of school attendance the CCDC youths' average improvement in reading was 2.6 months, for spelling, 1.9 months, and for math, 2.2 months.

Another alternative to the medical model has been the application of behaviorally oriented approaches to the youthful probationer. An excellent example of the work in this field is demonstrated by the community-based, family-style treatment home called *Achievement Place* (Phillips, 1968). This is a behavioral–intervention type of program. It was conceptualized and implemented in Lawrence, Kansas for 12- to 16-year-old Anglo and Black youths referred by the Department of Probation as a result of a variety of delinquent acts. The treatment program centers around teaching parents. A married couple is responsible for the administration and delivery of the program which is conducted on a small scale consisting of six to eight youths in a renovated home in a quiet residential community. Therefore, the youths receive considerable individualized attention and treatment in their own environments. The program was also designed to permit the residents' participation in the direction and operation of the home through self government, by means of monitoring each other's behavior and participating in "family conferences." Because of the success of the original Achievement Place, the model has been replicated in different locations throughout the country. One such program was comprised entirely of Mexican-American teenagers in a rural Southern California community.

The program, known as Welcome Home (Liberman et al., 1975) was carried out in a family-style home in Santa Paula, a small agricultural town of 20,000 inhabitants in Southern California. It housed a total of 16 delinquent youths, all of whom were Mexican-American, and a married couple who served as teaching parents. The teaching parents were Mexican Americans with high school educations, some college, and two years' experience in counseling young people. In addition to receiving training in behavioral techniques through a variety of workshops and professional consultations, the teaching parents attended an intensive, week-long workshop sponsored by the original Achievement Place program on treatment and administrative aspects of running the home. While operating Welcome Home, they received weekly consultations with a psychologist and also attended weekly meetings led by another behavioral psychologist aimed at teaching simple reinforcement methods to the parents of the delinquent youths.

The boys at Welcome Home were committed by the Juvenile Court and supervised by the County Probation Department while in placement. They ranged in age from 12 to 16 years of age, and seven was the maximum census at any one time. Their delinquent activities ranged from "beyond parental control" to offenses that would have been classified as felonies had they been committed by adults. Generally, the youths were from low-income families with only one parent in the home. Their average stay in Welcome Home was 6 months, with a range of 3 to 15 months.

The behavioral treatment approach used was that of a token economy. The youngsters earned points for appropriate social, self-care and academic behavior and lost points for inappropriate behavior. They received specific instructions from the teaching parents in acquiring behaviors that were absent and in improving those that were deficient. Points were earned or lost on a daily or weekly basis, depending upon progress through the program. The points could be exchanged for privileges such as snacks, television time, allowance, permission to attend special social events, and weekends in their own homes.

A typical day at Welcome Home started at 7:00 A.M. The boys showered, dressed, and cleaned their bedrooms and bathrooms before breakfast. After breakfast, they cleaned up the kitchen and went to school, where they earned points for academic and social performance. After school, they returned home where they had a snack if they had earned that privilege. They then began chores which were usually finished by 4:00 P.M. Until dinner at 6:00 P.M., the boys studied or engaged in activities they had earned. After dinner, a family meeting was held for the purpose of teaching self-governing skills. Grievances were aired, rules infractions reported, appropriate consequences enacted, and individual accomplishments praised and rewarded. Changes in household operations and program policies were also discussed and made. At 10:00 P.M. the boys retired for the evening.

Several objective studies of the effectiveness of various components of the treatment program have been conducted. These involved assessing the effectiveness of methods for changing behaviors in directions thought to be important for the youths' successful adaptation to their home and school environments. Some of the specific behaviors studied were decreasing annoying interruptions of conversations, performing chores, and increasing promptness. Since talking-out inappropriately in class and other social situations is a common problem with delinquent youth, an intervention was designed which fined the boys for interrupting ongoing conversations. It was determined that this approach significantly reduced incidences of inappropriate talking-out. The performance of chores was increased by rewarding the youths for the performance of specified tasks. After an initial phase of using points as rewards, they were gradually discontinued and replaced with warm encouragement and attention from the teaching parents which sufficed to maintain a high level of task completion. A common problem among delinquents is the lack of promptness at school and in meeting family schedules for meals and time home. Therefore, a program was devised in which the boys were fined for being late to dinner or other agreed-upon times. Again, it was found that this method significantly reduced tardiness. In addition to the above specific improvements, the boys at Welcome Home made important gains in their academic records and their successful completion of probation.

The above described social and community interventions and behavioral approaches share some general features. First, they focus far more on concrete observable behaviors than do traditional approaches. Thus, the assessment of the effects of the interventions becomes an ongoing process which permits inappropriate strategies to be discarded while effective ones are maintained. A second feature is that they share organizational structures and modes of delivery that are in full view of the community they serve, thus permitting them to reflect the needs and values of the people they serve. Third, their goals, in addition to effecting more adaptive coping styles for the probationers, also include effecting institutional and community change. Fourth, they deal with problems of living directly in the natural environments of those in which these problems occur. Finally, they use the resources of the community and the talents of nonprofessionals in carrying out the delivery of service.

CONCLUSION

The juvenile justice system was seen as having four interacting components: the police, probation, the Juvenile Court, and placement institutions. Three trends appear to be evolving in the handling of juvenile offenders: more lenient dispositions (out of court) of those who commit very minor crimes, sometimes called status offenders; the effort to divert from the juvenile justice system offenders who might benefit from community-based treatment alternatives; and harsher treatment of juveniles who commit serious crimes. Some surveys have shown that minority juveniles are not receiving equal treatment and that juvenile correctional programs disproportionately represent the minority population.

The police, as "gatekeepers," were seen as having the most influence in determining that juveniles are kept out of, or in, the juvenile justice system. Stereotypic beliefs regarding clothing and lifestyle about minority juveniles, reinforced by field deployment patrol policies, greatly increase the likelihood of those persons being arrested by police. These police-initiated preventive patrol arrests increase minority community crime statistics, generate the need for more police, and prematurely introduce minority youth into the juvenile justice system. It also makes it more difficult for minority youth to qualify for more lenient, diversion processing.

Probation Department referral statistics revealed that there was an overrepresentation of Black and Hispanic youth. These statistics further indicated that, contrary to common belief, white juveniles had their fair share of serious offenses, even surpassing minority groups in the number of manslaughter incidents. However, it was surprising to see that Blacks comprised 85 percent of those minors detained at Juvenile Hall awaiting a court hearing. Hispanics and whites represented the remaining 15 percent of those in detention. It was not specifically clear what forces were at work which caused such a gross overrepresentation of Blacks. This finding supported other evidence in the country showing that minorities are overrepresented in juvenile corrections programs. The answer appears to be related to institutional racism.

The case study of minorities in Juvenile Hall detention demonstrated an almshouse-like standard of care which constituted basically a custodial milieu. Serious behavioral problems, which in adolescents often indicate depression, hyperkinesis, mental retardation, learning disorders, and even psychosis, did not result in psychiatric referrals. Often this was due to staff not being adequately trained to detect these problems. The policies and procedures of the institution appeared to operate for the convenience of the institution rather than for the biological, social and psychological needs of the juvenile inmates. Perhaps the most tragic finding was that at least half of those juveniles, mostly minority, being subjected to those inhuman conditions were subsequently released by the Court because their petitions were not sustained (found not guilty)!

Social and community and behavioral intervention types of programs were discussed as being particularly helpful to juvenile minority offenders. These programs have also worked well with white youths. Rather than following a medical model focusing on individual, psychological treatment, these programs follow a residential approach *in the community* and reflect the needs and values of the people they serve. They also have the advantage of using available resources in the minority community, and the skills and talents of minority nonprofessionals in carrying out the delivery of services.

REFERENCES

Beck, R. "White House conference on children: An historical perspective." *Harvard Educational Review*, 1973, 43(4), 653–668.

Crewe, H. J. "Fears and anxiety in childhood." *Public Health*, 1973, 87(5), 165–171.

Fink, A., and Kosecoff, J. *An Evaluation Primer*. Washington, D.C.: Capitol Publications, 1978.

Friendship Station Newsletter, Los Angeles, California, 1978, p. 2.

Geis, G. "Statistics concerning race and crime." (Unpublished paper submitted to the U.S. Commission on Civil Rights, September 13, 1962, p. 6.)

Glueck, S., and Glueck, E. *Family Environment and Delinquency*. Boston: Houghton Mifflin, 1962.

Kahn, C., and Piockowski, G. "Conditions promoting creativity in group rearing of children." *Psychoanalytic Study of the Child*, 1974, 29, 231.

Kanner, L. "Outline of the history of child psychiatry." In *Child Psychiatry*, 4th ed. Springfield, Ill. Charles C. Thomas, 1972.

Klein, M. W., Teilman, K. S., Styles, J. A., Lincoln, S. B., and Labin-Rosensweig, S. "The explosion in police diversion programs: Evaluating the structural dimensions of a social fad." In M. W. Klein ed., *The Juvenile Justice System*. Beverly Hills: Sage Publications, 1976, pp. 107–108.

Liberman, R. P., Ferris, C., Salgado, P., and Salgado, J. "Replication of the achievement place model in California." *Journal of Applied Behavior Analysis*, 1975, 8, 287–299.

Lipsey, M. W., and Johnston, J. E. "The impact of juvenile diversion in Los Angeles County." A report to the Los Angeles County (AB90) Justice System Advisory Group, July, 1979, p. ii.

Los Angeles Times, Monday, February 27, 1978a.

Los Angeles Times, October 8, 1978b.

Los Angeles Times, Calendar, March 18, 1979a, p. 38.

Los Angeles Times, Part I, April 2, 1979b, p. 3.

Mayo, J. A. "The significance of sociocultural variables in the psychiatric treatment of black outpatients." *Comprehensive Psychiatry*, 1974, 15, 471–482(a).

Miller, J. G. "Professional dilemmas in corrections." *Seminars in Psychiatry*, 1971, 3(3), 357–362.

Morales, A. "Police deployment theories and the Mexican American." In J. H. Skolnick and T. C. Grey (eds.), *Police in America*. Boston: Educational Associates, 1975, pp. 118–125.

Morales, A. "Institutional racism in mental health and criminal justice." *Social Casework*, (July 1978) 59(7), 391–392.

Nelson, S. H., Wolff, B., and Batalden, P. B. "Manpower training as an alternative to disadvantaged adolescent drug misuse." *American Journal of Public Health*, 1975, 65, 599–603.

Phillips, E. L. "Achievement place: Token reinforcement procedures in a home-style rehabilitation setting for 'pre-delinquent' boys. *Journal of Applied Behavior Analysis*, 1968, 1, 213–223.

Polier, J. W. "Myths and realities in search for juvenile justice. *Harvard Educational Review*, 1974, 44(1), 112–124.

President's Commission on Law Enforcement and Administration of Justice. *The Challenge of Crime in a Free Society*. Washington, D.C.: U.S. Government Printing Office, 1967, p. 247.

Probation Automated Intake Data System, Los Angeles County Probation Department, 1978.

Report of the Joint Commission on Mental Health of Children. *Crisis in Child Mental Health: Challenge for the 1970's*. New York: Harper and Row, 1969.

Sarri, R. C., and Vinter, R. D. "Justice for whom? Varieties of juvenile correctional approaches." In M. W. Klein ed., *The Juvenile Justice System*. Beverly Hills: Sage Publications, 1976, p. 180.

Schwitzgebel, R. K. "Limitations on the coercive treatment of offenders." *Criminal Law Bulletin*, 1972, 8, 269–319.

Sendi, I. B., and Blomgren, P. G. "A comparative study of predictive criteria in the predisposition of homicidal adolescents. *American Journal of Psychiatry*, 1975, 132(4), 423–427.

Statistical Summary, Los Angeles County Sheriff's Department, Fiscal year, 1974–75, pp. 80, 97.

Street Gangs. Copy in the possession of the ACLU Foundation of Southern California, 1980, pp. 11, 15. Also see Attorney General George Deukmejian's *Report on Youth Gang Violence in California*. Department of Justice, State of California, June 1981, pp. 21, 22, 24, 25.

Wertham, C., and Piliavin, I. "Gang members and the police." In J. H. Skolnick and T. C. Gray eds., *Police in America*. Boston: Educational Associates, 1975, pp. 155–168.

Worsfold, V. L. "A philosophical justification for children's rights." *Harvard Educational Review*, 1974, 44(1), 142–157.

CHAPTER 18

The Impact of Macro Systems on Puerto Rican Families

Emelicia Mizio

PREFATORY COMMENT

This chapter by Emelicia Mizio highlights the importance of understanding the cultural heritage of Puerto Ricans and the extent of each familiy's identification with Puerto Rican or Anglo American culture. A unique blending of these cultural factors is found in many of these families and individuals which is also flavored by socioeconomic class factors. Since cultures rarely remain static, it is particularly important to be aware of evolving male/female roles and their functional and dysfunctional aspects as it concerns subordination patterns. As is the case with most Hispanic cultures, Puerto Ricans also value the extended family and this should not be seen as a threat to a person's individuality. Mizio offers suggestions for the social worker in helping Puerto Ricans deal with oppressive external social systems through joint advocacy aimed at systems change.

Healthy families are the *sine qua non* of a healthy society. Well integrated families are critical to the preservation of our societal structure and its effective functioning. Families cannot exist in isolation and cannot maintain their health without societal supports. There is a reciprocity which must be recognized between society and its members (Zimmerman, 1976).

To understand a family and its operations, one must study its transactions with its environments. The family is an extremely vulnerable institution impacted by and responsive to societal conditions. The degree of a family's vulnerability relates closely to its socioeconomic status. The effects of poverty have been well documented in terms of physical and mental malaise and the overwhelming sense of helplessness, hopelessness and alientation. The generally poor, low-status Puerto Rican family is consequently in extreme jeopardy because its extended family system and differences in its values place it in conflict with a sociolegal system in this country which addresses itself

From: Gloria Johnson Powell, Joe Yamamoto, Annelisa Romero, Armando Morales (Eds.), *The Psychosocial Development of Minority Group Children* (New York: Brunner/Mazel, Inc., 1983).

basically to the nuclear family. Our society, in turn, jeopardizes itself when it does not meet the needs of its citizenry or provide necessary supports; hence, the problems of our inner cities. Major cities such as New York, Chicago, Philadelphia, Cleveland, Newark, and Boston have large Puerto Rican (and other minority) populations. The quality of life for Puerto Ricans (and other minorities) in key urban centers must be viewed as inextricably linked to the general quality of life in those cities (U.S. Commission on Civil Rights, 1976).

A coherent and just national family social policy must evolve and address itself to ethnic differences. Social policy deals with the kinds of benefits that are to be distributed, with the people to whom they are to be distributed, with the amount to be distributed, with the way in which they are to be financed, and with the cost of providing the specific benefit (Zimmerman, 1976). Ethnicity is defined as conscious and unconscious processes fulfilling a deep psychological need for security, identity, and sense of historical continuity. Within the family, it is transmitted in an emotional language, and it is reinforced by similar units in the community (Giordano, 1974). Ethnicity refers to a common culture. It operates on both conscious and unconscious levels and shapes basic values, norms, attitudes, and life styles of the group's members even as it is modified by such factors as class, race, religion, sex, region and generation (Giordano, 1976a). Social policy experts and planners and service-delivering professionals must make certain that they take these ethnic differences into account. Considerable research is now being conducted in this area (Giordano, 1976b).

THE EXTENDED FAMILY IN A NUCLEAR FAMILY SOCIETY

The family has been viewed as a goal-oriented, task-performing system. It has the following functions: (1) physical care and maintenance of its members; (2) addition of new members through reproduction and their relinquishment when they mature; (3) socialization of children for various roles as spouses, parents, workers, citizens, and members of social groups; (4) maintenance of order within the family and between the family and outside groups; (5) maintenance of family motivation and morale to facilitate performance of tasks in the family and other social groups; (6) production as well as distribution of services and goods necessary for maintaining the family (Zimmerman, 1976).

There are also different family types characterized by common residence. The one with which we are most familiar in the United States is the "model American family," a nuclear family where special emphasis is placed on the conjugal bond. Typically, a nuclear family consists of wife and husband, and their offspring; kin are generally excluded (Murdock, 1968). In a nuclear family the family's decision making and reciprocal controls are weak since few mandatory exchanges are required (Goode, 1964). In the search for upward mobility, the nuclear family structure has freed its members to seek their fortunes without consideration of in-laws or other kin. It is often said that economic factors have shaped the "ideal" American family pattern.

A specific type of American humor centers around interfering in-laws who attempt to violate the sanctity of the nuclear family. Many mental health practitioners have not placed a high value on extended family ties. They have often correlated a successful analysis or course of treatment with the independence of individuals and their own procreated families from their families of origin. A study by the Jewish Family Service in New York showed that social workers often attempt to help the family change its kin relationships—usually in the direction of less involvement. Social workers were also found to be less kin-oriented than their clients. This fact leads to issues about the significance of value differences in therapeutic practice as well as, of course, in society (Leichter and Mitchell, 1967).

Policy makers, as well as mental health practitioners working with Puerto Rican families, must realize that the Puerto Rican family, in contrast to the American family, is an extended one, with strong ties that are in no way considered or experienced as pathological.

An extended family is a composite form of the nuclear family (Leichter and Mitchell, 1967). It is characterized by intense and frequent relationships. The Puerto Rican family is patriarchal, and roles are clearly defined and strictly monitored. There are important reciprocal obligations and strict fulfillment of each person's role responsibilities. Scheele (1969), for example, writes that a person in Puerto Rico, whether bootblack or bank president, by successfully fulfilling the expectancies of his or her various statuses, maintains *Dignidad*—one of the most important Puerto Rican values. The elderly are respected and have a place in this society. Children are deeply loved; they are not held accountable for the parents' "sins."

To visualize the Puerto Rican family, it is important to understand the interrelated Puerto Rican cultural values of *Dignidad, Respeto,* and *Personalismo*. For a fuller discussion of important Puerto Rican values, see Mintz (1973), Wagenheim (1970), Fitzpatrick (1971). A person automatically possesses *Dignidad* (dignity in a broadened sense). This is a belief in the innate worth and inner importance of each individual. The spirit and soul are more important than the body. The focus is on the person's qualities, uniqueness, goodness and integrity.

Persons are born into their socioeconomic roles and therefore, cannot be held accountable for their status. There is often a *fatalismo* (fatalism) about their position in life. Fatalism and Puerto Rican values should be examined in the context of Catholicism and colonialism. The notion of a "colonialized personality" is found throughout a good part of the literature. Some acquaintance with the history would be essential to an understanding of the Puerto Rican situations. (The beginning reader is referred to Wagenheim, 1970. For an interpretation from an independent point of view, see Maldonado–Denis, 1972. For an understanding of how fatalism comes into play in the helper/client relationship, see Vasquez de Rodriquez, 1973). They may see life's events as inevitable (*"Lo que Dios manda"*—What God wills). They feel themselves at the mercy of supernatural forces and are resigned to their fate. This life view is illustrated by a conversation between Piri Thomas, a Puerto Rican raised in the U.S., and his mother, who had spent her formative years in Puerto Rico. "Our parents were resigned to their life. But we, the youngsters, would say, 'Has this life gotta be for us forever?' I remember my own mother's answer one day when I asked her. 'Why can't we have a nice house like this?' showing her a picture in a magazine . . . 'Of course, we can have it in heaven someday'" (Thomas, 1974).

It does not matter, therefore, what people have in this life or what their stations in life are. They possess status simply by existing. Rewards will come in heaven. A person is, however, entitled to be treated in this life with *respeto* ("respect" in a broadened sense) as long as they fulfill their role requirements and adhere to Puerto Rican values and norms. *Respeto* is the acknowledgement of an individual's personal attributes, uninfluenced by wealth or social position (Abad, Ramos and Boyce, 1974). *Respeto* also connotes hierarchal relationships. Elders and superiors of one form or another, are to be accorded respect. The superior, in turn, must always be cordial. There are prescribed cultural rituals to show respect. Puerto Ricans are very sensitive to affronts which would violate their *dignidad*. People who have been insulted must always handle themselves in an honest, dignified, and upright manner. An attempt is made to settle the situation *a la buena* (in a nice way). Generally, an attempt is made to avoid direct confrontation, with *"pelea monga"* ("passive resistance") often employed. Aggression is permitted when a man's machismo is challenged.

As previously stated, tied in with *dignidad* and *respeto* is the concept of *personalismo*, a strong preference for face-to-face contact and primary relationships. As an illustration of the importance and extent of this preference, while the supermarket may be a much cheaper place to shop, the *bodega* (neighborhood grocery store) is much more popular in many communities in the states, taking on the characteristics of a primary social institution (Vasquez, 1974). It is the individual in the organization or institution one trusts and deals with. The concept of a collective welfare generally has little meaning. One thinks instead of adverse or favorable effects on Pablo, José, and Juan. Even in terms of their ties to the church, Puerto Ricans experience special and individualistic relationships with the saints. Puerto Ricans do not want their unique personalities absorbed into committees and bureaucracies. Their participation in groups will depend on strong ties to individual group members rather than on ties to a cause per se (Roger, 1971). Puerto Ricans seem to seek charismatic leadership. A recent study comments on the high rate of participation in elections together with the tendency to idolize their leaders and to leave too much policy making and implementation to those they have elected. This relates as well to other leaders, labor and religious (Brameld, 1976). *Personalismo* requires that all social, economic, political relationships proceed on the basis of known face-to-face contact (Mintz, 1973).

Puerto Ricans feel most comfortable with a family style in their relationships. It is not surprising that the Puerto Rican extended family encompasses not only those related by blood and marriage, but also those tied to it by custom in reciprocal bonds of obligation and feeling. Important parts of the Puerto Rican family system are the *Compradazgo* and *hijos de crianza*.

The *Compradazgo* is the institution of *compadres* ("companion parents"), a network of ritual kinship whose members have a deep sense of obligation to each other. These responsibilities are taken quite seriously and include economic assistance, emotional support, and even personal correction. Sponsors of a child at baptism and confirmation take on the role of *Padrinos* ("godparents") to the child and *compadres* to the parents. Also assuming this role are witnesses at a marriage or close friends (Fitzpatrick, 1971). The relationship develops a significant religious and even mystical quality.

Hijos de crianza ("children of the upbringing") is the cultural practice of accepting responsibility for another's child, without the necessity of blood or even friendship ties. This child is raised as if it were one's own. Neither the natural parent nor the child is stigmatized for the relinquishment. There is also no stigma attached to an illegitimate child. Following the Roman legal tradition, there is no concept of illegitimacy; the child is viewed as a natural child (Fitzpatrick, 1971). This institutional practice serves as an economic and emotional safety valve for the family and often makes it possible for the child to enjoy a better life. The family, in all likelihood, will not be able to produce documents for the child. As Hidalgo (1972) points out, the helping professional must be prepared, if necessary, to battle the legal system. Previously stated and important to reiterate is that the Puerto Rican family is placed in immediate jeopardy as a result of described differences in family structure and values, bringing it into conflict with the socio-legal system of the U.S., which addresses itself basically to the nuclear family. Consider social security and income tax provisions as illustrations. Income tax regulations do not allow tax deductions for *Compadres* or consensual unions. In many parts of Puerto Rican society, consensual unions are a common and acceptable practice. Consensual unions must, however, be examined in the context of the economic situation. When one owns no property, there is little need for legal entanglements. It is interesting to note that with the rise of the middle class in Puerto Rico the percentage of consensual marriages has dropped and it is basically a phenomenon of the poor (Fitzpatrick, 1971).

Support of the *hijo de crianza* is credited by the Internal Revenue Service if the contribution has been more than half the year's total support. Social Security benefits are not paid to any of these groups. For those few fortunate Puerto Ricans who hold health insurance policies, coverage is defined without reference to the Puerto Rican concept of family.

There is a gross inequity in the amount of societal benefits and residual services provided to the Puerto Rican population. Young and old receive little from society. One need only look at the conditions in ghetto schools, hospitals, outpatient clinics and housing, at the lack of recreational facilities and activities, at the limited amount of police protection, at the types of jobs available and their salary range, along with the unemployment figures, to be struck by the harsh reality of the Puerto Rican condition. A society which provides so little to the Puerto Rican community also serves in many ways to render the minority impotent in its self-help efforts. Under existing societal conditions, mutual assistance, both financial and emotional, is essential. Puerto Ricans in the United States have been described as having lost their social assets; they are removed from the customary support of tradition, kin, and esteem of hometown neighbors. Housing patterns in New York show that Puerto Ricans scattered throughout the city at a faster rate than was true of other ethnic groups upon their arrival. Housing is not as easy to find as it was in the past. Puerto Ricans are thus exposed to the host culture more intensively and sooner. Isolation from their ethnic groups has been associated with increased rates of mental illness in minorities (Rabkin and Struening, 1976). It is imperative, therefore, that any remaining semblance of the extended family be preserved. Public policy and programs must lend support to the extended family. The extended family system should be viewed as important not only to the Puerto Rican, but to other ethnic groups as well. Moreover, the value placed on the extended family should not be assumed to be solely related to a poverty status. An examination of Anglo-American alternative life styles will frequently reveal attempts to create such an extended family group (Beck, 1976).

Society's restrictions on self-help affect the nearly two million Puerto Ricans and their descendants on the Mainland, most of whom live in New York City (*New York Times*, 1977). New York City Housing Authority regulations prohibit the public housing dweller from extending the traditional hospitality of an open door to their "kin" in need of a start in the new land; neither can they share the rent when it would be mutually beneficial in financial and child-caring terms. Among Puerto Rican families living in poverty, nearly 60 percent are headed by a woman. (U.S. Commission on Civil Rights, 1976). The need for mutual aid arrangements within such families is especially critical. Lack of child care facilities for their children inhibits the participation of Puerto Rican women in the labor force (U.S. Commission on Civil Rights, 1976). Restrictions on apartment sharing occur at a time when it is virtually impossible to obtain an apartment in a project or to rent a decent apartment elsewhere. In attempting to qualify as foster parents, Puerto Rican families find that they face a serious problem in lack of housing space. Institutional care, rather than foster home care, is stressed by child welfare agencies (Valle Consultants Ltd., 1973). Can institutional care be considered better than the loving concern of a *Madrina* (Godmother) for an *hijo de crianza*, even if in substandard housing? To solve both the housing and child care problems, abandoned buildings in local neighborhoods might be refurnished and made available on a nonprofit basis to families who qualify as foster parents (Valle Consultants Ltd., 1973).

On the other hand, the author does not believe self help efforts alone can suffice, nor is sharing a cramped apartment in New York. The Puerto Rican Family Institute in New York has found that migrants may overstay their welcomes when they are unable to find a job or secure housing. Reliance for too long on a *Compadre* may lead to tension between the host and the newly arrived family (Gorbea, 1975). Certainly, day care or institutional programs are needed; however, their use should be dictated by need and cultural preference. Most importantly, the author should not be interpreted as denying society's responsibility to provide a humane standard of living for its poor. But if the poor are not to be helped, let them not be hindered in their communal efforts to solve the problems of their poverty.

SOCIETAL STRAINS ON THE PUERTO RICAN FAMILY

Points of tension in the Puerto Rican family have been classified as:

1. A traditional system of relationships based on social class and family background versus an industrial system based on competition, initiative, and conspicuous consumption as a basis for status.

2. High aspirations and low achievement.

3. The value of dignity, pride, and honor contrasted with the increasing emphasis on material wealth and consumption.

4. A value system that reveres the *jibaro* (an idolized folk hero of the Puerto Rican) (Wagenheim, 1970) as opposed to one that reveres the successful entrepreneur.

5. The present commitment to democracy compared to the traditional methods of power that prevailed in the colonial system (Vasquez de Rodriquez, 1971).

One cannot truthfully write about the Puerto Rican family living in the United States or in Puerto Rico as if a universal model existed. Families are affected by and deal with potential strains in different ways. The Puerto Rican family system must be viewed along a continuum from the extended family system to the American nuclear family system. There are many possible variations in between. It may be helpful to understand differences in Puerto Rican family structure and values as influenced by industrialization on one hand and by the penetration of the Anglo-American culture on the other (Mintz, 1973). Strains may be caused by either stream of influence. Traditional patterns are also often augmented by other friendships, such as work relationships (Wagenheim, 1970). Business firms may be quite paternalistic and highly centralized in authority, following a preindustrial form (Scheele, 1969). A study dealing with acculturation among Puerto Rican women on the Mainland showed that even among those who score high on acculturation there is still respect for an adherence to traditional family-related values (Torres–Matrullo, 1976).

These points of tensions exist in Puerto Rico as well as in the United States. Under the impact of American colonialization, industrialization, and urbanization, the family in Puerto Rico has undergone considerable shock. Before emigrating, the poor family has often moved from a rural community to an urban area, where traditional values may have encountered "Americanization," and the effects of a clash of values may have already begun. The life style in a prosperous urban area in Puerto Rico is different from anything in their past experience. Families often find themselves living in urban shanties, sometimes in the shadow of sleek new office buildings. They exist by doing odd jobs and collecting meager welfare payments (Wagenheim, 1970).

The urban area stateside, especially in New York, is considerably more complex than in Puerto Rico. Lack of proficiency in English, limited education and occupational skills, and possible dark skin add to the problems of Puerto Ricans. Because they are automatically United States citizens, there is little preparation required for emigration to the States. They find themselves suddenly transplanted to an unfamiliar environment, and are expected to know how to negotiate business immediately in an American urban setting and to resolve the complexities of such a life style. The Puerto Rican Family Institute in New York has found that the newly arrived migrant needs assistance in dealing with the vital areas of housing, health, education, employment, and home management (Canabal and Goldstein, 1975). It is to be expected that many migrants would not know how to maneuver in this complicated environment that is so different in culture and institutional arrangements.

Families must be able to deal with an urban environment as well as to cope with major changes in values. These changes usually mean an increase in role failures. Family members will differ in their interpretations of role obligations, and strained relations may well ensue. Family members have not been prepared to fulfill the new expectations. Previously, roles in the Puerto Rican family had been clearly defined. In rural settings there was a sharp division of labor, with wage earning activities generally relegated to men. Women's freedom was severely limited and their relationships with men were limited to kin. The cults of virginity and machismo were combined, with men as innately superior to women, a view reinforced through the societal structure. Boys and girls in Puerto Rico had been basically segregated from each other and this pattern continued in adulthood. Parents had viewed their children as completely dependent, demanding obedience from them. Children should be quiet, submissive, and respectful; achievement is less important than conformity. These concepts were especially applicable to girls. In the middle and upper classes there is less emphasis on these subordination patterns, but they are still interwoven into the overall fabric of Puerto Rican society (Bucchioni, 1965; Stycos, 1952; Wagenheim, 1970). Wagenheim (1970) points to a phenomenon that was once taboo, that of a suburban wife in Puerto Rico driving and shopping alone; while she now shops alone, the same woman today will not venture out alone at night without her husband. While the double standard continues its hold among all classes in Puerto Rico, it is decreasing most rapidly in the urban class. The virginity cult, however, remains largely unmodified, even by the impact of more flexible continental standards (Brameld, 1976).

The traditional family structure and value system come into immediate conflict with the demands of the stateside environment. Women must act independently, work, and carry the same types of burdens as men. They are forced to deal with external systems such as school, police, hospitals, etc., and to be involved with non-kin men in lively interactions. Men cannot protect their women from external pressure. Children must also become assertive in order to survive and often continue this pattern by challenging parental views. While these exchanges and others like them need not become crises, they become critical when compounded by a society that denies access to resources which an individual needs to adequately play the newly defined role. American society denies such access to Puerto Ricans and then judges them by what they have been denied. This is indeed a crucial dilemma for Puerto Ricans. Rabkin and Struening's (1976) review of research on mental illness among New York City residents revealed that epidemiological studies consistently show higher rates of mental illness for Puerto Ricans than for other ethnic groups or for the total population.

It is important to note that the available statistics might not reflect accurately the degree of the problem. Puerto Ricans have great tolerance for the "peculiarities" of others and will lend support to keeping the person at home and in the community. Also, many Puerto Ricans have a belief system which differs from that of Anglos. Spiritualism flourishes hand in hand with Catholicism, the predominant religion of Puerto Ricans. Spirits are believed to be the cause of illness, and a person feeling his or her defenses tumbling may see a spiritualist and attend a seance. Such persons may find community support in dealing with their psychic problems, the origins of which are considered spiritual. However, for some not seeking psychiatric help may quickly precipitate a more severe breakdown. It is crucial for health practitioners working with the Puerto Rican population to have an understanding of this belief system, as well as of the way in which professionals can cooperate with spiritualism (Lubchansky, Egri and Stokes, 1970; Ruiz and Langrod, 1976).

Rabkin and Struening (1976) write that the development of mental illnesses in migrant populations relates to the amount of social change experienced in the transition from one setting to another. They view alterations in life style, family organization and role assessment, membership in social networks, and extent of community supports as each contributing to the individual's vulnerability to the experience of stress and illness. We have already noted the great number of social changes experienced by the Puerto Rican migrant. In general, all families handle stress differently. The fact that the great majority of families cannot be classified as mentally ill is a testimony to human resiliency. There are great differences in family structure and value systems. In the case of Puerto Ricans, differences relate in part to whether formative years were spent in the United States or in Puerto Rico, as well as to the level of education. When viewing Puerto Rican families along the continuum described earlier, one should not expect to find too many families at either the traditional or nuclear end. It is important to note, however, that certain Puerto Rican families in the United States may remain in a more traditional form than families in Puerto Rico because of their isolation from the wider society. This tendency may reflect needs to cling to the security of the familiar and to reject what appears to be so unaccepting of them.

To understand variations between families and family members, it is imperative that in our assessments we go beyond ego strength and pathology. It is critical to take into consideration the external systems with which the family and its members have been in transaction. How much stress can any family be expected to tolerate and still maintain a viable homeostatic balance? Families are open social systems and as "living systems are acutely dependent upon their external environment" (Katz and Kahn, 1966).

Sociologists have classified the family as having the following functions fundamental to social life: sexual, economic, reproductive, and educational (Murdock, 1968). The family, along with meeting instrumental needs, must be able to meet the expressive and affective needs of its members. One cannot evaluate the Puerto Rican family's ability to perform its functions or the way in which Puerto Rican culture structures these tasks without examining the environment of the Puerto Rican family in the United States. Goode (1964) pointed out that a family can continue to exist only as it is supported by the larger society. The society, as a larger social system, furnishes the family, as a smaller social system, with the conditions necessary for its survival.

THE PUERTO RICAN AS A MINORITY MEMBER

We have seen that the Puerto Rican family finds itself in a hostile environment which makes life a struggle for existence. Racist practices, along with a highly technological, stratified, closed society, inhibit the upward mobility of Puerto Ricans and relegate them and their family to the lower caste. The Puerto Rican family finds itself defined as a minority group, whereas in Puerto Rico it was part of a majority. Minority is synonymous with an out-group whose worth, culture, values, and life styles are deprecated and stereotyped. Minority is synonymous with blocked access to the fraternity of the in-group and the full benefits of the American way of life. Erickson (1959) notes that the shock of American adolescence is the standardization of individuals and the intolerance of difference. This destructive parochialism permeates the whole American scene. Society even attempts to force Puerto Ricans into defining themselves as white or black, the standardized categories for color in the United States, with no allowances for the Puerto Rican's mixed Indian, Spanish, and African heritage.

In fact, the Puerto Ricans' chances for success seem related to their ability, as individuals and families, to obscure their differences from the majority group. Puerto Ricans who, by placing themselves into the proverbial "melting pot," are able to metamorphose as white with an Anglicized name and lifestyle can provide their families with an American standard of living. The price they must pay is denial of self and heritage, and sacrifice of personal integrity. Whether or not society permits them self-definitions, as white or black they are faced with an identity problem. There is no intention here to stigmatize or blame the victims, a procedure Ryan (1969) defines as an "intellectual process whereby a social problem is analyzed in such a way that the causation is found to be in the characteristics of the victim rather than in any deficiencies or structural defects in his environment."

As Longres (1974) points out, the racial experience in the United States goes beyond the individual and family and must be viewed as a collective one where all are forced to confront and question their racial identity. The color question persists as a psychological dilemma even among the seemingly assimilated. It is as if each day the Puerto Rican issue and color question come up even for those who can pass as Anglo. Again and again, one needs to decide whether to confront or let a remark about Puerto Ricans go by. Always at issue is how much racism one can accept in one's "friends." Also ubiquitous is the need to reassess the "fit" of the Puerto Rican stereotype and to place oneself and others in perspective.

This racism and its internalization also threaten Puerto Rican unity and can serve to divide Puerto Ricans along racial lines. For some a negative internalization of self may work against the interests of their own group in an attempt to deny their own heritage and to secure their new "chosen" identity.

The havoc society wreaks and the problems it creates for the individual and for the family by its measurement of worth in terms of color are vividly portrayed in *Down These Mean Streets*. Thomas's (1967) autobiography describes how his painful identity problem and destructive relationships with his siblings and father were related to the differences in color between him and his siblings and to feelings about self and others tied to these color differences:

> It wasn't right to be ashamed of what one was. It was like hating Momma for the color she was and Poppa for the color he wasn't . . . Man do you know what it is to sit across a dinner table looking at your brothers that look exactly like paddy people? True, I ain't never been down South, but the same crap's happening here. So they don't hang you by your neck. But they slip an invisible rope around your balls and hang you with nice smiles, and "If we need you, we'll call you." I wanna feel like a "Mr." I can't feel like that just yet and there ain't no amount of cold wine and pot can make my mind accept me being a "Mr." part time . . . You and James (his brothers) are like houses painted white outside and blacker'n mother inside. And I'm close to being like Poppa—trying to be white on both sides. (p. 8)

Thomas's identity crisis is unfortunately not atypical. How intense this crisis can be is indicated by the fact that admission rates to mental hospitals for non-white Puerto Ricans are the highest among the Puerto Rican group. Second generation Puerto Ricans have a higher total admission rate than their parents. This finding is surprising in its contrast to the usual pattern among immigrant groups (Rabkin and Struening, 1976). It may well be, however, that not being subject to minority status throughout one's formative years provides better insulation than growing up as a minority "non-person." First generation parents can probably maintain their *dignidad* and find comfort in their recollections of their past.

Identifying oneself as Anglo-white, black, or Puerto Rican serves as a focus of orientation to concepts of self and others, to values and to life styles. The kinds of identifications, confusions, and ambivalences experienced by Thomas unfortunately reflect malignancies in our society because individuals and their families comprise vulnerable and open social systems.

It is futile to enter into a debate about whether Puerto Ricans uncontaminated by American society are themselves racist. It is also futile to attempt to determine whether the prejudice observed in Puerto Rico relates to class, as is claimed, rather than to color. What is certain is that Puerto Ricans are totally unprepared to deal with the discrimination to which they are subjected upon arrival in the United States. Both in statistics and in literature, the devastating effects of color discrimination and ghetto existence on the Puerto Rican family in this country are clear. Thomas's excruciatingly painful identity struggle over what and who he was and his pathological relationships with his family over color differences would not have happened in Puerto Rico.

THE SEARCH FOR THE POT OF GOLD

The United States has traditionally attracted immigrants seeking their fortunes. Though the Puerto Rican has not found a fortune in the United States, Anglo-Americans have found a fortune in Puerto Rico. Puerto Ricans have filled labor shortages in many important stateside industries: in Illinois, electronic industries; in Wisconsin foundries; in the steel mills of Ohio, Indiana, and Pennsylvania; in East and Midwest farms; and in the textile and garment industries of New York (Migration Division, 1975). Puerto Ricans initially were recruited to serve as a source of cheap labor. Some employers now consider minorities an "excess population" because machines are increasingly being substituted for low-level positions. Current migration therefore differs from previous immigration in that the opportunities for work are no longer available.

White immigrants did not have to deal with the degree of racism that permeates our society with respect to "rainbow" people. There are other important differences which should be noted. For example, the Puerto Rican migration is an airborne one. It has a back and forth flow significant in that the feeling of need to adjust to the stateside environment tends to be less than if travel were more difficult. In fact, it is difficult to find a Puerto Rican adult who has not spent some time in the United States (U.S. Commission on Civil Rights, 1976).

Though Puerto Ricans come to the States for many reasons, migration has been seen to have an economic regulator (Migration Division, 1975) that serves as the primary motivation for migration. Puerto Rico's economic situation at present is devastating. It should be noted that the means of production, resources, and capital in Puerto Rico are mainly in the hands of North Americans. The dollar value of United States business holdings in Puerto Rico is exceeded only by its holdings in Britain, Germany, and Canada. Strategic considerations are also critical in Puerto Rico's proximity to Cuba and the Panama Canal. Also, Puerto Rico may prove in the future to be an oil resource, as preliminary seismic studies show potential deposits off the northwestern coast (*New York Times*, 1977).

In Puerto Rico present conditions are deplorable. The myriad of economic problems necessitate a continuation of patterns that are cruel and divisive to the family. It is not uncommon to find wives separated from husbands and children, or vice versa, with children cared for an ocean away from their parents. With part of the family in Puerto Rico and part in the United States enough is earned to keep the family from starving. Yet, "stateside," the Puerto Rican is by no means doing well. Puerto Ricans have had the dubious distinction of being poorer, having less education, and being more dependent upon welfare than the national average (U.S. Commission on Civil Rights, 1976). In the general population, about 64 percent of all persons 25 years old and over were high school graduates compared to 30 percent in the Puerto Rican population. By 1976, in the overall population, about 3.8 percent of all persons had completed less than 5 years of school; the figure was 18.7 percent for the Puerto Rican population (U.S. Bureau of Census, 1976).

We should, however, take note that official census figures often belie existing conditions. As an illustration, a 1966 report by the U.S. Department of Labor stated that the unemployment rate for Puerto Ricans in slum areas in New York was 33.1 percent, which contrasted with the 10 percent official unemployment rate (U.S. Commission on Civil Rights, 1976).

With reference to education, the dropout problem becomes acute in the 18–24 age group. In Chicago, a study showed that the dropout rate for Puerto Ricans in grammar and high school was 71.2 percent; 12.5 percent dropped out of grammar school while 58.7 percent dropped out of high school. It is important to understand that reasons for dropping out are not purely academic. Of the 30 percent of the Puerto Rican U.S. high school students who drop out each year, one-third have already completed most of their required courses and are in their senior year. Most dropouts are bored, feel the need to find a job, or find the school unresponsive to their cultural background.

Studies of schools in Chicago and New York revealed that schools with heavy Puerto Rican enrollments had students with reading averages lower than predominantly black or Anglo Schools. Lags increased with each succeeding grade. Birthplace, language, and dropout rate were interwoven. Young Puerto Ricans born on the Island are more likely to be doomed to a life of poverty (U.S. Commission on Civil Rights, 1976). The Chicago report discussed its interviews of 140 dropouts (better termed "pushouts"). The pushout's personal reason for leaving school was a major crisis in self-identity that made staying in school more and more difficult. The pushout had learned that his or her position in society was clearly lower than that of an Anglo. This newly acquired consciousness of societal rejection was in violent opposition to the internalized sense of *respeto* and *dignidad*. "Social schizophrenia," a conflict of great intensity, resulted. The easiest way out was to dissociate oneself from school, a major establishment symbol. Aspirations for the future decreased and a sense of defiance developed. Some students joined gangs, which provided an environment where they could find recognition, new respect, and leadership roles. Such students concluded that academic achievement often does not bring the expected reward (Lucas, 1974).

While census figures and findings paint a grim picture of the Puerto Rican condition, what is perhaps of even greater concern is the fact that the situation has worsened greatly.

> The . . . stresses and strains burdening the Puerto Rican family have resulted in an escalating increase in children without homes, delinquent children, addicted youth, and youth poorly prepared to compete for higher education or employment. It remains rather amazing that, despite these burdens, the majority of Puerto Rican families have been able to make an adjustment to their new environment, recreate some of their cultural ambience (for example, food, religion, and recreation), and create communal institutions and organizations that contribute to the community's well-being and progress. It is a strong, vibrant community, often resisting forces that attempt to assimilate it or eradiate it, linguistically or culturally. One commentator has suggested that the tenacity to exist as a distinctive group has been stubbornly embedded in Puerto Ricans as a result of 450 years of colonialism (Miranda, 1973).

To round out the picture, we should note that the situation is not uniformly bleak. One hundred and four thousand Puerto Ricans earned $10,000 or more in 1974. About 25,000 earned in excess of $15,000 and around 5,000 had earnings in excess of $25,000. Thousands of mainland Puerto Ricans are high school and university graduates. The figures for 1975 show 198,000 high school graduates, 12,000 college graduates, and more than 17,000 enrolled college students. Forty-two thousand Puerto Ricans held professional, technical, or managerial jobs in 1975. Three-fourths of the Puerto Rican families on the mainland are entirely self-sufficient and do not receive any government aid (U.S. Commission on Civil Rights, 1976).

Nevertheless, the overall statistical picture is a dismal one. The figures in human terms mean that it is often difficult for a Puerto Rican man or woman to find employment. When secured, jobs are frequently seasonal or temporary, and the norm is dead-end employment. Doors are often closed for reasons having nothing to do with willingness to work. Qualifications are unrelated to the task at hand. As an illustration written examinations for some sanitation workers require a college education; high school diplomas are required of airplane maintenance personnel; there is a height requirement for police personnel; Puerto Ricans in union construction jobs are token workers (U.S. Commission on Civil Rights, 1976); fluency in English is required for dishwasher jobs, etc. For a Puerto Rican seeking employment, discrimination exists at all levels, not only in the private sector but in public service as well as in employment and training programs. Discriminatory practices in government are well documented by the United States Commission on Civil Rights (1976). This is a matter of gravest concern, for how can Puerto Ricans expect to make gains in the private sector if they cannot rely on the governmental sector to set an example and enforce its own regulations.

A minority group woman can at times secure employment more easily than a man, perhaps as a sewing-machine operator or as a domestic, because our society still needs to have these functions performed. In those instances where a husband must stay at home to care for young children, family roles are reversed. Recall that in the Puerto Rican family system the male is expected to be the breadwinner and a dominant figure. Hence, role reversal is of tremendous importance in a family system where *machismo* is valued; the extent of valuation, of course, varies with the family. American psychiatrists have ethnocentrically defined *machismo* as "belligerent masculinity" and "sexual dominance" that such men are expected to display under any possible challenge or situation. They have viewed *machismo* in terms of sexual overcompensation, and as related to generic problems in masculine identification (Group for the Advancement of Psychiatry, 1970). *Machismo*, however, in its ramifications does not appear to be too different from the combination of male chauvinism, with its implications for female-male roles and rewards, and the double standard of sexuality (Sirjamaki, 1969).

The difference seems to be that Latin American *machismo* is not disguised or subtle so that its impact is more readily discernible. *Machismo* in its individualized expression can be viewed in the context of a society denying a male his manhood by societal castration. This situation has been found by social workers to create panic, confusion, marital discord, and the breakdown of family ties (Giordano, 1976a, 1976b).

A man needs to work. The significance of work to a man's self-concept is well understood. Peter Drucker states:

> Social effectiveness, citizenship, indeed even self-respect depend on access to a job. Without a job, a man in industrial society cannot possibly be socially effective. He is deprived of his citizenship, social standing, and of the respect of his fellow man, if not his family, and finally of self-respect (Mayfield, 1972, p. 108).

A man needs avenues for achievement. Being a *macho completo* (complete man) provides an avenue of gratification when there are few other opportunities for status or reward. This sense of being a *macho* must go hand in hand, however, with being able to provide for and protect one's family. It is not necessary that these functions be a man's exclusive domain. It is recognized that government has taken over more and more family functions. Consequently, the family's authority in relation to such concerns as parental discipline and legal systems has lessened. A Puerto Rican man with no employment, power, or status can be expected to be impotent in protecting his family in relation to these external systems. A principal strain on Puerto Rican family life is the disparity between the presumed dominance of the male and the actual facts of the situation (Group for the Advancement of Psychiatry, 1970).

Some women may experience contempt for their husbands because they can no longer view them as *machos*. A husband can be expected to strive to reassert his dominance, but due to all the external pressures, he will often in the end experience defeat and lose his sense of *dignidad*. Many women feel torn apart at seeing the men they love destroyed by forces over which they have no control. Children, experiencing the friction in the home, seeing the family structure undermined, and probably having had no contact with successful Puerto Rican families, internalize contempt of parents, Puerto Ricans, and themselves. Funnye and Shiffman (1967) note that the ghetto imposes a pervasive sense of worthlessness on its children, with implications of undesirability and inferiority. There are situations in which the impact of these feelings is such that even after the parents' struggle to provide the child with a college education, the child is fearful of leaving the ghetto to achieve in the larger community.

In working with a group of Puerto Rican adolescents at Aspira, the author learned that for many youths the image of what a family should be was related to models derived from television. Media influences often mean that Puerto Rican parents and children, literally and figuratively, do not speak the same language in speech or in values. In the adolescent's eyes the Puerto Rican family can never be expected to compete with families in programs such as Life with Father. Studies conducted by Hickel among Afro-Americans revealed that young black television viewers regard whites as more competent than blacks, and model their conduct accordingly (*Newsweek*, 1977). Models on TV have been changing, with minorities, particularly Afro-Americans, being depicted in a more positive light. Yet the harsh realities of ghetto existence seem in many ways to be romanticized in the TV programming. Even with the limited changes, however, neither Afro- nor Anglo-American models are Puerto Rican models.

There are few Puerto Rican professionals in any area with whom the adolescents have contact and can identify. It is hoped that the further development of bilingual, bicultural school programs will help these adolescents establish goals for themselves and to recognize the worth of their family and their group. This author will never forget her first day on a job in a settlement as a Field Instructor of a student unit and as an Assistant Professor from a University. A youngster came running after her and said in disbelief, "Are you really Puerto Rican?"

Puerto Rican adolescents in contact with external systems in the larger society have been stripped of their cultural heritage.

> When Juan Ortiz began bringing his homework back from the second grade in Brooklyn, his mother noticed he had changed the spelling of his first name. "Well," the nine-year-old explained, "My teacher tells me my name isn't Juan, it's John." (*New York Times*, 1972).

The stripping process continues today. Many professionals are inadvertently guilty of taking part in this without any awareness of the racism involved. On one occasion the author served as speaker and discussion leader at a program designed to help social workers deliver relevant services to the Puerto Rican community. Under discussion were the difficulties students encountered in school in terms of both cultural and language issues. One day-care worker pointed out proudly how the children who were in her program would never face those difficulties, since from early infancy only English was spoken and Anglo values were stressed. The other professionals seemed convinced that the solution to Puerto Rican problems was socialization in the Anglo culture during infancy or at least in early childhood. They appeared taken aback when the author pointed out the racism in such an approach.

> Our definition of cultural pluralism must include the concept that our language and our culture will be given equal status to that of the majority population. It is not enough simply to say that we should be given the opportunity to share in the positive benefits of modern American life. Instead, we must insist that this sharing will not be accomplished at the sacrifice of all those traits which make us what we are as Puerto Ricans (U.S. Commission on Civil Rights, 1976).

In the futile search for the "pot of gold," children may often experience their parents' pain and feel tremendously responsible for the family's burdens and "failures." They often have had to learn to negotiate various systems for the family and may be crushed in the process. Some children exhibit acting-out behavior which may have primarily sociological determinants and great sociological and psychological ramifications (Cressey and Ward, 1969). Whatever the antecedents of Puerto Rican delinquency for example, the authority of the parents, especially of the father, is destroyed. Clearly, not all families disintegrate. Great credit must be given to those families that maintain their strength and balance in a society where the "pot" discovered is not filled with gold but is a melting pot filled with stereotypes of the middle class Anglo-American family unit.

CASE ILLUSTRATIONS OF FAMILIES IN TRANSACTION WITH THEIR ENVIRONMENT

Several case vignettes from the files of family agencies demonstrate some of the transactions of the Puerto Rican family with the stateside environment.*

*The agencies are not being identified in the interest of protecting further the identity of the client. The author, however, would like to thank these agencies for their cooperation.

No claim is made that these cases are a statistically representative sample of the Puerto Rican population stateside, but the situations are not atypical. Nor should these family agency clients be viewed as more or less pathological because of their relationship with the agency. Identifying data have been disguised so as to protect the client's right to confidentiality.

Case #1 (Gonzales)

Mr. and Mrs. Gonzales both came from Puerto Rico as adults. Both have some college education. Their financial situation is adequate in that their combined income makes it possible for them to live comfortably with their two children. They had just come back from a Florida vacation when they made contact with the family agency social worker. Mrs. Gonzales was working in a semi-professional position in a day-care center, in an Eastern city, where a family agency worker served as a consultant. When her 16-year-old daughter was arrested for shoplifting, she immediately turned for help to the family agency worker. An unsuccessful attempt was made to involve the father in the family sessions. Coming for help, especially to a female worker, seemed to be too great an affront to his machismo. His wife was quite accepting of the male-female role dichotomy in the home. Nevertheless, from the content of the sessions it was clear that Mr. Gonzales was very much involved in the counseling process and with his family. His affection and concern were very evident to the worker despite his difficulty in expressing his feelings directly.

The need for that clear communication by this family of feelings, ideas, and needs was also apparent to the worker. The daughter Dolores was feeling extremely lonely and misunderstood, and the parents in turn were feeling quite hurt. Dolores experienced herself as different from all her friends. She had stolen some clothing in order to dress like all the other teenagers and so that she could go to a school dance. The parents were very strict in keeping with the tradition of protecting the female. They did not approve of the typical teenage attire and the freedoms allowed to Anglos.

The parents came to see that they had to accept the reality of the stateside culture and that they would cripple their daughter were they to continue to deny her the right to participate in teenage activities. They gave up setting limits in an automatic way and tried to balance the traditional value system with the needs of their teenage daughter in an Eastern city environment. The 16-year-old daughter had internalized the traditional Puerto Rican value system with some modifications. Her rebellion against her heritage did not mean she was truly desirous of throwing it all off. She needed to feel she had options. She assessed her group of friends and recognized certain behaviors of which she did not approve. Nor did she herself truly wish to dress in any extreme fashion. The daughter was able to modify her dress in the way that was satifactory to all. She pleased her parents and willingly went to family affairs. (All age groups socialize together in the Puerto Rican culture.) The parents recognized she needed to be allowed her own separate life.

Basically, what happened in this situation was a cultural clash that went beyond a clash of generations typical in families with teenagers. The family was able to handle a crisis by opening up channels of communication and build upon their foundation of love and caring. Fortunately, this was not a situation where poverty compounded the difficulties.

Case #2 (Garcia)

The Department of Public Assistance of an Eastern city referred Mr. Garcia to the family agency for a number of problems. The client was drinking heavily and showed no interest in the W.I.N. program to which he had been referred for employment. He needed assistance with his medicaid eligibility and had great difficulty taking care of his 9-year-old daughter who was acting out. Also, they were living in a deplorable housing situation. Mr. Garcia, a man in his early fifties, had come to the States eight years ago, leaving a decent civil service job as a foreman in construction. His wife had moved herself and five children to the States against her husband's wishes.

Mrs. Garcia had insisted that in the States the family would have better economic and educational opportunities. Hoping to get his family to return to Puerto Rico, he took out a loan from a credit union and bought a home in Puerto Rico. Not succeeding in getting his wife to relent, he came to the States. His wife died from alcoholism shortly after his arrival. While in Puerto Rico he had had no idea of his wife's condition. The money that was left after selling the home in Puerto Rico and repaying the loan was used for her funeral expenses. The family had been receiving supplemental assistance while he was in Puerto Rico, as what he had been able to send was insufficient for their basic needs. He decided after his wife's death against returning to Puerto Rico and was able to secure a construction job to which he had to commute daily. Though his income was still inadequate, he withdrew the family from welfare on the basis that ". . . if I can work to take care of my family, I don't want them acting like beggars." He had a series of layoffs and when he was no longer eligible for unemployment benefits he had to go on assistance. He tried hard looking for work. He picketed with the Puerto Rican construction workers for more jobs, having met up with job discrimination. When some jobs did finally open up, he was not able to obtain one because of his age. He was so defeated and depressed that he increasingly took to drink.

Mr. Garcia feels that basically he has been a happy man. He equates happiness with being in Puerto Rico where he feels he can function at his best. Puerto Rico is a memory which triggers a smile on his face. He does not speak, however, of returning to Puerto Rico. His children are very important to him and they intend to remain. His depression is clearly a reactive one.

It is not unusual for part of a family to come to the States and the other member(s) to feel forced to follow. A woman may very well take the lead in such a situation. Mrs. Garcia wanted what she thought would be the best for her family. She was especially concerned about educational opportunities. Puerto Ricans value education. Mr. Garcia valued his family and, despite the upheaval he knew it would cost him, came to reunite himself with his family.

Little by little the force of circumstances and the environment tore this proud man down. All he had was in his past and like many Puerto Ricans he turned to his past for solace. He had not come to the States looking for handouts. He responded well to the combination of counseling, advocacy efforts and the concrete interventions of the family service worker. Importantly, through the worker's efforts he was again able to resume construction work, which gives him a sense of well being. His daughter is doing well. It is a sad commentary on this society that a man should have to depend on a social worker to obtain employment.

Case #3 (Santos)

The Santos family was referred to the family service agency by the school their 11-year-old daughter attends. The mother was acting in a bizarre fashion and was interfering with the teacher's functioning and her daughter's schooling. The father is a factory worker. The mother was a former practical nurse in Puerto Rico and because of her inability initially to speak English worked on an assembly line for a while. Mrs. Santos has had a mastectomy, is terminally ill and undergoing chemotherapy. Due to her irrational behavior, there is fear that she may hurt herself as she wanders about or that she may hurt others as she is easily upset. When she takes her medication, she is under better control.

Mrs. Santos has always been a devoted mother and has become obsessed with her daughter. Until her illness the mother functioned well. She now no longer allows her daughter to visit girlfriends and limits all her activities.

The Santos are members of a Pentecostal congregation. The mother carries a Bible in her pocketbook and says, "God will help me," but will not discuss her condition. The minister and his congregation have been extremely supportive of the family. All the Santos find comfort and draw strength in the church experience. The minister takes the daughter to school and in an effort to contain and watch over Mrs. Santos the minister's wife has tried to stay with her during the day. Mr. Santos cannot continue to miss days from work without jeopardizing his job. If money is secured from Cancer Care, a member of the congregation will stay with Mrs. Santos. Plans are for the daughter to go and live with an aunt in Puerto Rico upon the death of her mother.

Mr. Santos is deeply concerned about his wife. He is at a loss about how to handle her. Under no circumstance, however, does he wish her institutionalized.

This family has ties to the Puerto Rican community in its affiliation with the Pentecostal Church, which is serving as a sustaining force in a difficult situation. The Pentecostal Church, a storefront variety, is a native organization and an important social institution both as a religious force and a community resource. This family, as many other Puerto Ricans have done, is able to draw emotional support from the religious experience. Mrs. Santos' belief that God will help her reflects the resignation to their fate that is not uncommon to many members of the Puerto Rican community.

Puerto Ricans, in general, have a wide tolerance for idiosyncratic behavior, which explains the acceptance of Mrs. Santos' irrationality. Families are willing to put up with a great deal and are not quick to institutionalize their own even when this seems absolutely necessary. A Puerto Rican social worker in New York recently reported to me how difficult it is to get familes to accept placing the elderly in nursing homes when they, under their living conditions, cannot possibly care for them. There is tremendous guilt to work through. Nevertheless, it is my understanding from her that there is a long waiting list in Puerto Rico for nursing homes. Changes are clearly taking place. The hope is that the changes will reflect need and not the Anglo rejection of the elderly.

As to be expected, their daughter upon her mother's death will be cared for by family. Puerto Ricans are very protective of their female children. Mrs. Santos has become irrationally protective of her daughter. It is understandable that her anxiety over her impending death would manifest itself in this way.

Case #4 (Castro)

The family was referred to the family agency by the Visiting Nurse Association. The family is known to just about every social agency in the community, including protective services. Mrs. Castro's husband had deserted the family about a year ago, just prior to the birth of the youngest child. The oldest child is five years old. All children and Mrs. Castro appear retarded. The children have totally lacked stimulation. Mrs. Castro refuses to allow the children out of her sight. She is quite paranoid and has had a number of psychiatric hospitalizations. This is not to deny that some paranoia in a minority person is necessary for survival. Mrs. Castro carries a knife constantly in her skirt pocket and people are frightened of her. She has tremendous difficulty managing the care of her home which is in chaos. A student social worker had finally managed to gain Mrs. Castro's trust and, hopefully, there will be some changes in the home.

The family agency has tried to no avail to involve Mrs. Castro's blood kin and inlaws in an attempt to provide her with the emotional support of family, to avoid the possibility of placement, and in the hope of providing the children with the warmth of family contact and interaction. They say she is too crazy and refuse to involve themselves with her or to assume any responsibility at any level for the children. The relatives feel greatly burdened by their own difficult circumstances. They clearly state they do not want to take on anyone else's troubles or to involve themselves at all with this nuclear family. In fact, it is felt that Mrs. Castro's sister has actually stolen food stamps from her in the past. The extended family system has clearly broken down in this situation and traditional values seem to have no place. Neither is there stateside a community that can serve as a mechanism of social control which demands the meeting of one's obligation to one's family if one is to remain in good standing and in turn obtain community support. Environmental pressures can exert such force that the culture of poverty seems to have greater impact than ethnic roots and may destroy the humanity of people. This must not be allowed to continue to happen.

Many social agencies are now involved with this family and it is costing society huge sums of money for these residual type services. Society will pay thousands to keep an individual in jail but not one cent for a guaranteed income. We can only speculate at this point about the kind of environmental and psychological stress that made Mr. Castro a runaway husband. One also needs to ask how much of the retardation of Mrs. Castro and the children relates to nutritional factors and how much to lack of intellectual development because of inadequate early stimuli. Projects such as the highly successful and replicated one originated by the Family Service Association of Hempstead, New York, need expansion. Trained personnel go into homes of two- and three-year-old children and attempt to foster verbal interaction by teaching mothers to play with their children. They demonstrate the use of toys and books. They work toward the development of a closer mother-child involvement and improvement of mother's self-image. The children's I.Q. scores have been shown to rise through such efforts. Preventive societal supports at all levels can enable familes to make their proper contribution to society.

SUMMARY AND CONCLUSIONS

In attempting to understand the Puerto Rican family, it is important to gain knowledge of its cultural heritage and the degree of each family's identification with the Puerto Rican or Anglo cultures. A unique blending is found in each individual and family. Class factors enter into this blending. Gordon (1964) has formulated the term, "ethclass," a subsociety created when ethnicity and social class intersect. He speaks of two types of ethnic identification: historical, which primarily focuses on the ethnic group, and participational, which focuses on the ethclass. He points out that members of similar ethnic groups from different social classes share peoplehood (historical identification) but do not necessarily have similar behavioral styles (participational identification).

All classes in Puerto Rican society seem to maintain both the historical and participational identifications. The degree of the identifications varies with the individual and family. On the mainland, it is, of course, difficult to identify the numbers of those who have completely assimilated into an Anglo life style. No culture will remain static, especially if it is to remain viable. In addition, all cultures have functional and dysfunctional aspects. As in all societies, subordination patterns in male-female roles must continue to undergo changes without females developing into superwomen. Extended families remain critical to individual members in an alienated world. This should not, however, negate a person's individuality. The humanitarian value system of the Puerto Rican needs to influence Anglo culture. Nevertheless, Puerto Ricans should not accept that the fruits of their efforts will be rewarded only in heaven. A humane standard of living must be available to all.

Caution must be taken not to stereotype any individual, class or group.

The author affirms Cafferty's and Chestang's (1976) view that it is as dangerous to ignore an individual's ethnic identity as it is to assume certain behavioral characteristics based on that identity.

Therefore, the characteristics of the Puerto Rican culture that have been discussed in this chapter should be utilized as guidelines for comparisons and applied with a respect for the differences and similarities among Puerto Ricans and Anglo-Americans.

Most of what is written in the literature and experienced by the Anglo in relation to the Puerto Rican relates to the lower-class Puerto Rican. Because this is the case, it is critical to recognize that our knowledge of Puerto Rican culture, even with attention to ethclass, is insufficient without reference to the Puerto Rican's transaction with the environment. We know that external macro systems furnish the conditions for a family's existence. As members of a minority group, Puerto Ricans have suffered greatly from institutionalized racist practices.

Mayfield's (1972) definition of powerlessness distinguishes the type of powerlessness imposed from without. The ecological conception and redefinition of pathology are also relevant to the Puerto Rican family situation. Behavior is not seen as sick or well, but as transactional, the outcome of reciprocal interactions between specific situations and the individual (Kelly, 1969).

Admittedly, the helping professions by themselves cannot restructure society and achieve a more equitable distribution of opportunities and rewards. The helping professions can, however, help the Puerto Rican family deal with suffocating external systems and, through joint advocacy efforts, work toward systems change. Helping professionals are certainly in a position to examine with honesty their own delivery system to the Puerto Rican consumer, noting the ways in which their services are functional, dysfunctional, or nonexistent. Services must be culturally syntonic and not geared to an Anglo value system.

To avoid continued polarization between groups in our society (McGready, 1976), the helping professions must work toward an acceptance of the concept of social utilities as developed by Kahn (1969), building on the Wilensky and Lebeaux (1958) concept of institutional and residual services in social welfare. We need to accept that by the very nature and complexity of modern society, services and supports will be necessary. A social utility, then, is a social invention, a resource or facility designed to meet a generally experienced need in living. These services must be accessible and be non-stigmatized, in the manner of public utilities.

Social utilities must be delivered in culturally relevant ways. Flexibility must be allowed for in their neighborhood design and implementation. Minimally, the helping professions must advocate a public social policy and a delivery system which takes ethnic factors into account. This includes working toward helping the Puerto Rican community have a part in its definition of its problem. Solutions must not be superimposed.

The Puerto Rican family must be permitted and assisted to utilize its own strength, draw upon its humanitarian values, and support its kin and the Puerto Rican community at large. The helping professions must work as agents of change if they are to be instrumental in the Puerto Rican family's efforts to manage its tasks effectively, in harmony with its values and life style, as well as with the realities of the mainland environment and urban existence.

REFERENCES

Abad, V., Ramos, J., and Boyce, E. "A model for delivery of mental health services to Spanish-speaking minorities." *American Journal of Orthopsychiatry*, 1974, 44, 584–595.

Beck, D. *Marriage and the Family Under Challenge. An Outline of Issues, Trends and Alternatives*, 2nd ed. New York: FSAA, 1976.

Betances, S. "Race and the mainland Puerto Rican." in A. P. Campos ed., *Puerto Rican Curriculum Development Workshop: A Report*. New York: CSWE, 1974, pp. 55–66.

Brameld, T. "Explicit and implicit culture in Puerto Rico: A case study in educational anthropology." In J. I. Roberts and Akinsanya eds., *Sociology in the Cultural Context*. New York: David McKay, 1976, pp. 44–57.

Bucchioni, E. "Home atmosphere and success in school. A sociological analysis of the functioning of elementary education for Puerto Rican children." (Unpublished doctoral dissertation, New School for Social Research, 1965, pp. 55–66.)

Cafferty, P. S. J., and Chestang, L. eds., *The Diverse Society: Implications for Social Policy*. Washington, D.C.: NASW, 1976.

Canabal, J., and Goldstein, D. "The Puerto Rican family institute: A laboratory for therapeutic techniques to aid Spanish-Speaking familes." In D. J. Curren ed., *Proceedings of Puerto Rican Conferences on Human Services*. Washington, D.C.: The National Coalition of Spanish Speaking Mental Health Organizations, 1975, pp. 61–85.

Cressey, D. R., and Ward, D. A. *Delinquency, Crime and Social Process*. New York: Harper & Row, 1969, especially pp. 244–253.

Erikson, E. *Identity and the Life Cycle*. New York: International Universities Press, 1959.

Fitzpatrick, J. J. *Puerto Rican Americans: The Meaning of Migration to the Mainland*. Englewood Cliffs, N. J.: Prentice-Hall, 1971.

Funnye, C., and Shiffman, R. "The imperatives of deghettoization: An answer to Piven and Cloward." *Social Work*, 1967, 12, 5–11.

Giordano, J. "Ethnics and minorities: A review of the literature." *Clinical Social Work Journal*, 1974, 2, 207–220.

Giordano, J. "Introduction. Group identity and mental health." *International Journal of Mental Health*, 1976(a), 5, 3–4.

Giordano, J. "Ethnicity and community mental health." *Community Mental Health Review*, 1976(b), 1, 4–14.

Goode, W. J. *The Family*. Englewood Cliffs, N.J.: Prentice-Hall, 1964.

Gorbea, C. "The institute's program for new arrivals." In D. J. Curren ed., *Proceedings of Puerto Rican Conferences on Human Services*. Washington, D.C.: The National Coalition of Spanish Speaking Mental Health Organizations, 1975, pp. 73–79.

Gordon, M. *Assimilation in American Life*. New York: Oxford University Press, 1964.

Group for the Advancement of Psychiatry. *The Case History Method in the Study of Family Process*. New York: Group for the Advancement of Psychiatry, 1970.

Hidalgo, H. *Ethnic Differences, Series #4*. Washington, D.C.: National Rehabilitation Association, 1972.

Kahn, A. *Theory and Practice of Social Planning*. New York: Russell Sage Foundation, 1969.

Katz, D., and Kahn, R. *The Social Psychology of Organizations*. New York: John Wiley and Sons, 1966.

Kelly, J. Ecological constraints on mental health services. In A. Bindman and A. Spiegel, eds., *Perspectives in Community Mental Health*. Chicago: Aldine, 1969, pp. 93–100.

Leichter, H. J., and Mitchell, W. E. *Kinship and Casework*. New York: Russell Sage Foundation, 1967.

Longres, J. F., Jr. "Racism and its effects on Puerto Rican continentals." *Social Problems*, 1974, 55, 67–75.

Lubchansky, I., Egri, G., and Stokes, J. "Puerto Rican spiritualists view mental health: The faith healer as a paraprofessional." *American Journal of Psychiatry*, 1970, 127, 88–97.

Lucas, I. "A profile of the Puerto Rican dropout in Chicago." in A. P. Campos, ed., *Puerto Rican Curriculum Development Workshop: A Report*. New York: CSWE, 1974, pp. 20–30.

Maldonado–Denis, M. *Puerto Rican: A Socio-Historic Interpretation*. New York: Vintage Books, 1972 (Translation).

Mayfield, W. "Mental Health in the black community." *Social Work*, 1972, 17, 106–110.

McGready, W. "Social utilities in a pluralistic society." In P. S. J. Cafferty and L. Chestang eds., *The Diverse Society: Implications for Social Policy*. Washington, D.C.: NASW, 1976, pp. 13–25.

Migration Division, Department of Labor, Commonwealth of Puerto Rico. *Puerto Ricans in the United States*, 1975 (Xerox).

Mintz, S. W. "Puerto Rico: An essay in the definition of national culture." In F. Cordasco and E. Bucchioni eds., *The Puerto Rican Experience: A Sociological Sourcebook*. Totowa, N.J.: Littlefield, Adams, 1973, pp. 26–90.

Miranda, M. ed., *Puerto Rican Task Force Report*. New York: CSWE, 1973.

Murdock, G. P. "The universality of the nuclear family." In N. Bell and E. Vogel eds., *A Modern Introduction to the Family*. New York: The Free Press, 1968, pp. 37–44.

Newsweek, February 21, 1977.

New York Times, Jan. 9, 1977.

New York Times, July 30, 1972.

Rabkin, J. G., and Struening, E. L. *Ethnicity, Social Class and Mental Illness*, Working Paper Series No. 17. New York: Institute on Pluralism and Group Identity, 1976.

Roger, L. *Migrant In the City: The Life of a Puerto Rican Action Group*. New York: Basic Books, 1972.

Ruiz, P., and Langrod. "The role of folk healers in community mental health services." *Community Mental Health Journal*, 1976, 12, 392–398.

Ryan, W. "Fretting about the poor." In W. Ryan ed., *Distress in the City*. Cleveland: The Press of Western Reserve University, 1969, pp. 262–267.

Scheele, R. "The prominent families of Puerto Rico." In J. Steward, ed., *People of Puerto Rico*. Urbana: University of Illinois Press, 1969, pp. 418–462.

Sirjamaki. J. "Cultural configurations in the American family." In R. J. R. King, ed., *Family Relations: Concepts and Theories*. Berkeley, Cal.: The Glendessary Press, 1969, 42–54.

Stycos, J. M. "Family and fertility in Puerto Rico." *American Sociological Review*, 1952, 17, 572–580. National Council on Family Relations, Reprint.

Thomas, P. "Puerto Ricans in the promised land." *Civil Rights Digest*, January 1974, 6.

Thomas, P. *Down These Mean Streets*. New York: New American Library, 1967.

Torres–Matrullo, C. "Accumulation and psychopathology among Puerto Rican women in mainland United States." *American Journal of Orthopsychiatry* 1976, 46, 710–719.

U.S. Bureau of the Census. *Current Population Reports*. Persons of Spanish origin in the United States, March 1975, Series P-20, No. 290. Washington, D.C.: U.S. Government Printing Office, 1976.

U.S. Bureau of the Census. *Current Population Reports.* Persons of Spanish origin in the United States, March 1976. Series P-20, No. 302. Washington, D.C.: Printing Office, 1976.

U.S. Commission on Civil Rights. *Puerto Ricans in the Continental United States: An Uncertain Future.* October, 1976.

Valle Consultants Ltd. *What Holds Sami Back: A Study of Service Delivery in a Puerto Rican Community.* New York: Valle Consultants Ltd., 1973.

Vasquez de Rodriquez, L. *Needs and Aspirations of the Puerto Rican People, Social Welfare Forum,* 1971. New York: Columbia University Press, for the National Conference on Social Welfare, 1971, 15–22.

Vasquez de Rodriquez, L. "Social work practice in Puerto Rico." *Social Work,* 1973, 18, 32–40.

Vasquez, J. D. "La Bodega—A social institution." In A. P. Campos, ed., *Puerto Rican Curriculum Workshop: A Report.* New York: CSWE, 1974, pp. 31–36.

Wagenheim, K. *Puerto Rico: A Profile.* New York: Praeger, 1970.

Wilensky, H. L., and Lebeaux. *Industrial Society and Social Welfare.* New York: Russell Sage Foundation, 1958.

Zimmerman, S. "The family and its relevance for social policy." *Social Casework,* 1976, 57, 547–554.

CHAPTER 19

Social Work with Native Americans

Ronald G. Lewis and Man Keung Ho

PREFATORY COMMENT

This article is primarily addressed to social workers who are, or might someday be, working with American Indians, many of whom prefer to be called Native Americans. The authors perceive shortcomings in the educational process of social work training because students are not specifically trained to work with Native Americans. Because literature on social work with Native Americans is almost nonexistent, Ronald G. Lewis and Man Keung Ho urge researchers and educators to devote more effort to identifying how social workers can more effectively serve Native Americans.

Social workers have lacked success in working with Native Americans because they do not understand Native American culture, they retain stereotyped images of Native Americans, and they use standard techniques and approaches in trying to help them. Since each tribe's culture is unique, there is no single Native American culture, and no social worker can be familar with the cultures of some 200 tribes. However, some customs are generally characteristic of all Native Americans, and the authors suggest that social workers become familiar with these. The concepts of sharing, time, acceptance of suffering, and optimism, to name a few cultural traits common to most tribes, differ significantly from Anglo traits. Social workers must realize these differences and proceed accordingly.

The Native American cultural concept of noninterference—that is, not interfering with or imposing oneself on the life of another—may result in problems in client-worker relations for the social worker who practices aggressive intervention. Because most Native American clients tend to reject aggressive social workers they must exercise great sensitivity when working with Native Americans. In working toward this goal, careful application of communication techniques and skills such as restating, clarifying, summarizing, reflecting, and empathizing may be particularly helpful.

Lewis and Ho conclude that it is impossible for a social worker always to know precisely how to respond to Native Americans. Social workers must be willing to admit their own limitations, listen carefully, avoid drawing conclusions prematurely, and anticipate that their presuppositions will be corrected by clients. They must genuinely want to know what the problem is and must be receptive to being taught. Perhaps the

*most important key to working with Native Americans, according to Lewis and Ho,
is an unassuming and unobtrusive humanistic attitude in the social worker.*

In the past, the social work profession has failed to serve effectively an important segment of the population—the Native Americans. Although social workers are in sympathy with the social problems and injustices long associated with the Native American people, they have been unable to assist them with their problems. This lack of success on the part of social workers can be attributed to a multitude of reasons, but it stems, in general, from the following: (1) lack of understanding of the Native American culture, (2) retention of stereotyped images of Native Americans, (3) use of standard techniques and approaches.

Currently, the majority of social workers attempting to treat Native Americans are whites who have never been exposed to their client's culture. Even when the social worker is a Native American, if his education and training have been in an environment that has completely neglected the Native American culture, there is still the possibility that he has drifted away from his people's thinking. Social workers with no understanding of the culture may have little or no sympathy for their Native American clients who fail to respond quickly to treatment.

Furthermore, Native Americans continue to be stereotyped by the current news media and often by the educational system. In all likelihood, the social worker will rely on these mistaken stereotypes rather than on facts. As Deloria explained, "People can tell just by looking at us what we want, what should be done to help us, how we feel, and what a 'real' Indian is like."[1] If a worker wishes to make progress in helping a Native American, he must begin by learning the facts and discarding stereotypes.

The ineffectiveness of social workers in dealing with Native Americans can often be attributed directly to the methods and techniques they use. Naturally, social workers must work with the tools they have acquired, but these may have a detrimental effect on a Native American. For example, the concept of "social work intervention" may be consistent with much of the white man's culture, but it diametrically opposes the Native American's cultural concept of noninterference.[2] There is a great need for social workers to examine carefully those techniques they plan to use in treating their Native American clients. If the worker discovers any that might be in conflict with the cultural concepts of the Native American, he should search carefully for an alternative approach. To do this, of course, the social worker must be aware of common Native American cultural traits.

Although there is no monolithic Native American culture—because each tribe's culture is unique to that individual tribe, and no social worker could be expected to be familiar with the cultures of some two hundred tribes—the worker should familiarize himself with those customs that are generally characteristic of all Native Americans. Only after a worker has gained at least an elementary knowledge of Native American customs and culture can he proceed to evaluate the various approaches and techniques and choose the most effective ones.

NATIVE AMERICAN TRAITS

The concept of sharing is deeply ingrained among Native Americans who hold it in greater esteem than the white American ethic of saving. Since one's worth is measured by one's willingness and ability to share, the accumulation of material goods for social status is alien to the Native American. Sharing, therefore, is neither a superimposed nor an artificial value, but a genuine and routine way of life.

In contrast to the general belief that they have no concept of time, Native Americans are indeed time conscious. They deal, however, with natural phenomena—mornings, days, nights, months (in terms of moons), and years (in terms of seasons or winters).[3] If a Native American is on his way to a meeting or appointment and meets a friend, that conversation will naturally take precedence over being punctual for the appointment. In his culture, sharing is more important than punctuality.

Nature is the Native American's school, and he is taught to endure all natural happenings that he will encounter during his life. He learns as well to be an independent individual who respects others. The Native American believes that to attain maturity—which is learning to live with life, its evil as well as its good—one must face genuine suffering. The resilience of the Native American way of life is attested to by the fact that the culture has survived and continues to flourish despite the intense onslaught of the white man.

One of the strongest criticisms of the Native Americans has been that he is pessimistic: he is presented as downtrodden, low-spirited, unhappy, and without hope for the future. However, as one looks deeper into his personality, another perspective is visible. In the midst of abject poverty comes "the courage to be"—to face life as it is, while maintaining a tremendous sense of humor.[4] There exists a thin line between pathos and humor.

The Native American realizes that the world is made up of both good and bad. There are always some people or things that are bad and deceitful. He believes, however, that in the end good people will triumph just because they are good. This belief is seen repeatedly in Native American folktales about Iktomi the spider. He is the tricky fellow who is out to fool, cheat, and take advantage of good people. But Iktomi usually loses in the end, reflecting the Native American view that the good person succeeds while the bad person loses.[5] Therefore, the pessimism of Native Americans should instead be regarded as "optimistic toughness."

Those who are unfamiliar with the culture might mistakenly interpret the quiet Native American as being stoical, unemotional, and vulnerable. He is alone, not only to others but also to himself. He controls his emotions, allowing himself no passionate outbursts over small matters. His habitual mien is one of poise, self-containment, and aloofness, which may result from a fear and mistrust of non-Native Americans. Another facet of Native American thought is the belief that no matter where any individual stands, he is an integral part of the universe. Because every person is fulfilling a purpose, no one should have the power to impose values. For this reason, each man is to be respected, and he can expect the same respect and reverence from others. Hence, the security of this inner fulfillment provides him with an essential serenity that is often mistaken for stoicism.

Native American patience, however, can easily be mistaken for inactivity. For instance, the Kiowa, like other Native American tribes, teach their young people to be patient. Today, when the young Native American has to go out and compete in another society, this quality is often interpreted as laziness. The white man's world is a competitive, aggressive society that bypasses the patient man who stands back and lets the next person go first.

The foregoing are only a few of the cultural traits that are common to most Native American tribes, but they represent important characteristics about which the effective social worker must be informed. The concepts of sharing, of time, acceptance of suffering, and optimism differ significantly from the white man's concepts. In dealing with a Native American client, the social worker must realize this and proceed accordingly. He must be familiar with the Native American view that good will triumph over evil and must recognize that Native Americans are taught to be patient and respectful. If the worker fails to do this, he is liable to make false assumptions, thus weakening his ability to serve his client effectively.

CLIENT–WORKER RELATIONS

A social worker's ability to establish a working relationship with a Native American will depend on his genuine respect for his client's cultural background and attributes. A worker should never think that the Native American is primitive or that his culture and background are inferior.

In the beginning, the Native American client might distrust the worker who is from a different race and culture. He might even view the worker as a figure of authority, and as such, the representative of a coercive institution. It is unlikely that he will be impressed with the worker's educational degrees or his professional title. However, this uncompromising attitude should not be interpreted as pugnacity. On the contrary, the Native American is gregarious and benevolent. His willingness and capacity to share depend on mutual consideration, respect, and noncoercion.

Because their culture strongly opposes and precludes interference with another's affairs, Native Americans have tended to regard social work intervention with disfavor. Social workers usually are forced to use culturally biased techniques and skills that are insensitive to the Native American culture and, therefore, are either detrimental to these clients or, at best, ineffective.

In an effort to communicate more fully, a social worker is likely to seat himself facing the client, look him straight in the eye, and insist that the client do likewise. A Native American considers such behavior—covert or overt—to be rude and intimidating; contrary to the white man, he shows respect by not staring directly at others. Similarly, a worker who is excessively concerned with facilitating the display of inner feelings on the part of the client should be aware of another trait. A Native American client will not immediately wish to discuss other members of his family or talk about topics that he finds sensitive or distressing. Before arriving at his immediate concern (the real reason he came to the worker in the first place), the client—particularly the Native American—will test the worker by bringing up peripheral matters. He does this in the hope of getting a better picture of how sincere, interested, and trustworthy the worker actually is. If the worker impatiently confronts the client with accusations, the client will be "turned off."

Techniques of communication that focus on the client—that is, techniques based on restating, clarifying, summarizing, reflecting, and empathizing—may help a worker relate to the client who sometimes needs a new perspective to resolve his problem. It is important that the worker provide him with such information but not coerce him to accept it. The worker's advice should be objective and flexible enough so that its adoption does not become the central issue of a particular interview.

For the Native American, personal matters and emotional breakdown are traditionally handled within the family or extended family system. For this reason, the client will not wish to "burden" the worker with detailed personal information. If the client is estranged from his family and cultural group, he may indirectly share such personal information with the worker. To determine the appropriate techniques for helping a Native American client deal with personal and psychological problems, the worker should carefully observe the client's cultural framework and his degree of defensiveness. The techniques of confrontation traditionally associated with the psychoanalytic approach and the introspective and integrative techniques used by the transactional analysts tend to disregard differences in culture and background between a client and worker.

FAMILY COUNSELING

In view of the close-knit family structure of Native Americans, along with the cultural emphasis to keep family matters inside the family, it is doubtful that many social workers will have the opportunity to render family counseling services. In the event that a Native American family does seek the worker's help, the family worker should be reminded that his traditional role of active and manipulative go-between must be tempered so that family members can deal with their problems at their own pace.[6] Equally important is the worker's awareness of and respect for the resilience of Native American families, bolstered in crisis by the extended family system. The example of the Redthunder family serves as illustration.

The Redthunder family was brought to the school social worker's attention when teachers reported that both children had been tardy and absent frequently in the past weeks. Since the worker lived near Mr. Redthunder's neighborhood, she volunteered to transport the children back and forth to school. Through this regular but informal arrangement, the worker became acquainted with the entire family, especially with Mrs. Redthunder, who expressed her gratitude to the worker by sharing her homegrown vegetables.

The worker sensed that there was much family discomfort and that a tumultuous relationship existed between Mr. and Mrs. Redthunder. Instead of probing into their personal and marital affairs, the worker let Mrs. Redthunder know that she was willing to listen should the woman need someone to talk to. After a few gifts of homegrown vegetables and Native American handicrafts, Mrs. Redthunder broke into tears one day and told the worker about her husband's problem of alcoholism and their deteriorating marital relationship.

Realizing Mr. Redthunder's position of respect in the family and his resistance to outside interference, the social worker advised Mrs. Redthunder to take her family to visit the minister, a man whom Mr. Redthunder admired. The Littleaxe family, who were mutual friends of the worker and the Redthunder family, agreed to take the initiative in visiting the Redthunders more often. Through such frequent but informal family visits, Mr. Redthunder finally obtained a job, with the recommendation of Mr. Littleaxe, as recordkeeper in a storeroom. Mr. Redthunder enjoyed his work so much that he drank less and spent more time with his family.

Obviously, treating a family more pathogenic than the Redthunders might necessitate that the social worker go beyond the role of mediator. Nevertheless, since Native Americans traditionally favor noninterference, the social worker will not find it feasible to assume the active manipulative role that he might in working with white middle-class families. The social work profession needs new and innovative approaches to family counseling that take into account social and family networks and are sensitive and responsive to the cultural orientation of Native American families.[7]

GROUP WORK

Groups should be a natural and effective medium for Native Americans who esteem the concept of sharing and apply it in their daily lives. Through the group process, members can share their joy, intimacy, problems, and sorrows, and find a means of improving their lives. Today's society tends to foster alienation, anomie, disenfranchisement, dissociation, loneliness, and schizoid coolness.[8] People wish for intimacy but at the same time fear it.[9] The new humanistic approaches to counseling and psychotherapy have developed a wide variety of powerful techniques for facilitating human growth, self-discovery and interpersonal relations.[10] The effectiveness of these approaches in cutting through resistance, breaking down defenses, releasing creative forces, and promoting the healing process has been amply demonstrated. However, such approaches are highly insensitive to the cultural orientation of Native Americans. These people consider such group behavior to be false; it looks and sounds real but lacks genuineness, depth, and real commitment.

As the worker uses his skills in forming the group, diagnosing the problems, and facilitating group goals, he may inevitably retain certain elements of manipulation. However, if he is committed to recognizing individual potential and to capitalizing on the group model of mutual assistance, he should come close to meeting the needs of Native Americans who value respect and consideration for oneself as well as for others.[11]

To avoid manipulation and coercion, a group worker needs to utilize indirect and extra-group means of influence that will in turn influence the members. Thus the worker may act upon and through the group as a mediating structure, or through program activities, for the benefit of his clients.[12] The success of the worker's influences and activities is related to his knowledge and acceptance of Native American culture, its formal and informal systems and norms.

Regardless of whether the purpose of the group is for effecting interpersonal change or social action, such Native American virtues as mutual respect and consideration should be the essential components of the group process. Using the group to pressure members who are late or silent will not only jeopardize and shorten the group's existence, but will cause alienation and withdrawal from future group activities.

In view of the vast cultural difference between Native Americans and other ethnic groups, especially whites, it is doubtful that a heterogeneous grouping of members will produce good results. Similarly, group activities that are action oriented may be contradictory to Native Americans who view the compulsion to reduce or ignore suffering as immaturity.

COMMUNITY WORK

Because of the Native Americans' experience of oppression and exploitation—along with their emphasis on noninterference and resolute acceptance of suffering—it is doubtful that a social worker, regardless of his racial identity, could bring about any major change in community policies and programs. The only exception might be the social worker who is accepted and "adopted" by the community and who agrees to confine himself to the existing system and norms. A worker's adoption by the Native American community will depend on his sincerity, respect, and genuine concern for the people. This concern can best be displayed through patience in daily contact with the community as well as through his efforts to find positive solutions to problems.

A worker who uses the strategy of trying to resolve conflict as a means of bringing about social change will undoubtedly encounter native resistance and rejection. On the other hand a worker who shows respect for the system, values, and norms of the Native American eventually places himself in a position of trust and credibility. Only through mutual respect, and not through his professional title and academic degree, can the worker produce meaningful social change.

Obviously, social work with Native Americans requires a new orientation and focus on attitudes and approaches. The term Native American encompasses many tribes, and within these there are intratribal differences; furthermore, individuals within each subtribe may react differently to problems or crises. Therefore, it is impossible for a social worker always to know precisely how to respond to a Native American client or group. The worker must be willing to admit his limitations, to listen carefully, to be less ready to draw conclusions, and to anticipate that his presuppositions will be corrected by the client. The worker must genuinely want to know what the problem or situation is and be receptive to being taught. Such an unassuming and unobtrusive humanistic attitude is the key to working with Native American people.

The social worker who can deal most effectively with Native Americans will be genuine, respectful of their culture, and empathic with the welfare of the people. By no means does the Native American social worker have a monopoly on this type of attitude. In fact, the Native American social worker who has assimilated the white man's culture to the extent that he no longer values his own culture could do more harm than good.

Recognizing the distinct cultural differences of the Native American people, those who plan social work curricula and training programs must expand them to include specific preparation for workers who will be dealing with Native American clients. Literature on the subject is almost nonexistent, and researchers and educators would do well to devote more study to how social workers can serve Native Americans. More Native Americans should be recruited as students, faculty, and practitioners in the field of social work. All persons, regardless of race, should be encouraged to develop a sensitivity toward Native Americans whom they may have the opportunity to serve. Social work agencies that deal primarily with Native American clients should intensify and refocus their in-service training programs.

A worker has the responsibility of acquiring knowledge that is relevant to the Native American culture so that he is capable of providing this effective treatment. A joint effort on the part of all those involved is required to give the service to the Native Americans that they justly deserve.

ENDNOTES

1. Vine Deloria, Jr., *Custer Died for Your Sins: An Indian Manifesto* (New York: Macmillan Co., 1969), p. 45.
2. For a detailed discussion of noninterference, see Rosalie H. Wax and Robert K. Thomas, "Anglo Intervention vs. Native Noninterference," *Phylon* 22 (Winter 1961): 53–56; and Jimm G. Good Tracks, "Native American Noninterference," *Social Work* 18 (November 1973): 30–34.

3. Good Tracks, op. cit., p. 33.
4. Clair Huffaker, *Nobody Loves a Drunken Indian* (New York: David McKay Co., 1967).
5. See John F. Bryde, *Modern Indian Psychology* (Vermillion, S.D.: Institute of Indian Studies, University of South Dakota, 1971), p. 15.
6. See Gerald Suk, "The Go-Between Process in Family Therapy," *Family Process* 6 (April 1965): 162–178.
7. Ross V. Speck, and Carolyn L. Attneave, "Social Network Intervention," in Jay Haley, ed., *Changing Families* (New York: Grune & Stratton, 1971), pp. 17–34.
8. Rollo May, "Love and Will," *Psychology Today* 3 (1969): 17–24.
9. Edward A. Dreyfus, "The Search for Intimacy," *Adolescence* 2 (March 1967): 25–40.
10. See Bernard Gunther, *Sense Relaxation: Below Your Mind* (New York: Macmillan Co., 1968); Abraham Maslow, "Self-Actualization and Beyond," in James F. Bugental, ed., *Challenges of Humanistic Psychology* (New York: McGraw-Hill Book Co., 1967); H. Oho, *Explorations in Human Potentialities* (Springfield, Ill.: Charles C. Thomas, 1966); Carl Rogers, "Process of the Basic Encounter Group," in James F. Bugental, ed., op. cit.
11. For further discussion of a reciprocal model, see William Schwartz, "Toward a Strategy of Group Work Practice," *Social Service Review* 36 (September 1962): 268–279.
12. For further discussion of indirect and extra-group means, see Robert Vinter, *Readings in Group Work Practice* (Ann Arbor: Campus Publishers, 1967), pp. 8–38.

CHAPTER 20

Social Work Practice with Asian Americans

Man Keung Ho

PREFATORY COMMENT

"Social Work Practice with Asian Americans" is a chapter developed for the fifth edition of this volume by Man Keung Ho, who is a leading scholar on Asian Americans. He reminds readers that Asian Americans are not homogeneous and are actually comprised of several subgroups (Chinese, Filipino, Japanese, Korean, Vietnamese, Samoan, Guamanian), each having its own unique language and culture. Although there are some cultural characteristics common to Asian Americans such as filial piety, respect for elders, and placing a high value on the traditional family, there can be differences involving seeking physical health, mental health, and social services. Some Asian American groups feel shame in talking to strangers about personal problems.

Some Asian Americans have their own unique psychotherapy models such as "Morita therapy" developed by the Japanese. This therapy emphasizes a "here and now" orientation with a focus on behavior rather than moods and feelings. Social workers need to become more aware of these cultural differences and therapeutic models if they are to become effective with Asian American clients.

Asian Americans are often perceived as sharing the same or similar characteristics, but they actually are comprised of many diverse groups: Chinese, Japanese, Korean, Filipino Americans, Samoans, Guamanians, Hawaiians, and other Pacific Islanders. Other groups include recent immigrants and refugees from Vietnam, Thailand, Cambodia, Laos, and Indonesia, persons from India, Pakistan, and Ceylon, and children of mixed marriages in which one parent is Asian.[1] There are obvious language, historical, social, and economic differences. Generational status (new immigrants versus third and fourth generation) among groups and individuals should not be overlooked. Before micro (direct) and macro (indirect) social work practice with Asian Americans is introduced, current demographics and ecosystems of Asian Americans are reviewed.

CURRENT DEMOGRAPHICS

Population

The Asian American population has doubled since 1970, now comprising about 2 percent of the total U.S. population (3.5 million) and continues to increase. The population distribution of Asian Americans in 1970 and 1980 is shown in Table 20–1.

In 1970 the most populous Asian American group was the Japanese (591,290), followed by the Chinese (435,062) and the Filipinos (343,060). In 1980, however, the Chinese were the most numerous (806,042), followed by the Filipinos (774,652) and the Japanese (700,974). The Koreans showed a fivefold increase from an estimated 70,000 in 1970 to 354,593 in 1980. Other Asian groups identified by the U.S. Census, but who are not included in Table 20–1 are the Asian Indians (361,531) and the native Hawaiians (166,814). The Immigration Act of 1965 and the U.S. policy on refugees that resulted from the Vietnam War are primarily responsible for the rapid Asian American population increase in this country. Most Asian Americans live in West coast and East coast urban areas and in Hawaii. There was a concentrated effort by the U.S. government to scatter recent Southeast Asian immigrants throughout the country. The majority were resettled in California (135,308), Texas (36,198), and Washington State (16,286).

Socioeconomic Issues

Selected socioeconomic characteristics of Asian Americans are provided in Table 20–2.

Asian American families are more likely than either black or white families to have children under age 18. One out of every ten Asian American households is headed by a female whose spouse is not present. Asian American households that are headed by women are less likely to include children than households headed by black and Hispanic women. Asian Americans make up the smallest proportion of people without a high school diploma and the largest proportion of those with at least one college degree.

Despite comparatively high national unemployment rates, a relatively large proportion of Asian Americans are part of the labor force. Asian American women are less likely to be employed outside the home than men. The median income of an Asian American household is $2,000 above the national average. Proportionally, Asian Americans own fewer homes than their white counterparts.

Health and Mental Health Risk Factors

Asian American patients have been found to be similar to white patients in mental health diagnoses, except they are more likely to receive psychotic diagnoses.[2] This difference may be explained by the fact that less severely disturbed Asian Americans avoid using mental health services.

Many investigators have suggested that Asian Americans as a group consume less alcohol and have fewer cases of alcoholism than whites and other ethnic groups.[3] This is attributed to the genetic-racial differences in alcohol sensitivity and aversion and Asian American attitudes and values toward the

TABLE 20–1 Asian Americans in the United States, 1970 and 1980

YEAR	CHINESE	FILIPINO	JAPANESE	KOREAN	VIETNAMESE	SAMOAN	GUAMANIAN
1970	435,062	343,060	591,290	70,000[a]	N.A.[b]	N.A.	N.A.
1980	806,042	774,652	700,974	354,593	261,729	41,948	32,158

Source: U.S. Bureau of the Census, "U.S. Summary," Characteristics of the Population: 1980 (Washington, D.C.: U.S. Government Printing Office, May 1983), Vol. 1. pp. 9–20.

[a] Estimated.

[b] N.A. = not available.

TABLE 20–2 Selected Socioeconomic Characteristics of Racial and Ethnic Groups in the United States, 1980 (percentages)

	ETHNIC AND RACIAL GROUPS			
CHARACTERISTICS	WHITE	BLACK	ASIAN AND PACIFIC ISLANDERS	HISPANIC
Family Type				
Families with children under 18 years	49.4	61.0	61.5	67.8
Female-headed households; no husband present	11.1	37.3	10.9	19.8
Female-headed households with children under 18 years	56.1	68.8	56.5	72.6
Education				
Persons 25 years or older with less than a high school degree	31.3	49.4	25.8	56.7
Persons 25 years or older with at least a college degree	17.2	8.4	32.5	7.6
Employment				
Persons 16 years or older in labor force	62.2	59.2	66.3	63.4
Unemployed persons 16 years or older	5.8	11.7	4.8	9.1
Females 16 years or older in labor force	41.5	48.4	45.0	39.1
Income				
Median income	$20,840	$12,618	$22,075	$14,711
Persons living below poverty level in 1979	9.4	30.2	13.9	23.8
Persons who own homes	67.8	44.4	51.5	43.5

Source: U.S. Bureau of the Census, 1980 Census Population Supplementary Reports PHC 80-S1-1-Provisional Estimates of Social, Economic, and Housing Characteristics: States and Selected Standard Metropolitan Statistical Areas (Washington, D.C.: U.S. Government Printing Office, 1982), pp. 47, 100.

use of alcohol. Some observers have predicted that alcoholism among Asian Americans may increase in the future in response to urbanization, cultural conflict, and changes in family structure.

At the First National Asian American Conference on Drug Abuse Prevention, participants generally felt that drug abuse is as prevalent in Asian American communities as in other communities.[4] Lyman believes organized drug dealings in San Francisco's Chinatown provided revenues for the tongs (Chinese Associations) and gained a foothold.[5] Among many of the early Chinese immigrants who were lonely and uncared for, Sung found that the suicide rate of Chinese Americans in San Francisco is four times greater than the rate for the city as a whole.[6] More Chinese American women than men resort to suicide as a means to resolve their personal and interpersonal problems. A high suicide rate may be attributable to the fact that Asian Americans tend to direct family discord and unhappiness inward toward the self.

Crime and juvenile delinquency is low in Asian American communities.[7] However, it is generally recognized that criminal acts in Chinatowns and other urban Asian American communities are underreported.[8] Youth gangs' violent activities have increased recently in various Chinatowns throughout the country. Lyman attributes the increased formation of gangs to: (1) an increase in the number of immigrant youths; (2) frustration over racism and powerlessness; (3) inability to succeed in school because of English-language problems and cultural conflicts; and (4) the financial gains obtained through gang activities.[9] Asian American gangs are discussed in Chapter 16.

The process of immigration and cultural transition has created a severe health and mental health risk factor for Asian Americans. Immigration itself necessitates a large number of life changes over a short period of time that are associated with lowered well-being.[10] Five major factors have been identified as contributing directly or indirectly to the immigrational and cultural transitional difficulties that, in turn, increase physical and mental health risks of Asian Americans.[11] These factors include: (1) economic survival, (2) U.S. racism, (3) loss of extended family and support systems, (4) major cultural conflicts, and (5) cognitive reactive patterns to a new environment.

Two physiological systems, respiratory and digestive, have been found to be primary somatic targets for Asians experiencing immigrational stress.[12] Denial is the defense mechanism most frequently used by recent Vietnamese refugees. This denial defense is congruent with the Asian cultural values of self-sacrifice, submission for the common good, harmony, and consignment to fate. When the use of denial fails to protect a refugee from some of the harsh realities of immigration and when previous support systems are unavailable, psychosocial destruction such as psychosis may occur.[13] A national Mental Health Needs Assessment found some alarming facts concerning stress among immigrants: (1) mental health problems among Southeast Asian immigrants who arrived in 1975 only began to surface several years later; (2) depression was the most frequently reported problem; (3) anxiety, marital conflict, and intergenerational conflict were prevalent; and (4) the stress of the uprooting and cultural adjustment led to many emotional problems.[14]

ECOSYSTEMS PERSPECTIVE

The practice of social work focuses on the interaction between the person and the environment. The goal of social work practice is to enhance and restore the psychosocial functioning of persons or to change oppressive or destructive social conditions that negatively affect the mutually beneficial interaction between persons and their environment. In assessing Asian Americans' needs for services, the social worker should seek to understand clients' feelings and attitudes about those oppressive and destructive factors and their negative impacts.

The ecosystem model of practice developed and advanced by Meyer, Germain, and Morales and Sheafor, is adopted for analysis of psychological factors impacting on Asian Americans.[15,16,17] The ecosystem consists of five interconnected levels: (1) historical, (2) environmental–structural, (3) cultural, (4) family, and (5) individual. Analysis of each level as it affects the lives and social conditions of Asian Americans follows.

Historical Influences

The Chinese were the first immigrants from Asia to arrive in the United States during the 1840s. Their immigration from China was encouraged by the social and economic unrest in China at that time and by overpopulation in certain provinces.[18] During this period there was a demand in the United States for Chinese to help build the transcontinental railroad. However, a diminishing labor market and fear of the "yellow peril" made the Chinese immigrants no longer welcome. Chinese men were robbed, beaten, and murdered, especially if they tried to compete with whites in the mining districts of Western states. This anti-Chinese sentiment culminated in the passing of the Federal Chinese Exclusion Act of 1882, the first exclusion act against any ethnic group. This racist immigration law was not repealed until 1943 as a gesture of friendship toward China, who was an ally of the United States during the Second World War. The Immigration Act of 1965 finally abolished national-origin quotas. "Old-timer" immigrants were characterized as primarily uneducated peasants, unskilled laborers, and men. Post-1965 immigrants have been well-educated, urban families.[19]

Early Japanese immigrants came to the United States from 1890 to 1924 after the Chinese exclusion laws were passed. They left a rapidly industrializing country as "contract laborers" for the plantations in Hawaii. Legislation similar to the anti-Chinese acts was passed against the Japanese. Anti-Japanese prejudice culminated in the forced removal in 1942 of over 110,000 Japanese, 75 percent of them U.S. citizens, to guarded relocation centers. Unlike the Chinese, Japanese immigrants were allowed to start families employing the "picture bride" (bride selected by photograph) method of marriage. Consequently, the acculturation process of their U.S.-born children occurred much earlier than for immigrant Chinese children. Hence, in general, the

Japanese are more acculturated than the Chinese, even though the Chinese have been in this country for a longer time.

The Filipino population in the United States grew most rapidly after the Immigration Act of 1965. As a result of the Spanish American War and the Treaty of Paris (1899), the Philippines at one time was actually a possession of the United States until the Tydings–McDuffie Independence Act conferred commonwealth status on the Philippines. Filipinos then became aliens for the purpose of U.S. immigration. The earliest Filipino immigrants were unskilled laborers or students who were encouraged by the U.S. colonial government to attend U.S. colleges and universities.[20] Immigrants who came in the 1960s were mostly young professionals, both men and women. Many of them experienced difficulties in obtaining U.S. licenses to practice their profession. The majority of the surviving early Filipino immigrants are now retired, living in cheap one-room hotels and apartments. They experience health care problems, limited recreational opportunities, and physical and psychological isolation.

The number of Korean immigrants just prior to the Immigration Act of 1965 was slightly over 7,000.[21] A high proportion of them were Christian, because U.S. missionaries in Korea played a major role in Korean immigration. Kim estimated that 90 percent of the Korean immigrants have been here less than fifteen years—since the Immigration Act of 1965 went into effect in 1968. The largest Korean community, with a population over 150,000 is in Los Angeles.[22] Generally, Korean post-1968 immigrants have had to endure less hostility and structural discrimination than the early Chinese and Japanese immigrants.

The Pacific Islanders include groups such as Samoans, Tongans, Guamanians, and a small number from Tahiti and the Fuji Islands. Samoan immigration began to increase from 1951 when the U.S. Navy closed its island base. Guamanian immigration was facilitated by the 1950 Organic Act, which conferred U.S. citizenship on inhabitants of the territory of Guam. Because of their ties with the Church of Jesus Christ of Latter-Day Saints, many Tongans have settled near Salt Lake City, Utah. The Pacific Islanders as a group are relatively few in number and have no visible strong ethnic community in the United States in the 1980s.

Southeast Asians from Cambodia, Laos, and Vietnam came to this country primarily as refugees. Statistics of 1980 indicate 415,238 Indochinese were in the United States, of which 78 percent were from Vietnam, 16 percent from Cambodia, and 6 percent from Laos. The majority of them have settled in California, Texas, and Washington.[23] Cambodia, Laos, and Vietnam were part of the old French colonial empire and were lumped together as French Indochina. Cambodian culture was influenced by India, whereas, the people of Laos are mainly ethnic Thai. The Vietnamese culture was heavily influenced by China. The exodus of Vietnamese refugees began in 1975 with the fall of Saigon and U.S. withdrawal from the country. The first wave of refugees were mostly professionals and well-educated. A second wave was admitted to the United States after 1975 and consisted of less-educated people. The latter group has experienced more difficulty than the first group in adjusting to the United States.

Environmental–Structural Factors

The designation of Asian Americans as a minority group that has experienced prejudice and discrimination is misunderstood by many who fail to assess accurately the status of Asian Americans and to conceptualize racial discrimination. Asian Americans have had a history of exploitation and racism in the United States.[24] Federal legislation has often restricted Asian immigration, or as in the case of the 1924 Immigration Act, prohibited their immigration entirely. Asian immigrants were placed in the category of "aliens ineligible for American citizenship." Alien land laws completed the nightmare in that "aliens ineligible for citizenship" were denied the right to own property. Antimiscegenation laws, which prohibited interracial marriages, were passed. More than 110,000 Japanese Americans were relocated in detention camps during the Second World War.

Restrictions against Asian Americans covered many other areas of life as well. Employment and housing opportunities were limited, and the full use of public and private facilities was denied. Such structural, social, and psychological constraints relegated Asian Americans to second-class status.

Gains in civil rights and civil liberties occurred only after the Second World War. Today Asian Americans are often considered "model" minorities, but many still face discrimination and prejudice.[25,26]

Asian American Culture

Social workers should focus on understanding the cultural values, belief systems, and societal norms of U.S. culture as well as Asian traditional culture. In an attempt to understand Asian American clients and to work effectively with this unique ethnic group, Ho lists seven salient cultural values operating among Asian Americans.[27] These indigenous cultural values are described below.

(1) *Filial piety.* The respectful love of parent is the cornerstone of morality and is expressed in a variety of forms. Oya–KoKo, a Japanese's version of filial piety to parents, requires a child's sensitivity, obligation, and unquestionable loyalty to lineage and parents. An Asian child is expected to comply with familial and social authority even to the point of sacrificing his or her own desires and ambitions.

(2) *Shame as a behavioral influence.* Shame (*tiu lien* in Chinese) and shaming are used traditionally to help reinforce familial expectations and proper behavior within and outside the family. If an individual behaves improperly, he or she will "lose face" and also may cause the family, community, or society

to withdraw confidence and support. In Asian societal structures, where interdependence is very important, the actual or threatened withdrawal of support may shake a person's basic trust and cause him or her considerable anxiety at the thought of facing life alone.

(3) *Self-control.* Self-discipline is another concept highly valued by Asian Americans. The value "enryo" requires a Japanese individual to maintain modesty in behavior, be humble in expectations, and show appropriate hesitation and unwillingness to intrude on another's time, energy, or resources. To "Yin–Nor" for a Chinese is to evince stoicism, patience, and an uncomplaining attitude in the face of adversity, and to display tolerance for life's painful moments.

(4) *Middle-position virtue.* In training children Asian parents emphasize a social norm that cultivates the virtues of the middle position, in which an individual should feel neither haughty nor unworthy. Middle-position virtue is quite different from perfectionism and individualism highly valued by the middle-class white U.S. population. Asian American emphasis on middle-position brings an individual in step with others, instead of ahead or behind others. Thus, it fosters the individual's sense of belonging and togetherness.

(5) *Awareness of social milieu.* An Asian's concern for the welfare of the group also is related to his or her acute awareness of social milieu, characterized by social and economic limitations and immobility. The individual is highly sensitive to the opinions of peers and allows the social nexus to define his or her thoughts, feelings, and actions. In the interest of social solidarity, one subordinates himself or herself to the group, suppressing and restraining any disruptive emotions and opinions. Despite an individual's wealth and social status compliance with social norms, which provide him or her with social esteem and self respect, is strictly observed.

(6) *Fatalism.* Constantly buffeted by nature and by political upheaval over which they had little control, Asian Americans adopted a philosophical detachment. This resignation allowed people to accept their fate with equanimity. Other than trying to philosophize or ascertain underlying meaning in life events, the Asian met life pragmatically. It is unfortunate that this pragmatic adaptability, the very factor that contributed to success in the United States, later became a serious handicap. The Asian American's continuing silence only let him or her fall further behind in an alien U.S. culture that encouraged, and indeed demanded, aggressiveness and outspoken individualism. This fatalistic attitude of Asian Americans has partly contributed to their unwillingness to seek outside professional help. Unfortunately, the Asian's pragmatic adaptability is often misconstrued as resistance by some mental health and social services providers.

(7) *Inconspicuousness.* Fear of attracting attention was particularly acute among the thousands of Asian immigrants who came to the United States illegally. Experiences with racist segments of U.S. society further convinced

the Asian immigrant of the need for and value of silence and inconspicuousness. Fear and distrust still linger today among the descendants of early
immigrants. It is understandable why Asians are extremely reluctant to turn
to government agencies for aid, even in cases of dire need. Asian Americans'
silence and inconspicuousness tend to make them verbally passive members
in politics, group work, and community activities.

Family Structure

The cohesive extended network of the traditional Asian American family is
structured and prioritized, fed with male dominance and having parental ties
paramount. A male child has distinct obligations and duties to his parents
that assume a higher value than obligations to his siblings, children, or wife.
Sibling relationships are considered next in priority and are frequently acknowledged through cooperative adult activities. Concepts and teachings,
such as working hard, responsibility, family obligations, and collaborations,
pervade parent–child relationships. Members of the older generation are responsible for transmitting guidelines for socially acceptable behavior, educating younger people in how to deal with life events, and serving as a source
of support in coping with life crises.[28] A traditional Asian American family
becomes the primary caretaker of its members' physical, social, and emotional
health.

The traditional Asian American family structure provided stability, interpersonal intimacy, social support, and a relatively stress-free environment
for its members.[29] However, the process of immigration and cultural transition exerts a severe blow to these families. Relatives and close friends are
often no longer available to provide material and emotional support to needy
members. The traditional hierarchical structure and rigidity of family roles
often make the expression and resolution of conflicts within the nuclear family
very difficult. Little or no interpersonal interaction outside the nuclear family,
in turn, forces greater demands and intense interaction *within* the nuclear
family. This can leave members highly vulnerable and with many unresolved
conflicts. Discrepancies in acculturation between husband and wife and between parents and children negatively affect the decision making and functioning of a family. An individual's acceptance of and compliance with Western values such as individualism, independence, and assertiveness, especially
in attitudes related to authority, sexuality, and freedom of choice, make the
hierarchical structure of a traditional Asian American family dysfunctional.

While an Asian American family undergoes several stages in its attempt
to help its members, different families may have different service needs and
help-seeking patterns. Generally, there are three types of Asian American
families in the United States.[30]

Recently Arrived Immigrant Families Initial requests for services by this
type of family tend to be predominantly requests for information and referral,
advocacy, and other concrete services such as English-language instruction,

legal aid, and child care. Due to cultural differences, unfamiliarity with mental health resources, and language barriers, these families seldom seek personal or psychological help.

Immigrant–American Families These families are characterized by for-eign-born parents and U.S.-born children and the great degree of cultural conflict between them. They usually require help in resolving generational conflicts, communication problems, role clarification, and renegotiation.

Immigrant–Descendant Families These families usually consist of second (Japanese Nisei) or third (Japanese Sansei) generation U.S.-born parents and their children. They speak English at home and are acculturated to Western values. They can seek help from mainstream human service agencies, mental health centers, and private practitioners with some degree of comfort.

The Individual

Asian Americans face different problems with cultural conflict. Jones believes many forms of culture conflict are really manifestations of cultural racism.[31] Although there is nothing inherently wrong in acculturation and assimilation, he believes "when it is forced by a powerful group on a less powerful one, it constitutes a restriction of choice; hence, it is no longer subject to the values of the natural order." Sue and McKinney found young Chinese clients ex-hibited anxiety over the inability to reconcile the Western values of inde-pendence with their feelings of filial piety and family obligation.[32] Also re-ported were feelings of social isolation and feelings of passivity in social situations.

In an attempt to combat social isolation and gain a feeling of belonging and acceptance, an Asian American is forced to find reference groups in the United States. The Asian American may identify entirely with traditional Asian culture or reject Asian culture as old fashioned and dysfunctional. He or she may adopt U.S. values exclusively or become bicultural. Unfortunately, regardless of what value system an individual adopts, there are potential adjustment problems.

INTERVENTION STRATEGIES

Social workers who provide direct service, or micro level social work inter-vention, and indirect service, or macro level societal intervention, with Asian Americans need to have first-hand knowledge of how this unique ethnic minority group has traditionally responded to mental health and social ser-vice. It is also advisable for social workers to be familiar with traditional help-seeking behaviors of Asians. Many authors have warned that the client's orientation to the process of help-seeking and the "fit" between traditional paradigms and those utilized by providers may be critical to successful process and outcome.[33]

Mental Health and Social Service for Asian Americans

Studies indicate that Asian Americans seeking mental health treatment were more severely disturbed than Caucasians.[34] There is a tendency for Asian Americans to somatize so that stress and tension are frequently turned into physical complaints.[35] In personality measures Asian Americans have indicated more feelings of isolation, loneliness, anxiety, and emotional distress than Caucasians.[36]

In spite of their many mental health and social service needs, Asian Americans do not generally turn to these institutions and services for assistance. Literature on minority counseling and social service indicates that Western modes of service delivery have not been effective.[37] Low utilization and early termination of services by Asian Americans support this premise.[38] Miranda and Kitano have identified several barriers to Asian American clients' utilization of mental health and social services.[39] They include: (1) fragmentation of services, so that clients are referred from one worker to another; (2) discontinuity between the life of the professional and that of the client; (3) inaccessibility of services, and (4) the primary focus of the professional on being accountable to fellow professionals rather than to the ethnic community.

Traditional Asian American Approach to Treatment of Psychological Problems

There are a number of therapeutic models traditionally used by Asians that should be of interest to social workers who provide mental health services to this group. Morita therapy is probably the best known Japanese therapeutic model for psychological problems. Morita therapy emphasizes a here and now orientation, behavior over moods and feelings, and the interdependence among individuals.[40] Further, Morita therapists place little emphasis on searching for the origins of neuroses, discourage verbal rumination of one's problems, and do not recommend elaborate treatment plans for recovery.

The Ajase complex developed by the Japanese psychoanalyst Kosawa is based on a figure described in Buddhist scriptures.[41] The most important concept of the Ajase complex is that of the ambivalent mother–child relationship, especially mother to son. During the process of separation and individualization, the child develops a resentment based upon his or her interpretation that the mother was unwilling to let go and disappointment that he or she could not totally let go of the mother. The child's feeling of ambivalence is resolved upon the mother's unconditional forgiveness.

Naikan therapy focuses on enabling the individual to recapitulate significant others, especially the mother's influence upon him or her in the development of personhood.[42] Through the therapeutic process the sensei (teacher or therapist) guides the individual to a better understanding of his or her relationship with these significant others. Reciprocal role performance, obligation, indebtedness, forgiveness, and self-sacrifice also are focused on as integral parts of the therapeutic process. Through discussion and guidance the individual gains insight into his or her selfishness, which is considered the root of personal and interpersonal problems.

Ho'oponopono is a family-centered therapeutic approach practiced by Hawaiians to resolve family conflicts. Ho'oponopono is defined as "setting to right . . . to restore and maintain good relationships among family, and family and supernatural powers.[43] The therapeutic process of ho'oponopono is outlined as follows:

(1) *Beginning phase* characterized by prayer offering; general problems of identification, partialization of problems according to order of importance.

(2) *Middle phase* characterized by problem solving through open discussion with minimized confrontation and negative emotional expression; sincere confession of wrongdoing; seeking forgiveness and restitution if necessary.

(3) *Ending phase* characterized by a summary of the therapeutic process by the leader, who is always a respected elder; reaffirmation of the family's strengths; commitment to the basic unit; closing prayer and family sharing food together.

Help–Seeking Patterns and Behaviors

To assist Asian Americans successfully, social workers need to understand their traditional cultural values toward dysfunctional behavior. The process of acculturation may have altered an individual's or a family's cultural values, but as Mass indicates, the influence exerted by the value patterns that were acquired throughout childhood is often considerable, even among those whose behavior is highly Westernized.[44] Asian Americans feel a stigma and shame in talking about personal problems. The terms Hajj for the Japanese, Hijj for the Filipinos, Tiu lien for the Chinese, and Chaemyoun for the Koreans indicate the shame and loss of face these Asian groups feel when talking about personal issues.[45] Most Asian Americans do not seek psychiatric dynamics and psychological theories to account for behavioral difficulty.[46] Instead, social, moral, and organic explanations are used. When an individual behaves dysfunctionally, he or she commonly identifies external events such as physical illness, death of a loved one, or the loss of a job. The individual, therefore, is not to blame. Interpersonal duties and loyalties are held sacred by many Asian Americans. The dysfunction or suffering of an Asian American individual may be attributed to his or her violation of some duty, such as filial policy. Community elders or family members may be expected to exhort the individual to improve. In surveying a sample of Asian Americans in Los Angeles regarding their attitude toward mental health seeking behavior, ministers, relatives, friends, and family doctors were mentioned as resources more frequently than professional workers.[47] Over one-half the sample indicated they would prefer to work out emotional problems on their own.

The following case examples are presented to illustrate how direct (micro) and indirect (macro) social work practice can be utilized to restore and enhance the psychological and social functioning of Asian American clients.

DIRECT (MICRO) SOCIAL WORK PRACTICE

The Tran family was brought to the attention of the Transcultural Family Institute by a complaint from Mrs. Tran that their fourteen-year-old son Fen had been missing for more than three days. The intake interview with Mrs. Tran revealed that the family immigrated to the United States in 1975 after the fall of Saigon. The Tran family resides in a run-down neighborhood in Oklahoma City. There are about thirty Asian families in Tran's neighborhood. Most of them are refugees, some Cambodians, a few Laotians. Before the refugees moved in, the neighborhood was heavily populated with blacks and a few Hispanics.

Mr. Tran is fifty-one years old, a dentist trained in Saigon, and speaks fairly good English. Because he received his professional training in Vietnam, he has been unable to obtain a license to practice dentistry in Oklahoma City. Mr. Tran works as a store clerk in a neighborhood Asian food store.

Mrs. Tran was a housewife and never worked outside the home in Saigon. She is now employed in a day-care center serving mainly Vietnamese pre-schoolers. She has attended several English classes offered at her church.

The Trans have three children: A twenty-two-year-old daughter who is married and lives with her Vietnamese husband in Dallas, Texas; a nine-year-old daughter who Mrs. Tran describes as "very nice," and Fen. "Our son Fen is just the opposite of our nine-year-old. He gets into fights all the time at school and with neighborhood kids, especially the black kids," volunteered Mrs. Tran. Both Fen and his younger sister were born in Texas. The Trans moved to Oklahoma City two years ago when Mr. Tran got his present job. Mrs. Tran also feared that Fen and his father "may hurt each other." "The men in our family are of a violent type," continued Mrs. Tran.

One day after the interview, Mrs. Tran called to inform the worker that Fen had returned home voluntarily and that her husband and Fen had gotten into a "big physical fight." Mrs. Tran asked if the worker would talk with her and her family before "something terrible" happened. I replied that I would assist the family and I indicated to Mrs. Tran that I would like to see Mr. Tran alone for the first meeting. I also suggested to Mrs. Tran that I would telephone Mr. Tran for the appointment.

When I telephoned Mr. Tran for an appointment next day, he expressed appreciation of my willingness to help. However, he said he doubted he could get off work and that he didn't know where my agency was located. I volunteered to meet with him at a Vietnamese restaurant two blocks from where he worked. He accepted my invitation.

Mr. Tran, a frail but gentle looking man, was early for the appointment and he graciously ushered me a to a corner table that was quieter. I expressed to him regret that I couldn't speak Vietnamese. Mr. Tran reciprocated by informing me that despite his Chinese/Vietnamese ancestry, he could speak only a few words of Chinese. (Perhaps his wife had informed him that I was Chinese.) As Mr. Tran was relating his background to me, he avoided eye contact by helping me with tea.

I asked Mr. Tran if his work at the store kept him busy. He immediately played down the importance of his present job. I empathized by letting him know that he must feel frustrated at not being able to practice his profession. Mr. Tran sighed that "my best years are over—they have been for quite sometime." I remained silent but at the same time helped Mr. Tran with tea.

Mr. Tran continued to relate to me his immigration experiences, his love for his lost home and country, his extended family members who were left in Vietnam, and finally his beloved vocation as a dentist in Vietnam.

"I am happy for you that you still have your immediate family with you," I commented. "That's my greatest problem now," complained Mr. Tran. Mr. Tran then proceeded to tell the difficulty he was experiencing with his son, Fen, who was fluent in English but doing marginal work at school, not getting along with neighborhood kids, and refusing to defer to him as father. Mr. Tran also complained that his wife had not been treating him with respect. He attributed this to his wife's "Americanization" and financial independence. Mr. Tran also disclosed that recently he had developed a colitis problem and that medication prescribed by the doctor did not help.

Before my interview with Mr. Tran ended, I summarized my understanding of his personal problems and family problem. Mr. Tran quickly told me his personal problems did not matter; it was his family problems he needed help with. I respected and supported his views and explained to him the manner in which I could assist the family, especially his son. Mr. Tran then related to me that his son had told him he would never see "no shrink" or social worker. I comforted Mr. Tran by letting him know that Fen's behavior could change without his actually seeing me. I emphasized that since Mr. Tran was the head of the family, I would need his help the most in order to help the family. Mr. Tran responded very positively and he assured me he would do whatever was needed in order to restore family harmony.

Over the following two weeks I saw Mr. Tran individually four times at my office. Our conversations centered around four major issues: (1) immigration and relocation experiences, (2) his father role and relationship with his son, (3) his role and relationship with his wife, and (4) his activities in the workplace, neighborhood, and home.

Having an opportunity to ventilate the loss associated with immigration and relocation, Mr. Tran realized he had a great deal of grief and unexpressed anger. Mr. Tran admitted that "I have been a walking time bomb for sometime." His pent-up feelings coupled by his disappointment with his present job and his wife's lack of deference toward him made him especially eager to assume the authoritarian, disciplinary father role toward his teen-age son.

Mr. Tran was helped to realize that he had been displacing all his disappointment and frustration onto his son. To support Mr. Tran and to help him understand adolescent characteristics, I reframed the situation by saying to him that he must have done a good job for his son to be adult enough to say "no" to him. Mr. Tran began to realize that Fen also was having a difficult time adjusting to family, school, friends, and the "American way of life." As I encouraged Mr. Tran to list the positive features about Fen he relaxed more and commented, "Fen is not a bad boy, after all." I gave Mr. Tran positive strokes as a responsible and caring father, but he suddenly stopped and commented, "But I cannot allow Fen to say 'no' to me. If I had done that as a child, my father would have knocked my head off." I responded by agreeing that some Asian parents felt violence was the only way to control their children and get their children to mind them. I challenged that such disciplinary action may be antithetical to the love and care we originally intended to provide for our children. I later provided Mr. Tran with some other ideas and ways to discipline. I challenged him to exercise self-control in order for these new disciplinary ideas to work. Mr. Tran accepted my challenge.

At our last session, Mr. Tran invited his wife to come with him. Mrs. Tran was elated and volunteered that Fen was getting along well at home and at school. Fen and her husband had had no fights at all, and she and her husband also got along much better. The Trans invited me to their home for dinner as a way of expressing their appreciation. I accepted the invitation and had a wonderful dinner. As the evening ended, Mr. Tran told me he no longer had "stomach problems."

INDIRECT (MACRO) SOCIAL WORK PRACTICE

Three months after my last home visit with the Tran family, Mr. Tran called me at the office requesting a private (individual) meeting. When we met, Mr. Tran was anxious to inform me that the "old" family problem was not why he called me. He insisted that everybody in the family was doing well and that he and his son Fen were getting along well. The reason for his wanting to talk with me was neighborhood disturbances, which had resulted in several violent incidents over the past months. In one of these incidents three Vietnamese and two black youths were badly hurt in a fight that required police intervention.

Additionally, there were more than three neighborhood vandalism cases involving both black and Vietnamese men. The Vietnamese, especially the women, were terrified by the violence and they did not feel safe walking alone on the streets.

Mr. Tran was very distressed over the unsafe environment in his neighborhood and that he lacked the means to relocate to another community. Mr. Tran insisted that nothing constructive in the prevention of crime had been accomplished, even though the police had been called each time. In fact, Vietnamese–black racial tension seemed to intensify each time after the police left the scene. Mr. Tran concluded that he was not sure if I could be of any assistance to him or to his neighborhood, but he needed to talk to somebody. I responded empathetically to him and to his situation and explained that I would call him back in a couple of days with some suggestions.

After Mr. Tran left my office, I consulted with a black colleague who had a good rapport with some of the black families in the Tran's neighborhood. My colleague was well aware of the racial tension there. He and I decided to work as a team to help reduce neighborhood racial tension and violence.

First, we each identified respected leaders among the blacks and the Asians in the refugee community. My colleague visited individually with the black leaders and I did the same with the Asian leaders. A meeting for all leaders (five blacks and five Asians) was set up initially to identify and explore the problems as both sides perceived them. My colleague and I served as mediators for this first meeting. Each ethnic group felt others were as concerned as they were in establishing a harmonious and safe community.

It should be noted that care was taken in selecting the five Asian leaders. Mr. Tran, who served as a leader, helped me identify four other Asians. We sought community leaders who spoke English fluently and who were not afraid to express themselves, despite traditional Asian values like inconspicuousness.

The next joint meeting centered around plans and implementation strategies for improving black–Asian relationships. Prior to that meeting I met separately with the Asian representatives to prepare them. In addition to brainstorming for plans and implementation strategies, I prepared the Asian group for arriving at some consensus. We also rehearsed the actual presentation of ideas. Mr. Tran was elected spokesperson for the Asian group. My colleague held preparatory meetings with the black representatives.

The second black–Asian joint meeting proceeded smoothly, and the group had no difficulty in arriving at a consensus. Specifically, the group decided to employ education as a tool to break down racial stereotypes and prejudices. The Asian group initiated an invitation for the blacks to attend their Lunar New Year celebration. The blacks invited the Asians to their churches and concerts. Two Asian representatives, who were owners of a restaurant and a food store, agreed to employ black youths. A representative from the black group who coached baseball invited Asian youths to join the team. Each group's spokesperson served as a liaison and coordinator for these activities. My colleague and I agreed to serve as consultants when needed. The group decided to meet bimonthly until concrete improvements had been made.

The group met five more times in the next two and one-half months. Two youths, one from each racial group, were added to the group to insure youth input. During the first two weeks the group met, there were two mild incidents between black and Vietnamese youths. Representatives from each group took part in mediating the event after it happened. There has been no violence reported since. Some blacks and some Asians actually began socializing, at churches, at baseball fields, and in stores and restaurants. Representatives from both groups made a conscious effort to socialize with each other, and this may have set the tune and direction for the rest of the community to follow. When both racial groups had shown signs of improvement in collaborative harmonious living, they decided to meet only when there was a need.

EMERGING ISSUES AND TRENDS

Using socioeconomic criteria to interpret Asian Americans' success image is inadequate for understanding the complex experiences of this group in the United States. Both native and foreign-born Asian Americans have been shown to be segregated into certain occupations, industries, and for specific firms.[48] Asian Americans generally experience a serious problem in transforming their high educational achievement into favorable occupations in the labor market, resulting in underutilization of their education. Asian Americans who are employed experience great difficulty in obtaining promotions and other benefits associated with career advancement.[49] Limited human capital resources are often blamed for minorities' labor market problems. Asian American experiences, however, indicate that high educational achievement and related human capital resources are insufficient to overcome minority status in the U.S. labor market.

Physical health, mental health, and welfare needs among Asian Americans have been underestimated. The appropriateness of the treated-case method of determining service needs is questionable. The untreated case method would be more valid with Asian and Pacific Americans. Social work practice with Asian Americans has progressed past the general "descriptive-issues" stage. Drug abuse, alcoholism, bicultural identity, youth gangs, suicide, child abuse, and family violence are common problems social workers must help with.

With the large influx of Indochinese over the past decade unique problems and issues are emerging. Due to different political climate and economic conditions these new immigrants are experiencing more difficulties than old immigrants of the 1800s. The newer Indochinese population is widely scattered around the United States and around both urban and rural areas. It is expected that immigrants who settled in the Midwest or Southwest, where fewer Asians have traditionally lived, may have more adjustment problems than immigrants in East and West coast urban centers.

As the Asian American population increases, its traditional "success image" becomes more visible and often more threatening to whites and other ethnic minorities. Interracial tensions and conflicts between Asian Americans and other minorities, especially blacks, have surfaced particularly in the Southwest. The Indochinese's sudden, traumatic uprooting experience, lack of natural support systems, language difficulties, and hostile host environment, have made their settlement experience more difficult.

As the population and service needs of Asian Americans mount, resources available to them have dwindled because of cutbacks in federally funded programs. Because of language difficulties and cultural value conflicts, Asian

Americans, especially newly arrived immigrants and refugees, need more bilingual and bicultural mental health and social service workers. Again cutbacks in federal education funds have reduced the number of bilingual and bicultural workers. To combat the resources shortage and to provide services consistent with the needs and desires of Asian Americans, social workers are challenged to strengthen or build "natural" resources within the community. Natural resources are those individual skills and strategies, interpersonal (family and friends) support systems, and institutional systems (churches, herbalists, family doctors, folk healers, etc.) available in everyday life and needed in times of stress. This concept of natural resource is by no means strange to Asian Americans. Murase and Kim observed that existing indigenous organizations within the Asian community, such as churches, family associations, hometown clubs, and credit unions, and community caretakers, including ministers, physicians, teachers, merchants, and elders, have provided care for Asians in distress or in need of help.[50,51]

Asian Americans experience a multitude of social service needs. As with any other segment of the population, some of these needs are constant and familiar; others are unique and just emerging. Social work practitioners, educators, and students must be up-to-date on development trends and sensitive to Asian cultural values to ensure that all Asian American clients receive the help they deserve and have a right to.

ENDNOTES

1. J. Marishima, "The Asian American Experience: 1850–1975," *Journal of Ethnic and Special Studies* 2 (March 1978): 8–10.
2. S. Sue, "Community Mental Health Services to Minority Groups: Some Optimism, Some Pessimism," *American Psychologist* 32 (June 1977): 616–624.
3. E. Gomberg, "Special Populations," in *Alcohol, Science, and Society Revisited*, edited by E. Gomberg and J. Carpenter (Ann Arbor: University of Michigan Press, 1982): 337–354.
4. Multicultural Drug Abuse Prevention Center. First National Asian American Conference on Drug Abuse Prevention (Los Angeles: Multicultural Resource Center, 1976).
5. S. Lyman, "Chinese Secret Societies in the Occident: Notes and Suggestions for Research in the Sociology of Secrecy," in S. Lyman, ed., *The Asian in North America*, (Santa Barbara, Calif.: ABC–Clio, 1977).
6. B. Sung, *The Story of the Chinese in America* (New York: Macmillan, 1967).
7. H. Kitano, *Japanese Americans: The Evolution of a Subculture* (Englewood Cliffs, N.J.: Prentice-Hall, 1976).
8. W. Petersen, "Chinese Americans and Japanese Americans," in T. Sowell, ed., *Essays and Data on American Ethnic Groups*, (Washington, D.C.: Urban Institute, 1978).
9. Lyman, "Chinese Secret Societies,": 136.
10. T. Holmes and M. Masuda, "Life Change and Illness Susceptibility," in B. Dohrenwend, ed., *Stressful Life Events: Their Nature and Effects*, (New York: John Wiley, 1974).
11. M. Ho, *Family Therapy with Ethnic Minorities* (Newbury Park, Calif.: Sage, 1987).
12. Holmes and Masuda, "Life Change,": 161–186.

13. M. Pfister–Ammeude, "Mental Hygiene in Refugee Camps," in C. Zwingmann, ed., in *Uprooting and After*, (New York: Singer Publishing Co., 1973).

14. Bureau of Research and Training, *National Mental Health Needs Assessment of Indochinese Refugee Populations* (Philadelphia: Pennsylvania Department of Public Welfare, Office of Mental Health, 1979).

15. C. Meyer, "What Directions for Direct Practice?" *Social Work* 24 (July 1979): 267–272.

16. C. Germain, "An Ecological Perspective in Casework Practice," *Social Casework* 54 (January 1973): 323–330.

17. A. Morales and B. Sheafor, *Social Work: A Profession of Many Faces*, 4th ed. (Boston, Mass.: Allyn and Bacon, 1986).

18. G. DeVos and K. Abbott, "The Chinese Family in San Francisco," MSW dissertation (Berkeley, University of California, 1966).

19. H. Lai, "Chinese" in S. Thernstrom et al., *Harvard Encyclopedia of American Ethnic Groups*, (Cambridge, Mass.: Harvard University Press, 1980): 217–334.

20. H. Melendy, "Filipinos" in S. Thernstrom et al., *Harvard Encyclopedia of American Ethnic Groups*, (Cambridge, Mass.: Harvard University Press, 1980): 354–362.

21. H. Kim, "Koreans" in S. Thernstrom et al. *Harvard Encyclopedia of American Ethnic Groups*, (Cambridge, Mass.: Harvard University Press, 1980) 601–606.

22. Ibid., p. 602.

23. D. Montero and I. Dieppa, "Resettling Vietnamese Refugees: The Service Agency's Role," *Social Work* 27 (February 1982) 74–82.

24. Lyman, "Chinese Secret Societies": 182.

25. Asian American Advisory Council: Report to the Governor on Discrimination Against Asians (Seattle: State of Washington, 1973).

26. B. Kim, *The Asian Americans: Changing Patterns, Changing Needs* (Montclair, N.J.: Association of Korean Christian Scholars in North America, 1978).

27. M. Ho, "Social Work With Asian Americans," *Social Casework* 57 (March 1976): 195–201.

28. G. Coelho and J. Stein, "Change, Vulnerability, and Coping: Stresses of Uprooting and Overcrowding," in G. Coelho, ed., *Uprooting and Development*, (New York: Plenum Press, 1980) 21.

29. F. Hsu, *American Museum Science Book* (Garden City, N.Y.: Doubleday, 1972).

30. Ho, *Family Therapy with Ethnic Minorities*: 35–36.

31. J. Jones, *Prejudice and Racism* (Reading, Mass.: Addison-Wesley, 1922): 166.

32. S. Sue and H. McKinney, "Asian Americans in the Community Mental Health Care System," *American Journal of Orthopsychiatry* 45 (September 1975): 111–118.

33. See N. Mokuau, "Social Worker's Perceptions of Counseling Effectiveness for Asian American Clients," *Social Work* 32 (August 1987): 331–335; T. Owan, "Southeast Asian Mental Health: Transition from Treatment Service to Prevention—A New Direction," in T. Owen, ed., *Southeast Asian Mental Health: Treatment, Prevention, Services, Training, and Research* (National Institute of Mental Health): 142–167.

34. D. Okimoto, *Asian Key Person: Survey on Drug Abuse*. Task Force Report of Seattle King County Drug Commission (Seattle, Washington 1975).

35. S. Sue and D. Sue, "Chinese American Personality and Mental Health," *Amerasia Journal* 1 (September 1971) 1: 36–49.

36. D. Sue, S. Ino, and D. Sue, "Nonassertiveness of Asian-Americans: An Inaccurate Assumption," *Journal of Counseling Psychology* 30 (March 1983): 581–588.

37. M. Bromerly, "New Beginnings for Cambodian Refugees or Further Disruptions?" *Social Work* 32 (June 1987): 236–239; N. Mokuau, "Social Worker's Perceptions of Counseling Effectiveness for Asian American Clients," *Social Work* 32 (June 1987): 331–335.

38. D. Sue, *Counseling the Culturally Different: Theory and Practice* (New York: Wiley, 1981).

39. M. Miranda and H. Kitano, "Barriers to Mental Health: A Japanese and Mexican Dilemma," in N. Herandez, ed., *Chicanos; Social Psychological Perspectives*, (St. Louis: C.V. Mosby and Co.; 1976).

40. M. Miura and S. Usa, "A Psychotherapy of Neurosis: Morita Therapy," in T. Lebra and W. Lebra, eds., *Japanese Culture and Behavior*, (Honolulu: University Press of Hawaii, 1974): 407–430.

41. K. Okonogi, "The Ajase Complex of Japanese," *Japan Echo* (March 1978) 5: 88–105.

42. T. Murase, "Naikan Therapy," in T. Lebra and W. Lebra, eds., *Japanese Culture and Behavior*, (Honolulu: University Press of Hawaii, 1974): 431–442.

43. M. Pukui, E. Haertig, and C. Lee, *Nana I Ke Kumu* (Honolulu: Hui Hana, 1972): 85; L. Paglinawan, "Ho'Oponopono," in E. Shook, ed., *Ho'Oponopono*, (Honolulu: University of Hawaii, 1983).

44. A. Mass, "Asians as Individuals: The Japanese Community," *Social Casework* (March 1978) 57: 160–164.

45. B. Kim, "The Asian American," p. 198.

46. L. Lapuz, *A Study of Psychopathology* (Quezon City: University of the Philippines Press, 1973).

47. Y. Okano, *Japanese Americans and Mental Health* (Los Angeles: Coalition for Mental Health, 1977).

48. A. Cabezas, *Disadvantaged Employment Status of Asian and Pacific Americans* (U.S. Commission on Civil Rights, 1979): 434–444.

49. W. Kuo, "On the Study of Asian Americans: Its Current State and Agenda," *Sociological Quarterly* 20 (June 1979): 279–290.

50. K. Murase, "State and Local Public Policy Issues in Delivering Mental Health and Related Services to Asian and Pacific Americans," in U.S. Commission on Civil Rights, *Civil Rights Issues of Asian and Pacific Americans: Myths and Realities*, (Washington, D.C.: U.S. Government Printing Office, 1980).

51. T. Kim. "Statement on Census Issues—Impact and Reaction," in U.S. Commission on Civil Rights, *Civil Rights Issues of Asian and Pacific Americans: Myths and Realities*, (Washington, D.C.: U.S. Government Printing Office, 1980).

CHAPTER 21

Social Work with Mexican Americans

**Armando Morales
and Ramon Salcido**

PREFATORY COMMENT

This chapter was written specifically for this book. Mexican Americans are conspicuously absent from social work literature; only twenty-one articles concerning this distinct ethnic group appeared in the literature from 1964 to 1981. Eighty-one percent of these were written between 1971 and 1975. Most of the articles have been concerned with social justice for Mexican Americans rather than practice issues; that is, how to work with and help Mexican Americans.

The authors maintain that Mexican Americans do have mental health needs and do avail themselves of direct services when they are provided at minimum cost, in their primary language (Spanish), and near their homes. Given the regressive social and economic policies of the Reagan administration in relation to the poor, Mexican Americans, specifically the "undocumented" Mexican immigrant, will be especially affected.

Armando Morales and Ramon Salcido offer practice suggestions, which have implications for macro social work in the barrio, mobilizing various indigenous social support systems, such as churches, neighbors, and the family. They also recommend the intervention strategy of advocacy in reducing institutional barriers to services for Mexican Americans.

Meeting the ever-increasing social service needs of disadvantaged groups, which are often isolated by class and cultural differences, is a continuing challenge to social work. If the social work profession hopes to be more viable among disadvantaged groups, especially among the Mexican American population, human service institutions must modify their service delivery systems. Moreover, social workers must understand the dynamics of both individual and institutional racism, which have discouraged or prevented Mexican Americans from availing themselves of existing services. At times those services have appeared impersonal and even nonsupportive.

Despite the recent attention focused on the special needs of Mexican Americans, any explanation of their situation is complicated by the difficulty of defining this population as to size and demographic characteristics. More has to be learned about the variations within this group and its immigration pattern.

MEXICAN AMERICANS: A HETEROGENEOUS POPULATION

Mexican Americans are one of the most diverse ethnic groups in the United States in comparison to white ethnic groups and minority groups of color. On the one hand, like American Indians, Mexican Americans were an indigenous people who resided in the Southwest, were overpowered by Anglo settlers, and are therefore one of the *oldest* minorities. On the other hand their continuing immigration from Mexico to the United States also makes them one of the *newest* and *largest* immigrant groups. Some are fully assimilated into Anglo society, and some reside almost exclusively in *barrios*.[1] Some retain strong ties to Mexico and return there frequently, while others prefer to remain in the United States. There are also those who partially integrate without assimilating but do not center their interactions exclusively within the *barrio*.[2]

With the Treaty of Guadalupe Hidalgo in 1848, most of the Southwest, including California, became the possession of the United States. The actual number of Mexicans in the new Territory of the Southwest was relatively small. Harry Kitano reports that all laborers who were Mexicans, whether they were "pure" Spanish or not, were perceived as "half-breeds" and inferior by Anglos.[3] By 1900 these people were already a subordinated population; they lived in segregated enclaves, and were controlled by the Anglos. From 1848 to 1910 very few Mexicans migrated to the United States. The relative ease of entry across a long, 3,000-mile border; the difficulty in distinguishing between Spanish-speaking, U.S.-born people and Spanish-speaking immigrants from Mexico, both legal and illegal; and dubious official data make precise quantification impossible. However, the following official census figures on immigration of Mexicans to the United States are of some use:

to 1900	28,000
1901–1910	50,000
1911–1920	219,000
1921–1930	460,000
1931–1940	22,000
1941–1950	59,000
1951–1960	319,000
1961–1970	453,000

Significant migration of Mexicans to the United States did not take place until after 1910. It is estimated that fully 10 percent of the Mexican people immigrated to the United States early in the twentieth century, and the vast majority of them assumed agricultural work in the Southwest. This migration peaked in the 1920s but was curtailed during the years of the Great Depression, when large numbers of Mexicans, including those born in the United States, were repatriated (deported) by social service and immigration agencies. Many of those deported were U.S.-born children of the Mexican immigrants: U.S. citizens!

Moreover, as the Mexican American population of the United States grew, it remained highly localized, with almost 90 percent of the people located in the five Southwestern states. California's share of this population steadily increased, as Table 21–1 shows.

The next large influx of migrants arrived in the post-Second World War period. The needs for agricultural laborers and for unskilled workers to keep pace with economic expansion of the post-war years made Mexican immigration attractive to businesses and small industries. Business was the only contact between the two cultures; U.S. society was not concerned with housing conditions, lack of schooling, or availability of social services for Mexican Americans. This neglect, coupled with racism, caused Mexicans as well as Mexican Americans to maintain a distance from institutions and governmental agencies. Certain social demographic characteristics have made the Mexican American experience unique in comparison to those of Europeans and Asians. This population is the second largest minority of color that is both indigenous and immigrant in character. Because of geographical proximity to Mexico, Mexican-born persons have followed a wide variety of migration patterns to the United States since the early part of the century. Generally,

TABLE 21–1 Mexican Population in the United States, 1910–1980

YEAR	U.S. BUREAU OF THE CENSUS DEFINITION	TOTAL U.S.	TOTAL CALIFORNIA	PERCENT IN CALIFORNIA
1910	Mexicans of foreign-born and mixed parentage	382,002	51,037	13.4
1920	Mexicans of foreign-born and mixed parentage	731,559	86,610	17.4
1930	Mexicans	1,282,883	368,013	29.3
1940	Spanish mother tongue	1,570,740	416,140	32.9
1950	Spanish surname	2,281,710	591,540	35.8
1960	Spanish surname	3,464,999	1,141,207	40.1
1970	Spanish surname	9,600,000	2,222,185	23.1
1980	Spanish origin	14,605,883	4,543,770	31.1

immigration to the United States has been greater from Mexico than from any other country in recent years. For example Mexico has been the primary source of both legal and illegal immigration to the United States since the 1950s.

The Mexican American population comprises at least three major subgroups: those who are born in the United States, those who are born in, and emigrate legally from Mexico, and those who are born in, and emigrate illegally from Mexico. The term *Mexican American* will be used to designate anyone having a Mexican heritage, regardless of time or place of arrival in the United States. During the highly political period of the 1960s and early 1970s, many persons of Mexican descent preferred the term *Chicano* rather than Mexican American. Some still prefer this designation today.

DEMOGRAPHIC PROFILE

The 1970 census showed that 9.6 million people of Spanish origin lived in the United States.[4] The 1975 population report showed an increase to 11.2 million Spanish people, and by March, 1987 census reports showed a jump to 18.7 million.[5,6] The 1987 population reports recorded that 11.8 million of the Hispanic populace were of Mexican origin; 2.3 million, Puerto Rican; 1.0 million, Cuban; and 2.1 million, of Central and South American origin.[7] Added to these figures are an estimated 6 million undocumented aliens predominantly from Mexico.[8] Although statistics vary widely on the basis of base lines and possible growth rates, demographers predict that Hispanics will be this country's largest minority by 1990, that half the population in California and a third in Texas may be Spanish-speaking by the same date, and that Hispanics could be the majority population group in three states by the year 2000.[9]

The Mexican American population is much larger than most figures indicate primarily because of census undercount and continued immigration, both legal and illegal, to the United States from Mexico. Mexican Americans make up about 60 percent of the Hispanic population in the United States, and their numbers grew by 75 percent in the last decade. A recent government census found that Mexican Americans now make up 19 percent of California's population and 28 percent of Los Angeles County, making Los Angeles the largest urban concentration of Mexicans outside Mexico City.[10]

The majority of Mexican Americans live in the states of California, Texas, and New Mexico. However, there are significant numbers in other states of the Southwest as well as in the Northwest and Midwest. Illinois, with its availability of manufacturing and agricultural jobs, has become home to many Mexican American migrants. Furthermore, contrary to stereotypes, the vast majority live in urban areas with 46.3 percent residing in central cities, 34.7 percent residing in the suburbs, and the remaining 19 percent residing in rural areas.[11]

Compared to Anglos, Mexican Americans are a relatively young population. The median age of Mexican Americans is 19.8 years compared to 28.6 years for the overall population.[12] Moreover, the 1975 census showed that the proportion of Mexican Americans over age 65 was only 4 percent compared to 11 percent for the general population. The fact that there are few elderly Mexican Americans is a startling statistic.[13]

There is clear evidence that Mexican Americans have large families, a characteristic of lower socioeconomic status. National statistics show that the mean for Mexican Americans is 4.06 number of children and for non-Hispanics, 1.07. More specifically, statistics show that 41.9 percent of families of Mexican origin have three or more children versus 22.3 percent of the total families in the United States.[14] Because of the large number of children, there are eighty persons in the dependent-age range (those under sixteen years old and over sixty-five years old) for every 100 Mexican American persons of working age; this compares to sixty-five persons in the dependent-age range for every 100 Anglos. The high rate of fertility among Mexican American women, especially combined with large family size, implies a high health risk for both mothers and children in this ethnic group.[15]

The reported income level for 1970 shows that 13.8 percent of Mexican Americans had incomes of less than $3,000, while only 5.7 percent of Anglos reported such low incomes.[16] The median family income for families identifying themselves as "of Mexican origin" in the 1975 population survey was $9,559 compared to $12,836 for all U.S. families.[17] The gap widened further: the 1980 median income for Hispanics was $12,952 compared to $19,116 for the entire population of the United States.[18] Furthermore, in 1978 about 2.5 million Hispanics (60 percent Mexican American), or 22 percent of the total Hispanic population, were below the poverty level in income compared with 11 percent for the entire population of the United States.[19] Those reported incomes must be considered in view of the fact that Mexican American families are larger than Anglo families.

Most Mexican Americans have occupations of low prestige. The 1975 population study conducted by the U.S. Bureau of the Census found that more than 60 percent of the occupations held by men of Mexican origin sixteen years of age and older were classified as blue collar workers.[20] According to the 1978 U.S. Census, there were half as many white collar workers among employed Mexican American males (18 percent) as among Anglo males (42.9 percent).[21]

The unemployment level of Mexican Americans generally is higher than that of the Anglo population. During recessions, the unemployment rate difference becomes more exaggerated. In 1975, Hispanic unemployment (60 percent Mexican American) was 12.9 percent compared to eight percent for the white work force, and in 1976 Hispanic unemployment stood at 11.8 percent of this ethnic population versus 8.9 percent of the white work force.[22] The disparities are even greater for youth. For instance, in 1974, 30 percent of Hispanic youth sixteen to nineteen years of age were unemployed compared to 18.4 percent of white youth.[23] In addition, according to the National Urban League, in the first quarter of 1978 teenage unemployment by race and ethnicity showed that 22.1 percent of Hispanic youth were unemployed compared to 15.7 percent of Anglo youth.[24] Some reasons for the above average unemployment among most groups of Hispanics, especially Mexican Americans, include educational disadvantages, language barriers, and discrimination. Furthermore, a significant number of Mexican American youth are employed as migratory farm workers, a sector of the economy that has high seasonal unemployment.

Despite the relative youth of the Mexican American population, school enrollment data indicate a low educational attainment. Although 67 percent of non-Mexican American or non-Hispanic adults completed high school, only 34.3 percent of Mexican American adults completed high school.[25] Data concerning adults with less than five years of schooling again show this group trailing other minorities and Anglos. *U.S. News and World Report* stated that "a drop-out rate as high as 85 percent in some cities to achievement scores that are two grade levels or more below national averages" are found in this population.[26]

Language usage is another important characteristic of the Mexican American population. According to information obtained from the 1976 *Survey of Income and Education Data*, 80 percent of Hispanic Americans lived in households where Spanish was spoken.[27] While there are few studies on Spanish language usage, the small amount of data that do exist clearly illustrate the importance of language use by this group. The report of the National Center for Education Statistics entitled *The Condition of Education for Hispanic Americans* states, "the language one speaks is related to one's place of birth."[28] Among Mexican Americans born in Mexico, about two-thirds spoke Spanish as their primary language. Among those of corresponding heritage who were born in the United States, less than 20 percent usually spoke Spanish. The rest of the population of corresponding heritage either was monolingual or bilingual.

MEXICAN AMERICANS IN SOCIAL WORK LITERATURE

A survey of social work literature discussing mainly Mexican Americans and written between January 1964 and February 1981 serves to exemplify the trends and volume of literature available to the social work profession concerning this group. Much that has been written about Mexican Americans is of a descriptive nature, focusing upon the value differences between Mexican American groups and the majority culture, and racism. The articles surveyed were obtained from the *Journal of Education for Social Work, Social Casework,* and *Social Work*; articles appearing in books or in non-social work journals were not included.[29] The selection of articles was based on titles and abstracts specifically stating Mexican American or Chicano content. Using this criterion may have excluded other social work articles used in practice. Although this survey does not encompass all social work has to say about Mexican Americans, it does allow some inferences to be drawn about the state of Mexican American literature in the social work practice.

Of the twenty-one articles about Mexican Americans published between 1964 and 1984, 81 percent were written between 1971 and 1975 (see Table 21–2). The remaining 29 percent were spread over eight of the fifteen years studied, with a greater number of articles written during the last years of the 1960s and fewer articles written during the last half of the 1970s. No articles were published about Mexican Americans during the middle 1960s. Considering the civil rights movement of the 1960s, it appears that the social work profession was slow to recognize the need to help Mexican Americans and to react in complying with that need. Recognition that this population did receive in the early 1970s rapidly diminished as the seventies came to a close.

The mid-1970s offered the most hope for achievement both within and outside the profession. The articles appearing between 1972 and 1976 were mostly concerned with social justice for Mexican Americans. The articles specifically emphasized the bilingualism and biculturalism of Mexican Americans, almost to the exclusion of other topics of interest to the profession. For example, one article focused on the elderly Mexican American. No articles were written about ex-offenders or gangs. Nor were any articles published about problems such as divorce, desertion, child abuse, wife abuse, and physical health/mental health needs. This pattern suggests that some subgroups and typical subjects of social work concern may have been overlooked because of the values and interests of the authors.

Table 21–3 clearly shows that cultural differences, experiences of racism, and family structure appeared more frequently than any other topics in the literature. These topics were for the most part not related to a discussion of how the social worker can use his or her knowledge of them in seeking to help Mexican Americans. Only one article discussed the application of knowledge in reporting a study of clients' perceptions of helping relationships formed with social workers of different ethnic backgrounds from their own. The study revealed that Anglo clients and Mexican American clients reacted positively to initial helping relationships with workers of different cultural backgrounds from their own. However, all the clients who spoke Spanish were excluded from the sample as were documented and undocumented immigrants. Nor were the clients asked if they preferred social workers of the same ethnic background. No doubt all these factors would have influenced the results of the study had they been included.

Similar conspicuous absences appeared in articles about social work practice. Only three articles gave general suggestions for working with Spanish-speaking Mexican Americans but offered no general framework. Only one

TABLE 21–2 Number of Articles on Mexican Americans/Chicanos by Years

ARTICLES	1964–67	1968–71	1972–75	1976–80	TOTAL
Mexican Americans/ Chicanos	0	9 (43%)	8 (38%)	4 (19%)	21

TABLE 21–3 Major Themes of Knowledge

THEMES	MEXICAN AMERICAN/ CHICANO
Cultural Differences	6
Language	1
Warmth, Empathy, Genuineness	1
Experience of Racism	6
Social System Theory	1
Politics	0
Community Structure	1
Family Structure	3

article presented a training model describing how knowledge of Mexican Americans could be applied to mental health training and incorporated in schools of social work. The lack of articles prescribing methods is one of the major shortcomings of the available literature.

Although the literature is limited in usable practice frameworks, it is rich in identifying those areas of knowledge the authors deemed to be most significant for social work intervention. The authors were profoundly concerned with the effects of racism and cultural differences. These concerns provide the profession with practice knowledge regarding Mexican American issues that can be incorporated by social workers in their work with this population.

INTERVENTION STRATEGIES

The central task for a social worker is to help persons resolve existing or potential problems in psychosocial functioning. This process may involve helping the client resolve problems within themselves or with other people, such as spouse, parent, children, friends, or coworkers. This focus is called *direct service* or *micro* level social work intervention. Intervening in behalf of clients with larger social structure (such as the neighborhood, organizations, community, or even broader community—in effect all those social work activities that fall outside the domain of direct services) is referred to as *indirect service* or *macro* level social work intervention. In work with the poor who are often at the mercy of various social, economic, and political forces in society, both levels of intervention, micro and macro, are necessary for optimal helping effectiveness.

Direct Service Intervention

Direct service intervention has various modes, one of which is treatment, or *clinical* intervention. This is not to say that the poor are poor because of psychological problems; rather, their impoverished status may contribute to and exacerbate their stress. Indeed, it becomes a difficult task to help someone work through separation feelings regarding the loss of a loved one when they are starving, have no place to live, or are freezing to death. In this respect, certain basic human needs related to food, clothing, and shelter are universal, and a person's emotional response to stress also has universal qualities. The specific nature of that response and how it is handled, however, are related to the societal cultural context in which it occurs.

History of Treating Mental Illness Societies throughout the world have developed various approaches for treating persons suffering from psychological problems. Three basic explanations and corresponding intervention strategies pertaining to psychological problems can be traced back to the earliest times: (1) the attempt to explain diseases of the mind in physical terms; that is, the organic approach ("It's in your blood/chemistry"); (2) the attempt to deal with inexplicable events through spiritual or magical approaches ("The devil/spirits made you do it"); and (3) the attempt to find a psychological explanation for psychological problems ("It's all in your mind"). Hippocrates (460–377 B.C.), the father of medicine, pioneered the organic approach, believing that black bile caused depression. Several centuries later, Cicero, the Roman statesman and attorney (106–43 B.C.), objected to the black bile theory, maintaining that depression was the result of psychological difficulties. He proclaimed that people were responsible for their emotional and psychological difficulties: in a psychological sense, *they* could do something about them. Cicero laid down the theoretical foundations for psychotherapy. The magical/spiritual approach found early man treating the afflicted person through appeasement, confession, incantations, magical rituals, or exorcism,[30]

The effectiveness of the treatment approach often depends upon the suggestibility of the person on whom the approach is worked, the suggestive power of the influencing practitioner, and the sympathetic connection (similarity) between the practitioner and the person seeking assistance. If a person strongly believes, for example, his or her headache, stomachache, or depression has as its basis a physical or chemical factor and that only a medical person can help, a physician or psychiatrist who prescribes medication may have the greatest likelihood of relieving that person's symptom. If, on the other hand, the person believes he or she is suffering certain symptoms because he or she has sinned and that only a minister or priest can help, the Church's representatives may indeed have the greatest impact. And, if the person believes his or her symptom has a psychogenic basis and can only be alleviated by talking to someone who can be "objective" in understanding the symptom or problem, the psychiatrist or perhaps social workers may offer the best help.

Mexico's Approach to Treating Mental Illness Mexican society like other societies, also developed approaches to help people with psychological problems. The ancestors of Mexican Americans, the Aztecs, numbering twenty million persons in Central Mexico in the fifteenth century, created a wealthy, powerful, and progressive empire. Their culture was highly developed, and in that intellectual atmosphere flourished highly advanced forms of psychiatry and psychotherapy. Translations of Aztec literature reveal that Aztec therapy was provided by competent personnel and in institutions of high repute. They had an amazing grasp of psychology and developed concepts about ego formation similar to those advanced by Freud almost 500 years later. Those concepts appear in an Aztec document about dream interpretation. The Aztec psychiatrists knew how to recognize persons who were manic, schizoid, hysterical, depressive, or psychopathic—mental disorder major classifications not unlike the ones used today. Aztec patients were treated by a variety of methods including an early form of brain surgery, hypnosis, "talking out" bad things in one's mind, and specific herbal potions for specific disorders.[31]

With the colonization of Mexico by Spain in the early sixteenth century came Spanish medicine based on European concepts. Spanish colonial physicians still held primitive ideas about the causes of disease, believing disease was a punishment for sins caused by devils who had taken possession of the patient's body and spirit. Because military might was associated with racial superiority, Spanish medicine was also believed by Spaniards to be superior to that of the Aztecs. Had Spanish oppression not occurred, Aztec psychiatry might have made a very significant contribution to the mental health practices of the Western world. In spite of this overt conflict and clash over psychiatric approaches, however, the first hospital for the mentally ill was founded in North America in Mexico City in 1567.[32] The first hospital for the mentally ill in the United States was founded 185 years later in 1752 in Philadelphia, Pennsylvania.[33] The United States established two additional hospitals for the mentally ill during this period, one in Williamsburg, Virginia, in 1773, and the Bloomingdale Asylum in New York in 1821. In a comparable period, Mexico also established a hospital in Yucatán in 1625, the "Manicomio de lä Canoa" in Mexico City in 1687, the "Hospital Civil" in Guadalajara in 1739, "Belém" in 1794, and the "Divino Salvado" in Mexico City in 1796.

Other mental health milestones found Mexico establishing its first department of psychiatry in 1860 in Jalisco; the United States began its first program in 1906. Mexico began the systematic training of physicians in psychiatry in 1910; the United States initiated its training program in 1937. Mexico launched its community mental health movement in 1951 by establishing mental health programs in health centers. The United States initiated community programs in 1964 with the passage of the Federal Community Mental Health Act.[34] Today in Mexico the major mental health trends and various theoretical orientations are similar to those in other Western countries. No single therapy orientation prevails, and as in the United States, psychiatrists are by and large in control of mental health programs, with psychologists, social workers, and psychiatric nurses having lesser roles. From the standpoint of mental health resources, the United States, being a much wealthier country than Mexico, far overshadows Mexico in terms of mental health resources and manpower. The United States, for example, has 12.4 psychiatrists per 100,000 versus less than one psychiatrist per 100,000 in Mexico.[35]

Mental Health Treatment for Mexican Americans   In the United States persons of Mexican descent have found it very difficult to obtain mental health services. One of the nation's first community mental health programs specifically for persons of Mexican descent was established in East Los Angeles in 1967. The staffing pattern included four psychiatrists, four psychiatric social workers, three nurses, a clinical psychologist, a rehabilitation counselor, a community services coordinator, a community worker, and six secretaries. All but one of the staff were bilingual. In applying one measure of utilization (the percent of Spanish surname population in the area—76 percent), the program was successful in that 90 percent of the clients seen had a Spanish surname. Clearly here there was an overutilization of services by Hispanics. The program offered traditional mental health services provided in the clients' primary language and at a fee ranging from 50 cents to $15.[36] There are a few other, rare examples of overutilization of mental health services by Hispanics,[37] but overall, the utilization rate by this population rarely exceeds 50 percent. In other words, Hispanic receipt of services is one-half or less of their representation in the population.[38]

There are a number of reasons proposed to explain this underutilization. The literature is now making it increasingly clear that the major factors involved are structural in nature and pertain to the availability, accessibility, and acceptability of services in terms of their relevance to the very heterogeneous bilingual, bicultural characteristics of Hispanics.[39] When Hispanics finally do receive services, they are often of inferior quality, with diagnoses often based on assessment procedures developed for the middle-class Anglo population that have no validity or applicability to these people. Furthermore, Hispanics are more likely to receive somatic and medication treatment and less individual or group therapy. These experiences can and do result in premature treatment termination.[40] Another important factor accounting for premature termination or resistance to treatment is whether the Hispanic is a *voluntary* client seeking help for a problem *he* or *she* defines or an *involuntary* client being referred for treatment regarding a problem of concern to the referring agency.[41] Racist and political policies and economic decisions (raising fees) by mental health agencies to deny services to "undocumented" or poor persons are other growing, contributing factors related to the underutilization of services by Hispanics.

Indirect Service Intervention

A major problem in achieving practice goals for Mexican Americans is the conceptual constraints imposed by social work methods. In other words social workers, as Judith Nelsen points out, perceive phenomena exclusively and narrowly through the lenses of the methods in which they have been trained.[42] Often the focus is mainly a clinical or direct service one. Carol Meyer believes the use of any methodological model as an anchoring or conceptual point of reference is like viewing something through the wrong end of the telescope—the view is too restricted and narrow to account for the breadth of the phenomena to be captured.[43]

Meyer adds that for years social work has been offering its well-honed methods only to those who could use them, instead of first finding out what was needed and then selecting the method from its intervention repertoire or inventing new methods. She believes the methods framework has been functional in maintaining social work's denial of what has to be done with regard to broader social problems. Meyer proposes the use of an ecosystems orientation to practice.[44]

Ecosystems Model Social work practice focuses on the interaction between the person and the environment. The term *person* may refer to an individual or may represent people in the context of a family, large or small group, organization, community, or even larger structure of society. Social work intervention might be directed at the person, the environment, or both. In each case, the social worker seeks to enhance and restore the social functioning of people or to change social conditions that impede the mutually beneficial interaction between people and their environment.[45]

This orientation involves the application of ecology and general systems theory to professional tasks. In explaining the ecosystems perspective, Meyer points out that it allows social workers to look at psychological phenomena, account for complex variables, assess the dynamic interplay of these variables, draw conceptual boundaries around the unit of attention or the case, and then generate ideas for interventions.[46] At this point methodology enters in, because in any particular case—meaning a particular individual, family, group, institutional unit, or geographical area—any number of practice interventions might be needed.

This model of practice can promote social workers' understanding of: (1) the psychosocial problems experienced by Mexican American people, (2) the crippling effects of institutional racism, and (3) the oppressive environments in which these people struggle to survive. The application of this model to a specific case is highlighted in Chapter 11.

The Ethnosystem Assuming that social work abandons its constricted methods framework and adopts the ecosystems perspective, then this question must be asked: What other knowledge is needed in understanding the psychosocial problems of Mexican Americans that is specific in terms of their ethnic background? Barbara Solomon's framework provides one option for integrating Mexican American concerns into a practice framework.[47] She utilizes the ethnosystem and empowerment concepts as major integrative concepts. The *ethnosystem* is defined as a society that comprises groups which vary in modes of communication, in degree of control over material resources, and in the structure of their internal relationships or social organization.[48] Moreover, these groups must be in a more or less stable pattern of relationships that have characteristics transcending any single group's field of integration; for example, the ethnosystem's political, educational, or economic subsystems. Solomon defines *empowerment* as a process whereby persons who belong to a stigmatized social category throughout their lives can be assisted to develop and increase skills in the exercise of interpersonal influence and the performance of valued social roles.[49]

The ethnosystems are the natural networks, the primary patterns of interaction, survival, and adjustment indigenous to societies. As used here, the concept of *natural networks* has its origins in several disciplines: social work, sociology, social psychology and anthropology, as well as in the mental health "community support—significant others" literature.[50] Social workers also need to be aware that these natural networks and primary systems exist apart from the usual modes of secondary interactions that Mexican Americans have developed for survival within Anglo-urbanized systems, including the social establishment. There is a basic similarity between the ethnosystem with secondary interaction for coping with the Anglo society and the concept of two environments, the immediate or nurturing environment and the wider environment. When, as Dolores Norton notes, the larger societal system rejects the minority group's immediate environment or ethnosystem, there is incongruence between the two (Solomon refers to this as negative valuation of a stigmatized collective), and power blocks are directed toward the minority individuals, groups, and communities.[51]

Barrio Service Systems   Mexican Americans have been immigrating to *barrios* in U.S. urban areas in great and small waves. The *barrio* is a microcosm of the dominant society as well as an ethnosystem. Although the communities interrelate with external institutional structures, such as the law enforcement system, the school system, and the public welfare system, *barrios* also have indigenous service systems that provide mutual aid and psychological support in time of need. Indigenous support systems include churches, neighbors, and friends, the family, and alternative services.[52]

Many Mexican Americans, especially the elderly and immigrant groups, have strong religious ties and attend church on a regular basis. The church, whether Roman Catholic or Protestant, is an important spiritual support for many Mexican Americans and, in addition, is a vehicle for disseminating information about *barrio* activities and services, reaching individuals who would be largely inaccessible to public agencies. There is trust in the church. For example, the parish priest or minister often knows of potential adoptive parents, who would provide an excellent home for an unwed mother's child.

Concerned neighbors and friends also provide aid and act as a resource. Perceived as confidential sources of advice, these significant persons act as referral agents. Tsiaiah Lee's study on the use of the services of a model neighborhood health center by Mexican Americans observed that some groups sought primary groups such as friends and neighbors as their major source of information about health care services.[53]

The family unit clearly plays an important role in providing economic, social, and psychological supports. Families also serve as adoptive parents for family members who are no longer able to care for their children. Especially in the case of older children, grandparents may care for them and eventually adopt them. Other relatives, or the child's godparents, or *compadres*, may also accept the responsibility of raising the child or children. Infants, of course, may also be adopted in the same manner. However, no matter how effective this network may be, it is the welfare agency, rather than the network itself, which has access at all times to the greatest amount of provision and the greatest number of providers in the greatest geographical area; it is the agency that has legal responsibility for bringing services to the community.

As a result of the Chicano movement in the 1960s and 1970s, alternative service systems are being developed within the *barrio* to deal with the special needs of the Mexican American community. Although there are variations in the services offered in each *barrio*, common patterns in both structure and function are observable. Self-help groups, social action organizations, and specialized service agencies staffed exclusively by bicultural and bilingual personnel are considered the most essential aspects of the alternative service system.

Max Siporin writes that the ecological perspective is an "effort to improve the functioning and competence of the welfare service system of natural self-help mutual aid networks, and to improve the social functioning and coping competence of individuals and their collectivities."[54] This approach calls for the practitioner to broaden his or her view of the client. Intervention involves assessment of the total social, physical, psychological needs of the client and of his or her network system. Intervention also calls for advocacy in the amelioration of identified problems related to barriers created by social welfare systems. Intervention strategies are initiated in anticipation of resolving psychosocial problems. Two examples of such macro level strategies include networking and advocacy.

Support Networks Alice H. Collins and Diane L. Pancoast refer to *networks* as consisting of people and relationships.[55] The social network is relatively invisible, though it is a real structure in which an individual, nuclear family, or group is embedded. The term *support systems*, as used here, parallels Gerald Caplan's conceptualization.[56] He states: "Support systems may be of a continuing nature, intermittent or short-term in the event of an acute need or crisis." Both enduring and short-term supports are likely to consist of three elements:

1. The significant others help the individual mobilize his psychological resources and master his emotional burdens;

2. They share his tasks; and

3. They provide him with extra supplies of money, materials, tools, skills, and cognitive guidance to improve the handling of his situation.[57]

Individuals usually belong to several networks at the same time. Networks can be based on kinship, friendship, employment, recreation, education, politics, ethnicity, religion, or whatever interests or elements individuals find in common. The content of exchanges can also be varied.[58] Although the informal network is important, it cannot provide all the needs. Formal resources (social service agencies, medical services, and other service providers) are likely to be utilized. Social network intervention, therefore, is an approach to service delivery that involves significant individuals in the amelioration of identified psychosocial problems.

Social network intervention takes into consideration both formal and informal systems that are involved in the life of the family. Also of significance to Mexican Americans is that this approach incorporates the sociocultural components of the family. The utilization of support systems can be conceptualized into two main divisions: (1) To engage existing networks and enhance their functioning and (2) to create new networks or "attach" a formerly isolated person or family to a network.[59]

The approach considers both psychological and environmental stresses and incorporates them into the total reality of a family. It focuses on rallying the life-sustaining forces of the individual and family. This viable system of self-help continues to function after the professional helper has been disengaged.

In social network intervention, the goal is to deal with the entire structure by rendering the network visible and viable and by attempting to restore its function. The social network for Mexican American families may include extended kin, *compadres* (coparents), friends, *curanderos* (folk healers), and other concerned individuals. These subsystems are identified because of their potential to provide emotional strength, support, and other types of assistance to the family. Social network intervention, therefore, emphasizes engagement of the family's network of support systems.

Advocacy   In cases where adequate services do not exist or are not accessible, the social worker can assume an advocacy function. As an advocate, he or she is concerned with making the social welfare system responsive to the unmet needs of the client. According to Scott Briar, the social worker as advocate is the client's supporter, advisor, champion, and, if need be, representative in his or her dealings with the court, the police, the social agency, and other organizations that affect the client's well-being.[60]

Advocacy can be divided into five areas of practice: (1) family advocacy, (2) community advocacy, (3) legislative advocacy, (4) ombudsmanship, and (5) brokerage. In *family advocacy*, the social worker represents an individual or family and then fights the battle with the system; the ultimate goal is showing the client or family how to fight its own battles.[61] In *community advocacy*, on the other hand, a board or staff of an agency takes collective action to change a condition affecting the lives of the agency's clients. According to Rino Patti and R. B. Dear, *legislative advocacy* refers to any individual agency or organization that attempts to influence the course of a bill or other legislative measure. *Ombudsmanship*, the least familiar of the practices, can be used when practicing advocacy.[62] A recent report identifies ombudsmanship as an individual or office concerned with correcting administrative grievances and overcoming administrative problems and errors.[63] Finally, *brokerage*, based on knowledge of and experience with, existing services, is a commitment to help each client reach the appropriate services.[64]

Social workers engaged in advocacy must be capable of using all forms of advocacy and must be able to select the one or a combination of the five forms, which best fits the client's specific situation. Social workers employed in hospitals and other social service institutions possess the knowledge and professional skills to function well in an advocacy service. In addition to utilizing existing resources, social workers must organize the services within the boundaries of the social service agency and use bilingual personnel to provide the services. The following example illustrates how advocacy intervention strategies can be applied when one confronts environmental and institutional barriers.

Political action and brokerage advocacy are the strategies a social worker employs to deal with environmental barriers. The social worker would be a partisan advocate for changes in present restrictive benefits. By lobbying directly with groups in the Mexican American community for these changes, the social worker can influence the legislative process at a governmental level useful to his or her clients.

Brokerage, on the other hand, entails acting as an intermediary between the client and existing services in the community. Brokerage, in this context, recognizes the dependence of the individual on his or her social environment and facilitates change by maximizing the resources available to the client. For example, a Mexican American seeking social services may be faced with inadequate housing, no medical or Social Security benefits, and no alien documentation. In such a case, the social worker should review the client's existing resources. If none exist, the worker would then seek out adequate resources and act as an advocate for the client. In this way, brokerage expands the role of the advocate beyond the boundaries of the health care institution to ensure that the client reaches the appropriate services.

Advocacy services that confront the barriers erected by the institution are both direct and indirect. Ombudsmanship and family advocacy deal directly with clients within the health care institution. Ombudsmanship is concerned with correcting administrative problems and errors within the health care institution. Unlike the broker, the ombudsman does not link up resources for his or her clients but pinpoints obstacles the institution presents to clients. Ombudsmanship provides a mediator to assist clients who feel their needs are not being met because of red tape or because the staff is insensitive to them.

Similarly, family advocacy is designed to improve life conditions for whole families or individual family members by linking direct and expert knowledge of family needs with a commitment to institutional change. According to Ronald Riley, family advocacy deals with institutional systems rather than with individuals.[65] Its purpose is to ensure that the institutional systems in closest contact with the clients work for them, rather than against them. Supportive networking, political action, brokerage, and family advocacy are all active practices in which social workers can engage and reasonably pursue within the social welfare system to insure the maximum utilization of existing services.

The following case history demonstrates the efficacy of such a system. The services provided are supportive services and brokerage.

> Mr. A., age 60, is an illegal alien from Guadalajara, Mexico. He speaks only Spanish. He has no schooling, so cannot read in Spanish or English. Mr. A. has no family in the area, only the friend who rents him a small room, and with whom he shares food.

> Mr. A. has resided in the U.S. for more than twenty years and has paid Social Security and taxes from his pay as a dishwasher, just as native-born Americans do. He presently draws $80 a month from the odd jobs he does in the neighborhood. Mr. A. is sick, yet he feels that he is not entitled to health and welfare benefits he supported with his taxes and Social Security contributions. He also fears deportation by the Immigration and Naturalization Service. Fortunately, he came to the attention of a social worker at the community health center. With assurances that he would not be turned over to the INS and that the services were free, Mr. A. received health screening at the center. Later, diagnosis revealed Mr. A. had severe diabetes.[66]

The social worker gained Mr. A.'s trust and recognized that his lack of financial resources was the major obstacle to his seeking the health care and other services he needed. The worker advised Mr. A. about current immigration laws that might make him eligible for resident alien status. As a resident alien, he would be eligible for welfare and health care provisions. After identifying Mr. A.'s reasons for not seeking health care and informing him of his rights under immigration law and as a consumer, the worker used brokerage to resolve his medical problems and to begin the paperwork for residency and welfare benefits.

> The worker's first concern was to obtain medication for Mr. A. The worker purchased the medication with petty cash funds allotted for that purpose. The worker then accompanied Mr. A. to a United Way funded agency for assistance in applying for resident status. The worker acted as a translator and as an advocate for Mr. A.'s immigration needs. A week later, the worker accompanied Mr. A. to the welfare office to provide support and to make sure he understood the necessary forms before signing them.[67]

Although the advocacy approach met some of Mr. A.'s needs, the fact that a social network was not available emphasized the importance of linking the client with a support system. The friend was encouraged to become more directly involved with the well-being of the client by providing emotional support and by seeking further assistance from trusting neighbors.

Mr. A. was helped by his support system in the following manner. First, he was successful in obtaining part-time employment as a gardener and maintenance man for two elderly people in the neighborhood. Second, Mr. A.

was recruited by a *compadre* of the friend to provide cleanup service at a nominal fee at the family's restaurant. Finally, Mr. A. was linked by the social worker to a senior citizens program in the *barrio* where he had contact with persons who spoke Spanish and who would socialize with him.

Mr. A.'s case shows how the social worker recognized the client's problem, overcame the language difficulty and lack of education, informed him of his legal and consumer rights, and showed him how to obtain the necessary services from the appropriate institutions. Advocacy provided Mr. A. with the medical treatment he needed and serviced to connect him with a supportive network.

CONCLUDING COMMENT

Mexican Americans are one of this country's most diverse ethnic groups. Because they were an indigenous population in their own land prior to the Anglo American conquest of Mexico in 1848, they, like Native Americans, are one of the oldest minorities. On the other hand, continuing immigration from Mexico also makes them one of the newest and largest immigrant groups. They are a very heterogeneous Hispanic group, responding to all categories of any language and cultural scale. Mexican Americans primarily reside in urban areas in the Southwest and generally occupy a low socioeconomic status and have large families, a high unemployment rate, and low educational attainments—all symptoms of working class exploitation, sexism, and racism. Mexican Americans constitute a small elderly population (4 percent), almost one-third the proportion of elderly whites, and a very large youthful population. Because their age profile is the opposite of whites, their human services needs are different from whites, who are currently preoccupied with the needs of the elderly. As is the case with blacks, Hispanics are increasingly being caught up in the juvenile justice system, a field of practice in which social work has not expressed much of an interest.

The authors' survey of the social work literature pertaining to Mexican Americans revealed that much of it is of a descriptive nature, highlighting racism and value and cultural differences between Mexican Americans and whites. Only one article focused on the elderly Mexican American. There were no articles written specifically about juvenile and adult offenders, gangs, police–community conflict, stress caused by fear or deportation, divorce and separation, child abuse, family therapy, marital therapy, or mental health needs.

Mexican Americans *do* have mental health needs and many do avail themselves of direct services when they are provided at modest cost in their primary language, and near their homes. A rich psychiatric history originating almost 700 years ago with the Aztecs provides Mexican Americans with a foundation to build upon, both as consumers and as providers of mental health services. However, a current regressive trend in the United States, with its accompanying stresses, is creating new racism and poverty casualties among the poor and minorities. As their needs for services increase, there is a corresponding increased effort to "economize" by "phasing out" or denying services to the poor. Mexican Americans are particularly affected by these trends, especially new Mexican immigrants and the "undocumented."

Practice suggestions were offered that may have implications for macro social work in the *barrio*. The *barrio* as an ethnosystem is comprised of indigenous social support systems such as churches, neighbors, friends, alternative services (self-help groups), and the family. Applying the concept of social network intervention to Mexican Americans signifies the inclusion of extended family members, *compadres* (coparents), friends, coworkers, and other concerned persons in their support systems. These subsystems have the potential to provide emotional strength, support, and other types of assistance to the family.

Complimenting networking, the intervention strategy of advocacy and its five modes of practice (family advocacy, community advocacy, legislative advocacy, ombudsmanship, and brokerage) can assist Mexican Americans in reducing institutional barriers to human services.

SUGGESTED READINGS

Hernandez, Carroll A., Haug, Marsha J., and Wagner, Nathaniel N. *Chicanos: Social and Psychological Perspectives.* 2nd ed. St. Louis, Mo.: C.V. Mosby Co., 1976.

Casas, J. Manuel, and Keefe, Susan E. *Family and Mental Health in the Mexican American Community.* Los Angeles: Spanish Speaking Mental Health Research Center, UCLA, 1978.

"La Causa Chicana." *Social Casework* 52 (May 1971): 259–334.

Levine, Elaine S., and Padilla, Amado. *Crossing Cultures in Therapy: Pluralistic Counseling for the Hispanic.* Monterey, Calif.: Brooks/Cole Publishing Co., 1980.

Mangold, Margaret M., ed. *La Causa Chicana.* New York: Family Service Association of America, 1971.

Montiel, Miguel, ed. *Hispanic Families: Critical Issues for Policy and Programs in Human Services.* Washington, D.C.: National Coalition of Hispanic Mental Health and Human Services Organizations, 1978.

Morales, Armando. "The Mexican American Gang Member: Evaluation and Treatment" in *Mental Health and Hispanic Americans: Clinical Perspectives,* edited by Rosina Becerra, Marvin Karno, and Javier Escobar. New York: Grune and Stratton, 1982.

Rothman, Jack, Gant, Larry M., and Hnat, Stephen A., "Mexican American Family Culture," *Social Service Review* 59, No. 2 (June 1985): 197–215.

The President's Commission on Mental Health. *Report of the Special Populations Subpanel on Mental Health of Hispanic Americans.* Vol. III, appendix. Washington, D.C.: U.S. Government Printing Office, 1978.

ENDNOTES

1. For the purposes of this chapter, a *barrio* is defined as a neighborhood or community area of a town or city occupied predominantly by persons of Mexican descent.
2. Harry H. L. Kitano, *Race Relations* (Englewood Cliffs, N.J.: Prentice-Hall, Inc., 1976), p. 242.

3. Ibid.
4. U.S. Bureau of the Census, "Persons of Spanish Origin in the United States: March 1976," *Current Population Reports,* Series P-20, No. 310 (Washington, D.C.: U.S. Department of Commerce, March 1977).
5. Ibid.
6. "The Hispanic Populations in the United States: March 1986 and 1987 (Advance Report)," U.S. Department of Commerce, *Bureau of the Census,* Series P-20, No. 416, issued August, 1987, p. 5.
7. Ibid., p. 1.
8. Wayne A. Cornelius, *Illegal Mexican Migration to the United States* (Cambridge, Mass.: MIT Press, 1977).
9. *Business Week,* June 23, 1980, p. 86.
10. *Los Angeles Times,* August 4, 1981, pt. II, p. 1.
11. U.S. Bureau of the Census, *Current Population Reports,* 1980, p. 1.
12. Ibid., p. 1.
13. U.S. Bureau of the Census, *Current Population Reports,* 1977, p. 17.
14. U.S. Bureau of the Census, *Current Population Reports,* 1980.
15. Carmen A. Johnson, "Mexican American Women in the Labor Force and Lowered Fertility," *American Journal of Public Health* 66 (April 1976): 1186–1188.
16. U.S. Bureau of the Census, *Current Population Reports,* 1977.
17. Ibid., 1977.
18. U.S. Bureau of the Census, *Current Population Reports,* 1980.
19. U.S. Bureau of the Census, "Money, Income and Poverty Status of Families and Persons in the United States: 1978," *Consumer Income,* Series P-60, No. 120 (Washington, D.C.: U.S. Department of Commerce, November 1979).
20. U.S. Bureau of the Census, "Persons of Spanish Origin in the United States: March 1976," *Current Population Reports,* Series P-20, No. 310 (Washington, D.C.: U.S. Department of Commerce, July 1977).
21. U.S. Bureau of the Census, *Consumer Income,* 1979.
22. U.S. Bureau of Labor Statistics, Employment and Earnings (January 1978).
23. Ibid.
24. National Urban League, *Quarterly Economic Report of the Black Worker,* No. 11, First Quarter (June 1978).
25. U.S. Bureau of the Census, *Current Population Reports,* 1977.
26. *U.S. News and World Report.*
27. U.S. Department of Health, Education, and Welfare, National Center for Education Statistics, "Place of Birth and Language Characteristics of Persons of Hispanic Origin in the United States," *Survey of Income and Education Data,* No. 78–135 (Spring 1976).
28. National Center for Education Statistics, *The Condition of Education for Hispanic Americans* (Washington, D.C.: U.S. Department of Education, July 1980).
29. Lydia R. Aguirre, "The Meaning of the Chicano Movement"; Tomas C. Antencio, "The Survival of La Raza Despite Social Services"; John Florez, "Chicanos and Coalition as a Force for Social Change"; Alejandro Garcia, "The Chicano and Social Work"; Faustina Ramirez Knoll, "Casework Services for Mexican Americans"; Armando Morales, "The Collective Preconscious and Racism"; Phillip D. Ortego, "The Chicano Renaissance"; Faustina Solis, "Socioeconomic and Cultural Conditions of Migrant Workers"; and Marta Sotomayor, "Mexican American Interaction with Social Systems," all found in *Social Casework* 52, No. 5 (May 1971). See also Ignacio Aguilar, "Initial Contacts with Mexican American Families," *Social Casework* 17 (May 1972): 66–70; Miguel Montiel, "The Chicano Family: A Review of Research," *Social Work* 18 (March 1973): 21–23; R. J. Maduro and C. F. Martinez, "Latino Dream Analysis: Opportunity for Confrontation," *Social Casework* 55 (October 1974): 461–469; F. Souflee and G. Schmitt, "Education for Practice in the Chicano Community," *Journal of Education for Social Work* 10 (Fall 1974): 75–84;

L. A. Santa Cruz and D. H. Hepworth, "News and Views: Effects of Cultural Orientation on Casework," *Social Casework* 56 (January 1975): 52–57; Teresa Ramirez Boulette, "Group Therapy with Low Income Mexican Americans," *Social Work* 20, No. 5 (September 1975): David Maldonado, "The Chicano Aged," *Social Work* 20 (March 1975): 213–216: I. Aguilar and V. N. Wood, "Therapy through a Death Ritual," *Social Work* 21 (January 1976): 49; C. Medina and M. R. Neyes, "Dilemmas of Chicano Counselors," *Social Work* 21 (November 1976): 515–517; Armando Morales, "Institutional Racism in Mental Health and Criminal Justice," *Social Casework* 59 (July 1978): 387–396; Henry Ebihara, "A Training Program for Bilingual Paraprofessionals," *Social Casework* 60 (May 1970): 274–281; Ramon M. Salcido, "Undocumented Aliens: A Study of Mexican Families," *Social Work* 24 (July 1979); Ramon M. Salcido, "Problems of the Mexican American Elderly in an Urban Setting," *Social Casework* 10 (December 1979); 609–615.

30. Franz G. Alexander and Sheldon V. Selesnick, M. D., *The History of Psychiatry* (New York: Harper and Row, 1966), pp. 7–14.
31. Guido Belsasso, "The History of Psychiatry in Mexico," *Hospital and Community Psychiatry* 20 (November 1969): 342–344.
32. Ibid.
33. Alexander and Selesnick, *History of Psychiatry*, p. 120.
34. Belsasso, "History of Psychiatry in Mexico."
35. Ramon Parres, "Mexico," *World Studies in Psychiatry*, 2, No. 3 (Medical Communications, Inc., 1979).
36. Marvin Karno and Armando Morales, "A Community Mental Health Service for Mexican Americans in a Metropolis," *Comprehensive Psychiatry* 12, No. 2 (March 1971): 116–121.
37. Morales, "Institutional Racism in Mental Health," pp. 394, 395.
38. *Report to the President's Commission on Mental Health*, "Special Populations Sub-Task Panel on Mental Health of Hispanic Americans" (Washington, D.C.: U.S. Government Printing Office, 1978), p. 3.
39. Ibid.
40. Joe Yamamoto, Quinston James, and Norman Palley, "Cultural Problems in Psychiatric Therapy," *Archives of General Psychiatry* 19 (1968): 45–49.
41. Armando Morales, "Social Work with Third-World People," *Social Work* 26 (January 1981): 49.
42. Judith C. Nelsen, "Social Work's Fields of Practice, Methods, and Models: The Choice to Act," *Social Service Review* 49 (June 1975): 264–270.
43. Carol H. Meyer, "What Directions for Direct Practice?" *Social Work* 24 (July 1979): 267–272.
44. Meyer, "What Directions," p. 269.
45. Ibid., p. 271.
46. Ibid., p. 268.
47. Barbara Bryant Solomon, *Black Empowerment: Social Work in Oppressed Communities* (New York: Columbia University Press, 1976), p. 6.
48. Dolores G. Norton, *The Dual Perspective: Inclusion of Ethnic Minority Content on the Social Work Curriculum* (New York: Council of Social Work Education, 1978).
49. Solomon, *Black Empowerment*.
50. Ramon Valle, "Ethnic Minority Curriculum in Mental Health: Latino/Hispano Perspectives" (Paper presented at Mental Health Curriculum Development Conference sponsored by Howard University School of Social Work, November 16–18, 1979, Chicago, Illinois.)
51. Norton, *The Dual Perspective*.
52. Valle, "Ethnic Minority," p. 7.
53. E. P. Tsiaiah Lee, "The Pattern of Medical Care Use: Mexican American Patients at a Model Neighborhood Health Center in Los Angeles" (Doctoral Thesis, U.C.L.A., 1975).

54. Max Siporin, *Introduction to Social Work Practice* (New York: Macmillan, 1975).

55. Alice H. Collins and Diane L. Pancoast, *Natural Helping Networks: A Strategy for Intervention* (Washington, D.C.: National Association of Social Workers, 1976).

56. Gerald Caplan, *Support Systems and Community Mental Health* (New York: Behavioral Publications, 1974).

57. Caplan, *Support Systems.*

58. Collins and Pancoast, *Natural Helping Networks.*

59. Carol Swenson, "Social Networks, Mutual Aid and the Life Model of Practice," in Carel B. Germain, ed., *Social Work Practice: People and Environment and Ecological Perspective,* (New York: Columbia University Press, 1979), pp. 213–238.

60. Scott Briar, "The Current Crisis in Social Casework," *Social Work Practice 1967* (New York: Columbia University Press, 1967), p. 28. Also in Scott Briar, "The Casework Predicament," *Social Work* 13 (January 1968): 5–11.

61 Ronald V. Riley, "Family Advocacy: Case to Cause and Back to Case," *Child Welfare* 50 (January 1975): 374–383.

62. Rino J. Patti and R. B. Dear, "Legislative Advocacy: A Path to Social Change," *Social Work* 20 (March 1975): 108–109.

63. David Fritz, "The Advocacy Agency and Citizen Participation: The Case of the Administration on Aging and the Elderly" (Paper presented at the 1978 Annual Conference of the American Society for Public Administration, Arizona, 1978).

64. Ronald C. Federico, *The Social Welfare Institution: An Introduction* (Lexington, Mass.: D.C. Heath and Company, 1976), p. 262.

65. Riley, *The Social Welfare Institution.*

66. Ramon M. Salcido, "A Proposed Model of Advocacy Services for Mexican Aliens with Mental Health Needs," *Explorations in Ethnic Studies* 2 (July 1981): 210. (Published by the National Association for Interdisciplinary Ethnic Studies, California State Polytechnic University, 3801 W. Temple Ave., Pomona, California 91768).

67. Salcido, "A Proposed Model of Advocacy Services for Mexican Aliens with Mental Health Needs."

Social Work with Afro-Americans

Barbara Bryant Solomon

PREFATORY COMMENT

This chapter was written specifically for this book. The author, Barbara Bryant Solomon, states that people have a stereotypic view of the 25 million Afro-Americans residing in the United States; that is, that they are all criminally oriented. Like other minority group members, blacks are a very heterogeneous population with more than half residing in central cities. The process of <u>racism</u> and <u>discrimination</u>, rather than urbanization, according to Solomon, contributed to the creation of a <u>permanent underclass</u>.

Solomon suggests social workers can increase their effectiveness in working with blacks by becoming actively involved in their educational, political, and cultural lives. In discussing black family structures and dynamics, Solomon points out that black families share mainstream cultural values and in many cases do not differ from those of other U.S. families. She adds, however, that blacks must deal with experiences that many other families do not confront, such as employment and educational discrimination and helping their children understand and learn to cope with racism and the negative self-images it generates. For those who suffer from powerlessness in their social environment, Solomon recommends the intervention strategy of empowerment, whereby the social worker engages in a set of activities with the client to reduce the powerlessness created by negative valuations based on membership in a group oppressed by discrimination.

Solomon is critical of social work's preoccupation with person variables rather than system variables and believes this factor has been an obstacle in developing effective intervention strategies with Afro-American clients. It would appear, therefore, that poor, Third-World communities need a social worker who has the knowledge and skills to obtain needed direct services and who is also able to intervene in larger social and community systems.

Social work is a profession that by definition must be responsive to changing social realities. It is not surprising that the often <u>dramatic events</u> of the past two decades in regard to Afro-Americans in the United States <u>affects</u> the <u>profession's priorities</u> as well as its <u>practice models.</u> For example, all the following factors: the civil rights movement; urban riots and political discontent; the War on Poverty; affirmative action; school busing to achieve integration; the Voting Rights Act; the new numerical dominance of blacks in major U.S. cities, and the proliferation of black mayors, city council members, school board members, and state legislators, symbolize the ferment of a minority group in transition. More importantly these assaults on traditional social arrangements have required social workers to reappraise their emphasis on changing individuals versus changing collectives, on utilizing existing resources versus developing new ones, and on introspection versus systems analysis. In the process Afro-Americans have made it clear that social workers' old preoccupations with finding the source of problems in the individual psyche and in helping clients to "adjust" to inadequate social supplies are unacceptable.

WHO ARE THE AFRO-AMERICANS?

Police officers have often observed the predominantly black faces among the petty thieves, pimps, violence-prone families, and hardened felons with whom they are in constant contact and made a quantum leap to the erroneous conclusion that these people are representative of Afro-Americans in general.[1] Social workers are guilty of making a similar error. Since the probability is great that black clients are on welfare, on probation or parole, in poor housing, and in chaotic family situations, the generalization is made that all blacks share the same problems. The reality is that police officers, social workers, lawyers, or psychiatrists are most likely to encounter biased samples of the black population in their clientele. Knowledge of "other" blacks, that is, those for whom the client sample is not representative, is necessary if black persons are not to be perceived as acting out a predestined scenario.

Who, then, are these Afro-Americans who constitute 12 percent of the population of the United States—some 25,381,000 individuals?[2] They are first of all descendants of slaves brought to the United States during the period before and after the Declaration of Independence. They are also descendants of blacks who immigrated later to the United States from the Carribbean, Central and South America, and to a lesser extent, Africa. Early in the nation's history, black people were found in every state, though they were essentially a rural population located in the South. However, the first World War marked the beginning of a great migration as large, segregated communities of Afro-Americans developed within many U.S. cities. The trend has continued into the 1980s: most Afro-Americans reside in metropolitan areas, and more than half reside in central cities. George Gilder has even suggested that the large proportion of poor blacks who receive welfare in comparison to poor whites is the result of their concentration in urban areas where they are accessible to the pressures of social service bureaucracies that encourage their dependence.[3] Other authors have attributed this overrepresentation of blacks in welfare caseloads to the creation of a more or less permanent underclass through processes of discrimination and racism rather than to the process of urbanization.[4] Nevertheless, black urbanization has created a number of cultural, social, and political changes that have implications for social work practice.

Historically, the Urban League has been the social agency most clearly directed toward alleviating the negative conditions encountered by blacks in cities. The strong social work emphasis in the League and its local affiliates stimulated the development of a school of social work in predominantly black Atlanta University in 1921 as well as the provision of fellowships to black students for professional social work training in predominantly white universities.[5] Ironically, the League was strongly denounced during the 1960s and 1970s by more radical groups for its conservative approach to problems of racism and discrimination. For example, the League was more likely to use strategies of negotiation, advocacy, and coalition-building than those of confrontation and boycotts. Yet it can be argued that it was the League's support of social work education for Afro-Americans that provided the "critical mass" of social work professionals who moved into previously "lily white" social welfare settings and who finally answered the demands for more relevant services and more sensitive service providers among Afro-Americans.

Though migration patterns have been relatively easy to interpret, socioeconomic changes in the Afro-American population have been more difficult to characterize. For example, Ben Wattenberg and Richard Scammon contended in the early seventies that on the whole Afro-Americans had made considerable progress in the preceding decade and that, in fact, a majority could be considered "middle class."[6] This contention was based on 1970 census data and other statistics that attempted to demonstrate that during the preceding decade black family incomes had increased by nearly 100 percent in contrast to 69 percent for white family incomes. Similarly, George Gilder more recently has asserted that the income gap between blacks and whites has closed so that differences are due to factors other than discrimination despite the myths disseminated by "the politics of persecution."[7] On the other hand, Robert Hill has called this same data base "the illusion of black progress."[8] His analysis of the data indicates that during the 1970s the number of poor blacks increased, whereas the number of poor whites declined. Utilizing standard budgets for urban families provided by the U.S. Bureau of Labor Statistics, the National Urban League Research Department in 1979 classified 10 percent of black families with incomes above the "higher" level ($30,317), 26 percent with incomes above the "intermediate" level ($12,517), and 46 percent with incomes above the "lower" level ($2,585). In contrast, 74 percent of white families had incomes above the "lower" level.[9]

These data demonstrate the difficulties experienced by the social work practitioner who seeks to use social science information as the basis for developing intervention strategies. Social scientists disagree on the extent to which blacks experience discrimination as well as on the extent to which dramatic changes have occurred in the relative incomes of black and white individuals and families. These disagreements necessarily create differences in intervention strategies aimed at increasing the effectiveness of social functioning among black families. A belief in the negative impact of discrimination results in more advocacy and social action; a belief in the lack of capacity to utilize opportunities provided leads to more intrapsychic, person-centered strategies.

Perhaps the most important characterization of Afro-Americans is their heterogeneity. The *majority* are employed and do not present major problems in social functioning. On the other hand their overrepresentation among the poor implies that a disproportionate number are consumers of social services; that is, those programs made available by other than market criteria to ensure a basic level of health and welfare. Therefore, social workers who are the primary professionals in the social welfare field must be familiar with Afro-American culture, lifestyles, and help-seeking behavior if they are to be effective practitioners.

AFRO-AMERICAN CULTURE AND LIFE STYLE

The United States has been defined as an ethnosystem; that is, a composite of interdependent ethnic groups, each in turn defined by some unique historical and/or cultural ties and bound together by a single political system.[10] The largest ethnic group, the Anglos, has successfully assimilated some groups who were ethnically distinct at the time of their extensive immigration to this country—the Dutch, the German, the Scandinavian, and the Irish, for example. On the other hand, Afro-Americans for a variety of historical reasons have not been assimilated; the result has been the maintenance of a distinctive culture that possesses elements of the dominant culture, elements of other subcultural groups who have been oppressed, and elements that are a consequence of the unique Afro-American experience. This cultural distinctiveness may be observed in language and communication, in family structures, in religion, and in relationships with major social institutions. Knowledge of these distinctive cultural patterns should not encourage stereotyping but rather sensitize practitioners to a wide range of behavioral possibilities.

Language and Communication

There are different and sometimes conflicting ideas about how important it is to understand the vocabularies and communication styles of the various black subcultures from which Afro-American clients come. For example, since most blacks are at least bicultural, some assume that although the non-black social worker may not understand the subtle nuances of language and communication styles current in black communities, the black client will understand the majority language of the social worker. Thus, the majority language must be the medium of communication in problem solving activity. This attitude, however, ignores some dynamics of communication that transcend the simple issue of a common vocabulary. For example, a social worker is more likely to communicate feelings of warmth, understanding, and acceptance when clients views him or her as similar to themselves and as having problems, goals, and coping styles with which they can identify.[11] At the same time clients who view their counselors as similar to themselves tend to be more willing to freely disclose their thoughts, self-doubts, and concerns than they are with social workers whom they view as different from themselves.[12]

Carolyn Block has found that blacks may have a tendency to communicate ideas and feelings by analogy rather than analysis.[13] Feelings of depression may be described as, "I feel like I do not have a real friend in the world," rather than, "I have feelings of intense loneliness." The client's tendency to give examples of his or her experience of a problem rather than to isolate and analyze specific factors is often considered reflective of a lack of insight or ability to abstract, rather than a style of communication. Furthermore, the kind of response the social worker makes to the client may cause additional problems. There is evidence that blacks who come for help expect the social worker to offer certain values and opinions on issues they present. Though these opinions may differ from their own, clients expect that communication about differences will be a major aspect of the counseling process. The neutral counselor appears to be someone who has nothing to offer!

Barbara Lerner offers an example of the kind of consequences that can result when a helping person does not understand the language of the client served.[14] A white psychologist was required to make an evaluation of black school children. The evaluation procedures called for each child to be given one-half hour of unstructured play with blocks. Tinker Toys and beads were followed by a brief discussion between the child and psychologist about what the child had made. However, because the psychologist was unfamiliar with black dialect, he could not understand the child's answer to the question of what she had made. Thus, he repeated the question several times, thereby increasing the child's anxiety. When the child finally was able to make the psychologist understand the word "sticks," she was so relieved that she responded "sticks" whenever the question was asked, regardless of what she had actually made. After all, isn't it better not to frustrate the poor psychologist with words he cannot understand? Yet the child is likely to be assessed as having limited capacity to verbalize or limited ability to conceptualize on the basis of the psychologist's inability to communicate.

W. M. Banks has recommended that helping persons who work with black clients should recognize the heterogeneity of black culture and should become actively involved in the educational, political, and cultural life of different kinds of blacks.[15] Doing this would enhance the worker's ability to understand distinctive language patterns and communication styles, particularly if he or she spends some time in barbershops, churches, bars, and other places where people congregate within black communities. Social workers should familiarize themselves with these black communities and experience the texture of life so that they will be able to project a shared life space in verbal and nonverbal communication regardless of how words may be accented.

Family Structures and Dynamics

Perhaps more has been written about black families than any other aspect of black life in the United States. Since the late nineteenth century influence of the psychoanalytic movement on social work and other helping professions, there has been an emphasis on the significance of the family in the etiology of problem behavior. For example black families have been subject to sweeping generalizations about the effects of their behavior on problems experienced by family members. Much of the social science literature attempts to account for the overrepresentation of black families in certain problem categories (among the poor, the unskilled, the uneducated, and the poorly housed, for example). One view is that black and white families share the same cultural values and norms but differ because of socioeconomic class.[16] Another view is that lower socioeconomic class status is an outcome of culture rather than its determinant.[17] Therefore, black families have different values and norms based on the harsh and oppressive experience of slavery, which developed behavior patterns that have persisted into the present and that have impaired the family's ability for social functioning. However, the most likely view is that black culture contains elements of "mainstream" white culture, elements from traditional African culture, and elements from slavery, reconstruction, and subsequent exposure to racism and discrimination.[18] Biculturalism serves to explain both similarities and differences in comparing black families with non-black families.

Andrew Billingsley has pointed out that black families must teach their young members not only how to be human but also how to be black in a white society.[19] Elaine Pinderhughes has expanded on this idea by identifying what black families need in order to cope effectively with the "victim system" of racism, poverty, and oppression:

> What these families need are (1) flexible boundaries to deal with the outside systems and (2) a family structure and process that reinforce a high degree of differentiation; effective leadership; and the ability to communicate and negotiate, tolerate differences in values and perceptions among members, function biculturally and build and use strong support systems such as the extended family.[20]

The concept of an ethnosystem also incorporates the idea of biculturalism as the primary force in the dynamics of black family behavior. Black families share mainstream cultural values to the extent that in many cases their family structures and process are no different from those of other U.S. families. At the same time, however, blacks are required to deal with experiences with which many other families do not have to deal, such as discrimination in access to educational and employment opportunities or helping their children understand how to deal with racism and the negative self-images it generates.

Certain aspects of family functioning are more characteristically encountered in black families and should be mentioned here. For example, the extended family is a common family pattern in which "base households" and "affiliate households" are interconnected in an extensive mutual aid family network.[21] Although this structure and its various components vary from place to place and with the circumstances of individual families, it can serve to help identify possible sources of family support beyond the nuclear family, which is the essential functional family unit in middle-class, white culture. Studies of working-class and middle-class black families show that nurturing and provider roles in the family are frequently shared equally by husband and wife.[22] Black child-rearing patterns often emphasize individual uniqueness, assertiveness, early independence, and avoidance of early gender identity, all of which may create problems for the child in encounters with the white middle-class dominated school.[23] Finally, in families that have become unstable because of excessive exposure to negative valuation from the oppressive social institutions, a variety of dysfunctional behaviors may be observed—extreme lack of motivation to achieve, apathy, negativism, irresponsibility, and violence.[24] Although most Afro-American middle-class families are able to cope with oppression better and have more resources to cope with oppressive social institutions than poor Afro-American families,they do not escape entirely; thus, recognition of the vulnerability of their status has meant that middle-class black families do not function *exactly* as do white middle-class families.

Religion

No African religious cults were established in the United States during slavery. However, with the coming of Baptist and Methodist missionaries, the slaves found an avenue for the expression of emotion as well as bonds of kinship with their fellow slaves. After Emancipation, the enlarged church organizations played an even more important role in the organization of the Afro-American communities. They promoted economic cooperation for the purpose of erecting and buying churches, establishing mutual assistance and insurance companies, and building educational institutions.[25] As the main form or focus of organized social life, the church has been both a secular and a religious institution, a fact that may well account for its playing a broader role in Afro-American communities than in white communities.

The role of the church in community life far beyond its strictly spiritual mission is exemplified by the campaign of 400 black ministers in Philadelphia in 1958 to end rigid patterns of job discrimination against blacks. This alliance of ministers brought an end to the more blatant forms of job discrimination by simply having members of their congregation boycott companies that practiced discrimination. Since segregation had ensured that managers of the offending businesses were not members of the churches or their boards of trustees or even acquaintances, the ministers did not have to worry about pressure from these individuals. The strategy was effective, and the ministers, led by Reverend Leon Sullivan went one step further and established the Opportunities Industrialization Centers to provide black people with the skills and training needed to fill the jobs selective patronage would open. Reverend Sullivan has attributed the success of this movement to prayer, moral initiative, black unity, and the appreciation of money as a prime determinant in human behavior.[26]

The spiritual side of the black church is far more personal than that of the traditional white church: God is never an abstraction apart from the here and now. He is personalized and included in daily life situations. It is not uncommon to hear Afro-Americans relate a conversation they have had with God or with His son, Jesus Christ. Prayer is a frequent response to everyday crisis, even by those who do not profess to any deep religious convictions. Comments like, "I prayed that my husband would find a job," or "I prayed that my child would get well," may be heard. The church provides significant services in black communities that can be utilized by creative social work practitioners seeking to enhance social functioning in those communities. For example James Leigh and James Green point out that churches have served to develop leadership skills and mutual aid activities as well as to provide emotional catharsis for those in need of some release of emotional tensions.[27] If social workers routinely assess the significance of the church in the lives of black clients, they may find avenues for enhancing their service effectiveness through collaborative activity.

Relationships with Social Institutions

Although the family, neighborhood groups, and the church represent the primary institutions influencing the behavior of Afro-Americans, schools, social welfare agencies, health care institutions, and the justice system also influence the behavior of blacks. In contrast, however, these institutions are usually controlled by those committed to the dominant culture. Because Afro-Americans have had the historical experience of being subjected to negative valuations by these institutions, they are likely to view them defensively. For example the schools have frequently perceived Afro-Americans as less capable of developing cognitive skills than whites; yet research has indicated that school failure is often a self-fulfilling prophecy reinforced by students' acceptance of the judgment. Students fail to expend the effort required to succeed (even in those instances in which that effort could certainly lead to success). The consequence is a high dropout rate among blacks and the accusation that "they lack interest in or appreciation for education." Yet failure in school is not a culture-based phenomenon.

Because health care institutions have long discriminated against Afro-Americans, blacks exhibit considerable distrust of health care practitioners. Jacquelyne Jackson has suggested that mainstream medical practitioners are most effective in treating urban blacks in emergency or critical situations and least effective in treating them in situations where much of the management of the illness is really the responsibility of the patient or his or her guardian.[28] The influence of the physician in those instances is somewhat small.

Particular targets of distrust are social welfare agencies, which have been given primary responsibility to help poor and disadvantaged persons. The policies of these agencies have contributed to their negative valuation by blacks; for example, welfare departments of Southern states have employed differential payment schedules for white and black clients in the belief that "blacks do not need as much as whites who have been accustomed to a higher standard of living." In addition to distrust blacks exhibit feelings of anger, hostility, passiveness, and dependency in their dealings with welfare agencies. These constitute responses to the frustration and powerlessness that is experienced when opportunities are denied because of membership in a stigmatized collective. They do not reflect individual deficiency.

SOCIAL WORK INTERVENTION

Prior to the 1960s, *culture* in social work education and practice was primarily concerned with the esoteric groups and variables encountered in the works of Margaret Mead and Clyde Kluckhohn. Only token attention was given to the special problems or techniques of service delivery to blacks. When these concerns were discussed, the focus was more often on the effects of discrimination or the role of culture in general. Acts of discrimination were perceived as generating cultural attitudes and behaviors such as concern for immediate gratification, lack of interest in personal achievement, and lack of commitment to marriage and family. Moreover these supposed characteristics were viewed as deterrents to the involvement of blacks in problem-solving relationships with social work practitioners.

The civil rights movement and subsequent black power movement raised issues of self-determination and institutional racism that precipitated the development of more responsive social services and a more responsive social work profession. The literature of that era, which dealt with psychosocial services to blacks, focused primarily on consciousness-raising. However, the history of limited access to services and the ineffectiveness of traditional problem-solving processes received relatively little attention from the social work profession.

The rhetoric of the 1960s gave way during the 1970s to greater concern for the development of more appropriate theories of behavior and theories of practice for guiding social work intervention with black clients. James Leigh and James Green have identified three major criticisms of the existing theoretical frameworks:

1. Intervention based on psychodynamic theories is, at best, palliative and at worst counterproductive. Since the problems presented by black clients are most often not ones of personal deficiency but of personal reactions to oppressive social institutions, an exclusive focus on the mental state of the

black client or on the worker's own intellectual and emotional problems in relating to social issues diverts attention from system as source of the client's problem and from the possible reasons that the client came to the attention of the social worker in the first place.

2. The role of the black family as a source of strength rather than as a source of dysfunctional behavior patterns has been virtually ignored.

3. Indigenous social institutions, such as the black church, have also been overlooked as a natural support system for troubled black individuals and families. More effective strategies for social work intervention with black families would seek to remove the basis for these criticisms.[29]

Theoretical Frameworks

Recent social work literature has included several attempts to infuse a black perspective into existing theoretical frameworks so that they serve to explain behavior of blacks more accurately, especially in terms of how these people are influenced by the larger social environment. For example, in addition to viewing the social system in the United States as an ethnosystem, the literature now cites power as the primary force governing the interrelationship between the dominant Anglo group and negatively valued ethnic groups. Therefore, power is as significant a concept in understanding the individual or family's experience of problems in psychosocial functioning as anxiety, guilt, or some other psychodynamic concept. The interrelationship of power, powerlessness, and human growth and development can be discerned most clearly through the basic process whereby individuals develop skills in social functioning.

> The individual experiences a complex series of events monitored by the family or surrogate family which involves the self, significant others and the environment. These experiences result in the acquisition of personal resources such as positive self-concept, cognitive skills, health, and physical competence. These personal resources lead to the development of certain interpersonal and technical skills such as sensitivity to the feelings and needs of others, organizational skills and leadership ability. The personal resources as well as the interpersonal and technical skills can then be used to perform effectively in valued social roles such as employee, parent or community leader.[30]

Racism, discrimination, and the general negative valuation of blacks may act directly or indirectly to decrease the individual's power to deal effectively with psychosocial problems. For example, the negative valuations from more powerful white persons in their environment are reflected in the family processes of many rural and low-income urban blacks. Because these families accept society's label of inferiority, they are prevented from developing such optimal personal resources as a positive self-concept or certain cognitive skills. In other instances, powerlessness may be expressed in an inability to develop interpersonal or technical skills because of low self-esteem or underdeveloped cognitive skills, which, in turn, are a direct consequence of interaction in an oppressive society. The final step in this vicious circle would be a reduction of the black individual's effectiveness in performing valued social roles because of his or her lack of interpersonal and technical skills. Finally, the inability to perform valued social roles confirms and reinforces feelings of inferiority and of negative values, and the vicious circle begins again!

Some negative valuations do not result in powerlessness because strong family relationships or strong group relationships provide a cushion or protective barrier against them. Despite the experience of discrimination or disadvantages simply because they are black, some individuals are able to obtain and utilize a broad range of personal, interpersonal, and technical resources to achieve goals effectively. Not all blacks can be considered powerless or unable to function effectively in the wider social system. On the other hand, for those who do suffer that powerlessness, which has at least some of its source in the relationship between the individual and oppressive social institutions, empowerment is an important goal and process for social work with these clients.

> Empowerment is defined here as a process whereby the social worker engages in a set of activities with the client system that aim to reduce the powerlessness that has been created by negative valuations based on membership in a stigmatized group. It involves identification of the power blocks that contribute to the problem as well as the development and implementation of specific strategies aimed at either the reduction of the effects from indirect power blocks or the reduction of the operation of direct power blocks.[31]

This theoretical perspective on the relationship between blacks in the ethnosystem and its oppressive social institutions provides a basis for the generation of practice principles that are consistent with the definition of empowerment. These principles serve to specify the goals of social work intervention; that is, intervention should be directed toward:

1. Helping the client to perceive himself or herself as causal agent in achieving a solution to his or her problem or problems.

2. Helping the client to perceive the social worker as having knowledge and skills which he or she can use.

3. Helping the client to perceive the social worker as peer collaborator or partner in the problem-solving effort.

4. Helping the social worker to perceive the oppressive social institution (schools, welfare department, courts, and so forth) as open to influence to reduce negative impact.[32]

These objectives are not substitutes for other objectives that may be derived from other theoretical perspectives; for example, helping clients to gain insight into their emotional reactions to significant others in their social environment or helping them to extinguish some problem behavior. However, the objectives related to empowerment take into account the fact that the problem may be created or exacerbated by the actions of external social institutions.

Presenting Problems

The criticism that traditional theoretical frameworks were not relevant to problem solving with black clients suggests that there is some inherent difference in the nature of the problems brought by black clients to social work agencies or settings. Social work has identified a broad range of problems in social functioning as amenable to change if subjected to application of social work skills. These problems are encountered not only in primary social work agencies (such as family agencies and adoption agencies) but also in host settings in health, education, law and justice, and income maintenance. Regardless of the setting, however, most black clients come to these agencies because they perceive them as a means for obtaining some needed material assistance or because they have been sent by agents of social control—judge, doctor, or educator—who have defined a problem for the client. Because most practice theories assume that the client will express a "felt difficulty," they are not very useful when the client expresses no felt difficulty or a very concrete one that, if accepted, requires only the connection of the client to the resource. In such cases, traditional practice theories indicate few options for intervention because they assume that the client is not motivated to help himself or herself. However, given the black experience in the ethnosystem, which generates little trust for social institutions, including those considered to be helping agencies, it should be expected that the majority of black clients will fall into the following two categories: (1) those people who have a mild to severe emotional and or social dysfunction but who perceive the social work practitioner as having no expertise of real assistance; or (2) those people who perceive the "system" as a major contributor to the problem and who believe it is not amenable to change or behavior modification. The incorporation of an empowerment goal in social work means that the social worker must intervene to change these attitudes of the client.

The distinctiveness of the presenting problems of black clients is not merely in their resistance to presenting the problems at all. In addition, even when the problems are clearly articulated by the client and not very different from problems presented by non-black clients (parent–child conflict, adolescent school difficulties, inability to function effectively in the workplace, teen-age pregnancy, gang violence, marital conflict, schizophrenia or depressive reactions) the chances are good that the experience of the client or family with oppressive social institutions will have created either direct or indirect power blocks to satisfactory functioning. Thus, the parent-child problem is exacerbated by the child's membership in a peer group that is spawned because of its negative valuation in the inner-city environment. Similarly, employment

problems or adolescent school difficulties may be to some extent a consequence of low expectations and self-fulfilling prophecy. Depressive reactions
may be a consequence to some extent of the cumulative frustration encountered in efforts to deal with school, employers, and social agencies. Eventually
anger is turned inwards, and the depreciated self is created. The presenting
problems of these black clients all involve stress from external systems. If the
theoretical frameworks that serve to guide social workers all relate primarily
to intrapsychic functioning as the determinant of ability to cope with one's
environment and not to institutional factors that might need to be changed
instead or as well, the profession will have limited effectiveness in helping
Afro-Americans.

Assessing the Problem

The social worker's initial problem-solving task is to assess (1) those factors
that have contributed to the development and maintenance of the problem
situation, and (2) the client's particular personal and social assets and liabil-
ities that influence the problem-solving process. Black individuals and families are often perceived in biased ways that lead to erroneous conclusions
about the source of the problem (for example, personal deficiency rather than
environmental stress) and the degree to which they have the ego strengths
(cognitive skills, language skills, and ability to relate to others) necessary to
engage in effective problem-solving work. The social worker should operate
from an empowerment perspective and attempt to discern and overcome the
powerlessness felt by the client as a member of an oppressed minority group.
However, the social worker must also assess the extent to which intrapsychic
and or intrafamilial forces also contribute to feelings of powerlessness and
impaired social functioning. This assessment must be a two-pronged one:
that of the client's unique personal problems and of the effect on him or her
of negative valuation as a consequence of being black in a white-dominated
society.

Certain elements of personality in black individuals have been directly
connected with growing up black in a white-dominated ethnosystem. For
example, William Grier and Price Cobb have suggested several defensive
postures that often characterize black-white relationships:

1. Cultural paranoia that assumes that anyone white or any social institution
    dominated by whites will potentially act against a black's best interests.

2. Cultural depression that is a consequence of life experiences and serves to
    define a black as less capable, less worthy than whites.

3. Cultural antisocialism that develops from a black's experience with laws,
    policies, and institutional procedures, which have no respect for him or
    her as an individual or blacks as a group; the black, in turn, has no respect
    for, or obligation to conform to, these laws, policies or procedures.[33]

Each of these defensive postures can be represented by a continuum: at one end there is just enough defensive posture to reduce the person's vulnerability to a potentially hostile social environment; at the other end there is so much defensive posture that the person is prohibited from functioning effectively.

The idea that personality development in blacks involves the task of achieving a balanced response to the experience of racism and discrimination is also found in Leon Chestang's contention that blacks have dual personality components. One is a "depreciated" component that recognizes the low status that society has ascribed to him or her and responds with feelings of worthlessness and hopelessness. The other is a "transcendent" component that seeks to overcome this low status and to actualize the potential for successful psychosocial functioning. If either the depreciated or the transcendent component of the personality becomes too dominant, problems in social functioning are likely to arise. For example, the overly depreciated personality projects the image of the deserving victim, whereas the overly transcendent personality projects a false power that has no basis in reality.[34]

The attitudes and behaviors exhibited by many blacks who come for help to social agencies are often labeled resistance; instead, these behaviors really reflect attempts at coping with discrimination and powerlessness. For example, because blacks often perceive delays in provision of service when requested from a counseling agency as indicative of indifference and/or a low priority, they may not approach the agency again. Similarly, blacks may "drop out" because they view lengthy gathering of background information and nondirective, neutral counseling styles as signifying the social worker's disinterest in them or inability to deal with their problems. It is a mistake to label this dropping-out behavior as lack of motivation or resistance to dealing with the problem, since this behavior could just as easily signify resistance to the experience of negative valuation or being "put down" by those representing white-dominated social institutions or practice disciplines. Moreover, dropping out is not always the same as failure to cope with the problem. The client may have opted for a solution that may or may not be less functional; for example, attempting a self-help strategy or attempting to find help in the informal support network of family and friends.

In order to determine the *extent* to which the powerlessness expressed in a black individual or family's request for help stems from membership in the stigmatized collective, certain questions should be explored:

1. How has the client's family perceived the fact of being black in its life experiences (for example, quality of education, job opportunities, and marital relationships)?

2. What has been the interaction of social class and race in the formation of attitudes, beliefs, values, and behavior patterns?

3. How have formal and informal support systems within the black community been utilized by the individual and/or family?

4. To what extent does the individual consider it possible to change the outcome of his or her interactions with white-dominated social institutions?

In those instances where answers to these questions indicate that much of the powerlessness being experienced by the individual or family stems from negative encounters with social institutions, the social worker's role necessarily involved at least strengthening the client's ability to deal with these institutions and at most modifying the functioning of the institution.

Establishing a Working Relationship Most black clients who come to social agencies for assistance have been sent by others who have defined their problem as requiring some type of social work intervention. For the most part, a social worker is viewed as synonymous with a "welfare worker" so that he or she is considered the one who is in a position to determine whether the client can receive or continue to receive concrete benefits such as financial assistance, food stamps, housing subsidies, and emergency shelter or referrals for employment, medical care, or educational programs. The social worker is not perceived as a "therapist," nor is "therapy" often considered a solution to emotional problems. If the social worker insists upon defining the problem only in psychological terms (the need for changes in the individual's emotional functioning), the client is likely to reject this definition. On the other hand, if the social worker focuses only on deficiencies in basic social supplies (such as food, clothing, and shelter), then any provision of help is unlikely to break the cycle of dependency created by dysfunctional attitudes, impaired intrafamilial and interpersonal relationships, and intrapsychic conflicts. A satisfactory working relationship can only be established for black clients when there is an expressed willingness on the part of the social worker to consider the multiple problems of clients as an interrelated whole.

Another aspect of establishing a satisfactory working relationship with black clients is to recognize the basis upon which black individuals will permit the social worker to influence their life situation. Two major orientations to interpersonal relationships have been identified in sociological literature. One is the "gesellschaft" orientation that is most characteristic of white, urban, middle-class individuals and that identifies appropriate behavior according to the social status of the individuals involved. Therefore, these individuals would examine the social worker's educational attainment, credentials, and license in order to assess his or her competence to perform a helping role. Framed degrees or certificates, titles such as "doctor," and the location and decor of the offices would all have some bearing on the client's judgment of the practitioner. The other is the "gemeinschaft" orientation that is more characteristic of rural, low-income, minority individuals for whom relationships are based on personal attributes of the individuals involved. For example, for these individuals, the social worker's answers to personal questions about marital status, number of children, religious beliefs, or time spent in the community may determine whether or not he or she is perceived as competent.

Establishing rapport between client and social worker is particularly difficult when ethnic boundaries are involved. Barbara Draper has suggested ways in which developing such rapport with low-income black clients may be more readily achieved:

> The white worker must try to enter the life space of the black client. He/she must listen to the expression of black language, its sounds and meaning. Read black literature and newspapers. Listen to black radio stations to get with the tempo and temper of blacks' feelings. Leave the office and walk around in black neighborhoods—look at the parts that are slums, but also acknowledge the blocks that are kept with price. . . . Look at the addict and the pimp but also see those who carry themselves with dignity. Look at the hustler but also see the shopkeeper, the dentist, the doctor. Go with the black client to the hospital and the social service agency. Notice the very real differences in the way services are often given to black and white clients. . . . There is an infinite variety among blacks whether in the metropolis or the small town.[35]

A personalized approach to establishing relationships with black clients and a keen sensitivity to in-group diversity may overcome apparent obstacles. Attempts to encourage discussion of thought, feelings, and problems in an open manner by a white person may fail because of the black client's lifetime of conditioning in an opposite direction. The characteristic black-white relationship was based on white superiority and was not a peer relationship; that is, the black person was expected to defer to the white and to provide the white person with any information demanded but at the same time was constrained from expecting similar deference or any information from the white person in return. This kind of relationship must be rejected totally; a peer-collaborator relationship must be established instead in which there is mutual respect and mutual sharing of information.

THE PROBLEM-SOLVING PROCESS

Social workers who are committed to an empowerment perspective in their practice constantly apply specific strategies aimed at helping clients to achieve a sense of control over their lives. They are particularly concerned with developing clients' abilities to influence the decisions of social institutions when such decisions will affect their lives.

The sense of control is often impaired by specific agency procedures. For example, clients of most social agencies are invariably required to answer myriad questions often to satisfy the needs of the agency (for example, to identify client population). These questions have little relevance to the problem-solving process. Therefore, a client who comes to an agency to present a problem of parent–child conflict may in the initial session be required to indicate length of time in the community, place of employment, amount of family income, and religion—none of which at the time may be important to meeting the client's immediate need. Furthermore, revealing so much that may be negative (such as failed marriages, evictions, and last job) reinforces the client's sense of personal deficiency, which is often already a dysfunctional aspect of the personality of the Afro-American client. The helping process becomes a part of the problem rather than a part of the solution.

In order to counteract the problem, a guiding principle of social work practice from an empowerment perspective is to ask no questions that do not have direct bearing on the problem-solving work. This may mean that the social worker does not even ask the client for his or her telephone number. If arrangements have been made for a future appointment, the client may be asked, "In case anything happens and the appointment will have to be changed, is there a way that I can reach you?" Then the client has to option to give the telephone number, to indicate that he or she will call the agency to confirm the appointment, or take his or her chances. In such a case, clearly, the client, rather than the social workker, will control the flow of information.

A client's sense of power over his or her life situation is also enhanced when the relationship with the social worker is a peer relationship. Each party brings a degree of expertise to the problem-solving process; that is, knowledge and/or skills that are necessary but not sufficient to reach a solution. For example, the client brings to the process first-hand knowledge of the problem he or she is experiencing, the strengths and weaknesses of the key actors (family members of the support network), and the consequences of past attempts at reaching a solution. The social worker brings to the process an understanding of human behavior and of how people create problem situations, as well as how they can be influenced to change or modify them. It is the blending of separate areas of expertise that makes possible the eventual solution.

Because the problem-solving process is by definition a collaborative one, the client or client system must take responsibility for bringing about whatever change is sought. For example, if the problem is inability to maintain employment, the underlying reasons may include a variety of systemic forces (poor educational opportunities and discrimination in hiring, for example). If these forces are to be overcome, the client must take specific actions to counteract the negative impact of a hostile environment. These actions may be directed toward changes in the oppressive social institutions, such as the utilization of the legal and court systems to reduce discrimination or compensate for past discrimination. The social worker who is skilled in facilitating change at both the individual and larger system levels will have much more utility in black communities than the social worker who is only skilled and only comfortable in dealing with individuals or small groups.

The social worker's role with Afro-American clients in the problem-solving process often is one of consciousness-raising so that the multiple forces that created problem situations can be acknowledged in order to relieve the demoralizing powerlessness that stems from an unconscious or conscious sense of personal deficiency. The question may be asked. "Why am I unable to make it when other people seem to be able to do so very well?" This question has become particularly problematic in more recent years when the reduction in legalized discrimination has meant that some blacks have been able to take advantage of what Andrew Billingsley has referred to as "screens of opportunity." It is still necessary to educate many Afro-Americans about the systemic factors that mitigate against "winning" if one is poor and black in this society.

CONCLUDING COMMENT

There are unique issues involved in social work practice with Afro-American clients. Most blacks who come to social work agencies for help have been sent by schools, correctional authorities, or other agents of social control and do not have faith that the social worker has skills that can help in solving their social and emotional problems. It is not enough for the social worker to have an appreciation for cultural diversity; he or she must have basic knowledge regarding the life styles, communication patterns, and characteristic problems encountered by black individuals and families. This knowledge is required for accurate assessment of the client's strengths, resources, support network, and potential for collaborating in a problem-solving process. The preoccupation of social work practice with *person* variables rather than *system* variables is a particular obstacle in developing effective intervention strategies with Afro-American clients. Their problems are characteristically intertwined with the behavior of the oppressive institutions with which they come into contact. However, these institutions are not monolithic and invariant in the application of oppression; therefore, skills can be enhanced in dealing with these institutions. The goal of increasing a client's sense of control in the problem-solving process and in his or her life situation characterizes the approach to social work with Afro-American clients which has been identified as *empowerment*.

SUGGESTED READINGS

Billingsley, Andrew, *Black Families in White America.* Englewood Cliffs, N.J.: Prentice-Hall, Inc., 1968.
Billingsley, Andrew, and Giovannoni, Jeanne M. *Children of the Storm: Black Children and American Child Welfare.* New York: Harcourt Brace Jovanovich, 1972.
Gary, Lawrence E., ed. *Black Men.* Beverly Hills, Calif.: Sage Publications, 1981.
Gilbert, Gwendolyn C. "The Role of Social Work in Black Liberation." *The Black Scholar.* December 1974.
Glasgow, Douglas G. *The Black Underclass.* San Francisco: Jossey–Bass. 1980.
Miller, Henry. "Social Work in the Black Ghetto: The New Colonialism." *Social Work* 14 (July 1969).
Morales, Armando. "Social Work with Third-World People." *Social Work* 26 (January 1981): 45–51.
Solomon, Barbara Bryant. *Black Empowerment: Social Work in Oppressed Communities.* New York: Columbia University Press, 1976.
Special Issue, "Social Work and People of Color." *Social Work* 27 (January 1982).

ENDNOTES

1. Lawrence Rosen, "Policemen," in Peter I. Rose, Stanley Rothman, and William J. Wilson, eds., *Through Different Eyes: Black and White Perspectives on American Race Relations,* (London: Oxford University Press, 1973), pp. 257–290.
2. *Blacks and Hispanics in the United States,* Data Track 6 (Washington, D.C.: American Council of Life Insurance, 1979), p. 5.
3. George Gilder, *Wealth and Poverty* (New York: Bantam Books, 1981), p. 160.
4. Douglas G. Glasgow, *The Black Underclass: Poverty, Unemployment and Entrapment of Ghetto Youth* (San Francisco: Jossey–Bass, 1980).
5. Guichard Paris and Lester Books, *Blacks in the City: A History of the National Urban League* (Boston: Little, Brown and Co., 1971), p. 78.
6. Ben J. Wattenberg and Richard M. Scammon, "Black Progress and Liberal Rhetoric." *Commentary* (April 1973): 35–44.
7. Gilder, *Wealth and Poverty,* pp. 155–156.
8. Robert Hill, "The Illusion of Black Progress," *Social Policy* (November–December 1978): 14–25.
9. Robert Hill, "The Economic Status of Black Americans," in James D. Williams, ed., *The State of Black America: 1981,* (New York: National Urban League, January 14, 1981), pp. 58–59.
10. Barbara Solomon, *Black Empowerment: Social Work in Oppressed Communities* (New York: Columbia University Press, 1976), pp. 44–45.
11. A. A. K. Shapiro, E. Struening, E. Shapiro, and H. Barten, "Prognostic Correlates of Psychotherapy in Psychiatry," *American Journal of Psychiatry* (1976): 802–808.
12. R. R. Carkhuff and R. Pierce, "Differential Effects of Therapist Race and Social Class upon Patient Depth of Self-Exploration in the Initial Clinical Interview," *Journal of Consulting Psychology* 31 (December 1967): 632–634.
13. Carolyn B. Block, "Black Americans and the Cross-Cultural Counseling and Psychotherapy Experience," in Anthony J. Marsella and Paul B. Pedersen, eds., *Cross-Cultural Counseling and Psychotherapy,* (New York: Pergamon Press, 1979), p. 183.
14. Barbara Lerner, *Therapy in the Ghetto: Political Importance and Personal Disintegration* (Baltimore: Johns Hopkins University Press, 1972), pp. 159–161.
15. W. M. Banks, "The Black Client and the Helping Professionals," in R. James, ed., *Black Psychology,* (New York: Harper and Row, 1972), p. 210.
16. See particularly Jacquelyne Johnson Jackson, "Family Organization and Ideology," in Kent S. Miller and Ralph Mason Dreger, eds., *Comparative Studies of Blacks and Whites in the United States,* (New York: Seminar Press, 1973); and Jerold Heiss, *The Case of the Black Family: A Sociological Inquiry* (New York: Columbia University Press, 1975).
17. See Robert Staples, "Toward a Sociology of the Black Family: A Theoretical and Methodological Assessment," *Journal of Marriage and the Family* (February 1971): pp. 119–138.
18. Barbara Bryant Solomon and Helen A. Mendes, "Black Families from a Social Welfare Perspective," in Virginia Tufte and Barbara Myerhoff, eds., *Changing Images Of the Family,* (New Haven: Yale University Press, 1979), pp. 285–289.
19. Andrew Billingsley, *Black Families in White America* (Englewood Cliffs, N.J.: Prentice-Hall, Inc., 1968), p. 28.
20. Elaine Pinderhughes, "Family Functioning of Afro-Americans," *Social Work* (January 1982): 92.
21. Elmer P. Martin and Joanne Mitchell Martin, *The Black Extended Family* (Chicago: University of Chicago Press, 1978), pp. 5–16.
22. James W. Leigh and James W. Green, "The Structure of the Black Community: The Knowledge Base for Social Services," in James W. Green, ed., *Cultural Awareness in the Human Services,* (Englewood Cliffs, N.J.: Prentice-Hall, Inc., 1982), pp. 106–107.

23. Diane K. Lewis, "The Black Family: Specialization and Sex Roles," *Phylon* 36 (Fall 1975): 222.
24. Pinderhughes, "Family Functioning," pp. 92–94.
25. Leigh and Green, "The Structure of the Black Community," pp. 103–104.
26. C. Eric Lincoln, *The Black Church Since Frazier* (New York: Shocken Books, 1974), p. 121.
27. Leigh and Green, "The Structure of the Black Community," pp. 103–104.
28. Jacquelyne Johnson Jackson, "Urban Black Americans," in Alan Harwood, ed., *Ethnicity and Health Care*, (Cambridge, Mass.: Harvard University Press, 1981), p. 117.
29. Leigh and Green, "The Structure of the Black Community," pp. 97–99.
30. Solomon, *Black Empowerment*, p. 17.
31. Ibid., p. 19.
32. Ibid., p. 26.
33. William H. Grier and Price M. Cobb, *Black Rage* (New York: Basic Books, 1968), pp. 200–213.
34. Leon Chestang, *Character Development in a Hostile Environment*, Occasional Paper No. 3 (Chicago: School of Social Service Administration, University of Chicago, 1972), pp. 7–8.
35. Barbara Jones Draper, "Black Language as an Adaptive Response to a Hostile Environment," in Carel B. Germain, ed., *Social Work Practices, People, and Environments*, (New York: Columbia University Press, 1979), p. 279.

Part Five

The Future of Social Work

To examine the profession of social work thoroughly, one must not only study the past and current status of this field, but also seek a glimpse of the future. A few developing needs and trends offer some insight into the directions social work is likely to move in the next few years and suggest some challenges the profession will face as it continues to evolve in these areas.

Underlying discussion of the future of social work is the assumption that this profession will survive. Although several respected and knowledgeable social workers warn that social work may be eliminated as a significant helping profession,* there are strong arguments to refute this position.

First, although social work is still a relatively young profession, it has now achieved adequate maturity to allow social workers to become engaged in meaningful roles in a wide range of social agencies. This significant contribution is evident not only in agencies where social work is the primary discipline, such as family service agencies and public welfare departments, but also in hospitals, schools, and other agencies where social work is a guest discipline. Despite some problems to be remedied if social work is to become an increasingly viable profession, social workers hold an important place in the delivery system of social services through the impact of their helping activities; they cannot be easily dislodged; their services are badly needed by the general public.

Second, the focus of social work on reconciling existing or potential problems between the person and the environment is not being accomplished successfully by any other professional

* Harry Specht, "The Deprofessionalization of Social Work," *Social Work* 17 (March 1972): 3–15; and Willard C. Richan and Allan R. Mendelsohn, Social Work: The Unloved Profession (New York: New Viewpoints, 1973), pp. 42–56.

group. The trend toward increased specialization and technology in most professions (with notable exception, the trend toward family practice in medicine) has moved them to focus on their unique practice areas and to become less concerned about the match between the person and the environment. Yet there is evidence that some emerging occupational groups are moving into this practice arena. The maintenance of social work as the primary profession with knowledge and skill for preventing or resolving problems in social functioning is critical to the successful provision of a comprehensive battery of social services to U.S. citizens. Unless extreme economic or physical disaster should force U.S. national priorities toward strict survival considerations to the neglect of consideration for the quality of life, this function will continue to be required.

Finally, its breadth allows social work to adjust its field at any one time toward greater emphasis on helping the person work more effectively with the environment or, conversely, toward making the environment more responsive to the person. A major factor in the survival of social work so far has been this ability to emphasize particular methodologies depending on the temper of the times. It is apparent that a strong social action emphasis would have damaged the development of the profession in the 1940s, when the psychoanalytic approach prevailed in the whole field of helping services. Yet in the 1960s social work was able to bring its social action

skills out of mothballs to support the civil rights movement and anti-poverty programs. In the 1970s the swing was back to a more balanced approach, ranging from clinical to social action roles for the social worker. This flexibility enables social work to avoid a narrow practice approach that could lead to the demise of the profession if conditions supporting the validity of any single practice approach change.

The six practice issues and developing trends presented in Chapter 23 serve to highlight concerns that will be confronting social work in the late 1980s and early 1990s and directions in which the profession is likely to evolve. These issues and developments pertain to: (1) the concept of mental health primary prevention and how it can be applied in a cost-effective way to at-risk social welfare populations; (2) the role of social workers in ensuring a person's right to treatment, or non-treatment, and even preventing treatment abuse with involuntary clients; (3) the potential role of social work intervention in the prevention of violence and homicide in gangs; (4) the flow of social workers into industrial settings with a unique opportunity to implement primary prevention programs; (5) the application of advocacy and empowerment concepts in working with clients as a foundation to develop primary prevention strategies with non-client populations; and (6) the continued development and testing in the courts of *class action social work* as a mental health primary prevention tool.

Prevention as a New Direction: The Future of Social Work

PREVENTION: A CONCEPT FOR THE LATE 1980s AND 1990s

As human services budgets were drastically reduced during the 1980s, an increasing number of people continued to need services. Substance abuse, child abuse, crime and delinquency, and the breakdown of the family are social problems that are also increasing. Even in the most favorable economic periods for the human services, the mental health needs of the U.S. population have far surpassed the nation's financial and manpower resources to meet these needs. For example it is estimated that there are anywhere from one million to two million children in the United States each year who suffer physical or sexual abuse, or neglect. Considering that each case could cost society $7,000 to treat, the total treatment expenditure might amount to $14 billion. The Department of Health and Human Services spends less than $30 million per year for child abuse and neglect. Federal and state agencies spend approximately $500 million per year for alcohol treatment services and treat less than 10 percent of all addicted alcohol abusers.[1] Accepting the fact that financial and professional manpower resources are limited, additional but less costly interventive approaches impacting large numbers of people have to be developed. Theories of *prevention*, therefore, have to be developed and applied.

In its most basic definition, prevention simply means to keep something from happening. As a helping concept in the field of social welfare, prevention is over 115 years old and dates back to the 1874 New York Society for Prevention of Cruelty to Animals (SPCA) child abuse case of Mary Ellen Wilson, who was protected by the court under laws designed to protect animals. SPCA President Henry Bergh's work led to the establishment of approximately 150 private child abuse prevention organizations. Their main function was to place children in alternative care away from abusive families.[2] In 1915 when Flexner's famous paper "Is Social Work a Profession?" was highlighted at the Proceedings of the National Conference of Charities and Corrections, six papers on prevention were also presented. The prevention papers dealt with topics such as sterilization of the insane, more institutions for the "feeble-minded," and reduced immigration. By today's standards, prevention concepts of 1915, which recommended the sterilization of schizophrenics to "prevent" schizophrenia or restricting the flow of immigrants into the United States to solve the social problems of immigrants, appear crude.[3]

Mary Richmond was actually discussing prevention in 1918, when she remarked that a good social worker not only helps people out of a ditch, but tries to find out what has to be done to get rid of the ditch.[4] By 1930 Richmond was defining prevention as one of the end results of a series of processes that included research, individual treatment, public education, legislation, and administrative adaptations.[5] Richmond was generalizing the potential of prevention from a single case basis to a broad societal level; that is, she was considering the range from micro to macro preventive intervention. H. John Staulcup reports that Christian Carl Carstens, who served as the director of the Massachusetts Society for Prevention of Cruelty to Children from 1904 to 1920, and director of the Child Welfare League of America from 1920 to 1939, was a very persistent person, dedicated to preventing child abuse by seeking to strengthen the natural family. Staulcup believes the popularity of the Freudian psychoanalytic movement and the expansion and application of psychotherapy for the treatment of "social" psychosocial problems detracted from the development and refinement of prevention concepts until about the 1960s.[6]

Although there are various definitions of prevention that will be discussed later in greater detail, the concept has three basic stages: *primary prevention*, or the anticipation of future consequences and the purposeful manipulation to achieve desired ends or to prevent undesired ones; *secondary prevention*, which involves treatment; and *tertiary prevention*, which is rehabilitation. Within the framework of this definition Kathy V. Nance surveyed 762 articles in seven social work journals published between 1976 and 1980 and found that only eighteen articles pertained to primary prevention. Of the eighteen, two dealt with theory or research. The remaining sixteen articles described primary prevention as practiced through several social work methods. For example five articles described the use of group work, three casework, three community organization, and five articles dealt with "multiple methods." Nance was of the opinion that the articles were conceptually weak in the area of primary prevention and that social work literature reflected the same overall lack of emphasis on primary prevention as did the mental health literature.[7]

Contemporary mental health conceptual formulations of prevention have as their foundation public health prevention theories and practice. In public health terms, prevention, as previously noted, has three stages. *Primary prevention* indicates actions taken prior to the onset of a problem to intercept its cause or to modify its course *before* a person is involved. It is the elimination of the noxious agent at its source. Through systematic spraying of affected ponds, for example, malaria-carrying mosquitoes, their eggs, and larva are destroyed before they have the opportunity to infect humans. *Secondary prevention* involves prompt efforts to curtail and stop the disease in the affected persons and the spreading of the disease to others. *Tertiary prevention* involves rehabilitative efforts to reduce the residual effects of the illness, that is, reducing the duration and disabling severity of the disease. In its most succinct form, therefore, prevention has three stages: prevention, treatment, and rehabilitation.

In 1977 the National Institute of Mental Health established an Office of Prevention to stimulate and sponsor large-scale programs of research on prevention. This Office has also assisted the Council on Social Work Education prepare curriculum materials about prevention.[8] The Director of the Office of Prevention developed the following definition of primary prevention within a mental health context:

> Primary prevention encompasses activities directed towards specifically identified vulnerable high risk groups within the community who have not been labeled psychiatrically ill and for whom measures can be undertaken to avoid the onset of emotional disturbance and/or to enhance their level of positive mental health.[9]

Primary preventive programs were for the promotion of mental health as educational rather than clinical in conception and practice, with their ultimate goal being to help persons increase their ability for dealing with crises and for taking steps to improve their own lives.[10] Goldston identifies two goals in primary prevention: (1) to prevent needless psychopathology and symptoms, maladjustment, maladaptation, and "misery" regardless of whether the end point might be mental illness; and (2) the promotion of mental health by increasing levels of "wellness" among various defined populations.[11] This places an emphasis on strength and positive qualities, in contrast to the problem-centered focus found in the medical model.

In applying primary prevention to child abuse, for example, intervention program efforts can be developed at three different levels. On a macro social reform level, prevention interventions may include legislation to protect children's rights, abolishment of corporal punishment, advocacy for abortion, and a more equitable economic distribution of resources. A second level of primary prevention intervention, also macro in impact, may utilize educational approaches aimed at a variety of audiences. This may include, for example, educating and sensitizing society to basic issues in child abuse and its deterrents, the use of newsletters and "crash courses" to provide helpful information to young families, and teaching adolescents in public schools essential skills needed in their future parental roles. A more focused primary prevention practice strategy, which is directly concerned with the operation of intrafamilial variables, involves utilizing homemaker and home visitor services to provide support and crisis assistance to "at risk" families with young children. The visitors could be hospital-based personnel, day care, child support workers, or community volunteers.[12] "Natural helpers" exist for most families. They are usually friends, neighbors, or relatives and have a relationship with the family not based on specific needs or problems of the family. With the family's sanction and the natural helper's cooperation, in at-risk families experiencing multiple problems requiring services, a preventive services worker may function as a case manager or consultant and attempt to coordinate the efforts of the various service providers. Child abuse may be prevented by assisting and meeting the needs of the at-risk family.[13]

The remainder of this chapter will examine several practice areas of concern to the future of social work, within a context of prevention theory and concepts. These areas relate to the prevention of treatment abuse, homicide prevention, the prevention implications of social work in industry, client advocacy and empowerment as prevention, and finally, class action social work as a macro level strategy and tool.

PREVENTING TREATMENT ABUSE

In preparing the fifth edition of *Social Work: A Profession of Many Faces*, our survey of the literature and current trends in the helping professions suggested that the availability or lack of treatment is often linked to economic scarcity, political climate, and to the devaluation of human services by the Reagan administration during the 1980–88 period. It is interesting to note that concerned activists once advocated for a right to treatment and then later a right to "non-treatment." Today the picture is mixed. There are some persons such as the homeless (of whom 50 percent may be mentally ill) who need treatment and are not getting it, while some affluent white adolescents who do not want treatment are involuntarily committed to private psychiatric hospitals by their parents for behavioral problems. This paradox will be touched upon later following a discussion of the right to non-treatment.

The social worker must be increasingly concerned about the right of the client to refuse treatment. In order to understand the concept of the *right to non-treatment*, the concept of the *right to treatment* must first be considered. The latter concept was first publicly advocated for inmates of public mental institutions by lawyer–physician Morton Birnbaum in 1960. The constitutional basis for this concept is due process of law, that "a mentally ill person should not be deprived indefinitely of his liberty in what amounts to a mental prison if he is not receiving adequate care and treatment for his illness."[14]

One of the first landmark legal decisions inspired by the concept of a right to treatment appeared in *Rouse* versus *Cameron* in 1966. Speaking for the majority Chief Judge David Bazelon of the U.S. Court of Appeals for the District of Columbia affirmed the concept of a right to treatment for persons confined in public mental hospitals. He declared that the purpose of involuntary hospitalization was treatment, not punishment, since Congress had established a statutory right to treatment in the 1964 Hospitalization of the Mentally Ill Act.[15]

The first comprehensive attempt to establish and define a statutory right to treatment for mental patients in state institutions is best exemplified in a legislative bill entitled The Right to Treatment Law of 1968, introduced in the Pennsylvania General Assembly in December 1967. By 1969 ten states and the District of Columbia had recognized a statutory right to treatment. Most statutes, however, tended to lack enforcement provisions and were little more than statements of policy—that the patient is entitled to medical care and treatment in accordance with the highest standards of the medical profession, although in fact limited by the facilities, personnel, and available equipment.[16]

Many subsequent court decisions upholding the right of institutionalized mental patients to adequate treatment have been made since 1960, but no guidelines were promulgated. The right to treatment was not fully and conclusively applied until 1971–72, when the orders and decrees known as *Wyatt* versus *Stickney* were given in the U.S. Middle District Court of Alabama. In this historic case the court clearly defined the purposes of commitment to public hospitals for the mentally ill and mentally retarded, affirmed the right of patients or residents to specific services and opportunities once a commitment had been effected, and established minimum standards of care and rehabilitation. It also established standards of staff qualification and appropriate staff-resident ratios and indicated appropriate approaches to transitional care and post-institutional care. Commenting on the implications of *Wyatt* versus *Stickney* for social work, Charles Prigmore and Robert Davis stated:

> At one stroke, it seems that one of the cherished goals of social work—to provide a framework for individuals to attain their fullest potential—may have a good chance of early realization, at least for the institutionalized mentally ill and retarded.[17]

Prigmore and Davis pointed out that a footnote in the court decision raised the possibility that some day the court might be confronted with the question of whether the voluntarily committed resident, like the involuntarily committed resident, also has a right to treatment. Within the realm of that possibility, they believe it will probably follow that once government accepts responsibility for providing a social service, the recipient has a constitutional right to service that is adequate. They conclude that this responsibility may result in a restructuring and reorienting of U.S. social services.[18]

Thomas Szasz, however, sees several fallacies in the right to treatment concept. He states that publicly operated psychiatric institutions perform their services based on the premise that it is morally legitimate to treat "mentally sick" persons against their will.[19] The most fundamental and vexing problem, according to Szasz, is how a treatment that is compulsory can also be a right. He would prefer to ask the question, Which do involuntarily hospitalized mental patients need more—a right to receive treatments they do not wish or a right to refuse such interventions (that is, *the right to non-treatment*)? He felt the answer to such a question should come from the imprisoned patients rather than from the institutional psychiatrists.[20] Szasz noted:

> It seems to me that improvement in the health care of poor people and those now said to be mentally ill depends less on declarations about their rights to treatment and more on certain reforms in the language and conduct of

those professing a desire to help them. In particular, such reforms must entail refinements in the use of medical concepts, such as illness and treatment, and a recognition of the basic differences between medical intervention as a service, which the individual is free to seek or reject, and medical intervention as a method of social control, which is imposed on him by force or fraud.[21]

The concept of the right to treatment for the involuntarily committed patient is in many ways similar to the right to social services for the involuntary client. Both have as a goal a social control function. A social control process is present in the social services that a public welfare client receives—it's in the law! Upon the recommendations of the Ad Hoc Committee on Public Welfare, composed largely of social workers, Congress specified in the law in 1962 what was meant by *social services*. The services were defined by the purposes and qualifications of the personnel who provided them. The purposes were to strengthen family relations, to help families to become self-supporting, to rehabilitate dependent people, and to prevent dependency. The services were to be given by professionally trained social workers, and provision was made in the legislation to increase the supply of qualified workers. David McEntire and Joanne Haworth maintain that the fundamental logic of combining social services with public assistance lies in the ideas that people who must depend on this "last resort" source of income are reduced to that extremity by personal or familial defects and that the application of professional knowledge and skill can remedy such defects so that these persons will become able to support themselves in some other manner.[22]

Social services are a form of social control to the extent that they encourage a welfare client to give up one set of behaviors for another set considered more appropriate in society. Charles Cowger and Charles Atherton assert that when social workers help clients find a job, apply for public aid, or manage the use of alcohol or other drugs, they are engaging in the process of social control. The objective is to enable clients to get along better within the social order.[23]

Henry Miller perceives a "terrible dilemma" in the social work value of preserving the dignity and worth of the human being, which, at the same time, demeans the person by imposing upon him or her a social service:

> The wrong inheres in the assumption that we have a right to impose unsolicited advice upon another human being—*and he is not free to withdraw himself from the situation or even discount the advice*. If he is on welfare, his benefit is contingent on being counseled in the use of his money or more; if he is on probation or parole his physical freedom becomes a condition of his receptivity to counsel; if he hangs around on street corners, he is assaulted by the insinuations of the street workers; if he is insane and hospitalized, the duration of his confinement becomes a function of a willingness to be counseled.[24]

Miller believes through such actions the individual is deprived of the one primary freedom that endows people with the core of their dignity: the freedom to make a shambles of one's life. "This may sound like a strange doctrine," he states, "that people should be free to err, to make mistakes, to fail, to be 'ill.' "[25] He advocates that people be offered the possibility of choice—and that includes the choice of being maladaptive, deviant, or even ill. Thus, the individual has a right not to be treated. Charles Prigmore reports that in a Michigan case, *Kainowitz* versus *Department of Mental Health of the State of Michigan*, the court found that involuntary psychotherapy was unconstitutional. The case is significant "because the right to treatment should logically be complemented by a corresponding right *not* to have treatment."[26] This movement for change is also affecting public welfare; in some states welfare is dispersed through an income maintenance section, while social services are offered in a casework section. The client is free either to choose to be helped by social workers or to ignore the help and continue to receive a check as long as he or she is financially eligible. There are indications that welfare clients are not flocking to engage in therapy.[27]

Social workers are learning to live with the idea that their involuntary clients might not want their social services, and clients are not being penalized for refusing these services. In this respect, "the right to non-treatment," as a phrase, might be newer to social workers than their familiarity with the ideology and application of the concept.

The development of the concept of the right to non-treatment has occurred over a very short period. This right will possibly have broader implications for social work and society as more people—particularly involuntary clients—become aware of the social control and political implications related to the definition of "deviant" behavior. For discussion purposes, one area of social work practice where this concept may have the greatest reform impact—social work practice with individuals, groups, and families—will be considered. To avoid confusion, the term *social casework*, rather than "social work practice with individuals, groups, and families," will be used in the following discussion.

Social casework, a tool in treatment that may be defined as a primarily psychotherapeutic method consisting of interviews dealing with the client's problems as defined by the client, in the context of the worker-client relationship,[28] is the largest segment of the social work profession.[29] It is also the primary mode of intervention used in the context of social service as previously defined. Social casework has been criticized consistently and most dramatically for its failure to demonstrate a clear effectiveness in helping clients.[30] In an analysis of eleven controlled studies of the effectiveness of social casework, Joel Fischer found that nine of the studies clearly showed that professional caseworkers were unable to bring about any positive, significant, measurable changes in their clients beyond those which would have occurred without the specific intervention program or have been induced by nonprofessionals dealing with similar clients, often in less intensive service programs.[31] Fischer therefore concluded:

Thus not only has professional casework failed to demonstrate that it is effective, but lack of effectiveness appears to be the rule rather than the exception across several categories of clients, problems, situations, and types of casework.[32]

Fischer pointed out that he was presenting research findings related to practice rather than an analysis of practice per se, and that most of the studies concentrated on work with children, juvenile delinquents, and low-income clients. He argued that the high rate of failure could have been an artifact of caseworkers' general inability to help clients when other, more powerful, environmental forces hold sway and that although the problem was important, the methods used may have been outdated.[33]

More recent research related to social casework has revealed positive results, indicating that effectiveness of casework may be related more to the problem and the client than to the method itself. In an analysis of thirty-two controlled studies on the treatment outcomes of marital counseling, Dorothy Beck found statistically significant positive gains in all but one of the studies. The participants in many of the studies were young, white, and relatively well-educated middle-class couples.[34]

The clients in Beck's research represented a relatively homogeneous group dealing with one dominant social problem, in contrast to multi-problem families, and their principal problem did not require changes in the institutional structure or wider social context. With minor exceptions, the marital samples in the studies were restricted to couples who either were *actively seeking help* or were willing to volunteer.[35] In the Fischer studies, with one exception, all participants were involuntary clients. This evidence strongly suggests that when social workers do casework within a social control framework with involuntary clients, their interventive efforts are not as effective as when they serve voluntary clients who are actively seeking help with a specific problem.

In one instance, then, the state and its representatives—social workers—define the problem and goals for the involuntary client, while in the other, the voluntary client defines the problem and goals. Individuals who are not seeking to change their behavior usually do not change, whereas those who are seeking to change usually do. Imposing treatment upon involuntary clients with questionable results and perhaps even deterioration of the clients in slightly under 50 percent of the cases[36] (that is, iatrogenic effects of practice[37]) raises ethical questions for the social worker. Is the social worker performing a disservice to the involuntary client? Imposing treatment poses a dilemma for social workers because they are given legal sanction to carry out a social control function that does not have the sanction of the involuntary client and is inconsistent with the value social workers place on self-determination. Social workers, as representatives of the state, may feel more comfortable in intervening on behalf of the victim in a serious child abuse and maltreatment case than in interfering with a marijuana-smoking seventeen-year-old whose behavior is condoned by his parents. Preferably, imposed intervention as an act of social control should be related to the seriousness of the specific case.

Social workers have a responsibility to people in need and should not permit themselves to be caught by and to swing with the pendulum which is moved by political forces to extreme positions, ignoring the welfare of persons at risk. As Ladner cautioned social workers about the homeless:

> The civil libertarians leaned too far in ensuring the mentally ill's rights, so that now people are denied access to treatment even when they really need it and ask for it. I think we need to recognize people's right to treatment as well as to short-term voluntary or involuntary hospitalization. And some will have to be put in asylums. But we have to stop going from one extreme to the other.[38]

The American Psychiatric Association's estimate that 25 to 50 percent of the country's estimated three million homeless are mentally ill may be a conservative figure. Lutheran Social Services in Washington, D.C., places the figure closer to 90 percent. Perhaps the most important issues are that the homeless have a need for various services and that social workers—according to Mark Battle, the executive director of NASW—by far represent the largest number of professionals in one occupation who deliver these services.[39] Social workers have a key role to play on behalf of the homeless. On the one hand they may still have to advocate for a right to non-treatment for those homeless who are still functioning, although marginally, and keep them from being institutionalized. Those who are gravely psychiatrically disabled and unable to care for themselves may need to be institutionalized against their will following due process in the courts.

In spite of the large estimates concerning the percentage of mentally ill among the homeless, the homeless by and large are *not* a homogeneous group. They will vary from state to state and city to city, and even be different *within* a city. Their needs will vary requiring varied practice responses from the social worker. For example a 1984 Los Angeles study by Richard Ropers revealed that the homeless were not mostly "crazy, lazy, drunk or doped." Rather, Ropers saw them by and large as victims of deindustrialization, not deinstitutionalization, mental illness, substance abuse, or family problems. In comparing a Westside group to a downtown "Skid Row" group he found more reported drug use in the Westside group (70.5 percent to 50.3 percent). The Westside homeless group was younger and better educated (56 percent "some college" versus 33 percent), with a median age of thirty-two compared to thirty-nine for the Skid Row group. More than three-fourths were white compared to less than half on Skid Row, and twice as many were likely to be women. There were no significant differences in the two groups concerning mental health as about 20 percent reported previous psychiatric hospitalization; 28 percent had not seen a doctor or other professional for emotional or nervous problems, 14 percent reported they had been hospitalized for alcohol detoxification, 8 percent for drug detoxification and 7 percent reported suicide attempts the previous year. Citing their reasons for being homeless, 52 percent said lack of money, 36 percent said lack of work, while a third major reason was domestic violence against women.[40] The homeless are indeed a heterogeneous group with various needs, who appear to be casualties of Reaganomics and the reduction in funding of human services programs.

From a mental health prevention standpoint the moderately to severely psychiatrically impaired homeless will require tertiary prevention; that is, rehabilitation services to reduce the duration and disabling severity of their mental condition. For those with no prior or very little prior history of mental disorder who are now becoming symptomatic, secondary prevention (prompt treatment) will need to be initiated to curtail the emerging symptoms. Previously well-functioning homeless persons who temporarily find themselves out on the streets due to unforeseen circumstances beyond their control, who are not clinically symptomatic, would be provided primary prevention services. Primary prevention intervention for that high-risk group would involve, for example, helping the person obtain a job, re-enroll in school or return to their home town in order to prevent needless psychopathology symptoms, or maladjustment, and to increase their level of wellness.

Another at-risk population group with which social workers should be concerned are juveniles who in fact have *not* committed crimes yet are involuntarily coming to the attention of private psychiatric hospitals and the public juvenile justice system. Congress enacted the Juvenile Justice and Delinquency Prevention Act of 1974 as a decriminalization and deinstitutionalization effort designed to prevent young people from entering a "failing juvenile justice system," and to assist communities in developing more sensible and economical alternatives for youths already in the juvenile justice system.[41] The Act was successful as arrests for status offenses or "crimes," which, had they been committed by adults, would not have been considered crimes (such as truancy, running-away, or incorrigibility), declined 15.8 percent (569,481 arrests to 466,885 arrests) between 1974 and 1979.[42] The 1980s have presented a mixed picture as juvenile crime nationally has been decreasing yet more juveniles are being institutionalized. In Minnesota, for example, even though there has been a decrease in institutionalization in public juvenile training institutions, there has been a tremendous growth in the numbers of youths admitted "voluntarily" to inpatient psychiatric settings in private hospitals.[43]

In California there has also been a surge of these psychiatric facilities, related in part to California's 1977 Juvenile Reform Act, which, like the federal law, decriminalized status offenses. In Los Angeles alone there are twenty-eight such institutions with a total of 820 beds—many having waiting lists. A study by Patricia Guttridge and Carol Warren found that more than 70 percent of the admissions to these hospitals were for antisocial, depressive, runaway, drug abuse, or personality-disorder diagnoses. Less than one-fifth of the admissions were for psychosis.[44] The District Attorney's office questions the propriety of these hospitalizations, pointing out that experts do not agree on what exactly constitutes mental illness. A patients' rights advocate for the Los Angeles County Department of Mental Health believes hospitalization could create future and perhaps even more serious problems for the adolescent. They will suffer social stigma, especially from peers, and future employers may be reluctant to hire someone who had been in a "mental institution." Some view the adolescent's acting-out as symptomatic of the parents' relationship with the youth, considering that this relationship should be the focus of intervention. Many youths are admitted "voluntarily" to the hospital only because their parents volunteered them—perhaps as scapegoats. The admitting physician, who is also a hospital employee, is the person responsible to determine whether or not treatment is necessary.

The cost of hospitalization may range from $10,000–$20,000 per month, thereby making it the exclusive domain of the very affluent or well-insured. Insurance companies cover most of the cases and since most prefer to cover inpatient rather than alternative forms of treatment, hospitalization becomes economically more attractive, according to Guttridge and Warren. There is a concern that adolescent wards have become profit-making ventures subsidized by the insurance companies; this has brought the mental health and insurance professions under criticism. Many allege that poor adolescents who are genuinely mentally ill but whose parents do not have the economic resources or insurance coverage are not receiving the specialized treatment that affluent youths with less severe problems receive, and are tracked instead into the public juvenile justice system.[45] Setting aside the potential economic conflict of interest issue for the private hospitals and the double standard of treatment for the affluent and the poor, are the rights of the hospitalized, affluent adolescents being abused?

Saul Brown, head of psychiatry at Cedars-Sinai Medical Center in Los Angeles believes the issues of patients' rights is a misguided one and that giving adolescents the right to decide whether they need treatment abrogates a certain kind of parental reason. The United States Supreme Court ruled in 1979 that parents had the right to commit their children to a psychiatric facility if qualified medical professionals did the admitting. However, the ruling applied *only* to state hospitals. This situation has been referred to as a "legal twilight zone." The California Supreme Court has asked the legislature to conduct an inquiry into psychiatric facilities being used by parents as "private prison hospitals for their incorrigible children."[46]

On the one hand while some affluent white adolescents expressing behavioral disorder symptoms are being involuntarily committed by their parents to private psychiatric hospitals, risking the long-term psychosocio-political consequences of a psychiatric label, some poor adolescents—mostly minorities—who have not committed any crimes and are expressing behavioral disorder symptoms are being labeled criminal by law enforcement and tracked prematurely into the public juvenile justice system. They will have to suffer the long-term consequences of a "criminal" label. The U.S. Department of Justice has developed and funded the "SHODI" (Serious Habitual Offenders—Drug Involved) program in five cities: Oxnard and San José in California; Portsmouth, Virginia; Jacksonville, Florida; and Colorado Springs, Colorado. The purpose of the SHODI program, according to Oxnard Police Chief Robert Owens, is to (1) identify the most serious offenders, ages 13 to 17; (2) ensure they receive "stiff" sentences; and (3) keep the youths off the streets for the longest period of time. The criteria to be labeled a SHODI is three arrests in the last year and two previous arrests (three of the five arrests must be for felonies); or three arrests in the last year and seven previous arrests (eight of the ten arrests must be for petty theft, misdemeanor assault, narcotics, or weapons violations).[47]

The most controversial aspect of the program is that a juvenile who has never been convicted (on allegations found to be true and sustained in a juvenile court proceeding) of a crime could be classified by police as a habitual offender because criteria are based on arrests, *not convictions*! In Jacksonville, Florida, 22 percent of all youths classified as habitual offenders never appeared in court. With the "SHODI" label, probation officers are more likely to refer the case to court for prosecution. Judge James McNally, former presiding judge of the Ventura County Juvenile Court (Oxnard area) disagrees with basing the SHODI criteria on arrests and believes some judges may overreact in a punitive manner when faced in court by a SHODI. The Public Defender's Office complained that Ventura County had a preoccupation with punishment and did not have adequate rehabilitation and treatment facilities. Approximately half the SHODI youths had drug problems—some chronic paint sniffers—but there were no drug treatment facilities for juveniles in the county. Eighty-three percent of the SHODI juveniles in Oxnard were either Hispanic or black. ACLU President Peggy Johnson believes basing the program on arrests rather than convictions results in more minorities being labeled "SHODI" because minority youths are more likely to have contact with police.[48] This discriminatory practice was documented in Chapter 17, showing a case in which Hispanic youths were twenty-three times more likely to be arrested for loitering than whites even though both groups had similar crime rates.

With reference to the above two examples of affluent white and poor minority adolescents being prematurely labeled and tracked into the private psychiatric hospitals and public juvenile justice systems, the values social workers place on self-determination, a right to non-treatment, opposing discrimination, and treatment abuse may require social workers to assume a position and take action. Those adolescents who are definitely a danger to themselves or others, who are severely psychiatrically disabled, or who chronically damage property or commit acts of violence, based on *convictions*, may indeed have to be institutionalized for their and/or society's protection. Social workers must support these detentions and make sure the youths receive proper treatment rather than punishment. This role would be consistent with *tertiary prevention*. However, for those youngsters whose acting-out is not harmful or who have numerous arrests that are related more to police deployment practices rather than the pre-delinquent behavior of poor minority adolescents, social workers should assume a *secondary prevention* role as advocates encouraging intervention at the family and community level rather than harsher measures such as institutionalization. *Primary prevention* intervention involving educational and employment alternatives for at-risk families and youths might consist of evening workshops or seminars for affluent families concerning the stresses and pressures some affluent adolescents suffer; for example, the fear that they will not be able to achieve as well as their parents in a tight economy that places the cost of a home out of reach for many. For poor communities, primary prevention community education programs could focus on helping families learn to cope with the stresses of migration, urbanization, gangs, and drugs. Youths would be provided assistance in school or helped to obtain employment if they chose not to remain in school.

GANG VIOLENCE AND HOMICIDE PREVENTION

It was seen in Chapter 16 that the U.S. homicide rate was approximately 8 per 100,000 but that in a specific high-risk group—gangs in inner city communities—the rate can be in some areas like Los Angeles, as high as 600 per 100,000. A seventeen-year Chicago study involving 12,872 homicides reported that more than half of Hispanic youth victims were killed in gang-related altercations.[49] In 1985, 10.5 percent of 2,781 homicide victims in California were killed by gangs and in Los Angeles, twenty-four percent of 1,037 homicide victims were gang-related.[50] Other large urban areas with gangs also have significant numbers of persons being assaulted and/or killed by gangs. This violence exacts an extremely high toll in injuries, death, and emotional pain and adversely impacts the quality of life for thousands of poor residing in the inner cities.

The public health profession with its focus on epidemiologic analysis and prevention believes that it can make a substantial contribution to solving problems of interpersonal violence. Surgeon General C. Everett Koop stated that "violence is every bit a public health issue for me and my successors in this century as smallpox, tuberculosis and syphilis were for my predecessors in the last two centuries."[51] The health professions are making their initial bold entry into this major problem area following in the footsteps of criminology, sociology, and the criminal justice system. Psychiatry and psychology have been investigating the issue primarily from a biological (brain chemistry) and behavioral (modifying the behavior of *individuals*) perspective. Chapter 16 demonstrated how the social work profession with its micro to macro level knowledge and skills base, was ideally suited to apply its techniques with individual gang members, gang groups, and the community to reduce urban gang violence and homicide. In addition to employing social work's traditional approaches in dealing with the problem, the present task is to devise ways in which prevention theory with corresponding intervention models can be applied.

It was stated earlier that *primary prevention* in a public health context involves averting the initial occurrence of a disease, defect, or injury. Primary prevention in homicide requires national efforts to be directed at social, cultural, educational, technological, and legal aspects of the macro environment, which facilitate the perpetuation of the U.S.'s extremely high homicide rate—

indeed, a tall order. A national strategy would involve public education about the seriousness and ramifications about violence, contributing factors, high risk groups, and need for social policy as a physical health and mental health priority in the United States. The topic must become a higher priority in medical schools, and schools of nursing, social work, and psychology. At the community level community self-help groups, social planning councils, and other civic groups need to work toward educating U.S. citizens about the causal relationship of alcohol, illegal drugs, firearms, and television violence to homicide and violence.[52] In theory these strategies when directed at high-risk populations are supposed to reduce those conditions that are seen as contributing to violence and homicide.

Secondary prevention in a public health context concerns the cessation or slowing down the progression of a health problem. It involves the early detection and case finding by which more serious morbidity may be decreased. In application of this concept to homicide such case finding requires the identification of persons showing early signs of behavioral and social problems that are related to increased risk for subsequent homicide victimization. Variables such as family violence, childhood and adolescent aggression, school violence, truancy, and "dropping out" of school, and substance abuse, are early indicators of many persons who later become perpetrators of violence and homicide. Secondary prevention intervention strategies with individuals already exhibiting these early symptoms interrupts a pattern that would have later resulted in serious violence or homicide.[53]

Tertiary prevention pertains to those situations in which a health problem is already well established but efforts can still be made to prevent further progress toward disability and death. In the case of homicide the problems of greatest concern are those of interpersonal conflict and nonfatal violence, which appear to have a high risk for homicide. Aggravated assault is one early significant predictor related to homicide.[54] In a study in Kansas in 25 percent of the homicides either the victim or the perpetrator had previously been arrested for an assault or a disturbance.[55] Victims of aggravated assault such as spouses or gang members are especially at high risk for becoming homicide cases.

Attempts have been made in developing program models aimed at preventing youth violence and homicide—although some of these programs are not specifically aimed at *gang* homicide prevention. These educational, court, and community based programs seem to be functioning mainly at the primary (reducing conditions contributing to homicide) and secondary prevention (identifying persons showing early signs of sociobehavioral problems) levels. A few of these programs as examples of prevention models will be discussed.

Educational Prevention Models

The *Boston Youth Program* instituted in four Boston high schools had a curriculum on anger and violence. The ten-session curriculum provided: (1) information on adolescent violence and homicide; (2) the discussion of anger as a normal, potentially constructive emotion; (3) knowledge in developing alternatives to fighting; (4) role playing and videotapes; and (5) the fostering of nonviolent values. Following the completion of the program an evaluation of control group (no curriculum) and an experimental group (curriculum) revealed that there was a significant, positive change of attitude in the experimental group. The researchers cautioned, however, that further study had to delineate the actual impact the curriculum will have on actual *behavior* and the longevity of the impact.[56] The Boston Youth Program was directed at minority students, but it was not indicated whether any of these students were gang members.

Peer Dynamics is another school based program sponsored by the Nebraska Commission on Drugs, which was designed to reduce the incidence of destructive risk taking behaviors of juvenile delinquency and substance abuse among high school adolescents in fifty-six public schools. With the goal of developing improved self-esteem and better communication skills, the program trained and supervised students who participated in group interaction activities with other students. A follow-up evaluation found that in relationship to other students, program participants showed a noticeable drop in discipline referrals among students.

A final evaluation noted that Peer Dynamics affected each sex equally and that the greatest changes were noted in eighth, tenth, and eleventh grade students. No significant change in attitude toward themselves or others was reported in the control group.[57] Again, this was not a program designed specifically for gang youths although some gang members may have been participants. The question remains, however, whether improved attitudes result in less violence and homicide.

A third school based prevention program functioning in the City of Paramount in Los Angeles County is called the *Paramount Plan*. This was designed to be a "gang prevention" model and unlike the Boston Youth Program and Peer Dynamics, which target high school youths, it is an educational model directed at *all* elementary school fifth and sixth graders in the school district. The program consists of neighborhood parent meetings and an antigang curriculum taught to students in school for fifteen weeks. Prior to the program 50 percent of students were "undecided" about joining gangs. After the fifteen weeks, 90 percent said they would not join gangs.[58]

No mention was made about the 10 percent of students who did not change their minds about joining gangs. In poor urban areas where there are gangs, it is only 3 to 5 percent of youths who become delinquents and/or join gangs. In other words at least 95 percent of youths do not join gangs even without a gang prevention program such as the Paramount Plan. Further research is needed to determine if those in the 10 percent who did *not* change their minds about joining gangs actually do and secondly, whether or not they later become either perpetrators or victims of gang homicide. Perhaps one of the major research challenges is to be able to measure what was prevented.

Court and Community–Based Programs

In Baltimore, Maryland *Strike II* was developed as a court based program linking juvenile justice with health care. Its "clients" were court adjudicated first-time offenders (secondary prevention) for violent crimes, assault, robbery, arson, and breaking and entering. Noninstitutionalized probationers were eligible for the program, which was a probation requirement. This multidiscipline program employed paralegal staff, counselors, social workers, and psychiatrists. The juvenile probationers were involved in five programs: recreation, education, job readiness, and ongoing counseling and medical care as needed. These services were in *addition* to traditional probation supervision.

The recidivism rates for Strike II clients were only 7 percent compared to 35 percent statewide and 65 percent for those leaving corrections institutions. The basic cost (excluding medical and job readiness services) was $100 per client.[59] The Strike II program dealt in large part with violent juveniles with a physical health/mental health, educational, employment, juvenile justice program with resulting impressive results. Although gang members were not mentioned specifically, it would appear that with a reduction in recidivism, i.e., becoming less violent, these perpetrators would have also been at reduced risk for becoming a violence/homicide victim.

Another community based program aimed specifically at gangs was called *House of Umoja*, developed in Philadelphia in 1969. Initiated by two inner-city black parents whose son had joined a gang, fellow gang members were invited to live with the family following the model of an extended African family. In response to increased gang related homicides in 1974 and 1975, the House of Umoja spearheaded a successful campaign to reduce gang violence by obtaining peace pledges from eighty youth gangs. From this experience evolved a community agency called Crisis Intervention Network that worked toward reducing gang violence through communication with concerned parties and organizational efforts.[60] This approach later was called the "Philadelphia Plan."

In 1978 the state California Youth Authority reported its findings concerning its *Gang Violence Reduction Project* in East Los Angeles. The project's basic strategy was to: (1) promote peace among gangs through negotiation and (2) provide positive activities for gang members. Directors maintain they reduced gang homicides in East Los Angeles 55 percent; from eleven homicides in seven months one year, down to five homicides during a similar seven-month period the following year. The project researchers admitted that "any judgment that a relationship exists between the changes in a gang related homicide and violent incident statistics and the activities of the Gang Violence Reduction Project must be based on inference."[61]

Another community based, peace treaty program aimed at high-risk gang youth patterned after the "Philadelphia Plan" is the *Community Youth Gang Services Corporation* in Los Angeles. "CYGS" counselors in fourteen street teams were able to convince forty-four of 200 gangs they worked with to come to the table to develop a "peace treaty." During the period the peace agreement was in effect, from Thanksgiving of 1986 through the New Year's holidays of 1987, there was only *one* act of violence among the forty-four gangs. The "peace treaties" model can "buy time" for all concerned, but if society does not respond with the needed resources (jobs, training, physical health-mental health services, education), peace treaties are very difficult to maintain. Obviously, *all* the above approaches are needed.

Continuing efforts have to be made in further refining homicide prevention models in order for them to correspond more closely with the specific type of homicide one wishes to prevent. There are different types of homicide that vary according to circumstances. Robbery, spousal, and gang homicide are all different and require different prevention strategies. If, for example, Asians are at extremely high risk for being robbed and murdered at 2 A.M. in "Uptown, U.S.A.," through a community education effort, Asians would be informed about the high homicide risk in visiting "Uptown" at 2 A.M. Adhering to the warning could immediately reduce the number of Asian homicide victims.

In addition to attempting to get a "close fit" between the prevention model and the specific type of homicide, it is equally important that the high-risk person be clearly identified in order to maximize the impact of the prevention model. In the educational and community based violence prevention models previously discussed, the focus of intervention appeared to be more on the perpetrator or the "pre-perpetrator" (the person showing early behavioral signs indicating he or she *might* become a perpetrator) who was at high risk for committing a violent act. In theory all potential victims in an *unspecified* population are spared victimization when the perpetrator ceases to be violent. Furthermore, there did not seem to be specific prevention programmatic strategies focusing on the violence *victim* or the person most likely to become a victim. What seems to be needed is a guideline or framework that assists in the identification of high-risk gang members.

When California is used as an example, Table 23–1 represents a "general to specific" profile framework for identifying and "zeroing in" on the high-risk gang members who will be the target population for homicide prevention.

For our purposes, we will attempt to develop a hospital and community-based youth gang psychosocial homicide prevention model in which social workers play a key intervention role. The focus of this prevention model will be on the gang member who actually becomes a violence or homicide victim of a gang and goes or is taken to the hospital. In Table 23–1 these victims would be gang members found in items 2b and 2c. In this respect the prevention model is largely tertiary in nature. However, it becomes a primary prevention model when intervention strategies are aimed at younger children and latency age siblings of the victim who are not yet gang members. By preventing children in high-risk families from becoming future gang members, it may significantly reduce the likelihood of the children being killed since gang members are sixty times more likely to be killed than persons in the general population (600/100,000 versus 10/100,000).

TABLE 23-1 Area and Demographic Characteristics Related to Homicide Risk

I. United States	(one of the most violent countries in the world, ranked #5 out of 41 countries)[62]
II. California	(along with Southern states, ranks among the most violent states)[63]
III. Los Angeles	(among the more violent cities in the United States)[64]
IV. Inner City (L.A.)	(the poorest areas, often the scene of most violent crime)
A. Minority Groups	(overrepresented among the disadvantaged and poor, and those residing in the inner city)
1. Profile of Perpetrators and Victims	
a. Males	(4 to 5 times more likely than females to be killed)
b. Age	(15 to 25 age category at highest risk)
c. Substance Abuse	(found in 50 percent to 66 percent of cases)
d. Low Education	(50 percent school drop-out rate not uncommon)
e. Low Income	(high unemployment, many living in poverty)
2. Gangs	(quite prevalent in inner city and a product of social disorganization, classism, and racism)[65]
a. Minor Assaults	(gang members are at high risk for being assaulted)
b. Aggravated Assaults	(gang members are at high risk for being victims of aggravated assault; usually occurs 20 to 35 times more often than homicide)
c. Homicide	(gang members are at high risk for becoming a homicide victim, rate being 600 per 100,000 in the 50,000 gang member population)[66]

Health professionals in community clinics and hospitals are actually in the "trenches" dealing with thousands of violence and homicide casualties related to gang violence. These professionals are usually the first to touch these bodies and in medical settings, they function in a tertiary prevention role, literally trying to control the bleeding and save lives. Wounded gang victims of gang violence are in reality a "captive audience," which creates an excellent intervention opportunity for secondary prevention.

By the physician, social worker, nurse, or other health practitioners on the hospital emergency room team inquiring about *how* the victim was injured, which may also be confirmed by police, family members, or interested parties, professionals could ascertain if the violence incident was "gang related." Through staff in-service training concerning gangs and their culture, health staff would be able to determine whether or not the victim was a gang member. Specifically, gang dress codes, mannerisms, graffiti, language, tattoos, and other gang symbols could help establish or rule out the gang identity of the victim. Police, family members, peers, and/or witnesses could also be good sources for gang identity confirmation.

If the injuries were caused by gang members and the victim is a gang member, a designated health team member (the social worker) would be responsible for referring the matter to the hospital's "SCAN Team." "SCAN" Team refers to *Suspected Child Abuse* and *Neglect* or in some hospitals, it refers to *Supporting Child Adult Network*.[67] SCAN Teams, which are found in many hospitals, are composed of multidisciplinary health staff in which at least one member is a social worker. SCAN Teams were originally developed to investigate suspected child sexual or physical abuse or neglect cases coming to the team's attention in medical settings. In cases of suspected child abuse and for the protection of the child, SCAN Teams are required to take immediate action by involving law enforcement and the child's welfare department.

Our gang homicide prevention model would require that gang violence victims also become a SCAN Team intervention priority. However, one additional social worker on the SCAN Team would be a gang "specialist" and would have primary treatment coordinating responsibility with the gang victim, his or her family, and the community.

Although not intended the emergency room provides access to a high-risk population (victims and families) that often is too embarrassed, frightened, or reluctant to seek assistance from traditional social work agencies that make the anonymity of a large, busy, impersonal hospital less threatening.[68] Additionally, medical crises may make some persons psychologically vulnerable, hence, more amenable to change during the crisis period.

In working with gang members who have been seriously injured as the result of gang assault, the author has found that often this is when their psychological defenses are down as they are suffering adjustment disorder or post-traumatic stress disorder symptoms (PTSD). In the acute stage of PTSD symptoms, victims may have recurrent, intrusive distressing recollections of the event including nightmares, flashbacks, intense stress at exposure to events resembling the traumatic event, persistent avoidance of stimuli associated with the event, sleeping problems, hypervigilance, anxiety, and fear. They are sometimes reluctant to leave the home and even become fearful of their own friends in gang "uniform."

During this acute stage, which may last about six months, they are quite motivated to abandon "gang banging" (gang fighting). If the social worker is not the primary therapist, arrangements should be made for the youngster to receive prompt treatment for PTSD while hospitalized or not, as untreated PTSD may become chronic and last for years. It is at this point that the social worker can also obtain needed employment, educational, recreational, or training resources for the vulnerable gang member. The parents may also be emotionally vulnerable having just gone through an experience in which they almost lost their son. They may be more willing to accept services for themselves if needed, and/or for younger siblings who might be showing some early behavioral signs of problems (deteriorating school performance, truancy, aggressiveness). Helping the family and young siblings is a primary prevention role as these efforts may result in preventing future gang members (perpetrators or victims) from developing in this family-at-risk.

There may also be situations in which the wounded gang member arrives deceased at the hospital or dies during or after surgery. This case would still be referred to the SCAN Team social worker for service. The focus of help would be—with the family's permission—in helping the parents and children deal with grief and other assistance they made need in burying their loved one. If there are adolescent gang members in the family, they may be quite angry and want to retaliate and get "even" for their brother's or sister's death. If not already involved, the social worker would call upon community gang group agencies to assist in reducing further conflict. If there are younger

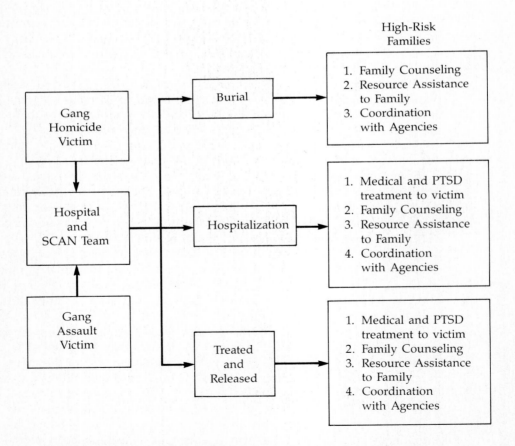

Figure 23–1 Gang Homicide Psychosocial Prevention Model

siblings in the family, an assessment would be made of their needs and efforts made to mobilize resources to meet these needs. These intervention strategies would have the objective of preventing future homicides in a high-risk family.

The preceding gang homicide prevention model operating from a medical-based agency, is presented to illustrate how social work may be able to have intervention impact on a very serious problem shortening the life of many poor, inner-city youths. Other models can be developed. Figure 23–1 demonstrates the various intervention strategies.

SOCIAL WORK IN INDUSTRY: PREVENTION IMPLICATIONS

It is ironic that as President Reagan's fiscal policies drove unemployment to 9.4 percent in April 1982, the highest since the 9.9 percent recorded in 1941, social workers began to find employment in business and industry.[69] The provision of social services in the business and industrial setting is a new practice arena for social work. This new practice turf is boundless considering the fact that there are at least 100 million workers in the United States. When family members are included, workers constitute a massive target population. Business and industry organizations could hire *every* graduating social worker and hardly dent their employee rolls.[70]

A brief look at the history of social work's involvement with industry shows social worker Jane Addams, founder of Hull House, helping clothing workers in a strike in 1910 against Hart, Schaffner and Marx in Chicago. During the 1930s some social workers, as union members, were active supporters of John L. Lewis' Congress of Industrial Organizations (CIO). Three social workers even managed to provide social services in the union halls of the National Maritime Union in New York. In the 1940s during the Second World War, federal funds made it possible to expand the number of social workers in industry. Large numbers of women and minorities were being hired, and federal contracts provided services for these inexperienced workers. Following the war, however, there was a federal cutback in these services, since the primary interest was in the rehabilitation of the psychiatrically disabled veteran. Although there were a few surviving social work practitioners of industrial social work after the 1940s, it was not until the 1960s and 1970s that the profession and the schools of social work began to take a more serious look at industry and business as an area of social work practice.[71]

The early 1960s saw the development of the Industrial Social Welfare Center at Columbia University's School of Social Work, which provided field placement opportunities for students in union settings. Industrial social work student placements were also offered at Boston College, Wayne State, and Hunter College School of Social Work in the late 1960s. In 1976 the Council on Social Work Education and the NASW introduced a nationwide project to examine business and industry as a potential area of social work practice intervention. Part of this effort resulted in the 1979 publication of *Labor and*

Industrial Settings: Sites for Social Work Practice, by the Council on Social Work Education.[72] Between 1976 and 1979 social work schools having a business/ industry social work practice concentration grew from four to fourteen.[73] These programs, both in schools and industry, are expanding rapidly and are providing more careers for social workers in the world of business.

Employee benefit programs fall into three areas: (1) extra pay for time worked (overtime, and work on holidays); (2) pay for time not worked (sick leave, vacations, and jury duty); and (3) payments for health, security, and welfare. Social work services provided to business and industry are within the framework of the third category.[74] There are five ways in which social services may be sponsored in industry:

1. Sponsorship by management in companies with or without a union.

2. Sponsorship by the union.

3. Sponsorship by both management and labor, with management employing social workers, and dual monitoring responsibility by management and labor.

4. Private consultantship by social worker under contract to union or management to provide services to workers and/or the organization.

5. Sponsorship by a community mental health center or family service agency having a specific contractual arrangement with the company.[75]

Social work intervention in the industrial setting may be on a micro and macro level. Micro level practice finds the social worker providing treatment to the client, his or her family, employer, union representative, and coworkers. The focus is helping employees with problems related to work, self, and others. Work-related problems may include those concerned with job performance, job dissatisfaction, absenteeism, and conflict with the supervisor or coworkers. Problems of self may relate to anxiety, depression, phobia, mental disturbance, and alcohol and drug abuse. Problems related to others may involve marital, parent–child, or family conflict.[76]

Macro level social work practice in business and industry involves organizational intervention. Here the social worker provides individual and group consultation to supervisors and managers at all levels regarding understanding human behavior. The focus is on the organization. For example worker dissatisfaction may be the result of the way work activities are organized. Intervention, therefore, might take the form of proposing a new job design to replace boring, tedious, assembly line work. One of the major goals of macro level intervention is to help management and employees achieve a common understanding, make decisions together, share and enjoy the fruits of their labor, and feel they have a common destiny.[77] At present the majority of social workers in business and industry are involved in micro level intervention activities. These practitioners report that casework is the most useful component in industrial social work.[78]

Considering the expansion of industrial social work courses in schools of social work and the increasing number of social work practitioners entering the business and industrial arena, one can definitely state that industrial social work will continue to be a trend for social work through the 1980s and 1990s. Giving impetus to this trend is the taxpayer revolt legislation, such as California's Proposition 13, in various states, Reagan's new federalism policies, and the related economic recession that is causing some social workers to lose their employment. Social workers, therefore, will be forced to seek new opportunities and territories of practice, such as the business and industry field.

This new opportunity and practice territory, however, presents several dilemmas for social work. Those favoring this new field for social work may argue that the working class is a population largely neglected by social services and that by providing services on the work site the profession begins to meet this need. Wherever there are people there is potential need.

Others may argue that the values of social work and industry are in conflict. Rosalie Bakalinsky states that what binds the social work profession:

> is a humanistic philosophy that stresses the inherent dignity and worth of people. Concern for the well-being of people, individually and collectively, historically has been social work's trademark. Industry, on the other hand, places its primary value on production and profits. Its people are viewed as a commodity having only instrumental value for the industry's central purpose. Detrimental conditions within industry are rarely considered in terms of the human cost involved. Or, more accurately, stressful and hazardous conditions may be considered, but their eradication is determined by financial rather than human cost.[79]

Social workers in business and industry inevitably face the risk of cooperation by rich and powerful representatives of the world of work. On the other hand Paul Kurzman and Sheila Akabas maintain the converse is equally likely. These authors believe social work in industry "holds promise of influencing not only the quality of work life, but the quality of life for workers and for *all* Americans."[80] In *theory*, this may be true and parallels the "trickle-down" economic theory; that is, if government provides business with sufficient economic advantages, business will flourish, profit, expand, hire more people, and generally contribute more to the economic well-being of the community and nation. So far the "trickle-down" economic theory apparently has not worked considering the duration of poverty and the massive number of poor people in the nation. In view of the current small number of social workers in industry, and even if they could be increased a thousandfold, it would appear to be quite a task for them to influence the quality of life for *all* people in the United States.

Another issue for social work as it enters the field of business and industry is the question of whether it wishes to deploy its critical available work force to a more affluent target population. In other words the new clients of industry social workers will have, according to new census data, a median annual income of approximately $24,000 compared to approximately $7,000 for the poor. Services therefore, would be directed at the *middle class* rather than the lower class. Some social workers entering private practice have attempted to deal with this dilemma by working part-time in a public agency with low socioeconomic clients and part-time with middle-class clients. Some, on the other hand, have chosen to have a full-time private practice and have accepted some low-fee clients. Social work practitioners in business and industry will not have this much flexibility available to them if they are employed full-time in an industrial setting. Perhaps a compromise is that social workers not enter the business and industry arena directly but provide services through existing resources such as family service agencies, community mental health centers, and private practitioners. These value dilemmas provide a challenge for the social work profession; given the new federalism policies that are resulting in a reduction of social work jobs, industry may offer social workers a temporary employment opportunity. Social work will survive; and when government once again makes a more vigorous commitment to help the poor, social workers will be ready to redirect their energies to this population.

In the meantime, industry offers social work a unique opportunity for primary, secondary, and tertiary prevention. Early detection and prompt treatment of employee problems as a secondary intervention measure may prevent some workers from becoming more serious casualties, losing their jobs, and ending up on the welfare rolls. Those who have developed serious problems such as chronic or acute substance addiction, for example, will require tertiary prevention intervention, that is, medical and psychosocial rehabilitation at a clinic or hospital facility. Primary prevention strategies in the workplace may take several forms. Educational programs and workshops for at-risk employees of the organization concerning topics such as learning about and coping with job-related stress, family and marital stress, substance abuse, and anxiety and depression, may be of benefit to many. If there are going to be large-scale layoffs, social workers could develop plans with management for new job training and placement at other companies as a means of softening the devastating emotional impact upon employees and families often brought on by abrupt termination.

ADVOCACY, EMPOWERMENT, AND PREVENTION

Webster's Third New International Dictionary defines the noun *advocate* as "one that pleads the case of another" or "one that argues for, defends, maintains, or recommends a cause or a proposal." Scott Briar defines the social worker advocate as one who is:

> his clients' supporter, his advisor, his champion, and if need be, his representative in his dealings with the court, the police, the social agency, and other organizations that affect his well-being.[81]

On the other hand, George Brager sees the social worker advocate as one who:

> identifies with the plight of the disadvantaged. He sees at his primary responsibility the tough-minded and partisan representation of their interests, and this supersedes his fealty to others. This role inevitably requires that the practitioner function as a policitcal tactician.[82]

Briar's concept represents advocacy on behalf of an *individual*, whereas Brager's concept represents advocacy on behalf of a group or *class* of people; the latter concept is similar to the role social workers would perform in *class action social work*, discussed later in this chapter.

Neil Gilbert and Harry Specht report that advocacy as a social work role (social change versus psychological change) has presented a dilemma for generations of social workers. Each generation redefines this issue in its own terms. For example in 1909 Mary Richmond defined the issue in terms of the "wholesale" versus the "retail" method of social reform. Porter R. Lee approached it in 1929 as "cause" versus "function," and in 1949 Kenneth Pray perceived it as "workmanship" versus "statesmanship." In 1962 Clarke A. Chambers conceptualized the matter in terms of "prophets" versus "priests," and in 1963 William Schwartz analyzed this conflict in terms of providing a service as opposed to participating in a movement.[83] In 1977 in a special issue of the journal *Social Work* on conceptual frameworks for practice, Armando Morales perceived the issue differently. He saw social workers as persons armed with appropriate knowledge and skills that enabled them to do clinical work in poor communities as well as to intervene via social action and advocacy in larger community systems.[84] Chapter 10 provides a detailed case illustration as to how such intervention can be accomplished.

The NASW has taken a clear position regarding the social worker as advocate. Its Ad Hoc Committee on Advocacy voiced the profession's commitment to advocacy:

> The obligation of social workers to become advocate flows directly from the social worker's Code of Ethics. Therefore, why should it be difficult for a profession that is "based on humanitarian democratic ideals" and "dedicated to service for the welfare of mankind" to act on behalf of those whose human rights are in jeopardy.[85]

The committee highlighted three dilemmas concerning the advocacy role in social work. First, in promoting a particular client's interests, the social worker may be injuring other aggrieved persons with an equally just claim. Neil Gilbert and Harry Specht suggest that a hard and fast rule should be followed, which is encompassed in the concept *primum non nocere*, a medical aphorism meaning "first of all, do no harm."[86] This dictum, no doubt, would apply to not harming other clients. But effective advocacy *is* going to cause harm to someone when any redistribution of power or resources is accomplished.

Because of *Serrano* versus *Priest*, for example, poor children will ultimately benefit by increased educational resources that result from a more equitable tax structure, and affluent children will be "hurt" as their privileges are eroded. This will be discussed in *class action social work*.

The second dilemma mentioned by the committee involves conflict between two types of advocacy—on behalf of client or class. Because there are no hard-and-fast rules to govern these situations, social work advocates will have to be guided by ethical commitments and professional judgment.

The third dilemma presented by the committee concerns the choice between direct intercession by the worker and mobilization of clients on their own behalf.[87] Some would argue that it is a disservice to clients when social workers participate in advocacy on the clients' behalf because it only makes them more dependent. There are cases for which this argument might be true, but advocacy on behalf of some powerless special populations, such as dependent children or mentally ill jail inmates, might be appropriate. Where it is not appropriate, however, social workers can help clients help themselves through the application of concepts such as *empowerment*.

A new trend evolving in social work pertains to the concept of client empowerment. Barbara Solomon defines *empowerment* as:

> a process whereby persons who belong to a stigmatized social category throughout their lives can be assisted to develop and increase skills in the exercise of interpersonal influence and the performance of valued social roles. Power is an interpersonal phenomenon; if it is not interpersonal it probably should be defined as "strength." However, the two concepts—power and strength—are so tightly interrelated that they are often used interchangeably.[88]

According to Solomon, empowerment as a social work practice goal in working with black clients or other persons living in oppressed communities implies the client's perception of his or her intrinsic and extrinsic value and the client's motivation to use every personal resource and skill, as well as those of any other person that can be commanded, in the effort to achieve self-determined goals. Solomon attempts to develop a conviction in the client that there are many pathways to goal attainment and that failure is always possible, but the more effort one makes the more probable success must be.[89]

Solomon suggests three practitioner roles that hold promise for reducing a client's sense of powerlessness and leading to empowerment: the resource consultant role, the sensitizer role, and the teacher/trainer role. The resource consultant role finds the practitioner linking clients with resources in a manner that enhances the clients' self-esteem and problem-solving capacities. Anne Minahan and Allen Pincus identify five specific practitioner tasks for accomplishing this.[90] In the sensitizer role the practitioner incorporates all the role behaviors that are designed to assist the client gain the self-knowledge necessary for him or her to solve the presenting problem or problems. The teacher/trainer role, according to Solomon's conceptualization, finds the practitioner as manager of a learning process in which the principal aim is the completion of certain tasks or the resolution of problems related to social living.[91]

A *voluntary* relationship seems to be implied in Solomon's conceptualization when she speaks of the practitioner assisting the client gain self-knowledge to solve a problem or problems. The practitioner does not appear to be working from a social control perspective in which the presenting problem is defined by someone other than the client. Such "helping" transactions might make *involuntary* clients feel powerless.

Advocacy and empowerment, according to Brian O'Connell, are related from the standpoint that through effective advocacy, power is secured and used. He adds that it is also natural that the most important aspect of effective advocacy is now being described as empowerment.[92] The movement toward empowerment—to use and transfer power so that the groups in need of services gain their own political and economic power that will enable them to represent themselves effectively—in the final analysis is most important to society, since society benefits when *all* its members can contribute to the best of their ability.

In prevention theory a social worker helping *clients* through advocacy and empowerment concepts would seem to be using a secondary prevention strategy since the target population is already identified as persons with problems. The social worker has a significant role and performs specific key tasks in advocacy and empowerment efforts with the client. In applying advocacy and empowerment concepts toward primary prevention goals, however, the social worker's role is not central as it is in working with client populations. Rather, the role is multiple since the at-risk target population is comprised largely of non-clients or "normal" persons. The focus must be on strengths foremost in the target population as opposed to problems, weaknesses, and inadequacies.[93] One of the essential tasks of the social worker in working with an at-risk population toward primary prevention will be to network. *Network* may be defined as the process of developing multiple interconnections and chain reactions among support systems.[94] There are four levels of networking approaches: (1) personal networking, (2) networking for mutual aid and self-help, (3) human service organization networking, and (4) networking within communities for community empowerment.[95] The last approach will be highlighted as it has primary prevention goals.

The community empowerment model and process has several goals. The first is to create community awareness of neighborhood strengths and needs, with emphasis placed on strengths as perceived by the target population. The second goal is to strengthen neighborhood helping networks by developing linkages among natural helpers in the community, among helpers and neighborhood leaders, and among neighborhood residents themselves. A third goal is to strengthen the professional helping networks by organizing a professional advisory committee in the target population area to advise this community empowerment-directed process. Fourth, linkages are formed between the lay and professional helping networks. The fifth goal is to form linkages between the lay and professional helping networks and the macro system. In a mental health primary prevention context, mental health professionals would help the target population put together a data base of information regarding federal, state, county, and local mental health and human services plans, or the macro system. The sixth and final goal would be to institutionalize the networking process, thereby creating a new mental health constituency, integrated into but not assimilated or taken over by the larger, bureaucratic human services system. Through such a networking process leading to community empowerment and an improvement in the quality of life, those problem areas that the professional system traditionally ends by treating (secondary and tertiary prevention) rather than preventing, the at-risk population may be spared unncessary pain, stress, and anguish.[96]

CLASS ACTION SOCIAL WORK AND PREVENTION

The enormous mission of social work is to enhance the quality of life for all persons. Some of the injustices and obstacles that damage the quality of life are poverty, racism, sexism, and drug abuse; there are many more.[97] Social work's impact on these problems is sometimes limited by the clinical model, by inappropriate interventive strategies, or by the fact that it becomes too time-consuming and inefficient to try to help people on a case-by-base basis. On other occasions a referred client with a "problem" may not really have a problem. The problem may be in the referring system.

For example a school may refer a problem student to the social worker to help him or her adjust to the requirements of the school system. The school system, however, may have serious defects that are the primary cause of the student's problem. The goal of the social worker should then be to help tailor the school system to meet the educational needs of the student. The student in this situation may represent a *class* of people—other students in a similar predicament. Rather than the social worker working individually with each student to document the deficiencies in the school system; one student can represent all students in a *class action* suit to improve conditions in the school. Class action is a legal concept that has promising implications for social work. Closer working relationships will have to be cultivated with the legal profession to enable lawyers to conceptualize broad social work concerns and to translate these concerns into legal class action suits. Such an approach can be called *class action social work*. Victories in the courts could provide relief for thousands of poor people.

The precedent of an organized body of social workers and lawyers—with the potential for broader collaborative impact through class action suits on behalf of the poor—exists. Recognition of matters of natural interconnection and mutual interest between lawyers and social workers led in 1962 to the creation of the National Conference of Lawyers and Social Workers, a joint committee composed of sixteen members, eight appointed from each parent organization. The Conference met twice a year.[98] In 1967 the Conference developed goals for the professions to work toward cooperatively in serving the needy. Some of these goals included:

1. Identification of needs requiring their individual or joint professional competencies.

2. Resolution of situations that involve both social and legal problems—including recognizing and reconciling respective professional orientations, especially with regard to the adversary role.

3. The development of machinery and procedures for effective referral relationships.[99]

The nine papers in *Law and Social Work*, one of the Conference's publications, envisioned a rather narrow role for social workers working with lawyers, following the traditional clinical, case-by-case model. For example, social workers defined their function as providing "expertise in psychosocial diagnosis including evaluation of the *individual's* potential for social functioning."[100] The collaborative potential of class action suits to help the poor on a broad scale is not mentioned in this 1973 document. Let it again be emphasized that the central theme of the Conference—"lawyers and social workers, as close collaborators in situations involving both social and legal problems, should seek to utilize to the full the resources of each profession to help the poor"—provides the foundation for social work to have a greater impact on social reform.

In some states social workers have already made pioneering efforts to enter the legal arena. In California, for example, the Greater California Chapter of the NASW presented an award to John Serrano, a social worker, for his actions as a concerned citizen in the widely publicized *Serrano* versus *Priest* case, which argued that the quality of a child's education should not be dependent on the wealth of a school district.[101] The California Supreme Court, in this class action suit filed by the Western Center on Law and Poverty, Inc., ruled six to one that the California public educational finance scheme, which relies heavily upon local property taxes, violated the equal protection clause of the Fourteenth Amendment to the U.S. Constitution. The court held that the financing system invidiously discriminated against the poor. The court also asserted that the right to a public education was a fundamental interest that could not be dependent on wealth, and it therefore applied the strict equal protection standard. Finding no compelling state interest advanced by the discriminatory system, the court held the scheme unconstitutional.[102]

The significance of the *Serrano* versus *Priest* decision transcends California boundaries because all states except Hawaii use similar educational finance systems. Wealthier districts are favored to the detriment of poorer school districts. A direct relationship exists between the number of dollars spent per child and the quality of education available to that child. In *Serrano* versus *Priest* it was discovered that poor communities were paying two to three times as much school tax per $100 of assessed valuation as were wealthy com-

munities, yet wealthy communities received two to three times as many educational dollars per child from the state as did the poorer communities.[103]

In *Serrano* versus *Priest* the court's policy considerations focused on the
pervasive influence of education on individual development and capacity
within modern society and on education's essential role in the maintenance
of free enterprise democracy. It was considered that the combination of these
factors sufficiently distinguished education from other governmental services
for it to merit recognition as a fundamental interest.[104] No court had previously placed education within the framework of interests meriting strict equal
protection scrutiny, and this decision represents the first time that any type
of governmental service has been held to involve fundamental interests.[105]

Considering the *Serrano* versus *Priest* precedent, might not the areas of
welfare, health, and mental health services also represent a set of circumstances as unique and compelling as education? A right to public education
may not be maximally enjoyed if the child is poorly housed, impoverished,
malnourished, and in need of physical and mental health care. *Serrano* versus
Priest, as a social work class action concept has the potential to be the cutting
edge of social reform in a wide range of governmental services, including
several in which social workers already have knowledge and experience. In
view of the regressive social and economic policies of the Reagan administration, which even threaten legal services for the poor from time to time,
the opportunity for class action collaboration between law and social work
as a significant tool of intervention is somewhat constrained. However, the
class action social work concept still holds promise and its application is presently being tested by one of the authors in the courts as a mental health
primary prevention activity.

It was seen that *class action* is a legal procedural device for resolving issues
in court affecting many people. Those persons actually before the court represent the unnamed members of the class in a single proceeding in equity,
thereby avoiding multiple case by case actions. *Class action social work* is a
social work/legal profession collaborative litigation activity involving social
work concerns, with the goal of obtaining a favorable court ruling that will
benefit the social welfare of a group of socioeconomically disadvantaged persons. Class action social work in a mental health primary prevention context
finds social workers and attorneys pursuing a court ruling that will have a
positive psychosocial impact upon a disadvantaged class of people who, *prior
to the ruling*, were at risk in developing psychological or psychiatric disorders
or symptoms. Among the requirements needed to accomplish the primary
prevention goals are—to borrow from public health terminology—a small
sample of "infected" organisms, an identification of the suspected toxic agent,
and a laboratory procedural test to show whether or not the toxic agent caused
the infection in the organism. Translating this into class action mental health
primary prevention terms in an actual case (*Nicacio* versus *United States INS*),
the "infected organisms" were thirteen Hispanic plaintiffs (the injured, com-
plaining parties) who were exhibiting psychiatric symptoms allegedly
caused by stressful interrogations conducted by patrol officers of the United

States Immigration and Naturalization Service (INS). The courtroom becomes the laboratory in which the suspected toxic evidence (behavior of the INS officers) is analyzed as to its potential harm. If found to be harmful, the court can issue an order terminating the toxic behavior of the INS, which then prevents psychosocial harm (psychiatric symptoms) in a specific at-risk population (millions of Hispanics residing in the Southwestern states or the State of Washington area, depending upon court boundary definitions).

In *Nicacio* versus *United States INS*, the Hispanic plaintiffs brought suit contending that: (1) the border patrol agents of the INS were conducting roving motor vehicle stops in search of "illegal aliens" on the roadways of the State of Washington that were in violation of Fourth Amendment rights to be free from unreasonable searches and seizures, (2) that the actions of INS officials were unlawful, and (3) that the plaintiffs were entitled to money damages for humiliation, embarrassment, and mental anguish suffered as a result of a violation of their Fourth Amendment rights.[106] The facts of the case were that: (1) all plaintiffs were of Mexican descent and were either born in the United States, U.S. citizens or permanent resident aliens who resided in the Yakima Valley area of the State of Washington; (2) the plaintiff class was defined by the court as "all persons of Mexican, Latin, or Hispanic appearance who have been, are, or will be traveling by motor vehicle on the highways of the State of Washington"; (3) at the time the litigation was initiated, INS agents were regularly conducting roving patrol motor vehicle stops, detentions, and interrogations in the Yakima Valley area; (4) many of the stops were based solely on Hispanic appearance, or the agents' subjective feelings or intuition, or the suspected "illegal aliens' " innocuous behavior or appearance, traits; and (5) persons stopped were required in most cases to provide identification or documentation of legal presence in the United States.[107]

In attempting to document the amount of humiliation, embarrassment, and mental anguish suffered by the plaintiffs as a result of their contact with INS officers, plaintiffs' attorneys contacted one of the authors as an expert witness to conduct a mental health evaluation of all the plaintiffs. Having been sworn in by the court and qualified and accepted as an expert witness, the author rendered a DSM III diagnosis as to each plaintiff. The findings were that: (1) not one of the thirteen plaintiffs had ever been hospitalized or treated on an outpatient basis for a mental health problem, (2) eleven of the plaintiffs suffered adjustment disorder symptoms, either with depressed mood, anxious mood, or with mixed emotional features, (3) one plaintiff suffered acute post traumatic stress disorder symptoms, and (4) one plaintiff was symptom free.

The findings of the court were that: (1) the INS border patrol practices were unlawful, (2) plaintiffs and class action members were entitled to a declaratory judgment covering future conduct of INS officers in stopping vehicles upon public highways, and (3) plaintiffs were *not* entitled to recover money damages for their suffering since plaintiffs were unable to specifically identify the officers.[108] The favorable court ruling affected *all* persons of Mexican,

Latin, or Hispanic appearance residing only in the State of Washington rather than in the Southwestern states as had originally been requested by plaintiffs' attorneys. Even so, the court order stopped the noxious activities of the INS directed at Hispanics in the State of Washington. *All* Hispanics in the State of Washington, therefore, will be spared INS-provoked psychiatric symptoms in the future. This case shows the growing potential of class action social work with a mental health primary prevention goal and outcome.

CONCLUDING COMMENT

In comparison to law and medicine, social work is a relatively young profession that, despite various growing pains, has survived and continues to be a viable profession in U.S. society. Six issues and trends affecting social work in the late 1980s were discussed. These included: (1) the development and application of prevention concepts during a period of significant human need; (2) the prevention of treatment abuse while ensuring a person's right to treatment or nontreatment; (3) the role of social workers in gang violence and homicide prevention; (4) the growth of social workers in industry and their potential for mental health prevention work in industrial settings; (5) the further refinement of and application of people based helping concepts such as advocacy and client empowerment, and how these concepts can also result in primary prevention outcomes through networking; (6) the continued development of class action social work and its potential as a mental health primary prevention tool.

Although the forecast for social work was not stable in view of the fact that Reagan's economic policies were reducing government commitment to social welfare programs, there are a few factors indicating a continuing need for social workers now and in the near future. First of all, there will continue to be a growing public recognition that formal education in social work prepares people to provide higher quality human services; this recognition should encourage the demand for professional education as a prerequisite for employment. Evidence does show that standards are increasing given the fact that forty-five states are licensing social workers. Furthermore, although there was a beginning declassification of social workers in a few states, more specialized practice is being made available at the MSW level, such as gerontology and industrial social work, barring the encroachment of related disciplines into jobs emphasizing social work skills.

It is anticipated that social work will more fully incorporate the concept of a multiple-level profession over the next few years, whether or not social work's human resources increase. Appropriate knowledge, values, and skills will be brought to bear more effectively on the problems presented by clients. Along with greater acceptance in the field of a common base for social work practice has come the realization that a core of knowledge, values, and skills required for practice can be identified. The social worker with this core competence will be a generalist able to engage in practice ranging from individual services to social reform on the community level. It is anticipated that all professional social workers will have a generalist foundation upon which a methodological specialization can evolve through advanced education and practice experience. In this manner social work will incorporate both the generalist and the specialist approach to practice.

Escalating costs coupled with increasing need for human services and the fact that there will never be sufficient mental health practitioners to meet these needs requires the development and application of helping concepts such as primary prevention, designed to benefit large numbers of persons *before* they are symptomatic. Because social work is one of the helping professions most involved in interacting with and helping communities, it is anticipated that the profession will play an increasingly vital role in applying primary prevention concepts in the late 1980s and 1990s.

As social work emerges into multiple levels of practice, including both the generalist and the specialist approach, issues such as the right to treatment, the right to nontreatment, and efforts to prevent treatment abuse pose interesting challenges to the profession. Social workers are more effective with voluntary clients; most of the time workers fail with involuntary clients and even cause deterioration of the client's condition in slightly under 50 percent of cases. A social control framework restricts the therapeutic effectiveness of social work intervention. Involuntary clients, therefore, must have a right to nontreatment, and social workers must advocate this right. The only exceptions to this, however, involve persons such as infants, children, and gravely psychiatricially disabled persons or others who need help but are not capable of making treatment decisions for themselves.

Urban gang violence and homicide was highlighted in this chapter to indicate to the social work profession that from a historical practice experience standpoint, it is best suited among the health and mental health professions, to assume a leadership role in developing micro to macro intervention strategies to deal with this problem that is killing thousands of inner-city youths. Primary, secondary, and tertiary violence and homicide prevention programs were discussed and analyzed as to their impact on violence and gang homicide. A framework for identifying high-risk gang victims was developed to correspond to a suggested hospital based prevention program. Social workers are already employed in hospital emergency rooms and on SCAN teams and in these settings, there is potential for developing prevention models working with gang victims and their families. Special attention to meeting the needs of high-risk young siblings not yet gang members may prevent them from becoming future perpetrators or victims.

As social workers enter the business and industry arena to practice, they will be challenged by an interesting dilemma. Involuntary clients do not exist only in the public sector. When social workers are sponsored by industry, how will they help an employee who is referred by the supervisor and who feels he or she does not have a problem? The role of the social worker in these instances will be basically to communicate very clearly the rights and options available to the employee and the consequences of exercising their right to nontreatment. The final choice, therefore, is left with the employee. Treating employees away from the shop on a private practice basis may give both the client and the practitioner greater autonomy and reduce the resistance level among those referred for help by the employer.

More and more social workers are leaving the public welfare arena, going into private practice, and shifting their target population to the middle class. Lacking public agency bureaucratic constraints, they are potentially free to help the poor through social action activities such as writing proposals, conducting needs surveys, or building coalitions to apply pressure on government. Related strategies of advocacy and client empowerment may result in a transfer of power so that client groups in need of services gain and exercise their own economic and political might. A community empowerment model built with networking methods can, in the final result, produce a mental health primary prevention outcome.

Class action social work, which was first introduced into the literature in this text in 1977, continues to show promise as a macro level intervention strategy. *Serrano* versus *Priest*, a class action victory, established the precedent of a right to an equal education; it paved the road for the poor to fight for the right to health and welfare in order to maximize their new educational opportunity. Increasing an individual's opportunities through such assistance is in the best interests of the individual and society. The effectiveness of class action social work with a mental health primary prevention goal was demonstrated in *Nicacio* versus *United States INS*, in which a positive court ruling will have the effect of preventing literally thousands of at-risk Hispanics from developing psychiatric symptoms caused by discriminatory law enforcement practices. A rare opportunity for social work to help the poor on a broad scale seems very possible in light of *Serrano* and *Nicacio*. Collaboration with the legal profession should be vigorously pursued by social workers.

Social work has developed into a vital and important profession in the United States. The future of this profession and its success in helping people prevent or resolve problems in social functioning will depend on its ability to respond effectively to the challenges it faces today. The quality of that response can surely enhance the quality of life for many persons in the future.

SUGGESTED READINGS

Albee, George W., and Joffe, Justin M. *Primary Prevention of Psychopathology, Volume I: The Issues.* Hanover, New Hampshire: The University Press of New England, 1977.

Bailey, Roy, and Brake, Mike, eds. *Radical Social Work.* New York: Pantheon, 1975.

Barton II, Preston N., and Byrne, Bridget. "Social Work Services in a Legal Aid Setting." *Social Casework* 56 (April 1975): 226–234.

Beck, Dorothy Fahs. "Research Findings on the Outcome of Marital Counseling." *Social Casework* 56 (March 1975): 153–181.

Burris, Donald S., ed. *The Right to Treatment.* New York: Springer, 1969.

Cowger, Charles D., and Atherton, Charles R. "Social Control: A Rationale for Social Welfare." *Social Work* 19 (July 1974): 456–462.

Cox, Fred M., Erlich, John L., Rothman, Jack, and Tropman, John E. eds. *Tactics and Techniques of Community Practice*, 2nd ed. Itasca, Ill.: F.E. Peacock Publishers, 1984.

Fischer, Joel. "Is Casework Effective: A Review." *Social Work* 18 (January 1973): 5–20.

Fox, Jerry R. "Mission Impossible? Social Work Practice with Black Urban Youth Gangs." *Social Work*, January–February, 1985, Vol. 30, pp. 25–31.

Hopps, June Gary. "Violence—A Personal and Societal Challenge." *Social Work*, November–December, 1987, Vol. 32. No. 6, pp. 467–468.

Krisberg, Barry, and Schwartz, Ira. "Rethinking Juvenile Justice." *Crime and Delinquency* (July 1983): pp. 333–364.

Middleman, Ruth R., and Goldberg, Gale. "Social Work Practice with Groups." *Encyclopedia of Social Work*, 18th ed., Vol. II (Silver Spring, Md.: National Association of Social Workers, 1987), pp. 714–729.

Morales, Armando. "The Mexican American Gang Member: Evaluation and Treatment." In Rosina M. Becerra, Marvin Karno, and Javier Escobar, eds., *Mental Health and Hispanic Americans: Clinical Perspectives* (New York: Grune and Stratton, 1982).

National Association of Social Workers. "The Social Worker as Advocate: Champion of Social Victims." *Social Work* 14 (April 1969): 16–22.

National Association of Social Workers. *Law and Social Work*. Washington, D.C.: The Association, 1973.

Prigmore, Charles S., and Davis, Paul R. "Wyatt vs. Stickney." *Social Work* 18 (July 1973): 10–19.

Rein, Martin. "Social Work in Search of a Radical Profession." *Social Work* 15 (April 1970): 13–28.

Report of the Secretary's Task Force on Black and Minority Health, Vol. 5, U.S. Department of Health and Human Services, January 1986.

Sloane, Homer W. "Relationship of Law and Social Work." *Social Work* 12 (January 1967): 86–97.

Smith, Alexander B., and Berlin, Louis. "Self-Determination in Welfare and Corrections: Is There a Limit?" *Federal Probation* 38 (December 1974): 3–10.

Solomon, Barbara Bryant. *Black Empowerment: Social Work in Oppressed Communities*. New York: Columbia University Press, 1976.

Spergel, Irving A. "Violent Gangs in Chicago: In Search of Social Policy." *Social Service Review*, June, 1984, Vol. 58, No. 2, pp. 199–226.

Thrasher, Frederick M. *The Gang: A Study of 1313 Gangs in Chicago* (Chicago: The University of Chicago, 1963).

ENDNOTES

1. H. John Staulcup, "Primary Prevention," in Aaron Rosenblatt and Diana Waldfogel, eds., *Handbook of Clinical Social Work* (San Francisco: Jossey–Bass, 1983), p. 1059.
2. Ibid., p. 1060.
3. Ronald A. Feldman, Arlene R. Stiffman, Deborah A. Evans, and John G. Orme, "Prevention Research, Social Work and Mental Illness," *Social Work Research and Abstracts* 18 (Fall 1982): 2.
4. Edith Abbott, "The Social Caseworker and the Enforcement of Industrial Legislation," in *Proceedings of the National Conference on Social Work*, 1918 (Chicago: Rogers and Hall, 1919), p. 313.
5. K. A. Kendall, "Discussion," in *The Social Forum* (New York: Columbia University Press, 1969), p. 587.
6. Staulcup, pp. 1061–1062.
7. Kathy V. Nance, "Understanding and Overcoming Resistance to Primary Prevention," *Social Work Research and Abstracts* 18 (Fall 1982): 32–33.

8. Feldman, et al., p. 6.
9. Stephen E. Goldston, "Defining Primary Prevention," in George W. Albee and Justice M. Joffe, eds., *Primary Prevention of Psychopathology*, Volume I: The Issues (New England: The University Press, 1977), p. 20.
10. Ibid.
11. Ibid., p. 21.
12. Steven L. McMurtry, "Secondary Prevention of Child Maltreatment: a Review," *Social Work* 30 (January–February 1985): 43.
13. Juliua R. Ballew, "Role of Natural Helpers in Preventing Child Abuse," *Social Work* 30 (January–February 1985): 40.
14. Morton Birnbaum, "A Rationale for the Right," in Donald S. Burris, ed., *The Right to Treatment* (New York: Springer, 1969), p. 77.
15. As cited by Thomas S. Szasz, "The Right to Health," in *The Right to Treatment* p. 64.
16. Nicholas N. Kittrie, "Can the Right to Treatment Remedy the Ills of the Juvenile Process?" in *The Right to Treatment*, pp. 170–171.
17. Charles S. Prigmore and Paul R. Davis, "Wyatt vs. Stickney," *Social Work* 18 (July 1973): 17.
18. Ibid., p. 18.
19. Szasz, "The Right to Health," p. 66.
20. Ibid., p. 67.
21. Ibid., p. 69.
22. Davis McEntire and Joanne Haworth, "The Two Functions of Public Welfare: Income Maintenance and Social Services," *Social Work* 12 (January 1967): 23–24.
23. Charles D. Cowger and Charles R. Atherton, "Social Control: A Rationale for Social Welfare," *Social Work* 19 (July 1974): 457.
24. Henry Miller, "Value Dilemmas in Social Casework," *Social Work* 13 (January 1968): 29–30.
25. Ibid., p. 30.
26. Charles S. Prigmore, "Points and Viewpoints," *Social Work* 18 (November 1973): 99.
27. Alexander B. Smith and Louis Berlin, "Self-Determination in Welfare and Corrections: Is There a Limit?" *Federal Probation* 38 (December 1974): 5.
28. Ann Hartman, "But What Is Social Casework?" *Social Casework* 52 (July 1971): 416.
29. Joel Fischer, "Is Casework Effective? A Review," *Social Work* 18 (January 1973): 5.
30. Scott Briar, "The Current Crisis in Social Casework," in *Social Work Practice*, 1967 (New York: Columbia University Press, 1967), pp. 19–33, as cited by Fischer, "Is Casework Effective?"
31. Fischer, "Is Casework Effective?" pp. 13–14.
32. Ibid., p. 14.
33. Ibid., p. 18.
34. Dorothy Fahs Beck, "Research Findings on the Outcome of Marital Counseling," *Social Casework* 56 (March 1975): 167.
35. Ibid., p. 168 (Emphasis ours.)
36. Fischer, "Is Casework Effective?" pp. 14–16.
37. Iatrogenic is primarily a medical term denoting that a problem, condition, or disorder is induced, produced, or aggravated by the physician or healer—*iatro* (healer), *genic* (origin of).
38. *NASW News* 30, p. 8.
39. *NASW News* 30, p. 7.
40. *Los Angeles Times*, Westside, Part VIII, December 23, 1984, p. 6.
41. *United States Senate Committee on the Judiciary Ford Administration Stifles Juvenile Justice Policy* (Washington, D.C.: U.S. Government Printing Office, 1975), p. 2.

42. Barry Krisberg and Ira Schwartz, "Rethinking Juvenile Justice," *Crime and Delinquency* (July 1983): 340.
43. Ibid., p. 360–361.
44. Ron Schultz, "A New Prescription for Troubled Teens," *Los Angeles* Vol. 30, No. 1, January 1985, p. 159.
45. Ibid., p. 206.
46. Ibid., p. 205.
47. *Los Angeles Times* Part II, March 24, 1985, p. 2.
48. Ibid.
49. Carolyn Rebecca Block, "Lethal Violence in Chicago over Seventeen Years: Homicides Known to the Police, 1965–1981," Illinois Criminal Justice Information Authority, p. 69.
50. "Homicide in California, 1985," Department of Justice, Bureau of Criminal Statistics and Special Services, State of California, 1985, p. 17; "Fiscal Year 1985–86 Statistical Summary," Los Angeles County Sheriff's Department; Statistical Digest, 1986," Automated Information Division, Los Angeles Police Department.
51. N. Meredith, "The Murder Epidemic," *Science 84* December 1984, p. 42.
52. Report of the Secretary's Task Force on Black and Minority Health, Vol. 5, U.S. Department of Health and Human Services, January 1986, pp. 43–44.
53. Report of the Secretary, pp. 46–50.
54. Report of the Secretary, p. 50.
55. Police Foundation. Domestic Violence and the Police: Studies in Detroit and Kansas City. Washington, D.C., Police Foundation.
56. The Boston Youth Program, Boston City Hospital, 818 Harrison Ave., Boston, Massachusetts, cited in *Report of the Secretary's Task Force* pp. 235–236.
57. C. Cooper, "Peer Dynamics," Final Evaluation Report, 1979–1980, Nebraska State Commission on Drugs, Lincoln, Nebraska State Department of Health, Lincoln.
58. "Early Gang Intervention," Transfer of Knowledge Workshop, Department of the California Youth Authority, Office of Criminal Justice Planning, 1985, pp. 11–12. Also see Tony Ostos, "Alternatives to Gang Membership," (Unpublished paper, Paramount School District, Los Angeles County, California, October, 1987.)
59. "Strike II," Hopkins Adolescent Program, Johns Hopkins Hospital, Park Building, Baltimore, Maryland.
60. Fattah Falaka, "Call and Catalytic Response: The House of Umoja," in R.A. Mathias, P. De Muro, and R. S. Allinson, eds., *Violent Juvenile Offenders: An Anthology*. San Francisco National Council on Crime and Delinquency, 1984, pp. 231–237.
61. "Gang Violence Reduction Project Second Evaluation Report: October 1977–May 1978" Department of the California Youth Authority, November 1978, pp. i, iii.
62. Mark L. Rosenberg and James A. Mercy, "Homicide: Epidemiologic Analysis at the National Level," in *Bulletin of the New York Academy of Medicine* Vol. 62, No. 5, June, 1986, p. 382.
63. Mark L. Rosenberg, p. 390.
64. Harold M. Rose, "Can We Substantially Lower Homicide Risk in the Nation's Larger Black Communities?" in *Report of the Secretary's Task Force*, p. 191.
65. Irving A. Spergel, "Violent Gangs in Chicago: In Search of Social Policy," *Social Service Review*, Vol. 58, No. 2, June 1984, pp. 201–202.
66. Armando Morales, "Hispanic Gang Violence and Homicide." (Paper commissioned by the Research Conference on Violence and Homicide in Hispanic Communities, sponsored by the Office of Minority Health, Department of Health and Human Services, the National Institutes of Mental Health, and the U.S. Centers for Disease Control, University of California, Los Angeles, September 14–15, 1987, p. 13.)

67. T. Tatara, H. Morgan, and H. Portner, "SCAN: Providing Preventive Services in an Urban Setting," *Children Today*, November–December 1986, pp. 17–22.
68. Karil S. Klingbeil, "Interpersonal Violence: A Comprehensive Model in a Hospital Setting from Policy to Program," in *Report of the Secretary's Task Force*, p. 246.
69. *Los Angeles Times*, May 8, 1982, Part I, p. 1.
70. Paul A. Kurzman and Sheila H. Akabas, "Industrial Social Work as an Arena for Practice," *Social Work* 26 (January 1981): 52.
71. Lou Ann B. Jorgenson, "Social Services in Business and Industry," in Neil Gilbert and Harry Specht, eds., *Handbook of the Social Services*, (Englewood Cliffs, N.J.: Prentice-Hall, Inc., 1981), pp. 338–339.
72. Ibid., p. 340.
73. Ibid., p. 347.
74. Martha N. Ozawa, "Development of Social Services in Industry: Why and How?" *Social Work* 25 (November 1980): 464.
75. Copyright 1978, National Association of Social Workers, Inc. Reprinted with permission from "Industrial Social Work Movement Expanding; Practitioners Conference Planned for June," *NASW News* 23 (February 1978): 7.
76. Rosalie Bakalinsky, "People vs. Profits: Social Work in Industry," *Social Work* 25 (November 1980): 472.
77. Ozawa, "Development of Social Services," pp. 468–469.
78. Jorgenson, "Social Services in Business and Industry," p. 349.
79. Copyright 1980, National Association of Social Workers, Inc. Reprinted with permission, from *Social Work* 25 (November 1980): 474, excerpt.
80. Kurzman and Akabas, "Industrial Social Work," p. 58. (Emphasis ours.)
81. Briar, "The Current Crisis in Social Casework," p. 28.
82. George A. Brager, "Advocacy and Political Behavior," *Social Work* 13 (April 1968): 6.
83. Neil Gilbert and Harry Specht, "Advocacy and Professional Ethics," *Social Work* 21 (July 1976): 288.
84. Armando Morales, "Beyond Traditional Conceptual Frameworks," *Social Work* 22 (September 1977): 393.
85. The Ad Hoc Committee on Advocacy, "The Social Worker as Advocate: Champion of Social Victims," *Social Work* 14 (April 1969): 18.
86. Gilbert and Specht, "Advocacy," p. 291.
87. The Ad Hoc Committee, "Social Worker as Advocate," p. 19.
88. Barbara Bryant Solomon, *Black Empowerment: Social Work in Oppressed Communities* (New York: Columbia University Press, 1976), p. 6.
89. Ibid., p. 342.
90. Anne Minahan and Allen Pincus, "Conceptual Framework for Social Work Practice," *Social Work* 22 (September 1977): 348.
91. Solomon, *Black Empowerment*, p. 354.
92. Brian O'Connell, "From Service to Advocacy to Empowerment," *Social Casework* 59 (April 1978): 198.
93. Felix G. Rivera and John Erlich, "An Assessment Framework for Organizing in Emerging Minority Communities," in *Tactics and Techniques of Community Practice*, p. 106.
94. Lambert Maguire, "Networking for Self-Help: An Empirically Based Guideline," in *Tactics and Techniques of Community Practice*, p. 198.
95. Maguire, p. 199.
96. Maguire, pp. 206–207.
97. Scott Briar, "The Future of Social Work: An Introduction," *Social Work* 19 (September 1974): 518.
98. National Association of Social Workers, *Law and Social Work* (Washington, D.C.: The Association, 1973), p. vii.
99. Ibid., p. 15.

100. National Association of Social Workers, *Law and Social Work*, op. cit., p. 25. (Emphasis ours.)
101. NASW *Newsletter*, Greater California Chapter, April 1975, p. 1.
102. Robert B. Keiter, "California Educational Financing System Violates Equal Protection," *Clearinghouse Review* 5 (October 1971): 287.
103. Ibid., p. 297.
104. Ibid., p. 298.
105. Ibid., p. 299.
106. *Nicacio* versus *United States INS*, 595 F.Supp. 19 (1984), p. 19.
107. Ibid., p. 21.
108. Ibid., pp. 19, 25.

Name Index

Subject Index